W9-BZA-065

X Toolkit Intrinsics
Programming Manual

Volume Four

X Toolkit Intrinsics
Programming Manual

OSF/Motif 1.2 Edition
for X11, Release 5

by Adrian Nye and Tim O'Reilly

O'Reilly & Associates, Inc.

X Toolkit Intrinsics Programming Manual

by Adrian Nye and Tim O'Reilly

Editor: Adrian Nye

Printing History:

January 1990:	Athena First Edition.
September 1990:	Athena Second Edition. Revised for R4.
December 1990:	Motif First Edition. Customized for Motif 1.1.
August 1992:	Motif Second Edition. Revised for R5 and Motif 1.2.
April 1993:	Athena Third Edition. Revised for R5.
August 1993:	Motif Edition. Minor corrections.
February 1995:	Motif Edition. Minor corrections.

ISBN 1-56592-013-9

Table of Contents

Figures

Examples

Tables

Preface

Note that while Motif is used for most of the examples in this book, the techniques described are equally applicable to and provide a good introduction to programming with any other widget set based on Xt, such as Athena or Athena. It is not difficult to convert an application between any of the widget sets listed above, since all of them use the same Xt Intrinsics programming interface.

In the Preface:

Preface

This book describes how to write X Window System programs using the Xt Intrinsics library (or simply Xt). Xt is a standard established by the X Consortium that provides an object-oriented programming style in the C language.

OSF's Motif library provides user-interface objects to be used with Xt. Motif is not an X Consortium standard, though it may nevertheless become a de-facto industry standard. This book primarily describes the Xt Intrinsics, but it also provides an introduction to Motif and uses Motif for many of the examples.

The Xt Intrinsics together with a second library such as Motif are collectively called the X Toolkit.

Summary of Contents

The discussion of the X Toolkit is divided into four volumes: Volumes Four, Five, and Six of the X Window System Series available from O'Reilly & Associates, Inc. Volume 6 is split into two volumes, Volume Six A, *Motif Programming Manual*, and Volume Six B, *Motif Reference Manual*.

This is Volume Four, *X Toolkit Intrinsics Programming Manual*, *Motif Edition*. It provides an explanation of the X Toolkit, including tutorial material and numerous programming examples. Arranged by task or topic, each chapter brings together a group of Xt functions, describes the conceptual foundation on which they are based, and illustrates how they are most often used in writing applications. This volume is structured to be useful as a tutorial and also as a task-oriented reference.

Volume Five, *X Toolkit Intrinsics Reference Manual*, includes reference pages for each of the Xt functions, as well as for the widget classes defined by Xt, organized alphabetically for ease of reference; a permuted index; and numerous appendices and quick reference aids.

Volumes Six A and Six B, *Motif Programming Manual* and *Motif Reference Manual*, provide detailed, practical instructions for building real applications with the Motif widget set.

The four volumes are designed to be used together. To get the most out of the examples in Volume Four, you will need the exact calling sequences of each function from Volume Five. To understand fully how to use each of the functions described in Volume Five, all but the most experienced Toolkit "hacker" will need the explanation and examples in Volume Four. Volume Six gives you the specifics of using each Motif widget and guidance in practical programming.

Volumes Four and Five include material from the original Toolkit documentation provided by MIT, though in Volume Four this material is mostly limited to the appendices. We have done our best to incorporate all the useful information from the MIT documentation, to reorganize and present it in a more useful form, and to supplement it with conceptual material, tutorials, reference aids, and examples. In other words, this manual is not only a replacement but is a superset of the MIT documentation.

Each reference page in Volume Five includes a detailed description of the routine similar to that found in the Xt specification (*X Toolkit Intrinsics—C Language Interface*), plus in many cases additional text that clarifies ambiguities and describes the context in which the routine would be used. We have also added the definitions of structures and symbolic constants used as arguments or returned values by the function, as well as cross-references to related reference pages and to where additional information can be found in Volume Four.

Assumptions

This book makes no assumptions about the reader's knowledge of object-oriented programming or the X Window System. Readers should be proficient in the C programming language, although examples are provided for infrequently used features of the language that are necessary or useful when programming with the X Toolkit. In addition, general familiarity with the principles of raster graphics will be helpful.

However, even though the Toolkit is intended to hide the low-level X interface provided by Xlib, there are times in writing applications or widgets when Xlib functions will be necessary because no Xt feature exists to do the same thing. This book describes the most common occasions for using Xlib, but does not provide a reference to the particular functions involved. Additional documentation on Xlib, such as that provided by Volume One, *Xlib Programming Manual*, and Volume Two, *Xlib Reference Manual*, will be indispensable.

Related Documents

Several other books and a journal on the X Window System are available from O'Reilly & Associates, Inc.:

Volume Zero	*X Protocol Reference Manual*
Volume One	*Xlib Programming Manual*
Volume Two	*Xlib Reference Manual*
Volume Three	*X Window System User's Guide, Motif Edition and standard edition*
Volume Five	*X Toolkit Intrinsics Reference Manual*
Volume Six A	*Motif Programming Manual*
Volume Six B	*Motif Reference Manual*

Volume Seven	*XView Programming Manual*
Volume Eight	*X Window System Administrator's Guide*
Quick Reference	*The X Window System in a Nutshell*
PHIGS in X	*PHIGS Programming Manual*
	PHIGS Reference Manual
PEXlib	*PEXlib Programming Manual*
	PEXlib Reference Manual
The X Resource	*The X Resource* is a journal dedicated to X programming. It contains the latest information about X including articles, papers, and documentation.

The following documents are included on the X11 source tape (the X distribution from MIT):

X Toolkit Intrinsics—C Language Interface, by Joel McCormack, Paul Asente, and Ralph Swick

X Toolkit Athena Widgets—C Language Interface, by Chris D. Peterson

Xlib—C Language X Interface, by Jim Gettys, Ron Newman, and Robert Scheifler

The following Nutshell Handbooks published by O'Reilly & Associates, Inc. are useful when programming in C:

Checking C Programs with lint, by Ian Darwin

Managing Projects with make, by Andrew Oram and Steve Talbott

Using C on the UNIX System, by Dave Curry

Posix Programmer's Guide, by Donald Lewine

Practical C Programming, by Steve Oualline

Power Programming with RPC, by John Bloomer

Guide to Writing DCE Applications, by John Shirley

The following is the classic introduction to C programming:

The C Programming Language, by B. W. Kernighan and D. M. Ritchie

How to Use This Manual

Volume Four explains both application programming with widgets and widget programming (the design and coding of new widgets).

The first five chapters treat widgets largely as "black boxes," which is appropriate considering the object-oriented philosophy of the Toolkit. These chapters also provide an overview of many elements of the X Toolkit, and so are appropriate for all readers.

Chapter 1   *Introduction to the X Window System*, provides a discussion of the context in which X programs operate. Programmers who are comfortable programming with Xlib can skip Chapter 1.

Chapter 2   *Introduction to the X Toolkit, and Motif*, describes the conceptual foundations underlying Toolkit programming, and shows how to write simple programs that use widgets from existing widget sets. It introduces such fundamental Toolkit programming concepts as resources, the Translation Manager, callbacks, and actions.

Chapter 3   *More Techniques for Using Widgets*, describes how to use some of the more complex widgets found in applications, including composite widgets, constraint widgets, and popups. It also describes how to define application resources and command-line options, and how to hardcode the value of widget resources when you create a widget. Finally, it describes how to create multiple top-level windows, and how to use application contexts to create applications that are more portable.

Chapter 4   *An Example Application*, describes a complete application, in several iterations. First, it shows a simple version of the program, a bitmap editor, as it would be written assuming the existence of a BitmapEdit widget (which is actually developed in Chapter 6). Then, two refined versions are developed, each demonstrating additional Toolkit programming techniques. Finally, the same application is shown as it would be written if the bitmap editor were implemented in an application window rather than with the BitmapEdit widget, as it would be written if no BitmapEdit widget existed.

Chapter 5   *More About Motif*, describes and illustrates the widgets available in the Motif 1.2 widget set, and introduces the features and functions provided by Motif that add to the programming model defined by Xt. As mentioned earlier, this volume does not contain detailed reference information on each widget, and it gives examples using only a few of the widgets in the Motif widget set. Additional information on each Motif widget is presented in Volume Six, *Motif Programming Manual*.

The next two chapters describe widget internals and the process of creating new widgets. Although this information is not essential for all application programmers, many applications require a custom widget to implement their special graphics capabilities.

Chapter 6   *Inside a Widget*, describes the code inside a widget. Much of this code is common to all widgets. You can think of it as a framework that Xt uses to implement a widget's features. After reading this chapter, you should understand the procedure for creating your own widget around this framework.

Chapter 7   *Basic Widget Methods*, describes a widget's `initialize`, `expose`, `set_values`, `destroy`, `resize`, and `query_geometry` methods. (A widget's methods are internal routines called automatically by Xt to give the widget a degree of independence from the application.) The chapter explains when Xt calls each method, and describes in detail what should be in each of these methods. Among other things, these methods prepare for and do the drawing of graphics that appear in a widget. This chapter describes what the Toolkit adds to the graphics model provided by Xlib but does not describe in detail how to draw using Xlib; this topic is described in Chapters 5, 6, and 7 of Volume One, *Xlib Programming Manual*.

Later chapters treat various topics of interest to either application or widget programmers, or both. Some of these topics have been introduced in the earlier chapters and are explored more completely in the following ones.

Chapter 8   *Events, Translations, and Accelerators*, describes the complete syntax of translation tables, which allow the user to configure the mapping of event sequences into widget actions. It also describes accelerators, a mechanism for mapping events in one widget to actions in another.

Chapter 9   *More Input Techniques*, describes how to handle events with event handlers and how to use information from the event structure inside an event handler or action routine. It also describes how to get file, pipe, or socket input, how to use timeouts to call a function after a delay or at particular intervals, and how to use work procedures to do background processing. Finally, it discusses some low-level features of Xt for directly interacting with the event queue.

Chapter 10   *Resource Management and Type Conversion*, is a more thorough discussion of how resources work and how they should be used. This chapter describes in detail the resource file format and the rules that govern the precedence of resource settings. It also describes how to add your own type converter so that you can set application- or widget-specific data through resources. Finally, it describes subresources and how to use them.

Chapter 11   *Interclient Communications*, discusses communication through the X server between an application and the window manager, and between two applications. The application-window manager communication is performed by code in the Shell widget; the application sets shell resources to control this communication. Application-application communication is usually done with a process called selections; this form of communication is already implemented in most widgets that display text, but you may want to implement it in your own custom widgets. Selections can also pass other kinds of data such as graphics.

Chapter 12   *Geometry Management*, discusses how composite and constraint widgets manage the layout of widgets, and how to write your own simple composite and constraint widgets.

Chapter 13   *Menus, Gadgets, and Cascaded Popups*, describes how menus work and describes several ways to create menu widgets. One of these ways involves the use of windowless widgets, or gadgets. This chapter also describes how to use more advanced features of the Xt pop-up mechanism, including modal cascades, to implement cascading pop-up menus.

Chapter 14   *Miscellaneous Toolkit Programming Techniques*, describes various Xt functions and techniques that have not been treated elsewhere in the book. These include functions for error and warning handling, case conversion, using *editres*, and so on.

Appendix A   *Athena, OPEN LOOK, and Motif*, provides a comparison of the widgets available in AT&T's OPEN LOOK widget set and OSF's Motif. These widgets are contrasted with those in the Athena widget set.

Appendix B   *Specifying Fonts and Colors*, gives information on the values that can be used when specifying fonts and colors as resources.

Appendix C   *Naming Conventions*, describes a suggested set of conventions for naming widgets and elements within widget code.

Appendix D   *Release Notes*, describes the changes between Release 4 and Release 5. This manual describes Release 4 and Release 5.

Appendix E   *The xbitmap Application*, shows the complete code for an advanced version of the *xbitmap* application and the BitmapEdit widget, which are described in Chapters 6 and 7.

Appendix F   *Sources of Additional Information*, lists where to get the X software, lists companies that offer training in X programming, and describes additional books on the subject that have been or soon will be published.

Glossary   gives you somewhere to turn should you run across an unfamiliar term. Some care has been taken to see that all terms are defined where they are first used in the text, but not everyone will read the manual in sequential order.

Index   should help you to find what you need to know.

Volume Five consists of a permuted index, reference pages to each library function, and appendices that cover macros, structures, and defined symbols.

Font Conventions Used in This Manual

Italics are used for:

- UNIX pathnames, filenames, program names, user command names, and options for user commands

- New terms where they are defined

`Typewriter Font` is used for:

- Anything that would be typed verbatim into code, such as examples of source code and text on the screen

- The contents of include files, such as structure types, structure members, symbols (defined constants and bit flags), and macros

- Motif, Xt, Xaw, and Xlib functions

- Names of subroutines in the example programs

`Italic Typewriter Font` is used for:

- Arguments to functions, since they could be typed in code as shown but are arbitrary

Helvetica Italics are used for:

- Titles of examples, figures, and tables

Boldface is used for:

- Chapter and section headings

We'd Like to Hear From You

We have tested and verified all of the information in this book to the best of our ability, but you may find that features have changed (or even that we have made mistakes!). Please let us know about any errors you find, as well as your suggestions for future editions, by writing:

```
O'Reilly & Associates, Inc.
101 Morris Street
Sebastopol, CA 95472
1-800-998-9938 (in the US or Canada)
1-707-829-0515 (international/local)
1-707-829-0104 (FAX)
```

You can also send us messages electronically. To be put on the mailing list or request a catalog, send email to:

info@ora.com	(via the Internet)
uunet!ora!info	(via UUCP)

To ask technical questions or comment on the book, send email to:

bookquestions@ora.com   (via the Internet)

Bulk Sales Information

This manual is being resold by many workstation manufacturers as their official X Window System documentation. For information on volume discounts for bulk purchase, call O'Reilly & Associates, Inc., at 800-998-9938 or send e-mail to linda@ora.com (uunet!ora.com!linda).

For companies requiring extensive customization of the book, source licensing terms are also available. Terms for online distribution are also available.

Obtaining the X Window System Software

The X window system is copyrighted but freely distributed. The only restriction this places on its use is that the copyright notice identifying the author and the terms of use must accompany all copies of the software or documentation. Thanks to this policy, the software is available for a nominal cost from a variety of sources. See Appendix F, *Sources of Additional Information*, for a listing of these sources.

Obtaining Motif

If your hardware vendor is an OSF member, they may be able to provide Motif binaries for your machine. Various independent vendors also provide binaries for some machines: see Appendix F, *Sources of Additional Information*, for a listing of a few of these. Source licenses must be obtained directly from OSF. Call OSF at 617-621-7300 for ordering information.

Obtaining the Example Programs

The example programs in this book are available electronically in a number of ways: by *ftp*, *ftpmail*, *bitftp*, and *uucp*. The cheapest, fastest, and easiest ways are listed first. If you read from the top down, the first one that works for you is probably the best. Use *ftp* if you are directly on the Internet. Use *ftpmail* if you are not on the Internet but can send and receive electronic mail to internet sites (this includes CompuServe users). Use BITFTP if you send electronic mail via BITNET. Use UUCP if none of the above works.

FTP

To use FTP, you need a machine with direct access to the Internet. A sample session is shown, with what you should type in boldface.

```
% ftp ftp.uu.net
Connected to ftp.uu.net.
220 FTP server (Version 6.21 Tue Mar 10 22:09:55 EST 1992) ready.
Name (ftp.uu.net:kismet): anonymous
331 Guest login ok, send domain style e-mail address as password.
Password: kismet@ora.com (use your user name and host here)
230 Guest login ok, access restrictions apply.
ftp> cd /published/oreilly/xbook/xt
250 CWD command successful.
ftp> binary (Very important! You must specify binary transfer for compressed files.)
200 Type set to I.
ftp> get xtprogs3.tar.Z
200 PORT command successful.
150 Opening BINARY mode data connection for motifpg2.tar.Z.
226 Transfer complete.
ftp> quit
221 Goodbye.
%
```

The file is a compressed tar archive; extract the files from the archive by typing:

```
% zcat motifpg2.tar.Z | tar xf -
```

System V systems require the following tar command instead:

```
% zcat motifpg2.tar.Z | tar xof -
```

If *zcat* is not available on your system, use separate *uncompress* and *tar* commands.

FTPMAIL

FTPMAIL is a mail server available to anyone who can send electronic mail to and receive it from Internet sites. This includes any company or service provider that allows email connections to the Internet. Here's how you do it.

You send mail to *ftpmail@online.ora.com*. In the message body, give the FTP commands you want to run. The server will run anonymous FTP for you and mail the files back to you. To get a complete help file, send a message with no subject and the single word "help" in the body. The following is an example mail session that should get you the examples. This command sends you a listing of the files in the selected directory, and the requested example files. The listing is useful if there's a later version of the examples you're interested in.

```
% mail ftpmail@online.ora.com
Subject:
reply jerry@ora.com           (where you want files mailed)
open
cd /published/oreilly/xbook/xt
dir
get README
mode binary
uuencode                      (or btoa if you have it)
get motifpg2.tar.Z
quit
%
```

A signature at the end of the message is acceptable as long as it appears after "quit."

BITFTP

BITFTP is a mail server for BITNET users. You send it electronic mail messages requesting files, and it sends you back the files by electronic mail. BITFTP currently serves only users who send it mail from nodes that are directly on BITNET, EARN, or NetNorth. BITFTP is a public service of Princeton University. Here's how it works.

To use BITFTP, send mail containing your *ftp* commands to *BITFTP@PUCC*. For a complete *help* file, send HELP as the message body.

The following is the message body you should send to BITFTP:

```
FTP  ftp.uu.net  NETDATA
USER  anonymous
PASS your Internet email address (not your bitnet address)
CD  /published/oreilly/xbook/xt
DIR
BINARY
GET  motifpg2.tar.Z
QUIT
```

Once you've got the desired file, follow the directions under FTP to extract the files from the archive. Since you are probably not on a UNIX system, you may need to get versions of *uudecode*, *uncompress*, *atob*, and *tar* for your system. VMS, DOS, and Mac versions are available. The VMS versions are on *gatekeeper.dec.com* in */archive/pub/VMS*.

Questions about BITFTP can be directed to Melinda Varian, *MAINT@PUCC* on BITNET.

UUCP

UUCP is standard on virtually all UNIX systems, and is available for IBM-compatible PCs and Apple Macintoshes. The examples are available by UUCP via modem from UUNET; UUNET's connect-time charges apply.

You can get the examples from UUNET whether you have an account or not. If you or your company has an account with UUNET, you will have a system with a direct UUCP connection to UUNET. Find that system, and type:

```
uucp uunet\!~/published/oreilly/xbook/xtmotifpg2.tar.Z yourhost\!~/yourname/
```

The backslashes can be omitted if you use the Bourne shell (*sh*) instead of *csh*. The file should appear some time later (up to a day or more) in the directory */usr/spool/uucppub-lic/yourname*. If you don't have an account but would like one so that you can get electronic mail, then contact UUNET at 703-204-8000.

It's a good idea to get the file */published/oreilly/xbook/xtls-lR.Z* as a short test file containing the filenames and sizes of all the files in the directory.

Once you've got the desired file, follow the directions under FTP to extract the files from the archive.

Compiling the Example Programs

Once you've got the examples and unpacked the archive as described previously, you're ready to compile them. The easiest way is to use *imake*, a program supplied with the X11 distribution that generates proper Makefiles on a wide variety of systems. *imake* uses configuration files called Imakefiles which are included. If you have *imake*, you should go to the top-level directory containing the examples, and type:

```
% xmkmf
% make Makefiles
% make
```

All the application-defaults files are in the main examples directory. The application-defaults files are not automatically installed in the system application-defaults directory (usually */usr/lib/X11/app-defaults* on UNIX systems).† If you have permission to write to that directory, you can copy them there yourself. Or you may set the XAPPLRESDIR environment variable to the complete path of the directory where you installed the examples. The value of

---

† On Sun systems under OpenWindows it is usually */usr/openwin/lib/app-defaults*.

XAPPLRESDIR must end with a / (slash). (Most of the examples will not function properly without the application-defaults files.)

Acknowledgments

As mentioned before, this manual includes some material from the *X Toolkit Intrinsics—C Language Interface*, by Joel McCormack, Paul Asente and Ralph Swick. This is the document that defines the X Consortium standard for Xt, known as the Xt specification. Overt borrowings from the Xt specification are rare in this volume. However, the Xt specification document, as well as the sample code of Xt distributed with releases of X, provides the intellectual basis for most of what appears here. Many thanks to the X Consortium for their copyright policy that allows others to build on their work.

We'd like to thank Sony Microsystems for the loan of a Sony NEWS workstation running their implementation of the X Window System. The speed and power of the Sony workstation, and the support of Sony's staff, were a great help in developing these books. Additional development was done on a Sun-3 workstation running MIT's sample server, a Visual 640 X Display Station, and an NCD16 Network Display Station.

We would also like to thank the reviewers of the Alpha draft of this book, even though we almost had to start over because of their comments. They were David Lewis of Integrated Computer Solutions (ICS), Wendy Eisner of Sunquest Information Systems, Dan Heller of Island Graphics, Inc. (now working with O'Reilly & Associates), Miles O'Neal of Systems and Software Solutions, Inc., and Chris Peterson of MIT Project Athena (now of the X Consortium). Ian Darwin of SoftQuad and Bradley Ross of Cambridge Computer Associates reviewed the Beta draft. Extra thanks are due to Ralph Swick, Chris Peterson, and Robert Scheifler, who answered many questions during the development of this book.

Of course, we alone take responsibility for any errors or omissions that remain. Special thanks go to Mark Langley, who wrote an early draft of this book. He helped to educate us about the Toolkit, and his efforts to make the book a success did not go unnoticed.

Special thanks also go to Integrated Computer Solutions, for their assistance in preparing the Motif edition. Thanks to Chris Peterson for permission to use his material on *editres*.

Of course, the authors would like to thank Kismet McDonough, Len Muellner, Laura Parker, and Donna Woonteiler of O'Reilly & Associates for producing the book, Chris Reilley for creating the illustrations, and the staff of Cambridge Computer Associates, Inc., for lending their support. David Flanagan and Paula Ferguson provided much of the information on Release 5. and Motif 1.2.

Perhaps most of all, we would like to thank our readers and customers for their patience, which we tested by promising that this book would be finished next month—every month for the last eight months. These days, with word processors, it is easy to generate a book-length manuscript, but no easier than it ever was to carve that text into something worth reading. We have had that book-length manuscript for a year, but have not been satisfied until now that it presented the material in a clear, friendly, and authoritative manner. We hope that the extra time we have spent boiling down the facts about this very new and continuously advancing subject will prove worthwhile to you, the reader.

—Adrian Nye and Tim O'Reilly

1

Introduction to the X Window System

This chapter introduces many of the most important concepts on which the X Window System is based, and describes the environment in which the X Toolkit operates. This chapter assumes that you are new to programming the X Window System. If you already have some experience programming the X Window System, you may wish to skim this chapter for a brief review or even begin with Chapter 2.

In This Chapter:

1
Introduction to the X Window System

The X Window System (or simply X)† is a hardware- and operating system-independent windowing system. It was developed jointly by MIT and Digital Equipment Corporation, and has been adopted by the computer industry as a standard for graphics applications.

X controls a "bit-mapped" display in which each pixel on the screen is individually controllable. This allows applications to draw pictures as well as text. Until recently, individual control of screen pixels was widely available only on personal computers (PCs) and high-priced technical workstations. Most general-purpose machines were limited to output on text-only terminals. X brings a consistent world of graphic output to both PCs and more powerful machines. Figure 1-1 compares an X application to an application running on a traditional text terminal.

Like other windowing systems, X divides the screen into multiple input and output areas called *windows*. Using a terminal emulator, windows can act as "virtual terminals," running ordinary text-based applications. However, as shown in Figure 1-1, windows can also run applications designed to take advantage of the graphic power of the bitmapped display.

X takes user input from a *pointer*. The pointer is usually a mouse but could just as well be a track-ball or a tablet. The pointer allows the user to control a program without using the keyboard, by pointing at objects drawn on the screen such as menus and command buttons. This method of using programs is often easier to learn than traditional keyboard control because it is more intuitive. Figure 1-2 shows an application with a typical three-button pointer being used to select a menu item.

---

†The name "X Windows" is frowned upon by the developers of X.

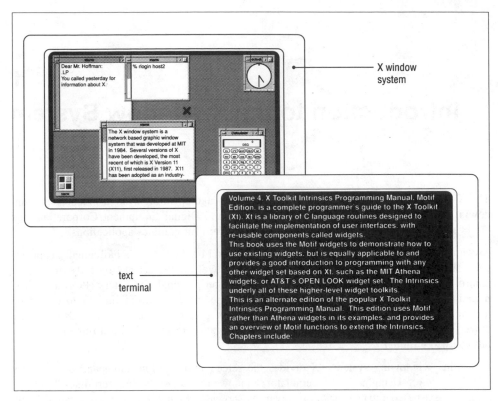

Figure 1-1. An X application, and an application on a traditional text terminal

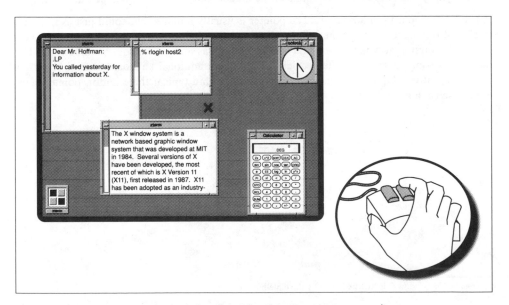

Figure 1-2. A three-button mouse directing the pointer to select a menu item

Of course, X also handles keyboard input. The pointer directs keyboard input from window to window. Only one window at a time can receive keyboard input.

In X, as in many other window systems, each application need not (and usually does not) consist of a single window. Any part of an application can have its own separate subwindow, which simplifies the management of input and output within the application code. Such *child windows* are visible only within the confines of their parent window.

Windows are rectangular and oriented along the same axes as the edges of the display.† Each window has its own coordinate system, with the origin in the upper-left corner of the window inside its border. The application or the user can change the dimensions of windows. Figure 1-3 shows a typical screen with several virtual terminals running. The screen also shows some applications, such as *xterm*, *oclock*, and *xcalc*, that run in their own windows.

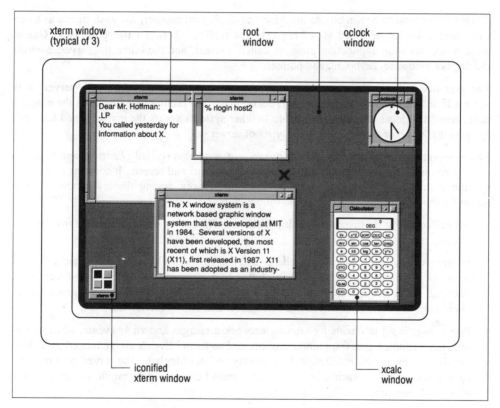

Figure 1-3. Screen layout of a typical user's X Window System

X supports both color and black-and-white displays.

---

†Note however that there is a standard extension, Shape, that supports non-rectangular windows.

Many of the above characteristics are also true of several other window systems. What is unusual about X is that it is based on a network protocol instead of on system-specific procedure and system calls. This network protocol enables X to be ported to different computer architectures and operating systems; it also allows programs to run on one architecture or operating system while displaying on another. Because of its unique design, X can make a network of different computers cooperate. For example, a computationally intensive application might run on a supercomputer, but take input from and display output on a workstation connected across a local area network. To the user, the application would simply appear to be running on the workstation.

1.1 The Server and Client

To allow programs to be run on one machine and display on another, X was designed as a network protocol—a predefined set of requests and replies—between two processes. One of these processes is an application program called a *client*, and the other, the *server*, controls the display hardware, keyboard, and pointer.

The user sits at the machine running the server. At first, this use of the word "server" may seem a little odd, since file and print servers normally are remote machines, but the usage is consistent. The local display is accessible to other systems across the network, and for those systems the X server does act like other types of server.

The X server acts as an intermediary between user programs (called *clients* or *applications*) and the resources of the local system such as the keyboard and screen. It contains all device-specific code, and insulates applications from differences among display hardware. The server (without extensions) performs the following tasks:

- Allows access to the display by multiple clients. The server may deny access from clients running on certain machines.

- Interprets network messages from clients and acts on them. These messages are known as *requests*. Some requests command the server to move windows and do two-dimensional drawing, while others ask the server for information. Protocol requests are generated by client calls to Xlib, either directly or through Xt and other function libraries.

- Passes user input to clients by sending network messages known as *events*, which represent key or button presses, pointer motion, and so forth. Events are generated asynchronously, and events from different devices may be intermingled. The server must pass the appropriate events to each client. The client must be prepared to handle any event it has selected at any time.

- Maintains complex data structures, including windows and fonts, so that the server can perform its tasks efficiently. Clients refer to these abstractions by ID numbers. Server-maintained abstractions reduce the amount of data that has to be maintained by each client and the amount of data that has to be transferred over the network.

In X, the term *display* is often used as a synonym for server, as is the combined term *display server*. However, the terms display and screen are not synonymous. A *screen* is the actual hardware on which the graphics are drawn. A server may control more than one screen. For example, a single server might control both a color screen and a monochrome screen, allowing users to debug an application on both types of screen without leaving their seat.

The user programs displaying on screens managed by a server are called its clients. There may be several clients connected to a single server. Clients may run on the same machine as the server if that machine supports multitasking, or clients may run on other machines in the network. In either case, the *X Protocol* is used by the client to send requests to draw graphics or to query the server for information, and is used by the server to send user input and replies to information requests back to the client.† All communication between client and server uses the X Protocol. The communication path between a client and the server is called a *connection*.

It is common for a user to have programs running on several different hosts in the network, all invoked from and displaying their windows on a single screen (see Figure 1-4). Clients running remotely can be started from the remote machine or from the local machine using the network utilities *rlogin* or *rsh*.

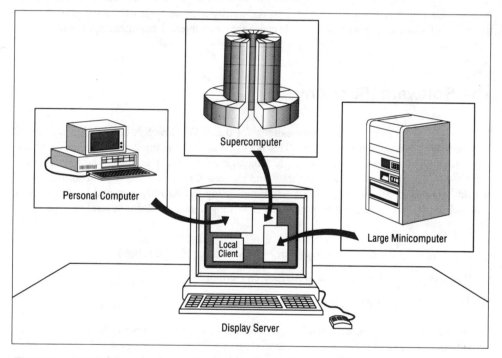

Figure 1-4. Applications can run on any system across the network

This use of the network is known as *distributed processing*. It allows graphic output for powerful systems that don't have their own built-in graphics facilities. Distributed processing

---

†The X Protocol runs on top of any lower-level network protocol that provides bidirectional communication, and delivers bytes unduplicated and in sequence. TCP/IP and DECnet are the most common low-level network protocols currently supported by X servers.

can also help solve the problem of unbalanced system loads. When one host machine is overloaded, users running clients on that machine can arrange for some of their clients to run on other hosts. Eventually there may be automatic load-balancing applications, but currently such remote execution is performed manually. It is not unusual to see users in the X environment having several *xload* load monitor applications running on various systems throughout the network but displaying on their screen, so that they can see the balance of loads throughout the network.

Before leaving the subject of servers and clients, we should mention PC servers and X terminals. Software is available that allows various types of PCs to operate as X servers.† X terminals are special-purpose devices designed to run just an X server, and to connect to remote systems over a local area network. PC servers and X terminals are the least expensive way to provide an X screen for a user. Since most PCs use single-tasking operating systems, they can't run any clients at the same time as the server. Therefore, they too require a network adapter to connect to another system where clients are run.

X terminals and PC servers both demonstrate the strength of X's client-server model. Even though PCs and X terminals aren't able to do multitasking on their own, they give the user the effect of multitasking workstations, because they can interact simultaneously with several clients running on remote multitasking systems.

1.2 The Software Hierarchy

This book is about writing client applications for the X Window System, in C, using the Xt Intrinsics library and a set of widgets. This is only one of the many ways to write X applications, since X is not restricted to a single language or operating system. The only requirement of an X application is that it generate and receive X protocol messages according to the X Consortium Protocol specification.‡ However, using the Xt Intrinsics and a widget set is, and is expected to be, the most common way of writing applications for several reasons:

- It is quite powerful.

- It results in applications that cooperate well with other X applications.

- It supports several popular user-interface conventions.

- The C Language is widely available.

Figure 1-5 shows the layering of software in an application that uses the Xt Intrinsics and a widget set. Notice that the Intrinsics are based upon Xlib, the lowest-level C-Language interface to X. Xlib provides full access to the capabilities of the X Protocol, but does little to

---

†Companies such as Graphics Software Systems, Interactive Systems, and Locus Computing offer server implementations for IBM-compatible PCs. White Pine Software offers an X server that runs under Multifinder on the Macintosh. An Amiga server is available from GfxBase/Boing. X terminals are available from Visual Technology, NCR, Network Computing Devices (NCD), Tektronix, Graphon Corp, and other companies. The number of X products on the market is growing rapidly.

‡Volume Zero, *X Protocol Reference Manual*, provides a conceptual discussion of the X Protocol and its detailed specification.

make programming easier. It handles the interface between an application and the network, and includes some optimizations that encourage efficient network usage.

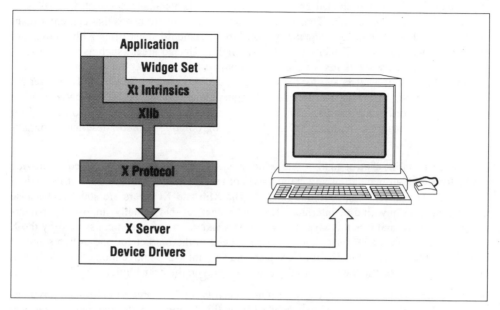

Figure 1-5. The software architecture of Xt Intrinsics-based applications

Xt is built upon Xlib. The purpose of Xt is to provide an object-oriented layer that supports the user-interface abstraction called a widget. A *widget* is a reusable, configurable piece of code that operates independently of the application except through prearranged interactions. A *widget set* is a collection of widgets that provide commonly used user-interface components tied together with a consistent appearance and user interface (also called *look and feel*). Several different widget sets are available from various vendors that are designed to work with Xt. The use of widgets separates application code from user-interface code and provides ready-to-use user-interface components such as buttons and scrollbars. Xt, widgets, and widget sets are described in much more detail in Chapter 2, *Introduction to the X Toolkit and Motif*.

In this book, we'll refer to the combination of the Xt Intrinsics and one widget set as the *X Toolkit* or just the *Toolkit*. When referring to the Xt Intrinsics layer alone, we'll use *Xt*, or *the Intrinsics*.

Applications often need to call Xlib directly to accomplish certain tasks such as drawing. Xt does not provide its own graphics calls, nor does it provide access to every X protocol feature. This book describes the features of Xlib that you may need from an Xt application, but it will not repeat the detailed description of Xlib programming found in Volume One, *Xlib Programming Manual*. You will find Volume One and Volume Two, *Xlib Reference Manual*, invaluable when you need to make Xlib calls.

Xlib, Xt, and several widget sets are available on MIT's public software distribution. The Motif and OPEN LOOK widget sets are not on the Release 4 or 5 distributions from MIT, but they are available for minimal cost from the vendors themselves (OSF, AT&T, or Sun, respectively.) The darkly shaded areas of Figure 1-5 indicate interfaces that are exclusive standards of the X Consortium. That Xlib is an exclusive standard means that computer manufacturers wishing to comply with the X Consortium standard must offer Xlib and cannot offer any other low-level X interface in C. The lightly shaded areas (such as the Xt Intrinsics) are nonexclusive standards—vendors are required to provide Xt but are also allowed to provide other toolkit-level layers for the C Language. For example, Sun and AT&T offer Xt, but they also offer XView as an alternate C-Language toolkit-level layer. XView was originally designed for porting existing SunView™ applications to X, but it can also be used for writing new applications. Volume Seven, *XView Programming Manual*, describes programming with XView.

X software is unlike that of many other window systems in that it was designed to provide mechanism without mandating any certain style of user interface. In the words of its designers, X provides "mechanism without policy." The Xlib and Xt layers are standard because they can support any kind of interface. It is the widget set that actually imposes user-interface conventions, and it is this layer for which no standard has yet been considered by the X Consortium. However, because there is a strong need in the market for one or two standard widget sets that provide consistent appearance and user-interface conventions, it is likely that one or two widget sets will emerge as de-facto standards in the near future.

It is important to note that the X Consortium standards for Xlib and Xt define the programming interface to each library (often referred to as the Application Programmer's Interface, or API), not the underlying code. This means that vendors are allowed to modify or rewrite the code to gain the best performance from their particular system, as long as they keep the programming interface the same. To you, the application writer and user of the Intrinsics, this means that you must always rely on documented behavior if you want your application to run on different systems. You must avoid accessing private structures, because they may be different in another vendor's release of the library, or they may be changed in a future release of X.

1.3 Event-driven Programming

Programming a graphically-based window system is fundamentally different from standard procedural programming. In traditional character-based interfaces, once the application starts, it is always in control. It knows only what kind of input it will allow, and may define exclusive modes to limit that input. For example, the application might ask the user for input with a menu, and use the reply to go down a level to a new menu, where the actions that were possible at the previous level are no longer available. Or a text editor may operate in one mode in which keyboard input is interpreted as editor commands, and another in which it is interpreted as data to be stored in an editor buffer. In any case, only keyboard input is expected.

In a window system, by contrast, multiple graphic applications may be running simultaneously. In addition to the keyboard, the user can use the pointer to select data, click on buttons or scrollbars, or change the keyboard focus from one application to another. Except in special cases (for example, where a "dialog box" will not relinquish control until the user provides some necessary information), applications are modeless—the user can suddenly switch from the keyboard to the mouse, or from one application area to another. Furthermore, as the user moves and resizes windows on the screen, application windows may be obscured or redisplayed. The application must be prepared to respond to any one of many different events at any time.

An X event is a data structure sent by the server that describes something that just happened that may be of interest to the application. There are two major categories of events: user input and window system side effects. For example, the user pressing a keyboard key or clicking a mouse button generates an event; a window being moved on the screen also generates events—possibly in other applications as well if the movement changes the visible portions of their windows. It is the server's job to distribute events to the various windows on the screen.

Event-driven window programming reduces modes to a minimum, so that the user does not need to navigate a deep menu structure and can perform any action at any time. The user, not the application, is in control. The application simply performs some setup and then goes into a loop from which application functions may be invoked in any order as events arrive.

1.4 The Window Manager

Because multiple applications can be running simultaneously, rules must exist for arbitrating conflicting demands for input. For example, does keyboard input automatically go to whichever window the pointer is in, or must the user explicitly select a window? How does the user move or resize windows?

Unlike most window systems, X itself makes no rules about this kind of thing. Instead, there is a special client called the *window manager* that manages the positions and sizes of the main windows of applications on a server's display. In Motif, this client is *mwm*. The window manager is just another client, but by convention it is given special responsibility to mediate competing demands for the physical resources of a display, including screen space, color resources, and the keyboard. The window manager allows the user to move windows around on the screen, resize them, and usually start new applications. The window manager also defines much of the visible behavior of the window system, such as whether windows are allowed to overlap or are forced to tile (side by side), and whether the keyboard focus simply follows the pointer from one window to the next window, or whether the user must click a pointer button in a window to change the keyboard focus.

Applications are required to give the window manager certain information to help it mediate competing demands for screen space or other resources. For example, an application specifies its preferred size and size increments. These are known as *window manager hints* because the window manager is not required to honor them. The Toolkit provides an easy way for applications to set window manager hints.

The conventions for interaction with the window manager and with other clients have been standardized by the X Consortium in a manual called the *Inter-Client Communication Conventions Manual* (ICCCM for short). The ICCCM defines basic policy intentionally omitted from X itself, such as the rules for transferring *selections* of data between applications, for transferring keyboard focus, for installing colormaps, and so on.

As long as applications and window managers follow the conventions set out in the ICCCM, applications created with different toolkits will be able to coexist and work together on the same server. Toolkit applications should be immune to the effects of changes from earlier conventions because the conventions are implemented by code hidden in a standard widget called Shell. However, you should be aware that some older applications and window managers do not play by the current rules.

1.5 Extensions to X

X is also *extensible*. The code includes a defined mechanism for incorporating extensions, so that vendors aren't forced to modify the existing system in incompatible ways when adding features. An extension requires an additional piece of software on the server side and an additional library at the same level as Xlib on the client side. After an initial query to see whether the server portion of the extension software is installed, these extensions are used just as Xlib routines and perform at the same level.

As time goes on, some extensions will become a basic part of what is called "X," and will become X Consortium standards themselves. For example, as of Release 5 the X Consortium has standardized three extensions: the non-rectangular window Shape extension, the X Input extension for supporting input devices other than the keyboard and mouse, and PEX for 3-D graphics. The only one of these libraries that is widely available on X servers, and is commonly used in conjunction with Xt, is the Shape extension. The C programming library used to access the Shape extension is –lXext.

2

Introduction to the X Toolkit and Motif

This chapter provides a conceptual introduction to the X Toolkit (including the Motif widget set), followed by a practical tutorial that starts with the most fundamental toolkit program, a "hello world" type application consisting of only a single widget. This application is successively refined until the major elements of any X Toolkit program have been introduced.

In This Chapter:

2

Introduction to the X Toolkit and Motif

It is difficult to build applications that have a graphical user interface using a low-level programming library such as Xlib. To simplify development, each of the user-interface elements of a graphical application—scrollbars, command buttons, dialog boxes, popup or pulldown menus (everything but the main application window)—should ideally be available ready-made, so the programmer need only integrate them with the application code.

The purpose of the X Toolkit is to provide such a simplified approach to graphical user-interface programming. However, in keeping with the X philosophy of "mechanism, not policy," the designers of the X Toolkit didn't develop a fixed set of components with a predefined look and feel. Instead, they created a general mechanism for producing reusable user-interface components so that these components can be built either by the application programmer himself, or by lower-level "object programmers" and then collected in libraries for use by the application. Motif is such a library of ready-to-use user-interface elements.

The heart of the Toolkit is a C library called Xt, also known as the X Toolkit Intrinsics. Xt provides routines for creating and using user-interface components called widgets. A typical application uses Xt along with a library of pre-built widgets (a widget set) such as Motif. This widget set includes menus, dialog boxes, scrollbars, command buttons, and so forth, which all work together to provide a consistent "look and feel" for an application.

2.1 Programming with Widgets

The simplest way to understand the role of widgets in an application is to look at a hypothetical application, as shown in Figure 2-1.

If you are at all familiar with graphical applications, you will recognize many of the widgets called out in the figure as standard user-interface elements:

- *Push buttons*, which initiate an action when clicked on with the mouse. (Pushbuttons are sometimes called command buttons in other widget sets, but in Motif a Command widget is used for typing in commands.)

- A *scrollbar*, which allows the user to scroll data visible in a display window. (The position of a "thumb" within the scrollbar indicates the position of the visible data within a

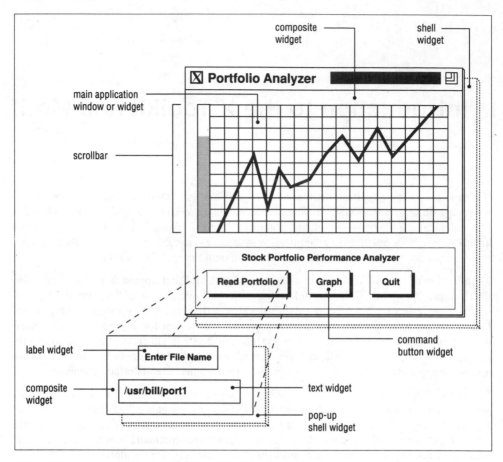

Figure 2-1. A widget-based application (simulated)

larger data buffer, and lets the user change the current position in the buffer by dragging the thumb with the mouse. Widget sets have various names for the scrollbar thumb.)

• A *data entry area*, in which the user can type information requested by the application.

Other widgets in the application may not be as obvious:

• *Composite widgets*, which are used to contain other widgets. In all widget sets, special classes of widgets manage the position (and possibly the size) of the *child* widgets they contain.

Composite widgets are an important part of any widget set, since they insulate the application programmer from having to place each widget individually, or from having to reposition or resize various widgets when the application is resized by the user. Composite widgets automatically adjust the layout of their children when child widgets are added or removed.

- *Shell widgets.* In any X Toolkit application, a special widget called a Shell widget is created by the call to initialize the Toolkit. This widget is used as the parent of all other application widgets (with the exception of popups, which receive their own transient Shell widget as a parent), and includes special functionality that allows it to interact with the window manager. The Shell widget is invisible, since it is overlaid by the main widget of the application (typically a composite widget), which is exactly the same size.†

- *A special-purpose application window.* Most applications have at least one window that has unusual characteristics not supported by an existing widget. For example, in our hypothetical application, the main application window is used to graph the performance of a stock portfolio.

  There are several ways to implement such windows. Which to use depends on the complexity of what you plan to draw, the types of input you want it to accept, and whether you know how to write a widget. You can add graphics to a DrawingArea widget. You can add functionality to an existing widget (usually called a Primitive widget) by adding actions as described in Chapter 4, *An Example Application*, or you can write your own widget, as described in Chapter 6, *Inside a Widget*. As you will see, no matter how you write application code to operate the special-purpose window, making a widget that does the same thing is mostly a matter of rearranging the code and changing variable names. Placing code into a widget gives you easier access to the configurability features of Xt, and neatly packages up the code to operate the special window.

- *A popup dialog box.* A *popup* is a widget that appears temporarily on the screen, until the user provides a certain kind of input. Popups are usually invisible when the application starts up. Using Xt, applications create popups very much like permanent widgets. The only difference is that a special kind of Shell widget called a *pop-up shell* needs to be created as the parent of the widget to be popped up. Many types of menus and dialog boxes (also referred to as "notices") are intended to be used as popups.

There is one other element in the figure that is not strictly part of the application, and is not provided by the widget set. This is the titlebar, which is added to the application by the window manager. Typically, the titlebar displays the window or application name, and also provides control areas for moving, resizing, and iconifying the application.

Although the titlebar isn't a widget, it is a window. The window manager adds the titlebar by "reparenting" the application. That is, it inserts another window between the application's top-level window and the root window. The visible portion of this window is the titlebar.

The titlebar in Figure 2-1 has been added by the *twm* window manager, which is standard in X11 R5 from MIT. Clicking on the small X logo in the left corner of the titlebar iconifies the application; dragging the pointer in the nested box symbol in the right corner resizes the window. The window can be moved by holding down the pointer anywhere else in the titlebar and dragging the window to a new location. Figure 2-2 shows the titlebar added by the *mwm* (Motif) window manager.

---

† The Shell widget is actually a type of composite widget, which is designed to have only one managed child widget. Its layout policy is extremely simple. It just makes its child widget exactly the same size as itself.

2.1.1 About Widget Sets

Shell widgets, and a few other base widget classes (Core, Composite, and Constraint) that are used to build more complex widgets, are defined by Xt. The special-purpose application window is written by the application programmer. All of the other widgets shown in Figure 2-1 come from a *widget set*—a library of pre-built user-interface components. Specifically, they are from the Athena widget set, developed at MIT.

The Athena widget set is distributed free along with the MIT X Window System distribution, and as a result, is the basis for many of the demonstration applications shipped by MIT and a great deal of public-domain X software. However, the Athena widget set was not intended to be complete—it was built mainly for testing and demonstrating the Intrinsics. Furthermore, the Athena widgets do not have a particularly attractive appearance nor user-interface conventions. For these reasons, we suggest that serious application development efforts should begin with a commercial widget set.†

Two commercial widget sets that are easily available and quite complete are OSF's Motif and AT&T's OPEN LOOK widgets. Both Motif and OPEN LOOK contain menus, scrollbars, command buttons, dialog boxes, and a wide variety of composite widgets. Both have an attractive appearance and consistent, well defined user-interface conventions. Each comes with a style guide that contains suggestions for designing applications to blend in well with other applications using that widget set.

In order to highlight some of the added value provided by a commercial widget set such as Motif, Figure 2-2 shows the same hypothetical application constructed with Motif widgets, and with a titlebar provided by the *mwm* window manager.

As you can see, Motif has a distinctive appearance, using shadowed outlines to simulate a 3-D appearance (buttons appear to be pushed in when you click on them, and so forth). What is more important, Motif has conventions about the use of its widgets that lead to a consistent look among all applications using Motif. The *OSF/Motif Style Guide* contains recommendations for application design and layout, and whenever possible, these recommendations are actually embodied in the design of the widget set. For example, the Motif MainWindow widget provides a menubar at the top of the application, which can contain titles for standard "pulldown" menus for file manipulation and on-line help, as well as for various application functions.

Motif also provides many more widgets than Athena, making it easy to create control areas such as radio boxes (groups of buttons, of which only one can be chosen at a time) or check boxes (groups of buttons that may be set independently of each other, say for making application configuration choices.) There are also convenience functions for creating many common combinations of widgets.

The *mwm* window manager provides similar functions to *twm*, but also always provides support for a help feature (invoked by clicking on the box in the upper right corner of the titlebar).

---

†The Athena widgets are described on reference pages in Volume Five, *X Toolkit Intrinsics Reference Manual*.

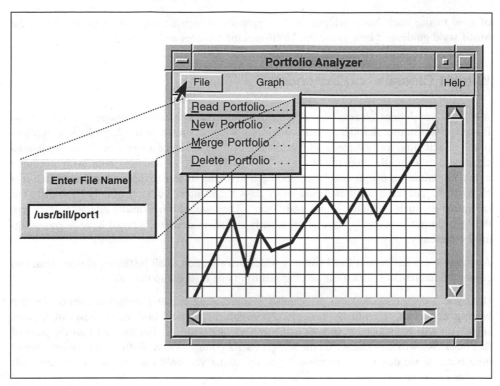

Figure 2-2. A Motif widget-based application (simulated)

The Motif widgets also support some advanced features for internationalization such as language-independent "compound strings," keyboard traversal (moving between widgets with keyboard keys rather than a mouse—this is very helpful for the design of data-entry applications), and mnemonic key equivalents for invoking menu commands.

This book provides examples that use the Motif 1.2 widget set. However, unless otherwise noted the techniques described in this book for using, modifying, and creating widgets are defined by Xt, and therefore are the same regardless of which widget set you use. You can use many of the same techniques to create applications using AT&T's OPEN LOOK widget set, or using the Athena widgets.

Note, however, that Motif provides many Xt-level functions (such as support for keyboard traversal and compound strings) that go beyond those provided by Xt. These features, are not portable to other widget sets. If you plan to write an application that will be portable between widget sets, you may wish to stay away from these Motif-specific features.

An important reminder here is that this is a book on the Xt Intrinsics, not primarily on Motif. Motif-specific features are introduced in Chapter 5 and in a few other places, but not described in minute detail. Moreover, Motif-specific features are carefully distinguished from the basic Xt features, to make it is easier to know what features are portable between widget sets. Volume Six, *Motif Programming Manual*, provides a more complete description of how to use each Motif widget, how to properly design an application according to the Motif style guide, and how to use the Motif-specific features and functions.

2.1.2 Widget Classes and Instances

A widget set defines *classes* of widgets. DrawingArea is a class of widget, as are Arrow-Button, PushButton, ScrollBar, and the various widgets shown in our hypothetical application.† Each time you create a widget, you create an *instance* of one of these predefined classes. For example, you might create several PushButton widgets, each with a unique name, containing a unique text label, and each invoking different application code when it is clicked on. All these widgets would be of class PushButton, but they usually have different string names such as "quit", "run", and "stop". They would have similar characteristics, but they would not necessarily look or act exactly the same since each could have been configured differently.

A widget class has certain fixed features which are common to all instances of that class, and certain characteristics which can be changed from one instance to the next.

How you view a class depends on whether you are using existing widget classes or are also writing new ones. Eventually you will thoroughly understand both these views of a class, since you will be competent in both using and writing widgets. For the first four chapters of this book, we will concentrate on the widget user's point of view. Both views are introduced here because we don't want to mislead you by telling you only the widget user's view, half the story of what a class is.

For a user of existing widget classes (a widget set), a widget class is a black box that has certain fixed features and certain configurable features, both of which are documented on the widget class's reference page. You need not know anything about how a class is implemented in Xt. You know that when you create an instance of that widget class, the instance will have the documented fixed features and that you can set the configurable features. A user of existing widget classes is most interested in the configurable features, since setting these is a big part of programming an Xt application. Each configurable feature is called a *resource*. Resources are more fully introduced in the next section.

If you are writing a widget class, or if you have written one and see things from that perspective, a class seems slightly different. To you, a widget class is a set of files in which the widget class is implemented. The widget class is no longer a black box—it is an open box. Knowing what widget class code looks like, you know that its fixed features and its configurable features are implemented in distinct sections of the code. You know that each resource is actually represented by a field in a structure. You know that each class has a structure (the class structure) that contains all the fixed features (both code and data) of that class. Even though you don't necessarily have access to the source code for a widget class, your definition of a class is based on how that class is implemented.

---

† The names of all Motif widget classes actually begin with Xm. However, to make the text more readable, we have omitted the Xm prefix when referring to these widgets, except in examples and discussions of code where the prefix must actually be used.

Figure 2-3 illustrates these two ways of viewing what a class is.

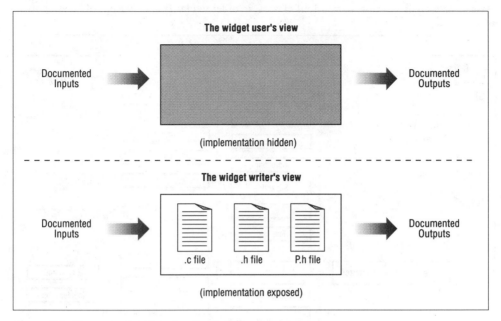

The widget user's view

Documented Inputs

Documented Outputs

(implementation hidden)

The widget writer's view

Documented Inputs

.c file   .h file   P.h file

Documented Outputs

(implementation exposed)

Figure 2-3. Two ways to think about a class

These two views of a class take on special relevance when looking at a characteristic of the Toolkit called class inheritance. Widget features and characteristics can be *inherited* from other, more basic classes of widgets. To a widget user, class inheritance is important only because it means that the resources (configurable features) of a widget class are defined not only by the class itself but also by the classes from which the class inherits features, called its *superclasses*. When you look up a widget class's features on its reference page, either all its superclass's resources will be described, or you will have to look up its superclass and look on that page also, and continue up the class inheritance hierarchy to the most basic widget, in order to get a complete list of its capabilities. This sounds difficult, but in reality you get to know the features of the most basic classes by heart, and the classes are not deeply nested.

From the widget writer's point of view, inheritance means that a new class of widget needs to define only its own unique features, and need not re-implement features common to all widgets, or already implemented by an existing superclass. All classes exist in a single-inheritance hierarchy that defines which other classes each class inherits features. (Note that the class hierarchy is completely different from the parent-child relationship of widget instances you create in an application. The class hierarchy of a particular widget set is fixed by the creators of the widget set, while the instance hierarchy is different in every application, and is determined solely by the writer of the application. The instance hierarchy specifies which widgets contain which other widgets on the screen.)

Figure 2-4 shows the class inheritance hierarchy for the Motif widget set. Classes defined by Xt (which are the same for all widget sets) are shaded gray.† This section describes the Xt classes, as well as the most basic Motif classes, in order to clarify the concept of classing as

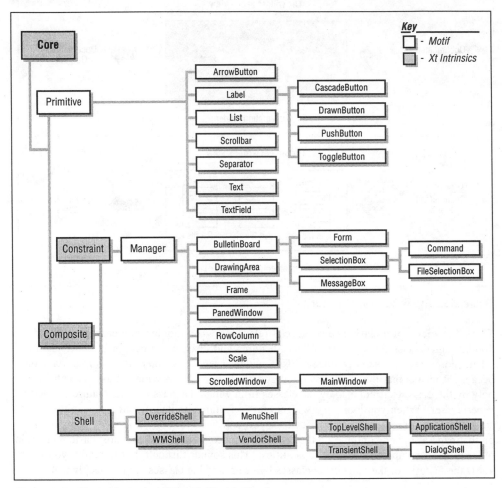

Figure 2-4. Class hierarchy of the Motif widget set

implemented in the Toolkit. A description and illustration of each of the Motif widgets is given later in the book. The Core widget class, defined by the Intrinsics, is the root of the hierarchy, from which all other classes descend. The Core class defines characteristics common to all widgets, such as size and position.

---

†Note that the X Toolkit supports only *single inheritance*. That is, characteristics can be inherited directly from only one superclass (though that superclass may itself have inherited characteristics from prior superclasses. A widget class can inherit only from the classes on a direct path upward from the class to Core.

The Motif Primitive widget class inherits basic widget features from Core and adds a few minor features of its own (for example, control of Motif style 3-D shadows) that are common to many Motif widgets. The Label widget in turn adds the ability to display a string or a pixmap, and adds mechanisms for changing the font and placement of the string. PushButton then inherits features from Label (including those already inherited from Core and Primitive) and adds more features, such as the ability to accept user input and highlight the button. PushButton is known as a *subclass* of Label, and Label is the *superclass* of PushButton. In general, lower classes in the hierarchy have more features.

The Composite class adds geometry-management capabilities to the basic characteristics defined by Core. Constraint is a further refinement of Composite that allows the application or the user to supply instructions on how the size and position of each child should be managed. All Motif geometry-managing widgets are subclasses of Manager, which is itself a subclass of Constraint. Manager is Motif's equivalent of Primitive for geometry-managing widgets—it adds features such as 3-D shadows so that they are available in virtually all Motif widgets.

Shell is a special class of Composite widget designed for interaction with the window manager.

New widgets can be subclassed by the widget programmer directly from Core, Composite, or Constraint, or can be subclassed from an existing widget in any widget set that has some of the desired behavior. For example, it is easy to imagine creating a subclass of Primitive in order to develop a custom graphics window.

As long as appropriate widget classes are available, the application programmer needs to know little or nothing about widget internals. In fact, even if widget internals are known, it is unwise to depend on them. Widgets should be treated as black boxes with documented inputs and outputs. If only these documented interfaces are used, the widget internals can be modified without affecting the application, and the application can be modified without affecting the widget.

2.1.3 Widget Configurability with Resources

To serve their purpose as reusable user-interface components, widgets must be highly configurable. For example, an application programmer must be able to define not only a separate label for each PushButton widget, but also the application function that is invoked when the button is clicked. The programmer will also want to let the user define additional attributes such as font and color.

To support this degree of configurability, widget classes can declare variables as named *resources* of the widget. The application can pass the value of widget resources as arguments to the call to create a widget instance, or can set them after creation using the Intrinsics call `XtSetValues()`. Even before that, though, as an application starts up, a part of Xlib called the *resource manager* reads configuration settings placed in a series of ASCII files by the user and/or the application developer, and Xt automatically uses this information to configure the widgets in the application. The collection of resource name/value pairs contained in the various resource files and set directly by the application is collectively referred to as the *resource database*.

Figure 2-5 shows several Label widgets configured with different resource settings, to show you how radically the appearance of even such a simple widget can be altered. Note that a widget's input characteristics can also be configured (although the Label class has no input characteristics to configure).

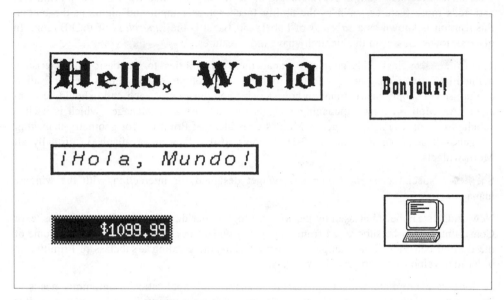

Figure 2-5. Several Athena Label widgets configured using resources

The resource manager provides a flexible mechanism for generalizing the behavior of widgets. The application developer can "hardcode" the value of those resources that must not be changed because they could cripple the application (as when changing the label of the Quit widget to Save), and can establish reasonable defaults for other resources, so that the user can configure all nonessential aspects of an application's look and feel.

Note that the term "resource" is used somewhat ambiguously in X. First, in the original documentation for Xlib and the X Protocol, various data structures that are maintained by the server and identified to clients only by an integer ID are referred to as resources. These data structures include windows, colormaps, fonts, and so forth. In this series, these are normally called *server resources* where there is possible confusion.

Second, the term is commonly used to refer both to a widget variable publicly declared as a widget resource, and to the name/value pairs in the resource database. In this book, we will use the term *resource* to refer to the actual variable and its current value in a widget instance, and the term *resource setting* to refer to a name/value pair in the database. The two are closely related, but may not be identical. For example, separate settings for the same resource may be requested in an app-defaults file and in an individual's user-preference file.†

---

†There are several possible sources of resource settings. If two or more contain resource settings for the same resource of the same widget, which will actually take effect is determined by rules of precedence that are described (along with the various sources of resource settings) in Chapter 10, *Resource Management and Type Conversion*.

Furthermore, the value of a resource may be set on the fly by a call to `XtSetValues()`, but this value is never saved in the resource database. (This value can be retrieved from within a widget or application by a call to `XtGetValues()`.)

2.1.4 Widget Independence

Each widget operates, to a large degree, independently of the application. Xt dispatches events to a widget, which performs the appropriate actions according to the design of its class, without application help. For example, widgets redraw themselves automatically when they become exposed after being covered by another window.† Widgets also handle the consequences when the values of their resources are changed. An instance of Label, for example, does not depend on the application that created it to determine its size. By default, Label will choose a size large enough to accommodate the current string in the current font. If the application changes the text or font in the Label widget with a call to `XtSet-Values()`, the Label widget itself will attempt to keep its own window large enough to accommodate the current string. (Of course, if necessary, the application can also explicitly choose the Label widget's size.) When the application tells a Label widget what font to display its string in, the widget knows how to load a new font, recalculate its own size, and redraw its string—the application doesn't have to micro-manage any of this. The application simply sets the font resource of the widget, and the widget does the rest.

Figure 2-6 and Figure 2-7 illustrate how a widget operates independently of the application and how `XtSetValues()` lets the application set how a widget operates itself.

---

†Redrawing is necessary because the contents of X windows are maintained by the X server only while they are visible. When one window is obscured by another, the contents of the obscured area of one of the windows is lost and must be redrawn when it later becomes exposed. X clients are responsible for redrawing the contents of their windows when this happens. Fortunately, Xt automatically redraws correctly written widgets at the appropriate times so that your application doesn't have to worry about this.

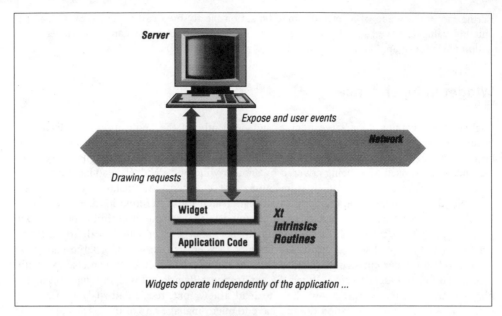

Figure 2-6. Widgets operate independently of the application

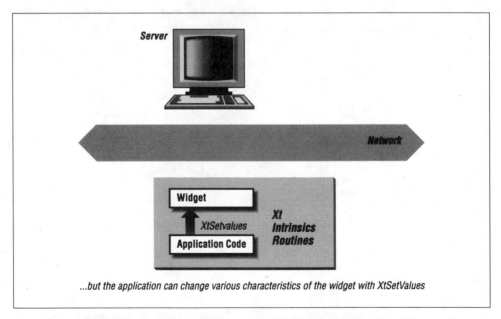

Figure 2-7. XtSetValues lets the application set how a widget will operate itself

2.1.5 Widget-Application Interaction

In the other direction, widgets are designed to let the user control the application. Therefore, widgets have the ability to invoke certain sections of application code—sections of the application's own choosing. Again, widgets will operate fine without invoking any application code, but if they don't invoke any, they won't do anything for the user.

One way that the application arranges for widgets to invoke application code is by registering application functions with Xt. Once the application is running, Xt will call these functions in response to some occurrence in the widget. For example, a PushButton widget usually invokes an application function when the user clicks on the widget. (Thus, the widget labeled "Quit" might invoke the code that checks whether data has been saved, and if so, exits the application.) Or the ScrollBar widget notifies the application when the user has moved the thumb, by calling a function that the application has registered with the widget for that purpose. Figure 2-8 and Figure 2-9 illustrate how an application registers a function during the startup phase, and how Xt then calls the function during the event-loop phase in response to a particular occurrence in the widget.

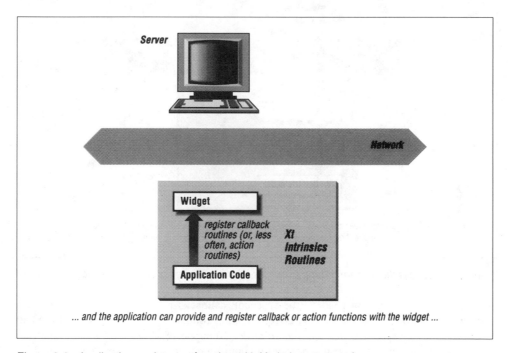

... and the application can provide and register callback or action functions with the widget ...

Figure 2-8. Application registers a function with Xt during startup phase

There are three separate mechanisms that can be used to link widgets and application functions: callbacks, actions, and event handlers.

Generally speaking, a widget expecting to interact with an application will declare one or more *callback lists* as resources; the application adds functions to these callback lists, which will be invoked whenever the predefined callback conditions are met. Callback lists are resources, so that the application can set or change the function that will be invoked.

Callbacks are not necessarily invoked in response to any event; a widget can call the specified routines at any arbitrary point in its code, whenever it wants to provide a "hook" for application interaction. For example, all widgets provide a `destroyCallback` resource to allow applications to provide a routine to be executed when the widget is destroyed. All callbacks have what Motif calls a *reason*—a well-defined occurrence of some kind that causes the callback to be triggered.

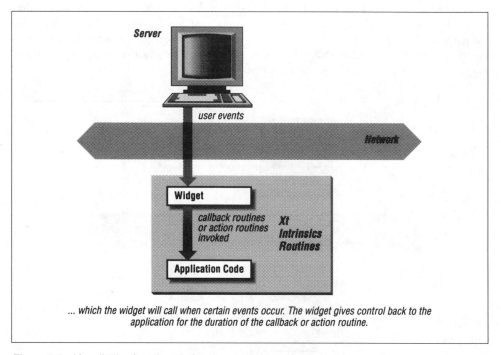

... which the widget will call when certain events occur. The widget gives control back to the application for the duration of the callback or action routine.

Figure 2-9. *Xt calls the function during the event-loop phase in response to an occurrence*

Although a callback reason need not be an event, callbacks are often invoked by widgets from within *actions*, which are event-driven. Action routines are called directly by Xt in response to events specified in a *translation table*. Xt supports a high-level event-specification syntax, which allows easy specification of complicated event sequences (such as double- or triple-clicks, or key- and button-press combinations) as the trigger for actions. Furthermore, the translation table is a resource, allowing the application developer or the user to configure the events that will invoke a given widget action.

Actions are usually internal to the widget and require no interaction with the application. (For example, in the Text widget, all editing operations are carried out entirely by the widget, using functions defined as actions. The only role required of the application is to read and write files.) However, an application can also add actions to a widget, which can function in much the same way as callbacks, but without the widget class having made provision for them.

The purpose of a well-designed widget set is to implement a particular user interface, which provides conventions designed to make all applications operate in the same way. A widget's callbacks are often designed to support the intended use of the widget, while adding actions to a widget can make it behave in ways the designer did not foresee and that the user might not expect. Nonetheless, there are cases in which the best way to implement the desired behavior is to add actions to an existing widget.

In addition to callbacks and actions, it is also possible for an application (or a widget) to implement *event handlers*, which use an event-selection mechanism similar to that used in Xlib. Event handlers are rarely used by application programmers, since actions are simpler and configurable without recompiling.

Some widgets also declare public routines, which can be used by an application to control aspects of the widget's behavior or to get widget data. Usually, the purpose of public routines is to provide a more convenient means for setting or getting widget data that would otherwise have to be accessed through resources.

2.1.6 Xt and Object-oriented Programming (OOP)

Xt provides an object-oriented programming (OOP) style, where the objects are widgets. However, since Xt is written in C, a language that provides no special support for OOP, Xt depends on programming conventions and programmer discipline to maintain the semblance of objects. It is very important that the programmer understand the goals and rules of OOP, because the language and the system won't enforce these rules, and if you don't follow them, you won't get the benefits. If you are familiar with another object-oriented system, you will need to understand Xt's particular implementation of OOP. On the other hand, if Xt is your first exposure to OOP, an explanation of its goals and concepts should make the whole system make a lot more sense.

Traditionally, object-oriented programming is defined in terms of the five words *object*, *method*, *message*, *class*, and *instance*, and the concept of *encapsulation*. We've already talked about classes and instances. This section describes the remainder of these terms.

2.1.6.1 The Object

In OOP, an object contains two elements: the data that represents a state, and code that reads or writes that data (called methods) and performs some action based on it. For example, the string displayed by a Label widget is part of its state data, and the code that actually draws the string on the window is a method that reads the state data and draws based on it. Inside widget code, the state data is represented as structure members, and the methods are represented as pointers to functions. Some state data members are public; they are resources that can be set or retrieved from outside the object. Other state data members are private; they cannot be read or written from outside, but they help the widget keep its own house in order.

2.1.6.2 Methods

What is called a method in traditional OOP is either a method or an action in Xt. In Xt, methods are a set of functions that are fixed for a particular class, triggered in fixed ways usually in response to Xt function calls made by the application (with one special case, the `expose` method, triggered directly by the `Expose` event). A widget's methods supply its most basic functions, such as the code needed to create a window, or to redraw itself. Actions, on the other hand, are called in response to the events specified in a translation table, and thus the events that trigger actions are user configurable. Actions supply most of the features of widgets, and these features can be added to or replaced by the application, as demonstrated in Sections 4.2 and 4.4.

From the widget writer's point of view, each method is just a function whose pointer has a place in the class structure. Each method has particular responsibilities in managing the basic functions necessary for a widget to be a widget. For example, every widget class must have a method that responds to calls to `XtSetValues()`. What each of the vital methods must do is described in Chapter 7, *Basic Widget Methods*. Each method has different arguments and returned values.

Every action, on the other hand, has the same set of arguments. Actions generally perform the features of the widget that are triggered by events. You could say that actions are the widget's occupation: it needs them to do anything useful but not to exist.

2.1.6.3 Messages

In pure OOP, input to objects and communication between them are called *messages*. In Xt, however, the forms of communication are function calls, events, actions, and callbacks. As you have seen, applications can communicate with widgets using function calls, such as to set or get widget resources using `XtSetValues()` and `XtGetValues()`. Widgets also respond directly to events from the user. Widgets contact the application when certain things occur using callbacks or actions. Widgets pass data back and forth using special kinds of events. All these types of communication can be thought of as forms of messages.

2.1.6.4 Encapsulation

Objects are intended to be black boxes with documented inputs and outputs. In other words, a program that uses an object must not depend on the internal implementation of the object, but instead only on the known inputs and outputs. This is called code *encapsulation*. The advantages of code encapsulation are that programmers can use the object without needing to understand its internal implementation (hiding details), and that the internal implementation of the object can be changed at any time because no other code depends on it. This can be stated in another way: it minimizes interdependencies. In large software projects, this one feature makes OOP worthwhile.

This encapsulation is very effective in Xt. You should be able to get a long way toward completing an application without even needing to know what the code inside a widget looks like, let alone the details that implement a particular widget. For that reason, in this book we don't show you what is inside a widget until Chapter 6, *Inside a Widget*. Even when you do know how widgets are implemented, it is a good idea to "forget" while writing application code, so that you are not tempted to depend on implementation details.

Each widget class has a public include file and a private include file. The application includes just the public include file, while the actual widget code includes the private (which happens also to include the public). The names of both include files are based on the class name of the widget, but the private include file adds the letter P to the end. For example, the Label widget's public include file is *Label.h*, while its private include file is *LabelP.h*. Application code should include only the public include file, to maintain the desired encapsulation. It is tempting for beginning Xt programmers to include the private include file, because it allows you to take shortcuts, but you should resist the temptation.†

2.2 Structure of Motif Applications

All Motif applications have the same basic structure, as follows:

1. Include *<Xm/Xm.h>*, the standard header file for Motif. (Note that *<X11/Intrinsic.h>* and *<X11/StringDefs.h>* replace *<Xm/Xm.h>* when using other widget sets.)

2. Include the public header file for each widget class used in the application. (Each widget class also has a private header file, which is used in the widget code. Do not include this file.)

3. Register the locale callback function with `XtSetLanguageProc()`. This function sets up internationalization support. This call is virtually always made with three NULL arguments. Always include it as boilerplate; exactly what it does is described in Chapter 14.

4. Initialize the Toolkit with `XtAppInitialize()` or `XtVaAppInitialize()`. (These two functions do exactly the same thing but have slightly different argument styles. The difference is described in Section 2.5.1. Many other Xt functions also have two versions with and without "Va" in their names. In the future, unless specifically stated otherwise, you can assume that when a sentence mentions one version it also applies to the other.)

5. Create widgets and tell their composite parent widget about them. This requires one call to `XtVaCreateManagedWidget()` for each widget. (Separate `XtVaCreate-Widget()` and `XtManageChildren()` calls can also be used to speed startup of applications with many widgets.) In Motif, there are also individual functions for creating many individual widgets and combinations of widgets. We use these "convenience functions" only for combinations of widgets, since `XtVaCreateManagedWidget()` is more general, more concise, and no more difficult to use.

6. Register callbacks, actions, and event handlers, if any, with Xt.

---

†In a language designed for OOP, such as C++, these shortcuts are generally prevented by the compiler or by the language itself.

7. Realize the widgets by calling `XtRealizeWidget()`. This function has to be called only once in the entire application, passing it the shell widget returned by `XtVaApp-Initialize()`. This step actually creates the windows for widgets and maps them on the screen. This step is separate from creating the widgets themselves, because it allows all interdependent widgets to work out their relative size and position before any windows are created. (For more on *geometry management*, see Chapter 12, *Geometry Management*.)

8. Begin the loop processing events by calling `XtAppMainLoop()`. At this point, Xt takes control of your application and operates the widgets. If any widgets are to call functions in your application, you must have registered these functions with Xt before calling `XtAppMainLoop.`

The four steps (3 through 6 above) of initializing the Toolkit, creating widgets, registering application functions with Xt, and realizing widgets, comprise the setup phase of the application. Your application should do as much of its work as possible in this phase, before calling `XtAppMainLoop()`, in order to speed up the second phase of the application (which is the event loop). This policy improves the response time to user events.† As we will see in Chapter 6, *Inside a Widget*, this policy also applies to the code inside a widget. It is basic to X, and indeed to any event-driven system.

2.3 A Simple X Toolkit Application

Some application code that uses the X Toolkit will go a long way to illustrate the basic concepts introduced above.

Figure 2-10 shows the actual window created by a minimal "hello, world" Toolkit application *xhello*, and Example 2-1 shows the code for it. *xhello* simply displays the string "hello" in a window.

Figure 2-10. xhello: appearance on screen

---

†In X Protocol terms, the setup phase consists of requests to the server that are generally long, and often require immediate replies, which tends to slow performance. The event loop phase, on the other hand, generally consists of short requests and very few "round-trip" requests. For a full description of this concept, see the introductory chapter to Volume Zero, *X Protocol Reference Manual*.

Most window managers add a decorated border above or surrounding the window; this is not part of the application. Likewise, the placement of the widget on the screen depends on the window manager. Since no coordinates are specified as resources for the widget, most window managers will require the user to place it interactively. Some window managers can be configured to place new windows at an arbitrary default location.

2.3.1 The Code

Example 2-1 shows the code for *xhello.c*.

Example 2-1. xhello.c: a minimal "hello, world" application

```
/*
 * xhello.c - simple program to put up a banner on the display
 */

/*
 * Header file required for all Motif programs is <Xm/Xm.h>.
 * In other Xt-based widget sets:
 * #include <X11/Intrinsic.h>
 * #include <X11/StringDefs.h>
 */
#include <Xm/Xm.h>      /* Standard Motif definitions */

/*
 * Public header file for widgets actually used in this file.
 */
#include <Xm/Label.h>      /* Motif Label Widget */

main(argc, argv)
int argc;
char **argv;
{
    XtAppContext app_context;
    Widget topLevel, hello;

    /* Register the default language procedure */
    XtSetLanguageProc(NULL, (XtLanguageProc)NULL, NULL);

    /* Initialize the Xt Intrinsics */
    topLevel = XtVaAppInitialize(
            &app_context,       /* Application context */
            "XHello",           /* Application class */
            NULL, 0,            /* command line option list */
            &argc, argv,        /* command line args */
            NULL,               /* for missing app-defaults file */
            NULL);              /* terminate varargs list */

    /* Create a widget */
    hello = XtVaCreateManagedWidget(
            "hello",            /* arbitrary widget name */
            xmLabelWidgetClass, /* widget class from Label.h */
            topLevel,           /* parent widget */
            NULL);              /* terminate varargs list */

    /*
     * Create windows for widgets and map them.
```

topLevel is a shell widget

Introduction to Xt
and Motif

Example 2-1. xhello.c: a minimal "hello, world" application (continued)

```
    */
    XtRealizeWidget(topLevel);

    /*
     *  Loop for events.
     */
    XtAppMainLoop(app_context);
}
```

Each of the Xt Intrinsics calls in *xhello* do more than meets the eye:

* **XtVaAppInitialize()** performs several important tasks. It reads the resource databases and merges in any command-line arguments so that Xt can use this information to configure widgets as they are created. It also opens a connection to the server, and creates a Shell widget that is designed to interact with the window manager and to be the parent for other widgets created in the application.

  The first argument to **XtVaAppInitialize()** passes the *address* of an **XtApp-Context**. An **XtAppContext** is an opaque pointer to a large structure in which Xt will manage all the data associated with the application. The only use of the **XtApp-Context** returned from **XtVaAppInitialize()** in a typical application is to pass it to **XtAppMainLoop()** and possibly a few other functions. The true purpose for the **XtAppContext** being a public variable is complicated and is discussed later.

  The second argument (a string) is the class name of the application. It is the string that can be used in resource files to set resources for this application, and it is also the name of the app-defaults file, in which the application writer establishes default resource settings for the application. By convention, the class name is the same name as the application name (the string typed to invoke the application), except with the first letter capitalized, or if the application name begins with X, the first two letters capitalized. For the current application, the class name is **XHello** since the application name is *xhello*.

  The remaining arguments have special purposes that are not used in this application. We will introduce them briefly here but reserve complete treatment of them for Chapter 3, *More Techniques for Using Widgets*. The third and fourth arguments are a pointer to and length of an array of application-specific command-line arguments that you can define. The fifth and sixth arguments are the common *argc* and *argv*—which **XtVaAppInitialize()** parses for a variety of standard X Toolkit options and the ones you defined in the previous arguments. The seventh argument is where you specify fallback resource settings in case the app-defaults file is not installed properly. The final argument terminates a variable-length argument list which can be used to customize the Shell widget with resources: this application uses the default Shell widget and therefore provides no resource settings in the list.

  The Shell widget returned by the call to **XtVaAppInitialize()** is used as the parent of the first widget created in the application.

* The **XtVaCreateManagedWidget()** call both creates the Label widget and tells the parent (the Shell widget) that the Label widget's geometry is to be managed. It is also possible to call **XtVaCreateWidget()** and either **XtManageChild()** or **Xt-**

`ManageChildren()` separately, but this is usually done only if you want to create many children of a single widget, then put them all under parental management at once.

`XtVaCreateManagedWidget()` is used for creating any class of widget. The first argument is the instance name, a string which Xt uses to look up settings in the resource database.† The second argument specifies the class of widget to create—this variable comes from the header file for that widget, and should always be found on the reference page for a widget. The third argument is the parent, which in this case is the Shell widget returned by `XtVaAppInitialize()`, but in a more complex example could be a composite widget deeper in a hierarchy of nested widgets. The fourth argument terminates a varargs list, unused in this example, that is for hardcoding widget resources. (More on varargs lists later.)

Notice that `XtVaCreateManagedWidget()` and `XtVaAppInitialize()` each return a value of type `Widget`. This type is an opaque pointer that is used to refer to a widget instance. It is used anywhere in the application that you need to refer to a particular widget. We sometimes refer to this as a *widget ID*, since even though it is a pointer to a structure, the individual fields in that structure should never be accessed from the application, so it can be treated just as a unique number.

• The steps of initializing the Toolkit and creating widgets seem logical. However, what does it mean to realize a widget? `XtRealizeWidget()` actually makes windows for the widgets, whereas creating the widgets simply creates and initializes various internal widget data structures.‡ Creation and realization of widgets are separate because some window geometries cannot be known until all the widgets are created and the composite widgets have determined their geometries. The realization step says "OK, all the widgets are created now; calculate their sizes and positions and make windows for them." However, note that it is acceptable to create additional widgets after calling `XtRealize-Widget()` as long as there is a good reason to do so (for example, when it cannot be known whether the widget would be needed until a certain user event arrives).

The realization step also maps all the widget windows. Mapping is an X concept, not something added by Xt. Mapping a window makes it eligible for display. For a window to actually become visible, all its ancestors must be mapped. Since `XtRealize-Widget()` is called for the widget created by `XtVaAppInitialize()`, which is the ancestor of all widgets in the application, the end result is that the entire application is displayed.§

• `XtAppMainLoop()` transfers control of the application to Xt. From this point on, Xt drives all the widgets in response to events, and it interacts with the application only at times the application has arranged ahead of time. *xhello* did not arrange any interaction

---

†The instance names for widgets need not be unique. However, if they are not unique then resources can only be set on all widgets with the same name at once. Instance names can also be " ", but then resources cannot be set at all. Instance names that include a period cannot be set from resource files.

‡A widget is a client-side object. It has no presence on the server other than as a normal X window. The Xt and widget set libraries running on the client side maintain the data that allow programs to work with the abstraction perceived as a widget.

§There are several other conditions that can prevent or delay a window from becoming visible, described in Section 2.2.4 of Volume One, *Xlib Programming Manual*. These will not affect your Toolkit application as long as you draw into windows at the right times, using one of the techniques described in Section 4.2 and Section 7.3.

with the widget, so Xt operates the Label widget without returning to *xhello*'s code. Example 2-3 demonstrates how to make such arrangements.

Xt programming is event-driven. `XtAppMainLoop()` dispatches events to widgets and functions in the order in which they occur. These events can be caused by user actions such as pressing a key or by window system actions such as displaying a new window. This is fundamentally different from procedural programming, where the application is in charge and polls for user input at certain points.

2.3.2 Compiling the Application

You can get the code for *xhello.c* and all the rest of the examples in this book via *uucp* or anonymous *ftp*, as described in the Preface. It is a good idea to compile and run each example as it is presented.

The example programs come with Imakefiles that should make building them easy if you have the *imake* program (which should already be in */usr/bin/X11* on UNIX-based systems that have X11 Release 4 installed), and you need the configuration files, in */usr/lib/X11/config* on most UNIX-based systems. The source for *imake* and the configuration files are also in the X11R4 distribution from MIT (see Appendix F, *Sources of Additional Information*, for how to get this distribution).

An Imakefile is a system-independent makefile that is used by *imake* to generate a Makefile. This is necessary because it is impossible to write a Makefile that will work on all systems. You invoke *imake* using the *xmkmf* program (also in */usr/bin/X11* and on the R4 distribution). Complete instructions for compiling the examples using *imake* are provided in a *README* file in the example source. Note that the examples are designed to work with Motif 1.1, and probably will not work with Motif 1.0.

To compile any of the examples on a UNIX system without using *imake*, use the following command line:

```
cc -O -o filename filename.c -lXm -lXt -lX11
```

If you want to do debugging, replace –O with –g in this command line. The order of the libraries is important. Xm relies on Xt, and both Xm and Xt rely on Xlib (the *–lX11* link flag specifies Xlib).

Note that unlike the Athena widget set, Motif does not use the Xmu miscellaneous utilities library, or the Xext extension library, both provided by MIT.

2.3.3 The App-defaults File

As mentioned above, the resource mechanism allows widgets to be customized. Widget resources can be set from any one of several sources, including a user's resource file, the command line, or an application-specific defaults file.

Is the X Toolkit Too Complex?
An editorial aside

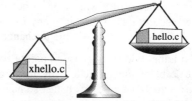

Window systems may be simple to use, but they are very complex to program. The first thing that strikes the novice X programmer is how complicated everything is. Learning to program the X Window System, even with the help of the X Toolkit, is a far cry from learning say, the C programming language, where the very first page of the tutorial presents a complete running program. The program itself is trivial, but this, the "hello world" program, has become a tacit benchmark of programmability. The assumption is "if you can't write 'hello world' simply, things are badly designed."

In fact, "hello, world" is a pathological example for X; it is a case where the stylized scaffolding outweighs the functional code. You've just seen an X Toolkit equivalent to "hello world," and it is nearly thirty lines long. But it is node-independent, does device-independent graphics, and can be customized by the user to control what font to use, and what color to use for the border, background, and text.

The "hello world" example is indeed a good benchmark of language complexity, but it is not necessarily a good general benchmark for overall programming complexity. It is an especially poor measure for a system that encompasses a generalized distributed software environment, network communication, and device-independent graphics. Most people write complicated applications, not trivial programs like "hello, world," and it is the ease with which a complicated program can be written that is the true test of a language.

For example, consider the difference in the number of lines of code between "hello world" and a text editor. Kernighan & Ritchie's C Programming Language, where "hello world" was first introduced, doesn't present an editor. However, Kernighan and Plaugher's Software Tools, an equally sacred reference from the same era, presents a text editor that contains well over one thousand lines. Furthermore, the editor is line-oriented, not screen-oriented. By comparison, because of the modular design of the Toolkit, and the development of widgets as reusable user-interface components, a programmer can construct a simple screen editor using the Motif Text widget in about 170 lines of code. This editor is user-configurable, device-independent, and based on a ready-made component that can easily be incorporated into any program needing to provide text-editing capabilities.

This is not to invite absurd comparisons of incommensurate programming tools, but to emphasize that the complexity of X is the outgrowth of added functionality, not unnecessary convolutions of straightforward algorithms. What really matters is what features are provided, how difficult is it to write the kind of application you want to write, and what performance can be achieved.

—Mark Langley

Each resource of a widget has a default value determined by the widget class that declared the resource. However, in many cases, the application wants a different default value, but still wants the user to be able to change the value of that resource.

The Label widget is a case in point. Example 2-1 (*xhello*) sets the default string displayed in the Label widget, "hello," by naming the widget `hello` in the call to `XtVaCreate-ManagedWidget()`. It just so happens that the Label widget uses its widget name as the string to be displayed if no other string has been specified in the resource database. However, this trick doesn't exist for the other resources of Label or of other widgets.

The application can provide a default value for resources by hardcoding them in the application source file using the fallback resources argument of `XtAppInitialize()`. However, changing these settings would require recompiling the source. Xt provides a better way.

To provide defaults, applications should always create an "app-defaults" resource file, which on UNIX systems is usually stored in the directory */usr/lib/X11/app-defaults*.† For any application, the name of this file should be the same as the *classname* argument to `XtVaApp-Initialize()`. By convention, this string is the same as the name of the application, with the first letter capitalized. If the application name begins with X, the first two letters should be capitalized. For *xhello* this is *XHello*.‡

Example 2-2 shows the contents of the app-defaults file necessary to make *xhello* display the string "Hello, World!" instead of the default "hello."

Example 2-2. XHello: the app-defaults file

```
*hello.labelString:     Hello, World!
```

The name of the widget instance whose string we are setting is `hello`, and the Label widget's resource that sets the string is `labelString`. After the colon is the string we want the widget to display. The string should not be quoted. White space after the colon is ignored.

All resource settings in app-defaults files should start with an asterisk, instead of specifying the application name or class (xhello or XHello). This is important as it allows the user to easily override this setting, for reasons described in Chapter 10 in the discussion of the ? wildcard.

The app-defaults file has the same format as all other resource database files. In brief, there are two types of resources: application resources and widget resources. (You already know about widget resources. Application resources are the same except that they apply to the application code instead of to individual widgets. Application resources are defined by the application writer—how to do this is described in Chapter 3, *More Techniques for Using Widgets*.)

---

†On Sun systems under OpenWindows the default location for the app-defaults files is the */usr/openwin/lib/app-defaults* directory. On all systems Xt provides a mechanism that allows you to provide a different app-defaults file for each language. This will be described in Chapter 10, *Resource Management and Type Conversion*.
‡Note that existing applications do not always follow this latter convention. For example, the app-defaults file for *xmh* is called *Xmh*, not *XMh*.

The syntax for specifying application resources in a resource file is simple:

> *application_name.resource_name*: *value*

Widget resources are more complicated since there may be multiple instances of the same widget class in an application. As a result, you must specify the name not only of the widget, but a pathname starting with the application name and containing the name of each widget in the widget hierarchy leading to the desired widget. For example, in the application *xhello*, the complete resource specification for the resource called *label* for the Label widget called *hello* would be:

> `xhello.hello.labelString:  Hello, World!`

The `xhello` refers to the widget created by `XtVaAppInitialize()`, and `hello` is its child created by `XtVaCreateManagedWidget()`. One possible source of confusion is that the shell widget instance returned by `XtVaAppInitialize()` is not named `xhello` by the arguments of that call (no instance name string is specified there at all—only its class name string `XHello`). Its instance name is the same as the name of the application (specified on the command line): `xhello`.

To simplify resource specifications, a wildcard syntax may be used, specifying an asterisk instead of a dot, and omitting one or more terms of the fully qualified name. For example, as we've shown above:

> `*hello.labelString:  Hello, World!`

or since there is no other Label widget in the application, even:

> `*labelString:  Hello, World!`

If you specify a widget correctly and the resource name correctly, but provide an illegal value, the widget should display an error message: the Motif widget set is fairly thorough about this. But the resource manager (the part of Xlib that processes resource specifications) silently ignores resource specification errors of any kind, so they can be difficult to track down. The kinds of errors that are not reported include:

* Misspelling any widget name or resource name.

* Leaving out a level in the hierarchy when using the . (period) binding.

* Setting a resource on a widget that doesn't exist.

* Setting a resource that doesn't exist for the widget.

You should also be aware that widget classes can be used in resource specifications. For example, instead of setting the `foreground` resource of each PushButton widget one at a time using their widget instance names, they can all be set with one line using the widget class name in place of the instance name:

> `*XmPushButton.foreground:  blue`

Because widget instance names take precedence over class names, however, one can override a class setting with a specific resource setting, by using a name for an individual widget instance. Therefore, you can set the foreground of all PushButtons to blue with one line, but then override that for one widget with one other line by setting the foreground using the widget's instance name.

Note that all resource specifications in files are given as strings, even though the data required for the resource may be of a different type. Xt automatically converts the string found in the resource database files into the appropriate destination type. For example, colors are specified as color names, which are automatically converted to the pixel values that are required for drawing. These converters are normally defined by Xt or the widget class.

Note also that in resource files, you and users specify the resource name as shown above. But in any Xt calls from source code, you always use symbolic constants of the form **Xm-**N*resourceName* (e.g., **XmNforeground**). (Standard Xt, as used for example with the Athena widget set, uses symbolic constants that begin with **XtN** instead.) Resource names are actually strings, and it improves compile-time checking to use symbolic constants instead of typing the string in directly.

The complete list of sources for resource database settings, the precedence rules used for establishing the actual resource value when there are conflicting settings in different database sources, and the mechanics of type conversion, are all described in detail in Chapter 10, *Resource Management and Type Conversion*. (See also Chapter 10, *Setting Resources*, in Volume Three, *X Window System User's Guide, Motif Edition*.) We'll also be returning to the topic of resources with each new example.

2.3.4 To Hardcode or Not to Hardcode

The resource settings you place in the app-defaults file for your application are, as the name suggests, only defaults. The user can place similar settings in a separate resource file, and these user settings override your app-defaults settings. This allows the user to customize the application.

There are pros and cons to applications that can be radically customized by the user through resources. The pros are quite clear:

- A flexible application will meet the needs of a wider audience.

- Users will have a wide variety of systems on which different colors and fonts will look best.

- Users may have a special job in mind for which the application can be customized.

Some of the cons are that:

- A user may make a mistake in the configuration that makes the application inoperable in some way.

- Documentation and technical support become more difficult.

A partial solution is to document the default resource specifications and require that users reinstall those default specifications before a technical support person tries to solve their problems. In some cases, dialog boxes can be added that require the user to confirm any irreversible actions.

In any case, you may eventually want to hardcode certain resources in the application so that they are not user-configurable. This would be done for resources that, if set incorrectly, would make your application operate in an unsafe fashion. Hardcoding a widget resource is done by placing the resource name and the desired value in the final arguments to `Xt-VaCreateManagedWidget()` or `XtCreateManagedWidget()`.

This technique is demonstrated later, because you won't need it until the later stages of developing your application. While an application is under development, it is better to leave as many resources as possible configurable from resource files, because this allows you to change them in the app-defaults file without recompiling the source.† When the code is stable and almost ready for release, then it's time to determine which resources need to be hard-coded, and then to hardcode them.

2.4 Connecting Widgets to Application Code

The Toolkit is designed so that the code that implements the user interface and the code that implements application features can be kept separate. This is an advantage, because it allows either part to be modified without affecting the other. However, these two pieces of code need to be intimately connected, because the user interface must drive the application code.

This section describes how to make this connection using callbacks. As mentioned earlier, the general idea is that the application registers functions to be called later by Xt in response to occurrences within certain widgets.

Callbacks are the method used when taking advantage of features of existing widgets. There are other methods, using actions in combination with translations or event handlers, but they are used primarily when adding functionality to widgets. The main purpose of actions is to modularize the code within a widget that responds to events. The use of actions in the application will be demonstrated in Chapter 4, and in widget code in Chapter 6.

A callback list is a widget resource. The application can add a callback routine to a widget using `XtAddCallback()` or `XtAddCallbacks()` only if the widget has declared a callback list as a resource. When a widget has a callback resource, it means that the widget writer foresaw that users of the widget would want to have application code called in response to a particular user behavior in that widget.

A widget class may have more than one callback resource. The Motif ScrollBar widget, for example, has eight, in addition to those defined by its superclasses Primitive and Core! Each callback resource represents a very specific occurrence in the widget. This allows you to specify a different function to handle each of these different occurrences. One of these resources, `XmNpageIncrementCallback`, is called when the user indicates that the information displayed should be paged down. `XmNincrementCallback` is similar but it indicates that the data should be moved a smaller amount. The purpose of the `XmNpage-DecrementCallback`, `XmNtoTopCallback`, and `XmNtoBottomCallback` should now be obvious. Each of these callbacks indicates a different kind of user behavior,

---

†There are a few resources in Motif that currently cannot be set from resource files. OSF may correct this in later releases.

and requires a different kind of movement of the data in the associated window. The callback function registered with each of these callback resources would actually move the data in the various ways. All widgets also have the callback **XmNdestroyCallback**, which is called when the widget is destroyed.

Note that a callback function is registered for a specific callback resource and on a specific widget instance. Therefore, two widgets can have different functions registered for the same callback resource.

The next section describes how to use callbacks, since they are by far the more often used of the two techniques to link the user interface with application code. The use of actions is demonstrated in Chapter 4, *An Example Application*.

2.4.1 Callbacks

To illustrate the use of callbacks from the application, we will write an application that uses the PushButton widget. Some analogue of this widget is present in every widget set. It contains a string or picture, and executes a command when a pointer button is clicked on it.

A PushButton widget calls an application function when you press and release the first pointer button (by default) in its window. When you press and hold the pointer button in the PushButton widget's window, the PushButton widget redraws the window in a slightly darker color, and swaps the colors of the two portions of the 3-D shadow surrounding the window. This gives the illusion that the button is actually being pressed into the screen. Moving the held button out of the window resets the widget without executing the command.

The *xgoodbye* program creates a single PushButton widget. It is very similar to *xhello*, but takes advantage of the callback provided by the PushButton widget. Clicking on the "Goodbye, Cruel World" button exits the program.

Figure 2-11 shows the window that *xgoodbye* creates if you have installed the suggested app-defaults file (otherwise, it will display "goodbye"). It is suggested that you compile and run *xgoodbye.c*, testing its response to moving the pointer in and out of its window, and clicking the various pointer buttons on its window.

Figure 2-11. The appearance of xgoodbye when the pointer is in the window

This example is not as frivolous as it seems. Many applications use code identical to this to implement their "Quit" button.

The code for *xgoodbye.c* is shown in Example 2-3.

Example 2-3. xgoodbye.c: complete code

```
/*
 * xgoodbye.c - simple program to put up a banner on the display
 *       and callback an application function.
 */

#include <stdio.h>
/*
 * Include file required for all Motif programs
 */
#include <Xm/Xm.h>   /* Standard Motif definitions */

/*
 * Public include file for widgets we actually use in this file.
 */
#include <Xm/PushB.h>     /* Motif PushButton Widget */

/*
 * Quit button callback function
 */
/* ARGSUSED */
void Quit(w, client_data, call_data)
Widget w;
XtPointer client_data, call_data;
{
    fprintf(stderr, "It was nice knowing you.\n");
    exit(0);
}

main(argc, argv)
int argc;
char **argv;
{
    XtAppContext app_context;
    Widget topLevel, goodbye;

    XtSetLanguageProc(NULL, (XtLanguageProc)NULL, NULL);

    topLevel = XtVaAppInitialize(
            &app_context,          /* Application context */
            "XGoodbye",            /* Application class */
            NULL, 0,               /* command line option list */
            &argc, argv,           /* command line args */
            NULL,                  /* for missing app-defaults file */
            NULL);                 /* terminate varargs list */

    goodbye = XtVaCreateManagedWidget(
            "goodbye",             /* arbitrary widget name */
            xmPushButtonWidgetClass, /* widget class from PushB.h */
            topLevel,              /* parent widget */
            NULL);                 /* terminate varargs list */

    XtAddCallback(goodbye, XmNactivateCallback, Quit,
            0 /* client_data */);
```

Example 2-3. xgoodbye.c: complete code (continued)

```
    /*
     *  Create windows for widgets and map them.
     */
    XtRealizeWidget(topLevel);
    /*
     *  Loop for events.
     */
    XtAppMainLoop(app_context);
}
```

And here is *xgoodbye*'s app-defaults file:

Example 2-4. XGoodbye: the app-defaults file

```
!
! Core resources
!
*goodbye.width: 200
*goodbye.height: 100
*goodbye.alignment: XmALIGNMENT_END
!
! Label resources
!
*goodbye.foreground: mediumblue
*goodbye.fontList: *courier-bold*180*iso8859-1
*goodbye.labelString:  Goodbye, Cruel World!
```

The differences between *xgoodbye* and *xhello* all apply to adding a callback function. In this example we have some application code (the `Quit` function) that we register with Xt as a callback function for the widget called `goodbye` using the `XtAddCallback()` call.

The `Quit` function is defined before `main`, so that we can use the function pointer `Quit` in the `XtAddCallback()` call. It is also legal in C to declare `Quit` as a function pointer early in the application, but actually to define it further down in the source code.

The `XtAddCallback()` call used to register `Quit` as the PushButton widget's callback is as follows:

```
    XtAddCallback(goodbye, XmNactivateCallback, Quit, 0);
```

The first argument, `goodbye`, is the widget that is to trigger the callback. The second argument, `XmNactivateCallback`, is a symbolic constant that identifies which of the widget's callback resources is being set. (This constant, like almost all resource names in Motif, is defined in the file *<Xm/Xm.h>*. Other widget sets define resource name constants in the public header files of individual widgets.)

The third argument of `XtAddCallback()` is the function the widget is to call, and the last argument is any data to be passed to the callback function. No data is to be passed to `Quit`. Later on we'll show many examples where this argument is used to pass data.

The `Quit` function itself, like all callback functions, takes three arguments:

```
    void Quit(w, client_data, call_data)
```

- The first argument is the widget that triggered the callback, as specified as the first argument in `XtAddCallback()`. You would use the value of this argument in your callback function if you registered the same function as a callback for two different widgets, and if you wanted to distinguish in the callback which widget the user clicked on.

- The second argument, *client_data*, is the value passed as the last argument of `XtAddCallback()`. This can be any data that you need in the callback function.

- The third argument, *call_data*, is a piece of data passed from the widget. Some classes of widget set this argument, but others do not. The documentation for the widget will specify the contents of this data if it is used. Most motif widgets pass a structure as *call_data*. The ScrollBar widget, for example, passes back the current position of the thumb.

If you are intentionally not going to use one or more of these arguments, you should place the comment `/* ARGSUSED */` on the line before the function. This prevents the C program checker *lint* from complaining about the unused arguments. The *lint* program can help you catch problems in your code that the C compiler can't detect. See the Nutshell Handbook *Checking C Programs with lint* for more details.

By convention, callback function names (and as you will see, action function names as well) are capitalized. This lessens the chance of collision with other variables names because callback functions are global in the source file. If this convention is not used, the most common collision is between callback functions and widget IDs of type `Widget`. It is tempting to call the quit callback function `quit`, and also to call the quit widget `quit`, but this will result in mysterious errors or a core dump. If you follow the convention that callback functions are given a capitalized name such as `Quit`, you avoid this potential problem.

2.5 More About Resources

You now have read about enough techniques to construct an application that uses widgets for its user interface and connects the widgets to application code. However, in order to really take advantage of any widget class, you have to learn about its resources, so that you can set the desired resources in the app-defaults file.

A class defines its own resources and also inherits the resources of all its superclasses. For example, PushButton supports not only its own resources but also the resources of its superclasses, Label, Primitive, and Core. The documentation for a widget class may describe only the resources for that class and list the name of the immediate superclass (which you can then look up), or it may list all the resources of that class and all superclasses.

2.5.1 Setting and Getting Resources from the Application

Resources are not just for customization of widgets at application startup. The application can change resources of widgets that have already been created, before or while the application is displayed. The application can also query the value of most resources. This section describes first how to set resources and then how to get them.

Setting resources is perhaps most often used for resetting strings in Label widgets. This can be very useful, but you should be aware that setting a resource from the application wipes out the app-defaults or user-specified value for that same resource (if any), unless you first query the resource, and then set it based on its earlier value. It is especially important not to hard-code strings if you want to be able to change the language used by the application simply by changing app-default files.

There are two parallel sets of functions that set or get resources. The two versions of each function have the same name except that one begins with **XtVa** and the other with **Xt** only. The arguments of both functions pass in or pass out resource name/value pairs, but they do it using a slightly different format of arguments. The **XtVa** style uses an ANSI C varargs list, which is a **NULL**-terminated list of resource name/value pairs. The **Xt** version takes an array of **Arg** structures (called an **ArgList**) and an array length. Each **Arg** structure contains a resource name/value pair. We will call these two styles the *varargs* style and the *ArgList* style.

The ArgList routines were the only interface until R4, and they can still be used. Using the ArgList form of call is slightly more efficient than the varargs form, since internally the varargs routines simply massage their arguments into the ArgList forms. However, the ArgList form is more verbose, hard to read, and error-prone, and lacks some of the features supported by the varargs form. The loss of efficiency of the varargs form is probably insignificant unless you depend on maximum speed in setting or getting resources many times in a loop. We use the varargs interface in most of this book, but will also show you how to use the ArgList form in the following sections so that you can understand existing applications written using them. Also, Motif provides only ArgList forms for some of its functions.

The following sections demonstrate how to set and get resources of an existing widget using the ArgList and varargs interfaces. The same form of arguments are used in many other functions that set resources, often while creating various types of widgets. Table 2-1 presents the parallel lists of Xt functions. The final arguments of all of these (many of which have not yet been described) are used in exactly the same manner as in the examples shown in Sections 2.5.1.1 and 2.5.1.2.

Table 2-1. Functions that Set Resources: ArgList and varargs Counterparts

ArgList	Varargs
XtSetValues()	XtVaSetValues()
XtGetValues()	XtVaGetValues()
XtCreateWidget()	XtVaCreateWidget()
XtCreateManagedWidget()	XtVaCreateManagedWidget()
XtAppCreateShell()	XtVaAppCreateShell()
XtGetSubresources()	XtVaGetSubresources()

ArgList	Varargs
`XtGetApplicationResources()`	`XtVaGetApplicationResources()`
`XtCreatePopupShell()`	`XtVaCreatePopupShell()`
`XtSetSubvalues()`	`XtVaSetSubvalues()`
`XtGetSubvalues()`	`XtVaGetSubvalues()`
`XtAppInitialize()`	`XtVaAppInitialize()`

2.5.1.1 Setting Resources with the Varargs Interfaces

The easiest way to set and get resources is to use the Xt functions `XtVaSetValues()` and `XtVaGetValues()`. Each of these functions takes a widget argument and a variable length list of resource name/value pairs, terminated by NULL. These interfaces are new to R4.

Note that the resource to set is called `XmNlabelString`, and its value must be a special type called a *compound string*, represented by a structure of type `XmString`. A single compound string can be multi-lingual, multiline, and multifont. A compound string contains a string, a character set, and a draw direction (left to right or right to left). The strings we specified in the app-defaults files for *xhello* and *xgoodbye* were automatically converted into compound strings by Xt. However, to set a string in the application code, we must do this conversion ourselves. This is done easily with the Motif function `XmStringCreate-Localized()`. (Motif also provides numerous other functions for manipulating compound strings.) `XmStringCreateLocalized()` replaces `XmStringCreate-Simple()` which was used in Motif 1.1. `XmStringCreateLocalized()` interprets its string argument in the user's locale (the user's language and culture, usually based on data from files defined by ANSI-C). Therefore, all strings should be read from the resource database or from files, not defined in the code. For simplicity, however, we have shown the strings defined in the code.

Example 2-5 shows the code needed to change the string of a Label widget—this will work any time after the widget has been created, either before or after the widget is realized.

Example 2-5. Using XtVaSetValues to set a widget resource

```
static String new_label = "Hi there."
XmString text;
    .
    .
    .
text = XmStringCreateLocalized(new_label);

XtVaSetValues(w,                            /* widget being modified */
        XmNlabelString, text,               /* resource setting */
        XmNalignment, XmALIGNMENT_END,      /* resource setting */
        NULL);                              /* terminate varargs list */

XmStringFree(text);
```

Introduction to Xt
and Motif

Note that a single `XtVaSetValues()` call can set any number of resources of a single widget instance. This example also changes the justification of the string (which by default is centered). (In order for justification to appear, the widget must be wider than the string being displayed. This can be arranged with the resource setting `*hello.width: 400`.)

The resource names used in the above example are `XmNalignment` and `XmNlabel-String`. The include file *<Xm/Xm.h>* contains these resource name symbolic constants. Resource names are actually strings. These strings are stored in symbolic constants to improve compile-time checking. If you misspell a symbolic constant, the compiler will note the error. If you misspell a string, on the other hand, the error will go unnoticed by the compiler and go unnoticed at run time as well, but the resource setting will do nothing. Therefore, all resource names are specified using constants of the form `XmNname`, where *name* is the resource name.

When you use a widget set other than Motif, you include *<X11/StringDefs.h>* instead of *<Xm/Xm.h>*. In *StringDefs.h* the same set of strings are given symbolic constants that begin with `XtN`. Motif has redefined these symbols just so that all its symbols and functions begin with `Xm`.

Also note that the value specified for each resource setting must be the type expected by the widget for that resource, or an error will occur. In this case, the type is `XmString`. If you were to attempt to pass a normal `char *` as the value, the widget would report the error at run time. In `XtVaSetValues()` calls (and `XtSetValues()` calls described in the next section), conversion from strings to the appropriate type does not happen automatically as it does for settings in resource files. However, you can arrange for it to happen by placing special arguments in the `XtVaSetValues()` call, as described in Section 3.8.2. (Note that this is a feature of the varargs interfaces that is not supported by the ArgList interfaces.)

NOTE

Don't set resources of type `float` using the `XtVaSetValues()` interface. On some systems `float` is widened to `double` (as specified in the Kernighan & Ritchie C manual). When this widening occurs, half the bytes are read by the Intrinsics as a `float`, and the next 4 as the string name of another resource. This can point into invalid memory, and cause a segmentation fault. Use `Xt-SetArg()` and `XtSetValues()` to avoid the problem. However, since the `value` field of the `Arg` is a `long` which may not be the same size as a `float`, use the following approach:

```
Arg arg;
union {
    int     int_value;
    float      float_value;
} value;

value.float_value = 3.2;
XtSetArg (arg, "name", value.int_value);
```

2.5.1.2 Setting Resources with the ArgList Interfaces

As mentioned above, the use of the ArgList interfaces is less elegant than the varargs interfaces just described, and ArgList interfaces lack the ability to use Xt's value conversion mechanism. However, the ArgList interfaces were the only interfaces until R4, and therefore are used in most existing applications. Example 2-6 shows how to set resources using `Xt-SetValues()`.

Example 2-6. Using XtSetValues to set a widget resource

```
Arg arg;
static String new_label = "Hi there."
XmString compound;
      .
      .
      .
compound = XmStringCreateLocalized(new_label);

XtSetArg(arg, XmNlabelString, compound);
XtSetValues(w, &arg, 1);

XmStringFree(compound);
```

The `Arg` type is defined as a structure containing the name and value pair that defines a resource:

```
typedef struct {
    String      name;
    XtArgVal    value;
} Arg, *ArgList;
```

The definition of `XtArgVal` differs depending on architecture—its purpose is precisely to make code portable between architectures with different byte sizes. Its use in application code is demonstrated in Section 3.8.2. All resource values (in all varargs and ArgList calls) are limited to the size of `XtArgVal`, which is the largest of `char *`, `caddr_t`, `long`, `int *`, and `proc *`. This means that for larger pieces of data, a pointer must be used. For example, data of type `float` or `double` must be passed as pointers. The documentation for a widget class that declares a resource with a large value should document the fact that a pointer must be passed rather than the value itself.

`XtSetArg()` is a macro that makes it more convenient to set the two members of the `Arg` structure. If desired, you can also set the `Arg` structure members like any other C structure by using the `.` or `->` syntax.

Note that the first member of `Arg` is of type `String`, but should be set to one of the `XmN` resource name constants.

`XtSetValues()` is the call that actually changes the widget resource. You pass it the widget to be reconfigured, a list of `Arg` structures, and the length of the list. Example 2-6 sets only one resource, so the list length is 1.

`XtSetValues()` can set any number of resources of a single widget instance. Example 2-7 shows the code necessary to set two resources. Compare this to Example 2-5 to see how much clearer the varargs interfaces are.

Example 2-7. Code fragment to set multiple resources of a widget

```
static String new_label = "Hi there."
XmString compound;
Arg args[3];
int i;
       .
       .
       .
compound = XmStringCreateLocalized(new_label);

i = 0;
XtSetArg(args[i], XmNalignment, XmALIGNMENT_END);   i++;
XtSetArg(args[i], XmNlabelString, compound);   i++;
XtSetValues(w, args, i);

XmStringFree(compound);
```

Note that the counter i cannot be incremented inside the **XtSetArg()** macro, because that macro references its first argument twice. Therefore, the counter is customarily incremented on the end of the same line, so that additional resource settings can easily be added.

2.5.1.3 Getting a Resource Value

It is also useful to be able to get the current value of a widget resource. One use of this is in finding out what value the user has specified for a particular resource, so that it can be modified with application data. Because C-Language arguments are passed by value, and some resource values are not actual values but pointers to them, it is important to thoroughly understand pointers while getting widget values. Example 2-8 shows how to get a pointer to the current string in a Label widget, using the varargs interface. This has to be done in two steps: first query the **XmNlabelString** resource to get the compound string, and then extract the character array from the compound string. Querying other resources is easier.

Example 2-8. Code fragment to get a widget resource using XtVaGetValues

```
#define MAXLEN 256
       .
       .
       .
    Widget hello;
    String p;            /* NOTE - memory for array not allocated */
    XmString      compound;
       .
       .
       .
    /* XmLabel widget named hello created here. */
    XtVaGetValues(hello,
            XmNlabelString, &compound,
            NULL);

    (void) XmStringGetLtoR(compound, XmFONTLIST_DEFAULT_TAG, &p);
    XmStringFree(compound);

    /* use string p */

    XtFree(p);
```

The type `String` is defined by Xt to be `char  *`. In the Athena widgets, a string queried from a resource must not be modified or freed by the application, since it points directly to private widget data. In Motif, the compound string returned from `XtVaGetValues()` (or `XtGetValues()`, of course) should be freed after use with `XmStringFree()` or `XtFree()` (they are equivalent), since Motif widgets pass a pointer to a copy of the resource value stored in the widget, not to a pointer to the widget's internal data.

Example 2-9 shows how to query a widget resource using the ArgList interface, `XtGetValues()`.

Example 2-9. Code fragment to get a widget resource using XtGetValues

```
#define MAXLEN 256
        .
        .
        .
    Widget hello;
    Arg arg;
    String p;      /* NOTE - memory for array not allocated */
    XmString compound;
        .
        .
        .
    /* Label widget named hello created here. */
    XtSetArg(arg, XmNlabelString, &compound);
    XtGetValues(hello, &arg, 1);

    (void) XmStringGetLtoR(compound, XmFONTLIST_DEFAULT_TAG, &p);
    XmStringFree(compound);

    /* use string p */

    XtFree(p);
```

Note, however, that some resources are not designed to be queried. For example, translation tables and callbacks are compiled into an internal representation, so it is pointless to try to read them.

2.5.2 Core Resources

The most basic widget class defined by Xt is Core. All widgets are subclasses of Core. Therefore, the resources of the Core class are available for all widgets. Table 2-2 shows the Core resources. Note that the resource name constants all begin with *Xm*. These constants are defined in the file *<Xm/Xm.h>*. In standard Xt, the resource name constants begin with *Xt*, and are defined in *<X11/StringDefs.h>*.

Table 2-2. Core Resources

Name	Type	Default
XmNx	Position	0
XmNy	Position	0
XmNwidth	Dimension	0
XmNheight	Dimension	0
XmNscreen	Pointer	from Display
XmNcolormap	Pointer	from parent
XmNdepth	int	from parent
XmNbackground	Pixel	White
XmNbackgroundPixmap	Pixmap	NULL
XmNborderWidth	Dimension	1
XmNborderColor	Pixel	Black
XmNborderPixmap	Pixmap	NULL
XmNtranslations	XtTranslations	NULL
XmNaccelerators	XtTranslations	NULL
XmNmappedWhenManaged	Boolean	True
XmNdestroyCallback	Pointer	NULL
XmNsensitive	Boolean	True
XmNancestorSensitive	Boolean	True

The fact that size and position are resources of all widgets means that your app-defaults file can control the layout of the application. You should always resize widgets by setting these resources—never resize or move a widget's window using Xlib calls since this would make Xt's knowledge of window geometries inaccurate. Nor should you use the Xt functions **Xt-ConfigureWidget()**, **XtMoveWidget()**, or **XtResizeWidget()** from the application. These routines are intended to be used only by geometry-managing composite widgets.

The **XmNscreen**, **XmNcolormap**, and **XmNdepth** resources hold the default screen, colormap, and depth (the number of bits per pixel used for indexing colors in the colormap). The top-level shell widget gets the screen from the DISPLAY environment variable or –*display* command-line option; other widgets inherit that value and cannot change it. The top-level shell widget gets the root window's depth, visual, and default colormap; other widgets inherit these attributes from their parent, so unless an intervening widget has set these attributes differently, a widget will inherit the root window's attributes by default. Normally you will set the depth, visual, and colormap resources only on Shell widgets and only when your application has special color requirements.

The **XmNbackground**, **XmNbackgroundPixmap**, **XmNborderWidth**, **XmNborderColor**, and **XmNborderPixmap** widget resources control the background and border of the window created by a widget. The background and border of a window are maintained by the X server, and setting these resources causes an immediate change in the window on the screen. You can set either a background color or a background pixmap, but not both. Whichever is set later takes priority. The same applies to the border. Details on the possible values to which these may be set are in Chapter 4 of Volume One, *Xlib Programming Manual*.

A *pixmap* is similar to a window but is off-screen. It is an array of pixels. When used as a background or border, a pixmap is *tiled* by laying out multiple copies of it side by side, for the purpose of patterning. Pixmaps are also used for icon patterns, in drawing, and as a temporary drawing surface later copied to a window.

The **XmNbackground** and **XmNborderColor** resources can be set using either a color name string or a hexadecimal color specification. (See Appendix B, *Specifying Fonts and Colors*, for more information on acceptable forms of color specification.)

The value of the **XmNbackgroundPixmap** and **XmNborderPixmap** resources should be a pathname to a file containing the bitmap, or to a bitmap created in your program. On UNIX systems, standard X bitmaps are stored in the directory */usr/include/X11/bitmaps*. See Appendix C in Volume Three, *X Window System User's Guide, Motif Edition*, for information on these standard bitmaps.

XmNtranslations is the resource that contains the translation table that maps events into actions. As is described exhaustively in Chapter 8, *Events, Translations, and Accelerators*, by setting this resource you can change the events that trigger a widget's actions or the actions your application has registered. **XmNaccelerators** contains an accelerator table. (Accelerators are an extended form of translations that allow events in one widget to be bound to actions in another.)

XmNmappedWhenManaged is a resource used by geometry-managing widgets to specify whether a widget should be eligible for display (i.e., mapped to the screen) as soon as it is placed under parental geometry management, or whether this should not happen until some later time. We'll talk more about this concept in Chapter 12, *Geometry Management*.

The **XmNdestroyCallback** resource, as mentioned in Section 2.4.1 above, lets you provide an application function to be called when a widget is destroyed. This is infrequently used, since the Toolkit normally handles the job of freeing widget data structures and any server resources.

The **XmNsensitive** resource controls whether a widget responds to user input. This allows you to turn on or off user input in a certain widget at will. For example, if you have a PushButton widget whose command is not allowed at certain times, you would set **XmNsensitive** to **False** during the period the command is not allowed. The PushButton widget changes its own look to indicate that it is invalid.

The **XmNancestorSensitive** resource specifies whether the widget's parent (or earlier ancestor) is sensitive. Sensitivity is automatically propagated downward, such that if any ancestor is insensitive, a widget is insensitive. This resource rarely needs to be set, but is sometimes useful to query.

2.5.3 Other Inherited Resources

Besides the resources inherited from Core, a widget inherits resources from each of its superclasses. For example, the PushButton widget used in *xgoodbye* inherits resources from its superclass, the Label widget class, and from Label's superclass, Primitive. As shown in Table 2-3, these include, in addition to the label itself, a font list, a foreground color, spacing above and below the string, and a value specifying how the string should be placed in the widget. (Note that there are many other resources not listed.)

Table 2-3. Label Resources

Name	Type	Default
XmNfontList	XmFontList*	the default font
XmNforeground	Pixel	XmForegroundColorDefault
XmNhighlightOnEnter	Boolean	False
XmNmarginHeight	Dimension	2 (pixels)
XmNmarginWidth	Dimension	2 (pixels)
XmNalignment	unsigned char	XmALIGNMENT_CENTER
XmNlabelString	XmString (compound)	NULL

It is a worthwhile exercise to experiment with the resources available to an application through its widgets, even with such a simple example as *xgoodbye*. For example, consider the resource settings for *goodbye* shown in Example 2-10.†

Example 2-10. Alternate resource settings for xgoodbye

```
! Core resources
!
! The following two lines don't work, but demonstrate a point
*goodbye.x: 100
*goodbye.y: 100
!
! Even though the following specification syntactically applies to
! all widgets in the application, and all windows have borders, the
! borderWidth resource value is only used by certain widgets.
! PushButton is not one of them, so this instruction is ignored.
!
*borderWidth: 10
!
*goodbye.width: 250
*goodbye.height: 100
*goodbye.alignment: XmALIGNMENT_END
!
! Label resources
!
*goodbye.foreground: red
*goodbye.fontList: *courier-bold*180*iso8859-1
*goodbye.labelString:  Click on me.
```

---

†See Appendix B, *Specifying Fonts and Colors*, for more information on the font resource specification shown in the example.

Note that an exclamation point (!) in column zero begins a comment line in a resource file. The number sign (#), the standard UNIX comment symbol, should not be used.

These settings can either be placed in an *.Xdefaults* file in your home directory, or you can save them in any file you like and load them into the server using the *xrdb* client, as follows:

```
xrdb -merge resource_file
```

(If you want to repeat the experiment with different values, you should be aware that once resources are set with *xrdb*, they remain in effect. Subsequent invocations of *xrdb -merge* will replace settings for the same resources, but won't remove any others that were set before. To start with a clean slate, use *xrdb -load* instead. Note, however, that this will replace *all* of your resource settings, including those for other applications. See Chapter 10, *Setting Resources*, of Volume Three, *X Window System User's Guide, Motif Edition*, for more information on using *xrdb*. See Chapter 10 of this book for more information on other possible sources of resource settings.)

The window that results when you run *xgoodbye* with these resource settings is shown in Figure 2-12.

Figure 2-12. xgoodbye run with new resource settings

If you spend some time playing with different resource settings, you will find some unexpected behavior. For instance, setting the value of the **x** and **y** resources has no effect. Regardless of their value, the *xgoodbye* application is simply placed at the current pointer position.

The reason for this is that these resources set the widget position relative to its parent, and since the **goodbye** widget is a child of an identically sized Shell widget, they are meaningless. In its geometry-management policy, the shell widget ignores the value of these resources.

If instead you use the **x** and **y** resources to try to set the position of the application:

```
xgoodbye.x:   100
xgoodbye.y:   100
```

they are ignored also, for a similar reason. It is customary for the window manager to assert control over the position of the main application window (in this case the Shell widget **goodbye**), and take the value of these resources, whether set by the application or by the user, simply as "hints" to the desired behavior. There is no guarantee that the window manager will honor these hints. The application is generally free to move widgets within its own window, but not to move itself. The basic X philosophy is that the user (through the window manager), not the application, should be in control. (Kill the window manager, or run a window manager that honors application position hints, and the resource specifications shown just above will work.)

Likewise, you will find that specifying:

```
*goodbye.borderWidth:   10
```

has no effect, while:

```
*borderWidth: 10
```

works. The reason for this behavior is that while the PushButton widget inherits the **borderWidth** resource from Core, it does nothing with its value. Only certain widget classes (Shells) use the **borderWidth** resource to set the border width of their window. Just because a resource is inherited by a widget does not mean that the widget's methods do anything to use its value.

Another surprising fact appears if you set the **foreground** resource to the same color as the background. No text appears in the window, and it does not highlight itself when you move the mouse inside. However, if you click a button, you will find that the widget is still working. What is happening is that the background and foreground colors are now both white, and therefore there is no contrast with which to see the widget's drawing. The widget is not sophisticated enough to check that its two colors are not the same. (Adding this simple check would be easy, but it is much more difficult to tell whether two colors that are not the same contrast enough.)

The cautionary point is that there may be unexpected interactions between resources in widget code. Like programs in general, widgets tend to do what you say, not what you mean. A well-designed widget will minimize ill effects, but given the amount of customization that is possible, it may take some time to uncover all the possible pitfalls. Unfortunately, the documentation for most existing widgets doesn't always do a good job of explaining how resources are used inside the widget.

2.6 Advice on X Programming

The X Window System is a very complex collection of software, not to try your patience, but to do things that no programming tools have done before. Not only does X provide tools to build a nice user interface, but it does so with network transparency, so that programs can run on any hardware and operating system and display on any other.

Probably the best feature of all from the application developer's point of view is the portability of the source between hardware and operating systems. It is worth a lot of aggravation to be able to write just one version of a piece of software, and have it able to compile and run on anything from a PC-compatible to a Cray.

The price you pay for these features is additional complexity. The key to programming X successfully is to keep things as simple as possible by keeping this complexity hidden.

By choosing to use Xt and Motif, you have taken a first step to isolate your application from the details of the lower levels of X software. In general, use the highest-level tools available. Use Motif functions instead of Xt functions when equivalents are available, and Xt functions instead of Xlib functions.

Also beware of configuring widgets too extensively. Every widget has many resources, and the number of possible permutations in even one widget makes it impossible for OSF to test them exhaustively. At the same time, programmers tend to abuse this flexibility by overly configuring widgets. Often developers try to make Motif applications work in a particular way that Motif's developers didn't intend or foresee. One way to avoid this problem is to make sure your intended interface conforms to the conventions specified in the *OSF/Motif Style Guide*.

Although Motif will undoubtedly be improved to support even more varied interfaces, this will take time, and there will always be features that Motif will not support without contortions. If you can compromise a little on the details of how your interface should work, you will be better off. With Motif, you can get 90 percent of what you want in a very short time. Think twice before spending lots of time trying to get the last 10 percent. First think if there is some other user interface design that can fulfill your needs while being more consistent with Motif style. If you still insist on having that functionality, think carefully about the best way to implement it (and consult with someone who knows X intimately, because such a decision may require an understanding of Motif, Xt, and the lower levels of X).

To be advised to compromise in this fashion may rub some programmers the wrong way. Most programmers program systems where they have total control over their environment. Many have the whole screen to play with, and worry about only one target system. In these environments, it is more practical to learn everything there is to know about the system, so that you can implement exactly what you want. Since X is a much larger piece of software than the operating system or toolbox of any one computer, it is less practical to obtain a complete understanding of every level of it. That's why it is better to use your creativity to design a good interface that can be implemented easily, using existing components in the ways they were designed to be used.

2.7 Debugging Xt Applications

Debugging Xt applications can be difficult because errors caused by your code can end up causing the program to abort somewhere deep in the Xt Intrinsics. There are, however, several techniques that can help.

One problem is that the standard error handlers exit so that you won't get a stack trace to tell you where the problem occurred. The workaround is to register your own Xlib and Xt error handlers that divide by zero after reporting the error (instead of exiting). See Chapter 14 for information on registering Xt error handlers, and Volume One, *Xlib Programming Manual* for Xlib error handlers.

If your application generates X protocol errors, then the problem is probably Xlib calls with improper arguments. Because of the asynchronous X protocol, the program will not exit at the error in the code. By running the application with the −sync command-line option, Xlib operates in synchronous mode and Xlib errors are reported immediately.

The *editres* application is useful for debugging widgets, testing resource settings, and for viewing the widget hierarchy of complex applications. The uses of the *editres* application are described in Chapter 14.

You are not normally allowed to see the data stored inside widget data structures. But you can view the data from a debugger if you specify the private header file for the widget in your source file. For example, instead of including *<Xm/Xm.h>* and *<Xm/XmPushB.h>* in *xhello.c*, we would include *<Xm/XmP.h>* and *<Xm/XmPushBP.h>*.

Finally, an integrated code development and debugging environment such as CodeCenter is invaluable in writing toolkit application and finding bugs in them.

3

More Techniques for Using Widgets

This chapter describes how to use some of the more complex widgets found in applications, including composite widgets, constraint widgets, and popups. It also describes how to define application resources and command-line options, and how to hardcode the value of widget resources when you create a widget.

In This Chapter:

3

More Techniques for Using Widgets

The techniques described in Chapter 2, *Introduction to the X Toolkit and Motif*, will get you started writing applications. But there are more tools at your disposal. This chapter describes the following techniques:

- How to use composite and constraint widgets to create a hierarchy of widgets in an application. This section describes how to use these different kinds of geometry-managing widgets so that the application can be resized and still look good. It also shows how to set resources for a widget hierarchy in the app-defaults file.

- How to build one style of application that conforms to the Motif style guide conventions.

- How to use popup widgets such as dialog boxes and menus.

- How to use callback lists (instead of single callback functions), and how to pass data to callback functions.

- How to make your applications easier for the user to customize by defining application-specific resources and command-line arguments.

- How to hardcode the value of resources when you create a widget.

- How and why you should use application contexts.

3.1 Using Composite Widgets

The examples in Chapter 2, *Introduction to the X Toolkit and Motif*, were atypical because they contained only one widget. Because any real application has several widgets, some way of laying them out is needed. This is tedious to do manually. Therefore, the first widget you create after calling `XtAppInitialize()` is usually a composite widget, whose job it is to manage the layout of a group of child widgets. The parent of this composite widget is the Shell widget created by `XtAppInitialize()`, usually called `topLevel`.

This chapter's first example is a small application, *xrowcolumn*, that creates two PushButton widgets contained in a RowColumn widget. Figure 3-1 shows how the application looks on the screen.

Example 3-1 shows the code that implements *xrowcolumn*.

Figure 3-1. xrowcolumn: appearance on the screen

Example 3-1. xrowcolumn.c: complete code

```
/*
 *  xrowcolumn.c - simple button box
 */

/*
 *  So that we can use fprintf:
 */
#include <stdio.h>

/*
 * Standard Motif include file:
 */
#include <Xm/Xm.h>

/*
 * Public include files for widgets used in this file.
 */
#include <Xm/RowColumn.h>
#include <Xm/PushB.h>

/*
 * quit button callback function
 */
/*ARGSUSED*/
void Quit(w, client_data, call_data)
Widget w;
XtPointer client_data, call_data;
{
    exit(0);
}

/*
 * "Press me!" button callback function
 */
/*ARGSUSED*/
void PressMe(w, client_data, call_data)
Widget w;
XtPointer client_data, call_data;
{
    fprintf(stderr, "Thank you!\n");
}

main(argc, argv)
int argc;
char **argv;
```

Example 3-1. xrowcolumn.c: complete code (continued)

```
{
    XtAppContext app_context;
    Widget rowColumn, quit, pressme, topLevel;

     XtSetLanguageProc(NULL, (XtLanguageProc)NULL, NULL);

    topLevel = XtVaAppInitialize(
            &app_context,         /* Application context */
            "XRowColumn1",        /* Application class */
            NULL, 0,              /* command line option list */
            &argc, argv,          /* command line args */
            NULL,                 /* for missing app-defaults file */
            NULL);                /* terminate varargs list */

    rowColumn = XtVaCreateManagedWidget(
            "rowColumn",              /* widget name */
            xmRowColumnWidgetClass,   /* widget class */
            topLevel,                 /* parent widget */
            NULL);                    /* terminate varargs list */

    quit = XtVaCreateManagedWidget(
            "quit",                   /* widget name */
            xmPushButtonWidgetClass,  /* widget class */
            rowColumn,                /* parent widget */
            NULL);                    /* terminate varargs list */

    pressme = XtVaCreateManagedWidget(
            "pressme",                /* widget name */
            xmPushButtonWidgetClass,  /* widget class */
            rowColumn,                /* parent widget */
            NULL);                    /* terminate varargs list */

    XtAddCallback(quit, XmNactivateCallback, Quit, 0);
    XtAddCallback(pressme, XmNactivateCallback, PressMe, 0);

    XtRealizeWidget(topLevel);

    XtAppMainLoop(app_context);
}
```

Example 3-1 creates a RowColumn widget called `rowColumn` as a child of `topLevel`, and then creates each PushButton widget as a child of `rowColumn`. Notice how the parent argument of each generation of widgets is used. Also notice that the Shell widget `topLevel` is exactly the same size as `rowColumn` and therefore is not visible.

Example 3-1 creates only two children of its RowColumn widget. If your application creates many children for a single widget, it may be preferable to create the children with `Xt-VaCreateWidget()`, and then manage all the children of that parent with a single call to `XtManageChildren()` (instead of calling `XtVaCreateManagedWidget()` for each child).†

---

† Just a reminder that all statements about functions such as `XtVaCreateWidget()` also apply to the other version of these same functions, such as `XtCreateWidget()`, unless specifically stated otherwise.

At the same time, if you are creating a lot of widgets, it pays to consider using gadgets instead of widgets. A *gadget* is a windowless widget, with somewhat reduced features. Motif provides gadget versions of many of its smaller, simpler widgets, such as PushButton. The gadget version of PushButton is PushButtonGadget. For the most part, gadgets are created and used just like widgets. Since a gadget has no window, it loads the server and the network less and can attain better performance. For example, one of the Motif demos, *xmfonts*, creates over 100 PushButtonGadgets as children of a single RowColumn widget. In that case, it definitely makes sense to use gadgets. Probably the most common use of gadgets in applications, though, is for the panes in menus. Therefore, we will reserve our major discussion of gadgets until Chapter 13, *Menus, Gadgets, and Cascaded Popups*.

3.1.1 Setting Resources for an Instance Hierarchy

You have already seen how an app-defaults file can set the string for a PushButton widget. However, *xrowcolumn* has an instance hierarchy that contains a RowColumn widget with two PushButton widgets as children. It is worth seeing how to set the PushButton widget labels in this new situation. (We will be returning often to the subject of setting resources, because it is so important to Toolkit programming. Each time, new ideas will be presented.)

Example 3-2 shows an app-defaults file for *xrowcolumn*.

Example 3-2. XRowColumn: app-defaults file

```
*pressme.labelString:      Press Me
*quit.labelString:         Quit
*XmPushButton.fontList:    variable
*XmRowColumn.background:   green4
```

When an application contains multiple widgets of the same class, resource specifications can either identify individual widget instances by name or can use wildcards or widget class names to reference more than one widget. The first two specifications in the example identify the `pressme` and `quit` widgets by instance name. The third specification uses the class name `PushButton` to set the font of both PushButton widgets in the application. This line shows that resources of groups of widgets can be set with a single line. The fourth specification uses the class name `RowColumn` to set the background of the RowColumn widget (but not the PushButton widgets) to the color green. Whenever you use a class name, it will match all widgets of that class in the application, even ones we add later in a later revision of the application.

By changing the period in the fourth specification to an asterisk, the specification will change the background color of not only all RowColumn widgets in the application, but also all their children, and their children, recursively. Remember from Chapter 2 that an asterisk matches zero or any number of intervening widget instance names or class names. In *xrowcolumn*, this setting will make the background of the RowColumn and PushButton widgets green. Try not to get careless with asterisks, though. They lead you to think you don't have to remember the instance hierarchy in your application, but this can backfire, because it is easy to set resources on more widgets than you realize.

Note that you need to know the instance name for each widget in the application in order to set its resources individually. This is true for all resource files, including the ones customized by the user. Therefore, in the documentation for your application, be sure to include the name and class of each widget in your instance hierarchy. To be thorough, also include a description of the resources of each class, and specify which resources the user can customize.

The first argument of each `XtVaCreateManagedWidget()` call is the widget instance name. This is the name used to set resources for this widget in the resource databases. Most programmers make the widget instance name the same as the variable name of type `Widget` that holds the widget ID. This lexical connection is not mandatory, but it is highly recommended because it reduces confusion by helping you to remember the connection between entries in the app-defaults file and the widget instances in the application.

3.1.2 Geometry Management in Practice

The purpose of geometry managing widgets is two-fold:

1. They take most of the tedium out of determining the initial positions of widgets.

2. They recalculate the positions of all the widgets when the user resizes the application, so that the application still looks good.

Build and run *xrowcolumn*, and then try resizing it to see how the RowColumn widget deals with various geometries. This is the default behavior of RowColumn—it can be customized with resources to use many different layout rules. Try adding the following resource settings to its app-defaults file, run it again, and try out its resizing characteristics.

```
*rowColumn.packing: XmPACK_TIGHT
*rowColumn.orientation: XmHORIZONTAL
```

Two of the resulting geometries are shown in Figure 3-2.

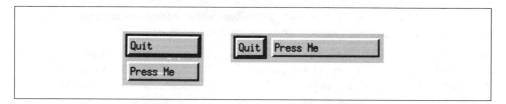

Figure 3-2. Two configurations of xrowcolumn

What happens if you use resource settings in the app-defaults file to directly set the size or position of a widget that is being managed by a geometry managing widget? Depending on the specific geometry managing widget, you may not get the desired effect. For example, trying to set the size of the PushButton widgets managed by RowColumn may not work. For example, if you added the resource setting `*pressme.height: 400`, it would have no effect on the height of the `pressme` widget unless `allowShellResize` is also set to *True* (if you are using mwm). This is because the RowColumn widget needs to ask its parent, the shell widget, to be resized, and this will be denied unless the window manager allows the shell to resize itself. However, it is possible to set things like geometries in the application code, as will be demonstrated later in this chapter.

Every widget's size and position is ultimately under the control of the window manager.† A RowColumn widget attempts to make itself just big enough to hold its children, using the resources provided by the application as a guide, but the window manager can override anything the widget or the application does.

What happens when the user resizes an application is only part of the picture. The application itself may need to resize one of its widgets in order to display more widgets. Or the application may tell a widget to display more data and the widget will have to ask its parent to be resized. For example, what happens when the application changes the string in one of the PushButton widgets while the application is displayed? The PushButton widget attempts to resize itself to display the current string, by asking its parent for permission.

Whether this request is granted depends on the position of the widget in the instance hierarchy, the resizing policy imposed by each composite widget in the hierarchy, and the window manager. This is because each widget, from the PushButton widget on up, negotiates with its parent when the PushButton widget requests a new size. The PushButton widget tries to change size to accommodate the new string (larger or smaller), and the RowColumn widget must approve this change. Since the RowColumn widget is already the same size as the Shell widget, RowColumn can't get any larger without asking Shell. The Shell widget is responsible for negotiating with the window manager.

The *mwm* window manager will allow applications to resize themselves only if the user has set the `allowShellResize` resource to `True`. (Some other window managers, such as *twm*, never allow it.) Otherwise, the RowColumn widget will reject the resize request unless the original change made the PushButton widget smaller. If the new size is rejected, the PushButton widget will still display the new string, but it may not show all of the string (if the new string is longer than the old one) or there may be extra space left over (if the old string was longer).

Fortunately, all this negotiation is done by the widgets themselves. The application doesn't need to do anything. However, you should be aware that any widget resource change that results in a widget size change may not work unless there is enough room in the application for the change to be granted without resizing the top-level window.

The RowColumn widget is Motif's most comprehensive and powerful geometry managing widget. It is widely used for managing groups of small widgets in many settings. (Some of these uses of RowColumn are under other names, such as CheckBox, PullDownMenu, and MenuBar.) However, it treats all its children the same, and therefore isn't appropriate for widgets of radically different geometries. Such situations make RowColumn's decisions about where to place the widgets inappropriate. Figure 3-3 shows the results upon resizing of a RowColumn widget that is attempting to manage two ScrollBar widgets and a BitmapEdit widget.‡

---

† BulletinBoard creates an exception to this rule. Since BulletinBoard never resizes its children, the window manager controls which of these children are visible, but does not resize them.

‡ The BitmapEdit widget is not part of the Motif widget set. It is used to build an application in Chapter 4, *An Example Application*, and written from scratch in Chapter 6, *Inside a Widget*, and Chapter 7, *Basic Widget Methods*.

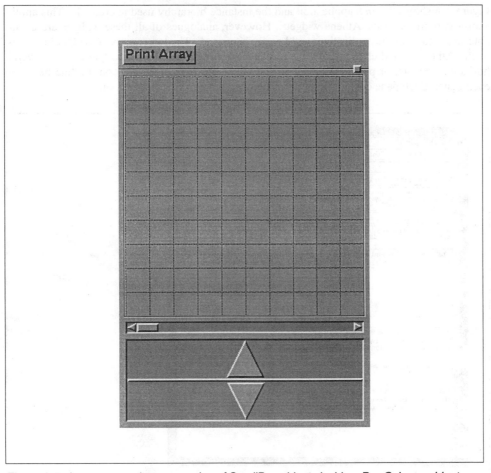

Figure 3-3. Incorrect results upon resize of ScrollBar widgets inside a RowColumn widget

Those two large triangles are actually ArrowButtons on the ends of a very wide but short ScrollBar! It might be possible to use the RowColumn resources to make this application look better, but it would be difficult to keep it good looking after resizing.

Because no single geometry managing widget can satisfy all needs, there are several different types of composite widgets in most widget sets, each with different rules about how it places children. Many widget sets, including Motif, have a widget specifically designed to place scrollbars next to a main window. In Motif, this widget is called ScrolledWindow.

Applications are not limited to using only one composite widget. It is quite common for the application's main window to be a large composite widget which contains several smaller composite widgets, each of which in turn contains certain groups of related widgets. You'll need to design the layout of widgets in your application, decide where in the instance hierarchy to place composite widgets, and experiment to find out which composite widgets provide the best appearance when the application is resized. The following application shows how several kinds of geometry managing widgets can be used together in an application.

Figure 3-4 shows the *xmh* application and the instance hierarchy used to create it. This application is built using the Athena widgets. However, analogues of all these widgets are available in Motif, and the application could easily be ported. The top composite widget in *xmh* is of the Athena Paned class (equivalent to PanedWindow). The Paned widget creates several horizontal panels, or panes, one for each child, with a sash positioned on the line between each pane. Each pane contains a different functional area of the application.

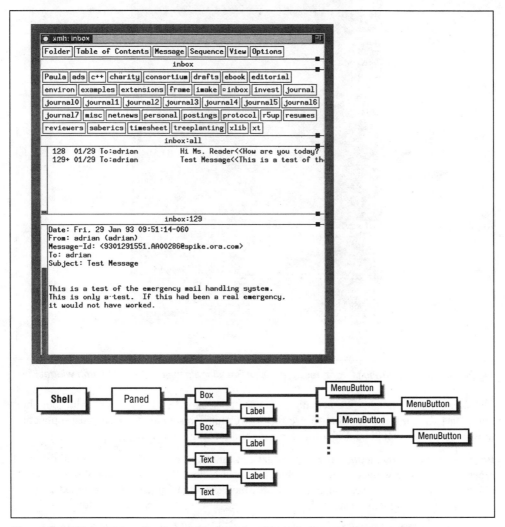

Figure 3-4. The xmh application and its instance hierarchy

- The top pane is a menubar (implemented with a Box widget, a simpler version of Row-Column) containing Athena MenuButton widgets (equivalent to CascadeButton).

- The next pane is a Label widget (equivalent to the Motif Label widget).

- The third pane is another Box widget containing Command widgets (equivalent to Push-Button). (Command and MenuButton widgets look the same, but do different things when clicked.)

- The fourth pane is another Label widget.

- The fifth pane is a geometry managing widget called a Viewport (equivalent to Scrolled-Window) containing a Text widget (equivalent to Text).

So, you see, there are three different kinds of geometry managing widgets in this application: Paned, Box, and Viewport. In a Motif port of this application, they would be PanedWindow, RowColumn, and ScrolledWindow.

Box and Viewport are relatively simple geometry managing widgets that are subclasses of the Composite class. The Paned widget is a more complex kind of geometry managing widget which is a subclass of the Constraint class. Both Composite and Constraint are basic classes defined by the Xt Intrinsics.

3.2 Using Constraint Widgets

Constraint widgets, like composite widgets, manage the layout of children. The difference is that constraint widgets let the application provide layout information for each child. This is a more powerful way to arrange children because it allows you to provide different rules for how each child will be laid out.

In an application, you create a constraint widget just as you would any other widget. But you don't just set resources of the constraint widget to specify how each child is laid out. You also set resources of each *child* of the constraint widget. Once any child widget is placed under the management of a constraint widget, the child suddenly has a special set of resources defined by the constraint widget, which controls its layout. As usual, these resources can be set from the app-defaults file, from any other resource database file, or in the application code.

We'll demonstrate how constraint widgets work by replacing the RowColumn widget in *xrowcolumn* (Example 3-1) with an Motif Form widget (a constraint widget). This example is called *xform* in the example source code. We won't show this code, because the differences from *xrowcolumn* are slight. The basic change is that all occurrences of `rowColumn` and `RowColumn` are changed to `form` and `Form`, respectively. The real difference between *xrowcolumn* and *xform* lies in the setting of resources.

The Form widget defines a number of constraint resources, which to the user appear to be resources of the child widgets managed by the Form. Looking at these resources gives you a good idea of the kinds of things that can be done with constraints.† Each edge of each child can be positioned in one of four ways. Different children can use different rules at the same time, and in fact different edges of the same child can be positioned using different rules.

---

† Note that even though the Motif Form widget and the Athena Form widget are both constraint widgets and have similar names, they have radically different constraint resources.

The following is a summary of what you can do with Form constraints. For details, see Volume Six, *Motif Programming Manual* because the complete behavior of Form is quite complicated.

For brevity, the following lists the various ways the left edge of a child can be positioned. You can substitute right, top, and bottom in any of the following.

1. Relative to one edge of the Form widget. To do this, you set the XmNleftAttachment to XmATTACH_FORM. This child edge will then be positioned the default distance from the same edge of the Form. You can specify a different distance from the edge of Form with the XmNleftPosition or XmNleftOffset resources. The latter is a fixed distance that won't change after resizing.

2. Relative to an edge of one of the other children. To do this, you set the XmNleft-Attachment to XmATTACH_WIDGET, and set XmNleftWidget to the Widget ID of the other child you want this child to be next to. XmNleftWidget can only be set in the application code, not in resource files.

3. To a percentage position within the Form widget (i.e., 50% would place the edge in the center of the Form widget, and upon resizing the edge would always be centered.) Set XmNleftAttachment to XmATTACH_POSITION, then set XmNleftPosition and XmNfractionBase so that XmNleftPosition / XmNfractionBase is the fraction of the width of the Form where the edge should be located.

4. To a percentage position established by the child's initial position within the Form widget. For example, if the application code initially positioned the child edge 20 pixels horizontally from the Form origin, and XmNfractionBase is set to 100 to represent the initial width of the Form, then the child edge will always be kept at 20% of the width of the Form. Set XmNleftAttachment to XmATTACH_SELF, then set Xm-NfractionBase so that the current XmNx position divided by XmNfractionBase is the fraction of the width of the Form where the edge should be located. The difference between XmATTACH_POSITION and XmATTACH_SELF is only that the former requires the setting of XmNleftPosition, while the latter takes the initial position directly from the child.

Note that the XmNresizable resource is a constraint that controls whether a child is allowed to resize itself, or be resized by the application. It does not affect whether the Form widget will resize that widget—Form is always allowed to resize any of its children.

The Form also has a number of normal resources (that are set on the Form, as opposed to constraint resources that are set on its children) that control default distances and so on. One of these is XmNrubberPositioning, which governs how unattached edges of children behave.

OSF in Motif 1.2 has made more Form constraints settable from the app-defaults file. In particular, they have added a String-To-Widget converter which allows the setting of resources such as XmNleftWidget. Testing and debugging constraints is much easier when done from resource files since you avoid recompiling every time a new combination of Form constraints is to be tried. Example 3-3 shows the resource settings in a resource file.

Example 3-3. XForm: app-defaults file

```
*quit.labelString:    Quit
*Command.background: orange

*pressme.labelString:     Press Me
*pressme.leftAttachment: XmATTACH_WIDGET
*pressme.leftWidget: quit
```

NOTE

Note that the order of creation of widgets affects the constraint resource settings that will position them. For the above resource file to work properly, `quit` must be created before `pressme`, because the resource setting `*pressme.left-Widget: quit` is evaluated when the `pressme` widget is created. Since this resource setting refers to `quit`, otherwise you will get the message:

`X Toolkit Warning: Cannot convert string "quit" to type Widget`

and the `pressme` widget will not be positioned properly.

Example 3-4 shows the resource settings in C code (*xform.c*) that position the two PushButton widgets within the Form. This technique for setting resources in code is described in Section 2.3.4. As we've said earlier, it's best not to set these in resource files instead of in the code, at least while the application is under development.

Example 3-4. xform: constraint resource settings added

```
}
    Widget quit, pressme;
      .
      .
    /* create quit widget here */
      .
    pressme = XtVaCreateManagedWidget("pressme", /* widget name */
            xmPushButtonWidgetClass,            /* widget class */
            form,                               /* parent widget */
            XmNleftAttachment, XmATTACH_WIDGET, /* resource setting */
            XmNleftWidget, quit,                /* resource setting */
            NULL);    /* terminate varargs list of resource settings */

    /* (Must not create quit here, or above resource setting will fail.) */
      .
      .
      .
}
```

Notice that since these are constraints, these resources are being set on the `quit` child of Form, but the Form will actually use this information. It is actually an instruction for the Form widget about where to place the `quit` widget relative to the `pressme` widget. The effect of this resource setting is shown in Figure 3-5. Note that both widgets referenced in a constraint must be child widgets of the same constraint widget, in this case the Form widget. If they are not, Form will print a message at run time.

If you run this program, you can compare its behavior on resize with the behavior of *xrowcolumn*, and you can experiment with different resource settings for the Form widget.

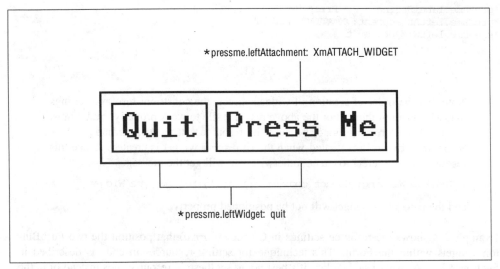

Figure 3-5. Effect of the Form's XmATTACH_WIDGET constraint resource

Both the Form and RowColumn widgets are able to resize the PushButton widgets in addition to or instead of moving them. In the Athena widget set there is a composite widget, Box, that moves but never resizes its children. Note that the difference between composite and constraint widgets is not their ability to resize children; it is that constraint widgets allow different layout rules for each child.

Without constraint settings, Form widgets pile up their children. This can also happen if you make an error in setting the constraints. Sometimes this can make it appear that one of the widgets has completely disappeared!

3.3 The Standard Motif Instance Hierarchy

Most Motif applications have a standard screen layout, which leads to a certain amount of boilerplate code in every application. This section describes that code. Figure 3-6 shows an example application, *xmainwindow*, which has this standard layout. Of course, in a real application the lower area would be more than an empty box.

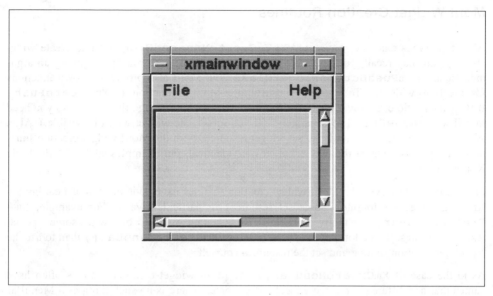

Figure 3-6. xmainwindow: an application with standard Motif screen layout

Customarily, the first widget created in a Motif application (after the one created by `XtApp-Initialize()`) is a MainWindow widget. A MainWindow is a geometry managing widget designed to manage a work area (often a custom window) with scrollbars, and optional menubar and Command widgets. In a drawing application, the drawing area would be the custom window, and MainWindow would automatically manage scrollbars that would allow the user to draw in an area larger than the application's total screen area. In our first example that includes a MainWindow, the work area will be simulated with a Frame widget, which is an empty box with a 3-D appearance.

Most Motif applications also have a menubar across the top of the main window. Visually, the menubar contains labels which indicate the titles of the menus available. In widget terms, each of these labels is a CascadeButton, which is similar to a PushButton except that CascadeButton is specifically designed to invoke a pulldown menu or dialog box instead of an application function. Two of the most common labels visible in a menubar are File and Help. The File button brings up a menu that includes the commands for reading and writing files, if any, and also the command to quit the application. According to the Motif style guide, the File button has the position at the far left in the menubar, and the Help button has the far right.† The Help button brings up a menu containing topics; selecting a topic brings up a dialog box which contains help text appropriate for the current situation.

A Command widget is another horizontal band across the application, just below the work area. A Command widget contains two windows, one that allows you to type in commands, and the other that shows you the history of prior commands. The Command widget is optional in a MainWindow and is less common than the menubar.

---

†The menubar and the File menu are common features of window-based graphical applications using other widget sets and other window systems, including the Macintosh.

Using Widgets

3.3.1 Motif Widget Creation Routines

All the previous examples have used `XtVaCreateManagedWidget()` to create widgets. As you may recall, you specify which type of widget you want by supplying an argument such as `xmPushButtonWidgetClass`. But Motif also provides its own functions for creating widgets. To create a PushButton, Motif's function is `XmCreatePushButton()`. Note, however, that Motif's function does not manage the widget, so you need to call `XtManageChild()` separately. (If you forget, the widget won't be visible.) Also, as you will see later, it is harder to set widget resources with the Motif widget creation functions. In the cases where the two techniques are identical, our examples stick with the basic Xt routine.†

In some cases, however, the Motif widget creation routines have code beyond just calling the Xt widget creation routine. Some set resources in particular ways. For example, `Xm-CreateMenuBar()` actually creates a RowColumn widget, but with some special resource settings. It is a lot more convenient to use `XmCreateMenuBar()` than to use the Xt widget creation routine and set the resources yourself.

As in the case of `XmCreateMenuBar()`, the Motif widget creation routines often have names that are different from the widgets they create. There is no such thing as a MenuBar widget. Remember this when you look up a widget's resources in the Motif reference manual. If you are unsure of the widget class, look on the page for the Motif widget creation function first.

Other Motif widget-creation functions actually create a combination of widgets. More will be said about this later.

3.3.2 Building a Main Window

With that introduction, we are ready to show you the code needed to implement a standard Motif MainWindow and its usual children. Example 3-4 shows a portion of *xmainwindow.c*, the code for implementing the application shown in Figure 3-6.

Example 3-4. xmainwindow.c: code for implementing standard Motif screen layout

```
/*
 *  xmainwindow.c - main window with help and quit
 */

/* Standard Motif include files: */
#include <Xm/Xm.h>
#include <Xm/RepType.h>

/*
 * Public header files for widgets used in this file.
 */
#include <Xm/MainW.h>          /* MainWindow */
#include <Xm/RowColumn.h>      /* for MenuBar (actually a RowColumn) */
```

---

†This is less verbose, less prone to error, and saves one function call.

```
#include <Xm/Frame.h>      /* Frame (simulated custom widget) */
#include <Xm/PushB.h>      /* PushButton (for menu buttons) */
#include <Xm/CascadeB.h>   /* CascadeButton (for menubar labels) */
#include <Xm/MessageB.h>   /* MessageBox dialog (for help) */

 /* callback functions defined here */

main(argc, argv)
int argc;
char **argv;
{
    XtAppContext app_context;
    Widget topLevel, mainWindow, menuBar, frame;
    Widget fileButton, fileMenu, quit, help, helpButton,
           helpMenu, helpBox;

    XtSetLanguageProc(NULL, (XtLanguageProc)NULL, NULL);

    topLevel = XtVaAppInitialize(
           &app_context,       /* Application context */
           "XMainWindow",      /* application class name */
           NULL, 0,            /* command line option list */
           &argc, argv,        /* command line args */
           NULL,               /* for missing app-defaults file */
           NULL);              /* terminate varargs list */

    /* create main window */
    mainWindow = XtVaCreateManagedWidget(
           "mainWindow",       /* widget name */
           xmMainWindowWidgetClass, /* widget class */
           topLevel,           /* parent widget */
           NULL);              /* terminate varargs list */

    /* register converter for setting tearoff menus from resource files */
    XmRepTypeInstallTearOffModelConverter();

    /* create menubar along top inside of main window */
    menuBar = XmCreateMenuBar(
           mainWindow, /* parent widget */
           "menuBar",  /* widget name */
           NULL,       /* no arguments needed */
           0);         /* no arguments needed */
    XtManageChild(menuBar);

    frame = XtVaCreateManagedWidget(
           "frame",            /* widget name */
           xmFrameWidgetClass, /* widget class */
           mainWindow,         /* parent widget */
           NULL);              /* terminate varargs list */

    /* Set MainWindow areas */
    XmMainWindowSetAreas (mainWindow, menuBar, NULL, NULL, NULL,
           frame);
       .
       .
       .
}
```

This code creates a MainWindow that contains two widgets: a menubar (which is actually a kind of RowColumn configured as a menubar via resources automatically set by the convenience function used to create the widget) and a Frame. Note that the *parent* arguments of functions that create the menubar and the Frame are both `mainWindow`.

We use `XtVaCreateManagedWidget()` to create the main window, but `XmCreate-MenuBar()` to create the menubar, for the reasons described above. Notice that widget name and widget parent arguments are in a different order in the two functions.

The menubar must be managed with a separate call to `XtManageChild()`, because `Xm-CreateMenuBar()` does not manage it.

`XmMainWindowSetAreas()` tells the main window which of its children should be treated as the menubar (placed across the top of the application), and which as the work area (at the bottom, with scrollbars if needed). The work area in this case is the Frame widget. The three unused arguments, here set to NULL, allow you to tell MainWindow which widget is the Command window, and which widgets are the scrollbars that will control the work area.

You might ask, why does MainWindow need to be told which widget is which, since it has access to its list of child widgets? This is done mainly for added flexibility, so that you can switch work areas or other children.

The purpose of the scrollbar arguments in `XmMainWindowSetAreas()` is a common point of confusion. MainWindow is a subclass of ScrolledWindow. That means that Main-Window has all the features of ScrolledWindow, plus more. Therefore, MainWindow automatically creates its own scrollbars and uses these scrollbars to control the work area. Why, then, should `XmMainWindowSetAreas()` allow you to tell MainWindow which scrollbars to use, when MainWindow already has its own scrollbars and knows how to use them? The answer is that in some cases an application wants to provide its own code to handle the callbacks that connect its scrollbars with its work region. In practically all cases, however, an application can use the scrollbars created automatically by MainWindow or ScrolledWindow, even if it wishes to manually connect those widgets with the work area.

A resource setting is necessary in order to make MainWindow display scrollbars and use them to control the custom window. Here is the portion of the *XMainWindow* app-defaults file that applies to the code shown so far:

```
! Set initial size of application
*XmMainWindow.width:  200
! Frame will be bigger that application, thus requiring scrollbars
*XmFrame.width:  300
*XmFrame.height:  300
! Make MainWindow display scrollbars and use them to
! pan around in the frame.
*XmMainWindow.scrollingPolicy:  XmAUTOMATIC
```

The remaining part of the boilerplate code in a standard Motif application is to build the File menu and Help button in the menubar, that you see in *xmainwindow*. This is described in the next section.

3.4 Using Popups

A *popup* is a widget that is displayed on the screen for short periods, instead of being permanently visible.

The two most common kinds of popup widgets are menus and dialog boxes. Menus are familiar to most people, but dialog boxes are less so. A dialog box is a box on the screen that contains a message, or asks for user input, or both. Sometimes a dialog box provides a way to get input that is needed only occasionally and therefore doesn't deserve a place in the permanently visible user interface. Fitting into this category is the Motif file selection box, which is commonly used as a dialog box. At other times, a dialog box requires immediate response by the user before the application can continue. For example, many applications that write files are capable of displaying a dialog box that says "Warning: file exists. Do you wish to overwrite?"

A menu becomes visible when the user presses a mouse button while the pointer is in one of the CascadeButtons in the menubar. It becomes invisible again once the user has selected an item from the menu, released the button outside the menu, or moved into another Cascade-Button in the menubar. Dialog boxes usually become visible either because a button such as Help was clicked on by the user, or because the program needs occasional user input that is best supplied through a temporary window instead of as a permanently visible part of the application user interface. Dialog boxes become invisible when the user clicks on the OK or Confirm button in the dialog box, or provides the input that the dialog box is requesting.

Popups are not a kind of widget, but rather a way of using widgets. Any widget can be used as a popup. However, some classes of widgets are more commonly used as popups, and Motif has simplified the interface by providing routines that not only create these widgets, but also prepare them for use as popups. For example, Motif provides `XmCreatePopup-Menu()` for creating an empty popup menu. Internally, this routine creates a special parent widget called an OverrideShell, and then creates a RowColumn widget inside it, with special resource settings. It is then your job to create widgets (or gadgets) to appear in the menu.

A Motif menubar, as described in Section 3.3, usually contains a File menu and a Help button that brings up a dialog box. We'll discuss creating the File menu first, and then the Help dialog box.

3.4.1 Creating a Basic Menu

Motif provides three different types of menu: Popup, Pulldown, and Option. Popup menus have no on-screen presence until you press a certain button or key-button combination while in a certain widget. Pulldown menus and Option menus have buttons on the screen—when you press the button the menu appears below (for Pulldown) or over (for Option) the button. Option menus remember the most recent previous selection. RadioBox and CheckBox can also be thought of as kinds of menus. The menus that are invoked from the menubar are Pulldown menus.

It's also worth mentioning that Motif 1.2 supports tear-off menus. This allows the user to move any menu which has its **XmNtearOffModel** resource set to **TEAR_OFF_ENABLED** from the location where it first appears anywhere on the screen, and semi-permanently post it there. This makes it quicker to use commonly-used menus (especially since the menus mnemonics—keyboard shortcuts—are only active while a menu is displayed.

The application can call **XmRepTypeInstallTearOffModelConverter()** to support setting of the **XmNtearOffModel** resource from resource files. This allows menus to be torn off and posted permanently.

Figure 3-7 shows *xmainwindow* with the File pulldown menu displayed. The techniques for creating all three types of menus are very similar, but we'll reserve discussion of the other types until Chapter 13, *Menus, Gadgets, and Cascaded Popups.*

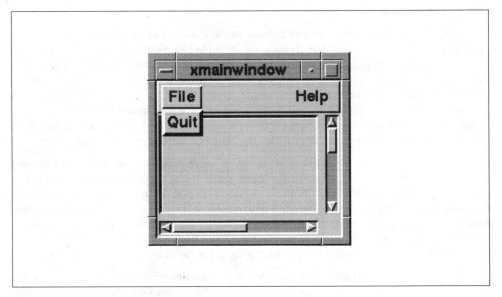

Figure 3-7. *xmainwindow with the File pulldown menu displayed*

Creating a pulldown menu is a four-step process:

1. Create a CascadeButton as a child of the menubar. This will be the button in which the user will click in order to pull down the menu.

2. Create an empty menu with **XmCreatePulldownMenu()** as a child of the menubar. This actually creates a RowColumn with certain resource settings.

3. Create PushButtons or PushButtonGadgets for each menu item, as children of the pull-down menu.

4. Tell the CascadeButton that just created the ID of the menu, it should pop up. This can't be done until step 2 is done.

In Motif, the RowColumn widget created by `XmCreatePulldownMenu()` is called a menu *pane*, and the buttons contained by that menu are called menu *items*.

This process sets up the popup widget, but does not put it on the screen. Somewhere in your code you need to call `XtManageChild()` to pop up the widget. This is typically done in the `XmNactivateCallback` callback routine of the CascadeButton. Motif takes care of popping down the menu at the appropriate times according to its conventions.

Example 3-5 shows the code needed to add a File menu containing only a quit button to an existing menubar.

Example 3-5. Adding a File menu to an existing menubar

```
/*
 * quit button callback function
 */
/*ARGSUSED*/
void Quit(w, client_data, call_data)
Widget w;
XtPointer client_data, call_data;
{
    exit(0);
}

main(argc, argv)
int argc;
char **argv;
{
    Widget fileMenu, fileButton, quit;
        .
        .
        .
    /*
     *  CREATE FILE MENU AND CHILDREN
     */

    /* create the File button in the menubar */
    fileButton = XtVaCreateManagedWidget(
            "fileButton",                   /* widget name */
            xmCascadeButtonWidgetClass,     /* widget class */
            menuBar,                        /* parent widget */
            NULL);                          /* terminate varargs list */

    /* create menu (really a Shell widget
     * and RowColumn widget combo) */
    fileMenu = XmCreatePulldownMenu(
            menuBar,                        /* parent widget */
            "fileMenu",                     /* widget name */
            NULL,                           /* no argument list needed */
            0);                             /* no argument list needed */

    /* Notice that fileMenu is intentionally NOT managed here */

    /* create button in menu that exits application */
    quit = XtVaCreateManagedWidget(
            "quit",                         /* widget name */
            xmPushButtonWidgetClass,        /* widget class */
            fileMenu,                       /* parent widget */
            NULL);                          /* terminate varargs list */
```

Example 3-5. Adding a File menu to an existing menubar (continued)

```
    /*
     * Specify which menu the fileButton will pop up.
     */
    XtVaSetValues(fileButton,
            XmNsubMenuId, fileMenu,
            NULL);

    /* arrange for quit button to call function that exits. */
    XtAddCallback(quit, XmNactivateCallback, Quit, 0);
        .
        .
        .
}
```

This code sample exactly matches the four steps listed above for creating a menu. First it creates the button that pops up the menu, followed by the menu pane itself, followed by a button that will appear in the menu. Finally, it tells `fileButton` that it should pop up `fileMenu` whenever activated.

There are several important things to remember about this example. Note that `fileMenu` is not managed after it is created, unlike the widgets in all previous examples. Motif itself will manage the widget when it comes time to pop it up. Also note how, by setting the `XmNsub-MenuId` resource, we connect the `fileButton` widget with `fileMenu`. Finally, note that both `fileButton` and `fileMenu` are children of the menubar, while `quit` is a child of `fileMenu`. This instance hierarchy is important.

3.4.2 Creating a Basic Dialog Box

Motif has even more different types of dialog boxes than it has menus. Luckily, they are also more uniform in the way they are created! This section will demonstrate creating a dialog box to provide help. Chapter 13, *Menus, Gadgets, and Cascaded Popups*, describes the variations in how to use other types of Motif dialog boxes. Figure 3-8 shows *xmainwindow* with the Help dialog box displayed.

This dialog box is a MessageBox widget. Motif doesn't provide a dialog widget that is ideal for providing help, since MessageBox provides Help buttons and Cancel buttons that are normally not needed in Help dialog boxes.

A Help button is created just like the `fileButton` in the previous example. It is a CascadeButton created as a child of the menubar. The dialog box that will contain the text is created with `XmCreateMessageDialog()`.

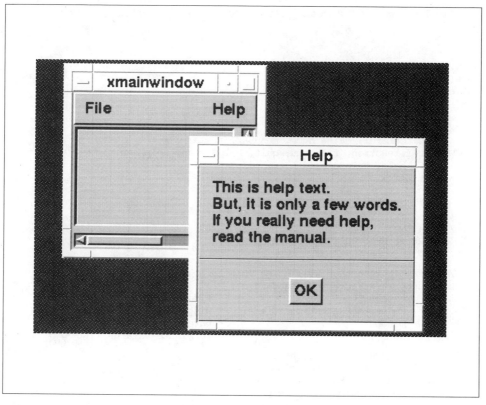

Figure 3-8. xmainwindow with the Help dialog box displayed

Example 3-6 shows the code required to add a Help button and dialog box to *xmainwindow*. Note that the OSF/Motif Style Guide specifies that the menubar can contain only menus. Therefore, we cannot just put a help button on the menubar. Instead, we need to create a help menu, and then put the help button on the menu. In a real application, the help menu might list various topics for which help is available.

Example 3-6. xmainwindow: creating a Help button and Help dialog box

```
    .
    .
    .
/*
 * callback to pop up help dialog widget (or any other dialog)
 */
/*ARGSUSED*/
void ShowHelp(w, client_data, call_data)
Widget w;
XtPointer client_data;
XtPointer call_data;
{
    Widget dialog = (Widget) client_data;
    XtManageChild(dialog);
}
```

```
        .
        .
        .

main(argc, argv)
int argc;
char **argv;
{
    XtAppContext app_context;
    Widget topLevel, mainWindow, menuBar, frame;
    Widget fileButton, fileMenu, quit, helpButton, helpMenu,
            help, helpBox;
    Widget temp;
        .
        .
        .
    /*
     *  CREATE HELP BUTTON AND BOX
     */

    /* create button that will bring up help popup */
    helpButton = XtVaCreateManagedWidget(
            "helpButton",                  /* widget name */
            xmCascadeButtonWidgetClass,    /* widget class */
            menuBar,                       /* parent widget */
            NULL);                         /* terminate varargs list */

    /* tell menuBar which is the Help button
     * (will be specially positioned. */
    XtVaSetValues(menuBar,
            XmNmenuHelpWidget, helpButton,
            NULL);

    /* create menu (really a Shell widget with a RowColumn child) */
    helpMenu = XmCreatePulldownMenu(
            menuBar,    /* parent widget */
            "helpMenu", /* widget name */
            NULL,       /* terminate argument list (none needed) */
            0);         /* terminate argument list (none needed) */

    /* create help button in the menu */
    help = XtVaCreateManagedWidget(
            "helpMenu"  /* widget name */
            XmPushButtonWidgetClass,  /* widget name */<
            helpMenu,     /* parent widget */
            NULL);        /* terminate argument list (none needed) */

    /* Specify which menu helpButton will pop up */
    XtVaSetValues(helpButton,
            XmNsubMenuId, helpMenu,
            NULL);

    /* create popup that will contain help */
    helpBox = XmCreateMessageDialog(
            help,     /* parent widget */
            "helpBox", /* widget name */
            NULL,      /* no arguments needed */
            0);        /* no arguments needed */
```

```
    temp = XmMessageBoxGetChild (helpBox, XmDIALOG_CANCEL_BUTTON);
    XtUnmanageChild (temp);
    temp = XmMessageBoxGetChild (helpBox, XmDIALOG_HELP_BUTTON);
    XtUnmanageChild (temp);

    /* arrange for help button to pop up helpBox */
    XtAddCallback(help,            /* widget that takes user input */
            XmNactivateCallback, /* callback resource */
            ShowHelp,            /* callback function */
                                 /* data passed as client_data
                                  * to callback function */
        .
        .
        .
}
```

As shown in Example 3-6, the first step in creating a Help feature is to create a Cascade-Button widget as a child of the menubar. Then, you set the **XmNmenuHelpWidget** resource of the menubar to tell the menubar that this particular CascadeButton is the Help button. This is necessary because the menubar treats the Help button specially; it is a Motif convention that the Help button appears at the extreme right of the menubar. Third, you create the dialog box with **XmCreateMessageDialog()**. Finally, you register a callback function, here called **ShowHelp**, with the CascadeButton widget. **ShowHelp** simply calls **XtManageChild()** to put the dialog widget on the screen. (If you have several dialog widgets, they can all share this callback function because it doesn't have any code that depends on any particular type of dialog widget.)

If you get a run-time error that says "Error: Attempt to manage a child when parent is not Composite," it may mean that you have used **XmCreateMessageBox()** instead of **Xm-CreateMessageDialog()**. **XmCreateMessageBox()** creates a widget with the same appearance, but it does not create the Shell widget parent that allows the message box to be used as a popup. This can also happen with file selection boxes, radio boxes, selection boxes, and check boxes.

The parent of the dialog box can be any widget in the application, since it is only used to determine on which screen to create the dialog. However, it is useful to use some consistent system of parenting, to make it easier to keep track of the purpose of each dialog. In this case, the parent is the CascadeButton widget that pops up the dialog, **getHelp**.

XmCreateMessageDialog() actually creates two widgets for you, an OverrideShell and a MessageBox as its child. The OverrideShell handles communication with the window manager, and the MessageBox displays the help text and creates the OK button that pops down the dialog. By default, a MessageBox (and most Motif dialogs) contains three buttons, that read by default OK, Cancel, and Help. Since we are providing help, we have no need for the Cancel and Help buttons. Unfortunately, Motif does not provide a dialog widget with just the OK button. But it is easy enough to take the Cancel and Help widgets off the dialog by unmanaging them. We get their IDs with the Motif function **XmMessageBoxGet-Child()**, and then unmanage them with **XtUnmanageChild()**. The MessageBox widget then automatically centers the OK button.

Note that the help text is not specified anywhere in the application code. At least until the application is final, it can be specified in the app-defaults file. Example 3-7 shows this portion of the app-defaults file for *xmainwindow*.

Example 3-7. XMainWindow: setting help text in the app-defaults file

```
*helpBox.messageString:  This is help text.\n\
But it is only a few words.\n\
If you really need help,\n\
I'm afraid you'll have to read the manual.
! The following used if the window manager titles the dialog.
*helpBox.dialogTitle:  Help
```

By ending lines with \n\, you can use a multi-line string as a resource value.

3.4.3 Popup Window Hierarchy

You may notice that dialog boxes can extend outside the application. This is because their Shell widgets are child windows of the root window, not the top-level window of the application, no matter which widget you supply as parent. By default in Xt, a child of the root is positioned at the top-left corner of the screen. However, Motif automatically positions most menus and dialog boxes in a suitable location in or over the application before popping them up. Dialog boxes or menus that are not triggered by a mouse button press, though, need to be positioned by the application. How to do this will be described in Chapter 13, *Menus, Gadgets, and Cascaded Popups*.

Figure 3-9 shows the widget instance hierarchy of *xmainwindow*, and its X window hierarchy. Note that the only difference between the two is the parentage of the dialog and menu widgets.

Note that when you create a PulldownMenu, you are actually creating a Shell widget with the menu as its child. The same is true of MessageDialog. Each separate window hierarchy has a shell widget at the top.

If you have a popup widget that might never be used, or whose characteristics are not known until just before it is popped up, you can create the popup shell and widget just before popping it up, in the callback function or action that pops up the widget. This technique makes the startup time of the application marginally faster, but slows the pop up time the first time the popup is used.

Popups, and menus in particular, will be described in much more detail in Chapter 13, *Menus, Gadgets, and Cascaded Popups*.

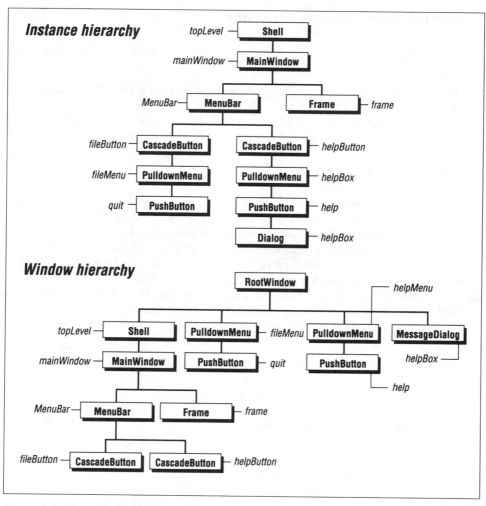

Figure 3-9. The widget instance and X window hierarchies are different only for popups

3.5 More About Callbacks

As you may recall, a callback is a function that your application wants called in response to a certain occurrence in a certain widget. The application simply declares the callback function and then calls `XtAddCallback()`. While Chapter 2, *Introduction to the X Toolkit and Motif*, discussed the concept of callbacks and demonstrated the most common use, it did not completely describe all the useful tricks. You can pass application data to callback functions. You can arrange for more than one callback function to be called (in a particular order) when the callback is triggered, and add and remove functions from this list at will. You can declare callbacks statically using a callback list instead of calling `XtAddCallback()` or `Xt-AddCallbacks()`.

3.5.1 Passing Data to Callback Functions

A callback function is called with three arguments: *widget*, *client_data*, and *call_data*.

The *widget* argument is necessary if you have registered the same callback function for two widgets, and you need to know which widget called the function. It also may be used in routine ways, such as for the argument of macros. The application determines the use of *client_data*, whereas the widget determines the use of *call_data*.

3.5.1.1 The client_data Argument

You may pass a single piece of data as the *client_data* argument, or pass a pointer to a structure containing several pieces of data. You may ask, "Why bother with passing data to a callback when I can just declare a global variable?" For one thing, it is a general principle of good C coding to use a global variable only where the variable is needed in several functions and the arguments would otherwise prove unwieldy. Secondly, using the *client_data* argument makes clear the purpose of your variable, whereas it is difficult to trace where a global variable is set or referenced. However, if you find it necessary to change the *client_data* argument in a number of functions in the application, you will need a global variable anyway, and there is nothing that says you must use *client_data* (but be sure to document what you are doing!).

Example 3-8 demonstrates how to pass a single piece of data into a callback function.

Example 3-8. Passing a single value to a callback function

```
/*ARGSUSED*/
void PressMe(w, client_data, call_data)
Widget w;
XtPointer client_data, call_data;
{
    fprintf(stderr, "%s\n", client_data);
}

main(argc, argv)
int argc;
char **argv;
{
    Widget pressme;
      .
      .
    /* XtAppInitialize, create pressme widget */
      .
      .
    /* last argument is client_data */
    XtAddCallback(pressme, XmNactivateCallback, PressMe, "Thanks");
      .
      .
}
```

Example 3-9 demonstrates passing a pointer to a structure into a callback function. `Xt-Pointer` is a generic pointer type with an implementation-dependent definition. It is used just like the standard C-type `caddr_t`.

Example 3-9. Passing a pointer to a structure to a callback function

```
typedef struct {
    String name;
    String street;
    String city;
} app_stuff;

/*ARGSUSED*/
void PressMe(w, client_data, call_data)
Widget w;
XtPointer client_data;    /* to be cast to app_stuff */
XtPointer call_data;
{
    /* cast required in ANSI C */
    app_stuff *address = (app_stuff) client_data;

    fprintf(stderr, "%s\n%s\n%s\n", address->name, address->street,
            address->city);
}
main(argc, argv)
int argc;
char **argv;
{
    XtAppContext app_context;
    Widget box, quit, pressme, topLevel;

    static app_stuff stuff = {
        "John Doe",
        "1776 Constitution Way",
        "Philadelphia, PA 01029"
    };
        .
        .
        .
    /* XtVaAppInitialize, create pressme widget */
        .
        .
    XtAddCallback(pressme, XmNactivateCallback, PressMe, &stuff);
        .
        .
}
```

Note that two coding conventions are required by ANSI C and should be followed, even though many compilers will not complain if they are not used. The first is that all three arguments of the callback must be declared, even if the trailing ones are not used. Many compilers will work fine if unused trailing arguments are omitted from the definition of the callback function. The second is that many compilers will automatically cast `XtPointer` to the type you want if you declare the callback function arguments using that type. The cast on the first line of the `PressMe` callback is required by ANSI C. Example 3-10 shows a definition of the above callback function that works on many compilers but is not ANSI C conformant. Compare Example 3-10 with Example 3-9.

Example 3-10. ANSI non-conformant callback function definition

```
/*ARGSUSED*/
void PressMe(w, address /* call_data omitted */)
Widget w;
app_stuff *address;       /* ANSI non-conformant cast */
/* third arg omitted - ANSI non-conformant */
{
    fprintf(stderr, "%s\n%s\n%s\n", address->name, address->street,
            address->city);
}
```

3.5.1.2 The call_data Argument

The *call_data* argument is passed in to the callback function from the widget itself. This argument's value is described in the documentation for the widget class unless it is not used. In the Motif widgets, this argument is usually a structure named after the widget that is performing the callback. For example, the structure passed by the PushButton widget is **Xm-PushButtonCallbackStruct**. Example 3-11 shows this structure.

Example 3-11. The XmPushButtonCallbackStruct structure

```
typedef struct {
    int     reason;
    XEvent  *event;
    int     click_count;
} XmPushButtonCallbackStruct;
```

Every Motif callback structure contains **reason** and **event** fields. Remember that widgets often have several callback resources. The **reason** field tells you which callback resource was triggered. For example, the PushButton widget has three callback resources, each of which has a different **reason** value:

* **XmNactivateCallback**, a commonly used resource, triggered when the user presses and releases the first mouse button on the PushButton. The callback function invoked is passed a **call_data** structure with the **reason** field set to **XmCR_ACTIVATE**.

* **XmNarmCallback** resource, which is triggered when the first mouse button is pressed and held on the PushButton. The callback function invoked is passed a **call_data** structure with the **reason** field set to **XmCR_ARM**.

* **XmNdisarmCallback** resource, which is triggered when the first mouse button is released outside the PushButton. The callback function invoked is passed a **call_data** structure with the **reason** field set to **XmCR_DISARM**.

Application callback functions rarely have to read the **reason** field since separate functions are usually registered for the different callback resources. In other words, an application that registers callback functions for all three of PushButton's callback resources would not need to use the **reason** field in any of the callback functions unless it registered the same function for two or more of the callbacks.

Most callback functions don't use the `event` field passed to the callback function either, but it is potentially useful, since it contains a lot of data about the user event that triggered the callback. If a button press or release triggered the callback, this event structure will be an `XButtonEvent` structure. This structure can be passed to `XmMenuPosition()` to position a menu created with `XmCreatePopupMenu()`, as will be described in Chapter 13, *Menus, Gadgets, and Cascaded Popups*. If the triggering event was a key press or release, an `XKeyEvent` would be passed. In some cases it may be useful to process this event to determine which key was pressed. Remember that due to Motif's keyboard interface, most callback functions can be invoked by either a keyboard or a mouse command. When this is the case, your callback function must be written so that it can handle either type of event.

Other widget sets do not use the *call_data* argument as heavily as Motif. For example, the Athena Widgets rarely use it at all.

3.5.2 Callback Lists

You may register any number of callback functions for a single widget callback resource. In other words, when a callback is triggered by a user event, all the functions in the current callback list for that callback for that widget instance will be called, one at a time. Multiple callback functions are not needed in many applications, but can be useful if applied carefully.

There is no guarantee that the functions on a callback list will be called in the specified order. Therefore, each callback function must be independent of all other callback functions on the list. This dramatically reduces the usefulness of multiple callback functions.

Remember that most widgets also have more than one callback list, each triggered by a different occurrence. What we are talking about here is that you can register a series of functions to be called in response to one occurrence.

Let's take an example of how a callback list might be used. Perhaps you have the functions A, B, and C, and you need to be able to call them separately in response to events in three different PushButton widgets, or to call all of them in response to events in a fourth PushButton widget. How should we structure the callback for the fourth PushButton widget? The first approach is to have a callback list including the functions A, B, and C. This is preferred if A, B, and C can be called in any order, since you can pass a different piece of data into each routine. The other approach is to register a single callback, function D, that calls A, B, and C. In this case you are assured that A, B, and C will be called in the desired order.

You can also call the same function more than once in a callback list.

NOTE

Never use `XtRemoveAllCallbacks()`. Widget sets such as Motif add their own callback functions to many of the widgets, and depend on these functions to operate properly.

One way to add more than one callback function is to call **XtAddCallback()** more than once. Another way is to call **XtAddCallbacks()**, which takes an **XtCallbackRec** array as an argument. This array is usually initialized at compile time, as shown in Example 3-12. The final **NULL, NULL** entry terminates the list. (This particular list registers the functions **do_A** and **then_B**, and passes them both 0 as *client_data*.)

Example 3-12. Initializing a callback list

```
XtCallbackRec quit_callback_list[ ]={
    {do_A, 0},
    {then_B, 0},
    {(XtCallbackProc) NULL, (XtPointer) NULL}
};
```

This form of **XtCallbackRec** list can also be used to replace a callback list with **XtSet-Values()** (but not to *get* a callback list, because Xt compiles the list into an internal form). An **XtCallbackRec** list can also be used to register one or more callbacks when creating a widget.

3.6 Application Resources

You already know that widgets declare resources that can be configured through the resource mechanism. In addition, the application itself may have variables that it wants the user to be able to configure from the resource databases, even though these variables have nothing to do with widgets. These are called *application resources*.

Application resources are just like widget resources except that they apply to application code, not to the widgets it creates.

There are three steps for adding application resources. You must:

1. Create an application data structure containing the variables to be set via the resource mechanism.

2. Create a resource table defining the type and default value for each variable.

3. Call **XtGetApplicationResources()** with pointers to the application data structure and resource table as arguments. When this function returns, the application data structure will contain the current settings from the resource databases.

To demonstrate how to get application resources, we will jump ahead and describe a portion of the code for the *xbitmap4* bitmap editor example described in Chapter 4, *An Example Application*. Because this application draws into a widget using Xlib, it needs two colors with which to draw. The bitmap editor also allows the user to specify the dimensions of the bitmap in cells, and the size of each cell in pixels. And, for general utility, it includes a debug flag that can be set in a resource file to invoke or ignore debugging code without recompiling.

3.6.1 The Application Data Structure

The structure type that contains all the application variables to be set through resources is commonly called **AppData**. Once this structure type is declared, memory can be allocated for a structure called **app_data**. Example 3-13 shows the code that defines the structure type and then allocates memory for the actual structure.

Example 3-13. xbitmap: getting application resources

```
typedef struct {
    Pixel copy_fg;
    Pixel copy_bg;
    int pixmap_width_in_cells;
    int pixmap_height_in_cells;
    int cell_size_in_pixels;
    Boolean debug;
} AppData;

AppData app_data;
```

As usual in C, the members of the **app_data** structure will be referenced throughout the application code using the dot format. For example, the value of the **debug** field of **app_data** will be referenced with **app_data.debug**.

3.6.2 The Resource List

The resource list looks complicated, but it is easy to understand and even easier to write because it conforms to a consistent pattern. Each field in the application data structure has an entry in the resource list. Each resource entry in turn has seven fields, which describe the name of the resource, its type and default value, and various other information.

The resource list controls Xt's value conversion facilities. Since user resources are always strings, and application data structure fields can be any type, a conversion may have to take place. Xt has built-in converters to convert from string to most common types needed by applications. These types are called *representation types* by Xt, and they are indicated by constants starting with **XmR** in Motif, or **XtR** in standard Xt. The representation type of a string (**char ***) is **XmRString**. A Motif compound string is **XmRXmString**. You control the conversion simply by specifying a resource as a certain representation type in the resource list.

It is possible to represent the same value in several different representation types. For example, a color may be represented as an ASCII color name such as "blue," as a structure containing Red, Green, and Blue values, or as a pixel value (an index into a colormap). Also note that a representation type is different from a C-Language type. It is also possible for two different representations of something to both use the same C-Language type. For example, two hypothetical representation types might be **XtRInch** and **XtRMeter**. Both represent distances and both would probably be integers or floating point numbers, but each would have a different value for the same distance.

Using Widgets

See Chapter 10, *Resource Management and Type Conversion*, for a description of the standard representation types, as well as information on how to write your own converter routine.

Example 3-14 shows the resource list for *xbitmap4*, followed by a description of each of the fields in each entry.

Example 3-14. The resource list for xbitmap4

```
/*
 * The following could be placed in a "xbitmap.h" file.
 */
#define XtNdebug "debug"
#define XtCDebug "Debug"
#define XtNpixmapWidthInCells "pixmapWidthInCells"
#define XtCPixmapWidthInCells "PixmapWidthInCells"
#define XtNpixmapHeightInCells "pixmapHeightInCells"
#define XtCPixmapHeightInCells "PixmapHeightInCells"
#define XtNcellSizeInPixels "cellSizeInPixels"
#define XtCCellSizeInPixels "CellSizeInPixels"

static XtResource resources[ ] = {
    {
        XtNforeground,
        XtCForeground,
        XtRPixel,
        sizeof(Pixel),
        XtOffsetOf(AppData, copy_fg),
        XtRString,
        XtDefaultForeground
    },
    {
        XtNbackground,
        XtCBackground,
        XtRPixel,
        sizeof(Pixel),
        XtOffsetOf(AppData, copy_bg),
        XtRString,
        XtDefaultBackground
    },
    {
        XtNpixmapWidthInCells,
        XtCPixmapWidthInCells,
        XtRInt,
        sizeof(int),
        XtOffsetOf(AppData, pixmap_width_in_cells),
        XtRImmediate,
        (XtPointer) 32,
    },
    {
        XtNpixmapHeightInCells,
        XtCPixmapHeightInCells,
        XtRInt,
        sizeof(int),
        XtOffsetOf(AppData, pixmap_height_in_cells),
        XtRImmediate,
        (XtPointer) 32,
    },
```

Example 3-14. The resource list for xbitmap4 (continued)

```
    {
        XtNcellSizeInPixels,
        XtCCellSizeInPixels,
        XtRInt,
        sizeof(int),
        XtOffsetOf(AppData, cell_size_in_pixels),
        XtRImmediate,
        (XtPointer) 30,
    },
    {
        XtNdebug,
        XtCDebug,
        XtRBoolean,
        sizeof(Boolean),
        XtOffsetOf(AppData, debug),
        XtRImmediate,
        (XtPointer) False,
    },
};
```

A resource list entry has the following fields:

- The first two fields of each entry are the name and class of the resource; both strings. These are specified as symbolic constants to improve compile-time checking, and should be selected from *<Xm/Xm.h>* if any there have an appropriate name, or they can be defined in your application's own include file. For the debug resource entry, the resource name and class strings would be "debug" and "Debug", respectively defined in the application's include file as `XtNdebug` and `XtCDebug`. Note that in this case we have chosen to spell the symbols `XtN` instead of `XmN`. This is just to highlight the fact that these are not built-in Motif symbols. You can use `XtN`, `XmN`, or your own prefix.

- The third field is the representation type. A representation type is a symbolic constant, beginning with `XtR` or `XmR`, that defines the data type of a resource. Because user resource specifications are always in the form of strings while the actual resources may be of any type, Xt uses resource converters to convert the string representation to the actual target type. If necessary, you can define your own representation type in your application include file, but you will also have to provide Xt with a way to convert from string to this type with a type converter function, as described in Chapter 10, *Resource Management and Type Conversion*. Table 3-1 lists the correspondence between some of the representation types defined in *<Xm/Xm.h>* and actual C data types and structures.

- The fourth field, the size of the representation, is specified using the C macro `sizeof` with the actual C type as an argument. For example, when the representation type is `XmRBoolean`, the size field is `sizeof(Boolean)`.

- The fifth field identifies the place in your application's data structure where Xt is to place the converted value. In Example 3-15, the structure is called `AppData`. This field for the debug resource entry is specified using the `XtOffsetOf()` macro as `XtOffsetOf(AppData, debug)`. Note that the field name in the application data structure is often the same as the resource name, except with all word transitions marked with an underscore instead of a capital letter.

- The sixth field specifies the representation type of the default value (the seventh field). Xt has routines for converting data between types. They are used to translate strings from the resource databases into certain representation types. Therefore, you can specify the default value as a string (among other things) and if the default value is needed Xt will convert it to the representation type you specified in field three. If the representation type in field three is not standard in Xt or Motif, you will have to write the conversion routine that converts from **XmRString** to that representation, as described in Chapter 10, *Resource Management and Type Conversion*. You can also use the special constant **XmRImmediate** here, which indicates that the value in field seven can be used without conversion. Using **XmRImmediate** should lead to faster startup.

- The seventh field is the default value, using the representation type specified in field six. This default value will be set into the application data structure field if there is no setting for this resource in the resource database.

Table 3-1 lists Motif and standard Xt resource types and the C data types they represent.

Table 3-1. Motif Resource Type Strings

Motif Resource Type	Standard Xt Resource Type	Data Type
XmRAcceleratorTable	XtRAcceleratorTable	XtAccelerators
XmRBoolean	XtRBoolean	Boolean
XmRBool	XtRBool	Bool
XmRCallback	XtRCallback	XtCallbackList
XmRColor	XtRColor	XColor
XmRCursor	XtRCursor	Cursor
XmRDimension	XtRDimension	Dimension
XmRDisplay	XtRDisplay	Display*
XmRFile	XtRFile	FILE*
XmRFloat	XtRFloat	float
XmRFont	XtRFont	Font
XmRFontStruct	XtRFontStruct	XFontStruct*
XmRFunction	XtRFunction	(*)()
XmRInt	XtRInt	int
XmRPixel	XtRPixel	Pixel
XmRPixmap	XtRPixmap	Pixmap
XmRPointer	XtRPointer	XtPointer
XmRPosition	XtRPosition	Position
XmRShort	XtRShort	short
XmRString	XtRString	char*
XmRTranslationTable	XtRTranslationTable	XtTranslations
XmRUnsignedChar	XtRUnsignedChar	unsigned char
XmRWidget	XtRWidget	Widget
XmRWindow	XtRWindow	Window
XmRXmString		XmString

3.6.3 Getting the Resources

Once the application data structure and resource list are set up, you pass pointers to them to `XtGetApplicationResources()`, just after calling `XtAppInitialize()`. `XtGetApplicationResources()` will search the databases for any matching resource settings and set the fields in the application data structure.

The last requirement is that you check the values specified by the user to make sure they are acceptable. Example 3-15 shows these two steps from *xbitmap4*.

Example 3-15. Calling XtGetApplicationResources and checking values

```
        .
        .
        .
AppData app_data;
        .
        .
        .
main(argc, argv)
int argc;
char *argv[ ];
{
    XtAppContext app_context;
    Widget toplevel, vpane, buttonbox, quit, output;
        .
        .
        .

    /* call XtAppInitialize here */

    XtVaGetApplicationResources(toplevel,
            &app_data,
            resources,
            XtNumber(resources),
            /* varargs list here for making
             * application resources
             * non-user-configurable */
            NULL);          /* terminate varargs list */
    /*
     * We must check the application resource values here.
     * Otherwise, user could supply out of range values.
     * Conversion routines do this automatically, so
     * colors are already checked.
     */
    if ((app_data.pixmap_width_in_cells > MAXBITMAPWIDTH) ||
            (app_data.pixmap_width_in_cells < MINBITMAPWIDTH) ||
            (app_data.pixmap_height_in_cells > MAXBITMAPHEIGHT) ||
            (app_data.pixmap_height_in_cells < MINBITMAPHEIGHT)) {
        fprintf(stderr, "xbitmap: error in resource settings:",
                "bitmap dimension must be between %d and %d cells\n",
                MINBITMAPWIDTH, MAXBITMAPHEIGHT);
        exit(1);
    }

    if ((app_data.cell_size_in_pixels < MINCELLSIZE) ||
```

```
            (app_data.cell_size_in_pixels > MAXCELLSIZE)) {
        fprintf(stderr, "xbitmap: error in resource settings:",
                "cell size must be between %d and %d pixels\n",
                MINCELLSIZE, MAXCELLSIZE);
        exit(1);
    }
    .
    .
    .
}
```

Because Xt automatically converts the user's color specifications (such as "blue") into the form required by X, it warns the user when an unknown color is specified.† Therefore, your code doesn't need to check this kind of validity for values that Xt or Motif converts. However, you may need to check for other kinds of validity of the same values. For example, you may wish to check that two colors are not the same by comparing values after conversion. In this case, only the bitmap dimensions and cell size are checked, since they are critical to the application's operation.

3.7 Command-line Options

You already know that Xt automatically customizes widgets according to the resource database, but this is not the whole story. Users often expect command-line arguments for the most important aspects of an application. By default, **XtAppInitialize()** understands only a minimal set of command-line arguments; more need to be added so that application resources and certain widget resources can be set from the command line.

There is no point, however, in trying to make every widget resource settable from the command line, because that's the purpose of the resource database. You should concentrate on the resources that the user is most likely to want to have different between two simultaneous instances of the application (since it is difficult to arrange this with the resource database).

Before describing how to define your own command-line arguments, we need to describe what command-line arguments **XtAppInitialize()** already handles.

---

†That is, if the resource in a database file is specified properly, but the value is not, Xt will warn the user. However, if the resource is not specified properly, Xt has no way of knowing that the resource was intended to specify a color, and therefore, no message will be issued. For example, "*background: grein" will elicit a warning message because grein is an unknown color, but "*background: green" will not, because the resource identifier is unknown. Unknown resource identifiers are simply ignored, because they could apply to some other widget or even some other application.

3.7.1 Standard Command-line Options

First of all, `XtAppInitialize()` recognizes the *–xrm* option for setting any widget or application resource. For example:

```
spike% xhello —xrm '*background: blue'
```

This command-line argument sets all widget resources and application resources that are named background to blue. This option style is awkward. Not only is it long, but *csh* users must quote the string with right-handed single quotes so that the asterisk (*) is not interpreted by the shell.

`XtAppInitialize()` also understands some command-line options that were considered so basic that they should be the same for all applications. The above *–xrm* command line can be replaced by:

```
spike% xhello —background blue
```

or:

```
spike% xhello —bg blue
```

`XtAppInitialize()` also understands any unique abbreviation of an option name, such as:

```
spike% xhello —backg blue
```

These resources will work with any application written using the X Toolkit—with any widget set. Try the command line above if you have a color screen. If not, try specifying a different font, using the *–fn* or *–font* option.

Table 3-2 lists the complete set of standard options.† Resources starting with a dot rather than an asterisk indicate that that option affects only the application's top-level Shell.

Table 3-2. Standard Command-line Parameters

Option	Resource	Value	Sets
–bg	`*background`	Next argument	Background color
–background	`*background`	Next argument	Background color
–bd	`*borderColor`	Next argument	Border color
–bw	`.borderWidth`	Next argument	Width of border in pixels
–borderwidth	`.borderWidth`	Next argument	Width of border in pixels
–bordercolor	`*borderColor`	Next argument	Color of border
–display	`.display`	Next argument	Server to use
–fg	`*foreground`	Next argument	Foreground color
–fn	`*font`	Next argument	Font name

†There is no legitimate way for the application to access this parse table, which is necessary to show the user an error in a parameter. Furthermore, this table is in the source for Xt and therefore not available online to some Toolkit users. However, this parse table is not expected to change radically in new releases. Therefore it can probably be safely copied from this document into application code to provide a synopsis of valid options, if desired. Most current applications simply say "This application understands all standard X Toolkit command-line options."

Using Widgets

Table 3-2. Standard Command-line Parameters (continued)

Option	Resource	Value	Sets
`−font`	`*font`	Next argument	Font name
`−foreground`	`*foreground`	Next argument	Foreground color
`−geometry`	`.geometry`	Next argument	Size and position
`−iconic`	`.iconic`	"on"	Start as an icon
`−name`	`.name`	Next argument	Name of application
`−reverse`	`*reverseVideo`	"on"	Reverse video
`−rv`	`*reverseVideo`	"on"	Reverse video
`+rv`	`*reverseVideo`	"off"	No Reverse Video
`−selectionTimeout`	`.selectionTimeout`	Null	Selection timeout
`−synchronous`	`*synchronous`	"on"	Synchronous debug mode
`+synchronous`	`*synchronous`	"off"	Synchronous debug mode
`−title`	`.title`	Next argument	Title of application
`−xrm`	value of argument	Next argument	Depends on argument

Note that many of these command-line options set the resource of every widget in the application to the same value. A few of them set the resources only of the application's top-level Shell widget.

Also note that there is no standard command-line option for the **XtNfontSet** resource (new in R5). You must use −xrm to set this on the command line.

3.7.2 Defining Your Own Command-line Options

Supplying your own command-line options allows you to simplify the customization of your application. It also allows the user to customize things that are difficult with the resource database (such as setting different values for the same resource in two instances of the application).

You make **XtAppInitialize()** understand additional command-line options by initializing a **XrmOptionDescRec** structure (called the *options table*) and passing it as an argument to **XtAppInitialize()**. Example 3-16 shows the code that implements command-line options for the application resources added in Example 3-14.

Example 3-16. xbitmap: specifying command-line options

```
/* include files, etc. */
    .
    .
    .
#define MINBITMAPWIDTH   2
#define MAXBITMAPWIDTH   1000
#define MINBITMAPHEIGHT   2
#define MAXBITMAPHEIGHT   1000
#define MINCELLSIZE   4
#define MAXCELLSIZE   100
```

Example 3-16. xbitmap: specifying command-line options (continued)

```
static XrmOptionDescRec options[ ] = {
    {"-pw",            "*pixmapWidthInCells",   XrmoptionSepArg, NULL},
    {"-pixmapwidth",   "*pixmapWidthInCells",   XrmoptionSepArg, NULL},
    {"-ph",            "*pixmapHeightInCells",  XrmoptionSepArg, NULL},
    {"-pixmapheight",  "*pixmapHeightInCells",  XrmoptionSepArg, NULL},
    {"-cellsize",      "*cellSizeInPixels",     XrmoptionSepArg, NULL},
    {"-fg",            "*foreground",           XrmoptionSepArg, NULL},
    {"-foreground",    "*foreground",           XrmoptionSepArg, NULL},
    {"-debug",         "*debug",                XrmoptionNoArg, "True"},
};

static void Syntax(argc, argv)
int argc;
char * argv[ ];
{
    int i;
    static int errs = False;

    /* first argument is program name - skip that */
    for (i = 1; i < argc; i++) {
        if (!errs++) /* do first time through */
            fprintf(stderr, "xbitmap4: command line option unknown:\n");

        fprintf(stderr, "option: %s\n", argv[i]);
    }

    fprintf(stderr, "xbitmap understands all standard Xt\
        command-line options.\n");

    fprintf(stderr,"Additional options are as follows:\n");
    fprintf(stderr,"Option          Valid Range\n");
    fprintf(stderr,"-pw             MINBITMAPWIDTH to\
        MAXBITMAPWIDTH\n");
    fprintf(stderr,"-pixmapwidth    MINBITMAPWIDTH to\
        MAXBITMAPWIDTH\n");
    fprintf(stderr,"-ph             MINBITMAPHEIGHT to\
        MAXBITMAPHEIGHT\n");
    fprintf(stderr,"-pixmapheight MINBITMAPHEIGHT to\
        MAXBITMAPHEIGHT\n");
    fprintf(stderr,"-cellsize       MINCELLSIZE to\
        MAXCELLSIZE\n");
    fprintf(stderr,"-fg             color name\n");
    fprintf(stderr,"-foreground     color name\n");
    fprintf(stderr,"-debug          no value necessary\n");
}

main(argc, argv)
int argc;
char *argv[ ];
{
    XtAppContext app_context;
    Widget toplevel, vpane, buttonbox, quit, output;
        .
        .
        .
    toplevel = XtVaAppInitialize(&app_context;
        "XBitmap4",
```

Using Widgets

Example 3-16. xbitmap: specifying command-line options (continued)

```
            options,              /* command line option table */
            XtNumber(options),
            &argc,
            argv,

            NULL,
            NULL);

    /* XtVaAppInitialize always leaves at least prog name in args */
    if (argc > 1)
        Syntax(argc, argv);
        .
        .
        .

}
```

Each options table entry consists of four fields:

- The option to be searched for on the command line. As with standard command-line options, Xt will automatically accept any unique abbreviation of the option specified here. For example, the option *–pixmapWidthInPixels* will be recognized if typed on the command line as *–pixmapW*. However, if you wanted the option *–pw* to set the same resource, then you would need another entry, since **pw** is not the leading string of **pixmapWidthInPixels**.

- The resource specification. This must identify a widget resource or an application resource, but not provide a value. Since it has the same form as allowed in the resource databases, it may apply to a single widget or to many widgets. If it applies to no widgets, no error message will be issued.

- The argument style. This field is one of seven constants describing how the option is to be interpreted. These constants are described below in Table 3-3.

- The value. This field is the value to be used for the resource if the argument style is **XrmOptionNoArg**. This field is not used otherwise. Note that this value must already be converted to the value expected for the resource (often not a string). You may be able to use Xt's type converter routines explicitly to convert this data to the right type (see Section 10.3.5).

The **enum** constants that specify the various command-line argument styles are as shown in Table 3-3.

Table 3-3. XrmOptionKind: Command-line Option Style Constants

Constant	Meaning
XrmoptionNoArg	Take the value in the **value** field of the options table. For example, this is used for Boolean fields, where the option might be *–debug* and the default value **False**.
XrmoptionIsArg	The flag itself is the value without any additional information. For example, if the option were *–on*, the value would be "on." This constant is infrequently used, because the desired value such as "on" is usually not descriptive enough when used as an option (*–on*).
XrmoptionStickyArg	The value is the characters immediately following the option with no white space intervening. This is the style of arguments for some UNIX utilities such as *uucico* where *–sventure* means to call system *venture*.
XrmoptionSepArg	The next item after the white space after this flag is the value. For example, *–fg blue* would indicate that "blue" is the value for the resource specified by *–fg*.
XrmoptionResArg	The resource name and its value are the next argument in *argv* after the white space after this flag. For example, the flag might be: **–res 'basecalc*background:white';** then the resource name/value pair would be used as is. This form is rarely used because it is equivalent to *–xrm*, and because the C shell requires that special characters such as * be quoted.
XrmoptionSkipNArgs	Ignore this option and the next N arguments in *argv*, where N is the value in the last field of this option table entry.
XrmoptionSkipArg	Ignore this option and the next argument in *argv*.
XrmoptionSkipLine	Ignore this option and the rest of *argv*.

Using Widgets

The options table is passed to **XtAppInitialize()** as its third argument, and the number of options table entries as the fourth. The **XtNumber()** macro is a convenient way to count the number of entries (this is only one of many contexts in which you'll see this macro used).

Note that you *cannot* override the standard options by providing options with the same names in your own parsing table. If you try this, your options with the same names will simply not be set to the values specified on the command line. Instead, the standard options will be set to these values. This was a design decision in Xt, one of the few cases where a user-interface policy is enforced. Uniformity in this basic area was deemed more valuable than flexibility.

Also note that there is no way to instruct Xt to interpret more than one argument format for the same option. For example, you cannot arrange for *–size 3* and *–size3* both to work.

`XtAppInitialize()` removes all the arguments it recognizes (including those in your options table) from *argv* and *argc*. If all goes well, only the application name will remain in *argv*, and *argc* will equal one. It is important to check whether there is more than one argument left after `XtAppInitialize()` has returned. Command-line options that `XtAppInitialize()` doesn't recognize will be left in *argv* and *argc*. This is your chance to catch this error and tell the user.† The **Syntax** function shown in Example 3-16 demonstrates code that informs the user of the proper syntax and the option that was not understood. (In response to incorrect command-line options, UNIX programs traditionally print only the correct calling sequence. However, you can be even nicer to the user by printing the option or options that were in error, by passing *argv* and *argc* into your **Syntax** function, as is done in Example 3-16.

Experienced UNIX programmers will note that Xt applications can (but usually don't) use the single-letter command-line arguments mandated by POSIX and the System V Interface Definition. As mentioned earlier, Xt automatically matches any unique abbreviation for any command-line option. For example, by default the *–display* option can be specified as *–d*, but only if you haven't included any other option in the options table that also begins with d. You can define the meaning of single-letter options simply by including them verbatim in the options table. In other words, if you specify that *–d* turns on a debugging resource, Xt will no longer try to match any other, longer option that also begins with *d*.

Note that the *argc* and *argv* arguments of `XtAppInitialize()` are in the same order as in the call to **main**. This is the opposite order of arrays and array lengths throughout other Motif, Xt and Xlib routine calls. Also note that the address of *argc*, not *argc* itself, is passed to `XtAppInitialize()`. This is so that `XtAppInitialize()` can decrement the count to reflect recognized options. Watch out for these snags.

---

†You can, of course, intentionally treat the arguments remaining after `XtAppInitialize()` as filenames or other pieces of data.

3.8 Preventing User Customization of Widget Resources

Although user customization is good to a certain degree, some resources need to be hard-coded to make sure that an application will run properly regardless of user configuration. This is particularly true of widget geometry resources and constraints. For example, it is easy to make a mistake with Form widget constraints such that some important widget is hidden behind others.

You prevent user customization of particular resources by setting them in the calls to `Xt-VaCreateManagedWidget()` or `XtCreateManagedWidget()`, using a varargs list or an argument list as was shown in `XtVaSetValues()` and `XtSetValues()` calls in Section 7.4. When you use a Motif widget creation function such as `XmCreateMenu-Bar()`, the easiest way to hardcode that widget's resources is to follow the creation call with a call to `XtVaSetValues()`. This section will review those techniques and show a few more tricks.

When resources are set in the calls to create widgets, the application can still modify these resources any time later using `XtVaSetValues()` or `XtSetValues()`. Therefore, this is hardcoding only from the user's perspective. Also note that Xt will not tell the user that you have hardcoded certain resources—your application documentation should do this.

The time to hardcode widget resources is when development of an application is almost finished, because until then the resource settings are still in flux and it is quicker to edit the app-defaults file than it is to recompile the application.

Motif itself prevents user customization of certain resources, because it does not allow them to be set from resource files.† These resources must be set in the code if they are to be set at all. This is unfortunate because these resource settings can't be debugged in the usual way, by modifying the app-defaults files or using *editres* (see Chapter 14). This leads to time-consuming recompilation.

Selecting which resources to hardcode is something we can't help you with, because there isn't enough experience to go on yet. Some application developers will hardcode almost everything, while others will hardcode almost nothing. Only time will tell where the proper balance lies. For example, there is a tradeoff between hardcoding strings such as "Quit" so that the user can't change them, and setting them in the app-defaults file so that they can be easily changed for operation in a different language.

3.8.1 Using the Varargs Interfaces

Setting widget resources in `XtVaCreateManagedWidget()` is the cleanest and most powerful way to do it. You have already seen the style of call shown in Example 3-17, but pay particular attention to the `XtVaTypedArg` entry. This example also shows the special technique required to set a Motif compound string in the code.

---

†Unfortunately, exactly which Motif resources can't be set from resource files is poorly documented. One sure sign is when Motif prints an error message telling you that there is no converter for that resource.

Example 3-17. The R4 varargs interface to creating a widget

```
main(argc, argv)
int argc;
char **argv;
{
    XtAppContext app_context;
    Widget topLevel, layout, quit;
    XmString text;
       .
       .
       .
    layout = XtVaCreateManagedWidget("layout", formWidgetClass,
            topLevel, NULL);

    text = XmStringCreateLtoR("Quit", XmFONTLIST_DEFAULT_TAG);

    quit = XtVaCreateManagedWidget("quit", xmPushButtonWidgetClass,
            topLevel,
            XmNwidth, 200,
            XtVaTypedArg,       XmNbackground,
            XmRString,          "red", strlen("red")+1,  /* cont'd */
            XmNsensitivity,     True,
            XmNlabelString,     text,
            NULL);

    XmStringFree(text);
       .
       .
       .
}
```

The standard varargs list entry is a resource name/value pair. The value must be already converted into the type required for that resource (documented on the widget's reference page). **XtVaTypedArg** (not **Xm . . .**) is a special symbol used just before a resource name, which, when encountered, indicates that the next four arguments specify a resource that needs to be converted.† In Example 3-17, the value "red" needs to be converted into a pixel value, which is the index to the colormap register that contains the correct RGB values to display on the screen. The argument **XmNbackground** is the resource to be set. **Xm-RString** is the type of the value to be converted. The final two arguments are the pointer to the value (or the pointer to the pointer to the value if not a string) and the size of the value pointed to in bytes. **XtVaTypedArg** can be used to convert any string that is valid in a resource file but is otherwise difficult to set in the source file. But don't use **XtVaTyped-Arg** unnecessarily, since it adds overhead.

The varargs interfaces will also accept an arglist as one item in the list, using the symbol **Xt-VaNestedList** as the resource name. **XtVaNestedList** allows you to create one argument list and pass it to a series of widget creation routines, instead of listing all the same resource settings in each widget creation routine. For more details on this, see Chapter 10, *Resource Management and Type Conversion*.

---

†Note that **XtVaTypedArg** does not begin with **Xm**. It is a symbol defined by Xt.

There is some extra overhead involved in using the varargs interfaces because they massage the arguments into an argument list and call `XtCreateWidget()`, `XtCreate-ManagedWidget()`, `XtSetValues()`, or `XtGetValues()`. However, the added convenience seems worth it. Furthermore, the `XtVaTypedArg` feature is not supported in the ArgList style of call (described in the next section).

Unless you use the `XtVaTypedArg` feature, no diagnostic is printed when you specify a resource value incorrectly in the argument list. Therefore, make sure you specify the resource values correctly, and recognize this as a possible place to begin looking for bugs. (This is another reason to hardcode resources only when the application is almost ready for release. If you do it all at once in a methodical fashion, you are less likely to make mistakes than if you are always adding, subtracting, and changing values in the argument lists.)

NOTE

If you use the varargs style of arguments, but forget to type the Va in the function name, you can get various types of errors. If you specify resources in the call, you will get a core dump at run time, but you can detect the problem with *lint*, which will note the function as having a variable number of arguments. If you don't specify resources in the call, the application will run but you will get the message:

```
Warning: argument count > 0 on NULL argument list
```

3.8.2 Using the Argument List Interfaces

Widget resources can also be hardcoded by creating an argument list containing the resources to be set and their values, and passing it to `XtCreateManagedWidget()`. This method of setting resources is less convenient that the varargs technique just described, but it was the only way until R4, and therefore many existing applications use it.

An *argument list* is just an array of `Arg` structures, of the same type as you set up to call `Xt-SetValues()` or `XtGetValues()`. Once set, this array is used as an argument to `Xt-CreateManagedWidget()`. Each `Arg` structure contains a resource/value pair. Attributes specified here override the same ones specified from the command line or from resource databases.

Example 3-18 shows an argument list that hardcodes the sensitivity of a PushButton widget and its callback list. Sensitivity is a good thing to hardcode for PushButton widgets, because if accidentally set by the user it could disable an application.† The callback list cannot be

---

†Sensitivity is a basic resource of all widgets. When set to `True`, the default, a widget accepts input and operates normally. When `False`, a widget displays itself in gray (or otherwise indicates insensitivity) and does not act on user input. The purpose of sensitivity is to allow the application to disable certain commands when they are not valid. If sensitivity were left configurable, the user could turn it off on some widgets and effectively cripple an application. It is hard to imagine the user doing this by accident, but it is not worth taking a gamble.

specified by the user anyway; setting it here is just an alternative to calling `XtAdd-Callback()`.

The `XtArgVal` type used in the callback list aids in porting Toolkit programs to different architectures. It allows the system manufacturer to select the type in the `typedef` for `Xt-ArgVal`, so that the application program need not worry about it. The `value` field of the `Arg` structure may be a number or a pointer.

Example 3-18. An argument list

```
Arg quit_args[ ] = {
    XmNsensitive,          (XtArgVal) True,
    XmNactivateCallback,        (XtArgVal) quit_callback_list,
};
```

An argument list can be used as an argument in the call to create a widget, as shown in Example 3-19.

Example 3-19. Using an argument list in widget creation

```
/* define quit_args */

main(argc, argv)
int argc;
char *argv[ ];
{
    Widget quit, box;

    /* create box */
      .
      .
      .

    quit = XtCreateManagedWidget(
            "quit",                    /* widget name */
            xmPushButtonWidgetClass,   /* widget class */
            box,                       /* parent widget */
            quit_args,                 /* argument list */
            XtNumber(quit_args)        /* arglist size */
            );
      .
      .
      .

}
```

Note the use of the `XtNumber()` macro to calculate how many arguments there are in the statically initialized argument list. This macro eliminates the need to keep track of the number of resources you have set.

Note also that the `value` field in the argument list must be in the correct representation type for that resource, which is often not a string. You may need to call `XtConvertAndStore()` to arrive at the right representation of the data to be placed in the argument list. For details on calling `XtConvertAndStore()`, see Chapter 10, *Resource Management and Type Conversion*. An easier way to do this is to use the `XtVaTypedArg` feature supported by the varargs interfaces.

As mentioned earlier, unless you invoke a converter, no diagnostic is printed when you specify a resource value incorrectly in the argument list. Therefore, make sure you specify these correctly.

3.8.2.1 Another Way to Set Arguments

Instead of creating the argument list as a static array, you can allocate storage at run time and use the `XtSetArg()` macro to set values into the storage. This is the coding style favored in Motif 1.0 applications.

`XtSetArg()` sets a single argument to a resource identifying a constant and a value. Example 3-20 shows the code that would create an argument list with the same contents as the one created in Example 3-18 above. Some people prefer this technique because it places the argument list setting closer to the `XtCreateWidget()` call, making the code easier to read. (However, it is still more difficult to read than when using the varargs interfaces.)

Example 3-20. Setting the argument list with XtSetArg

```
int i;
Arg args[10];
/* XtAppInitialize may be called before or after the XtSetArg calls */

i = 0;
XtSetArg(args[i], XmNactivateCallback, (XtArgVal)
        quit_callback_list); i++;
XtSetArg(args[i], XmNsensitive, (XtArgVal) True); i++;

banner = XtCreateManagedWidget(
        banner,                   /* widget name */
        xmPushButtonWidgetClass,  /* widget class from Label.h */
        toplevel,                 /* parent widget */
        args,                     /* argument list */
        i);                       /* arg list size from XtSetArg counter */
```

Notice that `i` is used as the number of arguments in the `XtCreateManagedWidget()` call, *not* `XtNumber()`. `XtNumber()` would in this case return the value `10`, the total length of the `Arg` array.

Remember that `i` must be incremented outside the macro, because `XtSetArg()` references its first argument twice. The following code will not work because `XtNresource2` will be set into `widget_args[2]` instead of `widget_args[1]`, as desired. Example 3-21 shows you how *not* to use `XtSetArg()`.

Example 3-21. Incorrectly setting the argument list with XtSetArg

```
Arg arg[10];
int num_args;

/* This example will NOT work correctly! */

num_args = 0;

/* The next two lines are wrong! */
XtSetArg(args[num_args++], XtNresource1, (XtArgVal) 10);
XtSetArg(args[num_args++], XtNresource2, (XtArgVal) 40);
        .
        .
        .
```

The `XtSetArg()` method has three advantages over static initialization:

- It moves the code that sets the argument list closer to where it is really used in the call to create a widget.

- It allows run-time value modification using the same method.

- The same storage can be used for multiple argument lists.

The disadvantages of the `XtSetArg()` method are as follows:

- It performs all assignments at run time, which slows startup slightly.

- It is possible to try to set more arguments than space has been allocated for, leading to a core dump.

- It is possible to misplace the counter increment, leading to improper operation.

- An argument list and a counter variable must be kept until the call to create the widget instance; the static method requires keeping only the argument list.

- It may waste a small amount of storage since the argument list array is usually initialized larger than the required size.

- Lots of `XtSetArg()` calls make for ugly code.

As you can see, these differences are mostly subjective. However, the varargs interfaces have many of the advantages of the `XtSetArg()` method, but none of its disadvantages. The only disadvantage of the varargs interfaces is the slight overhead they add. You may use whichever method you prefer, or some combination.

3.8.2.2 Merging Argument Lists

`XtMergeArgLists()` takes two argument lists and counts all arguments, allocates the storage for a single argument list big enough to hold them, and stores all the entries from both in the returned argument list. It does not remove duplicate entries. The calling application can use `XtNumber()` to determine the resulting argument count (or can add the original counts).

3.9 More About Application Contexts

We have used application contexts in the examples so far, but not discussed what they really are or what they are for.

An application context is a structure maintained by Xt that stores all the data associated with the application, including the functions registered by the application and other information about the application. Primarily, its purpose is to allow Xt applications to run without modification on certain operating systems that do not have a separate address space for each process. These systems include the Xerox Cedar environment, the Symbolics Genera environment, and the TI Explorer system. Although systems like this are not common, the goal of all X software in C is to be portable to any system that supports C.†

Why then is the `XtAppContext` exposed in the programming interface? It is possible, though difficult, to create more than one application context within a single program. This is rarely done and its implications are complex, so we will reserve discussion of it until Section 14.10.

The important thing to remember is that for maximum portability, you need to use the versions of routines that begin with `XtApp` instead of those that don't. For instance, use `XtAppInitialize()` instead of `XtInitialize()` and `XtAppMainLoop()`, not `XtMainLoop()`.

Of the routines you have seen so far in this book, only `XtVaAppInitialize()`, `XtAppInitialize()`, `XtAppMainLoop()`, and `XtAppAddActions()` use explicit application contexts. The complete list of routines that have equivalents is presented in Section 14.10.

Throughout this book we will continue to use the routines that use the explicit application context.

---

†It is almost a maxim that there is no such thing as portable software, only software that has been ported. The goal (and more or less the reality) of X is that the porting process should be much easier than it has traditionally been, and, most important, that only one version of a particular piece of software should need to be maintained. The various idiosyncrasies of particular compilers can be dealt with using conditional preprocessor directives (#ifdef). X features were designed specifically to provide ways to handle differences in screens and keyboards. The application context is an effort to provide a way to handle odd operating systems.

4

An Example Application

This chapter describes a complete application, in several iterations. First, it shows a simple version of the program, a bitmap editor, as it would be written assuming the existence of a BitmapEdit widget (which is actually developed in). Then, two refined versions are developed, each demonstrating additional Toolkit programming techniques. Finally, the same application is shown as it would be written if the bitmap editor were implemented in an application window rather than with the BitmapEdit widget.

In This Chapter:

4

An Example Application

Enough of these trivial programs! Now for an (almost) real application. This chapter describes the development of a bitmap editor. Although it is simple, it can be easily extended to be quite powerful without any new techniques.

We will show several versions of *xbitmap*, beginning with a simple version that assumes the existence of a BitmapEdit widget (which will actually be developed in Chapter 6, *Inside a Widget*, and Chapter 7, *Basic Widget Methods*). Subsequent versions add two widgets that display the bitmap in small scale (one normal, one reverse video), and finally implement the same application without the use of the specialized BitmapEdit widget.

These examples will demonstrate the techniques described in Chapter 2, *Introduction to the X Toolkit and Motif*, and Chapter 3, *More Techniques for Using Widgets*, as they would appear in a real application, and will bring up a number of new topics:

- The initial version introduces the bitmap editor application, and demonstrates the way the application can access the data within the BitmapEdit widget using a public function defined by the widget class. It also further demonstrates the most common method of linking widgets with application code: using callbacks.

- The second version demonstrates two ways of adding the small-scale bitmaps, one using a standard widget and one drawing into a Core widget from the application. This allows us to introduce actions and translations, another (less commonly used) way to link widgets with application code.

- The third version does not use the BitmapEdit widget, but instead implements its features by drawing into a Primitive widget. This demonstrates one way to prototype features while learning to write your own widget. It also allows us to describe the code necessary to implement the bitmap editor so that you will already understand this code when you see it in the internal framework of a widget described in Chapter 6 and Chapter 7. Note, however, that the proper way to implement functionality of this level of complexity (or greater) is to write a widget.

Many applications have at least one custom window for which no existing widget will suffice. This chapter demonstrates several of the ways to implement such a window, and describes the tradeoffs between the different options. Features can be added from the application code by building on a Motif DrawingArea widget, or creating a Core or Primitive widget to draw into. They can also be implemented by creating a custom widget. By the end of Chapters 6 and 7, you will have seen how to implement this application entirely with existing widgets and application code, how to implement it using custom widgets, and how to implement a mixture of the two.

4.1 xbitmap1: Bitmap Editor Using a BitmapEdit Widget

Most application programming is done entirely using widgets written by someone else. *xbitmap1* is such an application.

The screen appearance of *xbitmap1* is shown in Figure 4-1. As usual, it is a good idea to compile and run each example as it is discussed.†

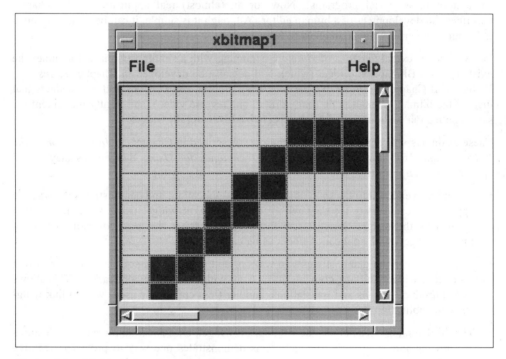

Figure 4-1. xbitmap1: how it looks on the screen

The BitmapEdit widget lets you set bits in the visible bitmap by clicking the first pointer button or dragging the pointer with the first button held down, lets you erase bits using the second button, or lets you toggle bits using the third button. The File menu contains a Print button which simply prints on the standard output an array of ones and zeroes representing the set and unset bits in the bitmap. (Code to read and write standard X11 bitmap files is added in a later version.) The File menu also contains a Quit button.

---

†How to get and compile the example source code is described in the Preface and Section 2.3.2.

xbitmap1 is implemented by adding a small amount of code to *xmainwindow*, described in Chapter 3, *More Techniques for Using Widgets*. We replaced the Frame widget with a BitmapEdit widget, and added the Print button to the menu. Of course, a callback for the print button also has to be added.

The code for *xbitmap1* is shown in Example 4-1. The only new technique shown in this example is the use of the public function **BitmapEditGetArray** defined by the Bitmap-Edit widget. **BitmapEditGetArray** gets a character array which represents the contents of the bitmap being edited, and the dimensions of the bitmap. This information is necessary for the application to print out the bitmap (or write it to a file). Although these values are widget resources that can be queried with **XtGetValues()**, this function makes it more convenient. Several Motif widgets also provide public functions to make it more convenient to set or get resources or manipulate internal widget data. All Motif public functions begin with **Xm**.

Example 4-1. xbitmap1: complete code

```
/*
 *  xbitmap1.c - bitmap in main window with help and quit
 */

/*  So that we can use fprintf: */
#include <stdio.h>

/* Standard Toolkit include files: */
#include <Xm/Xm.h>

/* Public include files for widgets used in this file.  */
#include <Xm/PushB.h>      /* push button */
#include <Xm/MainW.h>      /* main window */
#include <Xm/MessageB.h>   /* message box */
#include <Xm/RowColum.h>   /* row column (for menus) */
#include <Xm/CascadeB.h>   /* cascade button */

#include "BitmapEdit.h"

/*
 * The printout routine prints an array of 1s and 0s representing the
 * contents of the bitmap.  This data can be processed into any
 * desired form, including standard X11 bitmap file format.
 */
/* ARGSUSED */
static void
PrintOut(widget, client_data, call_data)
Widget widget;
XtPointer client_data;     /* cast to bigBitmap */
XtPointer call_data;       /* unused */
{
    Widget bigBitmap = (Widget) client_data;
    int x, y;
    int width_in_cells, height_in_cells;
    char *cell;

    cell = BitmapEditGetArray(bigBitmap, &width_in_cells,
            &height_in_cells);

    (void) putchar('\n');
    for (y = 0; y < height_in_cells; y++) {
```

Example Application

Example 4-1. xbitmap1: complete code (continued)

```
        for (x = 0; x < width_in_cells; x++)
            (void) putchar(cell[x + y * width_in_cells] ? '1' : '0');
        (void) putchar('\n');
    }
    (void) putchar('\n');
}
/*
 * callback to pop up help dialog widget
 */
/*ARGSUSED*/
void ShowHelp(w, client_data, call_data)
Widget w;
XtPointer client_data;
XtPointer call_data;
{
    Widget dialog = (Widget) client_data;
    XtManageChild(dialog);
}
/*
 * quit button callback function
 */
/*ARGSUSED*/
void Quit(w, client_data, call_data)
Widget w;
XtPointer client_data, call_data;
{
    exit(0);
}
main(argc, argv)
int argc;
char **argv;
{
    XtAppContext app_context;
    Widget topLevel, mainWindow, menuBar;
    Widget fileButton, fileMenu, quit, helpButton, helpMenu,
             help, helpBox;
    Widget temp;
    Widget bigBitmap, output;

    /* never call a Widget variable "exit"! */
    extern exit();

    static XrmOptionDescRec table[ ] = {
        {"-pw",          "*pixmapWidthInCells",  XrmoptionSepArg, NULL},
        {"-pixmapwidth", "*pixmapWidthInCells",  XrmoptionSepArg, NULL},
        {"-ph",          "*pixmapHeightInCells", XrmoptionSepArg, NULL},
        {"-pixmapheight","*pixmapHeightInCells", XrmoptionSepArg, NULL},
        {"-cellsize",    "*cellSizeInPixels",    XrmoptionSepArg, NULL},
    };

     XtSetLanguageProc(NULL, (XtLanguageProc)NULL, NULL);

    topLevel = XtVaAppInitialize( &app_context, "XBitmap1",
           table, XtNumber(table), &argc, argv, NULL, NULL);

    /* create main window */
```

Example 4-1. xbitmap1: complete code (continued)

```
mainWindow = XtVaCreateManagedWidget( "mainWindow",
        xmMainWindowWidgetClass, topLevel, NULL);

/* create menu bar along top inside of main window */
menuBar = XmCreateMenuBar( mainWindow, "menuBar",
        NULL, 0);
XtManageChild(menuBar);

bigBitmap = XtVaCreateManagedWidget("bigBitmap",
        bitmapEditWidgetClass, mainWindow,
        NULL);

/*  Set MainWindow areas */
XmMainWindowSetAreas (mainWindow, menuBar, NULL, NULL, NULL,
        bigBitmap);

/*
 *   CREATE FILE MENU AND CHILDREN
 */

/* create button that will pop up the menu */
fileButton = XtVaCreateManagedWidget("fileButton",
        xmCascadeButtonWidgetClass, menuBar, NULL);

/* create menu (really Shell widget-RowColumn widget combo) */
fileMenu = XmCreatePulldownMenu( menuBar,
        "fileMenu", NULL, 0);

/*
 *   CREATE BUTTON TO OUTPUT BITMAP
 */

/* create button that will pop up the menu */
output = XtVaCreateManagedWidget( "output",
        xmPushButtonWidgetClass, fileMenu, NULL);

XtAddCallback(output, XmNactivateCallback, PrintOut, bigBitmap);

/* create the quit button last so it's last in the menu */
quit = XtVaCreateManagedWidget( "quit",
        xmPushButtonWidgetClass, fileMenu, NULL);

/*
 * Specify which menu fileButton will pop up.
 */
XtVaSetValues(fileButton,
        XmNsubMenuId, fileMenu,
        NULL);

XtAddCallback(quit, XmNactivateCallback, Quit, 0);

/*
 *   CREATE HELP BUTTON AND BOX
 */

/* create button that will bring up help popup */
helpButton = XtVaCreateManagedWidget( "helpButton",
        xmCascadeButtonWidgetClass, menuBar, NULL);

/* tell menuBar which is the help button
 * (will be specially positioned. */
XtVaSetValues(menuBar,
```

Example Application

Example 4-1. xbitmap1: complete code (continued)

```
                XmNmenuHelpWidget, helpButton,
                NULL);

    helpMenu = XmCreatePulldownMenu(
            menuBar,    /* parent widget */
            "helpMenu", /* widget name */
            NULL,       /* terminate argument list (none needed) */
            0);         /* terminate argument list (none needed) */

    /* create help button in the menu */
    help = XtVaCreateManagedWidget(
                "helpMenu"  /* widget name */
                XmPushButtonWidgetClass,  /* widget name */
                helpMenu,   /* parent widget */
                NULL);      /* terminate argument list (none needed) */

    /* Specify which menu helpButton will pop up */
    XtVaSetValues(helpButton,
            XmNsubMenuId, helpMenu,
            NULL);

    /* create popup that will contain help */
    helpBox = XmCreateMessageDialog( help,
            "helpBox", NULL, 0);

    temp = XmMessageBoxGetChild (helpBox, XmDIALOG_CANCEL_BUTTON);
    XtUnmanageChild (temp);
    temp = XmMessageBoxGetChild (helpBox, XmDIALOG_HELP_BUTTON);
    XtUnmanageChild (temp);

    /* arrange for help button to pop up helpBox */
    XtAddCallback(help, XmNactivateCallback, ShowHelp, helpBox);

    XtRealizeWidget(topLevel);

    XtAppMainLoop(app_context);
}
```

You should recognize the command-line options table as the one described in Section 3.6.1. If there is anything you don't understand in Example 4-1, review Chapter 3, *More Techniques for Using Widgets*.

Adding a Print button to the menu is a simple matter of creating another PushButton as a child of `fileMenu`.

The `Printout` callback function gets the array of ones and zeroes from the BitmapEdit widget and prints them to the standard output. Some widget public functions like `Bitmap-EditGetArray` are provided simply because they are more convenient to use than calling `XtSetValues()` or `XtGetValues()`. Others are supplied by a widget class that wants certain data to be readable or writable by the application, but for some reason does not want the data both readable *and* writable as would be the case if it were a resource. Sometimes a widget class has features that it wants controllable from the application but never user-customizable (because they are meaningless at startup, for example), and therefore it provides a function for setting them.

4.1.1 XBitmap1 App-defaults File

Example 4-2 shows the app-defaults file for *xbitmap1*. This app-defaults file is identical to *XMainWindow* with the addition of resource settings to set an appropriate help message, the label Print Array for the new menu button, the size in cells of the bitmap, and the size in pixels of each cell in the bitmap.

Example 4-2. XBitmap1: app-defaults file

```
! BitmapEdit resources
*cellSizeInPixels:          30
*pixmapWidthInCells:        30
*pixmapHeightInCells:       30
! fonts
*fontList:                  variable
! strings
*helpButton.labelString:    Help
*help.labelString:          Editing Bitmaps
*quit.labelString:          Quit
*output.labelString:        Print Array
*fileButton.labelString:    File
!
*helpBox.messageString:     To set bits, press or drag\n\
the first mouse button.\n\
To clear bits, use the second mouse button.\n\
To toggle bits, use the third mouse button.
! The following used if the window manager titles the dialog:
! mwm does, twm doesn't
*helpBox.dialogTitle:       Help
! Turn on scrollbars
*XmMainWindow.scrollingPolicy:   XmAUTOMATIC
*XmMainWindow.width:        300
*XmMainWindow.height:       300
```

Note that by default the MainWindow will make itself big enough for only a few bitmap cells to be visible. The resource settings for the width and height of MainWindow make sure that the application has a reasonable initial size.

4.2 xbitmap2: Adding Graphics to Display the Bitmap

When you have some graphics to draw, you need a widget that is designed to allow you to draw into it; the DrawingArea widget.

In addition to displaying the bitmap in blown-up, editable form, a bitmap editor should display the bitmap in true scale, how the bitmap really looks when displayed on the screen. It is customary to present this bitmap in both normal and reverse video, and update it every time the user toggles a cell in the enlarged bitmap. Figure 4-2 shows the appearance of the application with this feature added.†

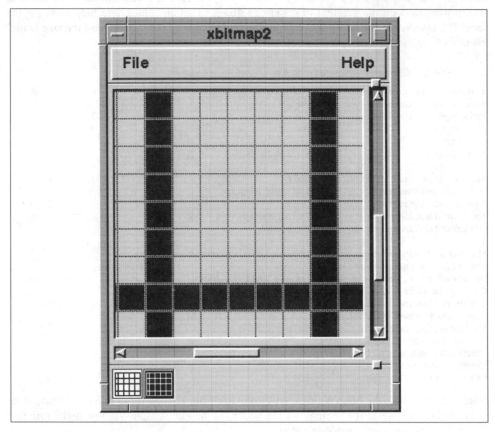

Figure 4-2. xbitmap2: true-scale normal and reverse bitmaps added

There are three ways to implement the small pixmap widgets. (All of them would look the same to the user.) One approach is to use the Label widget, which can display a pixmap instead of a string. However, it is then difficult to make the Label widget redraw the pixmap each time a cell is toggled. This is difficult because we are changing the contents of the pixmap (by drawing into it) without the Label widget's knowledge; therefore the widget does not know to redraw itself. The only obvious way to tell Label to redraw is to clear the widget's window; this generates an **Expose** event and forces the widget to redraw itself. However, this results in a flashing effect that is unacceptable. You can avoid flashing by

---

†You may notice that we have abandoned the MainWindow used in *xbitmap1*, and instead used PanedWindow as the main window of the application. This is because there is no easy way to fit the two additional small pixmap widgets into the layout scheme of MainWindow. (We originally intended to place the small pixmaps in the menubar, but it can accept only CascadeButton widgets. This restriction is intended to enforce the convention that the menubar is only for menus.)

synthesizing an **Expose** event (creating an **XExposeEvent** structure and filling it with values) and sending it to the Label widget using **XSendEvent()**. This is a bit of a kludge but it works. If Label provided a public function called **XmLabelRedrawPixmap**, we could more cleanly correct the flashing bug. Although adding this function to the widget code would be easy, we could no longer call the remaining widget class Label; we would be creating a new widget class.

Another way to display the small pixmaps is to use a DrawingArea widget, which is an empty widget that provides callbacks in which you can place drawing code. DrawingArea is useful for building simple custom windows that don't have complicated graphics or user input. This technique is implemented in *xbitmap2*.

The third possibility is to draw into a Core or Primitive widget. This would use code very similar to that in *xbitmap2*, but would link the application code with the widget using actions and translations instead of with callbacks. We will be demonstrating this technique in *xbitmap3* as an introduction to translations and actions.

4.2.1 Exposure Strategy

The redrawing technique used in *xbitmap2* works as follows. Two pixmaps (off-screen drawable areas) are created to record the current state of each bitmap. Whenever a cell is toggled, a pixel in each pixmap is changed by drawing into each pixmap. Then each entire pixmap is copied into the corresponding widget. The same routine that copies from pixmap to widget is used whenever the widgets become exposed. Figure 4-3 illustrates this technique.

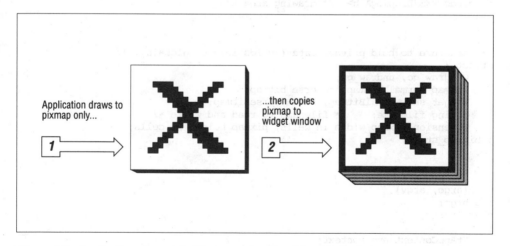

Figure 4-3. Application draws into Pixmap and copies it to widget window

In the actual code, two single-plane pixmaps are created during application startup, the same size as the bitmap displayed in the BitmapEdit widget. Each of the two bitmap display areas is implemented with a DrawingArea widget. DrawingArea provides a callback resource called **XmNexposeCallback**. The application calls **XtAddCallback()** to register a function with each of the two widgets for the **XmNexposeCallback** resource. This function, called **RedrawSmallPicture**, copies from the pixmaps into the widget's window. This function takes care of redrawing the widgets whenever exposure occurs, and it also can be called whenever a cell is toggled. The BitmapEdit widget has an **XtNtoggle-Callback** resource. The function registered for this widget and resource draws into the two pixmaps, and then calls **RedrawSmallPicture** to copy the updated pixmap information to the window (alternately, it could draw directly into window instead of copying from the pixmap).

Three new routines are needed: **RedrawSmallPicture**, **SetUpThings**, and **Cell-Toggled**. These three routines are primarily composed of Xlib calls that set up for and perform graphics. The **RedrawSmallPicture** routine copies a pixmap into a widget, **Set-UpThings** creates the pixmaps and the GCs (introduced in the next subsection, 4.2.2) needed to draw into these pixmaps, and **CellToggled** is a callback function registered with the BitmapEdit widget that updates the pixmaps whenever a cell is toggled. Code is also added to **main** to create the two DrawingArea widgets and register **RedrawSmall-Picture** with them. We'll show these routines one at a time. Example 4-3 shows the improvements to the **main** routine.

Example 4-3. xbitmap2: implementing small pixmaps with DrawingArea widgets

```
/*
 * Public include files for widgets used in this file.
 */
 .
 .
 .
#include <Xm/DrawingA.h>   /* drawing area */
 .
 .
 .
/* Structure to hold private data (avoids lots of globals). */
struct {
    GC draw_gc, undraw_gc;
    Pixmap normal_bitmap, reverse_bitmap;
    Widget showNormalBitmap, showReverseBitmap;
    String filename;    /* filename to read and write */
    Dimension pixmap_width_in_cells, pixmap_height_in_cells;
} bitmap_stuff;
 .
 .
 .
main(argc, argv)
int argc;
char **argv;
{
    XtAppContext app_context;
    Widget topLevel, mainWindow, menuBar;
    Widget fileButton, fileMenu, quit, helpButton, helpMenu,
            help, helpBox;
    Widget temp;
    Widget bigBitmap, output, smallPixmapBox;
    Widget scrolledWin, frame1, frame2;
      .
      .
      .
```

```
    .
    /*
     * Size of bitmap must be queried so that small pixmaps
     * of the right size can be created.
     */
    XtVaGetValues(bigBitmap, XtNpixmapWidthInCells,
            &bitmap_stuff.pixmap_width_in_cells,
            XtNpixmapHeightInCells,
            &bitmap_stuff.pixmap_height_in_cells,
            NULL);

    /*
     * Create pixmaps and GCs, draw initial contents into pixmaps */
     */
    SetUpThings(topLevel);
    .
    .
    .

    /* create RowColumn to hold small pixmap widgets */
    smallPixmapBox = XtVaCreateManagedWidget("smallPixmapBox",
            xmRowColumnWidgetClass, mainWindow,
            NULL);

    /* create Frame so small pixmap widget appears in box */
    frame1 = XtVaCreateManagedWidget("frameNormal",
            xmFrameWidgetClass, smallPixmapBox,
            NULL);

    /* create DrawingArea for small pixmap widget - must set size. */
    bitmap_stuff.showNormalBitmap = XtVaCreateManagedWidget(
            "showNormalBitmap", xmDrawingAreaWidgetClass, frame1,
            XmNwidth, bitmap_stuff.pixmap_width_in_cells,
            XmNheight, bitmap_stuff.pixmap_height_in_cells,
            NULL);

    /* create Frame so small pixmap widget appears in box */
    frame2 = XtVaCreateManagedWidget("frameReverse",
            xmFrameWidgetClass, smallPixmapBox,
            NULL);

    /* create DrawingArea for small pixmap widget - must set size. */
    bitmap_stuff.showReverseBitmap = XtVaCreateManagedWidget(
            "showReverseBitmap", xmDrawingAreaWidgetClass, frame2,
            XmNwidth, bitmap_stuff.pixmap_width_in_cells,
            XmNheight, bitmap_stuff.pixmap_height_in_cells,
            NULL);

    /* register RedrawSmallPicture as the redrawing function */
    XtAddCallback(bitmap_stuff.showNormalBitmap, XmNexposeCallback,
            RedrawSmallPicture, 0);

    XtAddCallback(bitmap_stuff.showReverseBitmap, XmNexposeCallback,
            RedrawSmallPicture, 0);

    /* Register CellToggled to be called whenever a cell is toggled. */
    XtAddCallback(bigBitmap, XtNtoggleCallback, CellToggled, 0);
```

Example Application

```
    XtRealizeWidget(topLevel);
    XtAppMainLoop(app_context);
}
```

The `main` routine registers `RedrawSmallPicture` as the `XmNexposeCallback` function for each DrawingArea widget. It also registers `CellToggled` as the `Xt-NtoggleCallback` for the BitmapEdit widget, to be called whenever a bitmap cell is toggled.

`SetUpThings` uses Xlib calls to create the pixmap that will be used as an off-screen copy of what will be displayed in the DrawingArea widgets. `SetUpThings` also creates GCs that will be used to draw into these pixmaps. `CellToggled` does the drawing, and `RedrawSmallPicture` performs the copying. These routines are shown in the next section, which describes how graphics work in Xt programs.

4.2.2 Graphics from the Application

Drawing in the X Window System is done by creating a *graphics context* (GC) that specifies such things as colors and line widths, and then calling a drawing routine that specifies what shape is to be drawn. These two steps are basic to X and required in programs written in any language with or without a toolkit. For example, the call to draw a line specifies only the start and endpoints of the line. The GC specifies everything else about how the server will actually draw this line.

A GC is a server-side object that must be created by the application. The purpose of the GC is to cache on the server side information about how graphics are to be executed by the server, so that this information doesn't have to be sent over the network with every graphics call. If X did not have GCs, every graphics call would have many arguments and this would waste network time (and be annoying to program). Instead, you create a small number of GCs before drawing (in the startup phase of the application). Each represents a particular color or line style you will need to draw with at some point. You then specify one of these GCs in each call to draw. For example, to draw text and be able to highlight it at will, it is customary to create two GCs, one for drawing in white on black, and one for drawing in black on white (where colors can be substituted for black and white on color screens).

Once created, a GC is referred to by its ID, of type `GC`. This ID is specified in calls to draw using that GC.

From the application, the Xlib routine `XCreateGC()` is usually used to create GCs. Xt also provides the `XtGetGC()` routine for creating GCs, but it is typically used only inside widget code when there could be many of the same GCs created. `XtGetGC()` is very similar to `XCreateGC()`, except that it arranges for GCs to be shared among widgets (within one application). `XtGetGC()` will be described in Section 7.1.

In *xbitmap2*, the `SetUpThings` routine is responsible for creating two pixmaps that act as off-screen drawing surfaces, and two GCs that will be used to draw and undraw pixels in the pixmaps. Whenever the DrawingArea widgets need to be updated, the pixmaps are copied into the widgets. This is only one possible exposure-handling approach. Another is to draw the required points directly into the DrawingArea widgets each time they need to be updated, keeping a record of the drawn points so that the entire widget can be redrawn in case of exposure. Example 4-4 shows `SetUpThings`, which creates pixmap and GCs and then initializes the pixmaps.

Example 4-4. xbitmap2: creating pixmaps and GCs

```
static void
SetUpThings(w)
Widget w;
{
    XGCValues values;

    bitmap_stuff.normal_bitmap = XCreatePixmap(XtDisplay(w),
            RootWindowOfScreen(XtScreen(w)),
            bitmap_stuff.pixmap_width_in_cells,
            bitmap_stuff.pixmap_height_in_cells, 1);

    bitmap_stuff.reverse_bitmap = XCreatePixmap(XtDisplay(w),
            RootWindowOfScreen(XtScreen(w)),
            bitmap_stuff.pixmap_width_in_cells,
            bitmap_stuff.pixmap_height_in_cells, 1);

    values.foreground = 1;
    values.background = 0;
    /* note that normal_bitmap is used as the drawable because it
     * is one bit deep.  The root window may not be one bit deep */
    bitmap_stuff.draw_gc = XCreateGC(XtDisplay(w),
            bitmap_stuff.normal_bitmap,
            GCForeground | GCBackground, &values);

    values.foreground = 0;
    values.background = 1;
    bitmap_stuff.undraw_gc = XCreateGC(XtDisplay(w),
            bitmap_stuff.normal_bitmap,
            GCForeground | GCBackground, &values);

    /* pixmaps must be cleared - may contain garbage */
    XFillRectangle(XtDisplay(w),
            bitmap_stuff.reverse_bitmap, bitmap_stuff.draw_gc,
            0, 0, bitmap_stuff.pixmap_width_in_cells + 1,
            bitmap_stuff.pixmap_height_in_cells + 1);
    XFillRectangle(XtDisplay(w),
            bitmap_stuff.normal_bitmap, bitmap_stuff.undraw_gc,
            0, 0, bitmap_stuff.pixmap_width_in_cells + 1,
            bitmap_stuff.pixmap_height_in_cells + 1);
}
```

Notice that GCs can only be used on windows or pixmaps with the same depth as the window or pixmap that is passed in the call to create the GC. In this case, the pixmaps created contain only one plane, even when running on a server with a color screen. These pixmaps are passed to `XCreateGC()` to set the depth of the GCs. These GCs can only be used to draw into the single plane pixmaps. As you will see in Example 4-6, a separate GC (the default GC) is used to copy from the pixmaps into the windows, since on color screens the windows have multiple planes. (You know you have done this incorrectly if you get an error only on color screens.)

Xt does not provide drawing calls of its own. You must call Xlib directly to draw. An Xlib drawing routine is known as a *primitive*. Under X, text is drawn by a graphics primitive, just as lines, arcs, and other graphics are drawn.

Colors are normally specified by the user as strings such as "blue," but the X server understands colors only when specified as numbers called pixel values. A pixel value is used as an index to a lookup table called a colormap, which contains values for the RGB (red-green-blue) primaries used to generate colors on the screen. However, a particular pixel value does not necessarily always map to the same color, even when run twice on the same system, because the contents of the colormap are configurable on most color systems. The wide variation of graphics hardware that X supports has required that the design of color handling in X be very flexible and very complex.

Fortunately, as long as your widget or application requires only a small number of colors, and you do not particularly care whether the colors you get are exactly the colors you requested, Xt provides a simplified interface. It hides the actual Xlib calls involved in the Resource Manager's converter routines. As described in Chapter 3, *More Techniques for Using Widgets*, if you specify application resources for colors in a resource list, Xt will automatically convert color names specified as resource settings into pixel values. If you need to do more advanced color handling, then you will need to make Xlib calls yourself. For a description of Xlib's color handling, see Chapter 7, *Color*, in Volume One, *Xlib Programming Manual*.

`xbitmap1` works either in color or monochrome, since the widgets it creates can have their color set by resources. All of *xbitmap2* except the small pixmaps we have been implementing also support color. To support color in the small pixmaps takes more work. We would need to add application resources to get the pixel values that will be set into the GCs used when drawing, as described in Section 3.6.

Example 4-5 shows the `CellToggled` routine. As you may recall, this routine is a callback function registered with the BitmapEdit widget, to be called whenever a cell is toggled.

Example 4-5. xbitmap2: the CellToggled routine

```
/* ARGSUSED */
static void
CellToggled(w, client_data, call_data)
Widget w;
XtPointer client_data;   /* unused */
XtPointer call_data;     /* will be cast to cur_info */
{
    /* cast pointer to needed type: */
    BitmapEditPointInfo *cur_info = (BitmapEditPointInfo *) call_data;
    /*
     * Note, BitmapEditPointInfo is defined in BitmapEdit.h
     */

    XDrawPoint(XtDisplay(w), bitmap_stuff.normal_bitmap,
            ((cur_info->mode == DRAWN) ? bitmap_stuff.draw_gc :
            bitmap_stuff.undraw_gc), cur_info->newx, cur_info->newy);
    XDrawPoint(XtDisplay(w), bitmap_stuff.reverse_bitmap,
            ((cur_info->mode == DRAWN) ? bitmap_stuff.undraw_gc :
            bitmap_stuff.draw_gc), cur_info->newx, cur_info->newy);
```

Example 4-5. xbitmap3: the CellToggled routine (continued)

```
    RedrawSmallPicture(bitmap_stuff.showNormalBitmap);
    RedrawSmallPicture(bitmap_stuff.showReverseBitmap);
}
```

Note that BitmapEdit passes a structure called `BitmapEditPointInfo` into the callback function as an argument. This structure is defined in the public include file, *BitmapEdit.h*, and it provides the information necessary to keep the small bitmaps displaying the same pattern as BitmapEdit. The fields of `BitmapEditPointInfo` are the mode (whether drawn or undrawn) and the coordinates of the point toggled. The `CellToggled` routine draws points into the pixmaps according to the information passed in, and then calls `Redraw-SmallPicture` to copy the pixmaps into each Core widget.

The first line of `CellToggled` casts the generic pointer `call_data` into the structure type defined by BitmapEdit, `BitmapEditPointInfo`. Under most compilers this can also be done (perhaps more clearly) by declaring the info argument as type `BitmapEdit-PointInfo` in the first place. However, ANSI C compilers require a cast.

The `RedrawSmallPicture` routine is shown in Example 4-6.

Example 4-6. xbitmap3: the RedrawSmallPicture routine

```
/*ARGSUSED*/
static void
RedrawSmallPicture(w, client_data, call_data)
Widget w;
XtPointer client_data;
XtPointer call_data;
{
    Pixmap pixmap;

    if (w == bitmap_stuff.showNormalBitmap)
        pixmap = bitmap_stuff.normal_bitmap;
    else
        pixmap = bitmap_stuff.reverse_bitmap;

    if (DefaultDepthOfScreen(XtScreen(w)) == 1)
        XCopyArea(XtDisplay(w), pixmap, XtWindow(w),
                DefaultGCOfScreen(XtScreen(w)), 0, 0,
                bitmap_stuff.pixmap_width_in_cells,
                bitmap_stuff.pixmap_height_in_cells,
                0, 0);
    else
        XCopyPlane(XtDisplay(w), pixmap, XtWindow(w),
                DefaultGCOfScreen(XtScreen(w)), 0, 0,
                bitmap_stuff.pixmap_width_in_cells,
                bitmap_stuff.pixmap_height_in_cells,
                0, 0, 1);
}
```

`RedrawSmallPicture` is called from `CellToggled`, and also by Xt in response to `Expose` events because we registered it as a callback for the DrawingArea widgets.

The use of one of two Xlib routines, depending on the depth of the screen, is an optimization. `XCopyArea()` is faster, but can be used for this job only on monochrome displays, because the pixmaps used here are one plane deep on all displays and must be translated into multiple planes with **XCopyPlane( )** on color displays.

See Volume One, *Xlib Programming Manual*, for details.

4.2.3 Writing a Bitmap File

Once we have pixmaps in our application that contain the current bitmap, it is a trivial matter to change the **printout** callback function to write a bitmap file instead of just printing an array of ones and zeroes to the standard output. This is easy because there is an Xlib function, **XWriteBitmapFile( )**, that writes the contents of a single-plane pixmap into a file. Example 4-7 shows the code that gets a filename from the command line and then writes the bitmap file.

Example 4-7. xbitmap2: writing a bitmap file

```
/* ARGSUSED */
static void
Printout(widget, client_data, call_data)
Widget widget;
XtPointer client_data, call_data; /* unused */
{
    XWriteBitmapFile(XtDisplay(widget), bitmap_stuff.filename,
            bitmap_stuff.normal_bitmap,
            bitmap_stuff.pixmap_width_in_cells,
            bitmap_stuff.pixmap_height_in_cells, 0, 0);
}

main(argc, argv)
int argc;
char *argv[ ];
{
        .
        .
    /* XtAppInitialize */
        .
        .
    if (argv[1] != NULL)
        bitmap_stuff.filename = argv[1];
    else {
        fprintf(stderr, "xbitmap: must specify filename\
            on command line.\n");
        exit(1);
    }

        .
        .
        .

}
```

Contrast this version of **Printout** to the one shown in Example 4-1.

Note that reading a bitmap file requires some more complicated Xlib programming, not Xt programming, so we will not take the space to describe it. If you are curious, the complete code for *xbitmap5*, which both reads and writes bitmap files, is shown in Appendix E, *The xbitmap Application*.

4.3 xbitmap3: Another Way to Create a Custom Window

The small bitmaps added in the last section provided a simple example of making a custom window by creating a DrawingArea widget and drawing into it from the application. DrawingArea also provides a callback for keyboard and pointer (mouse) input, so that you can implement simple user response from the application. However, you will quickly find that to implement a more complicated custom window you need more control than Drawing-Area gives you.

The next technique to consider for implementing features not supported by any existing widget is to add features to an empty widget such as Core or Primitive using actions and translations. This is simpler than writing a widget to do the same thing. It also uses less memory because you do not create a whole new widget class. This section describes how to implement the small pixmaps that way. But first, there are some new concepts involved.

4.3.1 Actions

So far in the book we have used callbacks to link widgets with application code. When you are implementing a custom window, callbacks are useless because they are defined by each widget class, and none of the existing widget classes has the callbacks or features that you need.

Therefore, you need to use a different technique for linking application code with widget code: the combination of actions and translations. You can use actions to add features to a Primitive or Core widget. (Actions are also used inside widget code to implement widget features.)

The action and callback techniques for linking the application with the user interface differ in the way that the registered function is invoked. For callbacks, the trigger is an abstract occurrence defined by the widget, which may or may not be event related. When this happens, the routines on one of a widget's callback lists are invoked by the widget code, using a call to `XtCallCallbacks()` or `XtCallCallbackList()`. Actions, on the other hand, are invoked directly by Xt's translation mechanism, as the result of an event combination.

In *xbitmap3* we will make the `RedrawSmallPicture` function into an action function instead of a callback function (this means just giving it different arguments). Then we need to arrange for Xt to call `RedrawSmallPicture` whenever one of the Primitive widgets becomes exposed. The general procedure for arranging this is the same as in *xbitmap2*—you register the function during the setup phase of the application, and then Xt will call it in response to Expose events. Registering an action, though, is quite different from registering a callback.

To register the action, you first declare an *actions table*, which maps action name strings to action function pointers. Then you must register the actions table with Xt by calling Xt-AppAddActions(). Finally you create a translation table and store it in the app-defaults file or hardcode it in the application. A translation table is a widget resource which contains a mapping between events or event sequences and action names. Figure 4-4 shows a translation table and an action table, and shows how each is used in the process of mapping events to action function calls. (The format of these two tables is described in the following sections and in Chapter 8, *Events, Translations, and Accelerators*.) This two-stage mapping is necessary so that translations can be specified in resource files. Since resource files contain only strings, a translation specified in a resource file can only translate an event into an action name. The action table, which can only be specified in the code, translates the action name into the actual action function pointer.

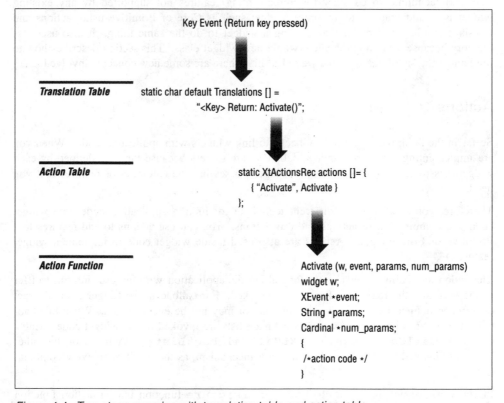

Figure 4-4. Two-stage mapping with translation table and action table

When an event arrives in a particular widget, Xt searches that widget's translation table resource. If that event is not found in the table, Xt does nothing. If the event is found, the matching action name is searched for in the action table. If the action name is found, the corresponding action function is called.

We'll describe the format of the action table and translation table, using *xbitmap3* as an example.

4.3.1.1 The Actions Table

The format of an actions table is defined as follows:

```
typedef struct _XtActionsRec{
    char *string;
    XtActionProc proc;
} XtActionsRec;
```

By convention, the string and the function name are identical, and begin with uppercase letters, as in the following example:

```
static void RedrawSmallPicture();

static XtActionsRec actions[ ] = {
    {"RedrawSmallPicture", RedrawSmallPicture},
    /* {"Quit", Quit}, */
};
```

The entry that is commented out in the action table shows how additional action functions would be specified in the table if they were needed. *xbitmap3* needs only one action function. In *xbitmap4* you will see a practical example of multiple action functions.

Action names and action functions should not start with Xt or xt: these are reserved for the Intrinsics.

Example 4-8 shows the code from *bitmap3* that creates the action table and registers it with `XtAppAddActions()`.

Example 4-8. xbitmap3.c: adding a feature to a Primitive widget

```
main(argc, argv)
int argc;
char **argv;
{
    /* other declarations */
        .
        .
        .
    static XtActionsRec actions[ ] = {
        {"RedrawSmallPicture", RedrawSmallPicture},
    };
        .
        .
        .
    /* XtAppInitialize */
        .
        .
        .
    XtAppAddActions(app_context, actions, XtNumber(actions));
        .
```

Example Application

```
        .
        .
    /* XtAppMainLoop */
}
```

Actions defined by a widget class are usable only by all instances of that widget class. Actions added with `XtAppAddActions()`, on the other hand, are global to the application context, and therefore usable by any widget instance of any class in the application. Which widgets they are actually used with is defined by the translation table, as described below.

The names of widget class actions and application actions do not conflict. For example, if an application were to define an action called **Move**, and some widget class in Motif already has an action by that name, the two actions would not conflict with each other.

When you map the action to events in a particular widget (using a translation table), the same is true, with a slight caveat. If you write an action called **Move**, and the widget you install it on already has a **Move** action, your version will be ignored. This implies that you are trying to replace a widget action with your own, and this is not allowed. You have to write a subclass of the widget to replace a widget action.

4.3.1.2 Format of an Action Function

An action function is just a pointer to a function with four arguments: a widget, an event, a string containing any arguments specified for the action in the translation table (described in Section 4.3.2.3), and the number of arguments contained in the string. Example 4-9 shows the action version of `RedrawSmallPicture`.

Example 4-9. An XtActionProc with widget and event arguments

```
/* ARGSUSED */
static void
RedrawSmallPicture(w, event, params, num_params)
Widget w;
XExposeEvent *event;
String *params;
Cardinal *num_params;
{
    Pixmap pixmap;

    if (w == bitmap_stuff.showNormalBitmap)
        pixmap = bitmap_stuff.normal_bitmap;
    else
        pixmap = bitmap_stuff.reverse_bitmap;

    if (DefaultDepthOfScreen(XtScreen(w)) == 1)
        XCopyArea(XtDisplay(w), pixmap, XtWindow(w),
                DefaultGCOfScreen(XtScreen(w)), event->x, event->y,
                event->width, event->height, event->x, event->y);
    else
        XCopyPlane(XtDisplay(w), pixmap, XtWindow(w),
                DefaultGCOfScreen(XtScreen(w)), event->x, event->y,
                event->width, event->height, event->x, event->y, 1);
}
```

Example 4-9. An XtActionProc with widget and event arguments (continued)

Action functions are directly passed the event structure that describes the event that triggered the action, in this case an XExposeEvent structure. This structure contains the position and dimensions of the area that was exposed. This version of RedrawSmallPicture copies only the necessary parts of the pixmap to refresh the areas that are exposed.

Under Motif (but not Athena) callback functions are passed the event structure as part of a larger structure, which is passed as the `call_data` argument (for example XmAny-CallbackStruct). Therefore, you have access to the event structure from within both callbacks and actions.

However, if you are allowing user configuration of the translation table (which is described below), an action may be called with different kinds of events. You should at least check the event type in the action routine and print an appropriate message if the user has arranged to call the action with the wrong type of event. We'll show how to do this in Chapter 8, *Events, Translations, and Accelerators*.

Note that for true ANSI C portability, all four arguments to the action function must be declared, even though many compilers allow you to leave off trailing arguments that are not referenced in the function. If some of the arguments are not used, you should be sure to include the *lint* comment /* ARGSUSED */.

Another difference between action functions and callback functions is that, unlike callbacks, there is no argument provided for passing in application data. You can only pass application data into an action function through global variables.

4.3.2 Translations

Once you have an action table registered, those actions are ready to be used by any widget in the application. But which widgets will they be used in, and which will trigger them? Translations determine these things.

You need to set a translation table resource, XmNtranslations, on any widget you want to be able to call an application action. In the case of *xbitmap3*, we want RedrawSmall-Picture to be called when Expose events occur in the widgets that are displaying the small pixmaps. This means that we need to set the XmNtranslations resource on those two widgets, and the value of the resource should be a translation that maps an Expose event into a RedrawSmallPicture call.

4.3.2.1 The Translation Table

Every widget that contains actions also has a default translation table that maps event combinations into those actions. The application can override, augment, or replace this table to make a widget call application-registered actions in addition to the widget's own actions. Registering actions with **XtAppAddActions()** makes them eligible for inclusion in translation tables.

Each line of a translation table maps a sequence of events to a sequence of actions. The entire translation table is simply a string consisting of one or more event specifications in angle brackets, with optional modifiers, followed by a colon and a function name string defined in an action table. Multiple translations can be specified as part of the same string. By convention, the string is continued on several lines, one for each translation, each line except the last terminated with a linefeed (\n) and a backslash (\).

We'll describe the details of event specification and other aspects of translation table syntax in Chapter 8, *Events, Translations, and Accelerators*. For now, an example should get the point across quite clearly.

The translation we need for *xbitmap3*, as it would appear in the application code, is shown in Example 4-10. This example also shows how the translation table must be converted into an internal form with **XtParseTranslationTable()** before it can be used to set an **Xm-Ntranslations** resource.

Example 4-10. A simple translation table

```
XtTranslations mytranslations;

static char transTable[ ] =
    "<Expose>:  RedrawSmallPicture()";
    .
    .
    .

bitmap_stuff.showReverseBitmap =
        XtVaCreateManagedWidget("showReverseBitmap",
        XmPrimitiveWidgetClass, frame2,
        XmNtranslations, XtParseTranslationTable(transTable);
        XmNwidth, bitmap_stuff.pixmap_width_in_cells,
        XmNheight, bitmap_stuff.pixmap_height_in_cells,
        NULL);
    .
    .
    .
```

The default translations for the PushButton widget (which are defined inside the widget implementation) are as follows:

Example 4-11. A complex translation table

```
static char defaultTranslations[ ] =
    "<Btn1Down>:            Arm()\n\
    <Btn1Down>,<Btn1Up>: Activate() Disarm()\n\
    <Btn1Down>(2+):      MultiArm()\n\
    <Btn1Up>(2+):        MultiActivate()\n\
    <Btn1Up>:            Activate() Disarm()\n\
```

Example 4-11. A complex translation table (continued)

```
<Key>osfSelect:      ArmAndActivate()\n\
<Key>osfActivate:    ArmAndActivate()\n\
<Key>osfHelp:  Help()\n\
~Shift ~Meta ~Alt <Key>Return:  ArmAndActivate()\n\
~Shift ~Meta ~Alt <Key>space:   ArmAndActivate()\n\
<EnterWindow>:       Enter()\n\
<LeaveWindow>:       Leave()";
```

Notice that this entire translation table is a single string. This translation table shows several useful techniques; all these techniques and more are described in full detail in Chapter 8, *Events, Translations, and Accelerators*:

- How to detect a button press followed by a release (second line).

- How to invoke two successive actions in response to an event sequence (second line).

- How to detect a double click (lines 3 and 4).

- How to detect the press of a particular key (lines 6, 7, and 8).

- How to detect a key press but only if certain modifier keys are not being held (9 and 10).

Like most other resources, translations can be specified in resource files. While debugging, it is a good idea to specify translation tables in files, to minimize recompiling. Example 4-12 shows the part of the app-defaults file for *xbitmap3* that sets the translation table.

Example 4-12. XBitmap3: specifying translations in the app-defaults file

```
*XmPrimitive.baseTranslations:\
    <Expose>:  RedrawSmallPicture()
```

Note that since resource files are strings, no quotation marks are needed. However, for multiple-line translation tables, you still need to escape the ends of each line with \n\.

The resource set here is `baseTranslations` (new in R5). (This resource has the same name for all widgets.) As you know, the contents of the app-default file consist solely of strings, so Xt processes the setting for `baseTranslations` into a translation table using what's called a resource converter. The resource converter calls `XtParseTranslation-Table()` for you when you specify translations in a resource file. Applications intended for both R4 and R5 should also set the `translations` resource. See Section 10.2.12 for more information.

In principle, you can modify the translations of existing widgets to customize their behavior. However, Motif discourages this practice since it tends to break user-interface conventions. In fact, some Motif widgets allow you to modify their translations (no error is generated), but they do not actually modify their behavior.† When modifying the translations of a widget with existing translations, you may specify a directive to control what happens when there are conflicts between your new translations and the existing translations. Xt recognizes one

---

† Which translation you cannot modify, and in which widget classes, is not precisely documented in Motif. In general, you should avoid modifying translation of existing widget classes altogether (with the exception of Primitive).

of three directives in a translation table, beginning with # on the first line, which tell how to handle existing translations (either set as widget defaults, or in other resource database files):

- #replace (the default if no directive is specified). Replace the old translations with the current table.

- #augment. Merge the new translations into the existing translation table, but not to disturb any existing translations. If a translation already exists for a particular event, the conflicting translation specification that appears in a table beginning with #augment is ignored.

- #override. Merge the new translations into the existing translation table, replacing old values with the current specifications in the event of conflict.

We used #override because this allows us to keep the translations for <EnterWindow> and <LeaveWindow> events in place. In addition, the PushButton widget's set and unset actions will also remain in effect for <Btn1Down> and <Btn1Up>. (For more details on why these aren't overridden by the new translations, see Chapter 8, *Events, Translations, and Accelerators*.)

The translation:

```
<Btn1Down>,<Btn1Up>:  confirm()
```

specifies that the confirm action should be called in response to a pair of events, namely a button press followed by a button release, with no other events intervening.

The translations:

```
<Btn2Down>:            set()\n\
<Btn2Down>,<Btn2Up>:   quit()
```

specify that the PushButton widget's internal set action should be invoked by pressing button 2, and that our own quit action should be invoked by clicking button 2. Note that we don't bother to bind the PushButton widget's unset action to <Btn2Up>, since the application will disappear as a result of the quit action. (The unset action is still used when the user presses button 2 and then moves the pointer outside the widget before releasing button 2. This is one of PushButton's default bindings that we have not overridden.) If we were using the widget for any other purpose, we would map <Btn2Up> to unset, so that the widget was restored to its normal appearance when our own action was completed.

4.3.2.2 Hardcoding Translations

There are cases in which an application may want not only to specify translations in an app-defaults file, but also to hardcode them into the application. When you specify translations only in the app-defaults file, the user has unlimited configurability; if the default translations are deleted or changed beyond recognition, the application may no longer work. But you can hardcode a minimum set of translations in the code, and then supplement these with a set of translations in the app-defaults file that you want to be user-customizable. Among resources, translations are unique because the final value can be the result of merging the values in the resource files with the values in the application (with other resources you get one or the other, but not a combination).

Three Xt functions are used for setting translation tables from the application code:

- `XtParseTranslationTable()` is used to compile a string translation table into the opaque internal representation `XtTranslations`. (For translations specified in resource files, this conversion is performed automatically by a resource converter.)

- `XtAugmentTranslations()` is used, like the `#augment` directive in a resource file, to nondestructively merge translations into a widget's existing translations.

- `XtOverrideTranslations()` is used, like the `#override` directive in a resource file, to destructively merge translations into a widget's existing translations.

Both `XtAugmentTranslations()` and `XtOverrideTranslations()` take as arguments a widget and a compiled translation table returned by `XtParseTranslationTable()`.

There is no function that completely replaces a widget's translations; however, you can do this by calling `XtSetValues()`, the general routine for setting resources (whose use is demonstrated later in this chapter) that set the value of a widget's `XmNtranslations` resource to a compiled translation table returned by `XtParseTranslationTable()`.

To set the same translations specified in the app-defaults file from the application itself, we would have used the following code:

Example 4-13. Code fragment: specifying translations in the program

```
static char defaultTranslations[ ] =
     "<Btn1Down>,<Btn1Up>:    confirm()\n\
     <Btn2Down>:             set()\n\
     <Btn2Down>,<Btn2Up>:    quit()";
XtTranslations mytranslations;
     .
     .
     .

mytranslations = XtParseTranslationTable(defaultTranslations);
XtOverrideTranslations(farewell, mytranslations);
```

As mentioned earlier, you will find it more convenient to place the translation table in the app-defaults file until the last minute, because this allows changes without recompiling the source.

4.3.2.3 Action Parameters

The *params* and *num-params* arguments of an action function are passed in from the translation table by Xt. For example, consider an action called *Move*, which can move some data left of right. A translation table that selects events that will invoke *Move* is shown in Example 4-14.

Example 4-14. A translation table with action parameters

```
*tetris.translations:\n\
<Key>Left: Move(l)\n\
<Key>Right: Move(r)
```

With this translation table, *Move* will be passed a *params* argument "l" when the left arrow key is pressed, and "r" when the right arrow key is pressed.

4.3.3 Adding Actions to Existing Widgets

It is also possible to add actions to widgets other than Core and Primitive, but it takes more care. Usually, when a widget does not provide a certain callback, it also does not provide various other characteristics that you want. For example, to make the Label widget work like PushButton (pretending that the PushButton widget didn't already exist), you would have to make it accept more kinds of input, add the drawing code to highlight the border and draw the window darker to simulate shadow, and add the ability to call an application function. All of this can be done with actions, but it would take a lot of work. What can make it difficult is that your code may interact with the widget's code in unpleasant ways. When the changes are major, it makes more sense to create a new widget subclass that shares some characteristics and code with its superclass. As we will see, that is exactly how PushButton is implemented, as a subclass of Label. The Primitive and DrawingArea widgets, on the other hand, have no input or output semantics at all, and therefore it is simpler to add actions to them without conflict.

4.4 xbitmap4: A Bitmap Editor Without a BitmapEdit Widget

Until you have experience working with widget code, it can be easier to prototype a custom window for your application by adding to a Primitive widget from the application code. Once this code is working, and you have read Chapter 6, *Inside a Widget*, and Chapter 7, *Basic Widget Methods*, you can easily move the code into a widget when you want to package it or take advantage of any of the features of Xt that are inaccessible from the application. The code for the BitmapEdit widget was originally written as an application (as described in this section) and later moved into a widget (with the result described in Chapters 6 and 7). Once you understand the structure of a widget, it becomes easier to write widgets directly than to build the same functionality in the application first.

The *xbitmap4* implements an application almost identical to *xbitmap1*, but without using the BitmapEdit widget. The custom bitmap editing window is done in a Primitive widget, with all the code in the application. This is an example of a custom window that could not be easily built using DrawingArea. This application is a culmination of everything you have seen so far. It is also a preview of what you will see in the next chapter. The same code in *xbitmap4* that is used to implement the bitmap editor will be moved into widget code in Chapters 6 and 7.

This example takes advantage of application resources to set the configurable parameters of the bitmap code. The code that sets up the application resources is described in Section 3.6. When moving the code into a widget framework, the same resource list will be used verbatim. The example also provides command-line options to set the important parameters of the bitmap code. The code for processing these options is described in Section 3.7. The code is the same whether used for setting application resources or widget resources, except no call equivalent to `XtGetApplicationResources()` is necessary in a widget.

The exposure strategy used for the bitmap editor is the same as for the small bitmaps in the previous section. The application creates a large pixmap of depth one that stores the current image of the bitmap being edited. Whenever the screen needs updating, the applicable part of the pixmap is copied to the Core widget in the `Redraw_picture` routine. Because this pixmap is much bigger than the ones in the last section, it is an important optimization that only the required parts of the pixmap are copied. (This is not the only possible exposure strategy. This particular strategy has very low network load, but uses a relatively large amount of server memory. For this reason it is not ideal for PC servers.)

The `SetUpThings` routine creates the pixmap, draws a grid into it that will persist for the life of the application, and creates three GCs. One GC is for copying from the pixmap to the window, and two are for drawing and undrawing cells in the pixmap. The `btn_event` routine draws and undraws cells in the pixmap according to pointer clicks and drags, and calls `Redraw_picture` to update the Core widget display.

`Redraw_picture` is called both from the application and from Xt. This is a common trick used to reduce the duplication of drawing code. Since `Redraw_picture` is an action, it has an event argument that is used by Xt to pass in the `Expose` event describing the area exposed. This application also uses this argument by constructing a fake event to pass in information about which part of the widget to draw.

The application adds actions and sets the `XmNtranslations` resource of the Core widget so that Xt calls the application routine `Redraw_picture` whenever `Expose` events arrive, and calls `btn_event` when `ButtonPress` or `MotionNotify` events arrive.

Example 4-15 shows the complete code for *xbitmap4*. You have seen all the techniques here in various examples before. You should work through the code and make sure you understand the purpose of each section. However, don't worry about the details of the Xlib calls, since they are specific to this application.

Example 4-15. xbitmap4: implementing the bitmap editor from the application

```
/*
 * xbitmap4.c
 */
#include <Xm/Xm.h>

#include <Xm/PanedW.h>
#include <Xm/RowColumn.h>
#include <Xm/PushB.h>
```

```
/* we use XmPrimitive, but no header file needed (in Xm.h) */

#include <stdio.h>

/* The following could be placed in an "xbitmap.h" file. */
#define XtNdebug "debug"
#define XtCDebug "Debug"
#define XtNpixmapWidthInCells "pixmapWidthInCells"
#define XtCPixmapWidthInCells "PixmapWidthInCells"
#define XtNpixmapHeightInCells "pixmapHeightInCells"
#define XtCPixmapHeightInCells "PixmapHeightInCells"
#define XtNcellSizeInPixels "cellSizeInPixels"
#define XtCCellSizeInPixels "CellSizeInPixels"

#define DRAWN 1
#define UNDRAWN 0

#define DRAW 1
#define UNDRAW 0

#define MAXLINES  1000

#define MINBITMAPWIDTH  2
#define MAXBITMAPWIDTH  1000
#define MINBITMAPHEIGHT  2
#define MAXBITMAPHEIGHT  1000
#define MINCELLSIZE  4
#define MAXCELLSIZE  100

#define SCROLLBARWIDTH 15

/*
 * Data structure for private data.
 * (This avoids lots of global variables.)
 */
typedef struct {
    Pixmap big_picture;
    GC draw_gc, undraw_gc; /* for drawing into the
                            * big_picture, 1-bit deep */
    GC copy_gc;            /* for copying from pixmap
                            * into window, screen depth */
    Widget bitmap;         /* this is the drawing surface */
    char *cell;            /* this is the array for printing output
                            * and keeping track of cells drawn */

    int cur_x, cur_y;
    Dimension pixmap_width_in_pixels, pixmap_height_in_pixels;
} PrivateAppData;

/* data structure for application resources */
typedef struct {
    Pixel copy_fg;
    Pixel copy_bg;
    int pixmap_width_in_cells;
    int pixmap_height_in_cells;
    int cell_size_in_pixels;
    Boolean debug;
} AppData;

AppData app_data;
PrivateAppData private_app_data;
```

```
/* resource list */
static XtResource resources[ ] = {
    {
        XmNforeground,
        XmCForeground,
        XmRPixel,
        sizeof(Pixel),
        XtOffsetOf(AppData, copy_fg),
        XmRString,
        XtDefaultForeground
    },
    {
        XmNbackground,
        XmCBackground,
        XmRPixel,
        sizeof(Pixel),
        XtOffsetOf(AppData, copy_bg),
        XmRString,
        XtDefaultBackground
    },
    {
        XtNpixmapWidthInCells,
        XtCPixmapWidthInCells,
        XmRInt,
        sizeof(int),
        XtOffsetOf(AppData, pixmap_width_in_cells),
        XmRImmediate,
        (XtPointer) 32,
    },
    {
        XtNpixmapHeightInCells,
        XtCPixmapHeightInCells,
        XmRInt,
        sizeof(int),
        XtOffsetOf(AppData, pixmap_height_in_cells),
        XmRImmediate,
        (XtPointer) 32,
    },
    {
        XtNcellSizeInPixels,
        XtCCellSizeInPixels,
        XmRInt,
        sizeof(int),
        XtOffsetOf(AppData, cell_size_in_pixels),
        XmRImmediate,
        (XtPointer) 30,
    },
    {
        XtNdebug,
        XtCDebug,
        XmRBoolean,
        sizeof(Boolean),
        XtOffsetOf(AppData, debug),
        XmRImmediate,
        (XtPointer) False,
```

Example Application

```
    },
};

/* Command-line options table */
static XrmOptionDescRec options[ ] = {
    {"-pw",            "*pixmapWidthInCells",    XrmoptionSepArg, NULL},
    {"-pixmapwidth",   "*pixmapWidthInCells",    XrmoptionSepArg, NULL},
    {"-ph",            "*pixmapHeightInCells",   XrmoptionSepArg, NULL},
    {"-pixmapheight",  "*pixmapHeightInCells",   XrmoptionSepArg, NULL},
    {"-cellsize",      "*cellSizeInPixels",      XrmoptionSepArg, NULL},
    {"-fg",            "*foreground",            XrmoptionSepArg, NULL},
    {"-foreground",    "*foreground",            XrmoptionSepArg, NULL},
    {"-debug",       "  *debug",                 XrmoptionNoArg, "True"},
};

/* callback function to print cell array to stdout */
/* ARGSUSED */
static void
PrintOut(w, event, params, num_params)
Widget w;
XEvent *event;
String *params;
Cardinal *num_params;
{
    /*
     * The absense of the small pixmaps in this version makes it
     * more difficult to call XWriteBitmapFile.  Therefore, we will
     * stick with the printed output for this version.
     */
    int x, y;
    putchar('\n');
    for (y = 0; y < app_data.pixmap_height_in_cells; y++) {
        for (x = 0; x < app_data.pixmap_width_in_cells; x++)
            putchar(private_app_data.cell[x + y *
                    app_data.pixmap_width_in_cells] ? '1' : '0');
        putchar('\n');
    }
    putchar('\n');
}

static void RedrawPicture(), DrawCell(), UndrawCell(), ToggleCell(),
        DrawPixmaps();

static void Syntax(argc, argv)
int argc;
char * argv[ ];
{
    int i;
    static int errs = False;

    /* first argument is program name - skip that */
    for (i = 1; i < argc; i++) {
        if (!errs++) /* do first time through */
            fprintf(stderr, "xbitmap4: command line\
                    option not understood:\n");
        fprintf(stderr, "option: %s\n", argv[i]);
    }
```

```
        fprintf(stderr, "xbitmap understands all standard Xt\
                command line options.\n");

        fprintf(stderr, "Additional options are as follows:\n");
        fprintf(stderr, "Option                Valid Range\n");
        fprintf(stderr, "-pw                   MINBITMAPWIDTH to\
                MAXBITMAPWIDTH\n");
        fprintf(stderr, "-pixmapwidth          MINBITMAPWIDTH to\
                MAXBITMAPWIDTH\n");
        fprintf(stderr, "-ph                   MINBITMAPHEIGHT to\
                MAXBITMAPHEIGHT\n");
        fprintf(stderr, "-pixmapheight         MINBITMAPHEIGHT to\
                MAXBITMAPHEIGHT\n");
        fprintf(stderr, "-cellsize             MINCELLSIZE to\
                MAXCELLSIZE\n");
        fprintf(stderr, "-fg                   color name\n");
        fprintf(stderr, "-foreground           color name\n");
        fprintf(stderr, "-debug                no value necessary\n");
}

main(argc, argv)
int argc;
char *argv[ ];
{
    XtAppContext app_context;
    Widget topLevel, vpane, buttonbox, quit, output;
    extern exit();
    /* translation table for bitmap core widget */
    String trans =
    "<Expose>:  RedrawPicture()                    \n\
        <Btn1Down>:    DrawCell()                   \n\
        <Btn2Down>:    UndrawCell()                 \n\
        <Btn3Down>:    ToggleCell()                 \n\
        <Btn1Motion>:  DrawCell()                   \n\
        <Btn2Motion>:  UndrawCell()                 \n\
        <Btn3Motion>:  ToggleCell()";

    static XtActionsRec window_actions[ ] = {
        {"RedrawPicture",   RedrawPicture},
        {"DrawCell",        DrawCell},
        {"UndrawCell",      UndrawCell},
        {"ToggleCell",      ToggleCell},
    };

      XtSetLanguageProc(NULL, (XtLanguageProc)NULL, NULL);

    topLevel = XtVaAppInitialize(
            &app_context,          /* Application context */
            "XBitmap4",
            options, XtNumber(options),
            &argc, argv,           /* command line args */
            NULL,                  /* for missing app-defaults file */
            NULL);                 /* terminate varargs list */

    /* XtInitialize leaves program name in args */
    if (argc > 1)
        Syntax(argc, argv);

    XtGetApplicationResources(topLevel,
```

```
            &app_data,
            resources,
            XtNumber(resources),
            NULL,
            0);

    /*
     * We must check the application resource values here.
     * Otherwise, user could supply out of range values and crash
     * program. Conversion routines do this automatically, so
     * colors are already checked.
     */
    if ((app_data.pixmap_width_in_cells > MAXBITMAPWIDTH) ||
            (app_data.pixmap_width_in_cells < MINBITMAPWIDTH) ||
            (app_data.pixmap_height_in_cells > MAXBITMAPWIDTH) ||
            (app_data.pixmap_height_in_cells < MINBITMAPWIDTH)) {
        fprintf(stderr, "xbitmap: error in resource settings:\
                dimension must be between %d and %d cells\n",
                MINBITMAPWIDTH, MAXBITMAPWIDTH);
        exit(1);
    }
    if ((app_data.cell_size_in_pixels < MINCELLSIZE) ||
            (app_data.cell_size_in_pixels > MAXCELLSIZE)) {
        fprintf(stderr, "xbitmap: error in resource settings:\
                cell size must be between %d and %d pixels\n",
                MINCELLSIZE, MAXCELLSIZE);
        exit(1);
    }

    /* begin application code */

    set_up_things(topLevel);

    private_app_data.cell = XtCalloc(app_data.pixmap_width_in_cells *
            app_data.pixmap_height_in_cells, sizeof(char));

    if (app_data.debug)
        fprintf(stderr, "xbitmap: pixmap dimensions are %d by %d\n",
                app_data.pixmap_width_in_cells,
                app_data.pixmap_height_in_cells);

    vpane = XtVaCreateManagedWidget("vpane", xmPanedWindowWidgetClass,
            topLevel, XmNwidth,
            private_app_data.pixmap_width_in_pixels, NULL);

    buttonbox = XtVaCreateManagedWidget("buttonbox",
            xmRowColumnWidgetClass, vpane, NULL);

    output = XtVaCreateManagedWidget("output", xmPushButtonWidgetClass,
            buttonbox, NULL);

    XtAddCallback(output, XmNactivateCallback, PrintOut, NULL);

    quit = XtVaCreateManagedWidget("quit", xmPushButtonWidgetClass,
            buttonbox, NULL);

    XtAddCallback(quit, XmNactivateCallback, exit, NULL);

    /* note: no header file needed to create xmPrimitive */
    private_app_data.bitmap = XtVaCreateManagedWidget("bitmap",
            xmPrimitiveWidgetClass, vpane,
```

```
            XmNtranslations, XtParseTranslationTable(trans),
            XmNwidth, private_app_data.pixmap_width_in_pixels,
            XmNheight, private_app_data.pixmap_height_in_pixels,
            NULL);

    XtAppAddActions(app_context, window_actions,
            XtNumber(window_actions));

    XtRealizeWidget(topLevel);

    XtAppMainLoop(app_context);
}

set_up_things(w)
Widget w;
{
    XGCValues values;
    int x, y;
    XSegment segment[MAXLINES];
    int n_horiz_segments, n_vert_segments;

    private_app_data.pixmap_width_in_pixels =
            app_data.pixmap_width_in_cells *
            app_data.cell_size_in_pixels;
    private_app_data.pixmap_height_in_pixels =
            app_data.pixmap_height_in_cells *
            app_data.cell_size_in_pixels;

    private_app_data.big_picture = XCreatePixmap(XtDisplay(w),
            RootWindowOfScreen(XtScreen(w)),
            private_app_data.pixmap_width_in_pixels,
            private_app_data.pixmap_height_in_pixels, 1);

    values.foreground = 1;
    values.background = 0;
    values.dashes = 1;
    values.dash_offset = 0;
    values.line_style = LineOnOffDash;

    private_app_data.draw_gc = XCreateGC(XtDisplay(w),
            private_app_data.big_picture, GCForeground | GCBackground
            | GCDashOffset | GCDashList | GCLineStyle, &values);

    values.foreground = 0;
    values.background = 1;
    private_app_data.undraw_gc = XCreateGC(XtDisplay(w),
            private_app_data.big_picture, GCForeground | GCBackground
            | GCDashOffset | GCDashList | GCLineStyle, &values);

    values.foreground = app_data.copy_fg;
    values.background = app_data.copy_bg;
    private_app_data.copy_gc = XCreateGC(XtDisplay(w),
            RootWindowOfScreen(XtScreen(w)),
            GCForeground | GCBackground, &values);

    XFillRectangle(XtDisplay(w), private_app_data.big_picture,
            private_app_data.undraw_gc, 0, 0,
            private_app_data.pixmap_width_in_pixels,
            private_app_data.pixmap_height_in_pixels);

    /* draw permanent grid into pixmap */
```

```
    n_horiz_segments = app_data.pixmap_height_in_cells + 1;
    n_vert_segments = app_data.pixmap_width_in_cells + 1;

    for (x = 0; x < n_horiz_segments; x += 1) {
        segment[ x ].x1 = 0;
        segment[ x ].x2 = private_app_data.pixmap_width_in_pixels;
        segment[ x ].y1 = app_data.cell_size_in_pixels * x;
        segment[ x ].y2 = app_data.cell_size_in_pixels * x;
    }

    /* drawn only once into pixmap */
    XDrawSegments(XtDisplay(w), private_app_data.big_picture,
            private_app_data.draw_gc, segment, n_horiz_segments);

    for (y = 0; y < n_vert_segments; y += 1) {
        segment[ y ].x1 = y * app_data.cell_size_in_pixels;
        segment[ y ].x2 = y * app_data.cell_size_in_pixels;
        segment[ y ].y1 = 0;
        segment[ y ].y2 = private_app_data.pixmap_height_in_pixels;
    }

    /* drawn only once into pixmap */
    XDrawSegments(XtDisplay(w), private_app_data.big_picture,
            private_app_data.draw_gc, segment, n_vert_segments);
}
/* ARGSUSED */
static void
RedrawPicture(w, event, params, num_params)
Widget w;
XExposeEvent *event;
String *params;
Cardinal *num_params;
{
    register int x, y;
    unsigned int width, height;

    if (event) {      /* drawing because of expose or button press */
        x = event->x;
        y = event->y;
        width = event->width;
        height = event->height;
    }
    else {  /* drawing because of scrolling */
        x = 0;
        y = 0;
        width = 10000;   /* always the whole window! */
        height = 10000;
    }

    if (DefaultDepthOfScreen(XtScreen(w)) == 1)
        XCopyArea(XtDisplay(w), private_app_data.big_picture,
                XtWindow(w), private_app_data.copy_gc, x +
                private_app_data.cur_x, y + private_app_data.cur_y,
                width, height, x, y);
    else
        XCopyPlane(XtDisplay(w), private_app_data.big_picture,
                XtWindow(w), private_app_data.copy_gc, x +
                private_app_data.cur_x, y + private_app_data.cur_y,
```

```
                    width, height, x, y, 1);
}

/* ARGSUSED */
static void
DrawCell(w, event, params, num_params)
Widget w;
XButtonEvent *event;
String *params;
Cardinal *num_params;
{
    DrawPixmaps(private_app_data.draw_gc, DRAW, w, event);
}

/* ARGSUSED */
static void
UndrawCell(w, event, params, num_params)
Widget w;
XButtonEvent *event;
String *params;
Cardinal *num_params;
{
    DrawPixmaps(private_app_data.undraw_gc, UNDRAW, w, event);
}

/* ARGSUSED */
static void
ToggleCell(w, event, params, num_params)
Widget w;
XButtonEvent *event;
String *params;
Cardinal *num_params;
{
    static int oldx = -1, oldy = -1;
    GC gc;
    int mode;
    int newx = (private_app_data.cur_x + event->x) /
            app_data.cell_size_in_pixels;
    int newy = (private_app_data.cur_y + event->y) /
            app_data.cell_size_in_pixels;

    if ((mode = private_app_data.cell[newx + newy *
            app_data.pixmap_width_in_cells ]) == DRAWN) {
        gc = private_app_data.undraw_gc;
        mode = UNDRAW;
    }
    else {
        gc = private_app_data.draw_gc;
        mode = DRAW;
    }

    if (oldx != newx || oldy != newy) {
        oldx = newx;
        oldy = newy;
        DrawPixmaps(gc, mode, w, event);
    }
}
```

Example Application

```
/* Private Function */
static void
DrawPixmaps(gc, mode, w, event)
GC gc;
int mode;
Widget w;
XButtonEvent *event;
{
    int newx = (private_app_data.cur_x + event->x) /
            app_data.cell_size_in_pixels;
    int newy = (private_app_data.cur_y + event->y) /
            app_data.cell_size_in_pixels;
    XExposeEvent fake_event;

    /* if already done, return */
    if (private_app_data.cell[newx + newy *
            app_data.pixmap_width_in_cells] == mode)
        return;

    XFillRectangle(XtDisplay(w), private_app_data.big_picture, gc,
            app_data.cell_size_in_pixels*newx + 2,
            app_data.cell_size_in_pixels*newy + 2,
            (unsigned int) app_data.cell_size_in_pixels - 3,
            (unsigned int) app_data.cell_size_in_pixels - 3);

    private_app_data.cell[newx + newy *
            app_data.pixmap_width_in_cells] = mode;

    fake_event.x = app_data.cell_size_in_pixels * newx -
            private_app_data.cur_x;
    fake_event.y = app_data.cell_size_in_pixels * newy -
            private_app_data.cur_y;
    fake_event.width = app_data.cell_size_in_pixels;
    fake_event.height = app_data.cell_size_in_pixels;

    RedrawPicture(private_app_data.bitmap, &fake_event);
}
```

Of particular interest in the code for *xbitmap4* is the **Syntax** function. Notice that it prints out the options that were not understood, in addition to printing out a list of valid options.

5

More About Motif

This chapter describes each widget in the Motif set that has not yet been introduced, and describes the features that Motif adds to the model provided by the Xt Intrinsics.

In This Chapter:

5
More About Motif

This book is primarily about how to program with the Xt Intrinsics, and has used the Motif widgets to demonstrate those techniques. It has so far not described many of the Motif widgets, and hasn't touched the surface of the topic of how to combine them to best advantage. Complete coverage of these topics is left to Volume Six, *Motif Programming Manual*. However, this chapter will acquaint you with the default appearance and general purpose of the Motif widgets we have not yet used. With this information, you should gain a general idea of the range of widgets you have to choose from.

Motif also provides many features that are roughly at the same level as those provided by Xt, but that go beyond those provided by Xt. Part of Motif, therefore, is a kind of extension of Xt. This chapter will provide sufficient introduction so that you know the purpose and capabilities of each of these features. This will enable you to determine whether these features will be useful in your application, and warrant further investigation. Again, more complete coverage of these features, with examples, will be left to Volume Six, *Motif Programming Manual*.

Note that Motif includes several components:

*   A widget set that works with the Xt Intrinsics library

*   A set of functions that provide additional Xt-level features.

*   The Motif Window Manager (mwm)

*   The User Interface Language (UIL) and Motif Resource Manager (MRM), which is a set of functions that works with Xt as well as a compiler that takes an ASCII file as input and generates a program-readable user interface description as output

*   A style guide which governs how a user interface should be put together in order to be certified as OSF/Motif compliant

We do not discuss the Motif Window Manager or style guide in any detail in this book. See Volume Six, *Motif Programming Manual* for more information.

5.1 The Remaining Motif Widgets and Gadgets

Let's begin with the primitive widgets that you haven't yet seen in examples in this book. These are widgets that do not manage child widgets. Although we have not explicitly created ArrowButton and ScrollBar widgets, you have seen them as part of MainWindow and ScrolledWindow. ArrowButton is the widget used at the ends of ScrollBars. ScrollBars, in turn, are created automatically by MainWindow and ScrolledWindow.

Command widgets are for keeping track of typed commands. The upper window shows the history of past commands typed, and the lower window shows the command currently being typed. Figure 5-1 shows a Command widget.

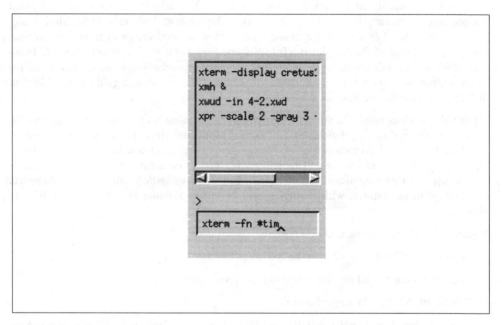

Figure 5-1. A Command widget

The FileSelectionBox is a complex widget which allows the user to move through the file system to select a file. See Volume Three, *X Window System User's Guide, Motif Edition*, for a description of how the user manipulates this widget. A FileSelectionBox can be created by itself without the buttons at the bottom (with **XmCreateFileSelectionBox()**) or it can be created as part of a dialog with **XmCreateFileSelectionDialog()**. Figure 5-2 shows a FileSelectionDialog widget.

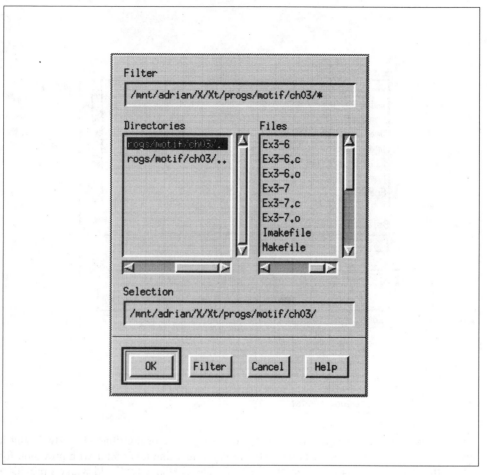

Filter

/mnt/adrian/X/Xt/progs/motif/ch03/*

Directories   Files

rogs/motif/ch03/.   Ex3-6
rogs/motif/ch03/..   Ex3-6.c
                           Ex3-6.o
                           Ex3-7
                           Ex3-7.c
                           Ex3-7.o
                           Imakefile
                           Makefile

Selection

/mnt/adrian/X/Xt/progs/motif/ch03/

OK   Filter   Cancel   Help

Figure 5-2. A FileSelectionDialog widget

A SelectionBox allows the user to choose from a list of alternatives. It provides a scrolled list, and a text area. The user can select from the list using the pointer, or type the name from the list. A SelectionBox can also be created as part of a dialog with **XmCreate-SelectionDialog( )**. Figure 5-3 shows a SelectionDialog widget.

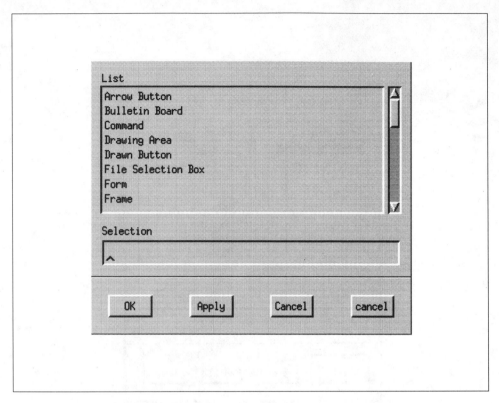

Figure 5-3. A SelectionDialog widget

Text is a text editor in a single widget. It can edit single line or multiline text. By default it uses Emacs-style editing commands. TextField is a single line text editor with provision for verification that the user supplied acceptable data. The Text and TextField widgets provide a multitude of functions for accessing and manipulating their contents from the application. The `XmCreateScrolledText()` function is used for creating a Text widget with ScrollBars. Figure 5-4 shows a TextField widget. A Text widget is similar but includes multiline editing capabilities.

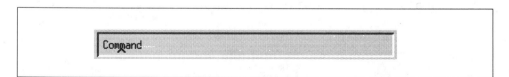

Figure 5-4. A TextField widget

The Separator widget is used to visually separate distinct areas within larger components. It just draws a line between widgets. Separators can be used to separate items in popup menus, action areas within dialog boxes, or simply adjacent geometry managing widgets. Usually you should use a SeparatorGadget instead. Figure 5-5 shows a menu containing elements separated with Separator widgets.

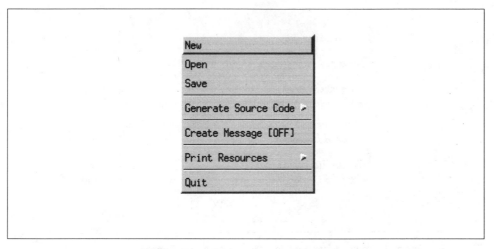

Figure 5-5. A menu containing buttons separated by Separator widgets

A ToggleButton sets a boolean value. ToggleButton is designed to be added in groups to a RadioBox or a CheckBox. See Figure 5-6. Both RadioBox and CheckBox are implemented using a RowColumn widget. The resources that distinguish these two types of user interface elements are automatically set when you use the `XmCreateRadioBox()` or `Xm-CreateSimpleCheckBox()` convenience functions. Each ToggleButton in a RadioBox has a diamond-shaped indicator, and only one ToggleButton at a time can be chosen. In a CheckBox, each ToggleButton has a square indicator and any number of the ToggleButtons can be selected at the same time.

A DrawnButton is a widget that works like a PushButton but it is empty except for a button shadow. It provides callbacks for exposure and resize events, so that you can provide your own drawing code. DrawnButtons are not often used, since PushButtons allow you to supply either text or a pixmap as its label. A DrawnButton can be used to implement an animated button (where the contents change frequently), or to draw text that is beyond the capabilities of a PushButton. Since a DrawnButton has no distinctive appearance, one is not shown.

The Scale is really a slider widget, which can be used for input or output. A Scale is shown in Figure 5-7.

The List widget provides an set of string choices. The List supports both single and multiple selection styles. Figure 5-8 shows a list widget containing numerous choices. `XmCreate-ScrolledList()` creates a specialized form of List that is for managing large lists.

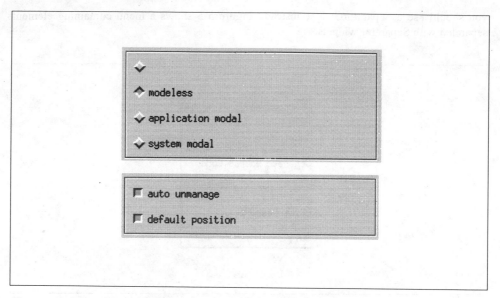

Figure 5-6. ToggleButton widgets used in a RadioBox and a CheckBox

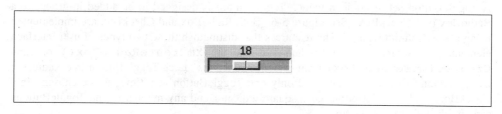

Figure 5-7. A Scale widget

Six types of simple widgets are also available as gadgets (window-less widgets): PushButton-Gadget, LabelGadget, ArrowButtonGadget, CascadeButtonGadget, SeparatorGadget, and ToggleButtonGadget. However, as of R5, you should avoid using gadgets since they can result in increased network load.

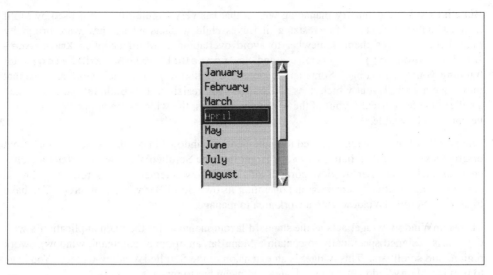

Figure 5-8. A List widget containing selectable strings

5.1.1 Geometry Managing Widgets

All Motif geometry managing widgets are subclasses of the Manager class. Instances of
Manager itself are never created. Manager serves the same purpose for geometry managing
widgets as Primitive does for graphics widgets. It provides the features common to all Motif
widgets, such as 3-D shadows, keyboard traversal, and so on.

Motif uses RowColumn very heavily. All of the following are not separate widget classes;
they are RowColumn widgets with certain resource settings:

- WorkArea—the default RowColumn type.

- CheckBox—a box designed to contain ToggleButtons, in which several can be selected
  at the same time.

- RadioBox—a box designed to contain ToggleButtons, in which only one can be selected.

- OptionMenu—appears as a button and an associated menu. The button shows the current
  selection from the menu. The menu appears over the button.

- PulldownMenu—a menu that appears just below a button that pops it up.

- PopupMenu—a menu that pops up at the pointer position.

- MenuBar—a horizontal bar across the top of the application's main window, containing
  CascadeButtons that post menus.

RowColumns do not have a three dimensional appearance, so they may be placed next to one
another without giving the user the impression that their sub-elements are grouped independently. However, they can be placed within Frame to generate a 3-D appearance.

BulletinBoard is a geometry managing widget that has very simple rules. It is used by Motif in most dialog widgets. After resizing, it leaves child widgets where they were originally placed, or it moves them somewhat to avoid overlapping. Motif supplies `XmCreate-BulletinBoard()` for general use and `XmCreateBulletinBoardDialog()` for building your own dialogs. Some applications use BulletinBoard as their work area, so that they have a static layout which does not change upon resizing. If a BulletinBoard is resized smaller than the current layout of the widgets it contains, the widgets are clipped and may not be completely visible.

The ScrolledWindow widget is used to implement a "window" into a data object (such as text or graphics). If the data being viewed is larger than the ScrolledWindow, scrollbars are attached to enable the user to view portions of the window interactively. ScrolledWindow is capable of automatically creating and operating its own ScrollBar widget children. You have to provide ScrolledWindow with a work area to manage.

The MainWindow widget acts as the standard layout manager for the main application's window. It is designed specifically to contain a MenuBar, an optional command window, a work region, and scrollbars. This widget is an extension of the ScrolledWindow widget. You have to provide MainWindow with a work area and menu bar to manage.

The Frame widget manages one child within a visible border that the Frame draws. It is most often used to provide a 3-D border for RowColumn and Form widgets, which otherwise have no 3-D look.

The PanedWindow widget manages its children in a vertically tiled format only. Its width fluctuates with the widest widget in its list of managed children. The widget provides a sash to allow the user to adjust the height of each pane.

The Form widget has an elaborate means of linking the edges of its children to itself and to one another. Different layout criteria can be specified for each child. Form widgets are good managers to use as children of DialogShells that you build yourself. Like RowColumn widgets, Forms have no border, allowing them to be placed next to other geometry managing widgets without giving the appearance that their items are grouped separately. A Frame widget is used to give Forms visible boundaries.

5.1.2 Dialog Widgets

DialogShell and MenuShell perform the window manager interaction as parent widgets of dialog widgets and menus respectively. DialogShell is created alone only when you are creating a custom dialog box that is not based on BulletinBoard or Form (since `XmCreate-BulletinBoardDialog()` and `XmCreateFormDialog()` exist). MenuShell is used when you are creating a menu that is not one of the standard types created by `Xm-CreatePulldownMenu()`, `XmCreatePopupMenu()`, `XmCreateOption-Menu()`, etc.

A simple Help dialog box was demonstrated in Section 3.4.2. This was a MessageBox created as a dialog using `XmCreateMessageDialog()`. A MessageBox widget can be configured to display a symbol that represents the kind of information being displayed. Motif defines five symbols for this purpose, and provides a widget creation function that creates a

MessageBox as a dialog for each symbol. They are `XmCreateErrorDialog()`, `Xm-CreateInformationDialog()`, `XmCreateQuestionDialog()`, `XmCreate-WorkingDialog()`, and `XmCreateWarningDialog()`. Figure 5-9 shows these five types of dialogs.

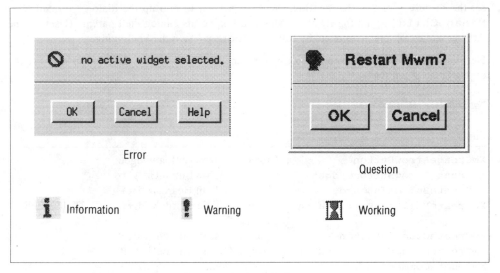

Figure 5-9. Dialog boxes with the five standard symbols

As noted in Chapter 3, *More Techniques for Using Widgets*, there is no standard dialog for help information. However, the InformationDialog seems most appropriate, once its Cancel button and possibly its Help button are unmanaged.

5.2 Widget Creation Functions

You have already seen a few of the functions Motif provides for creating widgets. For example, in Chapter 3 we used `XmCreatePulldownMenu()`, `XmCreateMenuBar()`, and `XmCreateMessageDialog()` in *xmainwindow*. As you may recall, these are very similar to Xt's widget creation functions except that in the Motif routines:

- The widget parent argument comes before the widget instance name argument (the reverse of the Xt functions).

- No widget class pointer is necessary (it is implied by the function name).

- A separate `XtManageChild()` call is required to display the widget.

There are many more of these functions. Some of them create single widgets, some create single widgets with certain special resource settings, and some create combinations of widgets.

For users of other widget sets such as Athena, the use of the IDs returned by Motif widget creation functions can be a bit confusing. The functions that create combinations of widgets don't always return the top level widget of the combination. For example, `XmCreate-MessageDialog()` returns the ID of the MessageBox widget, not the ID of the Dialog-Shell that `XmCreateMessageDialog()` creates as its parent. This allows you to easily set the resources of the MessageBox. When you want to pop up the dialog, you call `Xt-ManageChild()` with the ID of the MessageBox, not its DialogShell parent. (Users of the Athena widget set popup widgets by calling `XtPopup()` on the Shell widget.)

Here is a complete list of the `XmCreate*` functions, and a brief description of what the object created is intended for.

Table 5-1. XmCreate Functions

Function	Description
`XmCreateArrowButton`	Create an ArrowButton widget.
`XmCreateArrowButtonGadget`	Create an ArrowButtonGadget.
`XmCreateBulletinBoard`	Create a BulletinBoard widget.
`XmCreateBulletinBoardDialog`	Create BulletinBoard widget with DialogShell parent.
`XmCreateCascadeButton`	Create a CascadeButton widget.
`XmCreateCascadeButtonGadget`	Create a CascadeButtonGadget.
`XmCreateCommand`	Create a Command widget.
`XmCreateDialogShell`	Create a DialogShell widget.
`XmCreateDragIcon`	Create a DragIcon widget.
`XmCreateDrawingArea`	Create a DrawingArea widget.
`XmCreateDrawnButton`	Create a DrawnButton widget.
`XmCreateErrorDialog`	Create a MessageBox with error symbol.
`XmCreateFileSelectionBox`	Create a FileSelectionBox widget.
`XmCreateFileSelectionDialog`	Create a FileSelectionBox with a DialogShell parent.
`XmCreateForm`	Create a Form widget.
`XmCreateFormDialog`	Create a Form widget with DialogShell parent.
`XmCreateFrame`	Create a Frame widget.
`XmCreateInformationDialog`	Create a MessageBox with information symbol.
`XmCreateLabel`	Create a Label widget.
`XmCreateLabelGadget`	Create a LabelGadget.
`XmCreateList`	Create a List widget.
`XmCreateMainWindow`	Create a MainWindow widget.
`XmCreateMenuBar`	Create a RowColumn widget with resource settings for being a menubar.
`XmCreateMenuShell`	Create a MenuShell widget.
`XmCreateMessageBox`	Create a MessageBox widget.
`XmCreateMessageDialog`	Create a MessageBox with a DialogShell parent.
`XmCreateOptionMenu`	Create a RowColumn widget with resource settings for being an option menu.

Table 5-1. XmCreate Functions (continued)

Function	Description
XmCreatePanedWindow	Create a PanedWindow widget.
XmCreatePopupMenu	Create a RowColumn widget with resource settings for being a popup menu.
XmCreatePromptDialog	Create a SelectionBox widget with a DialogShell parent.
XmCreatePulldownMenu	Create a RowColumn widget with resource settings for being a pulldown menu.
XmCreatePushButton	Create a PushButton widget.
XmCreatePushButtonGadget	Create a PushButtonGadget.
XmCreateQuestionDialog	Create a MessageBox with question symbol.
XmCreateRadioBox	Create a RowColumn widget with resource settings to be a radio box.
XmCreateRowColumn	Create a RowColumn widget.
XmCreateScale	Create a Scale widget.
XmCreateScrollBar	Create a ScrollBar widget.
XmCreateScrolledList	Create a ScrolledWindow widget containing a List widget.
XmCreateScrolledText	Create a Text widget.
XmCreateScrolledWindow	Create a ScrolledWindow widget.
XmCreateSelectionBox	Create a SelectionBox widget.
XmCreateSelectionDialog	Create a SelectionBox widget with a DialogShell parent.
XmCreateSeparator	Create a Separator widget.
XmCreateSeparatorGadget	Create a SeparatorGadget.
XmCreateSimpleCheckBox	Create a RowColumn widget with resource settings to function as a CheckBox, and children.
XmCreateSimpleMenuBar	Create a RowColumn widget with resource settings to function as a MenuBar, and children.
XmCreateSimpleOptionMenu	Create a RowColumn widget with resource settings to function as a OptionMenu, and children.
XmCreateSimplePopupMenu	Create a RowColumn with resource settings to function as a popupMenu, and children.
XmCreateSimplePulldownMenu	Create a RowColumn widget with resource settings to function as a PulldownMenu, and children.
XmCreateSimpleRadioBox	Create a RowColumn widget with resource settings to function as a RadioBox, and children.
XmCreateText	Create a Text widget.
XmCreateTemplateDialog	Create a MessageBox configured as a template.
XmCreateTextField	Create a TextField widget.
XmCreateToggleButton	Create a ToggleButton widget.
XmCreateToggleButtonGadget	Create a ToggleButtonGadget.

More About Motif

Table 5-1. XmCreate Functions (continued)

Function	Description
`XmCreateWarningDialog`	Create a MessageBox with warning symbol.
`XmCreateWorkArea`	Create a RowColumn widget with resources to function as a WorkArea.
`XmCreateWorkingDialog`	Create a MessageBox with working symbol.

5.3 Compound Strings

Compound strings are designed to address two issues frequently encountered by application designers: the use of foreign character sets to display text in other languages, and the use of multiple fonts when rendering text.

Many character sets used by foreign languages are too large for the characters to be represented by the `char` type, as English can be. Compound strings solve this problem by representing characters as 16 bit values ("words") rather than the classic 8 bit values ("chars"). Also, since some languages such as Hebrew and Arabic are read from right-to-left, compound strings also store directional information for rendering purposes. Compound strings allow widgets to handle different languages transparently to the application. All the application has to do is not hard code any strings in the application. All strings should be external to the application, usually in resource files or XPG3 (X/Open) message catalogues, or if using UIL, in UID files. In this section, we demonstrate the simplest usages of compound strings, in a way not intended to be internationalized since the strings are hard coded.

A compound string is made of three elements: a font list element tag, a direction and text. Compound strings that incorporate multiple fonts are achieved by concatenating separate compound strings with different character sets together to produce a single string. A separator is placed between each compound string.

5.3.1 Simple Compound Strings

Almost all of the Motif widgets require a compound string when specifying text. Labels, PushButtons, Lists—all require their text to be given in compound string format, whether or not you require the additional flexibility compound strings provide.† Therefore, the most common use for compound strings in English-language applications is simply to convert standard C-style null-terminated text strings for use in a widget.

First of all, strings specified in resource files need not be converted, since Motif will automatically do the conversion.

---

†As of Motif 1.2 the Text widget does not use compound strings.

To do the conversion for strings specified directly in the application code, we use the function `XmStringCreateLocalized()`.

```
XmString
XmStringCreateLocalized(text)
    char *text;
```

The `text` parameter is a common C `char` string. The value returned is of type `XmString` which is an opaque type to the programmer.

As its name implies, `XmStringCreateLocalized()` converts a C string into a compound string using the current locale. You cannot specify a font, a string direction, or have multiple lines. As mentioned earlier, no strings should be specified in an internationalized application, although we do so here for simplicity.

```
XmString str = XmStringCreateLocalized("Push Me");

widget = XtVaCreateManagedWidget("widget_name",
    xmPushButtonGadgetClass, parent,
    XmNlabelString,  str,
    NULL);

XmStringFree(str);
```

`XmStringCreateLocalized()`, along with the other functions that create compound strings, allocates memory to store the strings created. Widgets whose resources take compound strings as values always allocate their own space and store copies of the compound string values you give them, so you must free your copy of the string after having set it in the widget resource. Compound strings are freed using `XmStringFree()`.

This three-step process is typical of the type of interaction you will have with compound strings. You create a string, set it in a widget, then free the string (unless you want to use it in another widget). However, this process involves quite a bit of overhead; memory is allocated by the string creation function, then again by the internals of the widget for its own storage, and then your copy of the string must be deallocated (freeing memory is also an expensive operation).

This process can be simplified by using the `XtVaTypedArg` feature in Xt. This symbol is used in variable argument list specifications for functions like `XtVaCreateManaged-Widget()` or `XtVaSetValues()`. It allows you to specify resources in any type—most likely a more convenient one—and have Xt do the conversion for you. In the case of compound strings, this method can be used convert between C strings and compound strings without having to do it yourself. The following code fragment has the same effect as the example shown above without the overhead of the three-step process.

```
widget = XtVaCreateManagedWidget("widget_name",
    xmPushButtonWidgetClass, parent,
    XtVaTypedArg,
      XmNlabelString, XmRString, "Push Me", strlen("Push Me") + 1,
    NULL);
```

`XtVaTypedArg` takes four additional parameters: the resource whose value is going to be set, the type of the value we are giving the resource, the value itself, and the size of the value's data type. (Note that this fourth parameter is the size of the value itself, not the size of the type!)

The resource is `XmNlabelString`, and its value is of type `XmString` (a compound string). We specify `XmRString` as the type of the value we are going to provide.† The string `"Push Me"` is that value, and it's length, including terminating `NULL`, is calculated with `strlen`.

5.3.2 Strings with Multiple Fonts

A common use of compound strings is to display a string using multiple fonts.

To incorporate more than one font in a single compound string, you must create a fontList that specifies multiple fonts or font sets. Then you must either create the compound text in *segments* using the function `XmStringSegmentCreate()` (a routine that allows you to control both the font list element tag and the direction of a compound string), or you must create separate compound strings using `XmStringCreate()` and then concatenate them with `XmStringConcat()`. This concatenated string will have information embedded in it to indicate font changes. Example 5-1 demonstrates how a compound string can be created to contain multiple fonts.

Example 5-1. xcomstring.c: code to use multiple fonts in a compound string

```
/*
 * Header files required for all Toolkit programs
 */
#include <X11/Intrinsic.h>      /* Intrinsics definitions */
#include <Xm/Xm.h>              /* Standard Motif definitions */

/*
 * Public header file for widgets we actually use in this file.
 */
#include <Xm/PushB.h>           /* Motif PushButton Widget */

main(argc, argv)
int argc;
char **argv;
{
    XtAppContext app_context;
    Widget topLevel;
    XmString text;
    XmString s1, s2, s3, s4;
    Widget hello;
    static String string1 = "Specify the ",
                  string2 = "character set ",
                  string3 = "in the code.";

    XtSetLanguageProc(NULL, (XtLanguageProc)NULL, NULL);

    topLevel = XtVaAppInitialize(
            &app_context,       /* Application context */
```

---

†This terminology can get confusing. Xt uses the typedef `String` for `char *`. The representation type used by Xt resource converters for this datatype is `XtRString` (`XmRString` in Motif). A compound string, on the other hand, is of type `XmString`, with the representation type used with resource converters specified as `XmRXmString`. You just have to read the symbols carefully. And it helps if you have a good understanding of the underlying mechanism of resource converters, which are described in detail in Chapter 9, *More Input Techniques*.

Example 5-1. xcomstring.c: code to use multiple fonts in a compound string (continued)

```
            "XComstring",           /* Application class */
            NULL, 0,                /* command line option list */
            &argc, argv,            /* command line args */
            NULL,                   /* for missing app-defaults file */
            NULL);                  /* terminate varargs list */
    s1 = XmStringCreate(string1, "tag1");
    s2 = XmStringCreate(string2, "tag2");
    s3 = XmStringCreate(string3, "tag1");

    s4 = XmStringConcat(s1, s2);
    XmStringFree(s1);
    XmStringFree(s2);

    text = XmStringConcat(s4, s3);
    XmStringFree(s3);
    XmStringFree(s4);

    hello = XtVaCreateManagedWidget(
            "hello",                /* arbitrary widget name */
            xmPushButtonWidgetClass, /* widget class from PushButton.h */
            topLevel,               /* parent widget */
              XmNlabelString, text,
            NULL);                  /* terminate varargs list */

    XmStringFree(text);

    XtRealizeWidget(topLevel);

    XtAppMainLoop(app_context);
}
```

Again, it's important to note that an internationalized application could not contain hard-coded strings as shown here. Instead, all strings would be external to the application (in resource files or message catalogues).

The output of this code fragment is shown in Figure 5-10.

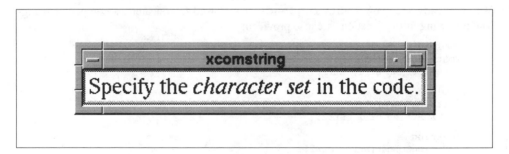

Figure 5-10. xcomstring.c: how it looks on the screen

The **XmNfontList** resource is specified to contain two fonts as shown in Example 5-2. Each string is created using **XmStringCreate()** with the appropriate text and font list element tag specified. Then, the strings are concatenated together using **XmString-**

`Concat()`, two at a time, until we have a single compound string that contains all the text and includes all the font changes.

It is possible to specify compound text strings (such as the **XmNlabelString** resource of the PushButton widget) in resource files as normal strings. This is possible because Motif takes care of the conversion to compound strings. However, when you want font changes within a string, you need to create compound strings or segments explicitly within the application as illustrated in Example 5-1.

Here is the app-defaults file for *xcomstring*.

Example 5-2. xcomstring: app-defaults file

```
*hello.fontList:      *times-medium-r*180*=tag1,\
                      *times-medium-i*180*=tag2
*foreground: black
*background: white
*bottomShadowPixmap: 75_foreground
*topShadowPixmap: 25_foreground
*highlightPixmap: 50_foreground
```

5.3.3 Manipulating Compound Strings

Most C programmers are used to dealing with functions such as **strcpy()**, **strcmp()**, and **strcat()**, to copy, compare and modify strings. However, these functions are ineffective with compound strings since compound strings are not based on a byte-per-character format and they have other types of information embedded within them (character sets, directions and separators). In order to accomplish some of these common tasks, you can either convert the compound string back into C strings or use the functions Motif provides to manipulate compound strings directly. Your choice depends largely on the complexity of the compound strings you have and the complexity of the manipulations you need to do.

We've already seen how **XmStringConcat()** is used to concatenate compound strings. The following utility functions are also provided:

```
    Boolean
    XmStringByteCompare(str1, str2)
        XmString str1, str2;

    Boolean
    XmStringCompare(str1, str2);
        XmString str1, str2;

    XmString
    XmStringConcat(str1, str2)
        XmString str1, str2;

    XmString
    XmStringNConcat(str1, str2, n)
        XmString str1, str2;
        int n;

    XmString
    XmStringCopy(str)
```

```
    XmString str;

XmString
XmStringNCopy(str, n)
    XmString str;
    int n;

int
XmStringHasSubstring(string, substring)
    XmString string, substring;

int
XmStringLength(str)
    XmString str;
```

The **XmStringNConcat()** and **XmStringNCopy()** functions differ from their "N-less" brethren in that they concatenate or copy, respectively, only *n* characters from the specified string. Otherwise, the purpose of these functions is readily apparent from their names. Note however that since a compound string includes various tags, direction indicators and segment separators, **XmStringLength()** cannot be used to get the length of the text represented by the compound string (i.e., it's not the same as **strlen()**).

5.3.4 Converting Compound Strings to Text

If the functions provided by the Motif routines in the previous section are inadequate, you can convert compound strings back into C strings. This process can be simple or complicated depending on the complexity of the compound string to be converted. If the compound string has one font list element tag associated with it and it has a left-to-right orientation, the process is quite simple. Fortunately, this is likely to be the case most of the time.

To make the conversion, you can use the function:

```
Boolean
XmStringGetLtoR(string, tag, text)
    XmString            string;
    char                *tag;
    char                **text;
```

The function takes a compound string and a font list element tag and converts it back into a C character string. If successful, the function returns **True** and the **text** parameter will point to a newly allocated pointer to a string.

The function only gets the text from the compound string that is associated with the font list element tag specified in *tag*. If the string contains multiple fonts, only the text associated with those segments with the same font is copied into the returned text.

As its name implies, this function gets only left-to-right oriented text. In order to convert compound strings that have either a right-to-left orientation or multiple fonts, you will have to scan through the elements of a compound string segment by segment (a process described in Volume Six, *Motif Programming Manual*).

5.3.5 Rendering Compound Strings

Motif always renders compound strings automatically within its widgets. More precisely, the widgets themselves manage compound string rendering. However, Motif provides convenient functions for doing the rendering which you may find useful if you are writing your own Motif-compatible widgets or extensions to Motif widgets.

For more information on this topic, see Volume Six, *Motif Programming Manual*.

5.4 Pixmap and Image Caching Functions

As you by now know, a pixmap is an off-screen drawable maintained by the server. It is accessed from the application using an ID. A pixmap can be created using a pattern defined in file, or drawn into, and copied to a window.

Motif's pixmap caching has a simple use and a more complicated use. The simple use is described in this paragraph. Motif provides `XmGetPixmap()`, which reads a bitmap file from disk and creates a pixmap of the default depth of the screen. `XmGetPixmap()` caches the pixmap so that subsequent requests for the same filename will return the original pixmap. The only thing slightly confusing about `XmGetPixmap()` is that you specify your filename (including path) in the *image-name* argument.

X also defines a client-side representation of a window area, called an *image*. An image is usually generated by grabbing a portion of an existing window or pixmap using `XGet-Image()`. An image is a structure that contains all the data from a window area, using the server's natural data format. The structure also includes fields that describe the combination of byte-order, bit-order, and image format used by the server. Unlike many other Xlib structures, the image structure is public—its fields are documented—since it is stored on the client side. Because of the many permutations of server formats that are possible, Xlib provides generalized functions for manipulating image data, though they are rather slow because they always convert the data into the client's natural format before processing it. An image can be dumped into a window or pixmap using `XPutImage()`.

Motif uses images to allow pixmaps to be specified in resource files, and to allow multiple instances of a widget to share one pixmap stored in the server. For example, you know that the MessageBox widget has several variations, with different symbols for information, warning, error, question, and working. Each of these symbols is created by MessageBox using `XmInstallImage()`. (This happens before any instances of the widget class are created, in the `class_initialize` method, which will be described later.) To install each image, first an image structure is created and filled with data in standard X11 bitmap file format. Then this structure is passed to `XmInstallImage()`. Also passed is the string name for this image, which will be used to used to refer to the image in resource files. For example, the question symbol is called `default_xm_question`.

When an instance of MessageBox is created using a call such as `XmCreateQuestion-Dialog()`, the `XmNdialogType` resource is automatically set to `XmDIALOG_QUES-TION`. In a switch statement, MessageBox maps this symbol into the corresponding image name, "default_xm_question." MessageBox calls `XmGetPixmap()` to get the pixmap specified by this image name. If the pixmap already exists because another QuestionDialog has already been created, then this pixmap is set into the `XmNsymbolPixmap` resource. If the pixmap does not yet exist, it is created, cached for later use by widgets of this type, and set into `XmNsymbolPixmap`. (You can also bypass this entire facility from the application by creating your own pixmap and setting `XmNsymbolPixmap` directly.)

Motif keeps reference counts in order to free these cached pixmaps when they are no longer needed. Therefore, MessageBox calls `XmDestroyPixmap()` when the `XmNsymbol-Pixmap` is set directly, when the dialog type is changed, or when the widget itself is destroyed. `XmDestroyPixmap()` just decrements the reference count to a pixmap—the pixmap is destroyed only if no other widgets are using it.

Motif defines a group of images that are pre-installed in the image cache. Each of these is converted into pixmaps when they are first used to set a widget resource, using the current foreground and background colors for that first widget. Table 5-2 lists and describes these pixmaps.

Table 5-2. Built-in Motif Pixmaps

Image Name	Description
`background`	Solid background.
`25_foreground`	25% foreground, 75% background.
`50_foreground`	50% foreground, 50% background.
`75_foreground`	75% foreground, 25% background.
`horizontal`	Horizontal lines of foreground and background.
`vertical`	Vertical lines of foreground and background.
`slant_right`	Up to right lines of foreground and background.
`slant_left`	Up to left lines of foreground and background.

Any of these pre-installed images or the images installed by Motif widgets such as Message-Box can be specified in resource files. For example, the following resource setting could appear in an app-defaults file:

```
*XmCascadeButton.backgroundPixmap: 25_foreground
```

This resource setting makes the background of CascadeButtons slightly darker than they usually are, which makes their outline visible over the menubar.

5.5 Dynamic Resource Defaulting

Most resources have a fixed default value determined by the widget class. However, several of the basic appearance resources supported by Primitive have defaults that are set at run time. Namely, the foreground, background, and the two shadow colors used by a widget are set dynamically depending on the type of screen being used and on the settings of each other. The highlight color, used to redraw the background when the user clicks on a PushButton, is also dynamically defaulted.

By default on a color screen, Motif chooses a light blue background, a black foreground, a very light blue-gray top shadow, a dark blue-gray bottom shadow, and a medium blue highlight color. These are carefully chosen to strengthen the 3-D effect of the interface. If the user sets the background color to sea green, Motif adjusts the foreground, background, shadow colors, and highlight color so that they work well with a green background. If the user chooses a dark color for the background, white instead of black is used for the text. However, the user should be informed that light colors work best for the background, since the highlight color must be darker than the background color to make buttons look pressed in.

On a gray-scale screen, Motif selects a black foreground, white background, and uses light gray and dark gray for the shadows. Medium gray is used for the highlight color. On a black and white screen, the same colors are used, but light gray and dark gray are simulated using pixmaps containing different percentages of white and black.

Dynamic resource defaults are implemented using a standard feature of the R4 Xt Intrinsics called `XmRCallProc` (called `XtRCallProc` in standard Xt). In the resource list, which has not yet been introduced, you can either specify a default value or a function to be called to calculate the default value. Motif does the latter for these resources.

5.6 Resolution Independence

As you know, the units for all Xlib and Xt calls are pixels. Motif allows you to set some resources using units such as inches, so that the size and spacing of widgets will appear the same size on any display, regardless of the pixel spacing on that display.

This resolution-independence is built into all position, dimension, spacing, padding, offset, and thickness resources of all Motif widgets. The interpretation of dimensions within each widget is controlled by the `XmNunitType` resource, which can be set anywhere where resources can be set, including in resource files.

For some applications, such as desktop publishing, resolution independence is important. For others, it is irrelevant, or in fact harmful, because while size of graphics will be the same on all screens, the quality of those graphics will vary. What is clear on a 1280 by 1024 screen may not be clear on a 640 by 480 screen if the graphics are the same size.

`XmNunitType` can be set to the following values:

- XmPIXELS—all values provided to the widget are treated as normal pixel values.

- Xm100TH_MILLIMETERS—all values provided to the widget are treated as 1/100 millimeter.

- Xm1000TH_INCHES—all values provided to the widget are treated as 1/1000 inch.

- Xm100TH_POINTS—all values provided to the widget are treated as 1/100 point. A point is a unit used in text processing applications and is defined as 1/72 inch.

- Xm100TH_FONT_UNITS—all values provided to the widget are treated as 1/100 of a font unit.

The font unit allows you to specify sizes based on a font that will be chosen at run time according to your specifications. The font used is the one the user specifies with the *–font* command-line option or by setting the `XmNfont` resource (not `XmNfontList`) in a resource file. (`XmNfont` is used only for this in Motif.) The font unit is calculated from the dimensions of the specified font. A font unit can also be set with `XmSetFontUnits()`. Note that once `XmNunitType` is set to `Xm100TH_FONT_UNITS`, and the font set, the actual numbers used to set resources are integral and generally large.

Unless `XmNunitType` is explicitly set, all widgets that are subclasses of Manager inherit the unit type of their parent. All widgets that are subclasses of Primitive have a default unit type of XmPIXELS. (They do not inherit their parent's unit type.)

Once a unit type is set, you can set resources using this unit type, and when you query them with `XtVaGetValues()`, you will get values that use this unit type. A one-time rounding error may occur, though, which could make the value you query slightly different from the value you set. Repeated queries and sets will not make the rounding error worse. (Internally, widgets still store all their values in pixels. This becomes important to you only when you begin to write widgets.)

Motif also provides `XmConvertUnits()` for converting between units. If you need to write your own widget that implements resolution independent custom graphics, you can use `XmConvertUnits()`, or you can use Xlib macros that give you the number of pixels and the size of the screen.

5.7 Keyboard Traversal and Focus

All Motif widgets are able to operate with keyboard input instead of pointer input. This is primarily so that people can use the keyboard to navigate forms conveniently, but it is also so that Motif applications can be run on systems that don't have a mouse.

Xt directs keyboard input to only one window at a time; this window has the keyboard focus. All Motif widgets and gadgets have code that gives them the ability to draw a highlight rectangle around themselves when they have the keyboard focus. (In practice, geometry managing widgets do not draw a highlight rectangle because they do not take user input.) The parent tells a gadget when to highlight, since gadgets can never get the focus themselves since they have no window.

The traversal works in two levels. The first level is movement between tab groups, and the second level is movement within a tab group. A tab group is one or more widgets. As you build the instance hierarchy of an application, Motif automatically links the widgets together into groups. By default, most simple widgets are a tab group by themselves. Most manager widgets are also tab groups, with all their children in the same tab group. For example, a MessageBox widget is really a Form widget containing a Label widget and three PushButton widgets; the Form, the Label, and the three pushbutton widgets are a tab group. However, since the Form and Label widgets set `XmNtraversalOn` to `False` since they don't take user input, they are not active in the tab group.

You can move the keyboard focus around in a tab group by using the arrow keys (also called navigation keys, since other keys may be mapped to this function).

Pressing the Tab key moves the focus to the first widget in the next tab group. Pressing Tab while holding the Shift key moves the focus to the first widget in the previous tab group.

Without doing anything, you should be able to negotiate your entire application using the keyboard, since Motif sets up default tab groups. However, you may want to tailor the order in which widgets are traversed within each tab group, and also the order in which tab groups are traversed.

The order of traversal of the widgets within a tab group is the same as the order in which the widgets were created. If a widget is normally included in a tab group, but you don't want it to be, set its `XmNtraversalOn` resources to `False`.

In Motif 1.1 you could modify the order of traversal between tab groups using `XmAddTab-Group()` and `XmRemoveTabGroup()`. Both functions just set the specified widget's `XmNnavigationType` resource. These functions are obsolete in Motif 1.2: now you just set the `XmNnavigationType` resource yourself to `XmEXCLUSIVE_TAB_GROUP` to add a widget to a tab group, or `XmNONE` to remove one. There are various other settings for this resource that you can use if you set the resource directly instead of using these functions.

You can also move the focus by clicking the pointer in a widget that can accept the focus (has `XmNtraversalOn` set to `True`). Within Motif applications, you can choose between a click-to-type model, which supports keyboard traversal, and a pointer-following model, which does not support keyboard traversal. The default is the click-to-type model. You can change this by setting the `XmNkeyboardFocusPolicy` resource of a Shell widget, but this is not recommended. Note that this resource sets the keyboard focus model within this one application; this is completely separate from the model you choose for *mwm*, although the two choices available in each case are the same.

List, ScrollBar, multiline Text widgets, and Option menus must be sole members of a tab group, because they use the arrow keys for other purposes.

Because keyboard traversal depends on Motif moving the keyboard focus around, applications should not set the keyboard focus explicitly. In other words, you should never call `Xt-SetKeyboardFocus()` or `XSetInputFocus()`. Instead you can call `XmProcess-Traversal()`.

Even Motif menus can be operated using the keyboard. A menu can be mapped by a mnemonic such as Alt-F typed anywhere in the application. Once mapped, the menu can be traversed with the arrow keys, and an item selected with the Return key. Alternately, if the strings in the menu have mnemonics defined, they will have letters underlined, and the user can type these letters to select the item. Finally, menu items can be selected without the menu being mapped by using accelerator keys, which are described in Chapter 8, *Events, Translations, and Accelerators*.

5.8 Motif Virtual Keyboard Bindings

The main alphabetic area of keyboards on different systems is very uniform, but the modifier keys such as Control, Alt, Meta, Hyper, and Super, and the function keys, are not uniform. The X keyboard model hides many of the differences between the different keyboards that are available on different systems. Each X server contains a mapping between the keycodes for each physical key, and keysyms, which are symbolic constants each of which represents a standardized meaning of a key combination. For example, there are separate keysyms `XK_A` and `XK_a` which represent the "a" key with and without the Shift key pressed. See Volume One, *Xlib Programming Manual*, for an extensive discussion of this model.

Motif adds another level of mapping to this system. Translation tables for Motif widgets reference keysyms not defined by the Xlib standard. For example, a line in the translation table of every Motif widget reads as follows:

```
static char defaultTranslation[ ] =
    .
    .
    <Key>osfHelp:    Help()";
```

The string `osfHelp` is in the position normally occupied by a keysym, but in this case it is a Motif virtual keysym. Motif then internally maps this string into a real keysym.

Motif maps virtual keysyms into real keysyms using the file *XKeysymDB*, which is usually in */usr/lib/X11* on UNIX-based systems. The contents of this file are different for each system, and installing this file is part of installing Motif. For example, on systems that have a Help key, `osfHelp` will be mapped to that key. On systems that don't have a Help key, some other key is chosen. The advantage of the Motif virtual binding system is that you can be assured that there actually is a key that performs the Help function, even if it isn't marked, and that all Motif applications on that system will use the same key. Also, on single user systems this gives the user the option of changing which key is used for each function.

Motif 1.2 provides a new function, `XmTranslateKey()`, to translate a keycode into a virtual key. This function allows applications that override the default `XtKeyProc` to handle Motif virtual keys. Motif 1.2 also includes a new client, *xmbind*, that configures the virtual key bindings for Motif applications. This action is performed by the Motif Window Manager (mwm) at startup, so you only need to use *xmbind* if you are not using *mwm* or if you want to reconfigure the bindings without restarting *mwm*.

5.9 Drag and Drop

Motif 1.2 introduces a new user interface for transferring data within an application or between applications, called *drag and drop*. From the user's perspective, data can be moved or copied by dragging an iconic representation of the data.†

Mouse button 2 is reserved for drag-and-drop. When the user begins a drag with button two over a "drag source", the pointer is replaced with a special drag icon. This icon indicates the type of data being dragged (text, pixmap, etc.), the drag operation (copy, move, or "link"), and whether the pointer is over a valid "drop site", an invalid drop site or no drop site. The drag icon may change as it enters and leaves drop sites, and drop sites themselves may change their visuals when the drop icon is within them. These changing graphics in drag icon and drop site are referred to as "drag over" and "drag under" visuals, respectively.

The type of data being dragged and the default operation (copy, move, or link) depends on the drag source. If the drag source supports multiple operations, the user can select an operation other than the default with the Shift and Ctrl modifiers.

The user can cancel a drag by pressing the Escape key. The user can request help on a drop site before dropping by pressing the F1 key.

Text, List, Label and Button widgets support drag and drop as drag sources, which means that text can be dragged from them. Text and TextField widget support drag and drop as drop sites, which means that text can be dragged to them. The Label class also supports dragging of `Pixmap` data. If you use existing widgets, therefore, there is no extra programming necessary to provide drag and drop. Custom drag and drop support can be added to any widget. Custom drag icons and drop site visuals can also be implemented. The details of implementing drag and drop in an application are beyond the scope of this book. See the *OSF/Motif Programming Manual* for more information.

5.9.1 Drag Protocol

In order to implement drag-over effects, the originator of the drag must know when it has entered a valid drop site. In order to implement customized drag-under effects, the process controlling the drop site must know when there is a drag icon inside of it. It is not possible to gracefully satisfy all of these requirements with X. To work around this, Motif drag-and-drop supports two different drag protocols with different tradeoffs. The protocol used depends on the preference of the user and on which protocols are supported by the initiating client and the drop site.

Preregister Protocol. In the "preregister" protocol, the client that initiated the drag is in complete control of the drag, and the clients controlling drop sites are never notified when the drag icon enters those drop sites. Therefore this protocol does not allow a drop site to implement custom drag-under visuals. In this protocol, the client that initiated the drag grabs the X server and implements the drag icon with a shaped window it moves around the screen.

---

†Dragging is the act of pressing a mouse button with the pointer over the object, moving the mouse with the button held down, and releasing the object in a new location by releasing the mouse button.

When the icon enters a top-level window, the initiating client reads a server property to determine the (preregistered) list of valid drop sites within that window. The initiating client can implement drag-over visuals when the icon enters a drop site, and can also implement simple drag-under visuals (such as highlighting the drop-site border) for the drop site.

Dynamic Protocol. In the "dynamic" drag protocol, the initiating client communicates (dynamically) with other clients to determine the list of valid drop sites and to notify then when the drag icon enters one of these drop sites. This notification allows these clients to implement custom drag-under visuals (which can include animation). The initiating client does not perform a server grab in this protocol, and the drag icon is implemented by specifying it as the hardware pointer. Many X servers restrict the maximum size of the pointer cursor, so this protocol may not work with large drag icons.

5.9.2 Drop Protocol

The drop protocol is primarily concerned with transferring the data from initiator to receiver, and is much simpler than the drag protocol. It is based directly on the Xt Selection mechanism used to implement standard Xt cut-and-paste.

The drag initiator registers a "convert proc" (of type `XtConvertSelectionIncr-Proc`) when it starts the drag with `XmDragStart()`. In Xt selection terms, starting a drag is analogous to calling `XtOwnSelection()`.

The receiving process registers each drop site along with a callback to invoke when something is dropped on that site. This callback registers a "transfer proc" (of type `Xt-SelectionCallbackProc`) as well as a list of target types that it would like the dragged data to be converted to and calls `XmDropTransferStart()`. In terms of the Xt selection mechanism, `XmDropTransferStart()` is analogous to `XtGet-SelectionValues()`. `XmDropTransferStart()` uses the underlying Xt Selection mechanism to transfer the data. The drag source's convert proc is called once for each target type, and the drop site's transfer proc is called once with the converted data for each target.

The drop protocol is also responsible for providing help. Each drop site should recognize when the user has requested help and post a dialog box explaining the consequences of dropping on that site. This dialog box must give the user the explicit options to continue with or cancel the drop.

5.9.3 Operations

Motif allows three drag-and-drop operations: copy, move, and link. The precise semantics of each operation will of course depend on the dragged data and the drop site. After a copy operation there should be two copies of the dragged data or object.

After a move, there should only be one copy. Note that the drop site is responsible for telling the drag source to delete its copy of moved data. It does this by sending a request to convert the data to the special target "DELETE". (This target is standardized by the ICCCM, described in Chapter 11.)

The semantics of the "link" operation are vague: "At the end of the operation, there is only one copy of the data, belonging to the initiator, but both applications have access to it". In the absence of shared memory, it is not clear what this means, but the link operation should presumably be used to establish any sort of "live link", or to enable dynamic data sharing between applications.

5.9.4 Application Programming Interface

Initiating a drag or registering a drop site or initiating a transfer once a drop has occurred each require a number of parameters (many of which are optional) to be specified. To avoid having functions with large number of arguments, Motif uses Xt Objects and allows these parameters to be specified with standard Xt arglists. Starting a drag with `XmDragStart()` creates an object of type `XmDragContext`. Registering a drop site with `XmDropSite-Register()` creates an object of type `XmDropSite`. Initiating a data transfer with `Xm-DropTransferStart()` creates an object of type `XmDropTransfer`. These objects have resources that control many of the visual effects of drag-and-drop, and also have callback list resources that provide hooks at many points during both the drag and the drop.

5.9.5 Summary: Drag and Drop in Applications

Programming with Motif drag-and-drop can become almost arbitrarily complex (the code for a single example in OSF's book is 65 pages). There are three general approaches to incorporating drag-and-drop into applications:

Do Nothing. Many of the standard Motif primitive widgets support drag-and-drop. Even if you do nothing, users will be able to perform basic drag-and-drop of text.

Add New Drag Sources and Drop Types. You can support additional drag sources by adding a translation/action pair that calls `XmDragStart()` and registers a convert proc to handle requests for the data once it is dropped. For example you might want to allow the user to drag the value from a Slider widget, or if you implemented a custom spreadsheet widget, you might want to allow the user to drag a column of numbers. To add a new drop site, call `XmDropSiteRegister()` and specify a callback to be called when a drop occurs. This callback should register a transfer proc to handle the dropped data and then call `XmDropTransferStart()` to fetch that data.

Customize Drag-and-Drop. There are many ways that you can customize drag-and-drop, most of which can be controlled through resources and callbacks. You can change the components of the default drag icon, or specify custom drag icon components for a particular drag source. You can also change the way that the components of the drag icon are combined or "blended." Using the `XtNdragCallback` callback list of the `XmDragContext` and `XmDropSite` objects, you can implements custom drag-over and drag-under visuals. If a drag site implements custom visuals, you can set resources to express a preference for the dynamic drag protocol which allows these visuals. You can specify a non-rectangular outline for a drag site, and specify the sort of highlighting should be done on that border when a drag icon enters it. You can specifying a stacking order for overlapping drop sites. You can only have one drop site for a widget, but with some extra coding work, you can implement a single drop site that appears and functions as a number of separate sites within the widget.

5.10 Tear-off Menus

Motif 1.2 supports tear-off menus. A tear-off menu appears with a dashed line across its top. Selecting this dashed line tears the menu off and allows the user to position it with the mouse. The torn-off menu becomes a top-level window subject to window manager control. Traversing to the torn-off menu follows standard window manager policy.

By default, menus do not allow themselves to be torn-off. To enable this behavior, set the new RowColumn resource **XmNtearOffModel** to **XmTEAR_OFF_ENABLED**. To disable it, set the resource to **XmTEAR_OFF_DISABLED**. **XmRepTypeInstallTearOffModelConverter()** registers the converter that allows this resource to be set from resource files. Note that some existing applications depend on receiving a callback when a menu is mapped; since torn-off menus are always mapped, these applications might fail if a user is able to enable tear-off menus from a resource file.

5.11 The Motif User Interface Language

Motif is a hybrid of technology developed by DEC, Hewlett Packard, IBM, and Microsoft. DEC's contribution was the Application Programming Interface (API) used in DECWindows. This included a tool called the User Interface Language, or UIL.

UIL is a language for describing a Motif user interface. It looks similar to a programming language except that it has no control flow. Part of it, stored in a separate library, is called the Motif Resource Manager (MRM). You specify your user interface in a file. The .c file is compiled in the standard fashion, and linked with the –lMrm library (in addition to –lXt, –lXm, and –lX11). The .uil file has to be compiled with a program called uil, to form a .uid file.

The .c file is similar to a standard Xt application, but after **XtAppInitialize()** you call **MrmOpenHierarchyPerDisplay()**, which reads the .uid file to create the hierarchy of widgets. The .c file is primarily boilerplate, except for the callback functions for the widgets in your application. Example 5-3 shows the .c file for a simple application built with UIL.

Example 5-3. The .c file for a simple UIL application

```
#include <stdio.h>
/*
 * Declare our callback functions.
 */
static void button_selected();

/*
 * Miscellaneous UIL boilerplate: next 8 lines
 */
```

Example 5-3. The .c file for a simple UIL application (continued)

```c
#include <Xm/Xm.h>                    /* Motif Toolkit */
#include <Mrm/MrmPublic.h>            /* Motif Resource Manager */

static MrmHierarchy     s_MrmHierarchy;    /* MRM database hierarchy ID */
static char      *vec[ ]={"hellomotif.uid"}; /* MRM database file list */
static MrmCode          class ;
static MrmCount           regnum = 1 ;
static MrmRegisterArg  regvec[ ] = {
    {"button_selected",(XtPointer) button_selected }
};
/*
 * Define our callback functions.
 */
static void button_selected(widget, call_data, client_data)
    Widget      widget;
    XtPointer client_data;
    XtPointer call_data;
{
    XmAnyCallbackStruct *data = (XmAnyCallbackStruct *) call_data;
    char *tag = (char *) client_data;

    printf("button selected\n");
}

int main(argc, argv)
int argc;
char **argv;
{
    XtAppContext        app_context;
    Widget topLevel, appMain;

     XtSetLanguageProc(NULL, (XtLanguageProc)NULL, NULL);

    /*
     *  Initialize the MRM
     */
    MrmInitialize ();

    topLevel = XtVaAppInitialize(
            &app_context,       /* Application context */
            "XUilDemo",         /* application class name */
            NULL, 0,            /* command line option list */
            &argc, argv,        /* command line args */
            NULL,               /* for missing app-defaults file */
            NULL);              /* terminate varargs list */

    /*
     *  Define the Mrm.hierarchy (only 1 file)
     */

    if (MrmOpenHierarchyPerDisplay(XtDisplay(topLevel),
            1,                  /* number of files */
            vec,                /* files */
            NULL,
            &s_MrmHierarchy)    /* ptr to returned ID */
            != MrmSUCCESS) {
        printf ("Mrm can't open hierarchy\n");
    }
```

Example 5-3. The .c file for a simple UIL application (continued)

```
    /*
     *      Register our callback routines so that the resource
     *      manager can resolve them at widget-creation time.
     */

    if (MrmRegisterNames (regvec, regnum)
            != MrmSUCCESS)
        printf("Mrm can't register names\n");

    /*
     * Call MRM to fetch and create the pushbutton and its container
     */

    if (MrmFetchWidget (s_MrmHierarchy,
            "helloworld_main",
            topLevel,
            &appMain,
            &class) != MrmSUCCESS)
        printf("Mrm can't fetch interface\n");

    /*  Manage the main window of the hierarchy created by Mrm.  */

    XtManageChild(appMain);

    XtRealizeWidget(topLevel);

    XtAppMainLoop(app_context);
}
```

This *.c* file stays essentially the same for a much more complicated application, with the exception of added callback functions and added event handlers for popping up popup widgets. The description of the hierarchy of widgets lies in one or more *.uil* modules. Example 5-4 shows the *.uil* module for the application whose C code is shown above.

Example 5-4. The .uil file for a simple UIL application

```
module helloworld
    version = 'v1.0'
    names = case_sensitive

procedure
    button_selected();

object
    helloworld_main : XmRowColumn {
    controls {
        XmLabel our_label;
        XmPushButton    our_button;
    };
    };

object
    our_button : XmPushButton {
    arguments {
        XmNlabelString = compound_string('Hello',separate=true)
                & 'World!';
    };
    callbacks {
        XmNactivateCallback = procedure button_selected();
    };
```

Example 5-4. The .uil file for a simple UIL application (continued)

```
    };
object
    our_label : XmLabel {
    arguments {
       XmNlabelString =
                compound_string('Press button once',separate=true) &
                compound_string('to change label;',separate=true) &
                'twice to exit.';
    };
    };
end module;
```

The question is: Should you develop your application with pure C code or use UIL?

The following is an attempt to weigh the benefits and disadvantages of each programming method.

UIL's benefits seem to be:

- More complete separation of user interface description from application code. The former is in the *.uil* file, and the latter in the *.c* file. Theoretically, different programmers can be working on each type of file, since they only interact in the names of callback functions.

- Better compile time checking than standard Xt programming. UIL checks your user-interface specification at compile time to make sure you don't try to set resources that don't exist on the widget you are setting them on, and checks that you are using the right type of value. It also issues a warning if you create a child under a parent that doesn't support that type of child.

- Forward references to widgets that have not yet been created are allowed. This can clarify a program, since the children of each widget are listed where the widget is created. In standard C code, you have to find out the variable of type **Widget** for the geometry managing widget, and then search throughout the code for widgets that use that widget as parent.

- Since the source code is boilerplate with the exception of callback functions, the application needs compiling and linking less often. The user interface can be modified by changing the *.uil* file, and compiling it with *uil*, which is fast.

- Complete description of the widgets UIL knows about in a syntax called the Widget Meta Language (WML). As of Motif 1.2, UIL now supports an extension that allows binary databases (WMD files) containing WML information to be read at run time. So custom widgets can be included in UIL files, and they are subject to the same runtime checking.

UIL's disadvantages are:

- You have to learn the UIL syntax. If you want to add custom widgets, you have to learn another syntax, WML, as well.

- Increase in executable file size. While a Motif "hello, world" program using pure C programming is about 820K bytes in size on my system,† the same application is 1400K in size using UIL. This size penalty is serious from the point of view of disk space, loading time, and memory utilization. On systems with shared libraries, however, there will be only one copy of the libraries in memory. This solves two of the above complaints, leaving only a slower linking time at run time.

- When the callbacks in the *.c* module must be changed, you have to recompile and relink, which takes longer (without shared libraries) than linking the same application using pure C programming. In my experiment, using the *time*(1) utility built into *csh* and */bin/time*, the UIL version takes about 50 percent longer. But as mentioned earlier, this is balanced by the fact that the *.c* module has to be recompiled less often.

- Longer startup time of the finished application.

When deciding whether to use UIL or standard C, it is also relevant to consider the other programming tools available. First of all there are User Interface Management Systems (UIMSs) and Interface Development Tools (IDTs) on the market. These are programs that let you build your user interface interactively, and then output either C code or UIL code that describes the interface. These eliminate the tedium of building the interface in C, and eliminate the need to learn UIL's syntax. UIMSs and IDTs also contain lists of Motif widgets and resources, but since they output C code you can easily add your own custom widgets.

Another tool worth researching is the Widget Creation Library (WCL), written by David Smyth and Martin Brunecky. This library performs a similar job as UIL, but allows you to specify the interface in resource files instead of using UIL syntax. This resource file is read at run time and therefore does not require compiling. The WCL library is much smaller than UIL.‡ There is a WCL tutorial in *The X Resource*, Issue 2, published by O'Reilly and Associates.

---

†A Sony NWS-841 workstation running BSD 4.3. Note that this is already quite big enough!

‡WCL is available via anonymous ftp from *expo.lcs.mit.edu*. As of publication, the *contrib* directory on *expo*, contains the following files:

```
Wcl.2.2.tar.Z
Wcl.ps.Z
```

The *.ps* files contain documentation in PostScript format. All files must be uncompressed, as described in the Preface.

6

Inside a Widget

This chapter describes the code inside a basic widget. Much of this code is common to all widgets. You can think of it as a framework that Xt uses to implement a widget's features. After reading this chapter, you should understand the procedure for creating your own widget around this framework.

In This Chapter:

6
Inside a Widget

This chapter reveals the framework of code common to all widgets. As an example, it describes the code for the BitmapEdit widget that was used in versions of the *xbitmap* applications early in Chapter 4, *An Example Application*. Later examples in that chapter described how to implement the bitmap editor without a BitmapEdit widget. Therefore, you have already seen the code that is specific to this widget, and can concentrate on the framework and how to place widget-specific code within this framework.

Some applications use only the standard user interface elements defined in the widget set. If you are writing an application like this, you have no need to write your own widgets, and no real need to understand the internals of widgets. However, many applications have at least one custom window which has features not supported by any existing widget. To implement such features, you can add to a Core or Primitive widget from your application code or you can write your own widget.

Placing specialized user-interface code into a widget has several advantages. For one, the widget becomes a self-contained module that can be modified and documented separately and used in other programs. Second, the code will take advantage of Xt's automatic dispatching of events to widgets, and several other features that you can't use from the application. Finally, it is a general premise of Xt that application code should be separated as much as possible from user-interface code.

It is important to remember that widget classes are never written from scratch. People always start from template files that contain the framework for a widget without the specific code, or even better, if possible, from an existing widget that has some similar characteristics. Therefore, you'll never have to type in the framework you're about to see. You'll only have to learn where to insert your code into it. The beauty of the widget framework is that the code within it is very modular—each module has a specific place and purpose. Once you understand the framework, you can locate these modules in existing code and use them as examples. Chapter 7, *Basic Widget Methods*, shows you how to write the most important modules within the framework.

Writing your own widget is also known as *subclassing* a widget, because you always build off the features of some existing widget class. It is possible to subclass any existing widget, to add or modify features of the existing widget. However, to subclass a widget with existing features, you have to understand in detail how these features are implemented. Therefore, subclassing a complicated widget such as Text is very difficult. To implement a custom window for an application, it is normally sufficient to subclass Core or Primitive.

By and large, a widget whose superclass is Core can operate under any widget set without modification. However, both the Motif widget set and the OPEN LOOK widget set have Primitive classes beneath Core that add some basic features common to all widgets in each set. In the case of Motif, by subclassing from Primitive you get support for keyboard traversal with highlighting, resolution independence, shadows, Motif's automatic color selection, and a Help key callback. These features are basic to Motif's user-interface conventions, and therefore a widget that doesn't use them would look out of place in a Motif application. In order to inherit these features, BitmapEdit is a subclass of Primitive; it not compatible with other widget sets. Converting it, however, is a trivial matter, and will be described later in the chapter.

6.1 Widget Source File Organization

A widget is implemented in two header files and an executable code file. Each of these files contains specific elements. The names of these files are derived from the name of the widget class, which in this case is BitmapEdit:

- The private header file, *BitmapEdiP.h*, defines the widget's class and instance structures, including pointers to the widget's methods.

- The implementation file, *BitmapEdit.c*, contains the actual code for the widget, including the widget's methods and actions.

- The public header file, *BitmapEdit.h*, contains declarations needed by the application to use the widget.

The final "P" in the include file name stands for Private. Only *BitmapEdit.c* and any modules that implement subclasses of BitmapEdit should include *BitmapEdiP.h*. If an application includes this file and references any of its contents, it is breaking the rules of encapsulation, and changes to this widget may affect the application.

An application program that uses a widget includes only *BitmapEdit.h*.

The implementation filenames (and all the filenames used by your application, for that matter) should have 12 or fewer characters so that the code can be copied easily to some System V systems.† That's why the "t" in *BitmapEdiP.h* is left out.

The next three major sections describe the contents of the three files that make up a widget. These files are treated in the order shown in the above list because they are generally developed in this order.

---

†These systems have a 14-character filename limit; the 12-character limit allows files to be placed under source control or compressed. The X Consortium keeps all filenames to a maximum of 12 characters. That limits the actual class name to 9 characters, to leave room for the P.h suffix. If the widget class name is longer than 9 characters, it is truncated in the filename. For example, the private include file for the Constraint class is *ConstrainP.h* (without the final t).

6.2 The Private Header File—BitmapEdiP.h

Xt implements classes and instances with two structures, the class structure and the instance structure. By definition of C structures, the fields in both structures are fixed at compile time. Both of these structures are defined in the private include file for the class, in this case *BitmapEdiP.h*.

There is only one copy of the class structure in the running application, which all instances share. But each instance has its own copy of the instance structure, whose fields are set by the resource database as the instance is created. Fields in the instance structure can also be set by `XtVaSetValues()` or read by `XtVaGetValues()`.

The class structure's fields contain pointers to methods and pieces of data that control how Xt handles instances of this class.

The instance structure carries a complete widget state, including everything that can be different between one instance and the next. For example, the instance structure of the Core class, which every widget inherits, has fields for *x*, *y*, *width*, and *height* values, which correspond to the size of the widget and its location relative to the top-left corner of its parent. These particular fields are public; they can be set from the resource database or with `XtVaSetValues()`, and their values can be read with `XtVaGetValues()`. Other instance structure fields are private, and are used only for convenience to make data globally available within the widget.

Actually, the instance structure is not global in the normal C sense. When Xt invokes a method, it passes the method a pointer to the widget instance structure. Methods do their work by using the public fields and changing the private fields in this instance structure. For example, a method that draws in the window can get the window's dimensions directly from the widget instance structure. When action functions are called, they also are passed a pointer to the instance structure. Therefore, the fields inside the instance structure are available just about everywhere in the widget code.

6.2.1 Parts and Records

The organization of both class and instance structures is determined by the hierarchy of widget classes from which the current widget class is derived. For example, in the code for the BitmapEdit widget whose class hierarchy is shown in Figure 6-1, the class structure begins with the class fields defined by the Core class, followed by the class fields defined by Primitive, followed by the class fields defined by BitmapEdit.

Xt supplies three basic classes that are used as the basis for custom widgets, Core, Composite, and Constraint.† Figure 6-1 also shows the relationship of these classes to each other. Core is the class upon which all widgets are based. It defines common characteristics of all widgets, such as their methods, and basic resources such as height and width. Even if your widget is unlike any existing widget, it will still inherit features from the Core widget. The

---

†Shell, the fourth Intrinsics-supplied widget class, is not usually subclassed by application or widget programmers.

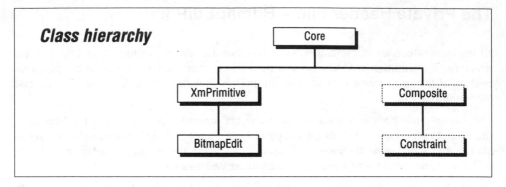

Figure 6-1. The class hierarchy of the BitmapEdit widget (with other classes shown dotted)

class and instance structures of a subclass of Composite such as Box begin with the fields from Core, continue with fields from Composite, and end with the fields defined by Box. Composite and Constraint are subclasses of Core that have additional methods that allow them to manage children; they are described in Chapter 12, *Geometry Management*. This chapter concentrates on the features of the Core widget.

Xt requires that you implement each class's new fields as a separate structure called a `Part`, and then combine this `Part` structure with each superclass's `Part` structure in the complete structure called a `Rec`, or record. In real code, these structures are called *widgetname*`ClassPart` and *widgetname*`ClassRec` for the class structure, and simply *widgetname*`Part` and *widgetname*`Rec` for the instance structure.

The reason for this "structure within a structure" design is primarily to reduce the changes in the code of subclasses that would be required if changes were made to the superclass's structures. As we will see later, only the portion of the *.c* file that initializes the class structure will need changing if a superclass class structure is changed. A second benefit of this design is that it reduces the amount of typing required to implement a new class.

6.2.2 Class Part and Class Record

Let's make these ideas concrete by showing the class structure for BitmapEdit. The complete class structure is called `BitmapEditClassRec`, and the partial structure is called `BitmapEditClassPart`. Their definitions from *BitmapEdiP.h* are shown in Example 6-1.

Example 6-1. BitmapEdiP.h: the class part and class record

```
/*
 * BitmapEditP.h - Private definitions for BitmapEdit widget
 */

/* protect against multiple including of this file */
#ifndef _ORABitmapEditP_h
#define _ORABitmapEditP_h

/*
```

Example 6-1. BitmapEdiP.h: the class part and class record (continued)

```
 * Include private header file of superclass.
 */
#include <Xm/PrimitiveP.h>

/*
 * Include public header file for this widget.
 */
#include "BitmapEdit.h"

/* New fields for the BitmapEdit widget class record */

typedef struct {
    int make_compiler_happy;     /* need dummy field */
} BitmapEditClassPart;

/* Full class record declaration */
typedef struct _BitmapEditClassRec {
    CoreClassPart       core_class;
    XmPrimitiveClassPart       primitive_class;
    BitmapEditClassPart       bitmapEdit_class;
} BitmapEditClassRec;
```

Like most widget classes, BitmapEdit provides no new fields in the class part, but it needs one dummy member to make the C compiler happy. A class defines new class part fields to allow a subclass to choose to inherit a function or to replace it. Most classes don't define fields here because they don't plan to have subclasses. This fine point is described in Section 12.4.5.

You need to include the private header file of the superclass at the top of your private header file. The **CorePart** and **CoreClassPart** structures are defined in Core's private header file *<X11/CoreP.h>*, which is included by *<Xm/PrimitiveP.h>*. **XmPrimitivePart** and **XmPrimitiveClassPart** are also defined in *<Xm/PrimitiveP.h>*. The header files begin with an **ifndef** statement that allows the preprocessor to make sure that no header file is included twice.

If the class structure contains a pointer to an extension structure, you can add to the class structure in later releases of your widget and maintain binary compatibility with subclasses. This feature is used in the basic Intrinsics classes Composite and Constraint, but is unlikely to be useful to you. However, when you do define an extension structure, you do so in the private header file. Extension structures are discussed in Section 14.13.

6.2.3 Instance Part and Instance Record

The instance record is built exactly like the class structure: by defining new fields in a part structure, and then by combining the instance parts of all superclasses in the instance record. **BitmapEditPart** defines BitmapEdit's new widget instance fields, and the entire widget instance record is **BitmapEditRec**. These structures are defined in *BitmapEdiP.h* (along with the class structures just shown) and are shown in Example 6-2. We've included several likely instance variables, but none of those shown is an essential part of the widget structure.

Example 6-2. BitmapEdiP.h: the instance part and instance record

```
/* New fields for the BitmapEdit widget record */
typedef struct {
    /* resources */
    Pixel   foreground;
    XtCallbackList  callback;/* application installed callback fns */
    Dimension  pixmap_width_in_cells;
    Dimension  pixmap_height_in_cells;
    int  cell_size_in_pixels;
    char *cell;              /* for keeping track of array of bits */
    Boolean showAll;         /* whether bitmap should display
                                entire bitmap */
    /* private state */
    int  cur_x, cur_y;       /* pstn of visible corner in big pixmap */
    Dimension  pixmap_width_in_pixels;
    Dimension  pixmap_height_in_pixels;
    Pixmap  big_picture;
    GC  draw_gc;             /* for drawing into pixmap */
    GC  undraw_gc;           /* for undrawing into pixmap */
    GC  copy_gc;             /* for copying pixmap into window */
} BitmapEditPart;

/*
 * Full instance record declaration
 */
typedef struct _BitmapEditRec {
    CorePart          core;
    XmPrimitivePart   primitive;
    BitmapEditPart    bitmapEdit;
} BitmapEditRec;

#endif                        /* _ORABitmapEditP_h */
```

Unlike the class part, which generally defines no new fields, the instance part of a widget almost always defines new instance variables. These variables control all the configurable elements of the widget, and they hold the widget's state.

Some of these instance variables are resources because they are listed in the resource list in the *BitmapEdit.c* file. (This resource list has exactly the same format as the resource list you saw in the application code in Section 3.6.2). These variables are known as public instance variables (because they are readable and writable from the application). By convention, the public instance variables are placed first in the instance part structure, and comments indicate which fields are public. When the application instantiates the widget, Xt sets the public fields based on the resource databases, the command line (the *–xrm* form), and the argument list passed to `XtVaCreateManagedWidget()`. Later on, the application may change these fields using `XtVaSetValues()`.

The private instance structure fields (not listed in the widget's resource list) are either derived from resource values or they hold some aspect of the widget's state (such as whether it is highlighted). As in Example 6-2, graphics contexts (GCs) are always found here as private fields if the widget draws any graphics. Graphics contexts are needed for doing drawing, and are derived from public instance structure fields such as colors and fonts, because it is the GC that actually carries color and font information to the X server. GCs were introduced in Section 4.2.2.

You may notice that the **Part** structures of the superclasses are referenced in the **Bitmap-EditRec** structure. As mentioned earlier, you get these by including the private include file of the immediate superclass, which in turn includes the private include file of its own superclass, and so on.

Both the class and instance structures defined in *BitmapEdiP.h* are **typedef** templates; they do not allocate storage. Xt allocates storage for the instance record when the application calls **XtVaCreateWidget()** or **XtVaCreateManagedWidget()** to create the widget. The class record, on the other hand, is initialized statically (at compile time) in the *.c* file. The compiler makes sure that the definition of the class record (in *BitmapEdiP.h*) and the initialization of the class record (in *BitmapEdit.c*) use identical structures, since *BitmapEdit.c* includes *BitmapEdiP.h*. If a field is accidentally left out of the class structure in either file, the compiler will catch the problem (but if the same member is left out of both files, the problem won't be caught and Xt will likely dump core).

BitmapEdiP.h contains an **extern** reference to the class structure initialized in *BitmapEdit.c*. This reference is shown in Example 6-3.

Example 6-3. BitmapEdiP.h: declaring the external class record

```
extern BitmapEditClassRec bitmapEditClassRec;
```

Because the private header file includes the public header file, there is no obvious reason for this **extern** declaration. But since all widget code seems to have it, we go along with the convention.

The naming conventions for the various structure declarations in the private header file are important, and can be confusing. A table summarizing the conventions for types and variables in the widget implementation files is shown in Section 6.6 (after the contents of the *.c* and *.h* files are shown).

That's all there is in the private header file! If you should need to refer back to the private header file for BitmapEdit, it is listed with the rest of the source for the widget in Appendix E, *The xbitmap Application*.

6.3 The Widget Implementation File—BitmapEdit.c

The central element of the *.c* file is the initialization of the class record. Remember that the **typedef** of the class record was declared in *BitmapEdiP.h*, but the record is allocated and the actual values in each field are set in *BitmapEdit.c*. When Xt takes over control of the widgets after the application calls **XtAppMainLoop()**, it is the values in this class record that supply Xt with all the information it uses to manage widget instances.

The organization of the *.c* file is quite simple. First, it defines everything that will be placed into the class record, and then initializes the class record, setting fields using these definitions. The major things that need defining are the functions that implement each method, the resource list, the translation table, and the actions table. It would be logical to define these four things at the beginning of the source file, and then put the class record last. This is almost the case, except that by convention the methods and actions are declared at the top of the source file and then defined at the end *after* the class record initialization. This actually makes the widget code clearer because the method declarations provide a complete list of the methods that will be defined later in the file, and the class record remains near the top of the file where it's easier to find. (Not all the methods have to be defined by a class, because some methods can be inherited or not used, as we will discuss in Section 6.3.6.) Figure 6-2 summarizes the conventional order of code in the *.c* file.†

6.3.1 Obligatory Include Files

The *.c* file begins with the standard includes:

- *<stdio.h>*, since `printf` always comes in handy for debugging purposes.

- *<Xm/XmP.h>*, which includes *<X11/IntrinsicP.h>* (which includes *<X11/Intrinsic.h>*) for the Xt supplied widget classes Core, Composite, and Constraint, declarations of Intrinsics functions, and several useful macros. *XmP.h* also includes *<Xm/Xm.h>* for the standard resource names used in defining the resource list.

- For widget sets other than Motif, include *<X11/IntrinsicP.h>* and *<X11/StringDefs.h>*.

- The private header file for this widget: *"BitmapEdiP.h"*.

Example 6-4. BitmapEdit.c: include files

```
#include <stdio.h>
#include <Xm/XmP.h>
#include "BitmapEdiP.h"
```

Remember that *BitmapEdiP.h* includes the private header file of the immediate superclass (which includes private header file of its own superclass, and so on), and each private header file includes the public header file for its class, so that all the information in all the public and private header files for all superclasses is available to this *.c* file as a result of this one include statement.

We'll look at *BitmapEdit.c* in seven parts, in an order corresponding to Figure 6-2.

---

†Here we use the terminology defined in Kernighan and Ritchie's *The C Programming Language* (Prentice-Hall 1978). A *declaration* announces the properties of a variable (its type, size, etc.), while a *definition* causes storage to be allocated. This distinction is important in the Toolkit because many things are declared and defined in separate steps.

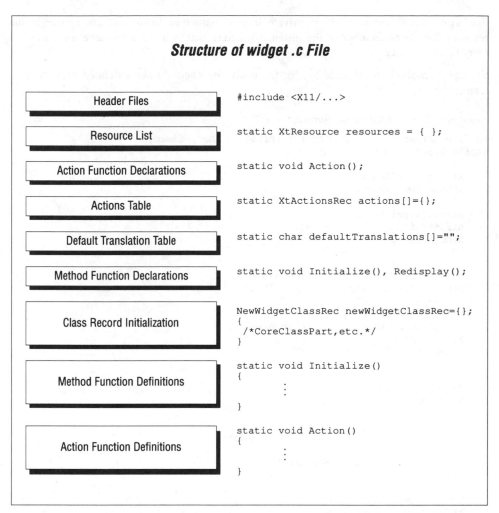

Figure 6-2. Order of code in widget .c file

6.3.2 Defining the Resource List

A widget inherits the resources defined by its superclasses, and it can also add its own resources by defining a resource list and setting it into the class structure. A widget resource list is identical to an application resource list, which you saw added to *xbitmap* in Chapter 4. The only difference is that a widget need not call **XtGetApplicationResources()**.

In creating an application resource list, we created a structure called **app_data** whose fields were to be set through resources. In widget code, the instance part structure is used just like `app_data`, except that the private instance structure fields will not appear in the resource list. Each member of the instance structure that is to be a resource must have an entry in the resource list.

Example 6-5 shows a resource list for the public instance variables defined previously in Example 6-2.

Example 6-5. BitmapEdit's resource list

```
#define offset (field) XtOffsetOf (BitmapEditRec, field)
static XtResource resources[ ] = {
    {
    XtNtoggleCallback,
    XtCToggleCallback,
    XtRCallback,
    sizeof(XtPointer),
    offset(bitmapEdit.callback),
    XtRCallback,
    NULL
    },
    {
    XtNcellSizeInPixels,
    XtCCellSizeInPixels,
    XtRInt, sizeof(int),
    offset(bitmapEdit.cell_size_in_pixels),
    XtRImmediate,
    (XtPointer)DEFAULT_CELL_SIZE
    },
    {
    XtNpixmapWidthInCells,
    XtCPixmapWidthInCells,
    XtRDimension,
    sizeof(Dimension),
    offset(bitmapEdit.pixmap_width_in_cells),
    XtRImmediate,
    (XtPointer)DEFAULT_PIXMAP_WIDTH
    },
    {
    XtNpixmapHeightInCells,
    XtCPixmapHeightInCells,
    XtRDimension,
    sizeof(Dimension),
    offset(bitmapEdit.pixmap_height_in_cells),
    XtRImmediate,
    (XtPointer)DEFAULT_PIXMAP_HEIGHT
    },
    {
    XtNcurX,
    XtCCurX,
    XtRInt,
    sizeof(int),
    offset(bitmapEdit.cur_x),
    XtRImmediate,
    (XtPointer) 0
    },
    {
    XtNcurY,
```

Example 6-5. BitmapEdit's resource list (continued)

```
      XtCCurY,
      XtRInt,
      sizeof(int),
      offset(bitmapEdit.cur_y),
      XtRString,
      (XtPointer) NULL
       },
       {
      XtNcellArray,
      XtCCellArray,
      XtRString,
      sizeof(String),
      offset(bitmapEdit.cell),
      XtRImmediate,
      (XtPointer) 0
       },
       {
      XtNshowEntireBitmap,
      XtCShowEntireBitmap,
      XtRBoolean,
      sizeof(Boolean),
      offset(bitmapEdit.showAll),
      XtRImmediate,
      (XtPointer) True
       },
};
```

The details of each field in a resource list entry is presented in Chapter 10, *Resource Management and Type Conversion*.

As mentioned earlier, a widget class inherits all the resources defined in the resource lists of its superclasses. If a resource is given the same name as a superclass resource, it overrides the superclass resource. One reason to create a new resource with the same name as a superclass resource is to give it a new, subclass-specific default value. The Primitive widget does this to replace Xt's default value for **XmNbackground** and **XmNbackgroundPixmap**. Another reason is to provide further processing on a resource value. For example, Primitive redefines the **XmNx** and **XmNy** resources so that it can add code to calculate these values using the current unit type (to implement resolution independence).

When defining a resource list, use constants defined in *<Xm/Xm.h>* whenever possible. However, any constant unique to this widget class can be defined in the public include file, as is described in the next section.

Table 6-1 summarizes the conventions for the constants used in the resource list.

Table 6-1. Resource List Constant Conventions

Prefix	First word capitalization	Description
XmN	Lower	Resource name
XmC	Upper	Resource class
XmR	Upper	Representation type

The representation type of a resource is a string that represents the type in which the widget stores the resource value. Xt constants and functions of all types use uppercase letters whenever a word break might otherwise be called for. Two examples of resource names following this convention are **XmNborderColor** and **XmNmappedWhenManaged**.

Example 6-6 shows how the resource list is entered into the class structure. You'll see this again in Section 6.3.5 where we show the entire class record and describe how to initialize it. The names of the fields in the class structure are shown in the comments at right.

Example 6-6. Setting the resource list into the class structure

```
BitmapEditClassRec bitmapEditClassRec = {
    {  /* Core class part */
        .
        .
        resources,              /* resources */
        XtNumber(resources),    /* resource_count */
        .
        .
    },
    {  /* Primitive class part */
        .
        .
        .
    },
    {  /* BitmapEdit class part */
        0,                      /* dummy_field */
    }
};
```

Note that a widget or an application can get the resource list for a class using **XtGet-ResourceList( )**, which returns a pointer to a resource list of the same form as shown above. This function isn't needed in most applications or widgets.

6.3.3 The Translation Table and Actions Table

You may recall that the translation table maps event sequences into string action names, and the action table then maps string action names into actual action functions. This is done in two steps so that the translation table is a single string that can be specified in the resource databases (since resource databases are always composed entirely of strings). The action table is not configurable through the resource database, but it can be added to the application or with **XtAppAddAction(s)**.

Like the resource list, the default translation table and the actions table have to be defined before the class record can be initialized. They determine which events this widget will respond to, and which functions defined in this source file will be triggered by those events.

The translation table is a resource defined by the Core class. It is a strange resource in several ways. It has no default value in the resource list. Instead, the default translation table is initialized into the class structure. Translations are not inherited like other resources—you do not get the sum of all the translation tables registered by the superclasses. Rather, the translation table you specify in the class structure is the only one (in the code) that matters. However, you can *choose* to use the immediate superclass's translation table instead of defining one, in which case you initialize the translation table field in the class structure to be `XtInheritTranslations`.

Each widget has its own action list, and if the application registers an action list, it is kept as a separate list. When an event combination occurs in a widget, Xt translates the event combination into an action string and searches that widget's action list. If the action string is found in the widget's action list, the search stops and that action function is called. If the action string is not found in the widget's action list, then the application's action list is searched. If neither list contains the appropriate action string, Xt prints a diagnostic warning. If the application and the widget both define the same action string in the actions table, the application's function mapped to that string will never be called. Two widget classes, however, may have the same action function name, and they will not conflict.

Example 6-7 shows a default translation table and an action table. Note that, like methods, the action functions are declared before being used in the actions table, but they will actually be defined later in the source file.

Example 6-7. The default translation table and the actions table

```
static void DrawCell(), UndrawCell(), ToggleCell();

static char defaultTranslations[ ] =
    "<Btn1Down>:    DrawCell()          \n\
     <Btn2Down>:    UndrawCell()        \n\
     <Btn3Down>:    ToggleCell()        \n\
     <Btn1Motion>:  DrawCell()          \n\
     <Btn2Motion>:  UndrawCell()        \n\
     <Btn3Motion>:  ToggleCell()";

static XtActionsRec actions[ ] = {
    {"DrawCell", DrawCell},
    {"UndrawCell", UndrawCell},
    {"ToggleCell", ToggleCell},
};
```

The pointers to the actions table and translation table are placed into the class structure just like the resource list (but of course into different fields), as shown in Example 6-8. The names of the fields in the class structure are shown in the comments at right. (You'll see this again shortly in the section on class structure initialization.)

Example 6-8. Translations in the Core class record

```
BitmapEditClassRec bitmapEditClassRec = {
    {  /* core class part */
        .
        .
        .
        actions,               /* actions */
        XtNumber(actions),     /* num_actions */
        .
        .
        defaultTranslations,   /* tm_table */
    },
    {  /* Primitive class part */
        .
        .
        .
    },
    {                          /* BitmapEdit class part */
        0,                     /* dummy_field */
    }
};
```

Note that the default translation table cannot be compiled with **XtParseTranslation-Table()** before being placed in the class structure, since the class structure initialization occurs at compile time. Xt compiles the default translations when the class is initialized.

The translation table and actions table are discussed more fully in Chapter 8, *Events, Translations, and Accelerators*.

6.3.4 Declaring Methods

Xt calls a method when the application calls a certain Xt function. For example, when an application creates a widget with **XtVaCreateManagedWidget()** (or any similar call), Xt calls the **initialize** method of that widget class. There are separate methods called when **Expose** events occur, when **XtVaSetValues()** is called, and when **Xt-DestroyWidget()** is called. Methods are distinct from actions in that methods are called in response to application function calls and **Expose** events, while actions are usually called in response to user-selectable events. Methods also each have their own field in the class structure, while actions are listed in a table that is stored in one field of the class structure. Pointers to action functions are placed in an action table which is then entered into the class structure, while a pointer to each method function is entered directly into its field of the class structure.

The widget's methods should be declared near the top of the *.c* file. This is so that the class structure initialization can appear before the method definitions. As usual in C, they should be declared as the actual type returned, such as **void** or **Bool**.† They should be declared static so that the scope of these variables is limited to this source file, eliminating possible

---

†Note that you cannot declare methods using the prototype procedure symbols Xt defines such as **XtExposeProc** (for the **expose** method), since these are defined to be pointers to functions that return the right type; they are not return types. Their only use is within Xt.

conflicts with other widget classes. Example 6-9 shows the method declarations from BitmapEdit.

Example 6-9. BitmapEdit.c: function type declarations

```
/* Declaration of methods */

static void Initialize();
static void Redisplay();
static void Destroy();
static void Resize();
static Boolean SetValues();
static XtGeometryResult QueryGeometry();

/* these Core methods not needed by BitmapEdit:
 *
 * static void ClassInitialize();
 * static void Realize();
 */

/* the following are functions private to BitmapEdit */
static void DrawPixmaps(), DoCell(), ChangeCellSize();

/* the following are actions of BitmapEdit */
static void DrawCell(), UndrawCell(), ToggleCell();
```

6.3.5 Initializing the Class Record

We've already shown you how to create the resource list, the translation table, and the actions table, and set into the class structure. A major part of the work is done. Now we just need to insert the method names we declared earlier into the class record, and set a few of the miscellaneous data fields.

As we saw in the discussion of the private header file, the BitmapEdit class record includes class parts for BitmapEdit itself and for each superclass of BitmapEdit, in this case Primitive and Core. To initialize the class record, each class part has to be initialized field by field. Fortunately this is easy because the majority of the fields are always initialized to the same values.

6.3.5.1 The Core Class Part

Since all widget classes are subclasses of Core, all need to initialize the Core class part. Example 6-10 shows the core part initialized as needed by the BitmapEdit widget. The actual name of each field is shown in the comment at left. Each field will be discussed after the example.

Example 6-10. BitmapEdit.c: initialization of Core class record

```
BitmapEditClassRec bitmapEditClassRec = {
    {                     /* core_class fields */
        /* superclass */           (WidgetClass) &xmPrimitiveClassRec,
        /* class_name */           "BitmapEdit",
        /* widget_size */          sizeof(BitmapEditRec),
```

```
        /* class_initialize */          NULL,
        /* class_part_initialize */     NULL,
        /* class_inited */              False,
        /* initialize */                Initialize,
        /* initialize_hook */           NULL,
        /* realize */                   XtInheritRealize,
        /* actions */                   actions,
        /* num_actions */               XtNumber(actions),
        /* resources */                 resources,
        /* num_resources */             XtNumber(resources),
        /* xrm_class */                 NULLQUARK,
        /* compress_motion */           True,
        /* compress_exposure */         XtExposeCompressMultiple,
        /* compress_enterleave */       True,
        /* visible_interest */          False,
        /* destroy */                   Destroy,
        /* resize */                    Resize,
        /* expose */                    Redisplay,
        /* set_values */                SetValues,
        /* set_values_hook */           NULL,
        /* set_values_almost */         XtInheritSetValuesAlmost,
        /* get_values_hook */           NULL,
        /* accept_focus */              NULL,
        /* version */                   XtVersion,
        /* callback_private */          NULL,
        /* tm_table */                  defaultTranslations,
        /* query_geometry */            QueryGeometry,
        /* display_accelerator */       XtInheritDisplayAccelerator,
        /* extension */                 NULL
    },
    {       /* Primitive class part */
        /* border_highlight */          _XtInherit,
        /* border_unhighlight */        _XtInherit,
        /* translations */              XtInheritTranslations,
        /* arm_and_activate */          NULL,
        /* syn_resources */             NULL,
        /* num_syn_resources */         0,
        /* extension */                 NULL,
    },
    {       /* BitmapEdit class part */
        /* extension */     0,
    },
};
```

If you are like most programmers, the core class part structure is the biggest structure you have ever seen! Don't worry, because many of the fields you will never have to worry about, and the rest you will gradually come to know as you need them. We will introduce all the fields here, but you are not expected to absorb all the details in a single sitting. Treat this section both as an introduction and as a summary to which you can turn back when you encounter a field you don't understand. Also, all of the methods and some of the data fields are described in more detail later in the book. These field descriptions reference the section in this book where you will find additional information about the field.

- The `superclass` field is set to a pointer to the superclass's class structure. This defines which widgets this class can inherit from. For a subclass of Core this would be `&core-ClassRec` (`widgetClassRec` was used in previous releases); for a subclass of Composite, `&compositeClassRec`; for a subclass of Constraint, `&constraintClass-Rec`, and so on.

- The next field, `class_name`, contains the name that will be used to set resources by class. In other words, this is the string that you want to appear in the resource database when setting resources for all instances of this class.

- The `widget_size` field is the size of the instance record. This should always be specified using `sizeof` with the complete instance record declaration for this class, defined in *BitmapEdiP.h*, as an argument. In this case the field is initialized to `sizeof(Bitmap-EditRec)`. Xt uses this field to allocate memory for instance records at run time.

- The next field, `class_initialize`, is the first of many pointers to widget methods. There are several issues regarding methods that require separate treatment, so we'll describe these in the next section. The complete list of methods in the Core part structure is as follows: `class_initialize`, `class_part_init`, `initialize`, `realize`, `destroy`, `resize`, `expose`, `set_values`, `set_values_almost`, `query_geometry`, and `accept_focus`.

- The `display_accelerator` field is used in conjunction with accelerators, which are a way of redirecting events to actions in different widgets, and will be discussed in more detail in Chapter 10, *Resource Management and Type Conversion*.

- The `class_inited` field is used internally by Xt to indicate whether this class has been initialized before. Always initialize it to `False`.

- The `initialize_hook`, `set_values_hook`, and `get_values_hook` fields are for use in widgets that have subparts. Subparts can have their own resources, and can load them from the resource databases as a widget can. The `initialize_hook` and `set_values_hook` are now obsolete, because their functionality can now be done in the `initialize` and `set_values` methods due to additional arguments added to those methods. The `get_values_hook` method is called immediately after the `get_values` method, and is for performing the same operations except on subparts. This field is described in Chapter 10. (Most widgets that used subparts have now been converted to use non-widget objects or gadgets instead.)

- The fields relating to resources, the default translation table, and the actions table have already been described. The only one of these fields without an obvious name is the `tm_table` field, in which you place the default translation table.

- The `xrm_class` field is used internally by Xt, and must always be initialized to NULLQUARK. This is a fixed initialization value.

- The `compress_motion`, `compress_exposure`, and `compress_enterleave` fields control the Toolkit's *event filters*. Basically, these filters remove events that some widgets can do without, thus improving performance. Unless a widget performs complicated drawing or tracks the pointer, `compress_exposure` should usually be Xt-

ExposeCompressMultiple and the other two fields should usually be `True`. These filters are described in Chapter 9, *More Input Techniques*.

- The `visible_interest` field can be set to `True` if your widget wishes to get `VisibilityNotify` events, which signal changes in the visibility of your widget. Normally this is set to `False`, because `Expose` events cause the widget to be redrawn at the proper times. For some widgets, however, `Expose` events are not enough. If your widget draws continuously, as in a game, it can stop computing output for areas that are no longer visible. There are other cases where `VisibilityNotify` events are useful.

- Xt uses the `version` field to check the compiled widget code against the library the widget is linked against. If you specify the constant `XtVersion` and it is different from the version used by the libraries, then Xt displays a run-time warning message. However, if you have intentionally designed a widget to run under more than one version of Xt, you can specify the constant `XtVersionDontCheck`.

- The `callback_private` field is private to Xt, and you always initialize it to NULL.

- The `extension` field is for later expansion of the widget while maintaining binary compatibility. When used, it is a pointer to an extension structure containing additional class structure fields.

The fields in the Primitive class part are there so that subclasses like BitmapEdit can inherit or replace certain features of Primitive. We are happy to inherit the relevant ones, and disable the rest by setting them to zero or NULL as appropriate. We inherit the `border_highlight`, `border_unhighlight`, and `translations` fields so that BitmapEdit can highlight itself and be a tab group. However, we turned these features off in the application that uses BitmapEdit (by setting `XmNtraversalOn` to `False` in *xbitmap1*) since there is not yet a keyboard interface for navigating within the bitmap.

6.3.5.2 Initializing the Core Methods

As you've just seen, there are several places for pointers to methods stored in the Core class structure. We will describe the purpose of each of these methods in the next section. But first, a word about how to set the method fields.

Fortunately, the Core class already defines some of the methods, and you can choose to inherit them instead of writing your own. In general, when you set out to write a widget, you will pick as your superclass the widget that has the most methods that you can inherit instead of writing from scratch.

Broadly speaking, there are two types of methods: self-contained methods and chained methods.

A *self-contained* method is one that is called alone—the methods of the same name in the widget's superclasses are not called. For example, `expose` is self-contained. When you write the `expose` method, you are writing all the drawing code for the widget. The `expose` method of the superclass will not be called even if it was designed to do drawing. Therefore, by writing an `expose` method you replace the `expose` method of the superclass.

A *chained method* is one that is not called alone—it is called either before or after all the methods of the same name in its superclasses and subclasses. Therefore, you can't replace any of the code in this method in the subclasses or superclasses, you can only add to it by writing your own.

Inheritance works differently for chained and self-contained methods. For self-contained methods, such as `realize` and `expose`, inheritance works almost as it does for default translations. When initializing a field in the class record that represents a self-contained method, you have three choices:

- You can define these methods in your widget code by placing the name of the function in the class record and defining that function somewhere in the source file.

- You can inherit that method from the immediate superclass by placing a special symbol beginning with `XtInherit` in that field in the class record.

- You can use the first technique, but reference the superclass's method in your method. This allows you to add features to the superclass's method without having to completely copy it and modify it.

These techniques are demonstrated in Section 6.3.8. Chained methods, on the other hand, use one of two flavors of inheritance. Some are *downward chained*, which means that the Core method is called first, followed by the same method in each subclass. Other methods are *upward chained*, which means that the Core class method is called last. For both upward and downward chained methods, your choice is whether to specify additional code by defining your own method, or to go with what the other classes have already defined. You cannot prevent the code from the other classes from being executed.

Here is how chaining works for the `initialize` method in BitmapEdit. Remember that BitmapEdit is a subclass of Primitive and then Core. The Core class record contains only the Core part structure. The Primitive class record contains the Core part structure and the Primitive part structure. The BitmapEdit class record contains the Core, Primitive, and Bitmap-Edit part structures. The `initialize` method is present in the Core part structure of all three classes. When an application creates an instance of the BitmapEdit widget, Xt calls the function specified in the `initialize` field in the Core class record first, followed by the one in the Primitive class record, and finally the one in the BitmapEdit class record. This is an example of downward chaining.

The `destroy` method, on the other hand, is upward chained. That is, the `destroy` method in BitmapEdit would be called first, followed by the `destroy` method for Primitive, and finally the one for Core.

If you specify NULL in your class structure for a method that chains upward or downward, it is equivalent to specifying a function that does nothing. The function for that method of the superclasses and subclasses will still be called normally.

Table 6-2 lists which methods fall into each type of inheritance. It also shows how translations, actions, and resources are chained.

Table 6-2. *Inheritance Style of Various Methods*

Self-contained	Upward chained	Downward chained
`class_initialize`	`destroy`	`class_part_init`
`realize`		`initialize`
`resize`		`set_values`
`expose`		`get_values_hook`
`accept_focus`		`set_values_hook`
`set_values_almost`		`initialize_hook`
`query_geometry`		
translations	actions	resources

6.3.6 Description of Core Methods

Here is a brief description of the purpose of each Core method, and where in this book the method will be described in detail. All these methods, except `realize`, can be set to NULL in the class record and the widget will still function. However, all widgets that draw into their window will also require the `expose` method, the `initialize` method, and usually the `resize` method. And to be good children, widgets should define a `query_geometry` method. The `realize` method is shown in Section 6.3.6, and the rest of the commonly-used methods immediately after that in Chapter 7, *Basic Widget Methods*.

This list describes *all* the methods, even those that are rarely used. There is a lot of detail here that you should not expect to absorb in a first reading. Like the list of Core class structure fields, treat this as an introduction and come back to it later for reference when you come across a method you don't know how to use, or if you have something you want to do and you don't remember in which method to do it.

- `initialize` sets initial values for all the fields in the instance part structure. This method is responsible for checking that all public fields have been set to reasonable values. This method is downward chained, so each class's `initialize` method sets the initial values for its own instance part structure. This method is described in Chapter 7, *Basic Widget Methods*.

- `initialize_hook` is called immediately after the `initialize` method of the same class. It is obsolete as of R4 (though still called for compatibility); its job has been added to that of `initialize`. It allows the widget to initialize subparts, and is used only in widgets that have subparts. Subparts have their own resources and are described in Section 10.5. `initialize_hook`, a downward chained method, is also described there.

- `class_initialize` is called once, the first time an instance of a class is created by the application. The widget registers type converters here, if it has defined any nonstandard ones. `class_initialize` is self-sufficient and is described in Chapter 10, *Resource Management and Type Conversion*.

- `class_part_init` is called once the first time an instance of a class is created by the application. It is different from `class_initialize` only in that it is downward chained. This method resolves inheritance of self-sufficient methods from the immediate superclass. It is needed only in classes that define their own methods in their class part (but is not present in Core, Composite, or Constraint, because Xt handles inheritance in these). This method is described in Chapter 14, *Miscellaneous Toolkit Programming Techniques*.

- `realize` is called when the application calls `XtRealizeWidget()`. This method is responsible for setting window attributes and for creating the window for the widget. It is self-sufficient, and is described in Section 6.3.6.

- `expose` redraws a widget whenever an `Expose` event arrives from the server (but note that Xt can coalesce consecutive `Expose` events to minimize the number of times it is called). This method is responsible for making Xlib calls to draw in the widget's window. The widget's instance variables are often used in the `expose` method to guide the drawing. This method is self-sufficient. This method is described in Chapter 7, *Basic Widget Methods*.

- `resize` is called when the parent widget resizes the widget. It recalculates the instance variables based on the new position and size of its window, which are passed into the method. This method is self-sufficient and is described in Chapter 7, *Basic Widget Methods*, and in Chapter 12, *Geometry Management*.

- `set_values` is called whenever the application calls `XtSetValues()` to set the resources of the widget. This method recalculates private instance variables based on the new public instance variable values. It contains similar code to the `initialize` method, but is called at different, and perhaps multiple, times. The `set_values` method is downward chained. This method is described in Chapter 7, *Basic Widget Methods*.

- `set_values_almost` is used to process application requests to change this widget's size. This field should never be NULL. Unless you've written your own `set_values_almost` method, this field should be set to `XtInheritSet-ValuesAlmost`. Most classes inherit this procedure from their superclass. This method is self-contained and is described in Chapter 12, *Geometry Management*.

- `set_values_hook` sets resource values in subparts. It is now obsolete (though still called for compatibility); its job has been added to that of `set_values`. This method is used only in widgets that have subparts, as described in Section 10.5. It is downward chained and is described in Chapter 10, *Resource Management and Type Conversion*.

- `accept_focus` is NULL for most widgets (or, at least, for all the Athena widgets). When it is present, this method should set the keyboard focus to a subwidget of this widget. This would be used, for example, to allow the application to set the input focus to the Text widget within a Dialog widget. This method is invoked when the application calls `XtCallAcceptFocus()`. This method is self-contained and is described in Chapter 14, *Miscellaneous Toolkit Programming Techniques*.

- `get_values_hook` is called just after `get_values` and is used to return the resources of subparts. This method is downward chained and is described in Chapter 10, *Resource Management and Type Conversion*.

- **destroy** deallocates local and server memory allocated by this widget. This is called when an application destroys a widget but remains running. This method is described in Chapter 7, *Basic Widget Methods*.

- **query_geometry** may be called when the parent widget is about to resize the widget. The method is passed the proposed new size, and is allowed to suggest a compromise size, or to agree to the change as specified. This method it self-contained. It is described in Chapter 7, *Basic Widget Methods*.

Initialization of the Composite and Constraint class parts, including the methods in those structures, is described in Chapter 12, *Geometry Management*, since this is necessary only in widgets that manage children.

6.3.7 Packaging the Class Record for Application Use

The final requirement of the *.c* file is a pointer to the class record, called **bitmapEdit-WidgetClass**, that applications use as an argument to **XtCreateManagedWidget()** to create instances of this widget class. This is shown in Example 6-11.

Example 6-11. BitmapEdit.c: declaring the class record pointer

```
WidgetClass bitmapEditWidgetClass = (WidgetClass) &bitmapEditClassRec;
```

bitmapEditWidgetClass is set to be a pointer to the **bitmapEditClassRec**, the complete class record. Remember that since the actual declaration of the class structure is in the private include file, the application cannot access class structure fields, and therefore this pointer is opaque to the application.

6.3.8 A Sample Method

Each method has a particular job to do, and is described in Chapter 7 or in the chapter that discusses that job. However, we'll describe the **realize** method now, because it is simple and demonstrates the two techniques of inheriting for self-contained fields that were described in Section 6.3.5.2. The **realize** method is responsible for creating the widget's window, and all widgets have a window.† The first technique is to inherit wholesale the method defined by the immediate superclass. The superclass may have its own **realize** method, or it may also inherit the method from its superclass, and so on. The Core widget's **realize** method creates a basic window.‡ In your subclasses of any of these widgets, you

---

†Gadgets don't have windows, and therefore don't have a **realize** method. The code to implement a gadget is described in Chapter 13, *Menus, Gadgets, and Cascaded Popups*.

‡If you have the source code for Xt, you may discover that the Core widget is actually an amalgamation of several other superclasses called WindowObj, RectObj, and so on. (You might also notice the include files for these classes in */usr/include/X11*.) The Core widget actually inherits the **realize** procedure from WindowObj. These classes are an implementation detail that will affect you only if you want to look in some of these superclasses to find the code that implements features normally attributed to Core. From application code or widget code, it is always safe to assume that Core is the top of the class tree. For gadgets, you need to know more about these "hidden" classes, so we'll discuss them in Chapter 13, *Menus, Gadgets, and Cascaded Popups*.

can inherit the Core `realize` method without modification by initializing the `realize` member of the Core class record to the symbolic constant `XtInheritRealize`, as shown in Example 6-12.

Example 6-12. BitmapEdit.c: inheriting a self-contained method

```
BitmapEditClassRec bitmapEditClassRec = {
    {                    /* Core class part */
          .
          .
          .
       XtInheritRealize,  /* realize */
          .
          .
          .
    },
    {  /* Primitive class part */
          .
          .
          .
    },
    {  /* BitmapEdit class part */
       0,                 /* dummy_field */
    }
};
```

Xt also defines symbolic constants for inheriting for every other self-contained method. They all begin with `XtInherit`, and in general continue with the capitalized name of the method field.

An important part of the process of creating an X window is the setting of window attributes. Therefore, a brief aside on window attributes is necessary. (You can skim the next page if you are already familiar with them.)

Window attributes are basic features of the way the server makes windows look and act. Window attributes can also be changed later if necessary, but the `realize` method is the place to set them initially. The Core class `realize` method sets some basic window attributes such as the window background and border colors or patterns, and it gets these values from Core resources. Here is a list of the window attributes that you may wish to set:

Background   Can be a solid color, pattern, or share bits with parent.

Border   Can be a solid color or pattern.

Bit Gravity   Determines how partial window contents are preserved when a window is resized. This is an optimization that can save redrawing.

Backing Store   Provides hints about when a window's contents should be preserved by the server even when the window is obscured or unmapped. This is useful for widgets that are very time-consuming to redraw. Not all servers are capable of maintaining a backing store. Check the value returned from the Xlib `DoesBackingStore` macro to determine whether this feature is supported on a particular screen on your server.

Saving Under   Provides hints about whether or not the screen area beneath a window should be saved while a window such as a popup menu is in place, to save obscured windows from having to redraw themselves when the popup is removed. Not all servers can save under windows. You can find out whether this feature is supported on a particular screen with the Xlib `DoesSaveUnders` macro.

Colormap Determines which virtual colormap should be used for this window. If your widget requires a lot of specific colors—for example, to draw a shaded image, it may need to create its own virtual colormap. In that case, it would set this attribute to the ID of the created colormap. For more information, see Chapter 7, *Color*, in Volume One, *Xlib Programming Manual*.

Cursor Determines which cursor should be displayed when the pointer is in this window. You must create this cursor before setting this attribute. This can be done with a standard type converter, as described in Chapter 14, *Miscellaneous Toolkit Programming Techniques*.

It may clarify the picture to describe the features that window attributes *do not* affect. Setting the window attributes does not determine a window's parent, depth, or visual. These are all set when a window is created, and are permanent. The window attributes are also not used for setting the size, position, or border width of a widget. These are set using `XtSet-Values()`. Window attributes do not determine how graphics requests are interpreted; this is the job of the graphics context (GC).

Note that some of the window attributes are not listed here because they should not be set directly by widgets, in the `realize` method or anywhere else. These include the `event_mask`, which controls which events are sent to this widget. Xt itself sets this window attribute based on the translation table. Another is `override_redirect`, which is handled by the Shell widget.

You could write a `realize` method that set your desired attributes and then called `XtCreateWindow()`. But this is slightly wasteful, since Core already has a `realize` method that creates a window and you can take advantage of it. This is the second inheritance scheme used for self-contained fields. You define your own `realize` method just as if you were going to write it from scratch, but then you call the superclass's `realize` method directly, as shown in Example 6-13.

Example 6-13. Inheriting by invoking the superclass method from a widget method

```
#define superclass        (&coreClassRec)

static void Realize(w, valueMask, attributes)
Widget w;
XtValueMask *valueMask;
XSetWindowAttributes *attributes;
{
    /* this is already set, but just for example */
    *valueMask |= CWBitGravity;
    attributes->bit_gravity = NorthWestGravity;

    /* use realize method from superclass */
    (*superclass->core_class.realize) (w, valueMask, attributes);
}
```

Xt passes to the **realize** method a set of window attributes based on Core instance structure values. You update these values as necessary, and then call the superclass's **realize** method, as shown.

See the **XtRealizeProc** reference page in Volume Five, *X Toolkit Intrinsics Reference Manual*, to find out the default settings of the window attributes as passed into the **realize** method.

You may wonder what happens if the superclass also inherited its **realize** method—does the code in Example 6-13 crash by assuming the superclass field contains a function pointer when it actually contains the constant **XtInheritRealize**? No. When the class is initialized, Xt reconciles all the inherited methods and resets the class record fields to be pointers to the right methods.

What is happening behind the scenes when you inherit the **realize** method is that the Core **realize** method calls the Toolkit function **XtCreateWindow( )**, which in turn calls the Xlib function **XCreateWindow( )**. You may need to call the Xlib routine yourself in the **realize** method if you want to use a visual other than the default. See the reference page for **XCreateWindow( )** in Volume Two, *Xlib Reference Manual*, and Chapter 7, *Color*, in Volume One, *Xlib Programming Manual*, for details on depth, visual, and the issue of color in general.

6.4 The Public Header File—BitmapEdit.h

The public header file defines the aspects of the widget that can be accessed from the application. Public header files tend to be short. The two obligatory features of the *BitmapEdit.h* file are:

- An external declaration of **bitmapEditWidgetClass**, the class record pointer used by applications in calls to **XtCreateWidget( )** to create an instance of this widget class.

- A pointer to the widget instance record, in this case **BitmapEditWidget**. Xt calls all methods and actions with an argument of type **Widget**. To access any of the fields in the instance structure, this pointer must be cast to type **BitmapEditWidget**. The easiest way to do this is to declare the argument of the method as type **BitmapEdit- Widget** (the other way is to cast in an assignment).

If your resource list uses **XmN**, **XmC**, or **XmR** constants not defined in *<Xm/Xm.h>* (*<X11/StringDefs.h>* for standard Xt applications), you must define them in the public include file. The definitions should have only a single space between the definition and the value, with no trailing comment or space. This reduces the possibility of compiler warnings from similar but not identical definitions in multiple classes. If you want, you can use a different convention for the symbol names, to distinguish your constants from those defined by Motif. For example, you could start them all with **Xo**.

If a widget offers any public functions, they would be declared **extern** here (and actually defined in the *.c* file). Public functions allow the application to read or change certain private data in certain more restricted or more convenient ways than is possible with resources. For example, the BitmapEdit widget provides the public function **BitmapEditGetArray** that applications can call to get the array of bits currently stored as private data in the widget. (This array is an attribute readable with **XtGetValues()**, but using this function is more convenient because it also returns the dimensions of the array.)

Example 6-14 shows BitmapEdit's public header file.

Example 6-14. BitmapEdit.h: complete public header file

```
#ifndef _ORABitmapEdit_h
#define _ORABitmapEdit_h

/* BitmapEdit Widget public include file */

/*
 * The public header file for the immediate superclass normally
 * must be included.  However, not in this case because the public
 * header file for Primitive is in Xm.h, which is already included
 * in all Motif applications.
 */

/* #include <Xm/Superclass.h>   */

/*
 * This public structure is used as call_data to the callback.
 * It passes the x, y position of the cell toggled (in units of
 * cells, not pixels) and a mode flag that indicates whether the
 * cell was turned on (1) or off (0).
 */
typedef struct {
    int mode;
    int newx;
    int newy;
} BitmapEditPointInfo;

#define XtNtoggleCallback "toggleCallback"
#define XtNcellSizeInPixels "cellSizeInPixels"
#define XtNpixmapWidthInCells "pixmapWidthInCells"
#define XtNpixmapHeightInCells "pixmapHeightInCells"
#define XtNcurX "curX"
#define XtNcurY "curY"
#define XtNcellArray "cellArray"
#define XtNshowEntireBitmap "showEntireBitmap"

#define XtCToggleCallback "ToggleCallback"
#define XtCCellSizeInPixels "CellSizeInPixels"
#define XtCPixmapWidthInCells "PixmapWidthInCells"
#define XtCPixmapHeightInCells "PixmapHeightInCells"
#define XtCCurX "CurX"
#define XtCCurY "CurY"
#define XtCCellArray "CellArray"
#define XtCShowEntireBitmap "ShowEntireBitmap"

extern char *BitmapEditGetArray(); /* w */
    /* Widget w; */

/* Class record constants */
extern WidgetClass bitmapEditWidgetClass;

typedef struct _BitmapEditClassRec *BitmapEditWidgetClass;
typedef struct _BitmapEditRec       *BitmapEditWidget;
```

Example 6-14. BitmapEdit.h: complete public header file (continued)

```
#endif /* _ORABitmapEdit_h */
/* DON'T ADD STUFF AFTER THIS #endif */
```

6.5 The Process of Widget Writing

The process of writing a widget generally begins with the same steps. They are:

- Copy all three files of an existing widget. If you are subclassing Core or XmPrimitive, it is generally easiest to copy the files of another subclass of Core or XmPrimitive, preferably the one most similar to the one you intend to write; pick one that has many methods defined so that you don't need to type them in. (It's easier to delete than to retype.) If you are subclassing a widget that has no existing subclasses, then you can use any set of widget template files. There is a widget in the Athena widget set called Template that is for this purpose.

- Globally change the widget class name in the files. The fastest way to do this under UNIX is with *sed*, using a script similar to the following:

    ```
    s/BitmapEdit/NewName/g
    s/bitmapEdit/newName/g
    ```

    Place this script in the file *sedscr*, and run the command:

    ```
    spike% sed -f sedscr file > newfile
    ```

    on each file. (Or write a simple `for` loop to run it on multiple files.)

- Start from the top of the *.c* file, and begin by writing the resource list. While writing the resource list, you may need to edit the public header file to define new resource names and classes (**XmN** and **XmC** symbols). While writing the resource list (and during the entire widget-writing process), you will also need to edit the private header file in order to add and remove instance part structure fields, as you determine a need for them while writing methods and actions. Later you will probably discover additional parameters that you want to define as resources.

- Design the output you expect your widget to draw. Your instance part structure fields must hold all the information necessary to redraw everything when the window is exposed—add the necessary fields.

- Design the user input you expect your widget to accept. Start with as many separate actions as you can—one for each distinguishable user input idiom. For example, Bitmap-Edit has three actions for changing one bitmap cell: **DrawCell**, **UndrawCell**, and **ToggleCell**. Even though these invoke almost identical underlying code, it is best to keep them as separate actions.

- Design a default translation table to have these actions called in response to the appropriate events. Help in this area is available in Section 8.1.2.

- Write the **expose** method and actions. How to do this is described in the next chapter. But in summary, both the **expose** method and actions often draw into the widget. The **expose** method must always be able to redraw what the actions drew. Therefore, it usually pays to have common elements of code called by both an action and the **expose** method. Neither the action nor the **expose** method pass arguments to this common code. Instead, the actions set instance variables that are read in the **expose** method or common code. The instance variables act as global variables because they are available almost everywhere in the widget code.

- Add parameters that allow your drawing code to work smoothly in any size window, and add a **resize** method that sets these parameters.

- Add the **initialize** method to check resource values that might have been user supplied and to initialize private instance variables.

- Add the **set_values** method to check application-supplied resource values and reset private instance variables based on the new resource values.

- Declare the methods and actions you have defined, near the top of the .c file.

- Enter all these functions and tables you have defined into the class structure initialization.

It is useful to have a simple application available for testing your widget as you develop it. One that simply creates the widget under construction and provides a Quit button is quite adequate. Then you can add code to the widget incrementally, assuring at each step that the program compiles, links, and runs without error.

As this list implies, it is a good idea to start simply by completing all the above steps for a small subset of the features you eventually want. Once you have a working widget that you can test, you can add features one at a time by going through the list again. If instead you attempt to write an ambitious widget in one pass, you will spend much longer debugging it.

Once you have learned how to write methods and actions in the next chapter, *Basic Widget Methods*, you should be ready to write a simple widget.

6.6 Summary of Conventions

The naming conventions for the various structure declarations in the widget source files can be confusing. Table 6-3 summarizes these conventions, using the BitmapEdit widget as an example, and describes where each type is used. This table is just to help you read the code. If you create a new class starting from an existing class, and globally change the names as described above, all of the definitions and references listed here will already be done for you.

Table 6-3. Summary of Xt Structure Name Conventions

Structure Name	Description
BitmapEditClassPart	Partial class structure typedef (usually dummy field only) used for defining **BitmapEditClassRec** in *P.h* file.
BitmapEditClassRec	Complete class structure typedef, declared **extern** in *P.h* file, used for initializing class structure in *.c* file.
bitmapEditClassRec	Name of complete class structure allocated in *.c* file, declared **extern** in *P.h* file, allocated in *.c* file, used as superclass in class record initialization of subclasses of this widget (*.c* file).
BitmapEditPart	Partial instance structure typedef, used for defining **BitmapEditRec** in *P.h* file.
BitmapEditRec	Complete instance structure typedef, also used to initialize **widget_size** field of class record in *.c* file.
_BitmapEditRec	Type of **BitmapEditRec**, used for defining **BitmapEditWidget** pointer in *.h* file.
_BitmapEditClassRec	Type of **BitmapEditClassRec**, used for defining **BitmapEditWidgetClass** pointer in *.h* file.
BitmapEditWidget	Pointer to **BitmapEditRec** (complete instance structure), used to reference instance structure fields in *.c* file (passed as argument to methods).
BitmapEditWidgetClass	Pointer to **_BitmapEditClassRec**, used to cast **bitmapEditClassRec** for superclass in class record initialization of subclasses of this widget (*.c* file).
bitmapEditWidgetClass	Of type **WidgetClass**, address of **bitmapEditClassRec**, used in **XtVaCreateManagedWidget()** calls to identify class to be created.

7

Basic Widget Methods

This chapter describes the initialize, expose, set_values, resize, query_geometry, and destroy methods. It explains when Xt calls each method, and describes in detail what should be in each of these methods. Among other things, these methods prepare for and do the drawing of graphics that appear in a widget. This chapter describes what the Toolkit adds to the graphics model provided by Xlib, but does not describe in detail how to draw using Xlib; this topic is described in Chapters 5, 6 and 7 of Volume One, Xlib Programming Manual. This chapter also describes how to write action routines that work in the widget framework.

In This Chapter:

7

Basic Widget Methods

This chapter describes the `initialize`, `expose`, `set_values`, `resize`, `query_geometry`, and `destroy` methods. These are the methods you need to write to make a functioning widget (although `destroy` is optional). The common thread in most of these methods is that they have a role in drawing graphics, although all but the `expose` method are also responsible for other things. We will describe all the responsibilities of these methods, but focus on the issues involving graphics because they are so important. Additional examples of each method are shown on the reference pages for each method in Section 4 of Volume Five, *X Toolkit Intrinsics Reference Manual*.

Three of these methods are called by Xt in response to application function calls:

- The `initialize` method is called when the application calls `XtVaCreate-ManagedWidget()`.

- The `set_values` method is called when the application calls `XtVaSetValues()`.

- The `destroy` method is called when the application calls `XtDestroyWidget()`.

A fourth method, `expose`, is called in response to `Expose` events, which occur whenever part or all of a widget's window becomes newly visible on the screen.†

When the parent widget, which is usually a geometry-managing Composite or Constraint widget, needs to resize one of its children, it may call the child's `query_geometry` method to find the child's opinion of the proposed change. Once the parent has actually resized the child, Xt calls the child's `resize` method, which is responsible for calculating private instance variables, so that the child is prepared to redraw itself in its new window size.

Applications that use the Toolkit should do all their drawing in widgets. Although it is possible to create normal X windows and draw into them from the application code, you lose the advantage of Xt's event dispatching, event filtering, and other features. It's just as easy to

---

†Note that `Expose` events are also handled through the translation mechanism like any other event. When they are present in the translation table, the action registered for `Expose` events will be called in addition to the `expose` method. Widgets do not normally include the `Expose` event in their translation table, because they already have the `expose` method. Applications might, conceivably, have `Expose` in their translation table to add drawing capability to a widget, although it is difficult to calculate where to do this drawing from the application since the widget's size may change.

draw in a widget, and it's easier to add processing of user input as described in Chapter 8, *Events, Translations, and Accelerators*.

7.1 The X Graphics Model Inside Widgets

Section 4.2.2 described the X graphics model and how drawing from the application is accomplished. In summary, the process consisted of creating GCs and then drawing from a function that Xt calls on receipt of **Expose** events. Drawing from inside a widget follows the same general procedure, but the code is organized differently.

Inside a widget, you normally create GCs with the Xt routine **XtGetGC()** or **XtAllocateGC** instead of the Xlib routine **XCreateGC()**. **XtGetGC()** is similar to the Xlib routine except that it arranges for the sharing of GCs among widgets within an application. This is important because each GC has some overhead and servers can achieve better performance when handling fewer GCs. Because Xt applications often have many instances of the same widget class, each needing the same GC characteristics (unless the user specifies a different color for each one), Xt arranges for them to share GCs when possible. The drawback with **XtGetGC()** is that no instance is allowed to modify the returned GC, because some other widget instance may be depending on it. **XtAllocateGC()** supports more flexible sharing. You specify which fields your widget wants the ability to change, and those that it doesn't care about, so that some other widget may get the same GC if it only needs to change the latter fields.

Xt organizes GC creation and drawing into separate methods. Setting initial values for the GC and creating the GC is done in the **initialize** method, and actual drawing is done in the **expose** method. This makes it very easy to find this code in existing widgets and straightforward to write this code for new widgets.

Since Xt allows resources to be changed during program execution by calling **XtVaSetValues()**, the widget code must be prepared to change the GC at any time if the GC components depend on resource values. The **set_values** method calculates the new values based on resource changes and updates the appropriate GCs.

The next six major sections discuss the code needed to implement the **initialize**, **expose**, **set_values**, **resize**, **query_geometry**, and **destroy** methods.

7.2 The initialize Method

As described in Section 6.3.5.2, the initialize method has basically one function: it sets instance structure members (also called instance variables).† This job has two parts: setting the initial values of private instance variables, and checking to make sure that the values of the public instance variables are valid (since they are user configurable). Since the initialize method is downward chained (defined in Section 6.3.5.2), the method for this class needs to initialize only the fields present in the instance part structure for this class. The exceptions are width and height. Even though they are instance variables of Core, they need to be checked by the subclass, because only this class knows its desired initial size.

Example 7-1 shows the initialize method from BitmapEdit.

Example 7-1. The initialize method

```
/* ARGSUSED */
static void
Initialize(treq, tnew, args, num_args)
Widget treq, tnew;
ArgList args;
Cardinal *num_args;
{
    BitmapEditWidget new = (BitmapEditWidget) tnew;
    new->bitmapEdit.cur_x = 0;
    new->bitmapEdit.cur_y = 0;
    /*
     *  Check instance values set by resources that may be invalid.
     */

    if ((new->bitmapEdit.pixmap_width_in_cells < 1) ||
            (new->bitmapEdit.pixmap_height_in_cells < 1)) {
        XtWarning("BitmapEdit: pixmapWidth and/or pixmapHeight\
                is too small (using 10 x 10).");
        new->bitmapEdit.pixmap_width_in_cells = 10;
        new->bitmapEdit.pixmap_height_in_cells = 10;
    }

    if (new->bitmapEdit.cell_size_in_pixels < 5) {
        XtWarning("BitmapEdit: cellSize is too small (using 5).");
        new->bitmapEdit.cell_size_in_pixels = 5;
    }

    if ((new->bitmapEdit.cur_x < 0) ||
            (new->bitmapEdit.cur_y < 0)) {
        XtWarning("BitmapEdit: cur_x and cur_y must be\
                non-negative (using 0, 0).");
        new->bitmapEdit.cur_x = 0;
        new->bitmapEdit.cur_y = 0;
    }
    /*
```

---

† As described in Chapter 12, *Geometry Management*, the initialize method can also be used for creating child widgets, to build a compound widget. This is a way of getting around Xt's geometry management scheme, and is not frequently done.

Example 7-1. The initialize method (continued)

```
 * Allocate memory to store array of cells in bitmap, if not
 * already done by application.
 */
if (new->bitmapEdit.cell == NULL)
    new->bitmapEdit.cell =
            XtCalloc(new->bitmapEdit.pixmap_width_in_cells
            * new->bitmapEdit.pixmap_height_in_cells,
            sizeof(char));
else
    new->primitive.user_data = True; /* user supplied cell array */

/* Calculate useful values */
new->bitmapEdit.pixmap_width_in_pixels =
        new->bitmapEdit.pixmap_width_in_cells
        * new->bitmapEdit.cell_size_in_pixels;

new->bitmapEdit.pixmap_height_in_pixels =
        new->bitmapEdit.pixmap_height_in_cells
        * new->bitmapEdit.cell_size_in_pixels;

/*
 * Motif Primitive sets width and height to provide enough room
 * for the highlight and shadow around a widget.  (This means
 * it does not honor user-specified sizes for widgets.)
 * BitmapEdit doesn't use these features.  A widget that did use
 * these features would *add* its desired dimensions to those set
 * by Primitive.  To use this widget with another widget set,
 * remove the following two lines.
 */
new->core.width = 0;
new->core.height = 0;

/* set initial size of window */
if (new->core.width == 0) {
    if (new->bitmapEdit.showAll == False)
        new->core.width =
                (new->bitmapEdit.pixmap_width_in_pixels >
                DEFAULTWIDTH) ? DEFAULTWIDTH :
                (new->bitmapEdit.pixmap_width_in_pixels);
    else
        new->core.width =
                new->bitmapEdit.pixmap_width_in_pixels;
}

if (new->core.height == 0) {
    if (new->bitmapEdit.showAll == False)
        new->core.height =
                (new->bitmapEdit.pixmap_height_in_pixels >
                DEFAULTWIDTH) ? DEFAULTWIDTH :
                (new->bitmapEdit.pixmap_height_in_pixels);
    else
        new->core.height =
                new->bitmapEdit.pixmap_height_in_pixels;
}

/* Tell Primitive not to allow tabbing to this widget,
 * since there is no keyboard interface for using it. */
XtVaSetValues(new,
```

Example 7-1. The initialize method (continued)

```
        XmNtraversalOn, False,
        NULL);

    CreateBigPixmap(new);

    GetDrawGC(new);
    GetUndrawGC(new);
    GetCopyGC(new);

    DrawIntoBigPixmap(new);
}
```

Even though the specific instance variables initialized here are particular to BitmapEdit, the techniques are common to all `initialize` methods. Some private instance variables, such as `cur_x` and `cur_y`, do not depend on resource settings and are simply initialized to a fixed value. Public instance variables are checked; if their values are out of range, `Xt-Warning()` is called to print a message on the standard output and they are instead initialized to a fixed value. Some private instance variables are set based on public instance variables. GCs are the most common example.

As you should recall from Chapter 6, *Inside a Widget*, all the variables set in `initialize` are declared in the `BitmapEditPart` instance structure in the private header file.

Note that most of the arguments of `initialize` are rarely used. When `initialize` is called, the *request* argument is an instance structure containing the same values as *new*. But as *new* is changed, *request* provides a sometimes useful record of the resource settings originally made by the user. The *args* and *num_args* arguments contain the resource settings provided in the call to `XtVaCreateManagedWidget()`. These are sometimes useful in distinguishing between settings made by the application (*args*) from settings made by the user (which already appear in *new* and *request*). The code in the `initialize_hook` method, described in Chapter 10, *Resource Management and Type Conversion*, can optionally be placed in the `initialize` method.

7.2.1 Creating GCs

In any widget that does drawing, some of the private instance variables will hold the IDs of GCs created in the `initialize` method. These variables will be read when the GCs are needed in the `expose` method, and will be reset if necessary in the `set_values` method. Example 7-1 called separate routines, `GetDrawGC`, `GetUndrawGC`, and `GetCopyGC` to create the GCs. Example 7-2 shows these routines.

A program prepares for creating a GC by setting the desired characteristics of the GC into members of a large structure called `XGCValues` (defined by Xlib), and specifying which members of `XGCValues` it has provided by setting a bitmask. This bitmask is made by ORing the GC mask symbols defined in *<X11/X.h>*. Each bitmask symbol represents a member of the `XGCValues` structure. Every GC field has a default value, so only those values that differ from the default need to be set. The default GC values are discussed in Volume One, *Xlib Programming Manual*.

Widget code normally creates a GC with the **XtGetGC()** call, not the Xlib analogue **XCreateGC()**. **XtGetGC()** keeps track of requests to get GCs by all the widgets in an application, and creates new server GCs only when a widget requests a GC with different values. In other words, after the first widget creates a GC with **XtGetGC()**, any subsequent widget that calls **XtGetGC()** to create a GC with the same values will get the same GC, not a new one. Using this client-side caching also reduces the number of requests to the server.

Xlib provides **XChangeGC()** to change the values in an existing GC. Xt provides no analogue. Because of the sharing of GCs allocated with **XtGetGC()**, you must treat them as read-only. If you don't, you may confuse or break other widgets. In cases where your widget creates a GC that needs changing in such a way that it is impractical to create a new GC each time, it may be appropriate to use the Xlib call **XCreateGC()** instead of the Xt call **XtGetGC()**.

BitmapEdit must use **XCreateGC()** for two of its three GCs because these GCs are for drawing into pixmaps of depth 1, while **XtGetGC()** always creates GCs for drawing into windows or pixmaps of the default depth of the screen. In other words, **XtGetGC()** would work on a monochrome screen, but not on color. However, this is an unusual situation. Most widgets can use **XtGetGC()** exclusively.

Example 7-2. Creating GCs from the initialize method

```
static void
GetDrawGC(w)
Widget w;
{
    BitmapEditWidget cw = (BitmapEditWidget) w;
    XGCValues values;
    XtGCMask mask = GCForeground | GCBackground | GCDashOffset |
            GCDashList | GCLineStyle;

    /*
     * Setting foreground and background to 1 and 0 looks like a
     * kludge but isn't.  This GC is used for drawing
     * into a pixmap of depth one.  Real colors are applied with a
     * separate GC when the pixmap is copied into the window.
     */
    values.foreground = 1;
    values.background = 0;
    values.dashes = 1;
    values.dash_offset = 0;
    values.line_style = LineOnOffDash;

    cw->bitmapEdit.draw_gc = XCreateGC(XtDisplay(cw),
            cw->bitmapEdit.big_picture, mask, &values);
}

static void
GetUndrawGC(w)
Widget w;
{
    BitmapEditWidget cw = (BitmapEditWidget) w;
    XGCValues values;
    XtGCMask mask = GCForeground | GCBackground;

    /* Looks like a kludge but isn't--see comment in GetDrawGC */
    values.foreground = 0;
```

Example 7-2. Creating GCs from the initialize method (continued)

```
    values.background = 1;

    cw->bitmapEdit.undraw_gc = XCreateGC(XtDisplay(cw),
            cw->bitmapEdit.big_picture, mask, &values);
}
static void
GetCopyGC(w)
Widget w;
{
    BitmapEditWidget cw = (BitmapEditWidget) w;
    XGCValues values;
    XtGCMask mask = GCForeground | GCBackground;

    values.foreground = cw->primitive.foreground;
    values.background = cw->core.background_pixel;

    /* This GC is the same depth as screen */
    cw->bitmapEdit.copy_gc = XtGetGC(cw, mask, &values);
}
```

As shown in Example 7-2, some GC components are set based on other instance variables, and some are just hardcoded. In this example, the foreground pixel value (color) in the GC is set to be the value of the **foreground** instance variable, which is derived from a resource of Primitive.† The background pixel value is derived from a resource of the Core widget. (Core defines a background resource but no foreground.) On the other hand, the **line_style** member of **XGCValues** is set to **LineOnOffDash** regardless of resource settings. In general, you hardcode the GC components that you don't want to be user customizable. (All these instance variables are defined in the *yourwidget*Part structure defined in *yourwidgetP.h*.)

Certain GC parameters are traditionally handled as resources rather than being hardcoded. Colors and fonts are the most basic examples. In the X Window System you can't use a color until you allocate a pixel value for it, and you can't use a font until you load it. The code that processes resources called by **XtAppInitialize()** automatically allocates and loads the colors and fonts specified as resources, and sets the instance variables to the right representation type as specified in the resource table. Therefore, it is actually easier to provide user customizability than to convert values to the representation types required to hardcode them.

How the resource conversion process works is described in more detail in Chapter 10, *Resource Management and Type Conversion*. To decide which GC settings you need for your application, see Chapter 5, *The Graphics Context*, in Volume One, *Xlib Programming Manual*.

---

†To work with the Athena widget set, BitmapEdit would have to define its own **XtNforeground** resource.

Basic Widget Methods

7.3 The expose Method

The **expose** method is responsible for initially drawing into a widget's window and for redrawing the window every time a part of the window becomes exposed. This redrawing is necessary because the X server does not maintain the contents of windows when they are obscured. When a window becomes visible again, it must be redrawn.

The **expose** method usually needs to modify its drawing based on the geometry of the window and other instance variables set in other methods. For example, the Label widget will left-justify, center, or right-justify its text according to the **XmNalignment** resource, and the actual position to draw the text depends on the widget's current size. The Label widget has an instance structure field called **alignment**, which is set initially in the **initialize** method, and is read in Label's **expose** method.

Another factor to consider when writing the **expose** method is that many widgets also draw from action routines, in response to user events. For example, BitmapEdit toggles bitmap cells in action routines. The **expose** method must be capable of redrawing the current state of the widget at any time. This means that action routines usually set instance variables when they draw so that the **expose** method can read these instance variables and draw the right thing.

Most widgets keep track of what they draw in some form of arrays or display lists. When they need to redraw, they simply replay the saved drawing commands in the original order to redraw the window. For example, BitmapEdit keeps track of the state of each bitmap cell in a character array. It could easily traverse this array and redraw each cell that is set in the array.

However, BitmapEdit does not use this strategy. In order to improve its scrolling performance, the **expose** method copies an off-screen pixmap into the window whenever redisplay is required. The actions draw into this off-screen pixmap (in addition to updating the character array), and then call the **expose** method directly to have the correct portion of the pixmap copied to the window.

The **expose** method is passed an event that contains the bounding box of the area exposed. To achieve maximum performance it copies only this area from the pixmap to the window. The BitmapEdit actions take advantage of this, too. They manufacture an artificial event containing the bounding box of the cell to be toggled, and pass it when they call **expose**. This causes the **expose** method to copy that one cell that was just updated to the window. Example 7-3 shows the **expose** method from the BitmapEdit widget.

Example 7-3. The expose method

```
/* ARGSUSED */

static void
Redisplay(w, event, region)
Widget cw;
XExposeEvent *event;
Region region;
{
    BitmapEditWidget cw = (BitmapEditWidget) w;
    register int x, y;
    unsigned int width, height;
```

Example 7-3. The expose method (continued)

```
    if (!XtIsRealized(cw))
        return;

    if (event) {  /* called from btn-event */
        x = event->x;
        y = event->y;
        width = event->width;
        height =  event->height;
    }

    else {/* called because of expose */
        x = 0;
        y = 0;
        width = cw->bitmapEdit.pixmap_width_in_pixels;
        height = cw->bitmapEdit.pixmap_height_in_pixels;
    }

    if (DefaultDepthOfScreen(XtScreen(cw)) == 1)
        XCopyArea(XtDisplay(cw), cw->bitmapEdit.big_picture,
                XtWindow(cw), cw->bitmapEdit.copy_gc, x +
                cw->bitmapEdit.cur_x, y + cw->bitmapEdit.cur_y,
                width, height, x, y);

    else
        XCopyPlane(XtDisplay(cw), cw->bitmapEdit.big_picture,
                XtWindow(cw), cw->bitmapEdit.copy_gc, x +
                cw->bitmapEdit.cur_x, y + cw->bitmapEdit.cur_y,
                width, height, x, y, 1);
}
```

Note that the **expose** method first checks to see that the widget is realized using **Xt-IsRealized()**. This is a precaution against the unlikely event that an instance of this widget is suddenly destroyed or unrealized by an application while **Expose** events are still pending. If this did happen, drawing on the nonexistent window would cause an X Protocol error.

Next, BitmapEdit's **expose** method sets the rectangle it will redraw based on the event passed in by Xt. We also call this method directly from the action that processes button presses. That action routine creates a pseudo-event to pass to **expose** to describe the area to be drawn.

If the **compress_exposure** field of the class structure is initialized to **XtExpose-CompressMultiple** (or one of a few other constants, described in Chapter 9, *More Input Techniques*), as it is in BitmapEdit, Xt automatically merges the multiple **Expose** events that may occur because of a single user action into one **Expose** event. In this case, the **Expose** event contains the bounding box of the areas exposed. BitmapEdit redraws everything in this bounding box. For widgets that are very time-consuming to redraw, you might want to use the third argument of the **expose** method, which is a region. The **Region** type is opaquely defined by Xlib (internally a linked list of rectangles). The **Region** passed into **expose** describes the union of all the areas exposed by a user action. You can use this region to clip output to the exposed region, and possibly calculate which drawing primitives affect this area. Xlib provides region mathematics routines (such as **XRectInRegion()**) to compare the regions in which your widget needs to draw with the region needing redrawing. If certain areas do not require redrawing, you can skip the code that redraws them, thereby saving valuable time. However, if this calculation is complicated, its cost/benefit ratio should be examined. Consider the arrangement of windows shown in Figure 7-1.

Window 1 and Window 3 are other applications, and Widget 2 is an application consisting solely of our widget.

Initially, Window 3 is on top, Window 1 is behind it, and Widget 2 is hidden completely behind Window 1. When Window 1 is lowered, Widget 2 becomes visible, except where it is still overlapped by Window 3. The newly-exposed area can be described by two rectangles; A and B. If `compress_exposure` is `False`, Widget 2's `expose` method will be called twice and passed an `Expose` event first describing Rectangle A, then Rectangle B. But if `compress_exposure` is `True`, Widget 2's `expose` method will be called just once, passed an `Expose` event describing the bounding box of all the original `Expose` events (which would be the entire widget in this case), and passed a `Region` which is the union of the rectangles described by all of the `Expose` events. The `region` argument of the `expose` method is unused unless `compress_exposure` is `True`. Each of these exposure-handling techniques may be the best for certain widgets. For a widget like BitmapEdit, any of the three methods will work, but the bounding box method is the most efficient and convenient. For a complete description of `Expose` event handling strategies, see Chapter 8, *Events*, in Volume One, *Xlib Programming Manual*.

The remainder of BitmapEdit's `expose` method shown in Example 7-3 consists of a single Xlib call to copy from a pixmap into the widget's window. As described in Chapter 4, *An Example Application*, BitmapEdit makes a large pixmap that is one plane deep and draws the

current bitmap into it. When needed in the `expose` method, this pixmap just has to be copied into the window. This approach was chosen for its simplicity. When scrollbars are added, the widget is able to pan around in the large bitmap quickly and efficiently. Note that one of two Xlib routines is called based on the depth of the screen. This is because `XCopy-Area()` is slightly more efficient than `XCopyPlane()` and should be used when running on a monochrome screen.

Note that instance variables are used for the arguments of the Xlib routines in Example 7-3. Don't worry about exactly what each Xlib routine does or the meaning of each argument. See the reference page for each routine in Volume Two, *Xlib Reference Manual*, when you need to call them in your code.

See Chapters 5, 6, and 7 in Volume One, *Xlib Programming Manual*, for more information on the GC, drawing graphics, and color, respectively. There is another example of an `expose` method on the `expose` reference page in Section 4 of Volume Five, *X Toolkit Intrinsics Reference Manual*.

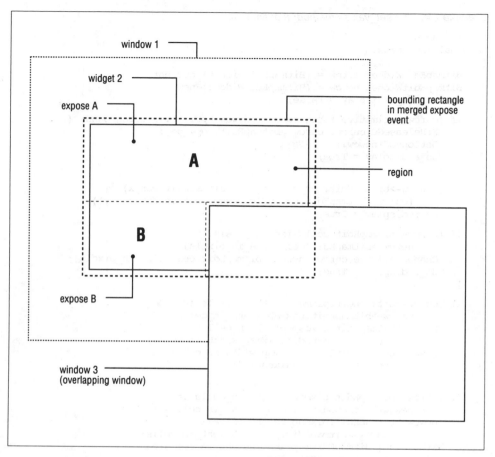

Figure 7-1. compress_exposure: 2 rectangles if XtExposeNoCompress; bounding box and region if XtExposeCompressSeries or XtExposeCompressMultiple

7.4 The set_values Method

When the application calls **XtVaSetValues()** (or **XtSetValues()**) to change widget resources during run time, Xt calls the **set_values** method. The **set_values** method is where a widget responds to changes in its public instance variables. It should validate the values of the public variables, and recalculate any private variables that depend on public variables that have changed.

Example 7-4 shows the **set_values** method for BitmapEdit.

Example 7-4. The set_values method

```
/* ARGSUSED */
static Boolean
SetValues(current, request, new, args, num_args)
Widget current, request, new;
```

Example 7-4. The set_values method (continued)

```
ArgList args;
Cardinal *num_args;
{
    BitmapEditWidget curcw = (BitmapEditWidget) current;
    BitmapEditWidget newcw = (BitmapEditWidget) new;
    Boolean do_redisplay = False;

    if (curcw->primitive.foreground != newcw->primitive.foreground) {
        XtReleaseGC(curcw, curcw->bitmapEdit.copy_gc);
        GetCopyGC(newcw);
        do_redisplay = True;
    }

    if ((curcw->bitmapEdit.cur_x != newcw->bitmapEdit.cur_x) ||
            (curcw->bitmapEdit.cur_y != newcw->bitmapEdit.cur_y))
        do_redisplay = True;

    if (curcw->bitmapEdit.cell_size_in_pixels !=
            newcw->bitmapEdit.cell_size_in_pixels) {
        ChangeCellSize(curcw, newcw->bitmapEdit.cell_size_in_pixels);
        do_redisplay = True;
    }

    if (curcw->bitmapEdit.pixmap_width_in_cells !=
            newcw->bitmapEdit.pixmap_width_in_cells) {
        newcw->bitmapEdit.pixmap_width_in_cells =
                curcw->bitmapEdit.pixmap_width_in_cells;
        XtWarning("BitmapEdit: pixmap_width_in_cells cannot\
            be set by XtSetValues.\n");
    }

    if (curcw->bitmapEdit.pixmap_height_in_cells !=
            newcw->bitmapEdit.pixmap_height_in_cells) {
        newcw->bitmapEdit.pixmap_height_in_cells =
                curcw->bitmapEdit.pixmap_height_in_cells;
        XtWarning("BitmapEdit: pixmap_height_in_cells cannot\
            be set by XtSetValues.\n");
    }

    return do_redisplay;
}
```

The **set_values** method is called with three copies of the widget's instance structure as arguments: *current*, *request*, and *new*. The *current* copy includes the current settings of the instance variables, and *request* includes the settings made through **Xt-VaSetValues()** but not yet changed by the superclasses' **set_values** methods. The *new* copy is the same as *request* except that it has already been processed by the **set_values** methods of all superclasses.

For each public variable, **set_values** compares the current value and the new value, and if they are different, validates the *new* value or changes any private values that depend on it. The *new* copy is the only one that the method changes; *request* and *current* are only for reference. As in the **initialize** method, you have to deal only with the instance variables for your subclass, and perhaps with width and height, because the **set_values** method is downward chained. Superclass **set_values** methods take care of setting all the superclass instance fields. However, if desired, you can change superclass fields in your method since it is called last. For example, this might be useful if your class has different criteria for determining valid values or dependencies.

The *request* copy of the instance variables is used only if your class needs to decide between a superclass setting and your widget's setting; disagreements about this usually occur over the size of the widget. For more information on when to use *request*, see the reference page for **set_values** in Volume Five, *X Toolkit Intrinsics Reference Manual*.

It is also important to notice that the **set_values** method, if it exists at all (that is, if it is not specified as **NULL** in the class structure), must return **True** or **False** to indicate whether the changes made to the state variables require the widget to be redrawn. If it is **True** for this class or any superclass, Xt calls the Xlib routine **XClearArea()** with the **exposures** argument set to **True** (to force the background of the widget to be redrawn, which normally occurs only after **Expose** events), and then Xt calls the **expose** method. In other words, you should make **set_values** return **True** whenever the changes to the instance variables will change what is drawn in the widget.

Note, however, that **set_values** should *not* return **True** if **width** and **height** change, because the X server automatically generates **Expose** events for a window when it is resized. If you do return **True** in this case, your **expose** method will be called twice.

Since the application may call **XtVaSetValues()** before the widget is realized, it is important not to assume in the **set_values** method that the widget has a window. In other words, the code must use **XtIsRealized()** to check whether the widget is realized before using the **XtWindow()** macro, such as in a call to set window attributes.

As mentioned earlier, some of the private variables are usually GCs. Whenever the public variable for a color or font is changed through **XtVaSetValues()**, a GC also has to be changed. This is an example of a private variable depending on a public one. GCs allocated with **XtGetGC()** should not be changed since they may be shared by other widgets. Therefore, the normal response to a change in one of the resources on which a GC depends is to release the GC with **XtReleaseGC()** and request a new one with **XtGetGC()**.

If some of your widget's GCs are unlikely to be shared by other widget instances in an application (either because each instance will use different values for the GC components or there will be only one instance), and the widget needs to be able to make changes to them, and the changes are not predictable enough or few enough to reasonably create a GC for each variation, then the **XtGetGC()/XtReleaseGC()** approach is not ideal. What happens in this situation is that **XtGetGC()** creates a new GC and **XtReleaseGC()** frees the old GC every time a change is made, even if the changes are small. It is more efficient in this situation to change the affected values in the existing GC. But this can be done only with an Xlib routine—there is no Toolkit routine for changing a GC. To implement this approach, you create, modify, and free the unusual GC using Xlib routines only. You call **XCreateGC()** in the **initialize** method to create the GC, **XChangeGC()** in the **set_values** method to change the GC, and **XFreeGC()** in the **destroy** method to free the GC. All of these Xlib routines are described in Chapter 5, *The Graphics Context*, in Volume One, *Xlib Programming Manual*.

`XtGetGC()` always creates a GC that can only be used on drawables (windows and pix-maps) of the default depth of the screen. Drawing into a pixmap of depth one using a GC created with `XtGetGC()` works on a monochrome display, but does not work on a color display. (The depth is the number of bits per pixel used to represent colors on the screen.) This is another situation in which you will need to call **XCreateGC()** instead of `XtGet-GC()`.

Note also that BitmapEdit does not allow two of its resources to be changed by `XtVaSet-Values()`; they can be set only until the widget is created. To disallow changes to a resource, the `set_values` method must actively set the value in the new widget (`newcw`) to the value in the current widget (`curcw`), wiping out the setting made through `XtVaSet-Values()`. It is also advisable that the widget print a message describing that the resource cannot be set through `XtVaSetValues()`.

The `XtWarning()` call used in the example is simply an alternative to calling **fprintf**, that helps to make all error messages uniform, and is described in Chapter 14, *Miscellaneous Toolkit Programming Techniques*. The code in the `set_values_hook` method, described in Chapter 10, *Resource Management and Type Conversion*, can optionally be placed in the `set_values` method.

7.5 The resize Method

When a widget is used in an application, it is created with a parent that will manage its geometry. Depending on the layout policy of this parent widget in the application, the widget's window may change size when the application is resized.† Most widgets need to recalculate the position and size of their graphics when their window changes size. This is the job of the `resize` method.

The `resize` method is passed only one argument, the widget instance structure pointer (of type `Widget`). This structure contains the new position, size, and border width of the widget's window. The method changes any instance part fields that depend on the size or position of the widget. When the `resize` method returns, Xt calls the **expose** method, regardless of whether or not the contents need redrawing. (It is a basic characteristic of the X server that it generates **Expose** events when a window is resized.)

A Label widget whose text is centered would reset the starting position of its text in the `resize` method.

In some widgets, it takes some thought to determine the correct response to resizing. Take BitmapEdit, for example. BitmapEdit can be configured to show only a portion of the bit-map, so that scrollbars can pan around in the complete bitmap. When the application is resized, should BitmapEdit show more cells or increase the cell size? Up to the point where the entire bitmap is shown, it is easier to increase the number of cells shown. When

---

†Also note that the application may be resized when it is first mapped on the screen, when the user sizes the rubber-band outline of the application provided by most window managers. (You may not think of this as resizing, but it is.) When this happens, the application has already created its widgets and the widgets have created windows. Therefore, the `resize` method of a widget will be called if its parent widget is forced to resize it.

BitmapEdit is resized larger than necessary to show the entire bitmap, it should probably increase the cell size. We will use this strategy in the **resize** method of the BitmapEdit widget, which is shown in Example 7-5.†

Example 7-5. BitmapEdit: the resize method

```
/* ARGSUSED */
static void
Resize(w)
Widget w;
{
    BitmapEditWidget cw = (BitmapEditWidget) w;
            /* resize does nothing unless new
             * size is bigger than entire pixmap */
    if ((cw->core.width > cw->bitmapEdit.pixmap_width_in_pixels) &&
            (cw->core.height >
            cw->bitmapEdit.pixmap_height_in_pixels)) {
         /* Calculate the maximum cell size that will
          * allow the entire bitmap to be displayed. */
        Dimension w_temp_cell_size_in_pixels,
                h_temp_cell_size_in_pixels;
        Dimension new_cell_size_in_pixels;

        w_temp_cell_size_in_pixels = cw->core.width /
                cw->bitmapEdit.pixmap_width_in_cells;
        h_temp_cell_size_in_pixels = cw->core.height /
                cw->bitmapEdit.pixmap_height_in_cells;

        if (w_temp_cell_size_in_pixels < h_temp_cell_size_in_pixels)
            new_cell_size_in_pixels = w_temp_cell_size_in_pixels;
        else
            new_cell_size_in_pixels = h_temp_cell_size_in_pixels;

        /* if size change mandates a new pixmap, make one */
        if (new_cell_size_in_pixels
                != cw->bitmapEdit.cell_size_in_pixels)
            ChangeCellSize(cw, new_cell_size_in_pixels);
    }
}

static void
ChangeCellSize(w, new_cell_size)
Widget w;
int new_cell_size;
{
    BitmapEditWidget cw = (BitmapEditWidget) w;
    int x, y;

    cw->bitmapEdit.cell_size_in_pixels = new_cell_size;

    /* recalculate variables based on cell size */
    cw->bitmapEdit.pixmap_width_in_pixels =
            cw->bitmapEdit.pixmap_width_in_cells *
            cw->bitmapEdit.cell_size_in_pixels;
```

†This resize strategy does have one problem; it never reduces the cell size. This is not a serious problem because BitmapEdit has a resource that controls the cell size. The application that uses this widget could provide a user interface for setting the cell size if the application writer was concerned about this problem.

Example 7-5. BitmapEdit: the resize method (continued)

```
    cw->bitmapEdit.pixmap_height_in_pixels =
            cw->bitmapEdit.pixmap_height_in_cells *
            cw->bitmapEdit.cell_size_in_pixels;

    /* destroy old and create new pixmap of correct size */
    XFreePixmap(XtDisplay(cw), cw->bitmapEdit.big_picture);
    CreateBigPixmap(cw);

    /* draw lines into new pixmap */
    DrawIntoBigPixmap(cw);

    /* draw current cell array into pixmap */
    for (x = 0; x < cw->bitmapEdit.pixmap_width_in_cells; x++) {
        for (y = 0; y < cw->bitmapEdit.pixmap_height_in_cells; y++) {
            if (cw->bitmapEdit.cell[x + (y *
                    cw->bitmapEdit.pixmap_width_in_cells)] == DRAWN)
                DoCell(cw, x, y, cw->bitmapEdit.draw_gc);
            else
                DoCell(cw, x, y, cw->bitmapEdit.undraw_gc);
        }
    }
}

static void
DoCell(w, x, y, gc)
Widget w;
int x, y;
GC gc;
{
    BitmapEditWidget cw = (BitmapEditWidget) w;
    /* otherwise, draw or undraw */
    XFillRectangle(XtDisplay(cw), cw->bitmapEdit.big_picture, gc,
            cw->bitmapEdit.cell_size_in_pixels * x + 2,
            cw->bitmapEdit.cell_size_in_pixels * y + 2,
            (unsigned int)cw->bitmapEdit.cell_size_in_pixels - 3,
            (unsigned int)cw->bitmapEdit.cell_size_in_pixels - 3);
}
```

Because of the two-phase resize strategy used by BitmapEdit, and because BitmapEdit uses a pixmap in its repaint strategy, this `resize` method is more complicated than most. When the widget is resized larger that necessary to show the entire bitmap in the current `cell_size`, it destroys the current pixmap and creates a new one. Since this should not happen very often and because resizing does not require extremely fast response, the time it takes to recreate the pixmap and draw into it is acceptable.

One difficulty in writing the `resize` method is that you do not have access to the old size or position of the window. The widget instance structure passed in has already been updated with the current size and position. If you need the old information, you can cache the old size in an instance part field, set first in the `initialize` method, and again at the end of the `resize` method.

It is also important to note that the `resize` method is not allowed to request that the parent resize the widget again to get a better size. (How to suggest properly to the parent that your widget be resized is described in Chapter 12, *Geometry Management*.)

7.6 The query_geometry Method

When your widget is used in an application, its parent widget will be a composite or constraint widget that manages its size and position. Parent widgets need to know the preferred size of a widget so they can make good decisions about the size of each child. The `query_geometry` method is called when the parent is about to make a size change to some of its children but is not yet sure which ones and by how much. (How geometry management works is described in Chapter 12, *Geometry Management*. For now, we are concentrating on what you need to do to write a simple widget.)

If your widget specifies NULL in the class structure for the `query_geometry` method, the parent will be told that your widget's current geometry is its preferred geometry. This is often wrong information. For example, if your widget has already been resized to be one-pixel-by-one-pixel because the user has resized an application to be very small, the parent would receive the message that your widget prefers to be that small. When the application is resized to be larger again, the parent will have no information on which to base its resizing decisions. Even if your widget has no particular preference for size, it is a good idea to specify the widget's default size in `query_geometry`. Then, at least, the parent has a ballpark figure for typical sizes for your widget. The parent could at least find out that BitmapEdit is intended to be larger than a Label widget.

The `query_geometry` method is passed pointers to two copies of the **XtWidget-Geometry** structure, one containing the parent's intended size for your widget, and the other to contain your reply to the parent's suggestion. The **XtWidgetGeometry** structure is shown in Example 7-6.

Example 7-6. The XtWidgetGeometry structure

```
typedef struct {
    XtGeometryMask request_mode;
    Position x, y;
    Dimension width, height;
    Dimension border_width;
    Widget sibling;
    int stack_mode;
} XtWidgetGeometry;
```

The `request_mode` field is a mask that indicates which other fields in the structure are set. It is a bitwise OR of any or all of the symbolic constants shown in Table 7-1.

Table 7-1. XtWidgetGeometry request_mode Symbols

Symbol	Description
CWX	The *x* coordinate of the widget's top left corner is specified.
CWY	The *y* coordinate of the widget's top left corner is specified.
CWWidth	The widget's width is specified.
CWHeight	The widget's height is specified.
CWBorderWidth	The widget's borderwidth is specified.

Table 7-1. XtWidgetGeometry request_mode Symbols (continued)

Symbol	Description
`CWSibling`	A sibling widget is specified, relative to which this widget's stacking order should be determined.
`CWStackMode`	A `stack_mode` value is present, specifying how this widget should be stacked relative to the widget identified as *sibling*.

The `sibling` and `stack_mode` fields are used together to indicate where in the stacking order of its siblings your widget will be placed. The symbols for `stack_mode` are **Above Below**, `TopIf`, `BottomIf`, `Opposite`, and `XtSMDontChange`. (These symbols are used singly, not combined with OR.) Their meanings are summarized in Table 7-2.

Table 7-2. XtWidgetGeometry stack_mode Symbols

Stacking Flag	Position
`Above`	*w* is placed just above *sibling*. If no *sibling* is specified, *w* is placed at the top of the stack.
`Below`	*w* is placed just below *sibling*. If no *sibling* is specified, *w* is placed at the bottom of the stack.
`TopIf`	If *sibling* obscures *w*, then *w* is placed at the top of the stack. If no *sibling* is specified, then if any sibling obscures *w*, *w* is placed at the top of the stack.
`BottomIf`	If *w* obscures *sibling*, then *w* is placed at the bottom of the stack. If no *sibling* is specified, then if *w* obscures any sibling, *w* is placed at the bottom of the stack.
`Opposite`	If *sibling* occludes *w*, *w* is placed at the top of the stack. If *w* occludes *sibling*, *w* is placed at the bottom of the stack. If no *sibling* is specified, then if any sibling occludes *w*, *w* is placed at the top of the stack, or if *w* occludes any sibling, *w* is placed at the bottom of the stack.
`XtSMDontChange`	Current position in stacking order is maintained.

Note that Xt's handling of stacking order is currently incomplete, and these symbols might not be honored. By default, the most recently created widget appears on the bottom.

One more issue about the `query_geometry` method must be raised before showing an example: the method's return value. The `query_geometry` method must return one of the three `enum` values `XtGeometryYes`, `XtGeometryAlmost`, or `XtGeometryNo`. `XtGeometryResult` is an `enum` name, and it is the returned type of `query_geometry`.

- If the proposed geometry is acceptable without modification, `query_geometry` returns `XtGeometryYes`.

- If the proposed geometry is not acceptable, your widget returns `XtGeometryAlmost` and sets its suggested changes to the proposed geometry back in the reply structure.

- If the proposed geometry is the same as the current geometry, `query_geometry` returns `XtGeometryNo`. This symbol is slightly misleading—think of it as `Xt-GeometryNoChange` (a symbol that is not defined). The symbol is `XtGeometryNo` because all three of these symbols are used in another context within composite and constraint widgets, as is described in Chapter 12, *Geometry Management*.

Note that, in all three cases, `query_geometry` must set any fields in the reply structure that it potentially cares about, even if it is only accepting the proposed geometry.

Example 7-7 shows the `query_geometry` method from BitmapEdit. All widgets should have at least this code in the method, substituting their initial size, or their current preferred size if known. (For example, a Label widget would set its preferred size based on the width and height of the current string.)

Example 7-7. BitmapEdit: the query_geometry method

```
static XtGeometryResult QueryGeometry(w, proposed, answer)
Widget w;
XtWidgetGeometry *proposed, *answer;
{
    BitmapEditWidget cw = (BitmapEditWidget) w;

    /* set fields we care about */
    answer->request_mode = CWWidth | CWHeight;

    /* suggest our default width or full size, whichever smaller */
    answer->width = (cw->bitmapEdit.pixmap_width_in_pixels >
            DEFAULTWIDTH) ? DEFAULTWIDTH :
            cw->bitmapEdit.pixmap_width_in_pixels;
    answer->height = (cw->bitmapEdit.pixmap_height_in_pixels >
            DEFAULTHEIGHT) ? DEFAULTHEIGHT :
            cw->bitmapEdit.pixmap_height_in_pixels;

    if (   ((proposed->request_mode & (CWWidth | CWHeight))
            == (CWWidth | CWHeight)) &&
            proposed->width == answer->width &&
            proposed->height == answer->height)
        return XtGeometryYes;
    else if (answer->width == cw->core.width &&
            answer->height == cw->core.height)
        return XtGeometryNo;
    else
        return XtGeometryAlmost;
}
```

7.7 The destroy Method

When a widget is destroyed by the application, its **destroy** methods are invoked in sub-class to superclass order. Therefore, the **destroy** method for any given class needs to free only the memory allocated by itself; it need not worry about memory allocated by super-classes.

Any server resources created by Xt (such as GCs requested through **XtGetGC()**) should be freed in the **destroy** method. In addition, if you called any Xlib routines, such as **XCreateGC()**, that allocate server- or client-side resources, be sure to free them here. BitmapEdit creates pixmaps for use in the drawing process, so it must free them. It must also free the GCs it allocated.

If this is not done, then the server resources allocated for the widget will not be freed until the application exits. This is not a fatal problem. It matters only in applications that destroy widgets and then continue running for a while before they exit, which is unusual. Example 7-8 shows the **destroy** method code from the BitmapEdit widget. It frees the pixmaps created in the **initialize** method shown in Example 7-1.

Example 7-8. The destroy method

```
static void
Destroy(w)
Widget w;
{
    BitmapEditWidget cw = (BitmapEditWidget) w;
    if (cw->bitmapEdit.big_picture)
        XFreePixmap(XtDisplay(cw), cw->bitmapEdit.big_picture);

    if (cw->bitmapEdit.draw_gc)
        XFreeGC(XtDisplay(cw), cw->bitmapEdit.draw_gc);

    if (cw->bitmapEdit.undraw_gc)
        XFreeGC(XtDisplay(cw), cw->bitmapEdit.undraw_gc);

    if (cw->bitmapEdit.copy_gc)
        XtReleaseGC(cw, cw->bitmapEdit.copy_gc);

    /* Free memory allocated with Calloc.  This was done
     * only if application didn't supply cell array.
     */
    if (!cw->primitive.user_data)
        XtFree(cw->bitmapEdit.cell);
}
```

If your widget allocated memory for any of its instance variables (or other global variables) using the Toolkit routines **XtMalloc()** or **XtCalloc()** (which operate just like the C library but add error checking), then it should free that memory here with **XtFree()**. Many widgets, including BitmapEdit, allow the application to supply the working memory, or the widgets can allocate it themselves. BitmapEdit maintains a flag (**user_allocated**) to indicate who originally allocated the memory.

If your widget called **XtAddEventHandler()** or **XtAddTimeOut()**, then you should call **XtRemoveEventHandler()** and **XtRemoveTimeOut()**, respectively (these routines are described in Chapter 9, *More Input Techniques*).

7.8 Actions in the Widget Framework

Although actions, strictly speaking, are not methods, writing them is part of the process of writing a simple widget. Fortunately, you have already seen action routines added from the application. Action routines look and work the same in the widget framework as in the application, except that they use instance structure fields as data instead of the application data structure fields. Example 7-9 shows the actions of BitmapEdit.

Example 7-9. BitmapEdit: action routines

```
/*ARGUSED*/
static void
DrawCell(w, event)
Widget w;
XEvent *event;
String *params;
Cardinal *num_params;
{
    BitmapEditWidget cw = (BitmapEditWidget) w;
    DrawPixmaps(cw->bitmapEdit.draw_gc, DRAW, cw, event);
}

/*ARGUSED*/
static void
UndrawCell(w, event)
Widget w;
XEvent *event;
String *params;
Cardinal *num_params;
{
    BitmapEditWidget cw = (BitmapEditWidget) w;
    DrawPixmaps(cw->bitmapEdit.undraw_gc, UNDRAW, cw, event);
}

/*ARGUSED*/
static void
ToggleCell(w, event)
Widget w;
XEvent *event;
String *params;
Cardinal *num_params;
{
    BitmapEditWidget cw = (BitmapEditWidget) w;
    static int oldx = -1, oldy = -1;
    GC gc;
    int mode;
    int newx, newy;

    /* This is strictly correct, but doesn't
     * seem to be necessary */
    if (event->type == ButtonPress) {
        newx = (cw->bitmapEdit.cur_x + ((XButtonEvent *)event)->x) /
                cw->bitmapEdit.cell_size_in_pixels;
        newy = (cw->bitmapEdit.cur_y + ((XButtonEvent *)event)->y) /
                cw->bitmapEdit.cell_size_in_pixels;
    }
    else  {
```

Example 7-9. BitmapEdit: action routines (continued)

```
        newx = (cw->bitmapEdit.cur_x + ((XMotionEvent *)event)->x) /
                cw->bitmapEdit.cell_size_in_pixels;
        newy = (cw->bitmapEdit.cur_y + ((XMotionEvent *)event)->y) /
                cw->bitmapEdit.cell_size_in_pixels;
    }

    if ((mode = cw->bitmapEdit.cell[newx + newy *
            cw->bitmapEdit.pixmap_width_in_cells]) == DRAWN) {
        gc = cw->bitmapEdit.undraw_gc;
        mode = UNDRAW;
    }
    else {
        gc = cw->bitmapEdit.draw_gc;
        mode = DRAW;
    }

    if (oldx != newx || oldy != newy) {
        oldx = newx;
        oldy = newy;
        DrawPixmaps(gc, mode, cw, event);
    }
}

static void
DrawPixmaps(gc, mode, w, event)
GC gc;
int mode;
Widget w;
XButtonEvent *event;
{
    BitmapEditWidget cw = (BitmapEditWidget) w;
    int newx = (cw->bitmapEdit.cur_x + event->x) /
            cw->bitmapEdit.cell_size_in_pixels;
    int newy = (cw->bitmapEdit.cur_y + event->y) /
            cw->bitmapEdit.cell_size_in_pixels;
    XExposeEvent fake_event;

    /* if already done, return */
    if (cw->bitmapEdit.cell[newx + newy *
            cw->bitmapEdit.pixmap_width_in_cells] == mode)
        return;

    /* otherwise, draw or undraw */
    XFillRectangle(XtDisplay(cw), cw->bitmapEdit.big_picture, gc,
            cw->bitmapEdit.cell_size_in_pixels*newx + 2,
            cw->bitmapEdit.cell_size_in_pixels*newy + 2,
            (unsigned int)cw->bitmapEdit.cell_size_in_pixels - 3,
            (unsigned int)cw->bitmapEdit.cell_size_in_pixels - 3);

    cw->bitmapEdit.cell[newx + newy *
            cw->bitmapEdit.pixmap_width_in_cells] = mode;
    info.mode = mode;
    info.newx = newx;
    info.newy = newy;

    fake_event.x = cw->bitmapEdit.cell_size_in_pixels *
            newx - cw->bitmapEdit.cur_x;
    fake_event.y = cw->bitmapEdit.cell_size_in_pixels *
```

Example 7-9. BitmapEdit: action routines (continued)

```
            newy - cw->bitmapEdit.cur_y;
    fake_event.width = cw->bitmapEdit.cell_size_in_pixels;
    fake_event.height = cw->bitmapEdit.cell_size_in_pixels;

    Redisplay(cw, &fake_event);
    XtCallCallbacks(cw, XtNcallback, &info);
}
```

Notice that as in methods, the widget instance pointer passed in is declared as type `Widget`, and then, in the first line of the action, cast to the desired type. This is necessary for ANSI C conformance.

An action routine in widget code can set and read fields in the widget instance structure passed in, while an action added from the application can access its own application data structure but not the widget's internal data structure because of the encapsulation rule (see Section 2.1.6.4). This is one of the advantages of moving this code into a widget.

You should now be ready to go back near the end of Chapter 6, *Inside a Widget*, and follow the directions to write your first widget. You will need to review parts of both Chapter 6 and this chapter as the process of actually writing a widget raises new questions in your mind.

8

Events, Translations, and Accelerators

This chapter describes the complete syntax of translation tables, and describes a mechanism called accelerators for mapping events in one widget to actions in another. Motif mnemonics, which are keyboard shortcuts for invoking menu items in visible menus, are also discussed.

In This Chapter:

8

Events, Translations, and Accelerators

Events drive the application. They send a great variety of information from the server to the client and from the user to the application. More knowledge of events is necessary both to use existing widgets successfully in large applications and to write widgets.

Events are sufficiently central to X that we've devoted two chapters in this book to them. This chapter provides a closer look at translations and actions; Chapter 9, *More Input Techniques*, looks at lower-level event handlers, as well as at other sources of input. Appendix C, *Event Reference*, in Volume Five, *X Toolkit Intrinsics Reference Manual*, will also be useful when you need details about any of the event types.

The basic concept and use of translations and actions has already been described. But translation tables have a complicated syntax which can be used to do much more than the simple mappings you have seen until now. Translation tables can detect user-interface idioms such as double- and triple-button clicks or key combinations such as Shift-Meta-M. This chapter focuses on the more advanced features of translation tables.

Next, we discuss a variation of translations called *accelerators*. Accelerators bind events that occur in one widget to actions in another. This is a flexible feature with many uses. One common use is to supply a keyboard interface to a normally pointer-driven application. By adding accelerators to the top-level window of the application, a keyboard event typed with the pointer anywhere in the application can be translated into an action in the correct widget. The name "accelerator" comes from the fact that many advanced users find it faster to use keyboard shortcuts instead of menus.

Both translations and accelerators are resources. Therefore they are normally set by default in the widget code, but can be replaced or overridden by user-defined settings in resource files or with *xrdb*. In R5, a new "psuedo-resource" called `XtNbaseTranslations` provides a new level of flexibility in modifying translations from resource files. Be sure to see Section 10.2.12 for an explanation of how translation resources should be set. As mentioned in Chapter 3, *More Techniques for Using Widgets*, it is a very good idea to specify translation tables and accelerator tables in the app-defaults file instead of hardcoding them in the application, especially while an application is under development. This lets you develop the translations and accelerators without recompiling the application every time you want to make a change.

8.1 Translation Table Syntax

If you are reading this book in sequence, you've already seen translations used many times. However, we haven't given a formal description of their syntax or a complete listing of the events you can translate.

A translation table consists of an optional directive, which specifies how the table should be merged with any other existing translation tables, followed by a series of production rules, of the form:

[*modifier_list*]<*event*>[,<*event*> *...*][(*count*)][*detail*]: *action*([*arguments*])[*action* *...*]

where brackets ([ ]) indicate optional elements, an ellipsis (...) indicates repetition, and italics indicate substitution of an actual modifier, event, detail, or action name.

At a minimum, a translation must specify at least one event, specified by a predefined event name or abbreviation enclosed in angle brackets; a colon separator; and at least one action. However, a sequence of events can be specified; likewise, more than one action can be invoked as a result. The scope of event matching can be limited by one or more optional modifiers, and, in the case of some events, by a "detail" field that specifies additional information about the event. (For example, for key events the detail field specifies which key has been pressed.) Repeated occurrences of the same event (e.g., a double-click) can be specified by a count value in parentheses. A colon and optional white space separates the translation and the action.

The examples below are all valid translations:

```
<Enter>:  doit()                    invoke doit() on an EnterWindow event
<Btn1Down>,<Btn1Up>:  doit()        invoke doit() on a click of Button 1
<Btn1Up>(2):  doit()                invoke doit() on a double-click of Button 1
Button1<Btn2Down>,<Btn2Up>:  doit()
        invoke doit() on a click of Button 2 while Button 1 is held down
Shift<BtnDown>:  doit()
        invoke doit() on a click of any button while the shift key is held down
<Key>y:  doit()                     invoke doit() when the y key is pressed
```

A translation table is a single string, even when composed of multiple translations. If a translation table consists of more than one translation, the actual newlines are escaped with a backslash (except for the last one), and character newlines are inserted with the \n escape sequence, as you've seen demonstrated in examples throughout this book.

The following sections provide additional detail on each of the elements of an event translation. We'll talk first about the directive, followed by event specifiers, details, modifiers, and counts. We'll also provide some pointers on the proper sequence of translations, and discuss what happens when translations overlap.

8.1.1 The Directive

As we've already seen, the three possible directives are **#replace**, **#override**, or **#augment**.

#replace says to completely replace the value of the **translations** resource in the widget. If no directive is specified, **#replace** is the default.

The difference between **#override** and **#augment** is more subtle. They differ in how they treat event combinations in the new translation that also appear in the old. With **#override**, the new translation takes priority, while with **#augment**, the old one does.

For example, say a widget has a default translation table that includes a translation for the Return key, and an application that uses this widget has an app-defaults file consisting of a translation table that applies to this widget. If the translation table in the app-defaults file began with **#override**, any translation for the Return key would take priority over the default translation for the Return key. On the other hand, if the translation table in the app-defaults file began with **#augment**, the default translations would take priority.

Remember that the difference between **#augment** and **#override** is only in the treatment of overlapping translations. Any translations added with either directive for events that do not already appear in the existing translation table will always be added.

Because of potential overlap between translations, when you are debugging your intended translations it is best to use **#replace** at first, then test with **#augment** or **#override** as appropriate once you are sure that the translations themselves have the desired effect.

8.1.2 Selecting the Events to Translate

An X event is a packet of data sent by the server to a client in response to user behavior or to window system changes resulting from interactions between windows. There are 33 different types of events defined by X. Most (though not all†) events can be thought of as occurring in a window: the pointer entering or leaving a window, pointer motion within a window, pointer button presses, key presses, and so on. However, most events are not sent to a window unless the window has explicitly selected that event type; events are selected on a per-window basis. In Xlib programming, events are selected by specifying an event mask as a window attribute. Some events, which are sent to all windows regardless of whether a window has selected them or not, are called non-maskable events. One of the most complex aspects of Xlib programming is designing the event loop, which must take into account all of the possible events that can occur in a window.

Xt's translation manager selects the events that are specified in the current translation table for each widget. In translations, events can be specified either by their actual names, as shown in Column 1 of Table 8-1, or by means of the abbreviations shown in Column 2. A

---

†Others reflect internal changes in the window system not related to any window. For example, a mapping **Notify** event occurs in response to a change in the mappings of keysyms (portable key symbols) to keycodes (actual codes generated by physical keys).

complete reference to each event type is provided in Appendix C, *Event Reference*, in Volume Five, *X Toolkit Intrinsics Reference Manual*.

Table 8-1. Event Type Abbreviations in Translation Tables

Event Type	Abbreviations	Description
ButtonPress	BtnDown	Any pointer button pressed
	Btn1Down	Pointer button 1 pressed
	Btn2Down	Pointer button 2 pressed
	Btn3Down	Pointer button 3 pressed
	Btn4Down	Pointer button 4 pressed
	Btn5Down	Pointer button 5 pressed
ButtonRelease	BtnUp	Any pointer button released
	Btn1Up	Pointer button 1 released
	Btn2Up	Pointer button 2 released
	Btn3Up	Pointer button 3 released
	Btn4Up	Pointer button 4 released
	Btn5Up	Pointer button 5 released
KeyPress	Key	Key pressed
	KeyDown	Key pressed
	Ctrl	KeyPress with Ctrl modifier
	Meta	KeyPress with Meta modifier
	Shift	KeyPress with Shift modifier
KeyRelease	KeyUp	Key released
MotionNotify	Motion	Pointer moved
	PtrMoved	Pointer moved
	MouseMoved	Pointer moved
	BtnMotion	Pointer moved with any button held down
	Btn1Motion	Pointer moved with button 1 held down
	Btn2Motion	Pointer moved with button 2 held down
	Btn3Motion	Pointer moved with button 3 held down
	Btn4Motion	Pointer moved with button 4 held down
	Btn5Motion	Pointer moved with button 5 held down
EnterNotify	Enter	Pointer entered window
	EnterWindow	Pointer entered window
LeaveNotify	Leave	Pointer left window
	LeaveWindow	Pointer left window
FocusIn	FocusIn	This window is now keyboard focus
FocusOut	FocusOut	This window lost keyboard focus
KeymapNotify	Keymap	Keyboard mappings changed
Expose	Expose	Part of window needs redrawing
GraphicsExpose	GrExp	Source of copy unavailable
NoExpose	NoExp	Source of copy available
ColormapNotify	Clrmap	Window's colormap changed
PropertyNotify	Prop	Property value changed
VisibilityNotify	Visible	Window has been obscured
ResizeRequest	ResReq	Redirect resize request to window manager

Table 8-1. Event Type Abbreviations in Translation Tables (continued)

Event Type	Abbreviations	Description
CirculateNotify	Circ	Stacking order modified
ConfigureNotify	Configure	Window resized or moved
DestroyNotify	Destroy	Window destroyed
GravityNotify	Grav	Window moved due to win gravity attribute
MapNotify	Map	Window mapped
CreateNotify	Create	Window created
ReparentNotify	Reparent	Window reparented
UnmapNotify	Unmap	Window unmapped
CirculateRequest	CircRec	Redirect stacking order change to window manager
ConfigureRequest	ConfigureReq	Redirect move or resize request to window manager
MapRequest	MapReq	Redirect window map request to window manager
MappingNotify	Mapping	Keyboard mapping changed
ClientMessage	Message	Client-dependent
SelectionClear	SelClr	Current owner is losing selection
SelectionNotify	Select	Selection is ready for requestor
SelectionRequest	SelReq	Request for selection to current owner

Many of these events are handled automatically by the Toolkit separately from the translation mechanism. For example, `Expose` events are automatically sent to the **expose** method of the appropriate widget. When there is also a translation for **Expose** events, the action is called in addition to the **expose** method. The only reason you would need a translation for `Expose` events is to add drawing to a Core widget. Because the Core widget doesn't have an **expose** method, there is rarely, if ever, a case where there is both an **expose** method and a translation for `Expose` events for the same widget. The point to remember is that any event can be specified in a translation, even when that event is also used in some other way by Xt.

`GraphicsExpose` and `NoExpose` events are useful when your application copies from a visible window with `XCopyArea()` or `XCopyPlane()`. They notify the application when part of the source of the copy is obscured. If you want `GraphicsExpose` and `No-Expose` events, you must explicitly select them by setting the `graphics_exposures` GC component in the GC used for the copy. Then you can provide a translation for them, or if you are writing a widget you can have them sent to your **expose** method by setting the `compress_exposure` field of the Core structure to a special value, as described in Section 9.7.2. (While *xbitmap* and BitmapEdit use `XCopyArea()` and `XCopyPlane()`, they copy from an off-screen pixmap that cannot be obscured, and therefore `GraphicsExpose` and `NoExpose` events are not needed. For a description of these events, see Chapter 5, *The Graphics Context*, in Volume One, *Xlib Programming Manual*.)

Several of the `*Notify` events are automatically handled by the Toolkit. Xt places this information in internal structures so that it can satisfy queries for widget positions and geometries without querying the server. `MappingNotify` events are automatically handled; Xt gets the current keyboard mapping from the server. `VisibilityNotify` events are handled automatically if the `visible_interest` field in the Core structure is set to `True` (see Section 9.5).

With the exception of `SelectionRequest`, the `*Request` events are intended for use only by window managers. The selection events are described in Chapter 11, *Interclient Communications*.

The keyboard traversal code built into the Motif Primitive class handles `EnterNotify`, `LeaveNotify`, `FocusIn`, and `FocusOut` events.

Whether or not they are already handled by Xt or in translations, events can also be selected explicitly by installing event handlers in a widget (as described in Chapter 9, *More Input Techniques*).

8.1.3 Details in Keyboard Events

As you've seen, Xt provides special event abbreviations to specify which pointer button was pressed or released. With key events, this approach would be a little impractical, since there are so many keys. Instead, the Translation Manager allows you to follow the event specification with an optional detail field. That is:

```
<Key>:  doit()
```

means that you want the `doit()` action to be invoked when any key has been pressed, while:

```
<Key>y:  doit()
```

means that you want the `doit()` action to be invoked only if the *y* key has been pressed.

What you actually specify as the detail field of a Key event is a keysym, as defined in the header file *<X11/keysymdef.h>*.† Keysyms begin with an `XK_` prefix, which is omitted when they are used in translations.

Before we explain any further, we need to review X's keyboard model, which, like many things in X, is complicated by the design goal of allowing applications to run equally well on machines with very different hardware.

The keyboard generates `KeyPress` events, and may or may not also generate `KeyRelease` events. These events contain a server-dependent code that describes the key pressed, called a *keycode*. *Modifier* keys, such as Shift and Control, generate events just like every other key. In addition, all key events also contain information about which modifier keys and pointer buttons were held down at the time the event occurred.

Xt provides a routine that translates keycode and modifier key information from an event into a portable symbolic constant called a *keysym*. A keysym represents the meaning of the key pressed, which is usually the symbol that appears on the cap of the key. For example, when the *a* key is pressed, the keysym is `XK_a`; when the same key is pressed while the Shift key is

---

†Note, however, that this file includes foreign language keysym sets that are not always available. Only the MIS-CELLANY, LATIN1 through LATIN4, and GREEK sets are always available.

held down, the resulting keysym is **XK_A** (uppercase). Note that even though both the *a* and the *A* events have the same keycode, they generate a different keysym because they occurred with different modifier keys engaged. (The mapping between keycodes and keysyms is discussed further in Section 14.5.)

You may specify either the keysym name, omitting the **XK_** prefix, or its hexadecimal value (also shown in *<X11/keysymdef.h>*), prefixed by **0x** or **0X** (zero followed by *x* or *X*).

This is fairly straightforward, though there are several provisos:

*   The keysym for nonalphanumeric keyboard keys may not always be obvious; you will need to look in *<X11/keysymdef.h>*. For example, the keyboard for the Sun workstation has keys labeled "Left" and "Right." Their keysyms are **XK_Meta_L** and **XK_Meta_R**, respectively. Fortunately, most common named keys have mnemonic keysym names (**XK_Return**, **XK_Linefeed**, **XK_BackSpace**, **XK_Tab**, **XK_Delete**, and so on) so you can often get by without looking them up. Notice, though, the small things that can trip you up: BackSpace, not Backspace, but Linefeed, not LineFeed. You can't count on consistency.

*   The definitions in *<X11/keysymdef.h>* spell out keysym names for punctuation and other special characters. For example, you'll see **XK_question** rather than **XK_?**, and so on. Nonetheless, you need not use this long keysym name; the Translation Manager will accept the equivalent single character, as long as it is a printing character. This is also true of digits. There are a few exceptions, namely the characters that have special meaning in a translation table. If you ever need a translation for colon, comma, angle brackets, or backslash, you'll have to use the keysym name rather than the single printing character.

*   The keycode-to-keysym translator built into the Translation Manager makes case distinctions only if the key event is prefaced with the colon (:) modifier. This means that **<Key>a** and **<Key>A** will be treated identically by default. We'll return to this subject when we discuss modifiers.

In sum, the following are all valid key event translations:

```
<Key>q:  quit()              invoke quit() when q or Q is pressed
:<Key>?:  help()             invoke help() when ? (but not /) is pressed
<Key>Return:  newline()      invoke newline() when the Return key is pressed
<Key>:  insert_char()        invoke insert_char() when any key is pressed
```

8.1.4 Details in Other Event Types

Key events are the most likely to require details, but details are also available for several other event types. They simplify your action function because they instruct Xt to call the action only when the event contains the matching detail. One type of detail, for **Motion-Notify**, actually affects the selection of events.

Trivially, the detail values `Button1` through `Button5` can be supplied as details for `ButtonPress` or `ButtonRelease` events; because of the available abbreviations, though, these button detail values should not often be necessary. It is easier to say:

```
<Btn1Down>: quit()
```

than:

```
<BtnDown>Button1:  quit()
```

The `EnterNotify`, `LeaveNotify`, `FocusIn`, and `FocusOut` events can take as details any of the notify mode values shown in Table 8-2.

Table 8-2. Notify Mode Values for Enter, Leave, and Focus Events

Detail	Description
Normal	Event occurred as a result of a normal window crossing.
Grab	Event occurred as a result of a grab.
Ungrab	Event occurred when a grab was released.

Normally, `EnterNotify` and `LeaveNotify` events are generated when the pointer enters or leaves a window, and `FocusIn` and `FocusOut` events are generated when a click-to-type window manager changes the keyboard focus window—the window that receives all keyboard input regardless of pointer position. In these cases the detail is `Normal`. But these events are also generated when the keyboard or pointer is grabbed by an application with a call to `XtGrabPointer()`, `XtGrabButton()`, `XtGrab-Keyboard()`, or `XtGrabKey()`. A *grab*, which is usually invoked by a popup window, also causes keyboard and/or pointer input to be constrained to a particular window. When these events are generated because of a grab or the release of a grab, the detail is `Grab` or `Ungrab`.

Details for additional events were added in Release 4. For `MotionNotify` events you can now select normal motion events or motion hints by specifying a detail of `Normal` or `Hint`. Normal motion events are used when you need a complete record of the path of the pointer. The `compress_motion` Core field, described in Chapter 9, is for use with normal motion events. Motion hints are used when you need only periodic pointer position updates. Each time you receive a motion hint you call `XQueryPointer()` (an Xlib call) to get the current pointer position. Note that the `MotionNotify` detail is the only one that affects event selection.

For `PropertyNotify`, `SelectionClear`, `SelectionRequest`, `Selection-Notify`, and `ClientMessage` events, the detail is an atom described in Table 8-3.

Table 8-3. Atom Details for Various Events

Event Type	Detail Atom
PropertyNotify	Property that is changing.
SelectionClear	Selection atom (such as PRIMARY).
SelectionRequest	Selection atom (such as PRIMARY).
SelectionNotify	Selection atom (such as PRIMARY).
ClientMessage	Message type.

For `MappingNotify`, the detail can be `Modifier`, `Keyboard`, or `Pointer`. Xt automatically does what is normally required to handle keyboard (and modifier) mapping changes. However, the *Pointer* detail might be used to make sure that the user has not disabled (by mismapping) any pointer button that is necessary for the safe operation of the application. You would simply write a translations such as `<Mapping> Pointer: ButtonMapCheck` and then call `XGetPointerMapping()` in the `ButtonMapCheck` action to make sure the pointer mapping is still acceptable.

The detail values for each event type corresponds to certain members of the associated event structure, as shown in Table 8-4. See Appendix C, *Event Reference*, in Volume Five, *X Toolkit Intrinsics Reference Manual*, for more details.

Table 8-4. Event Structure Fields Used As Translation Table Hints

Event Type	Event Structure Field
ButtonPress, ButtonRelease	button
MotionNotify	is_hint
EnterNotify, LeaveNotify	mode
FocusIn, FocusOut	mode
PropertyNotify	atom
SelectionClear	selection
SelectionRequest	selection
SelectionNotify	selection
ClientMessage	message_type
MappingNotify	request

8.1.5 Modifiers

Certain events include as part of their data the state of the pointer buttons and special keyboard modifier keys at the time the event was generated. The events for which this state is available include `ButtonPress`, `ButtonRelease`, `MotionNotify`, `KeyPress`, `KeyRelease`, `EnterNotify`, and `LeaveNotify`.

For these events, you can specify a desired modifier state using one or more of the modifier keywords listed in Table 8-5. An error is generated if you specify modifiers with any other types of events.

Table 8-5. Modifiers Used in Translation Tables

Modifier	Abbreviation	Description
Ctrl	c	Control key is held down.
Shift	s	Shift key is held down.
Lock	l	Caps Lock is in effect.
Meta	m	Meta key is held down.
Hyper	h	Hyper key is held down.
Super	su	Super key is held down.
Alt	a	Alt key is held down.
Mod1		Mod1 key is held down.
Mod2		Mod2 key is held down.
Mod3		Mod3 key is held down.
Mod4		Mod4 key is held down.
Mod5		Mod5 key is held down.
Button1		Pointer Button 1 is held down.
Button2		Pointer Button 2 is held down.
Button3		Pointer Button 3 is held down.
Button4		Pointer Button 4 is held down.
Button5		Pointer Button 5 is held down.

8.1.5.1 Physical Keys Used as Modifiers

The meaning of the `Meta`, `Hyper`, `Super`, `Alt`, and `Mod1` through `Mod5` keywords may differ from server to server. Not every keyboard has keys with these names, and even if keysyms are defined for them in *<X11/keysymdef.h>*, they may not be available on the physical keyboard.†

For example, the file *<X11/keysymdef.h>* includes the following definitions:

```
/* Modifiers */

#define XK_Shift_L          0xFFE1   /* Left shift */
#define XK_Shift_R          0xFFE2   /* Right shift */
#define XK_Control_L        0xFFE3   /* Left control */
#define XK_Control_R        0xFFE4   /* Right control */
#define XK_Caps_Lock        0xFFE5   /* Caps lock */
```

---

†The contents of *<X11/keysymdef.h>* are the same on every machine. What is different is the default mapping of keysyms to physical keycodes, which occurs in the server source. The only way to find out the mappings is through documentation (which is usually not available) or experimentation (as described in Chapter 11 of Volume Three, *X Window System User's Guide*, Second or Third Edition).

```
#define XK_Shift_Lock           0xFFE6   /* Shift lock */

#define XK_Meta_L               0xFFE7   /* Left meta */
#define XK_Meta_R               0xFFE8   /* Right meta */
#define XK_Alt_L                0xFFE9   /* Left alt */
#define XK_Alt_R                0xFFEA   /* Right alt */
#define XK_Super_L              0xFFEB   /* Left super */
#define XK_Super_R              0xFFEC   /* Right super */
#define XK_Hyper_L              0xFFED   /* Left hyper */
#define XK_Hyper_R              0xFFEE   /* Right hyper */
```

There are two things you must learn before you can use these modifiers:

1. Which physical key generates a given keysym, if it is not obvious from the name.

2. Which modifiers are valid on your server.

The best way to find out what keysym a key generates is with the *xev* client, which prints detailed information about every event happening in its window. To find out a keysym, run *xev*, move the pointer into its window, and then press the key in question.

On the Sun SparcStation, there is only one control key, on the left side of the keyboard. It generates the keysym `XK_Control_L`. There are two shift keys, one on each side, which generate the keysyms `XK_Shift_L` and `XK_Shift_R`. The Meta modifier is mapped to the keys labeled "Left" and "Right." Even though there is an Alternate keyboard key, which generates the keysym `XK_Alt_R`, this key is not recognized as a modifier. There are no Super and Hyper keys.

The list of valid modifiers can be displayed with the *xmodmap* client, as follows:

```
isla% xmodmap
xmodmap:  up to 2 keys per modifier, (keycodes in parentheses):

shift       Shift_L (0x6a),  Shift_R (0x75)
lock        Caps_Lock (0x7e)
control     Control_L (0x53)
mod1        Meta_L (0x7f),  Meta_R (0x81)
mod2
mod3
mod4
mod5
```

That is, either of the two shift keys will be recognized as the Shift modifier, the Caps Lock key as the Lock modifier, and either the Left or Right keys as the Meta modifier. The Left and Right keys are also mapped to the Mod1 modifier. The Alt key is not recognized as a modifier.

xmodmap also allows you to add keysyms to be recognized as the given modifier. For example, the following command would cause the F1 function key to be recognized as mod2:

```
isla% xmodmap -e 'add mod2 = F1'
```

For more information on *xmodmap* and *xev*, see Chapter 11 of Volume Three, *X Window System User's Guide, Motif Edition.*

8.1.5.2 Default Interpretation of the Modifier List

If no modifiers are specified in a translation, the state of the modifier keys and pointer buttons makes no difference to a translation. For example, the translation:

```
<Key>q:    quit()
```

will cause the `quit` action to be invoked when the *q* key is pressed, regardless of whether the Shift, Ctrl, Meta, or Lock key is also held, and regardless of the state of the pointer buttons.

Likewise, if a modifier is specified, there is nothing to prohibit other modifiers from being present as well. For example, the translation:

```
Shift<Key>q:    quit()
```

will take effect even if the Ctrl key is held down at the same time as the Shift key (and the *q* key).

There are a number of special modifier symbols that can be used to change this forgiving state of affairs. These symbols are shown in Table 8-6.

Table 8-6. Modifier Symbols

Symbol	Description
None	No modifiers may be present.
!	No modifiers except those explicitly specified may be present.
:	Apply shift (and lock) modifier to key event before comparing.
~	The modifier immediately following *cannot* be present.

The syntax of these special modifiers symbols is somewhat inconsistent, and made clearest by example.

8.1.5.3 Prohibiting a Modifier

The tilde (~) is used to negate a modifier. It says that the specified modifier may not be present. For example:

```
Button1<Key>:  doit()
```

says that `doit()` should be invoked by a press of any key when button 1 is being held down, while:

```
~Button1<Key>:  doit()
```

says that `doit()` should be invoked by a press of any key *except* when button 1 is being held down.

A ~ applies only to the modifier that immediately follows it. For example:

```
~Shift Ctrl<Key>:  doit()
```

says that `doit()` should be invoked when Ctrl is held down in conjunction with any key, except if Shift is depressed at the same time.

8.1.5.4 Requiring an Exact Match

An exclamation point at the start of a modifier list states that only the modifiers in that list may be present, and must match the list exactly. For example, if the translation is specified as:

```
!Shift<Key>q:  quit()
```

the translation will take effect only if the Shift key is the only modifier present; if Caps Lock were in effect, or if a pointer button were depressed at the same time, the translation would no longer work.

The modifier `None` is the same as `!` with no modifiers specified. That is:

```
None<Key>q:  quit()
```

or:

```
!<Key>q:  quit()
```

will invoke `quit` only if no modifier keys at all are pressed.

8.1.5.5 Paying Attention to the Case of Keysyms

The `:` modifier, like `!`, goes at the beginning of the modifier list and affects the entire list. This one is really in a category by itself, since it applies only to Key events.

Normally, the translations:

```
<Key>a:  doit()
```

and:

```
<Key>A:  doit()
```

have identical results: both will match either a lowercase or an uppercase *A*. Preceding the translation with a colon makes the case of the keysym significant. For example, to create commands like those in the UNIX *vi* editor, you might specify the following translations:

```
:<Key>a:  append()  \n\
:<Key>A:  appendToEndOfLine()
```

In this case, *a* and *A* are distinct. You could achieve somewhat the same result by specifying:

```
~Shift<Key>a:  append()  \n\
Shift<Key>a:  appendToEndOfLine()
```

However, this second example is both more complex and less effective. While the colon syntax will match an uppercase character generated as a result of either the Shift or Lock modifiers, the example shown immediately above will handle only Shift. You could use the following translation to prohibit both Shift and Lock from being asserted, but there is no way to specify that either Shift or Lock may be present:

```
~Shift ~Lock<Key>a:  append()  \n\
Shift<Key>a:  appendToEndOfLine()
```

Note that you cannot specify both the Shift or Lock modifier and an uppercase keysym. For example:

```
Shift<Key>A:  doit()
```

will have no effect, since you cannot further shift an uppercase character. The sequence !: at the beginning of a translation means that the listed modifiers must be in the correct state and that no other modifiers except the Shift and Lock keys may be asserted. In other words, !: by itself means the translation is triggered only if the specified key is pressed, considering case, and no other modifier is pressed.

For more details on how the Toolkit handles the ins and outs of case conversion, see Chapter 14, *Miscellaneous Toolkit Programming Techniques*. A more rigorous discussion of how the colon modifier works is also given in Appendix F, *Translation Table Syntax*, in Volume Five, *X Toolkit Intrinsics Reference Manual*.

8.1.6 Event Sequences

The left-hand side of a translation may specify a single event or a sequence of events that must occur for the action to be invoked. For example, we might want a certain action to be invoked only if the first button is clicked twice in succession.

Each event specified in the sequence is one of the abbreviations for an event type enclosed in angle brackets, optionally led by any set of modifiers and special characters, as described in Section 8.1.5. Each modifier-list/event pair in the sequence is separated by a comma.

For example, the translation to perform an action in response to a button press followed by a release of the same button (a button click) is the following:

```
<BtnDown>,<BtnUp> : doit()
```

Button press events may be specified in the translation table followed by a count in parentheses to distinguish a multiple click. The translation to detect a double click is:

```
<Btn1Down>(2) : doit()
```

or:

```
<Btn1Up>(2) : doit()
```

Notice that though they have the same effect for the user, these two translations are actually interpreted differently. The first is equivalent to saying:

```
<Btn1Down>,<Btn1Up>,<Btn1Down>:  doit()
```

while the second is equivalent to:

```
<Btn1Down>,<Btn1Up>,<Btn1Down>,<Btn1Up>:  doit()
```

A plus (+) may appear immediately after the count inside the parentheses to indicate that any number of clicks greater than the specified count should trigger the action.

The following translation detects two or more clicks:

```
<Btn1Down>(2+) : doit()
```

The maximum count that can be specified is 9.

Xt uses a timing technique to detect whether two or more clicks should be considered a multi-click or separate single clicks. The time is controlled by the `XmNmultiClickTime` application resource, which defaults to 200 milliseconds. If 200 milliseconds or more of idle time passes between clicks, Xt does not consider that a match. You can set this resource to different values for each display using `XtSetMultiClickTime()`.

For key events, you need to be careful when you want to make a particular key sequence invoke one action, and a subset of that key sequence to invoke another. For example, consider the following translation:

```
<Key>a,<Key>b : something()
<Key>        : else()
```

One might expect `<Key>b` events not preceded by `<Key>a` events to invoke the **else()** action. But instead, such `<Key>b` events are discarded. To get what you expected, use:

```
<Key>a,<Key>b : something()
<Key>b        : else()
<Key>         : else()
```

8.1.6.1 Special Considerations Involving Motion Events

Beware of interaction between pointer motion events and double clicking translations in the same table. If no motion events are specified in a translation table, these events are never selected, so there is no problem if they occur between other events. This allows a double click to be detected even if the user inadvertently jiggled the pointer in the course of the click. However, if motion events are selected for anywhere in the table, they may interfere with the expansion of events specified with the repeat notation. The suggested way to handle both motion events and double clicks in the same translation table is to have all clicks sent to one action procedure, then use the timestamps in the events to implement your own algorithm for differentiating single clicks from double clicks. For example:

```
<Btn1Down>: handleClicks()
Button1<Motion>: handleMotif()
```

The **handleClicks** action would handle both single and double clicks. As described in Section 8.1.7.3, this type of implementation also is useful when you want different semantics for single and double clicks.

Multiple motion events will match any single motion selected event in the translation. That is:

```
<Motion>: doit()
```

will cause `doit()` to be invoked many times, once for each motion event generated by the pointer movement, unless the `compress_motion` event filter is turned on in the Core class structure. (This filter is described in Section 9.7.2.)

8.1.6.2 Modifiers and Event Sequences

A modifier list at the start of an event sequence applies to all events in the sequence. That is:

```
Shift<BtnDown>,<BtnUp>:  doit()
```

is equivalent to:

```
Shift<BtnDown>,Shift<BtnUp>:  doit()
```

However, if modifiers and events are interspersed, the modifier applies only to the event immediately following. As an extreme case to demonstrate this behavior, consider the following translation:

```
Ctrl<Btn2Down>,~Ctrl<Btn2Up>: doit()
```

which requires that the Ctrl key be depressed when pointer button 2 is pressed; however, the key must not be depressed when the button is released.

8.1.6.3 Using Modifiers to Specify Button Event Sequences

Remember that there are modifiers for specifying the state of pointer buttons as well as modifier keys. These modifiers provide another way of expressing some event sequences. For example, the following translation would invoke the action when the F1 key is pressed while button 1 is being held down:

```
Button1<Key>F1:     doit()
```

This is equivalent to:

```
<Btn1Down>,<Key>F1:  doit()
```

The following translations could be used to call an action when both the first and second pointer buttons are down, regardless of the order in which they are pressed.

```
!Button1<Button2>:     doC() \n\
!Button2<Button1>:     doC()
```

8.1.6.4 Key Event Sequences

The Translation Manager specification provides a special syntax for specifying a sequence of Key events—as a string. That is:

```
"yes":  doit()
```

is theoretically equivalent to:

```
<Key>y,<Key>e,<Key>s:  doit()
```

We say "theoretically" because, at least in R4 and R5 sample implementations from MIT, the "yes" syntax does not work from resource files. It may or may not work in other implementations.

Within a sequence of key events expressed as a string (on systems where the "yes" syntax does work, if any), the special character ^ (circumflex) means Ctrl and $ means Meta. These two special characters, as well as double quotes and backslashes, must be escaped with a backslash if they are to appear literally in one of these strings.

8.1.7 Interactions Between Translations

One of the most difficult things to learn about translations is how to predict the interactions between overlapping translations.

8.1.7.1 Translations in Multiple Resource Files

Much more will be said about resource files and resource matching in Chapter 10, *Resource Management and Type Conversion*. However, it is important to make one point here.

If several resource files contain translation tables for the same widget, only the one that takes priority according to file precedence and resource matching will have any effect even if all of them specify **#augment** or **#override**. This is because the translation table is the value of the resource, and only one resource value will override all other values.

In other words, even if all the translation tables specify **#augment** or **#override**, a maximum of two translation tables are merged by Xt: the widget's default translation table and the one translation table that takes priority as determined by the process of reading and merging all the resource files (and the command line) and then the process of resource matching. If you call **XtOverrideTranslations()** or **XtAugmentTranslations()** in the application, this is a third level of merging, but it is unrelated to the resource files.

8.1.7.2 Order of Translations

The order of translations in a table is important, because the table is searched from the top when each event arrives, and the first match is taken. Therefore, more specific events must appear *before* more general ones. Otherwise, the more specific ones will never be reached.

For example, consider a text entry widget that wants to close itself and dispatch a callback once the user presses the Return key, indicating that entry is complete. The widget's translations might be:

```
<Key>Return:   gotData()    \n\
<Key>:         insertChar()
```

If the translations were specified in the reverse order:

```
<Key>:         insertChar() \n\
<Key>Return:   gotData()
```

insertChar() would be called in response to a press of the Return key, and got-Data() would never be called.

Keeping track of translation order is made more complicated when translations are merged. For example, if one of the above lines is in the default translations of a widget class, and the other is in a translation table in a resource file, in what order are the resulting translations? Though not documented in the Xt specification, it appears that the MIT implementation of Xt places the more specific translation first.

8.1.7.3   Event Sequences Sharing Initial Events

An exception to this rule of more specific translations being placed earlier in the translation table occurs with event sequences. One translation can contain an event or event sequence that appears in another translation. If the leading event or event sequence is in common, both will operate correctly. For example, the translations:

```
<Btn1Down>,<Btn1Up>:     actionB()\n\
<Btn1Down>:              actionA()
```

execute actionA() when button 1 is pressed and actionB() when it is then released. This is true regardless of which translation appears first in the table.

This is the reason, alluded to in Chapter 2, *Introduction to the X Toolkit and Motif*, why it is not possible to bind two different actions to a single and a double click of the same button in the same widget. Specifying:

```
<Btn1Up>(2):  quit() \n\
<Btn1Down>,<Btn1Up>:  confirm()
```

will invoke the confirm() action on a single click and both the confirm() and quit() actions on a double click.

This behavior was a design decision on the part of the X Consortium. Otherwise, the Intrinsics could never dispatch the single-click action until the double-click interval had passed, since it would have no way of knowing if a second click was coming. Applications needing to have single and double clicks in the same widget must do so by designing the two actions appropriately, rather than relying on the Translation Manager to make the distinction.

8.1.7.4   Event Sequences Sharing Noninitial Events

If a noninitial event sequence is common between two translations, each translation will match only event sequences where the preceding event does not match the other translation. Consider the translation:

```
<Btn1Down>,<Btn1Up>:     actionB()\n\
<Btn1Up>:                actionA()
```

When a Btn1Up event occurs, it triggers actionA() only if not preceded by Btn1Down.

The way this works is that Xt keeps a history of recent events. When each event arrives, Xt compares this event and its immediate history to the event sequences in a translation table. An event in the sequence may have already triggered an action, but that is irrelevant. Any translation whose final event in the event sequence matches the current event and whose earlier event sequence matches the event history is matched. If there are two translations that can match a particular event sequence, then the translations are considered overlapping, the latter will override the former, and Xt will print a run-time warning message at startup (not waiting for the overlapping actions to be invoked). This is an exception to the rule stated earlier that the translation manager executes the first match.

8.2 Accelerators and Mnemonics

As defined by Xt, accelerators are simply translation tables registered to map event sequences in one widget to actions in another. This is a general mechanism, but its name is based on a common use—adding keyboard shortcuts for widgets that are normally triggered by mouse button presses, such as PushButton widgets—because for advanced users a keyboard interface is often faster.

What Motif calls accelerators are implemented using Xt's accelerators, but the two are not at all the same. Motif implements a more convenient interface for providing keyboard shortcuts in menus, which it calls accelerators, but at the same time disables the more general accelerators feature in standard Xt. We will begin with a discussion of accelerators as defined by Xt, using the Athena widget set in the examples since they will not work in Motif. Then we will proceed with how Motif accelerators and mnemonics work. If you are interested only in how to program with Motif, then you can skip to Section 8.2.5.

8.2.1 Xt Accelerators

Every widget has an `XtNaccelerators` resource, inherited from the Core widget class. This resource contains an accelerator table, which is identical in format to a translation table; it maps event sequences to action sequences. Accelerator tables can be set into the `XtNaccelerators` resource in all the same ways translation tables can. The widget on which the `XtNaccelerators` resource is set is the widget whose actions are to be invoked from events in other widgets.

Once the `XtNaccelerators` resource of a widget is set, the application must call `XtInstallAccelerators()` or `XtInstallAllAccelerators()` to specify which widget will be the source of the events to invoke the actions specified in the accelerator table.

The MIT Intrinsics documentation refers to these two widgets as the *source* and *destination*. This can be confusing, especially since the arguments are referenced in reverse order in the call to `XtInstallAccelerators()`:

```
void XtInstallAccelerators(destination, source)
    Widget destination;
    Widget source;
```

Just remember that the source is the widget whose actions you want executed, and the destination is the widget you want the events to be gathered in. To understand the use of the phrase *install accelerators*, think of the accelerators as the `XtNaccelerators` resource of the *source* widget, together with the actions of that widget, and the ***destination*** as the widget to which these actions are transplanted (i.e., "installed").

`XtInstallAccelerators()` is always called from the application. (Widgets never install accelerators, because by definition they don't know about any other widgets.) In applications, accelerators can be installed any time, before or after the widgets are realized. Just before the `XtAppMainLoop()` call is a good place.

As an example, we'll add accelerators to the *xbox1* application, which is the Athena version of *xrowcolumn* from Chapter 3, *More Techniques for Using Widgets*. This application displays two Command widgets in a Box, as shown in Figure 8-1.

Figure 8-1. xbox1: two Command widgets in a Box

To add accelerators requires a single line of code—a call to `XtInstall-Accelerators()`, as shown in Example 8-1.

Example 8-1. Installing accelerators in an application

```
main(argc, argv)
int argc;
char **argv;
{
    XtAppContext app_context;
    Widget topLevel, box, quit;
        .
        .
        .

    /* allow quit widget's actions to be invoked by events in box. */
    XtInstallAccelerators(box, quit);

    XtAppMainLoop(app_context);
}
```

The actual value of the accelerator table is set through the resource mechanism. The `Xt-NAccelerators` resource is set for the widget whose actions are to be invoked from another widget. Xt stores this accelerator table, in compiled form, in the widget's instance structure when the widget is created. When the application calls `XtInstall-Accelerators()`, the accelerator table stored in the widget is merged with the translation table of the widget that will be capturing the events. (If `XtRemoveAccelerators` is called, the original translation table, prior to merging with the accelerators from the source widget, is restored.)

Example 8-2 shows a possible app-defaults file.

Example 8-2. Specifying the XtNaccelerators resource from the app-defaults file

```
*quit.label:   Quit
*pressme.label:  Press me
*quit.accelerators:\n\
        <KeyPress>q:     set() notify()
```

This resource setting will allow a *q* typed anywhere in the Box widget that comprises the *xbox1* application window to invoke the quit widget's `notify()` action (which, as you may recall from Section 2.4, in turn invokes the `Quit` callback installed by the application). Notice that the accelerators are specified as a resource of the source widget, even though the events that invoke them will come from the destination widget.

There are some differences in the translation tables that can be used for accelerators.

*   Abbreviations for event types are not valid. Only the event names that were shown in Column 1 of Table 8-1 may be used (although `Key` works in place of `KeyPress`).

*   The None, Meta, Hyper, Super, Alt, or ANY modifier symbols are not valid.

*   The default directive for accelerator tables is `#augment` rather than `#replace`. If specified, the `#replace` directive is ignored. It is important to realize that accelerators are merged with the source widget's translations. `#override` thus says that the accelerators take priority over any matching translations in the source widget, and `#augment` says that the accelerators have lower priority.

*   Parameters passed to actions must be quoted with double quotes.

8.2.2 Event Propagation

If you install accelerators in the Box widget as shown in Example 8-2, you will notice that even though the destination widget is Box, keyboard input will also be accepted in the children of **box**, including not only the quit widget but also the **pressme** widget. This is because of a characteristic of X called *event propagation*.

The server sends to the client only the types of events the client selects. Internally, Xt selects events using the Xlib call `XSelectInput()`. From a Toolkit application, this is hidden because the translation mechanism automatically selects the appropriate event types specified in the translation table. (As we will see in Chapter 9, *More Input Techniques*, Xt provides a low-level event-handling mechanism that exposes event selection more directly.)

Event selection reduces the amount of network traffic, the number of events the server has to generate, and the number of unneeded events the client must process only to throw away.

Most event types are selected on a per-window basis. Each selected event that arrives at the client contains the window ID of the window it was selected for. (Non-maskable events, the last five event types in Table 8-1, are the exception; they are selected using a different mechanism or are not selected at all.)

Pointer and keyboard events propagate *through* windows that have not selected them, as shown below in Figure 8-2. That is, if the **pressme** widget's window has not selected **KeyPress** events, any key events that occur in that window will be passed on to its parent, the Box widget. If the Box widget's window didn't select them either, they would be passed on to the window created by the top-level Shell widget, and so on. Events propagate through the window hierarchy all the way to the root window, until they reach a window that selected them. (If no window has selected them, they are never sent by the server.) Xt treats an event that originally occurred in some descendent widget just as if it actually happened in the widget that selected the event.

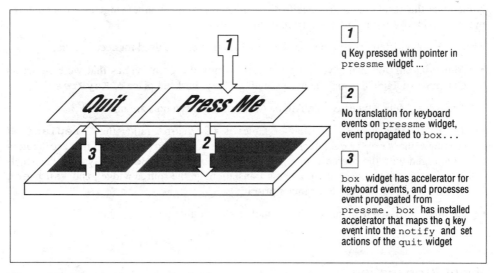

1
q Key pressed with pointer in pressme widget ...

2
No translation for keyboard events on pressme widget, event propagated to box...

3
box widget has accelerator for keyboard events, and processes event propagated from pressme. box has installed accelerator that maps the q key event into the notify and set actions of the quit widget

Figure 8-2. Key event propagation in xbox

Propagation is a characteristic of **ButtonPress**, **ButtonRelease**, **KeyPress**, **KeyRelease**, **MotionNotify**, **EnterNotify**, and **LeaveNotify** events only. As mentioned earlier, keyboard events are the events most often used as accelerators.

In the version of *xbox* we just looked at, keyboard events propagate through the Command widgets to the Box widget, because they are not selected by the Command widgets. When they reach the Box widget, they match the events specified in the accelerator table and invoke actions from the **quit** widget.

The Command widgets have a default translation table that includes pointer button events and enter/leave events. Xt, therefore, selects these events for each Command widget. Before accelerators are installed, the Box widget has no translation table and therefore has no events selected for it. When the accelerators are installed, the accelerator table is merged with the (nonexistent) translation table of the Box widget and becomes the Box's translation table. Xt then selects keyboard events for the Box widget.

But consider the resource settings in Example 8-3.

Example 8-3. Conflicting translations and accelerators

```
*quit.label:  Quit
*pressme.label:  Press me
*pressme.translations:  #override\n\
       <KeyPress>p:     set() notify()
*quit.accelerators:\n\
       <KeyPress>q:     set() notify()
```

No key event will propagate through a widget that has a translation for any key event. With the resource settings in Example 8-3, since **pressme** has a translation for the *p* key, the *q* key will not propagate through the widget. Therefore, it is often better to specify all key events as accelerators and install them on a common ancestor.

Accelerators are just merged into translations—they are not a completely different mechanism. The **#augment** (default) or **#override** directives used in accelerator tables specify whether the accelerator should override or augment existing translations for the destination widget. For example, if **box** had a translation of its own that matched the event sequence in the accelerator installed on the same widget, whether the translation or the accelerator would be invoked depends on whether **#augment** (the default) or **#override** had been specified as the accelerator directive. (This example is a little farfetched, since the Box widget defines no actions or translations—but it illustrates the point.)

When using or writing widgets, event propagation is usually important only for accelerators, because widgets are rarely layered in such a way that any of the ones that accept input are obscured.

8.2.3 Installing Accelerators in Multiple Widgets

If you want to install accelerators from more than one widget, you can call **XtInstall-Accelerators()** once for every widget whose actions you want executable from the destination. Alternatively, you can call **XtInstallAllAccelerators()** just once for a whole application, specifying the application's top-level window as both the destination and the source. **XtInstallAllAccelerators()** recursively traverses the widget tree rooted at the source, and installs the accelerators of each widget onto the destination.

For example, to install accelerators from both the quit and **pressme** widgets onto **box**, you could replace the call to **XtInstallAccelerators()** shown in Example 8-3 with:†

Example 8-4. Installing accelerators from both command widgets

```
XtInstallAllAccelerators(box, box);
```

_____

†In a more complex application, where the Box widget was not the main window but only a subarea containing command buttons, you might instead use the call:

```
    XtInstallAllAccelerators(topLevel, box);
```

which would make the actions from only the widgets contained in **box** available from anywhere in the application.

You could then define an app-defaults file such as the following:

Example 8-5. Accelerators resource settings for two widgets

```
*quit.label:  Quit
*pressme.label:  Press me
*pressme.accelerators:  \n\
      <KeyPress>p:    set() notify()
*quit.accelerators:     \n\
      <KeyPress>q:    set() notify()
```

Because you would be most likely to specify distinct **KeyPress** events to invoke the actions in each Command widget, you would normally specify each accelerator resource separately, as shown above. But in the unlikely case that you wanted actions of multiple Command widgets to be invoked by the exact same event, you could do this instead. For example:

```
*Command.accelerators:  \n\
      <KeyPress>:  set() notify()
```

would invoke the **set** and **notify** actions of every Command widget, but not of widgets belonging to other classes.

Or assuming that there were multiple Box widgets in an application, one containing options, and the other commands, you might specify something like this:

```
*optionsbox*accelerators:  \n\
      <KeyPress>:  set() notify()
```

to invoke the actions of every Command widget in **optionsbox** only.

The point is that, like any resource setting, an accelerator table can apply to only one widget, to a group of children of a widget, or to an entire class, depending on how you identify the widgets for which you are setting the **XtNaccelerators** resource.

8.2.4 Defining the Accelerator Table in the Code

If you want to install a default accelerator table from within a program, you must follow similar steps to those used for translations, but with the following differences:

*   You must set the **XtNaccelerators** resource instead of **XtNtranslations**.

*   Instead of using **XtParseTranslationTable()** to convert the ASCII translation table into Xt's internal form, use **XtParseAcceleratorTable()**.

*   There are no accelerator equivalents of **XtOverrideTranslations()** or **Xt-AugmentTranslations()**. Instead you can use **XtVaSetValues()** and use the accelerator directive by specifying **#augment** or **#override**.

8.2.5 Motif Accelerators and Mnemonics

Motif accelerators are keyboard shortcuts for menus, but they are used in a way that is completely different from that of the standard Xt accelerators just described.

When a RowColumn widget has been configured to operate as a popup menu or MenuBar, its `XmNmenuAccelerator` resource is activated. This resource can be set to a keysym which, when pressed, will pop up the popup menu or move the focus to the first item in the MenuBar. For example, the effective default value for `XmNmenuAccelerator` for the MenuBar is `<KeyUp>F10`.

RowColumn also has a subpart which has an `XmNbuttonAccelerators` resource. The `XmNbuttonAccelerators` resource is set to an array of keysyms, which when pressed will trigger the respective buttons. The `XmNbuttonAcceleratorText` resource is an array that lets you provide text that will appear in each button, to show the user the accelerator for each button.

All the resources that begin with `XmNbutton` can only be used when a menu is created with a function that begins with `XmCreateSimple` (there is one for each of the six types of Motif menus). These functions create a menu and populate it with children. Here are the other RowColumn subresources that configure the children as they are created:

- `XmNbuttonCount` specifies the total number of menu buttons, separators, and titles to create.

- `XmNbuttons` specifies a list of compound strings to use as labels for the buttons created. The list contains one element for each button, separator, and title created.

- `XmNbuttonType` specifies a list of button types associated with the buttons to be created. The list contains one element for each button, separator, and title created. If this resource is not specified, each button in a MenuBar is a CascadeButtonGadget; each button in any other type of RowColumn widget is a PushButtonGadget. Each entry in the button type array can have several possible values such as `XmPUSHBUTTON`.

These resources work only when set while creating a menu using `XmCreate-Simple*Menu` such as `XmCreateSimplePopupMenu()`. Setting them at any later time will have no effect. Some resources that configure the children of menus are not listed here.

8.2.5.1 Mnemonics

A *mnemonic* is a keyboard shortcut as well. However, a mnemonic is available only when a menu is visible, while an accelerator can invoke a menu entry even when the menu is not visible. Therefore, accelerators must be unique application-wide, while mnemonics only need to be unique within a single menu. Consequently, a mnemonic is a particular key regardless of modifiers, while accelerators are usually key combinations such as Ctrl-C.

A mnemonic is indicated in a button by underlining a character in the button label. Motif does this automatically as long as the mnemonic you choose appears in the label. The `Xm-NbuttonMnemonics` subresource of RowColumn specifies a mnemonic for each button created, but can only be used while creating the menu with one of the `XmCreate-Simple*Menu` routines. The list contains one element for each button, separator, and title created. The mnemonic for a particular button can also be set using the `XmNmnemonic` resource of any kind of button widget.

Further discussion of mnemonics is provided in the forthcoming Volume Six, *Motif Programming Manual*.

8.2.6 The display_accelerators Method

Xt calls the source widget's `display_accelerators` method when the accelerators are installed. The purpose of this method is to display to the user the installed accelerators. The method is passed a string representation of the accelerator table, which the method can theoretically manipulate into a form understandable by the user.

All Motif widgets just set this method to `NULL`. All of the Athena widgets inherit the Core widget's `display_accelerators` method by initializing the appropriate member of the class structure to `XtInheritDisplayAccelerators`. This default method, as implemented in the MIT distribution, does nothing.

9

More Input Techniques

This chapter describes how to handle events with event handlers, and how to use information from the event structure inside an event handler or action routine. It also describes how to get file, pipe or socket input, how to use timeouts to call a function after a delay or at particular intervals, and how to use work procedures to do background processing. Finally, it discusses some low-level features of Xt for directly interacting with the event queue.

In This Chapter:

9

More Input Techniques

In addition to translations, there is a lower-level mechanism called *event handlers*. Event handlers can be used from application or widget code. An event handler is a function registered with `XtAddEventHandler()` to be called in response to a particular event or group of events (but not an event sequence or detail, as is possible with translations). This is a low-level, non-user-configurable means of getting events. Event handlers provide no additional capabilities over translations and actions. But they allow Xt to skip the step of searching a translation table before dispatching the event to an event handler. This speed advantage is possibly significant for events that come in large numbers, such as pointer motion events, or in applications with large translation tables. (Despite this speed difference, good performance in tracking pointer motion can be achieved with translations.)

Both event handlers and actions are passed as an argument the actual event structure that caused them to be invoked. Many event handlers and actions use data in the event. For example, a routine handling motion events may want to obtain the current pointer position from the event structure. After describing how to add and remove event handlers, we discuss the event structures and show a routine that uses specific event data.

Next, this chapter discusses three ways to register functions Xt will call for input other than events, since some programs do not live by X events alone.

- `XtAppAddInput()` registers a procedure to be called when input is available from a file (or pipe or socket). This procedure can be used to perform code necessary when reads, writes, or exceptions are detected.

- `XtAppAddTimeOut()` registers a function to be called at a particular relative time. This function can be used to implement delays or to execute code repeatedly at known intervals.

- `XtAppAddWorkProc()` registers a work procedure. Work procedures are called when input from other sources is *not* available. They perform background tasks while the application is waiting for user input.

Finally, we provide more background on how the Toolkit dispatches events from `XtApp-MainLoop()`, and describe the low-level routines that can be used to construct your own main loop. We also describe Xt's event filters, which are controlled by flags in the Core class structure. These filters tell Xt whether or not to compress multiple motion, enter, leave, or expose events occurring in the same widget.

9.1 Event Handlers

An event handler is a function you provide to handle a particular type of event or group of event types. You register this function with a call to **XtAddEventHandler()** or **Xt-InsertEventHandler()**, specifying the widget in which the events are to be monitored. The difference between these two functions is described below.

You can later stop the function from being called with **XtRemoveEventHandler()**. On any widget, you can register as many event handlers as you want, each for the same or for different types of events. When more than one routine is registered for an event, the order in which they are invoked is undefined.

Within Motif applications, event handlers have one common use; they are used to pop up Motif popup menus. A popup menu is mapped where the user presses a mouse button in a particular widget, usually the application's main window. Since the application's main window probably doesn't have an **XmNactivateCallback** resource, the function that pops up the menu can't be registered as a callback. It can be registered as an event handler, however, because this requires no prior agreement from the widget. This function could also be added as an action from the application, but the required translations could interfere with the operation of the main window if it already uses ButtonPress events. Event handlers have the advantage that they work in parallel with Xt's other event dispatching mechanisms, and therefore they don't interfere. Example 9-1 shows how a typical application uses an event handler. The meaning of each argument will be described in a moment.

Example 9-1. Using an event hander to pop up a popup menu

```
static void
PostMenu (w, client_data, event)
Widget          w;
XtPointer       client_data;
XEvent          *event;
{
    Widget popup = (Widget) client_data;

    if (event->button != Button3)
        return;

    XmMenuPosition(popup, event);

    XtManageChild(popup);
}

main(argc, argv)
int argc;
char **argv;
{
    Widget mainW, Menu;

        .
        .
        .

    Menu = XmCreatePopupMenu(mainW, "popMenu", NULL, 0);

    XtAddEventHandler(mainW,        /* events sent to this widget */
            ButtonPressMask,        /* events desired */
            False,                  /* non-maskable events */
```

Example 9-1. Using an event hander to pop up a popup menu (continued)

```
        PostMenu,            /* function */
        Menu);               /* client_data passed to function */
            .
            .
            .
}
```

Within widget code, event handlers are used for various special requirements of individual widgets. For example, RowColumn uses an event handler to implement keyboard mnemonics in menus. Manager uses event handlers to generate synthetic events for its gadget children. (Since gadgets do not have windows, they would normally not get **EnterNotify** and **LeaveNotify** events. So the Manager widget class keeps track of the pointer position, and when the pointer enters one of the gadget children, Manager sends that child a synthetic **EnterNotify** event.)

In general, however, event handlers are infrequently used in application or widget code. None of the Athena widgets use them, and, out of the 40 applications in MIT's core distribution, only *xterm* and *xman* use them. As mentioned earlier, event handlers are useful for handling high-volume events, such as **MotionNotify** events, with maximum speed. An event handler for motion events would probably be the best way to implement a drawing program. However, translation tables provide good speed even for motion events on most systems.

Event handlers would also be useful when the type of events being handled changes frequently, because there is some overhead involved in compiling and merging translation tables. Event handlers can also be used to handle events for which the user-configurability of translations is not needed or wanted, such as **EnterWindow**, **LeaveWindow**, **FocusIn**, and **FocusOut** events.

Another possible use of event handlers is to speed the handling of certain events when there is a very large translation table. For example, editors typically have a large number of translations for various key combinations. If an editor was to accept pointer motion as well (to allow drawing of simple graphics), it might pay to handle motion events in an event handler instead of through translations.

The call to **XtAddEventHandler()** specifies which events trigger the event handler function. This is done with an *event mask* argument.† In an event mask, each bit represents one or more event types. Symbolic constants are defined by Xlib for each event mask bit. Multiple types of events can be selected at the same time by ORing together different masks with the bitwise OR operator (|). Note that there is not a one-to-one correspondence between event masks and event types. Some event masks select only one event, but others select multiple events. Furthermore, several of the masks select the same event type, but specify that it be delivered only when it occurs under special conditions. Table 9-1 shows the event masks and the event types they select.

---

†The event mask used in **XtAddEventHandler()** is the same as the one used in the Xlib call **XSelect-Input()**.

Table 9-1. Event Masks and Event Types

Event Mask	Event Type
KeyPressMask	KeyPress
KeyReleaseMask	KeyRelease
ButtonPressMask	ButtonPress
ButtonReleaseMask	ButtonRelease
OwnerGrabButtonMask	n/a
KeymapStateMask	KeymapNotify
PointerMotionMask	MotionNotify
PointerMotionHintMask	
ButtonMotionMask	
Button1MotionMask	
Button2MotionMask	
Button3MotionMask	
Button4MotionMask	
Button5MotionMask	
EnterWindowMask	EnterNotify
LeaveWindowMask	LeaveNotify
FocusChangeMask	FocusIn
	FocusOut
ExposureMask	Expose
(selected in GC by	GraphicsExpose
graphics_expose component)	NoExpose
ColormapChangeMask	ColormapNotify
PropertyChangeMask	PropertyNotify
VisibilityChangeMask	VisibilityNotify
ResizeRedirectMask	ResizeRequest
StructureNotifyMask	CirculateNotify
	ConfigureNotify
	DestroyNotify
	GravityNotify
	MapNotify
	ReparentNotify
	UnmapNotify
SubstructureNotifyMask	CirculateNotify
	ConfigureNotify
	CreateNotify
	DestroyNotify
	GravityNotify
	MapNotify
	ReparentNotify
	UnmapNotify
SubstructureRedirectMask	CirculateRequest
	ConfigureRequest
	MapRequest
(always selected)	MappingNotify

Table 9-1. Event Masks and Event Types (continued)

Event Mask	Event Type
(always selected)	`ClientMessage`
(always selected)	`SelectionClear`
(always selected)	`SelectionNotify`
(always selected)	`SelectionRequest`

The events that are always selected are called *nonmaskable events*. These can also be handled with an event handler, but not by specifying them in the event mask. An argument to the `XtAddEventHandler()` call, `non_maskable`, is a Boolean value that, if `True`, specifies that the event handler should be called for nonmaskable events. This event handler then must branch according to which of the seven types of nonmaskable events it is passed. A typical nonmaskable event handler is shown in Section 9.1.2.

9.1.1 Adding Event Handlers

Event handlers are added with a call to `XtAddEventHandler()` or `XtInsert-EventHandler()`. `XtAddEventHandler()` takes five arguments: the widget for which the handler is being added, an event mask, a flag that specifies whether or not this handler is for nonmaskable events (see below), the name of the handler, and optional client data. `XtInsertEventHandler()` takes these and one additional argument: the position, either `XtListTail` or `XtListHead`.

A list of event handlers can be registered for the same event; but the same function will appear only once in the list with the same `client_data`. If the same function/`client_data` pair is registered again with `XtAddEventHandler()`, nothing will happen except that the event mask for that function may change. But if the same function/`client_data` pair is registered again with `XtInsertEventHandler()`, the function will be moved to the beginning or the end of the function list.

`XtAddEventHandler()` or `XtInsertEventHandler()` may be called before or after a widget is realized. In application code, this means the call can appear anywhere before `XtAppMainLoop()`. In a widget, `XtAddEventHandler()` or `XtInsert-EventHandler()` calls are placed in the `initialize` or `realize` methods.

Example 9-2 shows the code from *xterm* that registers an event handler for `FocusIn` and `FocusOut` events, and a gutted version of the event handler itself.

Example 9-2. Registering an event handler, and the handler function itself

```
extern void HandleFocusChange();

static void VTInitialize (request, new)
XtermWidget request, new;
{
    .
    .
    .
```

More Input Techniques

```
    XtAddEventHandler(topLevel,      /* widget */
        FocusChangeMask,             /* event mask */
        False,                       /* non-maskable events */
        HandleFocusChange,           /* event handler */
        NULL);              /* client_data */

        .
        .
        .

}

/*ARGSUSED*/
void HandleFocusChange(w, unused, event, continue_to_dispatch)
Widget w;
register XFocusChangeEvent *event;
XtPointer unused;                        /* client_data */
Boolean *continue_to_dispatch;
{
    if (event->type == FocusIn) {
                                    /* process FocusIn */
        .
        .
        .
    }
    else {
                                    /* process FocusOut */
        .
        .
        .
    }
    /*
     * If subsequent event handlers registered for this event
     * should not be called, set *continue_to_dispatch = False;
     * This is not recommended.
     */
}
```

In typical usage, either the event mask argument is a mask and the *non_maskable* argument is set to `False`, or the event mask argument is set to zero and *non_maskable* is set to `True`. Example 9-1 demonstrated the former case; now we'll look at the latter.

9.1.2 Adding Nonmaskable Event Handlers

The *non_maskable* argument of `XtAddEventHandler()` specifies whether the specified event handler should be called in response to the events that can't be selected as described above. The nonmaskable events are `GraphicsExpose`, `NoExpose`, `Mapping-Notify`, `SelectionClear`, `SelectionRequest`, `SelectionNotify`, and `ClientMessage`. The first two of these events are selected using the `graphics_expo-sure` component of the GC, and the rest are always sent to the client whenever they occur. `MappingNotify` is automatically handled by Xt, so it isn't passed to event handlers and you don't need to worry about it. The selection events are described in Chapter 11, *Interclient Communications*.

Because there are several nonmaskable event types, a nonmaskable event handler must be sure to branch according to the type of event, and throw away any event types not handled. You need not have all the code to handle all the types in a single event handler. Instead, you can handle each type in a separate handler, each registered separately. However, each handler would still need to check the event type because the entire list of them would be called for every nonmaskable event.

Example 9-3 shows the registration of a nonmaskable event handler and the handler itself, from *xman*.

Example 9-3. Adding a nonmaskable event handler

```
static void
Realize(w, valueMask, attributes)
register Widget w;
Mask *valueMask;
XSetWindowAttributes *attributes;
{
    .
    .
    .

    XtAddEventHandler(w, 0, True,
            GExpose, NULL); /* Get Graphics Exposures */
} /* Realize */

/* ARGSUSED */
static void
GExpose(w, client_data, event)
Widget w;
XtPointer client_data;
XEvent *event;
{
    if (event->type == GraphicsExpose)
        Redisplay(w, event, NULL); /* call the expose method directly */
}
```

This event handler is sometimes used because Xt does not normally call the **expose** method in response to `GraphicsExpose` events. But in R4, another way to accomplish this has been introduced. If the `compress_exposure` field in the Core structure is set to **(Xt-ExposeCompressMultiple | XtExposeGraphicsExpose)**, Xt will call the **expose** method with these events.

9.1.3 Removing Event Handlers

`XtRemoveEventHandler()` takes the same arguments as `XtAddEventHandler()`; if there are parameter mismatches, the call is quietly ignored. For example, the client data argument may be used to distinguish between different event handlers; if the client data argument does not match that which was passed in the **XtAddEventHandler()**, then **Xt-**

`RemoveEventHandler()` will do nothing. `XtRemoveEventHandler()` is also silent about failing to remove a handler that was never added or a handler that was incorrectly specified.

9.1.4 Adding Raw Event Handlers

Xt also allows you to add event handlers without actually selecting events. The main purpose of this feature is for Xt to register functions before widgets are realized (because events can't be selected until windows are created during realization). Event handlers registered without selecting events are called *raw* event handlers, and are added with `XtAddRawEventHandler()` or `XtInsertRawEventHandler()`, which have the same calling sequences as `XtAddEventHandler()` and `XtInsertRawEventHandler()`. The event mask indicates which events the handler will be called in response to, but only when these events are selected elsewhere. Raw event handlers are supported mostly because they are used inside Xt. They are mentioned here only for completeness—you are unlikely to need them.

A raw event handler might be used to "shadow" another event handler (both added with the same event mask), such that until a primary event handler is added, the shadow handler will never be called. The primary handler will be added with `XtAddEventHandler()`, which will select events, and then both handlers will be called when the appropriate events occur.

However, the "shadowing" technique is not necessary to assure that multiple calls to `XtAddEventHandler()` don't result in wasted `XSelectInput()` calls in which the event mask has not changed. Xt keeps a cache of the event masks of each widget, and calls `XSelectInput()` only when it is necessary to change the window's event mask attribute in the server.

Raw event handlers are removed with a call to `XtRemoveRawEventHandler()`.

9.2 Writing Routines That Use Specific Event Data

An event is a packet of information that the server sends to the client. Xlib takes this packet from the network and places it into an `XEvent` structure and places it on a queue until the client program requests it. Xt requests events from this queue and dispatches the event to the appropriate action routine or event handler for the widget in which the event occurred. The event itself is passed as an argument to the routine.†

Actually, `XEvent` is a C-Language union of many event structures all the same size but with some different field names. The first member of the union, and of any of the individual event structures, is the event `type`. Table 9-2, later in this section, lists the event types and the matching event structure types.

---

†We'll look at the low-level routines Xt provides for directly manipulating the event queue later in this chapter.

Many action routines are intentionally written not to depend on the detailed information inside any particular type of event, so that the user can specify translations to call the action in response to different types of events. For example, it is useful for an action routine normally triggered by a pointer click to work when called in response to a key instead. Such an action should not depend on the event structure fields unique to button events.

However, many other action routines, and most event handlers, do use the detailed information inside event structures. The first member, `type`, identifies which type of event this structure represents, and hence implies which other fields are present in the structure.

To access event structure fields other than `type` you need to cast `XEvent` into the appropriate event structure type. If you are expecting only one type of event to trigger this action, then you can simply declare the argument as the appropriate type, as shown in Example 9-4.

Example 9-4. Casting the event structure by declaring action routine arguments

```
/*ARGSUSED*/
static void
ActionA(w, event, params, num_params)
Widget w;
XEvent *event;
String *params;
Cardinal *num_params;
{
    if ((event->type != ButtonPress) && (event->type != KeyPress)) {
        XtWarning("ActionA invoked by wrong event type.");
        /* possible exit here */
    }
        .
        .
}
```

When an action routine or event handler depends on the fields in a particular event structure, it is a good practice to check the event type in that action unless you are sure that the user can't change the translation (and thus the events used to invoke the action).

If you want the same code called for two event types, then you would do better to create two separate translations and two separate actions that each call a common routine. However, it is sometimes more convenient to have an action called by two different events. Example 9-5 shows the `ToggleCell` action from the BitmapEdit widget, which is called in response to either `MotionNotify` or `ButtonPress` events. This action inverts a pixel in the bitmap either if the pointer is clicked on a cell in the widget, or if it is dragged across the cell with the pointer buttons held down.

Example 9-5. Handling multiple event types in an action routine

```
static void
ToggleCell(w, event)
Widget w;
XEvent *event;
{
    BitmapEditWidget cw = (BitmapEditWidget) w;
    static int oldx = -1, oldy = -1;
    GC gc;
    int mode;
```

```
    int newx, newy;

    if (event->type == ButtonPress) {
        newx = (w->bitmapEdit.cur_x + ((XButtonEvent *)event)->x) /
                w->bitmapEdit.cell_size_in_pixels;
        newy = (w->bitmapEdit.cur_y + ((XButtonEvent *)event)->y) /
                w->bitmapEdit.cell_size_in_pixels;
    }
    else if  (event->type == MotionNotify) {
        newx = (w->bitmapEdit.cur_x + ((XMotionEvent *)event)->x) /
                w->bitmapEdit.cell_size_in_pixels;
        newy = (w->bitmapEdit.cur_y + ((XMotionEvent *)event)->y) /
                w->bitmapEdit.cell_size_in_pixels;
    }
    else
        XtWarning("BitmapEdit: ToggleCell called with wrong event\
                type\n");
        .
        .
        .
}
```

Notice that some code is repeated to cast the event structure to the two different event types. With the current MIT implementation of Xlib, the positions of the **x** and **y** fields in the **XButtonEvent** and **XMotionEvent** structures are the same, and therefore this casting is unnecessary on many compilers. However, for strict ANSI C conformance these casts are necessary, and furthermore it is improper to depend on any particular implementation of Xlib. The order of the fields in one of these events could be different in some vendor's implementation of Xlib.

9.2.1 Event Types and Structure Names

Table 9-2 lists the event types and the matching event structure types. The event descriptions in the table will give you a general idea of what each event is for. Many of these events are not often used in applications, and more of them are automatically handled by Xt. We've already discussed how to use the most common event types and their abbreviations in translation tables in Chapter 8, *Events, Translations, and Accelerators*. Appendix C, *Event Reference*, in Volume Five, *X Toolkit Intrinsics Reference Manual*, provides a complete reference to the circumstances under which each event is generated, what it is for, and the fields in each of the event structures. You will need this information to write action routines that use event-specific data.

Table 9-2. Event Types and Event Structures

Event Type	Structure	Description
KeyPress	XKeyPressedEvent	Key pressed.
KeyRelease	XKeyReleasedEvent	Key released.
ButtonPress	XButtonPressedEvent	Pointer button pressed.
ButtonRelease	XButtonReleasedEvent	Pointer button released.
KeymapNotify	XKeymapEvent	State of all keys when pointer entered.
MotionNotify	XPointerMovedEvent	Pointer motion.
EnterNotify	XEnterWindowEvent	Pointer entered window.
LeaveNotify	XLeaveWindowEvent	Pointer left window.
FocusIn	XFocusInEvent	This window is now keyboard focus.
FocusOut	XFocusOutEvent	This window was keyboard focus.
Expose	XExposeEvent	Part of window needs redrawing.
GraphicsExpose	XGraphicsExposeEvent	Source of copy unavailable.
NoExpose	XNoExposeEvent	Source of copy available.
ColormapNotify	XColormapEvent	Window's colormap changed.
PropertyNotify	XPropertyEvent	Property value changed.
VisibilityNotify	XVisibilityEvent	Window has been obscured.
ResizeRequest	XResizeRequestEvent	Redirect resize request to window manager.
CirculateNotify	XCirculateEvent	Stacking order modified.
ConfigureNotify	XConfigureEvent	Window resized or moved.
DestroyNotify	XDestroyWindowEvent	Window destroyed.
GravityNotify	XGravityEvent	Window moved due to win gravity attribute.
MapNotify	XMapEvent	Window mapped.
ReparentNotify	XReparentEvent	Window reparented.
UnmapNotify	XUnmapEvent	Window unmapped.
CirculateRequest	XCirculateRequestEvent	Redirect stacking order change to window manager.
ConfigureRequest	XConfigureRequestEvent	Redirect move or resize request to window manager.
MapRequest	XMapRequestEvent	Redirect window map request to window manager.
MappingNotify	XMappingEvent	Keyboard mapping changed.
ClientMessage	XClientMessageEvent	Client-dependent.
SelectionClear	XSetSelectClearEvent	Current owner is losing selection.
SelectionNotify	XSelectionEvent	Selection is ready for requestor.
SelectionRequest	XSelectionRequestEvent	Request for selection to current owner.

9.3 File, Pipe, and Socket Input

`XtAppAddInput()` allows a program to obtain input from a file. This is not merely reading the file once, but monitoring it for further activity. Under UNIX this can be used to get input from pipes and sockets, since they are variations of files. We will demonstrate getting file and pipe input in this section.

The `XtAppAddInput()` routine takes four arguments: a file descriptor, a flag (see below), your function, and `client_data`.

`XtAppAddInput()` returns an ID that uniquely identifies the `XtAppAddInput()` request. You can use the ID to cancel the request later with `XtRemoveInput()`.

One argument of `XtAppAddInput()` is a file descriptor (this file must be open before calling `XtAppAddInput()`). Since implementation of files varies between operating systems, the actual contents of the parameter passed as the file descriptor argument to these routines is operating system-dependent. Therefore, this code is inherently nonportable.

Possible values for the mask and their meanings are as shown in Table 9-3.

Table 9-3. Other Input Source Masks

Mask	Description
`XtInputReadMask`	File descriptor has data available.
`XtInputWriteMask`	File descriptor available for writing.
`XtInputExceptMask`	I/O errors have occurred (exceptions).
`XtInputNoneMask`	Never call function registered.

Calling these argument values masks is something of a misnomer, since they *cannot* be ORed together. However, you can call `XtAppAddInput()` additional times to register a separate function (or the same function) for each of these masks on the same file descriptor.

9.3.1 Getting File Input

In Example 9-6, a program called *xfileinput* reads new characters from a file whenever they appear. In other words, the program will initially print to the standard output the contents of the file specified on the command line, and it will print any characters that are later appended to that file. Try the program *xfileinput* as follows:

```
echo "test string" > testfile
xfileinput testfile &
echo "more text" >> testfile
```

A program such as this functions similarly to the UNIX command *tail –f*. It could be used to monitor system log files, or other similar files that grow.

The code shown in Example 9-6 opens the file and calls **XtAppAddInput()** in **main**. The `get_file_input` function registered with **XtAppAddInput()** reads and prints characters from the file.†

Example 9-6. Getting file input with XtAppAddInput

```
/* header files */
   .
   .
   .

/* ARGSUSED */
get_file_input(client_data, fid, id)
XtPointer client_data;      /* unused */
int *fid;
XtInputId *id;
{
    char buf[BUFSIZ];
    int nbytes;
    int i;

    if ((nbytes = read(*fid, buf, BUFSIZ)) == -1)
        perror("get_file_input");

    if (nbytes)
        for (i = 0; i < nbytes; i++)
            putchar(buf[i]);
}
main(argc, argv)
int argc;
char **argv;
{
    XtAppContext app_context;
    Widget topLevel, goodbye;
    FILE *fid;
    String filename;

     XtSetLanguageProc(NULL, (XtLanguageProc)NULL, NULL);

    topLevel = XtVaAppInitialize(&app_context, "XFileInput", NULL,
            0, &argc, argv, NULL, NULL);

    if (argv[1] == NULL) {
        fprintf(stderr, "xfileinput: filename must be specified on\
                command line.\n");
        exit(1);
    }

    filename = argv[1];
       .
       .
       .

    /* open file */
    if ((fid = fopen(filename, "r")) == NULL)
        fprintf(stderr, "xfileinput: couldn't open input file.\n");
```

---

†Note that the code for opening and reading files is probably not portable to operating systems other than UNIX.

Example 9-6. Getting file input with XtAppAddInput (continued)

```
    /* register function to handle that input, NULL arg
     * is client_data */
    XtAppAddInput(app_context, fileno(fid), XtInputReadMask,
            get_file_input, NULL);

    XtRealizeWidget(topLevel);

    XtAppMainLoop(app_context);
}
```

The function registered with **XtAppAddInput()** is called with *client_data* (used for passing in any application data), a pointer to the file descriptor, and the ID of the **XtApp-AddInput()** request. You can use a call to **XtRemoveInput()** in the function registered with **XtAppAddInput()** if that function is only to be called once. One argument of the **XtRemoveInput()** call is the ID of the **XtAppAddInput()** request.

Under some operating systems, the function registered with **XtAppAddInput()** is called very frequently even when no new input is available. This is because Xt makes a system call to detect whether the file is "ready for reading," and some operating systems say the file is ready even when there is nothing new to read. The example shown above works, but it loads down the system much more than necessary. You may wish to check the file every quarter second instead of continuously, by adding and removing your input handler periodically using timeouts (as described in Section 9.4). Under UNIX, this problem should happen only for files, not for pipes or sockets.

9.3.2 Getting Pipe Input

The code to get pipe input is almost identical to the code just shown that gets file input. The only difference is that we use *popen* instead of *fopen*, and change the various error messages. Now instead of treating the command-line argument as a filename, it is treated as a program run under a shell. This program's output is piped into our application. For example, here is an example of how to invoke this version of *xpipeinput*:

```
spike% xpipeinput "cal 11 1989"
    November 1989
 S  M Tu  W Th  F  S
             1  2  3  4
 5  6  7  8  9 10 11
12 13 14 15 16 17 18
19 20 21 22 23 24 25
26 27 28 29 30
```
(*Program continues to monitor pipe for further input until application exits.*)

Note that *xpipeinput* is reading the string "cal 11 1989" from the command line, invoking a shell, running the command specified by the string under this shell, reading the output of the shell, and then printing it on the standard output. This is an easy way to use all kinds of shell scripts and utilities from within a program.

If you want your application to accept standard input, this is even easier. Remove the code that reads the filename from the command line and remove the **popen** call to open the pipe, since the pipe from `stdin` is always open. Then use the **XtAppAddInput()** function as shown in Example 9-7.

Example 9-7. Reading stdin from an Xt application

```
XtAppAddInput(app_context, fileno(stdin), XtInputReadMask,
        get_file_input, NULL);
```

Once you have done this, you can invoke *xpipeinput* as follows:

```
spike% cal 11 1989 | xpipeinput
     November 1989
 S   M Tu  W Th  F  S
            1  2  3  4
 5   6  7  8  9 10 11
12  13 14 15 16 17 18
19  20 21 22 23 24 25
26  27 28 29 30
```
(*Program continues to monitor pipe for further input until application exits.*)

Note that in this case, *xpipeinput* is reading directly from stdin, and then printing the output to stdout. With more code, it could display this calendar in a Text widget instead.

9.4 Timeouts

A program may wish to be notified when a period of time has elapsed, while being able to do other things in the meantime. For example, a clock widget requires a periodic nudge to change the time it is displaying, but must also be able to redisplay itself at any time in case of exposure.

This is done by using **XtAppAddTimeOut()**. This routine is passed a time interval in milliseconds, and the address of a function to be invoked when the time interval expires. As usual, a `client_data` argument can also be registered. The **XtAppAddTimeOut()** routine returns a handle that can be used to cancel the timeout before it triggers, if necessary.

A timeout is automatically removed when the registered function is called. Therefore, to have a function called repeatedly, every *N* milliseconds, the registered function must add the timeout again by calling **XtAppAddTimeOut()**.

One of the major applications of timeouts other than clocks is in real-time games. Figure 9-1 shows the appearance of a game called *xtetris* after it has been played for a couple of minutes.

The object of the game is to steer falling blocks and rotate them so that they fit well into the existing fallen blocks.† The game is over when the blocks pile up to the top of the window.

---

†This game is provided with the example source code. It is an X version of a game available on the Macintosh called *Tetris*, trademark of AcademySoft-ELORG, copyright and trademark licensed to Andromeda Software Ltd. The original concept of the game is by Alexi Pazhitnov and Vadim Gerasimov.

Figure 9-1. xtetris in play

Every time a row is completely filled, it is removed and all the blocks above it move down one row. The window in which the blocks fall is a specialized widget. This game uses timeouts to time the falling of the blocks.

Example 9-8 is an excerpt from a widget used by *xtetris* that adds the timeout. The timeout function itself is also shown.

Example 9-8. xtetris: registering a timeout and the timeout function

```
static XtIntervalId timer;

static void
StartBlock(w)
TetrisWidget w;
{
    w->tetris.cur_x = 9;
    w->tetris.cur_y = 0;

    w->tetris.type = PickType();

    DrawBlock(w, DRAW);

    timer = XtAppAddTimeOut(XtWidgetToApplicationContext(w),
            w->tetris.delay, MoveDown, w);
}

static void
MoveDown(w, id)
BitmapEditWidget w;         /* client_data */
XtIntervalID *id;
{
    if (CanMoveDown(w)) {
        drawBlock(w, UNDRAW);
        w->tetris.cur_y++;
        DrawBlock(w, DRAW);
        CopyBlock(w);
        timer = XtAppAddTimeOut(XtWidgetToApplicationContext(w),
                w->tetris.delay, MoveDown, w);
    }
    else { /*block has hit bottom or other stationary blocks*/
        UpdateCellArray(w);
        KillRows(w);
        Score(w);
        w->tetris.delay -= 5;
        StartBlock(w);
    }
}
```

Notice that in widget code, the application context is specified using `XtWidget-ToApplicationContext()`.

Notice also that a timeout function is called with only one argument, *client_data*. Inside a widget, this argument is commonly used to pass in the widget instance pointer. Also notice that every time a block hits the bottom, the instance variable `delay` is decremented by 5, which reduces the number of milliseconds of delay used when `XtAppAddTime-Out()` is next called. In other words, the blocks fall progressively faster.

xtetris also needs to remove a timeout in one of its routines. The user can "drop" a block to score extra points (if there is enough time). Whenever a block is dropped, the block is immediately moved down as far as it will go, and a new block is started. If the `Drop` action did not remove the timeout, the new block would be started with a new timeout while an existing timeout was already in force. This would mean that the `MoveDown` timeout function would be invoked twice in quick succession when each of these timeouts expired. Example 9-9 shows the `XtRemoveTimeOut()` call in the `Drop` action.

More Input Techniques

Example 9-9. xtetris: calling XtRemoveTimeOut

```
/*ARGSUSED*/
static void
Drop(tw, tevent, params, num_params)
Widget tw;
XEvent *tevent;
String *params;
Cardinal *num_params;
{
    TetrisWidget w = (TetrisWidget) tw;
    XButtonEvent *event = (XButtonEvent *) tevent;
    XtRemoveTimeOut(timer);

    while (CanMoveDown(w)) {
        DrawBlock(w, UNDRAW);
        w->tetris.cur_y++;
        DrawBlock(w, DRAW);
        CopyBlock(w);
    }

    UpdateCellArray(w);
    KillRows(w);
    score++;
    Score(w);
    w->tetris.delay -= 5;
    StartBlock(w);
}
```

Notice that the `timer` ID returned from the calls to `XtAppAddTimeOut()` is a global variable. Xt calls the timeout function with only one argument, and that argument passes in the widget instance pointer. We could have created a structure containing the widget instance pointer and the timer ID and passed its pointer to the timeout function. But this wouldn't help, because the action routine in which we remove the timeout is passed with no `client_data` argument. (It has string parameters, but these are hardcoded in the actions table.) Therefore, we are forced to have a global variable for the timer ID.

Note that between the time when the timeout is registered and when it triggers, the application processes events in `XtAppMainLoop()`. Therefore, all the widget's actions and `expose` method are in operation between the invocations of the timeout function.

9.5 Visibility Interest

Timeouts operate regardless of the visibility of the application. Since it is pointless for most games to continue operating while obscured, it makes sense to remove the game's timeouts when the game is partially or fully obscured (or iconified). To do this, you can set the `visible_interest` field in the Core class structure to `True`, and then check the `visible` field of the Core instance structure periodically. When the application is fully obscured, you add a separate timeout to continue testing the visibility status. When the visibility status is satisfactory once again, the game can add its timeout again. All these changes are in the widget's *.c* file. First we set the `visible_interest` field to `True` in the Core structure:

```
TetrisClassRec tetrisClassRec  = {
    /* core_class fields */
    .
    .
    .
    /* visible_interest          */ True,
    .
    .
    .
}
```

Second we change:

```
timer = XtAppAddTimeOut(XtWidgetToApplicationContext
    (w), w->tetris.delay, MoveDown, w);
```

to:

```
if (w->core.visible == False)
        timer = XtAppAddTimeOut(XtWidgetToApplicationContext
            (w) 250, CheckVisibility, w);
    else
        timer = XtAppAddTimeOut(XtWidgetToApplicationContext
(w)
w->tetris.delay, MoveDown, w);
```

And finally, we add the timeout function that continues to check the visibility status.

```
static void
CheckVisibility(w)
BitmapEditWidget w;     /* client_data */
{
    if (w->core.visible == False)
        timer = XtAppAddTimeOut(250, CheckVisibility, w);
    else
        timer = XtAppAddTimeOut(w->tetris.delay,
            MoveDown, w);
}
```

Unfortunately, the Core **visible** field is **True** even if a tiny sliver of the widget is visible. The only way to get around this is to add an event handler (or translation) for **VisibilityNotify** events and to add an instance variable to maintain the visibility state. The event handler or action would check the **state** field of the event, and put the game into hibernation if the window is only partially obscured. However, this approach has the opposite problem; it disables the game even when only a sliver is obscured.

There is nothing you can do about the game continuing to run while being moved or resized with the window manager. However, using the Core **visible_interest** field does stop the game when it is iconified.

9.6 Work Procedures

A work procedure is an application-supplied function that is executed while an application is idle waiting for an event. Work procedures are registered with **XtAppAddWorkProc()**. They can perform any calculation that is short enough that the routine will return in a small fraction of a second. If the work procedure is too long, the user's response time will suffer.

If a work procedure returns **True**, then Xt will remove it and it will not be called again. But if one returns **False**, it will be called repeatedly every time there is idle time, until the application calls **XtRemoveWorkProc()**. A work procedure would return **True** if it performs a one-time setup such as creating a popup widget. It would return **False** if it were continuously updating a disk file as security against a system crash or server connection failure.

You can register multiple work procedures, and they will be performed one at a time. The most recent work procedure added has the highest priority. Therefore, for example, if you want to create ten popup widgets during idle time, you should add ten work procedures. The popup that you expect to need first should be added in the last work procedure registered.

The call to register a work procedure is shown in Example 9-10.

Example 9-10. Registering an Xt work procedure

```
static Boolean create_popup();
    .
    .
    .
main(argc, argv)
int argc;
char **argv;
{
    XtAppContext app_context;
    XtWorkProcId popup_work_ID;
    Widget topLevel;
        .
        .
    /* XtAppInitialize, create widgets, etc. */
        .
        .
    popup_work_ID = XtAppAddWorkProc(app_context,
            create_popup, topLevel);
        .
        .
    /*
     * popup_work_ID not actually needed because work proc
     * unregisters itself by returning True.
     */
    XtRealizeWidget(topLevel);
    XtAppMainLoop(app_context);
}
```

Notice that `XtAppAddWorkProc()` returns an ID of type `XtWorkProcId`, which is used only in any subsequent call to `XtRemoveWorkProc()`. You can cast the returned value to `void` if you do not intend to explicitly remove the work procedure.

The `client_data` argument passes application data into the work procedure. It is used just like the same argument in callback functions. Example 9-11 shows a work procedure to create a popup widget.

Example 9-11. A work procedure to create a popup widget

```
Widget getHelp;

/* work procedure */
Boolean
create_popup(client_data)
XtPointer client_data;
{
    Widget parent = (Widget) client_data;
    Widget helpBox;
    Widget temp;

    helpBox = XmCreateMessageDialog(parent, "message", NULL, 0);

    temp = XmMessageBoxGetChild (helpBox, XmDIALOG_CANCEL_BUTTON);
    XtUnmanageChild (temp);
    temp = XmMessageBoxGetChild (helpBox, XmDIALOG_HELP_BUTTON);
    XtUnmanageChild (temp);

    /* arrange for getHelp button to pop up helpBox */
    XtAddCallback(getHelp, XmNactivateCallback, PopupDialog, helpBox);

    return(True);    /* makes Xt remove this work proc automatically */
}
```

Remember that Xt cannot interrupt a work procedure while it is running; the procedure must voluntarily give up control by returning, and it must do so quickly to avoid slowing user response.

If your application has any big jobs that it must do, the only way to do them without resulting in long delays is to write the code that does the big job in a way that voluntarily interrupts itself and saves its state so that it can be restarted where it left off. One way to run such a task is as a work procedure, but this is only useful for tasks that need not be done before other application tasks can begin. If you want `Expose` processing to continue but no other application task to begin until your task is done, you would use the same type of code but place low-level event management routines in it, or make the rest of the application insensitive until the task is done.

9.7 Low-level Management of the Event Queue

As you know, an X Toolkit application simply calls `XtAppMainLoop()` to begin processing events. `XtAppMainLoop()` itself is quite simple: it consists of an infinite loop calling two lower-level routines, `XtAppNextEvent()` and `XtDispatchEvent()`. `XtAppNextEvent()` extracts the next event from the application's event queue; `XtDispatchEvent()` actually uses the event to invoke the appropriate actions or event handlers. (The functions registered by `XtAppAddInput()` and `XtAppAddTimeOut()` are dispatched directly by `XtAppNextEvent()`; if no events are available, `XtAppNextEvent()` flushes the X output buffer, and calls any work procedures registered by `XtAppAddWorkProc()`.)

An application can provide its own version of this loop, as shown in Example 9-12. For example, it might test some application-dependent global flag or other termination condition before looping back and calling `XtAppNextEvent()`. Or for fine-grained debugging, it might be worthwhile to insert a routine that prints out the type of each event dispatched.

Example 9-12. Skeleton of a custom main loop

```
void MyMainLoop(app_con)
XtAppContext app_con;
{
    XEvent event;

    for (;;) {
        XtAppNextEvent(app_con, &event);
        XtDispatchEvent(&event);

    /* Do application-specific processing here */

    }
}
```

9.7.1 XtPending and XtPeekEvent

All event sources depend on idle time in the application to return to `XtAppMainLoop()` where Xt can check to see if input is available from any of the various sources. If an application has long calculations to make, the program may not return to `XtAppMainLoop()` frequently enough to detect important input in a timely fashion. The application itself should, if possible, suspend lengthy calculations for a moment to check whether input is available. Then it can determine whether to process the input before continuing, or finish the calculation.

To detect whether input from any input source is available, you can call `XtPending()`. This function returns a mask composed of a bitwise OR of the symbolic constants `XtIMXEvent`, `XtIMTimer`, and `XtIMAlternateInput`. These constants refer to X events, timer events, and alternate input events, respectively.

To find out what the first event in the queue contains, you can call `XtPeekEvent()`. This function returns an event structure without removing the event from Xlib's queue.

It is also possible to remove and process a single event. `XtAppProcessEvent()` combines some (but not all) of the functions from `XtAppNextEvent()` and `XtDispatchEvent()`. That is, while `XtAppNextEvent()` takes the next event from the queue, whatever it is, `XtAppProcessEvent()` allows you to specify as a mask a bitwise OR of the symbolic constants `XtIMXEvent`, `XtIMTimer`, and `XtIMAlternateInput`. This lets you select only some of these event types for processing. In addition, `XtAppProcessEvent()` actually calls `XtDispatchEvent()` to dispatch X events, so only this one call is necessary.

9.7.2 Event Filters

As you saw in Chapter 6, *Inside a Widget*, the class structure contains three Boolean fields that control Xt's event filters. These are `compress_motion`, `compress_enterleave`, and `compress_exposure`. Widgets set these fields to `True` when repeated events of these types are unwanted. Each would be used in different situations. If turned on, they tell Xt to search Xlib's queue for a certain event sequence and then remove repeated occurrences of those events from the queue.

When the `compress_motion` filter is set to `True`, and there is a series of `MotionNotify` events on the queue (which occurs when the application gets behind in processing them), the filter throws out all but the last one (the most recent position). This is useful for widgets that need the most up-to-date position but do not need a complete history of pointer positions.

The `compress_enterleave` filter throws out all `EnterNotify`/`LeaveNotify` pairs on the same window in which there are no intervening events. This would be used by a widget that is interested in enter and leave events, but not if the application falls behind. For example, even the Command widget sets `compress_enterleave` to `True`. It highlights its border when the pointer enters, and clears it when the pointer leaves. But if for some reason the widget falls behind and has not highlighted the border by the time the `LeaveNotify` event arrives with no intervening events, the border will not be highlighted. To see this, move the pointer quickly across a large panel of Command widgets such as in *xmh*, and you will see that not all of them draw and then undraw the border.

The symbols used for setting the `compress_exposure` filter have changed in R4. If the field of this name in the Core class structure is set to `False` or `XtExposeNoCompress`, a widget's `expose` method is called once in response to each `Expose` event in a contiguous series. Each event specifies a different rectangle of the widget that needs redrawing.

With `compress_exposure` set to `True` or `XtExposeCompressSeries`, however, a contiguous series of events resulting from one user action is compressed into a single modified `Expose` event and the `expose` method is called only once. This modified `Expose` event contains the bounding rectangle of the union of all the rectangles in the individual events. In this case the `expose` method is also passed an Xlib `Region` that describes in detail the area exposed. Probably the most useful value for `compress_exposure` is `XtExposeCompressMultiple`, which compresses all the contiguous events resulting from multiple contiguous user actions.

When ORed with any of the `XtCompress*` symbols, the `XtExposeGraphicsExpose` symbol causes Xt to call the `expose` method with any `GraphicsExpose` events that occur. Remember that you must set the `graphics_exposures` component to `True` in the GC used in `XCopyArea()` or `XCopyPlane()` in order to get `GraphicsExpose` events. `XtExposeGraphicsExposeMerged`, when ORed with an `XtCompress*` symbol, merges contiguous `Expose` and `GraphicsExpose` events together before calling the `expose` method.

The `XtExposeNoExpose` symbol causes Xt to dispatch `NoExpose` events to the `expose` method. This doesn't make much sense; if you need `NoExpose` events it is better to add an event handler or translation to handle them.

The remaining symbol is `XtExposeCompressMaximal`. This symbol is dangerous and usually should not be used: it merges non-continuous `Expose` events into one event before calling the `expose` method. This is unwise because the intervening events could be `ConfigureNotify` events that change the size of the window. When this happens, the application will redraw itself, then receive the `ConfigureNotify`, but then it will not redraw itself in the new size because the `Expose` event that would trigger the drawing has already been removed from the queue.

Almost all widgets except those that display a large amount of text should set this filter to `XtExposeCompressMultiple`. Text widgets can very efficiently redraw only the needed parts of the window because each character is in a fixed location. (Characters are in fixed locations in the Text widget because it uses fixed-width fonts—this is not applicable to widgets that display proportional fonts.) Therefore, it can efficiently process all the `Expose` events one at a time.

9.7.3 Input Sensitivity

There are times when some widgets should be insensitive to events in which they are usually interested. For example, a Command widget should be insensitive when the command that it executes is already in operation.

Widget sensitivity is inherited. For example, if a parent widget is insensitive, then its children are too. In other words, an entire box full of widgets can be set insensitive by simply setting the box widget insensitive. Note, however, that this process can be a little slow because all the widgets in the box that honor sensitivity will redraw themselves dimmed or grayed. A widget is made insensitive from an application by calling `XtSetSensitive()` with the `sensitive` argument set to `False`, or using `XtVaSetValues()` on the `Xm-Nsensitive` resource (`XtSetSensitive()` is slightly faster).

Any widget that may need to be disabled for a time by the application should change its visible appearance when insensitive.

The widget that has one of the `XtCallback*` standard popup callback functions registered on its callback list will automatically be set insensitive when the callback is triggered. If the `XtCallbackPopdown()` callback function is registered on this widget it will automatically be set sensitive again when this callback is invoked.

10

Resource Management and
Type Conversion

*This chapter is a more thorough discussion of how resources work and how
they should be used. This chapter describes in detail the resource file format
and the rules that govern the precedence of resource settings. It also
describes how to add your own type converter so that you can have application or widget-specific data set through resources. Finally, it describes
subresources and how to use them.*

In This Chapter:

10
Resource Management
and Type Conversion

This chapter provides a thorough discussion of how resources work and how they should be used. First, we describe how to define resources, the complete syntax of resource files, and the rules that describe the precedence of one resource setting over another. For the sake of completeness, and to make sure that the ideas are presented in context, there is some repetition of material that has been presented earlier.

Next, the chapter describes the resource conversions performed automatically by Xt. As you may recall from the discussion in Chapter 2, *Introduction to the X Toolkit and Motif*, a value converter is invoked by Xt to convert a resource from the string form specified in resource files to the representation type actually used in the application or widget. For the representation types understood by Xt, simply listing the representation symbol (a constant beginning with XmR, or XtR in standard Xt) in the resource list is enough to make Xt automatically perform the conversion. But if you create a representation type unknown to Xt, you need to write a type converter routine and register it with Xt before the automatic conversion can take place. We discuss both the standard converters and how to write a new one.

Finally, the chapter describes a mechanism Xt provides whereby widgets or applications may have subparts with separate sets of resources. Special routines are provided for setting and getting these resources. The R3 Athena Text widget used subparts to implement replaceable units that provide the data storage and display for text data. This allowed the same central code to edit a disk file or a string. But using subparts is now out of favor; the Athena Text widget and the Motif Text widgets now use objects to accomplish the same modularity (see Chapter 14, *Miscellaneous Toolkit Programming Techniques*).

10.1 Review of Resource Fundamentals

As we've previously discussed, widgets and applications can declare some or all of their variables as resources. Not every variable need be a resource—only those for which values need to be supplied by the user (or for a widget, also by the application programmer) through the Resource Manager. Both applications and widgets may use nonresource variables for internal bookkeeping, or for storing values calculated or otherwise derived from resources.

Resources are defined using an `XtResource` structure, which is declared as follows:

```
typedef struct {
    String resource_name;       /* specify using XmN symbol */
    String resource_class;      /* specify using XmC symbol */
    String resource_type;     /* actual data type of variable */
    Cardinal resource_size;        /* specify using sizeof() */
    Cardinal resource_offset;  /* specify using XtOffsetOf() */
    String default_type; /* will be converted to resrce_type */
    XtPointer default_address;   /* address of default value */
} XtResource, *XtResourceList;
```

For example, Example 10-1 shows three of the resources defined by the Primitive widget:

Example 10-1. Three resources defined by the Motif Primitive widget

```
static XtResource resources[ ] = {
    .
    .
    .

    {
    XmNforeground,   /* Resource name is foreground */
    XmCForeground,   /* Resource class is Foreground */
    XmRPixel,        /* Resource type is Pixel */
    sizeof(Pixel),   /* allocate enough space to hold a Pixel value */
    XtOffsetOf(XmPrimitiveRec,
            primitive.foreground),        /* where in instance strct */
    XmRCallProc,     /* type of default value */
    _XmForegroundColorDefault /* Address of default value, or function */
    },
    .
    .
    .

    {
    XmNhighlightColor,
    XmCHighlightColor,
    XmRPixel,
    sizeof (Pixel),
    XtOffsetOf (XmPrimitiveRec, primitive.highlight_color),
    XmRString,
    "Black"
    },
    .
    .
    .

    {
    XmNtraversalOn,
    XmCTraversalOn,
```

Example 10-1. Three resources defined by the Motif Primitive widget (continued)

```
    XmRBoolean,
    sizeof (Boolean),
    XtOffsetOf (XmPrimitiveRec, primitive.traversal_on),
    XmRImmediate, (XtPointer) True
    },
        .
        .
        .
}
```

The fields in the `XtResource` structure are used as follows:

*   The resource name is usually similar to the name of the variable being set by the resource; by convention, the resource name begins with a lowercase letter, and no underscores are used to separate multiple words. Instead, the initial character of subsequent words is given in uppercase. For example, the resource name for a variable named **border_width** would be **borderWidth**, and the defined constant used to refer to this name would be **XmNborderWidth**.

    As previously described, the name, class, and representation type of resources are specified in the resource list (and elsewhere in Xt code, but not in user database files) using symbolic constants defined in *<Xm/Xm.h>* (or *<X11/StringDefs.h>* in standard Xt), and consist of the resource name, class, or type preceded by the characters **XmN**, **XmC**, or **XmR**, respectively. Use of these constants provides compile-time checking of resource names, classes, and types. Without the constants, a misspelling would not be noticed by the compiler, since resource names, classes, and representation types are simply strings. The misspelling would be considered a real resource at run time. Nothing would happen if it were set from the application, because no widget would actually use it. If, on the other hand, the misspelling were in the widget resource list, the application's setting of the intended resource would have no effect.

    Newly-defined resources may use a name, class, or type constant defined in *<Xm/Xm.h>* (or *<X11/StringDefs.h>* if not using Motif), if an appropriate constant exists. Otherwise, the constant is defined in the widget's public header file, or for application resources, in the application itself, or in the application header file, if any.

*   For many resources, the class name is simply the same as the resource name, except that the **XmC** prefix is used, and, the first letter of the name is conventionally capitalized. For example, the class name constant for the **XmNbackgroundPixel** resource is **XmCBackgroundPixel**. However, when appropriate, a single class can be used for a group of related resources. This allows a single setting in the resource database to control the value of multiple resources.

    For example, a widget can have several elements that use pixel values (i.e., colors) as resource settings: background, foreground, border, block cursor, pointer cursor, and so on. Typically, the background defaults to white and everything else to black. If the **background** resource has a class of **Background**, and all the other pixel resources a class of **Foreground**, then a resource file needs only two lines to change all background pixels to offwhite and all foreground pixels to darkblue:

```
*Background:      offwhite
*Foreground:      darkblue
```

- The representation type of the resource is specified by the **resource_type** field of the resource list, using a symbolic constant prefixed by **XmR**. Table 10-1 lists the correspondence between the **XmR** symbols defined by Xt, and actual C data types or X data types and structures.

Table 10-1. Resource Type Strings

Resource Type	Data type
XmRAcceleratorTable	XtAccelerators
XmRAtom	Atom
XmRBitmap	Pixmap (of depth one)
XmRBoolean	Boolean
XmRBool	Bool
XmRCallback	XtCallbackList
XmRCallProc	*see final bullet below*
XmRCardinal	Cardinal
XmRColor	XColor
XmRColormap	Colormap
XmRCursor	Cursor
XmRDimension	Dimension
XmRDisplay	Display *
XmREnum	XtEnum
XmRFile	FILE *
XmRFloat	float
XmRFont	Font
XmRFontStruct	XFontStruct *
XmRFunction	(*)()
XmRGeometry	String - format as defined by XParseGeometry()
XmRImmediate	*see final bullet below*
XmRInitialState	int
XmRInt	int
XmRLongBoolean	long
XmRObject	Object
XmRPixel	Pixel
XmRPixmap	Pixmap
XmRPointer	XtPointer
XmRPosition	Position
XmRScreen	Screen *
XmRShort	short
XmRString	char *
XmRStringArray	String *
XmRStringTable	char **
XmRTranslationTable	XtTranslations

Table 10-1. Resource Type Strings (continued)

Resource Type	Data type
XmRUnsignedChar	unsigned char
XmRVisual	Visual *
XmRWidget	Widget
XmRWidgetClass	WidgetClass
XmRWidgetList	WidgetList
XmRWindow	Window

As we'll discuss in detail in Section 10.3.5, Xt automatically converts values in the resource database (which always have the type `XmRString`, since resource files are made up entirely of strings) into the target type defined by `resource_type`.

- The `resource_size` field is the size of the resource's actual representation in bytes; it should always be specified as `sizeof(type)` (where `type` is the C-Language type of the resource) so that the compiler fills in the value.

- The `resource_offset` field is the offset in bytes of the field within the widget instance structure or application data structure. The `XtOffsetOf()` macro is normally used to obtain this value. This macro takes as arguments the data structure type, and the name of the structure field to be set by the resource.

- If no value is found in the resource database, the value pointed to by the `default_address` field will be used instead. The type of this default value is given by the `default_type` field. If the `default_type` is different from the `resource_type`, a conversion will be performed automatically in this case as well.

There are two special resource types that can be used only as the `default_type`. `XmRImmediate` means that the value in the `default_address` field is to be used as the actual resource value, rather than as a pointer to it (or in the case of a string, the value is a pointer to a string, rather than a pointer to a pointer to a string). The other special resource type, `XmRCallProc`, is a pointer to a function that will supply the default value at run time. We'll demonstrate the use of these values in Section 10.3.3.

10.2 How Xt's Resource Manager Works

Xt's resource handling is based on the resource manager built into Xlib, but Xt adds a great deal. While using the resource manager from Xlib is cumbersome, from Xt it is easy: to use resources in existing widgets, all you have to do is write the app-defaults file.

Xt's handling of resources occurs in two stages:

1. When the application starts up, with a call to `XtAppInitialize()`, Xt reads the app-defaults file, along with several other resource files, command-line options, and the RESOURCE_MANAGER property stored in the server by the user with *xrdb*. (Any, all, or

none of these may contain data.) It merges all these sources of data into one internal database per screen (per display in R4, per screen in R5) that is used when each widget is created.

2. Whenever you create a widget, the call to **XtVaCreateManagedWidget()** reads the resource database and automatically sets widget resources to the values in the database. In order to explain this stage more clearly, we further divide it into two separate steps in the sections that follow. First, Xt compares the settings in the database to the widget's class and instance hierarchy, to find which settings apply to the widget being created. Second, Xt decides which one of the (possibly conflicting) settings that apply to that widget should actually be used.

If the value of a resource is hardcoded by passing arguments to **XtVaCreateManaged-Widget()** or **XtVaSetValues()**, the hardcoded value overrides the value looked up from the resource database.

To retrieve the value of application resources from the database, an application must make an explicit call to **XtGetApplicationResources()**, as described in Section 3.6.3.

10.2.1 Basic Syntax of Resource Specifications

As discussed in Chapter 2, each entry in the merged database (and in the source databases) is a resource specification/value pair. For application resources, the specification is the application name followed by a period and the resource name. The value to which the resource is to be set follows, after a colon and optional white space.† For example:

```
xterm.scrollBar: on
```

An asterisk can be used as a "wildcard" in place of the application name. For example:

```
*scrollBar: on
```

would set a resource named **scrollBar** to "on" in any application that recognized a resource of that name.

For widget resources, the specification leading up to the resource name may contain a widget instance or class hierarchy (or a mixed instance/class hierarchy). Some examples are shown below. (Remember that instance names begin with a lowercase letter, while class names begin with an uppercase letter.)

specification	*value*	
`xbitmap.rowColumn.quit.labelString:`	Quit	*fully-specified instance hierarchy*
`XBitmap.RowColumn.PushButton.Foreground:`	blue	*fully-specified class hierarchy*
`XBitmap.RowColumn.quit.foreground:`	blue	*mixed class and instance hierarchy*

---

†Note the distinction between what we are calling the resource *specification* (the fully qualified name of the resource, up to the colon), and the *value* (the actual value to which the resource is to be set). We refer to both the specification and the value together as a *resource setting*.

An instance hierarchy describes the instance names of the widget's ancestors. A class hierarchy describes the class names of the widget's ancestors. This portion of the resource specification may consist of a mixture of instance names and class names (each of which describes one generation in the widget's hierarchy), separated by periods or asterisks.

- A period (.) is referred to as a *tight* binding.

- An asterisk (*) is referred to as a *loose* binding.

A tight binding means the left component must be the parent of the right component in the instance hierarchy. A loose binding means the left component must only be an ancestor of the right component; there can be any number of levels in the hierarchy between the two.

Loose bindings are preferable because they stand a better chance of working when the instance hierarchy changes. Tight bindings are rarely necessary at every position in the resource specification, since widget names are usually unique and single widgets can be identified by name. Furthermore, it takes more text to specify the complete instance hierarchy for every widget to be set.

Using loose bindings, the instance, class, or instance/class hierarchy may be abbreviated to the point where specifying the hierarchy as a single asterisk would indicate that any instance or class hierarchy (any widget in the application) will match. However, care should be taken when using loose bindings. One common mistake is to abbreviate a hierarchy too much, so that resource settings that were supposed to apply to only one widget now apply to several. This can be particularly serious (and hard to trace) when the resources being set are translation tables or constraints.

The resource name must be the string that appears in the resource name or resource class field in a resource list. This is the value of the XmN or XmC symbolic constant used in that field of the resource list.

Any entry that is not a resource specification/value pair or does not match any resource for any widget in the application or any application resource is quietly ignored (no warning message is printed). This means that a slight error in the resource specification of an entry will cause that entry to be quietly and completely ignored. It is often difficult to detect such errors.

Lines beginning with an exclamation point (!) are treated as comments. Some people have been using # instead, since it is currently supported in MIT's sample implementation of Xt. But # is not mandated in the Xt specification and therefore may be eliminated in future sample implementations from MIT or in a vendor's implementation. You are advised to use the exclamation point. (Even in the MIT implementation, # elicits warning messages from *xrdb*.)

10.2.2 Wildcarding Resource Component Names

R5 (and later) resource databases allow the character ? to be used to wildcard a single component (name or class) in a resource specification. Thus the specification:

```
xmail.?.?.Background: antique white
```

sets the background color for all widgets (and only those widgets) that are grandchildren of the top-level shell of the application `xmail`. And the specification:

```
xmail.?.?*Background: brick red
```

sets the background color of the grandchildren of the shell and all of their descendants. It does not set the background color for the child of the top-level shell or for any popup shells. These kinds of specifications simply cannot be done without the ? wildcard; sometimes the * wildcard does not provide the necessary fine-grained control. To set the background of all the grandchildren of an application shell widget without the ? wildcard, it would be necessary to specify the background for each grandchild individually.

There is one obvious restriction on the use of the ? wildcard: it cannot be used as the final component in a resource specification—you can wildcard widget names, but not the resource name itself. Also, remember that the wildcard ? (like the wildcard *) means a different thing in a resource file than it does on a UNIX command line.

The ? wildcard is convenient in cases like those above, but it has more subtle uses that have to do with its precedence with respect to the * wildcard, as discussed later. First, note the important distinctions between the ? and the * wildcards: a ? wildcards a single component name or class and falls between two periods (unless it is the first component in a specification), while the * indicates a "loose binding" (in the terminology of the resource manager) and falls between two component names or classes. A ? does not specify the name or class of a resource component, but does at least specify the existence of a component. The * on the other hand only specifies that zero or more components have been omitted from the resource.

10.2.3 Merging of Resource Files

`XtAppInitialize()` constructs the resource database by consulting the following sources of resource settings, in the order shown in the list below. The effect is that if there is a specification that applies to a particular resource of a particular widget instance in more than one of these locations, and these specifications are of equal precedence, then the first one in this list is the one used (the previous edition of this book presented this list in the reverse order). The unfamiliar topics touched upon in this list are discussed in detail in the following sections.

The list shows the R5 merging of files. This has changed since R4, but the result is the same accept as affected by the new `customization` resource or by the new screen-dependent resources. All filenames and environment variables are for a POSIX-based system.

1. If the application has defined any command-line options by passing an options table to `XtAppInitialize()`, values from the command line will override those specified by any other resource settings.

2. Any values specified on the command line with the *–xrm* option will be loaded for that instance of the program.

3. A temporary database is created by parsing the resources contained in the `RESOURCE_MANAGER` property on the root window of the default screen of the display. If this property does not exist, the contents of the file $HOME/.*Xdefaults* are used instead. The contents of the property or file are assumed to be entirely in the X Portable Character Set so that the database can be correctly parsed before the application's locale has been set. (See Volume One, *Xlib Programming Manual*, Third Edition, for information about locale and the X Portable Character Set.)

4. If a language procedure has been set with `XtSetLanguageProc()` (see Chapter 14, for more information on the language procedure and the internationalization of Xt programs), the application command line is scanned (but not actually parsed into a database) for the **–xnlLanguage** option or an **–xrm** option that specifies the **xnlLanguage** resource. (See Section 10.2.6 for a discussion of the language string.) Because the command line is scanned before the locale has been set, the value of this resource must be in the X Portable Character Set. If neither command-line option is found, the temporary database is queried for the value of the **xnlLanguage** resource. The value of this resource, or the empty string if it is not found, is passed to the registered language procedure which sets the locale and returns its name. The return value of the language procedure is associated with the display for future use (for example, by `XtResolve-Pathname()`). All future resource specifications will be parsed in the encoding of this locale, and resource databases will have the locale associated with them. `XrmLocale-OfDatabase()` will return the name of the locale.

5. The application command line is parsed, and the resulting resource specifications are stored in a newly created database. This database will be augmented with resources from a number of sources and will become the screen resource database.

6. If a language procedure has not been set, the value of the **xnlLanguage** resource is looked up in the screen database, the temporary database, and the environment variable `LANG`. This language string (or the empty string) is associated with the display for future use.

7. If the `XENVIRONMENT` environment variable is defined, the resource file it points to is merged into the screen database with `XrmCombineFileDatabase()`; the new resources do not override existing resource values in the database. If the environment variable does not exist, the file $HOME/.*Xdefaults-hostname* is used, if it exists. The difference between this and XAPPLRESDIR below is that this is a complete path name including the file name.

8. The per-screen specifications stored in the SCREEN_RESOURCES property are merged into the database. The new resources do not override existing values in the database. The user can set the SCREEN_RESOURCES property using *xrdb*. This is intended to be the method whereby the user specifies screen-wide resources (to apply to all clients no matter which system they are running on).

9. The temporary database which was created in step 1, and which contains the per-server RESOURCE_MANAGER resources is merged into the screen database. The resources in the temporary database do not override the resources in the screen database. The user can set the RESOURCE_MANAGER property using *xrdb*. This is intended to be the method whereby the user specifies server-wide resources (to apply to all clients no matter which system they are running on).

10. The screen database being built is associated with the display with a call to **XrmSetDatabase()**, and the old value of the "display database" is saved so that it can later be restored. The user's application specific app-defaults file is searched for, using **XtResolvePathname()** with the path specified by the **XUSERFILESEARCHPATH** environment variable if it exists. If this environment variable does not exist, a default path is used relative to the user's home directory and relative to the value of the **XAPPLRESDIR** environment variable, if that exists. **XtResolvePathname()** uses **XrmGetDatabase()** to find the current database of the display (which is the screen database created up to this step), and uses that database to look up the value of the **customization** resource for substitution into the path. If a resource file is found in one of these paths, the resource specifications in it are merged into the screen database using **XrmCombineFileDatabase()**. The new resources do not override the resources already in the database.

11. The application's app-defaults file is located using **XtResolvePathname()** and the path specified in **XFILESEARCHPATH**, or a default path if that environment variable does not exist. As above, **XtResolvePathname()** looks up the value of the **customization** resource in the screen database constructed so far. The resources from the app-defaults file are merged into the screen database using **XrmCombineFileDatabase()**, and do not override resource values already there. The original "database of the display," which had been stored away in step 8 above, is restored using **XrmSetDatabase()**.

12. If no app-defaults file is located in step 9 and the application has registered fallback resources with **XtAppSetFallbackResources()**, then those fallback resources are merged into the screen database without overriding the values already there.

The order in which these various sources are loaded, as shown in the list above, is the order of their priority. That is, those that are loaded first override those loaded later if both specifications have the same precedence and affect the same widget or widgets.

If a resource value is hardcoded in the arguments of the call to create a widget, that value takes precedence over any value for that resource in the resource database. If a widget is created and no setting exists in the database for a particular resource, the value pointed to by the **default_address** field of the resource list in the widget is used. This is also true for application resources and subresources.

Figure 10-1 shows where Xt looks for resource files and in what order, on most UNIX-based systems. The exact directories are operating system and implementation dependent. Remember that the app-defaults file is written by the application writer, and all the rest of the resource sources are for the user. In practice, few users use more than one or two of these sources of resource settings.

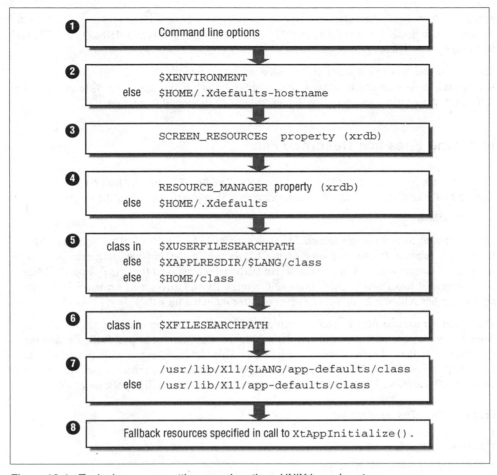

Figure 10-1. *Typical resource setting search path on UNIX-based systems*

10.2.4 Syntax of Environment Variables

The environment variables listed above that describe paths allow a special syntax involving % (the percent symbol) to substitute various elements into the path.

For example, the XFILESEARCHPATH environment variable is a colon separated path. Under Sun OpenWindows, the *openwin* script appends the string "/usr/openwin/lib/%T/%N%S" to the XFILESEARCHPATH variable. The effect is that app-defaults files are found in the directory */usr/openwin/lib/app-defaults*.

`XtDisplayInitialize()` reads the environment variables, makes the % syntaxes into paths with `XtResolvePathname()`, and uses the `XtFindFile()` to actually find the files. %T becomes the *type* arg of XtResolvePathname(), %S becomes the *suffix* arg, and %N is the *filename* arg. Type is a category of files, such as app-defaults, help or bitmap. Suffix is file suffix such as .txt. So in your example, %T is app-defaults, and %N%S is the complete filename.

This syntax can get much more complicated when it includes %l, %L, %t, and %c, all of which have to do with internationalization, and %C, which is for specifying different files for different types of displays (usually color and mono), as described in Section 10.2.11.

10.2.5 Including Files in a Resource File

The Xrm functions that read resources from files, `XrmGetFileDatabase()` and `Xrm-CombineFileDatabase()` (the latter new in R5), recognize a line of the form:

```
#include "filename"
```

as a command to include the named file at that point. The directory of the included file is interpreted relative to the directory of the file in which the include statement occurred. Included files may themselves contain `#include` directives, and there is no specified limit to the depth of this nesting. Note that the C syntax `#include <filename>` is not supported; neither Xlib nor Xt defines a search path for included files.

The ability to include files is useful when producing a special app-defaults file for use on a color screen, for example, you can simply include the monochrome app-defaults file and then set or override the color resources as you desire. This technique is particularly useful when producing app-defaults files for use with the customization resource described below. Example 10-2 shows a hypothetical color resource file for the "xmail" application.

Example 10-2. The resource file

```
! include the basic (monochrome) defaults
#include "XMail"

! and augment them with color
*Background: tan
*Foreground: navy blue
*Command*Foreground: red
*to*Background: grey
*subject*Background: grey
```

Do not confuse this file inclusion syntax with the `#include`, `#ifdef`, etc. syntax provided by the program *xrdb*. That program invokes the C preprocessor to provide C include, macro, and conditional processing. The include functionality described here is provided directly by Xlib.

10.2.6 The Language String

Xt's resource handling is designed to support resource files in different languages. The goal is to have all the language dependencies of an application in files, so that just by selecting a different set of resource files and localization files at run time, the application will operate correctly in another language.†

The language to use is selected with a *language string*, which is an application resource defined by Xt: "xnlLanguage" (no symbol **XmNxnlLanguage** is defined for it). The default language string is **NULL**, which makes Xt operate in English, with all files in the locations used prior to when the internationalization features were added. But when the **xnl-Language* resource, or the LANG environment variable, is set to a language name such as "spanish," Xt looks first in certain directories for the Spanish app-defaults and user defaults files, before defaulting to the normal app-defaults or user defaults directories.

Note that all app-defaults and user defaults files have the same name (the class name of the application); only the directory in which they are first examined for changes according to the language string. Therefore it is possible to have all the files for all the languages installed on a system at the same time.

The search path for resource files is implementation dependent, but it is always begins with a language string-based directory. Each app-defaults file on UNIX-based systems is normally in a directory */usr/lib/X11/$LANG/app-defaults*. When the user sets LANG to "spanish," for example, Xt looks for an app-defaults file first in */usr/lib/X11/spanish/app-defaults*.

The path searched for user defaults files (which have the same name as the app-defaults file) is more complicated. If the XUSERFILESEARCHPATH environment variable is defined, Xt follows that path. If it is not defined but the XAPPLRESDIR environment variable is defined, Xt will look in $XAPPLRESDIR/LANG first before looking in $XAPPLRESDIR. If XAPPLRESDIR is not defined either, Xt looks in $HOME/LANG and then $HOME.

The remaining resource setting sources are not affected by the language string. As described in the previous section, the next source of resource settings merged is the RESOURCE_MANAGER property set with *xrdb*, or if not set, *.Xdefaults*, followed by the file specified by the XENVIRONMENT environment variable, or if not set, the *.Xdefaults-host* file.

For a summary of the path of resource files searched by Xt, see Figure 10-1.

Most western languages other than English use characters with accents or other marks. These are non-ASCII characters, in the second half of the ISO Latin-1 character set. Most fonts now in the X distribution provide glyphs (bitmaps) for these characters. Therefore, all you have to do is specify these characters in your app-defaults file in the directory named for the desired language. However, most standard English keyboards do not provide a way to type non-ASCII characters (and some computers can't store them). Because of this, the resource file format has been augmented to provide a special syntax for specifying non-ASCII characters. Each character is specified using a backslash followed by a three-character octal number that represents the character. You can use *xfd* to determine the proper octal number

---

†See the discussion of internationalization in Chapters 10 and 11 of Volume One, *Xlib Programming Manual*, Third Edition.

to use. Just click on the desired character to have its index displayed. This index is the number you enter in the app-defaults file. For example, Example 10-3 shows a Spanish app-defaults for *xhello*.

Example 10-3. An app-defaults file for the Spanish language

```
*hello.fontList:      *courier-bold*18*iso8859-1
*hello.labelString:   \161Hola, Mundo!
```

The sequence \161 produces the inverted exclamation point that begins the Spanish exclamatory sentence. It is important to know for sure that the font you choose has the desired glyphs. Note that `iso8859-1` means ISO Latin-1, so that if you specify it in your font name, you are guaranteed to have all ISO-Latin-1 characters. Many of the fonts in the *misc* directory (such as the standard terminal fonts) do not include these characters. Also note that strings such as \161 may not work on systems that can only handle seven bit (ASCII) characters (they ignore the eighth bit).

10.2.7 Screen-specific Resource Strings and Databases

The (pre-R5) function, `XResourceManagerString()`, returns the contents of the RE-SOURCE_MANAGER property on the root window of the default screen of the display. This property contains the user's resource customizations in string form, and is usually set with the program `xrdb`. It is read by `XtDisplayInitialize()` when creating the resource database to be used by an application. Until R5 this single RESOURCE_MANAGER property contained resources for all screens of a display, and there was no way for a user to specify different resources for different screens (for example, color vs. monochrome).

In R5, xrdb can set resources in the SCREEN_RESOURCES property on the root window of each screen of a display. `XtDisplayInitialize()` reads the SCREEN_RESOURCES specifications and uses them to override the screen-independent RESOURCE_MANAGER specifications. The resource database that is created in this way is the database of the screen, rather than the database of the display. If the same application is executed on different screens of a display, or if a single application creates shell widgets on more than one screen of a display, a resource database will be created for each screen, and the application instances or shell widgets will find resources in them that are appropriate for that screen.

Recall that `XtDisplayInitialize()` creates databases using resources from a number of sources other than these window properties, so in many cases resource databases on different screens will contain substantially the same values. Note, however, that the SCREEN_RE-SOURCES property can be used to set the `customization` resource and thereby cause different app-defaults files to be merged into different screen databases. Screen-specific resource databases are created by Xt only as needed, so an application running exclusively on the default screen of a two-screen system will not have the overhead of maintaining two per-screen databases.

Two new functions support screen-dependent resources and resource databases. The contents of the SCREEN_RESOURCES property on the root window of a screen are returned by the function `XScreenResourceString()`. The database of a screen may be obtained with the function `XtScreenDatabase()`. The function `XtDatabase()`, which prior to R5 returned the (single) database of the display, is now specified to return the database of the default screen of the display.

The client **xrdb** has been rewritten for R5 to handle the new screen-specific properties. Any load, merge, or query operation can now be performed on the global RESOURCE_MANAGER property, a specific screen property, all screen properties, or all screen properties plus the global property. This last option is the default and "does the right thing"—the input file is processed through the C preprocessor once for each screen, and resource specifications that would appear in all of the per-screen properties are placed in the global property and removed from the screen-specific properties. With this new system, a defaults file which uses #ifdef COLOR to separate color from monochrome resource specifications can be used to correctly set the values of the screen-dependent and screen-independent properties for a two-screen monochrome-and-color display. An application can then be run on either screen and find the correct user defaults for that screen. Example 10-4 shows a user default file that takes advantage of the new **xrdb** functionality and the **customization** resource to set different defaults on color and monochrome screens.

Example 10-4. A user defaults file for color and monochrome screens

```
! generic, non-color resources
*Font: -*-courier-medium-r-*-*-*-180-75-75-*-*-iso8859-1
xclock.geometry: -0+0

#ifdef COLOR
! resources for color screens here
*Background: grey
*Foreground: navy blue
XTerm*Foreground: maroon
#else
! resources for monochrome screens here
XTerm*reverseVideo: true
#endif

! set the customization resource to get
! special app-defaults, if they exist.
#ifdef COLOR
*customization: -color
#else
*customization: -mono
#endif
```

When an Xt application creates a shell widget with **XtAppCreateShell()**, the value of the **XtNscreen** resource is used to determine what screen the shell should be created on and which screen's resource database should be used to look up the widget's resources. But the value of the **XtNscreen** resource must be looked up itself. The Xt specification resolves this circular problem by stating that the value of the **XtNscreen** resource is looked up first in the argument list passed to **XtAppCreateShell()**, and then in the resource database of the default screen of the display. If it is found, then all further resources are looked up in the resource database for that particular screen. If the **XtNscreen** is not found, then the widget is created on the default screen, using the database for that screen.

10.2.8 Fallback Resources

As you may recall from Chapters 2, 3, and 4, `XtAppInitialize()` has an argument in which you can specify fallback resources, which we didn't use. Many applications won't operate properly without their app-defaults file. *Fallback resources* are a defense in case the user doesn't install the app-defaults file, or if something happens to prevent access to it. They provide minimal application-specific resource settings that either allow the application to run safely or instruct the user to install the app-defaults file properly.

If your app-defaults file is small, you can (and should) put the whole app-defaults file in the fallback resources. However, if your app-defaults is large, it probably makes more sense just to set one or more labels in the application to tell the user that the app-defaults file is not installed properly or cannot be accessed. Remember that the fallback resources are used only if the app-defaults file is not found. Fallback resources are a NULL-terminated list of strings, each containing a resource setting. Example 10-5 shows how they are declared and then passed to `XtVaAppInitialize()`.

Example 10-5. Setting fallback resources in XtAppInitialize

```
main(argc, argv)
int argc;
char **argv;
{
    XtAppContext app_context;
    Widget topLevel, hello;

    static String fallback_resources[ ] = {
        "*hello.labelString: App-defaults file not installed or not\
            accessible.",
        "*hello.fontList: *courier-bold*18*iso8859-1",
        NULL,          /* Must be NULL terminated */
    };

      XtSetLanguageProc(NULL, (XtLanguageProc)NULL, NULL);

    topLevel = XtVaAppInitialize(
            &app_context,       /* Application context */
            "NoFile",           /* Application class */
            NULL, 0,            /* command-line option list */
            &argc, argv,        /* command line args */
            fallback_resources, /* for missing app-defaults file */
            NULL);              /* terminate varargs list */

    .
    .
    .
}
```

Note that there is also a separate function, `XtAppSetFallbackResources()`, that can be used to set the fallback resources separately from the `XtAppInitialize()` call.

10.2.9 Resource Matching Algorithm

When a widget is created, its expanded instance hierarchy and class hierarchy together with
its resource names and classes are compared to each entry in the merged resource database.
To demonstrate how matches are made, we'll look at a sample widget hierarchy and follow
the process of finding the value for one resource of one widget from the merged resource database. Figure 10-2 shows the widget instance hierarchy for the quit widget in the
xrowcolumn application shown in Chapter 3, *More Techniques for Using Widgets*. The figure
also shows the corresponding fully specified instance and class names for the quit widget.
This section describes how this widget's resources are set by the resource manager.†

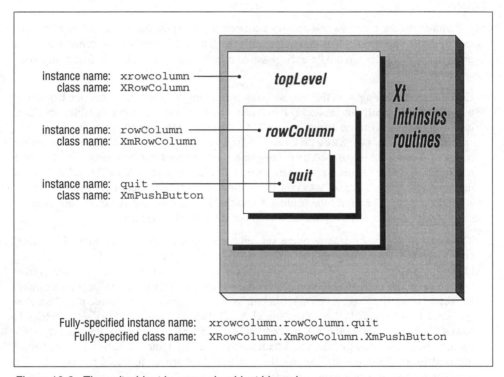

Figure 10-2. The quit widget in a sample widget hierarchy

We know that quit is a XmPushButton class widget and therefore that Xt will be searching the resource database for each resource in XmPushButton's resource list (and the resources in its superclasses' resource lists). It will search for one resource at a time. To demonstrate the conflicts that can occur, we'll use the Core resource XmNbackground, which is
common to all widgets. It will appear in the resource database as background.

---

†The actual algorithm used by Xt differs slightly from that described here, because there are shortcuts that the resource manager takes that are hard to follow even if you have the source code. However, the algorithm described
here gives the same result, with more clarity.

The matching process can be thought of as a process of elimination. Let's assume the merged resource database is as shown in Example 10-6.

Example 10-6. A sample merged resource database

```
*rowColumn.background:                 blue      (entry 1)
*background:                           red       (entry 2)
*quit.background:                      green     (entry 3)
*quit.labelString:                     Quit      (entry 4)
*XmPushButton.background:              yellow    (entry 5)
*XmRowColumn.XmPushButton.background:  violet    (entry 6)
*rowColumn*background:                 pink      (entry 7)
xrowcolumn.background:                 orange    (entry 8)
*?.background:                         purple    (entry 9)
```

Only resource database entries that specify **background** as the last element before the colon are possible matches. That eliminates entry 4. The fully specified instance and class hierarchies are then compared with each possible match, beginning with the first component in each hierarchy.

1. Every entry beginning with the asterisk wildcard binding (*) as well as the one beginning with **xrowcolumn**, matches **xrowcolumn**, the first component of the fully specified instance name. All those beginning with * also match the first component of the fully specified class name, **XRowColumn**. Since entry 8 actually contains the string **xrowcolumn**, the **xrowcolumn** component is removed for comparison at the next level. Entry 8 now begins with **.background**. Similarly, the R5 ? wildcard in Entry 9 matches any single instance or class in the hierarchy, so it matches **xrowcolumn** or **XRowColumn**. Therefore, the leading * and the ? in Entry 9 are removed for comparison at the next level. Entry 9 also now begins with **.background**.

2. The first component of each resource specification (after removal of previously matched components) is now compared to the second element in the widget's class and instance hierarchies. This should be either **rowColumn** or **XmRowColumn**. All the entries that begin with * still match, because * matches any number of levels in the hierarchy. However, there is no second element in entries 8 and 9, since the resource name **background** is not counted. Therefore, entries 8 and 9 are eliminated. Also, since entries 1, 6, and 7 actually contain the strings **rowColumn** or **XmRowColumn**, the leading asterisk and the strings **rowColumn** and **XmRowColumn** are removed before comparison of the next level. Example 10-7 shows the resource database as it would appear after the components and entries eliminated so far.

Example 10-7. Sample resource database with eliminated entries and components

```
.background:                  blue      (entry 1)
*background:                   red       (entry 2)
*quit.background:              green     (entry 3)
*XmPushButton.background:      yellow    (entry 5)
.XmPushButton.background:      violet    (entry 6)
*background:                   pink      (entry 7)
```

Note that entries 2 and 7 are now duplicates except for the resource value. The resource manager actually eliminates one of these entries based upon the levels at which each entry matched, whether the instance name or class name matched, whether a tight or loose binding was used, and which had more elements specified. These are the precedence rules to be described in the next section. In order to keep the example clearer, we'll pretend that the resource manager keeps the information necessary to apply all the precedence rules, and keeps all the entries, until the end.

3. Now the contents of the resource database are compared to the third component in the widget's instance and class hierarchies, **quit** and **XmPushButton**. As usual, anything beginning with an asterisk or anything beginning with a period (.) followed by either the expected class or instance name is a match. This matches all but entry 1, which is eliminated.

   Before going on to the next comparison, any components that matched specifically (a . or * followed by either string) are removed, which results in the resource database shown in Example 10-8.

Example 10-8. Resource database after final elimination of entries and components

```
*background:    red         (entry 2)
.background:    green       (entry 3)
.background:    yellow      (entry 5)
.background:    violet      (entry 6)
*background:    pink        (entry 7)
```

Now you see that we are left with only the resource names and tight or loose bindings. The matching process is finished, and the precedence analysis begins. The next section describes the precedence rules and then finishes this example to determine the priority of the finalist entries.

10.2.10 Resource Precedence Rules

Because of the way merging works, no two resource specifications in the merged resource database will be alike. (Remember that we are using the term *specification* for the part of the resource setting up to and including the colon.) For example, the merged database could never contain both of the following:

```
XBitmap*rowColumn*background: green
XBitmap*rowColumn*background: red
```

because the merging process would remove the setting that appeared earlier in the list of database sources (or that appeared later in a single file).

However, the database could contain two or more resource settings that apply to the same resource of the same widget, because of differences in the widget class or instance hierarchy or the bindings. For example, the database could contain:

```
XBitmap*rowColumn*background: green
XBitmap*quit.background: red
```

If the **quit** button is a child of **rowColumn**, both settings apply to the **quit** button's background.

The resource manager provides a set of rules that govern which setting takes precedence in cases where there are two settings for the same resource of the same widget. Here are the three rules:

1. A resource that matches the current component by name, by class, or with the **?** wildcard takes precedence over an resource that omits the current component by using a *****.

```
XBitmap*Form.quit.background:          and
XBitmap*Form.Command.background:       and
XBitmap*Form.?.background:             take precedence over
XBitmap*Form*background:
```

2. A resource that matches the current component by name takes precedence over a resource that matches it by class, and both take precedence over a resource that matches it with the **?** wildcard.

```
*quit.background:          takes precedence over
*Command.background:       takes precedence over
*?.background:
```

3. A resource in which the current component is preceded by a dot (**.**) takes precedence over a resource in which the current component is preceded by a *****.

```
*box.background:           takes precedence over
*box*background:
```

Situations where both rule 2 and rule 3 apply often cause confusion. In these cases, remember that rule 2 takes precedence since it occurs earlier in the list above. Here is an example:

```
*box*background:           takes precedence over
*box.Background:
```

To understand the application of these rules, let's return to our extended example. In the course of developing that example, we eliminated information about the level at which components occurred. However, the actual process of matching applies the precedence rules at each step. As a result, let's start again with the original appearance of the entries that pass the matching test. The remaining five as they appeared originally are shown in Example 10-9.

Example 10-9. Resource database finalists in original form

```
*background:                            red       (entry 2)
*quit.background:                       green     (entry 3)
*XmPushButton.background:               yellow    (entry 5)
*XmRowColumn.XmPushButton.background:   violet    (entry 6)
*rowColumn*background:                  pink      (entry 7)
```

From here on, we will determine not only which one of these five will take effect, but the actual precedence of the five. In other words, once the one with highest precedence is determined, we'll see which would take effect if that one was commented out, and so on.

The precedence rules are applied in order to determine the order of the finalist entries.

1. Rule 1 specifies that a specification that contains higher components in the instance or class hierarchy takes precedence over one that contains only lower ones. The highest components that appear in our example are rowColumn and XmRowColumn in entries 6 and 7. Therefore, these two have higher priority than any others.

2. To choose between these two, we continue to Rule 2. Instance names (rowColumn) take precedence over class names (XmRowColumn). Therefore, entry 7 has the highest precedence, followed by entry 6. Note that the precedence comparison of two finalists proceeds in the same manner as the original matching—from left to right in the entry, one component at a time.

3. To determine the precedence of the remaining three entries, 2, 3, and 5, we begin again with Rule 1. Rule 1 indicates that entry 2 is of lower priority than entries 3 and 5 because entry 2 has only an asterisk to specify widget, while in the same position entries 3 and 5 have instance (quit) and class (XmPushButton) names. Rule 2 specifies that the instance name quit takes precedence over the class name XmPushButton, and therefore entry 3 has higher priority than entry 5. Rule 3 does not apply, because no two entries are identical except for binding.

Therefore, the final precedence is as shown here:

```
1.   *rowColumn*background:                    pink      (entry 7)
2.   *XmRowColumn.XmPushButton.background:     violet    (entry 6)
3.   *quit.background:                         green     (entry 3)
4.   *XmPushButton.background:                 yellow    (entry 5)
5.   *background:                              red       (entry 2)
```

People get used to the fact that they can set the resources of all the children of rowColumn with something like entry 7, but then are shocked to find that nothing happens when they attempt to override entry 7 with entry 3—entry 3 seems more specific to them. Even the following entry (using a class name) takes precedence over entry 3 because the rule about being higher in the widget hierarchy carries more weight than the rule that instance names take precedence over class names:

```
*XmRowColumn*background:     pink          (entry 7)
```

Finally, a note about creating app-defaults files. Consider what happens when users specify a line like *Background: grey in their personal resource files. They would like to set the background of all widgets in all applications to grey, but if the app-defaults file for the application "xmail" has a specification of the form *Dialog*Background: peach, the background of the dialog boxes in the xmail application will be peach-colored, because this second specification is more specific. So if they really don't like those peach dialog boxes, (pre-R5) users will have to add a line like XMail*Background: grey to their personal resource files, and will have to add similar lines for any other applications that specify colors like "xmail" does. The reason this line works is rule 1 above: at the first level of the resource specification, "XMail" is a closer match than *.

This brings us to the specific reason that the **?** wildcard was introduced in R5: any resource specification that "specifies" an application name with a **?** takes precedence over a specification that omits the application name with a *****, no matter how specific the *rest* of that specification is. So in R5, the frustrated users mentioned above could add the single line:

```
?*Background: grey
```

to their personal resource files and achieve the desired result. The sequence **?*** is odd-looking, but correct. The **?** replaces a component name, and the ***** is resource binding, like a dot (**.**).

The solution described above relies, of course, on the assumption that no app-defaults files will specify an application name in a more specific way than the user's **?**. If the "xmail" app-defaults file contained one of the following lines:

```
xmail*Dialog*Background: peach
XMail*Background: maroon
```

then the user would be forced to explicitly override them, and the **?** wildcard would not help. To allow for easy customization, programmers should write app-defaults files that do not use the name or class of the application, except in certain critical resources that the user should not be able to trivially or accidentally override. The standard R5 clients have app-defaults files written in this way.

The moral of this story is that you should choose the bindings in your resource file to reflect how easy (or difficult) you want to make it for users to override your specifications. (But of course, even a specification containing only tight bindings can still be overridden by a user specification that also includes all tight bindings.)

Be careful with tight bindings, however. Since there are no messages telling you which resource specifications are actually being used, you can be tricked into thinking that you have set resources that you actually haven't.

A useful tool for figuring out the priority of resource files is the *appres* utility. You specify the class name of the application on the command line, and *appres* shows you what resource settings that application will see when run. Note, however, that this does not tell you how these resource settings will actually apply to the widgets in the application, since *appres* has no knowledge of the widget instance hierarchy in your application.

Another tactic in tracing resource settings is to build a routine into your application that gets and prints all the critical resources of a widget. Using **XtGetResourceList()** you can get the list of resources supported by a widget class. Then you can query each of those resources and print most of them out. Remember that certain resources are compiled into internal forms, so you can't print out translation tables, accelerator tables, or callback lists. It may also be difficult to interpret other values, since many of them will have already been converted from the string form in the resource file into the most convenient internal form. For example, colors will have been changed from strings such as "red" into a pixel value (a number which could change each time the application is run).

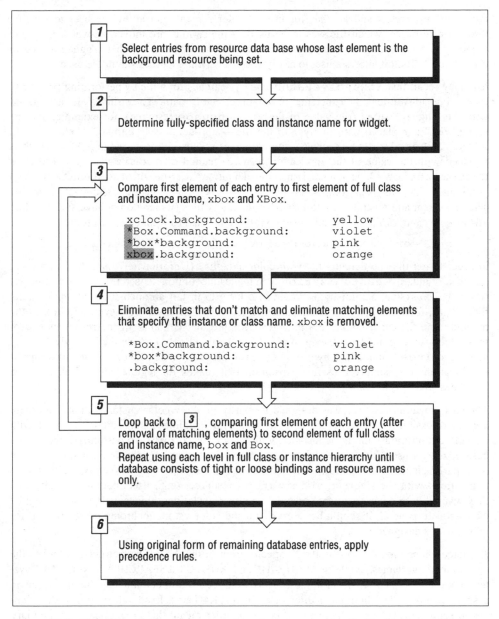

Figure 10-3. Steps in matching resource entries for one resource of widget being created

10.2.11 Customized Resource Files

In X11R4, it was possible to install an application with multiple app-defaults files so that users could use the **xnlLanguage** resource to specify what language the application should display itself in. But it was not possible to install one app-defaults file for use on monochrome screens and another for use on color screens and allow the user to specify, through a resource, which file was to be used. Applications are moved between color and monochrome environments far more often than they are ported to other languages, and in X11R5 the X Toolkit allows a user to easily specify which resources should be used.

You may recall that `XtResolvePathname()` searches for a file by performing `printf`-type string substitutions on a specified or default directory path. The string "%L" is replaced with the language string (the value of the `xnlLanguage` resource), for example, and the string "%T" is replaced with the type of the file—"app-defaults," "bitmap," "help," etc. In X11R5, `XtResolvePathname()` supports a new substitution variable "%C," which is replaced with the value of the application resource named `customization` and of class `Customization`. It is intended that the default or user-provided XFILESEARCHPATH will contain filename path components of the form %N%C%S—name, customization, suffix. Then a system administrator could install app-defaults files (which do not have suffixes) like *XMail-color* and *XMail-mono* and a user could run the `xmail` application as follows:

```
xmail -xrm "*customization: -color" &
```

in order to get the app-defaults file with color defaults. (Unfortunately, X11R5 Xt does not define a standard `-customization` command-line option to set the value of this resource.) The system administrator would also have to install an uncustomized app-defaults file, *XMail*, for use when no customization is set. This file could be a symbolic link to the monochrome file, or it could be a base resource file that contains all the resources except those that affect color. Then the customized files could simply include the base file with the new `#include` feature. The hyphen in the customization name (-color) is not part of the Xt specification; it is simply a useful convention that makes for legible customized resource filenames (like *XMail-color*).

The customization resource was designed primarily to allow color customizations, but there are other possibilities as well: app-defaults files with customized translations that work with a single-button mouse might be installed with a `-single-button` customization, or files customized for use within a specific group or department of an organization could be selected by department name. Note, however, that because there is no way to specify multiple customizations with the single `customization` resource, (e.g., users couldn't specify that they wanted both color resources and single button translations) this technique should not be overused. In general, it should be reserved for the color vs. monochrome customization for which it was designed.

A related change in X11R5 is to the Xt specification of the default paths to be used when the environment variables, XFILESEARCHPATH and XUSERFILESEARCHPATH (on UNIX systems), are not defined. In X11R4, these paths were required to contain specific directories in a specific order. The individual directories in X11R4 had a fixed substitution order: language (optionally), type, name, and suffix. This order meant that an application's auxiliary files (app-default, bitmaps, help text, etc.) had to be installed in scattered locations throughout a file system. In X11R5, the default paths still have a required number of entries in a specified order, but the order in which substitutions appear in these path entries is no longer specified. This means that vendors may choose default paths for their implementations that allow auxiliary files to be installed in a single directory. The MIT implementation retains the substitution order of X11R4, except for the insertion of the "%C" customization substitution between the name and suffix substitutions. When using a vendor-supplied X11R5, be sure to check your documentation for the default file search path. When writing a *Makefile* or *Imakefile* to distribute with an application, bear in mind that app-defaults files, bitmap files, help files, and so on may not be installed in the "usual" places on all systems.

10.2.12 The XtNbaseTranslations Resource

Until R5, there was an annoying problem with specifying translation tables as resources. Because a translation table is a multi-line resource, it is useful to be able to override or add individual lines to the table rather than always replace the table. Application developers often do this in their application's app-defaults file, using the **#override** or **#augment** directive as part of the **XtNtranslations** resource value. Sometimes, though, users would also like to add or override individual translations, but if they specify a value for the **XtNtranslations** resource in a personal resource file, it will take precedence over the resource in the application's app-defaults file, and the application's customizations will be lost from the database before the widget ever sees them. So until R5, users had to duplicate the application's translation settings in its app-defaults file and then modify their copy.

In R5, there is a new resource, **XtNbaseTranslations**, that can be used by an application developer to specify a base set of translations that will be correctly overridden, augmented, or replaced by the value of the **XtNtranslations** resource. Note that this is an **Xrm** resource, but is not a widget resource in the usual Xt sense of the word (the Xt specification uses the term "pseudo-resource")—it does not correspond to an instance field in **Core** or any other widget class, and it cannot be set with **XtSetValues()** or queried with **XtGetValues()**. The value of the **translations** field of the Core widget is handled specially by the Xt resource management code. The final value for a widget's translations are obtained as follows:

1. The default value of a widget instance's translations are obtained from the **Core** widget class field **tm_table**. These translations are specified by the widget writer.

2. When a widget is initialized, the Intrinsics' resource management code looks up the value of the **XtNbaseTranslations** resource for that widget, and if it exists, uses the translations it specifies to replace, override, or augment the widget's default translations. These translations are intended to be specified exclusively by the application developer in the application's app-defaults file.

3. Finally, the value of the **XtNtranslations** resource is looked up for the widget, and if it exists the value is used to replace, override, or augment the widget's translations (which may have once already been replaced, overridden, or augmented). These translations are intended to be specified by the end user of the application.

For maximum flexibility to the user, all R5 applications should specify translations in a resource file using the **XtNbaseTranslations** resource rather than with **XtNtranslations**. If the same resource file is to be used by applications compiled under both the R5 and R4 versions of the Intrinsics, then the resource file should specify the application's translations as the value of both resources. Under R4, the **XtNbaseTranslations** resource will be ignored, and under R5, any value of the **Xt-**

`Ntranslations` resource specified by the user will override the value specified in the application's app-defaults file.

10.3 Type Conversion

You already know that Xt is capable of converting resource values from the string representation specified in resource files to the actual type required in code. In fact, Xt does so automatically if the resource list is properly written. This section describes this process in more detail, and tells you how to create converters for converting your own data types.

In R4, a new set of interfaces for type converters was introduced. The new interfaces support display-specific conversions and better control of converted-value caching. This section describes these new interfaces, but does not describe the older ones. Be aware that many existing widgets and applications still use the older interfaces.

10.3.1 Conversions from XmRString

The primary purpose of converters is to allow resource files to contain string values for non-string program variables. (They are also used internally to convert default values that cannot be specified easily in the desired data type.) Secondly, converters confine the details of data conversion to a single routine that is registered with Xt. This is a big benefit because users of the converted types need not know the details of how the conversion takes place, or the internal definition of the target type.

Xt provides converters from `XmRString` to the representation types listed in Table 10-2. You can use these representation types as target types in resource lists in applications or widgets, without having to register them, if you want the user to be able to specify the resource in a resource file. Note that if you are using standard Xt, the various representation types begin with `XtR` rather than `XmR`.

Table 10-2. Built-in Type Converters from XmRString

Target Type	Description of Converter
XmRAcceleratorTable	Compiles a string accelerator table into internal accelerator format (no need to call `XtParseAccelerator-Table()`).
XmRAtom	Converts a string property name into the corresponding Atom.
XmRBoolean	Converts strings "true", "false", "yes", "no", "on", and "off" to corresponding Boolean value (case insensitive).
XmRBool	Same as for `XmRBoolean`.
XmRCursor	Given a standard X cursor name, returns a cursor ID.
XmRDimension	Converts a width or height value to a `Dimension`.
XmRDisplay	Given a display name, opens the display and returns a `Display` structure.

Table 10-2. Built-in Type Converters from XmRString (continued)

Target Type	Description of Converter
XmRFile	Given a filename, opens the file and returns the file descriptor.
XmRFloat	Converts a numeric string to floating point
XmRFont	Given a font name, loads the font (if it is not already loaded), and returns the font ID. See Appendix B, *Specifying Fonts and Colors*, for more information on legal values. The value **XtDefaultFont** will return the default font for the screen.
XmRFontSet	Given a base font name list, creates a font set needed to display text in the user's locale, and returns a font set ID and the list of missing charsets if any. The value **XtDefault-FontSet** will return the default font set determined by the user's locale.
XmRFontStruct	Given a font name, loads the font (if it is not already loaded), and returns a pointer to the **FontStruct** containing font metrics. The value **XtDefaultFont** will return the default font for the screen.
XmRGeometry	Given a standard geometry string, this converter simply copies a pointer to the string and calls it a new resource type.
XmRInitialState	Converts strings "Normal" or "Iconic" into the symbols **NormalState** or **IconicState**.
XmRInt	Converts a numeric string to an integer.
XmRPixel	Converts a color name string (e.g., "red" or "#FF0000") into the pixel value that will produce the closest color possible on the hardware. See Appendix B, *Specifying Fonts and Colors*, for more information on legal values. The two values **XtDefaultBackground** and **XtDefaultForeground** are always guaranteed to exist, and to contrast, on any server. However, Motif calculates its own colors to implement its four-color shadow scheme.
XmRPosition	Converts an **x** or **y** value to a **Position**.
XmRShort	Converts a numeric string to a short integer.
XmRTranslationTable	Compiles string translation table into internal translation table format (no need to call **XtParseTranslation-Table()**).
XmRUnsignedChar	Converts a string to an unsigned char.
XmRVisual	Converts a string specifying a visual class to a pointer to a supported visual structure of that class.

If there is no converter from **XmRString** to a particular resource type, it may not be possible to specify that resource type in a resource file. For example, there is no converter for **XmRCallback** since it would be meaningless to specify a function in a resource file. The only ways to set a callback resource are with **XtAddCallback()** or a static callback list declared in the application.

Most of the Xt converters allow the resources of the base classes Core, Composite, Constraint, and Shell to be set from resource files. Motif provides numerous converters that allow the resources of its widgets to be set from resource files. However, not all Motif widget resources can be set from resource files, because the needed converters are not provided. (As of Motif 1.2, Motif now includes a StringToWidget converter, which allows Form and other constraint resources to be set from resource files.) Motif provides converters from **Xm-RString** to **Widget, Window, Char, XmFontList, XmString, KeySym, HorizontalPosition, HorizontalDimension, VerticalPosition, VerticalDimension, BooleanDimension, CharSetTable, KeySymTable, ButtonType, XmStringTable, StringTable, AtomList,** and **Cardinal.**

In addition, the Xmu library contains several useful converters. For example, Xmu provides a converter that converts from a filename (string) to a bitmap suitable for use as an icon pixmap. Even though Xmu (like Xaw) is not part of the X Consortium standard, it is part of MIT's core distribution and is available on most systems. However, because the Xmu converters are not built into Xt, you need to register them with a call to **XtSetTypeConverter()** or **XtAddConverter()** (from widget code) or **XtAppSetTypeConverter()** or **XtAppAddConverter()** (from application code) before using them in an application or widget. (We'll describe the converters and show how to register them in Section 10.3.4.)

10.3.2 Other Built-in Type Conversions

While the conversions from **XmRString** are the most widely used, since they allow a resource to be specified from a resource file, there are also a number of built-in converters between other data types, for use internally within Toolkit programs.

Most commonly, these converters are used to convert between the **resource_type** and **default_type** fields of a resource definition.

Table 10-3 lists those converters automatically recognized by Xt.

Table 10-3. Other Built-in Converters

From	To	Description of Converter
XmRColor	XmRPixel	Converts an **XColor** structure to a pixel value.
XmRPixel	XmRColor	Converts a pixel value to an **XColor** structure.
XmRInt	XmRBoolean	Converts an int to a **Boolean**.
	XmRBool	Converts an int to a **Boolean**.
	XmRColor	Converts an int to an **XColor**.
	XmRDimension	Converts an int to a **Dimension**.
	XmRFloat	Converts an int to a **float**.
	XmRFont	Converts an int to a **Font**.
	XmRPixel	Converts an int to a pixel value.
	XmRPixmap	Converts an int to a **Pixmap**.

Table 10-3. Other Built-in Converters (continued)

From	To	Description of Converter
	XmRPosition	Converts an `int` to a `Position`.
	XmRShort	Converts an `int` to a `short`.
	XmRUnsignedChar	Converts an `int` to an `unsigned char`.

For example, the default value of the Core resource **XmNborderPixmap** is set as shown in Example 10-10.

Example 10-10. A resource definition converting an integer to a pixmap

```
static XtResource resources[ ] = {
    .
    .
    .
    {
    XmNborderPixmap,
    XmCPixmap,
    XmRPixmap,
    sizeof(Pixmap),
    XtOffsetOf(CoreRec, core.border_pixmap),
    XtRImmediate,
    (XtPointer) XtUnspecifiedPixmap
    },
    .
    .
    .
}
```

(Note that the code for the base classes defined by Xt use constants beginning with **Xt**, not **Xm**. However, the value of each of these constants is the same in both versions.)

The specified default value **XtUnspecifiedPixmap** is an integer defined to have a value that does not equal the constant **CopyFromParent** or any valid Pixmap ID. The **initialize** method for the Core widget class checks for this value, and does not set the **background** window attribute unless the application or a resource file has set the **XmNborderPixmap** resource to some value other than the default.

10.3.3 Special Resource Defaults That Do Not Use Conversion

There are two special values, **XmRImmediate** and **XmRCallProc** that can be used only in the **default_type** field of a resource definition. These values require no type conversion. The value provided in the **default_address** field must be of the correct type.

The type **XmRImmediate** means that the value in the **default_address** field is the default value itself, not its address. For a string, this means that the **default_address** field is a pointer to the string, not a pointer to a pointer.

In Example 10-11, the value in the `default_address` field of the **XmNheight** resource definition is the actual default—in this case, zero.

Example 10-11. A resource definition using XmRImmediate

```
static XtResource resources[ ] = {
    .
    .
    .
    {
    XmNheight,
    XmCHeight,
    XmRDimension,
    sizeof(Dimension),
    XmOffsetOf(RectObjRec, rectangle.height),
    XmRImmediate,
    (XtPointer) 0
    },
    .
    .
    .
};
```

The type **XmRCallProc** means that the value in the `default_address` field is a pointer to a function. This function is of type **XtResourceDefaultProc**,† and it is expected to retrieve the desired default value at run time. When the widget instance is created, the function is automatically invoked with these parameters: the widget ID, the resource offset, and a pointer to the **XrmValve** in which to store the result. The function should fill in the `addr` field of the **XrmValue** with a pointer to the default data in its correct type.

In Example 10-12, the value in the `default_address` field of the **XmNscreen** resource definition is the name of a function that retrieves the screen on which the widget is displayed.

Example 10-12. A resource definition using XmRCallProc

```
static XtResource resources[ ] = {
    .
    .
    .
    {
    XmNscreen,
    XmCScreen,
    XmRPointer,
    sizeof(int),
    XtOffsetOf(CoreRec, core.screen),
    XmRCallProc,
    (XtPointer) XtCopyScreen
    },
    .
    .
    .
};
```

Example 10-13 shows an example of an **XtResourceDefaultProc**.

---

†This function type is relevant primarily because the reference page in Volume Five, *X Toolkit Intrinsics Reference Manual*, that describes its calling sequence is listed under this name, **XtResourceDefaultProc**. This reference page is in the Prototype Procedures section in Volume Five.

Example 10-13. An example of an XtResourceDefaultProc

```
/*ARGSUSED*/
void XtCopyScreen(widget, offset, value)
    Widget          widget;
    int             offset;
    XrmValue        *value;
{
    value->addr = (XtPointer)(&widget->core.screen);
}
```

10.3.4 Registering Type Converters

As noted earlier, not every representation type symbol defined in *Xm.h* is supported by a built-in converter, though Motif and the Xmu library do provide some of the most important converters that are missing in Xt. In addition, you can define your own resource types, and write converter routines to convert from a string representation in a resource file to the appropriate data type. (You can write converters from any type to any other type, but converters from `String` are by far the most useful.)

Table 10-4 lists the converters from `XmRString` provided by the Xmu library.

Table 10-4. Xmu Converters

From	To	Description of Converter
XmRString	XmRBackingStore	The `XmuCvtStringToBackingStore` converter converts the strings "NotUseful", "WhenMapped", and "Always" (in any case) into the corresponding constants (in proper case) for use in setting the `backing_store` window attribute. (See Volume One, *Xlib Programming Manual*, for details on backing store.)
	XmRBitmap	The `XmuCvtStringToBitmap` converter takes the string filename of a file in standard X11 bitmap format and creates a one-plane pixmap containing that bitmap data.
	XmRCursor	The `XmuCvtStringToCursor` and `XmuCvtStringToColorCursor` converters convert one of the standard cursor names (from *<X11/cursorfont.h>*), a font name and glyph index of the form "FONT fontname index [[font] index]", or a bitmap file name as in `XmRPixmap` below, and converts it to an X `Cursor`.
	XmRGravity	
	XmRJustify	The `XmuCvtStringToJustify` converter converts the strings "right", "left", or "center", in any case, to an enumeration constant suitable for use by a justify resource. This converter is used by the Athena Label widget.

Table 10-4. Xmu Converters (continued)

From	To	Description of Converter
	`XmRLong`	Converts a string to a long integer.
	`XmROrientation`	The `XmuCvtStringToOrientation` converter converts the strings "horizontal", or "vertical", in any case, to an enumeration constant suitable for use by an orientation resource. This converter is used by the Athena Scrollbar widget.
	`XmRShapeStyle`	Converts the strings `ShapeRectangle`, `ShapeOval`, `ShapeEllipse`, and `ShapeRoundedRectangle` in shape style constants, for use in making Xmu calls that access the Shape extension.
	`XmRWidget`	The `XmuCvtStringToWidget` and `XmuNewCvtStringToWidget` converters convert a widget name into the corresponding widget ID. These are old-style and new-style converters respectively. This convert is commonly used to specify the relative positions of the children of constraint widgets, as in the Athena Form widget resources `fromHoriz` and `fromVert`. Motif 1.2 provides its own String-To-Widget converter.
`XmRFunction`	`XmRCallback`	Converts a function pointer to a callback list containing that function.

Whether defined in Xmu or in your own program, a converter other than those built into Xt or Motif must be registered with a call to `XtAddConverter()` or `XtSetTypeConverter()` before a resource list is used that references the converted types. Resource lists are used when widgets are created or when the application calls `XtGetApplicationResources()`. In the application, a converter must be registered after `XtAppInitialize()` but before `XtGetApplicationResources()`.

Within a widget, the `class_initialize` method is the standard place to register type converters. This method is responsible for doing processing that should be done only once when the first instance of a particular class is created.

Example 10-14 shows the code needed to register the `XmuCvtStringToJustify` converter in a widget. As noted above, this converter would be used for a resource (such as the Athena Label widget's `XtNjustify` resource) designed to give the user the option of justifying text (or a graphic object) to the right, left, or center of a widget.†

---

†While it may seem a little backwards to describe how to add a converter before we say how to write one, the availability of the Xmu converters makes it likely that you would in fact want to add converters you haven't written.

Example 10-14. Registering a type converter

```
static void
ClassInitialize()
{
        .
        .
        .
    XtSetTypeConverter(XmRString,      /* source type */
            XmRJustify,                /* target type */
            XmuCvtStringToJustify,     /* converter routine */
            (XtConvertArgList) NULL,
            /* args for converter routine */
            0                          /*# args for converter routine */
            XtCacheAll,                /* caching instructions */
            NULL);                     /* destructor function */

}
```

Note that `XtSetTypeConverter()` was added to Xt in R4. Its predecessor, **XtApp-AddConverter()**, is still available and can still be used, but has reduced functionality. `XtAppAddConverter()` cannot be used for conversions that require a server query (such as those involving colors or fonts), and does not provide the caching control provided by `XtSetTypeConverter()`. Note that the explicit application context version of the call (`XtAppSetTypeConverter()`) is not used in this case, because the **class_ini-tialize** method does not pass in a widget from which the application context could be determined.

The first two arguments of `XtSetTypeConverter()` are the source and target type, respectively, specified using **XmR** symbolic constants defined in *<Xm/Xm.h>* (or defined in an application header file or the widget public header file if the type is not standard in Xt).

The third argument is the name of the converter routine, which by convention contains the string **Cvt**. The Xmu converters all add the prefix **Xmu**.

The fourth and fifth arguments of `XtSetTypeConverter()` are an argument list that will be passed to the converter routine when it is called. Some converter routines require information about the context in which the converter is called. This is usually passed in via an **XtConvertArgRec** structure, as described in the next section. If no arguments are needed, the fourth and fifth arguments of `XtSetTypeConverter()` can be **NULL** and **0** respectively.

The sixth argument specifies whether the results of the conversion should be cached. The basic symbols are **XtCacheNone**, **XtCacheAll**, and **XtCacheByDisplay**. Expensive conversions should be cached. Xt caches resource values to avoid repetitive conversions of the same value, which are common in an application made up of many identical widgets. It is especially important to cache conversions that require round-trips to the server, such as color, font, and atom conversions. But it is wasteful of memory to cache silly conversions such as **XtCvtStringToGeometry**, which actually doesn't do any conversion or even validity checking. (The **XmRGeometry** representation type is a geometry string, as defined by **XParseGeometry()**. It takes no conversion to convert **XtRString** to **Xt-RGeometry**. The converter could at least test the string to make sure it looks like a geometry string.) Another benefit of caching is that Xt remembers unsuccessful conversions and efficiently generates warning messages without attempting any conversion more than once.

The symbol `XtCacheRefCount` can be ORed with any of the above values, in which case Xt keeps track of how many widgets still exist that used a converted value, and frees the cached value when the count reaches zero. The application, if it uses the converted value in a call to `XtGetApplicationResources()`, is also counted as one reference. Reference counting is needed only if an application destroys widgets whose resource values may take up extensive space. Because reference counting takes up space and requires time, it should not be done unless necessary. To control reference counting on a widget-by-widget basis, an application must explicitly set the `XmNinitialResourcesPersistent` resource to `False` for each widget whose conversions are to be reference counted. These should be widgets that might be destroyed before the application exits.

The seventh argument of `XtSetTypeConverter()` is a pointer to a procedure called a *destructor*. If the reference count for a particular resource reaches zero, Xt calls the destructor function, and removes the resource value from the conversion cache. The destructor will also be called when `XtCloseDisplay()` is called if the converter was registered with `XtCachePerDisplay`. Before calling `XtCallConverter()` or `XtConvertAndStore()` to convert a value, the client must allocate memory in which to place the result. The job of the destructor is to deallocate this memory. If you are allowing Xt to convert data automatically, by declaring a resource list, Xt allocates the memory, and you don't need a destructor (so specify `NULL`). If you plan to call `XtCallConverter()` from an application, and you allocate memory statically for the converted value, you don't need a destructor function and can specify `NULL` for this argument. A destructor is needed only if you allocate memory dynamically for an explicit call to `XtCallConverter()`. (Remember that reference counting happens only if the converter is registered with `XtCacheRefCount` set and `XmNinitialResourcesPersistent` set to `False` for at least one widget. If these conditions are not met, the destructor is only called when `XtCloseDisplay()` is called and if registered with `XtCachePerDisplay`.)

Xt provides several functions for manipulating reference counts, which are rather obscure and mentioned here only for completeness. `XtAppReleaseCacheRefs()` explicitly decrements the reference counts for resource values converted with `XtCallConverter()`. This would be used in the rare occasion where a value has been cached but you don't want it cached. If this is the last reference to the conversion, the registered destructor is called. Xt also defines two built-in callback functions that decrement reference counts, `XtCallbackReleaseCacheRef()` and `XtCallbackReleaseCacheRefList()`.

10.3.4.1 Passing Arguments to a Type Converter

Some type converters need to be registered with additional arguments that provide information needed during the conversion. For example, `XmuCvtStringToWidget` needs to be passed the parent of the current widget in the application, so that it can compare the name specified in the resource to the names of the children of the parent. Example 10-15 shows the code used by a widget to register the Xmu string-to-widget converter.

Example 10-15. Adding a converter with arguments

```
static void ClassInitialize(w)
Widget w;
{
    static XtConvertArgRec parentCvtArgs[ ] = {
        {
            XtWidgetBaseOffset,
            (XtPointer)XtOffsetOf(CoreRec, core.parent),
            sizeof(CoreWidget)
        }
    };
        .
        .
        .
    XtSetTypeConverter(XtRString,
            XtRWidget,
            XmuCvtStringToWidget,
            parentCvtArgs,
            XtNumber(parentCvtArgs),
            XtCacheAll,
            NULL);
}
```

The format of the argument list for **XtSetTypeConverter()** shown in Example 10-16 looks complicated, but in practice almost all converter argument lists will look very similar to the one in this example. The argument list is specified as an **XtConvertArgRec**:

```
typedef struct {
    XtAddressMode address_mode;
    XtPointer address_id;
    Cardinal size;
} XtConvertArgRec, *XtConvertArgList;
```

The **address_mode** field specifies how the **address_id** field should be interpreted. **address_id** itself is a pointer to the needed data, an offset within the widget instance structure to the data, or a function that provides the needed data. The **size** field specifies the length of the data in bytes.

By specifying the address mode as **XtWidgetBaseOffset** (see below), you can use **XtOffsetOf()** to find the offset of appropriate data in the instance structure.† All you have to do is change the name of the instance structure field (in this case **core.parent**), and the structure type that contains that field (in this case **WidgetRec**). Notice that a pointer to this structure type appears in the **sizeof** call (in this case **Widget**).

You have just seen the normal way of specifying the converter arguments. Using different **XtAddressMode** values you can also specify them in other ways. The enumerated type **XtAddressMode** (defined in *<X11/Convert.h>*) specifies the possible values for the **address_mode** field:

---

†You can also use **XtOffset()** instead of **XtOffsetOf()**, but it is less portable. The usage difference between the two is that **XtOffset()** takes a pointer to the structure type, while **XtOffsetOf()** takes the structure type itself.

```
typedef enum {
        /* address mode parameter representation */
        XtAddress,              /* address */
        XtBaseOffset,           /* offset */
        XtImmediate,            /* constant */
        XtResourceString,       /* resource name string */
        XtResourceQuark,        /* resource name quark */
        XtWidgetBaseOffset,     /* offset */
        XtProcedureArg          /* procedure to call */
} XtAddressMode;
```

- `XtAddress` causes `address_id` to be interpreted as the address of the data.

- `XtBaseOffset` causes `address_id` to be interpreted as the offset from the widget base address. `XtWidgetBaseOffset` (see below) is now slightly preferred, since it works with objects and gadgets as well as widgets.

- `XtImmediate` causes `address_id` to be interpreted as a constant.

- `XtResourceString` causes `address_id` to be interpreted as the name of a resource that is to be converted into an offset from the widget base address.

- `XtResourceQuark` causes `address_id` to be interpreted as a quark—that is, as an internal compiled form of an `XtResourceString`.

- `XtWidgetBaseOffset` is similar to `XtBaseOffset` except that it searches for the closest windowed ancestor if the object is not a subclass of Core. This must be used in the resource list of objects and gadgets, but can also be used for widgets.

- `XtProcedureArg` specifies that `address_id` is a pointer to a procedure to be invoked to return the conversion argument. `address_id` must contain the address of a function of type `XtConvertArgProc`. This function type takes three arguments: an object (or widget), pointer to size (Cardinal *), and a pointer to an `XrmValue`. The value is returned in the `XrmValue`.

In most cases, you will use `XtWidgetBaseOffset` in widgets, gadgets and objects, as shown in Example 10-15.

When registering a type converter in an application rather than a widget, the structure field specified in the argument list shown in the example would be a field of the `AppData` structure instead of the instance part structure, and `CoreRec` would be replaced by `AppData`.

10.3.5 Explicitly Invoking a Converter

Converters are normally invoked by Xt because the types they convert are specified in a resource list. But this is not the only way in which converters can be invoked. It is possible to manually invoke type converters, the easiest way being `XtConvertAndStore()`.† This

---

†`XtConvertAndStore()` replaced `XtConvert()` in R4. Both have the same arguments, but `XtConvert-AndStore()` returns `Boolean` while `XtConvert()` returns `void`. `XtConvertAndStore()`'s return value indicates whether the conversion succeeded or failed. `XtConvertAndStore()` also implements new display-specific conversion, caching and reference counting features.

may be useful in an application, such as for reading an icon pixmap from a file using a converter, or you may need to explicitly invoke a converter from within a converter you want to write. (Converter routines can themselves invoke other converters directly.)

One possible manual use of type converter routines is in the processing of the string parameters passed to action routines. Perhaps in the action routine itself it is more convenient to have some parameters converted to another form. For example, if an action is passed the string "True," the action code might prefer to convert this parameter to a Boolean value. The `CvtStringToBoolean` converter understands many strings that would be interpreted as Boolean, such as "Off," "On," "True," "False," "No," and "Yes," in upper, lower, or mixed case. It saves code to use the converter rather than comparing a string to all these strings in your own code. Example 10-16 shows an action routine of the Athena Text widget (modified for R4) in which a converter is manually invoked.

Example 10-16. Manually invoking a type converter

```
static void
DisplayCaret(w, event, params, num_params)
Widget w;
XEvent *event;              /* CrossingNotify special-cased */
String *params;             /* Off, False, No, On, True, Yes, etc. */
Cardinal *num_params;       /* 0, 1 or 2 */
{
    .
    .
    .
    if (*num_params > 0) { /* default arg is "True" */
        XrmValue from, to;
        from.size = strlen(from.addr = params[0]);
        if (XtConvertAndStore(w, XtRString, &from, XtRBoolean, &to)
                == False)
            XtAppError(XtWidgetToApplicationContext(w),
                    "DisplayCaret action: String to Boolean\
                    conversion failed");
        else {
            ; /*
             *          (*(Boolean*)to.addr) has boolean value;
             *                do something with it here */
             */
        }
    }
}
```

Note that the *from* and *to* arguments of **XtConvertAndStore()** are pointers to structures containing length/pointer pairs—they are not values. The actual data is passed as a pointer to a pointer. Thus the cast to Boolean (in the comment) must dereference the pointer twice.

The widget argument of **XtConvertAndStore()** is used internally by Xt as the argument for the **XtDisplay()** macro, to get the pointer to the display structure, and for other purposes. In normal applications you can pass any widget here. (For some converters, the widget may need to be realized.)

`XtConvertAndStore()` calls a lower-level routine called `XtCallConverter()`.† If you prefer, you can use this routine. Instead of passing it the widget and the source and destination type, you pass it a display, the name of the conversion routine, any arguments to the routine, and storage in which to place the cache reference count. See Volume Five, *X Toolkit Intrinsics Reference Manual*, for details.

10.3.6 Writing a Type Converter

If your application or widget has a data type that you would like the user to be able to set through resource files, and no Xt or Xmu converter exists, you will need to write (and register) a type converter from `XmRString` to your type.

The first step in creating a converter is to decide upon the characteristics of the string you will be converting from, and the C-Language type you will be converting to. Then you can copy an existing similar converter and fill in the code to convert to your desired type. Note that the R5 Athena widgets still use a mixture of the old-style (R3) and new-style converter interfaces. To use the current converter functions `XtConvertAndStore()` or `XtCall-Converter()`, or any of the cache reference counting features, you must define your converter using the type `XtTypeConverter`. The difference between new-style and old-style type converters is just that new-style type converters have a display as their first argument, and they must do a display-specific conversion when a server query is involved. The new-style converters also must return TRUE or FALSE to indicate whether the conversion succeeded.

Example 10-17 shows an Xmu converter that shows the essential elements of a converter. It has been modified to be compatible with the new-style resource conversion routines such as `XtSetTypeConverter()`. (The only difference is the presence of a leading `Display` argument and the return value.)

Example 10-17. A simple type converter

```
/* ARGSUSED */
#define done(type, value) \
        {                                                        \
            if (toVal->addr != NULL) {                           \
                if (toVal->size < sizeof(type)) {                \
                    toVal->size = sizeof(type);                  \
                    return False;                                \
                }                                                \
                *(type*)(toVal->addr) = (value);                 \
            }                                                    \
            else {                                               \
                static type static_val;                          \
                static_val = (value);                            \
                toVal->addr = (XtPointer)&static_val;            \
            }                                                    \
            toVal->size = sizeof(type);                          \
            return True;                                         \
        }
```

---

†`XtCallConverter()` superceded its rough equivalent R3 routine `XtDirectConvert()`.

Example 10-17. A simple type converter (continued)

```
Boolean XmuCvtStringToLong (display, args, num_args, fromVal, toVal)
    Display *display;
    XrmValuePtr args;
    Cardinal    *num_args;
    XrmValuePtr fromVal;
    XrmValuePtr toVal;
{
    static long l;

    if (*num_args != 0)
        XtWarningMsg("wrongParameters","cvtStringToLong",
                "XtToolkitError","String to Long\
                conversion needs no extra arguments",
                (String *) NULL, (Cardinal *)NULL);
    if (sscanf((char *)fromVal->addr, "%ld", &l) == 1) {
        done(&l, long);
        return(TRUE);
    } else {
        XtDisplayStringConversionWarning(display, (char *)
                fromVal->addr, XtRLong);
        return(FALSE);
    }
}
```

Note that Xt manages the cache of converted values: converter routines are not responsible for caching their own returned data. Notice that the `XrmValuePtr` arguments passed into the converter are pointers to structures, not values. The `XrmValue` structure contains an address field and a size field.

`XtDisplayStringConversionWarning()` takes as arguments a pointer to the `Display` structure, the string that could not be converted, and the type to which it could not be converted. It issues a warning message with name `conversionError`, type `string`, class `XtToolkitError`, and the default message string "Cannot convert "*src*" to type *dst_type*." (See Chapter 14, *Miscellaneous Toolkit Programming Techniques*, for more information on error and warning messages.)

Many converters need to compare multiple strings in order to convert a value. For example, Motif's string to arrow-direction converter has to determine whether a string matches XmARROW_UP, XmARROW_DOWN, XmARROW_LEFT, or XmARROW_RIGHT. Normally this would require several time-consuming string comparisons for each conversion. Instead, converters of this type use a shortcut based on quarks. A quark is a unique integer ID for a string, of type `XrmQuark` (defined by Xlib). A call to the Xlib routine `XrmStringToQuark` returns the quark for a string. A converter determines quarks for each of its reference strings (such as XmARROW_UP) only once during run time, and determines a quark for each string to be converted. Then quarks can be compared quickly since they are just integers. (See Volume Two, *Xlib Reference Manual*, for details on quarks.)

When a nonstandard type converter that uses quarks is defined and registered in widget code, the `XrmStringToQuark` calls are normally placed in the `class_initialize` method just before the `XtSetTypeConverter()` call.

10.3.6.1 Defining the Default Value

When performing conversions, such as from strings to fonts or colors, for which there is no string representation that all server implementations will necessarily recognize, a type converter should define some set of conversion values that the converter is guaranteed to succeed on, so that these can be used as resource defaults.

For example, Xt's default string-to-pixel converter recognizes the symbols `XtDefault-Foreground` and `XtDefaultBackground`. As part of its conversion, it tests for these values, and establishes the appropriate value based on the string value. The code is shown in Example 10-18.

Example 10-18. Testing for a special-case default value

```
/*
 * CompareISOLatin1 is an undocumented Xt function, allowed
 * since this converter is within Xt.  In your converters,
 * you would use XmuCompareISOLatin1.
 */
if (CompareISOLatin1(str, XtDefaultBackground) == 0) {
    *destructor_data = False;
    if (pd->rv)
        done(Pixel, BlackPixelOfScreen(screen))
    else
        done(Pixel, WhitePixelOfScreen(screen));
}
if (CompareISOLatin1(str, XtDefaultForeground) == 0) {
    *destructor_data = False;
    if (pd->rv)
        done(Pixel, WhitePixelOfScreen(screen))
    else
        done(Pixel, BlackPixelOfScreen(screen));
}
```

Although Motif uses Xt's string to pixel value converter when colors are specified in resource files, it uses its own algorithm to calculate the default value depending on the type of screen and on the colors that can be successfully allocated.

10.4 Subparts and Subresources

A subpart is a section of a widget that is replaceable but that cannot operate independently. It is just a further subdivision of the widget into smaller pieces. Gadgets and objects usually provide a more elegant way to do this.

Subresources allow subparts of a widget to have separate sets of resources. Since the R3 Athena Text widget was the only example of the use of subresources in MIT's core distribution, we'll describe how Text used subparts and subresources so you can understand the motivation behind them. You can then compare this concept with the current Athena Text widget which is implemented using objects. Motif 1.1 and 1.2 also use subresources to fetch data that isn't part of the primary widget structure. This happens for resource data that is shared among widgets (gadget caching) or that can't reside in the primary widget due to binary compatibility (e.g., VendorShell resources).

The R3 Text widget has three parts: the source, the sink, and the coordinator widget. The source subpart manages the storage of data and the sink subpart manages how it is displayed. The coordinator is the central widget that manages the communication between the source and the sink, and is inoperable without them. Both the source and the sink are replaceable pieces of code. Xaw provides only one source, which edits a string or disk file, and only one sink, which displays text in one color and in one font. The idea of providing the subparts in the first place is that they would allow enhancements to be made without changing the basic editor functionality that is in the coordinator. For example, only the source and sink would need replacing in order to implement a multifont and/or multicolor text widget.

Each subpart has its own resource list so that it truly can be replaced without any modifications to the central widget. These are the subresources.

0.4.1 The Hook Methods

The `initialize_hook`, `set_values_hook`, and `get_values_hook` methods are used by widgets that have subparts. They have the same function as their nonhook counterparts, except that they process only the resources of a subpart, and any subpart instance fields that depend on the subpart resources. These methods are called immediately after their nonhook counterparts.

However, the `initialize_hook` and `set_value_hook` methods have become obsolete in R4 because their arguments have been added to the `initialize` and `set_values` methods. The hook methods are still called for compatibility with existing widgets, but new widgets should move the code that would have been in the hook methods into `initialize` and `set_values`.

The `get_values_hook` method is passed a single copy of the widget instance structure (the *new* copy already modified in the nonhook methods), and the argument list passed to the Xt routine that triggered the method. The `set_values_hook` and `get_values_hook` methods simply take this widget ID and argument list and pass them to `XtSet-Subvalues()` or `XtGetSubvalues()` respectively. The `initialize` method uses the contents of the argument list to validate resource settings for subparts and to set non-resource subpart data.

The `get_values_hook` method is still used in R4. Example 10-19 shows the `get_values_hook` for the AsciiSrc subpart of the R3 Text widget (somewhat simplified to show the essential elements).

Example 10-19. Simplified get_values_hook method of the AsciiSrc subpart of the Text widget

```
static void
GetValuesHook(src, args, num_args)
XawTextSource src;
ArgList args;
Cardinal * num_args;
{
        .
        .
        .
```

```
    XtGetSubvalues((XtPointer) src,
            sourceResources,
            XtNumber(sourceResources),
            args,
            *num_args);
}
```

10.4.2 Managing Subresources

Managing subresources is very similar to managing application resources. Like the application, the subpart must have a structure containing the fields to set through resources. In the application you call XtGetApplicationResources() or XtVaGetApplication-Resources() to set these fields. In a subpart, the analogous calls are XtGetSub-resources() or XtVaGetSubresources(), which is called from the initialize method.

Like widgets, the resources of subparts can be queried and set manually. XtVaGet-Subvalues() or XtGetSubvalues() queries the values, and XtVaSet-Subvalues() or XtSetSubvalues() sets them. However, because subvalues are not part of any widget, these calls cannot identify what object is being queried or set simply by passing the widget ID. These calls have different arguments than XtSetValues() and XtGetValues(). Instead of the widget ID, you pass the pointer to the data structure, the resource list, and the number of resources. Therefore, XtSetSubvalues() and XtGet-Subvalues() can be invoked only from within the widget or subpart. Actually, all these routine do is set or get the value in the specified structure.

Any application using the widget will set or get subresources using XtSetValues() and XtGetValues() as for normal resources, specifying only the coordinating widget as the first argument. These calls are translated into XtSetSubvalues() and XtGet-Subvalues() calls by the set_values and get_values_hook methods. These methods are passed the arguments from the XtSetValues() or XtGetValues() calls and translate them into XtSetSubvalues() or XtGetSubvalues() calls by adding the data structure and resource list arguments. But in addition, the set_values method is responsible for validating the resource settings passed in before it calls XtSet-Subvalues(), and for changing any nonresource subpart structure fields like GCs that depend on resources.

11

Interclient Communications

This chapter discusses communication through the X server between an application and the window manager, and between two applications. The application—window manager communication is performed by code in the Shell widget. The application sets shell resources to control this communication with the window manager. Application—application communication is usually done with a process called selections. This form of communication is already implemented in most widgets that display text, but you may want to implement it in your own custom widgets. Selections can also pass other kinds of data such as graphics. How to use the Motif Clipboard is also described.

In This Chapter:

11
Interclient Communications

Applications share the server with other clients. Server resources, such as screen space and colormaps, must be used in a responsible, consistent manner so that applications can work effectively together. In most window systems, the window system itself embodies a set of rules for application interaction. However, the X Protocol, Xlib, and Xt were all specifically designed to avoid arbitrary conventions, so that they provide "mechanism, not policy."

Instead, the conventions covering interclient communication are described in a separate document, adopted as an X Consortium standard in July, 1989, called the *Inter-Client Communication Conventions Manual* (ICCCM). This chapter will not fully describe the ICCCM, because the job of implementing its rules is given over to a special client called the window manager and a special widget class called Shell and its subclasses.† As a result the details of the ICCCM are, for the most part, irrelevant to the application writer's needs. Widget writers may need to refer to it when implementing selections.

In X Toolkit programs, the Shell widget returned by `XtAppInitialize()` and used as the top-level window of the application automatically handles most of the required interactions with the window manager. However, the Shell widget needs additional information in certain areas. For example, the application needs to provide an icon pixmap so that the window manager can iconify it properly. The first section in this chapter describes how to set Shell resources to control how an application interacts with the window manager. This portion of the chapter is for application writers, regardless of whether you need to write widgets for your application.

The ICCCM defines the required information that must be sent by the client. The Shell widget class takes care of sending this information. However, *mwm*, the Motif Window Manager, also allows the application to send or be sent optional information. One set of information warns the application when it is about to be killed or when one of its windows is about to be destroyed. A separate set lets the application specify what kind of decorations it wants on its top-level shell widgets. The final set allows *mwm* to notify the application when a certain entry on its system menu has been selected. This entry is normally added to the user's *.mwmrc* as part of the application's installation procedure.

---

†If you do need to look up certain details of the ICCCM, see Appendix L, *Inter-Client Communication Conventions*, in Volume Zero, *X Protocol Reference Manual*. The ICCCM is also included in *troff* source form in the standard X distribution from MIT.

In X Toolkit applications, widgets can communicate with other widgets using a mechanism called *selections*, which in turn is based on an X mechanism for common storage called *properties*. Whether the widgets involved in transferring selections are part of the same application or different applications is irrelevant. The communication between widgets takes place without input from the application. However, it can be used as a means of communication between applications. The second major section in this chapter will describe these concepts and how to implement selections between your own custom widgets. Only if your application requires a custom widget that must communicate with other widgets should you actually have to write this code. Thus, this part of the chapter is primarily for widget writers.

Motif 1.2 introduces another layer of abstraction over selections, called *drag-and-drop*. This is an optional user interface feature where data can be moved or copied from one widget to another (in the same or different applications) by dragging an icon.† The most widely known implementation of the drag-and-drop concept is the Apple Macintosh finder where files can be moved from one folder to another by dragging them. The Motif implementation is more general however, since any type of data can be selected and dragged. Motif drag-and-drop is built-in to the Text, TextField, Label, List and most forms of Button widgets for transferring text. The details of how to implement drag-and-drop within a widget are beyond the scope of this book, see the *OSF/Motif Programming Manual*. That book provides 60 pages on the subject, as well as a 65 page example.

11.1 Window Manager Interactions

The window manager was introduced in Chapter 1, *Introduction to the X Window System*, but little mention of it has been made since then. You may recall that the window manager is just another client running on a server, except that it is given special authority to manage screen space and other limited server resources like colormaps.‡ To let the window manager do a better job of mediating competing demands of the various clients, each client gives the window manager information called *window manager hints*. These hints specify what resources each client would like to have, but they are only hints; the window manager is not obligated to honor them, and the client must not depend on them being honored.

Application code has little to do to interact properly with the window manager. The Shell widget returned by `XtAppInitialize()` takes care of setting the essential window manager hints. However, there are a number of optional window manager hints that the application may wish to have passed to the window manager. This is done mainly by setting resources of the Shell widget. Also, there are variations in window managers and it takes some effort to make some applications work equally well under all of them.

The next few sections describe the various resources of the Shell widget, including how and when they should be set. Because the Shell widget is part of the Xt standard, these resources are present when writing applications with any widget set.

---

†Dragging is the act of pressing a mouse button with the mouse over the object, and moving the mouse with the button held down. The object is finally released by releasing the mouse button.

‡Note that we are using the term *resources* here in a general sense, rather than implying its Xt-specific meaning.

11.1.1 Shell Subclasses

There are several types of Shell widgets. The Shell widget class itself, specified by the class structure pointer `shellWidgetClass`, is never instantiated directly in applications. Only its subclasses are used. You have seen two subclasses of the Shell widget used earlier in this books: the one used for the application's top-level widget and the one used for popups. The application's top-level widget is created by passing the class structure pointer `applicationShellWidgetClass` as the widget class argument to `XtAppCreate-Shell()`; this call is also made internally by `XtAppInitialize()`. Popup shells for dialog boxes are created by passing `transientShellWidgetClass` as the widget class argument to `XtCreatePopupShell()`. There are two other subclasses of Shell that are commonly used in applications. One is the **OverrideShellWidgetClass**, passed to `XtCreatePopupShell()` when the shell is used for popup menus. The convention is this: the shell should be an OverrideShell when the pointer is grabbed to prevent other windows from getting input while the popup is up, and the shell should be Transient-Shell for other popups. This is discussed further in Chapter 13, *Menus, Gadgets, and Cascaded Popups*.

The other additional subclass of Shell is `topLevelShellWidgetClass`, which is used to create additional, non-popup, top-level shells. Some applications have multiple permanent top-level windows. One of the top-level shells would be of the **applicationShell-WidgetClass**, and the rest would be of the `topLevelShellWidgetClass`. Each would have a separate icon.

11.1.2 Setting Shell Resources

Shell resources are primarily a way for the user and the application to send in data to be communicated to the window manager. These window manager hints control several major areas of window manager activity: they manage screen space, icons, and keyboard input. We'll discuss these areas one at a time in the following sections. Table 11-1 lists the Shell widget's resources with a brief description of what they control, and whether the application, the user, or Xt normally sets them.

As indicated in Column 3 of the table, some Shell resources are intended to be set only once. These set-once resources can be left to their default values, set in the app-defaults file, or they can be set in the code before the Shell widget is realized; but they should not be set with `XtSetValues()` after realization.

Table 11-1. Shell Resources

Resource	Purpose	When Settable
usually set by Xt or Shell itself, depending on the subclass:		
XmNargc	Command-line args count	–
XmNargv	Command-line args	–
XmNoverrideRedirect	Set for popup shells not to be decorated	–
XmNtransient	Set for popup shells	–
XmNwaitForWm	Whether to wait at all	–
XmNwindowGroup	Links popups to main window	–
XmNwmTimeout	Waiting time for slow wm	–
usually set by user:		
XmNiconX	Icon position	Before realization
XmNiconY	Icon position	Before realization
XmNiconic	Sets XmNinitialState to iconic	Before realization
XmNgeometry	Initial size and position	Before realization
XmNtitle	String for title bar	Anytime
usually set by application:		
XmNallowShellResize	Does shell ask wm for size change?	Anytime
XmNbaseHeight	Height of fixed components	Anytime
XmNbaseWidth	Width of fixed components	Anytime
XmNheightInc	Desired height increment	Anytime
XmNwidthInc	Desired width increment	Anytime
XmNiconMask	Mask used with icon pixmap	Before realization
XmNiconName	String for icon	Before realization
XmNiconPixmap	Picture for icon	Before realization
XmNiconWindow	Window for icon	Before realization
XmNinitialState	Whether normal or iconic	Before realization
XmNinput	Keyboard input model	Before realization
XmNmaxAspectX	Maximum aspect ratio x/y	Anytime
XmNmaxAspectY	Maximum aspect ratio x/y	Anytime
XmNmaxHeight	Maximum acceptable height	Anytime
XmNmaxWidth	Maximum acceptable width	Anytime
XmNminAspectX	Minimum aspect ratio x/y	Anytime
XmNminAspectY	Minimum aspect ratio x/y	Anytime
XmNminHeight	Minimum acceptable height	Anytime
XmNminWidth	Minimum acceptable width	Anytime
XmNsaveUnder	Should server save under when mapped	Before realization

Several of the Shell resources are set automatically by Xt or the window manager and under normal circumstances should not be modified by an application:

- The `XmNargc` and `XmNargv` resources are set by Xt to contain the command-line arguments used to invoke the application. These values may be used by the window manager or a session manager to allow the user to reinvoke the application using the same arguments.

- The `XmNwindowGroup` resource is used to link popup windows to an application's main window. If not set explicitly, `XmNwindowGroup` is automatically set to the top-level ancestor of the popup shell, which is usually the application's top-level shell.

- The `XmNtransient` and `XmNoverrideRedirect` resources are set automatically by Xt depending on what kind of Shell widget you create. For top-level application shells, both are set to indicate that the window manager should treat this window as a top-level window. For TransientShell popup shells, `XmNtransient` is set automatically to the shell specified in `XmNwindowGroup`. When the top-level window is iconified, the TransientShell popup will also be iconified. The TransientShell may also be decorated differently from main application shells.

- `XmNoverrideRedirect` defaults to `True` in the OverrideShell class, indicating that the popup can map itself completely without window manager intervention. This type of popup shell is typically used for popup menus, because they should not be decorated or interfered with by the window manager.

- The `XmNwaitForWm` and `XmNwmTimeout` resources control the response to delays by the window manager when responding to geometry change requests. By default,, `XmNwaitForWm` is `True`, and `XmNwm_timeout` is five seconds. When making a geometry request to the window manager, the Shell widget will wait for five seconds for a response. If a response does not arrive within five seconds, the Shell widget will set `XmNwaitForWm` to `False`, and assume that the window manager is not functioning. The Shell widget will continue without waiting for the event that would otherwise arrive to report the size of the window, and also without updating Xt's internal cache of window geometries. When this event does arrive later, Xt may set `XmNwaitForWm` back to `True` and update its internal cache. These resources should normally be left to their default values.

The `XmNgeometry` and `XmNiconic` resources are intended to be specified by the user. Only these two resources use standard command-line options. The `XmNgeometry` resource is settable using a command-line option of the form:

    –geometry [*width*{x}*height*][{+-}*xposition*{+-}*yposition*]

(Either the size or position portion of the geometry string may be omitted, as indicated by the square brackets. In specifying the *x* or *y* position, a positive value, indicated by a plus sign, is relative to the top or left side of the reference window, while a negative value, indicated by a minus sign, is relative to the bottom or right side.)

The *–iconic* command-line option, if present, sets the `XmNiconic` resource, indicating to the window manager that the application should start up as an icon.

The `XmNicon_x` and `XmNicon_y` icon position hints are best left specified by the user. Icons' positions are determined by the window manager based on these hints or on an icon-positioning policy. An application with several top-level windows could set the icon position hints in its app-defaults file so that the icons for each top-level window appear side-by-side.

We will discuss the remaining resources in related groups. Section 11.1.3 discusses the ones related to the size of the application's main window and other screen space issues. Section 11.1.4 describes the keyboard input model hint. Section 11.1.5 describes how applications should handle colormaps to cooperate with the window manager. Section 11.1.6 describes the ones that apply to the application's icon.

11.1.3 Screen Space

The Shell widgets of each application have windows that are children of the root window. These are called top-level windows. The window manager directly controls the size and position of the top-level windows of each application. The window manager does not control the geometry of other widgets that are the descendants of the Shells, except indirectly through the geometry management mechanism described in Chapter 12, *Geometry Management*.

The most basic size hint, the one that specifies simply the desired initial height and width, is automatically set by Xt based on the size of the child of the Shell widget. This hint is used by most window managers to display the outline of your application when it first appears on the screen, ready for the user to place and/or size the application. If your application does not have specific size needs, you need not set any additional resources.

The additional size hints specify the application's range of desired sizes, desired increments of sizes, and desired range of aspect ratios. These are set by the `XmNbaseHeight`, `XmNbaseWidth`, `XmNminWidth`, `XmNminHeight`, `XmNmaxWidth`, `XmNmaxHeight`, `XmNwidthInc`, `XmNheightInc`, `XmNminAspectX`, `XmNminAspectY`, `XmNmaxAspectX`, and `XmNmaxAspectY` resources.

Size increment hints are useful for applications that prefer to be in units of a particular number of pixels. Window managers that listen for this hint always resize the window to the base size (for each dimension), plus or minus an integral multiple of the size increment hint for that dimension. If the base size resource has not been set, the minimum size is used as the base. For example, *xterm* uses the font width and font height as width and height increment hints, because it prefers not to have partial characters or dead space around the edges. The bitmap editor application described in Chapter 4, *An Example Application*, should probably set both the width and height increments to the `cell_size_in_pixels`, since the bitmap cells are square.

Most applications that use size increment hints redefine the interpretation of geometry specifications (the `XmNgeometry` resource, settable through the *−geometry* standard command-line option) to reflect the size increments. For example, the width and height in *xterm* geometry specifications are in units of characters, not pixels. The Vt100 widget within *xterm* implements this by having an `XmNgeometry` resource separate from the shell geometry resource with that name. The entry for this resource in the widget resource list specifies the Vt100 instance structure field, not the shell instance structure field. Then the `realize` method for the Vt100 parses the geometry string with `XParseGeometry()` (an Xlib routine that returns four separate variables containing the size and position from the geometry string) and sets the width and height fields of the core structure and the various size hints according to the returned variables. (The Vt100 within *xterm* is not a real, self-sufficient widget. For one thing, it has no `set_values` method. For any real widget to implement this approach to interpreting geometry specifications, the `set_values` method would have to multiply the `XmNwidth` and `XmNheight` resource settings by the increment hints.)

An aspect ratio is the ratio of the width to height measurement or vice versa. The `XmNminAspectX` and `XmNminAspectY` resources are used together to determine one extreme of acceptable aspect ratios, and `XmNmaxAspectX` and `XmNmaxAspectY` determine the other extreme. For example, to suggest that the *xmh* application never be more than four times larger in one direction than it is in the other, the following values (as they would appear in the app-defaults file) would suffice:

```
xmh*topLevel.minAspectX:    1
xmh*topLevel.minAspectY:    1
xmh*topLevel.maxAspectX:    4
xmh*topLevel.maxAspectY:    4
```

Remember that every application must be able to do something reasonable given any size for its top-level window, even if the window is too small to be useful or if any of these hints are ignored by the window manager.

11.1.4 Input Model

Window managers also control which window keyboard input will be delivered to by setting the *keyboard focus window* (sometimes called just the *keyboard focus*) to an application's top-level window. The distribution of events according to the current keyboard focus is handled by the server; it is a basic feature of X, not of Xt. Some window managers, like *twm*, use the pointer-following (also called real-estate-driven) model of keyboard input; the window containing the pointer gets the keyboard input. Setting the keyboard focus once to the root window implements the pointer-following model. Other window managers use the click-to-type model, exemplified by the Macintosh™ user interface, requiring that the user click the pointer in the window where keyboard input is to go. The window manager sets the keyboard focus to the window the user clicks on. *mwm* lets the user select between these two focus models by setting a resource.

With some window managers other than *mwm*, how the window manager treats an application window can be modified by the input model hint, which is set by the `XmNinput` resource. Even though *mwm* doesn't use the value of this hint, Motif applications should set it in case they are used under a window manager that does use the hint.

If `XmNinput` is set to `True`, the window manager will set the keyboard focus to this application or not, according to its pointer-following or click-to-type model of keyboard input. However, if it is set to `False`, the window manager will not set the keyboard focus to this application. If the application sets this resource to `False` and wants input, it will have to forcefully take the keyboard focus, and then put it back to the original window when finished.

For historical (not logical) reasons, the Intrinsics default for the **XmNinput** resource is **False**. However, there is a special internal Shell widget class called VendorShell, which sets appropriate resources for a given widget set. The proper default for a given widget set (which usually has an accompanying window manager) is set by that widget set's Vendor-Shell. The majority of applications need **XmNinput** set to **True** unless they don't require keyboard input (and expect never to have accelerators).

There are four models of client input handling defined by the ICCCM:

- No Input. The client never expects keyboard input. *xload* is an example of such an output-only client. This type of client sets **XmNinput** to **False**.

- Passive Input. The client expects keyboard input but never explicitly sets the input focus. This describes the vast majority of applications that always accept keyboard input in the window that contains the pointer. This type of client sets **XmNinput** to **True**.

- Locally Active Input. The client expects keyboard input, and explicitly sets the keyboard focus, but only does so when one of its windows already has the focus. An example would be a client with subwindows defining various data entry fields that uses Next and Prev keys to move the keyboard focus between the fields, once its top-level window has received the keyboard focus. This type of client sets **XmNinput** to **True**.

- Globally Active Input. The client expects keyboard input, and explicitly sets the input focus even when the focus is in windows the client does not own. An example would be a client with a scrollbar that wants to allow users to scroll the window without disturbing the keyboard focus even if it is in some other window. It wants to temporarily set and then reset the keyboard focus when the user clicks in the scrolled region, but not when the user clicks in the scrollbar itself. Thus, it wants to prevent the window manager from setting the keyboard focus to any of its windows. This type of client sets **XmNinput** to **False**.

Note that even if the **XmNinput** resource is not set to **True**, your application will still work under some window managers, including *uwm*, *twm*, and *mwm*. This is because these window managers use the pointer-following keyboard focus model or ignore this hint. However, it is not wise to assume that all window managers will ignore this hint. Therefore, if your application expects keyboard input, and is not of the globally active type described above, you can use the code shown in Example 11-1 to set the **XmNinput** resource.

Example 11-1. Setting the XmNinput resource of a Shell widget

```
main(argc, argv)
int argc;
char *argv[ ];
{
    .
    .
    .

    /* create the Shell widget, setting resource */
    topLevel = XtVaAppInitialize(&app_context, "Xmh",
            table, XtNumber(table),
            &argc, argv, NULL,
            XmNinput, (XtArgVal)True,
```

Example 11-1. Setting the XmNinput resource of a Shell widget (continued)

```
        NULL);
    .
    .
    .
}
```

Note that the `XmNinput` resource should always be hardcoded, since the application may fail if the user is allowed to change the expected style of keyboard focus.

For a further discussion of the keyboard focus, see Section 14.4.

11.1.5 Colormaps

On most color systems, the display uses one or more hardware registers called *colormaps* to store the mapping between pixel values and actual colors, which are specified as relative intensities of red, green, and blue primaries (RGB values).

X allows virtual colormaps to be created by applications. Some high-performance systems even allow all virtual colormaps to be installed in hardware colormaps and used at the same time, even to the level of one colormap per window. Far more commonly, though, there is only one hardware colormap, and virtual colormaps have to be copied into the hardware colormap one at a time as needed. Copying a virtual colormap into the hardware colormap is called *installing* the colormap, and the reverse process where the default colormap is installed is called *uninstalling*. The window manager is responsible for installing and uninstalling colormaps.

If your application has standard color needs (decoration only), then you do not have to worry about the effects of colormaps being installed and uninstalled. Your application should use the standard `XmRString` to `XmRPixel` converter to translate color names into pixel values. If the colormap is full, or becomes full at any of the color allocations in the converter, the warning messages place the burden on the user to kill some applications in order to free some colormap cells. (If the converter cannot allocate the desired color, it prints a warning message, and the default for that resource is used. If the default is not `XtDefault-Foreground` or `XtDefaultBackground`, it also must be converted and this may also fail. If both allocations fail, the color will default to black. If this is not acceptable, then you will need to write your own type converter.)

If your application absolutely requires accurate colors, a certain number of distinguishable colors, or dynamically changeable colors, you will need to write your own converter to allocate colors. For example, if a color allocation for a known correct color name string fails, it means that all the colormap entries have already been allocated and no entry for that color is available. In this case, your converter might call the Xlib call `XCopyColormapAnd-Free()` to copy the allocations your application has already made into a new colormap. Then the converter would allocate the color (and all subsequent colors) from the new colormap.

See Chapter 7, *Color*, in Volume One, *Xlib Programming Manual*, for details of various color allocation techniques.

The window manager is responsible for installing and uninstalling colormaps according to its own policy. Typically, the policy is to install the colormap of the application that has the keyboard focus or that contains the pointer. When an application has created a new colormap on a system that supports only one hardware colormap, and that colormap is installed, all applications that were using the other colormap will be displayed using the new colormap. Since the pixel values from the old colormap have not been allocated in the new colormap, all applications that use the old colormap will be displayed with false colors. This is known as "going technicolor."

The window manager or some other client may also create standard colormaps to facilitate the sharing of colors between applications. A standard colormap is a colormap allocated with a publicly known arrangement of colors. The Xlib routine **XGetStandard-Colormap()** allows an application to determine whether the window manager has created a specific standard colormap, and it gets a structure describing the colormap. Xmu provides numerous utilities for creating and using standard colormaps—see Volumes One and Two for a description.

If your application requires more than one colormap, each installed at the same time in a different window, you need to tell the window manager about this so that these colormaps can be properly installed when the application is active. You do this by calling **XtSet-WMColormapWindows()**, specifying the ApplicationShell widget as the first argument, a list of widgets that need certain colormaps as the second argument, and the length of the list as the third argument. This instructs the window manager to read the **colormap** window attribute of each of the listed widgets, and to install that colormap in each widget (if possible) whenever the application is active. (Of course, any application that depends on the existence of multiple simultaneous colormaps is doomed to run on only a small percentage of existing systems.)

The **colormap** window attribute of a window is an unchangeable characteristic of that window, that is assigned when the window is created (when the widget is realized). The Core **realize** method sets it based on the **XmNcolormap** Core resource of the widget. Therefore, if a widget must have a certain colormap, you must set its **XmNcolormap** resource *while creating the widget*. Attempting to set **XmNcolormap** after a widget is created will have no effect on its colormap window attribute.

11.1.6 Icons

The window manager always manages the icons for each application. Depending on the window manager, these icons may simply contain a text string called the icon name, or they may contain a pattern that identifies the application, called the icon pixmap. The window manager is not obligated to display the application's icon pixmap (by default, *mwm* and *twm* do not display the icon pixmap). However, the window manager will always display at least the icon name.

An application may supply an icon name by setting the **XmNiconName** resource; if it does not, the window manager will usually use the application name or the value of the **Xm-Ntitle** resource.

The application should supply the pattern for the icon, in the form of a single-plane pixmap, as the `XmNiconPixmap` resource. There are two basic ways to do this: one is by including bitmap data, and the other is by reading it in at run time. The former is easy to do with an Xlib call; the code that needs to be added is shown in Example 11-2. The latter technique, because it involves building a filename and looking in a number of locations for the file, is better done with a converter defined by the Xmu library. This converter technique is more complicated because the converter has to be registered and called with the proper arguments. The example using a converter is provided in the example source code for this book (*xicon2*), but is not shown here. See Chapter 10, *Resource Management and Type Conversion*, for more information on invoking converters.

Example 11-2. Creating an icon pixmap, and setting XmNiconPixmap

```
      .
      .
      .
/*
 * The following needed if not using Motif:
 *   #include <X11/Shell.h>
 */

#include "icon"

main(argc, argv)
int argc;
char **argv;
{
    Pixmap icon_pixmap;
      .
      .
      .
    /* create topLevel here */

    icon_pixmap = XCreateBitmapFromData(XtDisplay(topLevel),
            RootWindowOfScreen(XtScreen(topLevel)),
            icon_bits,
            icon_width, icon_height );

    XtVaSetValues(topLevel, XmNiconPixmap, icon_pixmap, NULL);
      .
      .
      .
    /* realize widgets */
}
```

The included file, *icon*, is in standard X11 bitmap file format. You can create such a file using the *bitmap* application from the standard distribution, or *xbitmap5* from the examples for this book.

The window manager may have a preferred standard size for icons. If so, it will set a property. The application can read this property with the Xlib call `XGetIconSizes()`. To fully support a variety of window managers, an application should be capable of creating icon pixmaps of different sizes, depending on the values returned by `XGetIconSizes()`.

An application has the option of creating its own icon window, and then passing its ID to the window manager for management. This might be done so that the application can draw a multi-colored picture in the icon, instead of the traditional two-color bitmap, or animate the icon. However, as with all hints, the window manager is not guaranteed to honor your desires and may just ignore the icon window you provide. But if you want to try anyway, create the window using Xlib calls, and select input on it so that your application receives `Expose` events when they occur. Then set the ID of the window using the `XmNiconWindow` resource, before realizing the application. Then make sure your event loop redraws the icon when it receives `Expose` events on it. Accomplishing this will require writing your own modified version of `XtAppMainLoop()` to handle the icon events.

11.1.7 Window Manager Decorations

Virtually all current window managers decorate windows on the screen.† These decorations typically include a title bar for the window with gizmos for moving and resizing the window. Current decorating window managers include *twm*, *awm*, *mwm*, *olwm*, and *gwm*.

The way these decorations are implemented can have an impact on Toolkit applications. The window manager places the decorations in a window slightly bigger than the application, and then *reparents* the application's top-level window into the decoration window. Reparenting gives the top-level window a new parent instead of the root window. The window manager actually creates the frame window as a child of the root window, then reparents the application's top-level window into the frame, and then maps the frame window.

Reparenting affects the application mainly when you try to determine a global position (relative to the root window) from the `XmNx` and `XmNy` resources of the Shell widget. This is usually done in order to place popups. Under a nonreparenting window manager such as *uwm*, these coordinates are indeed relative to the root window, because the parent of the shell is the root window. However, under a window manager that reparents, the coordinates of the application's main Shell widget are relative to the decoration window, not the root window. Therefore, these coordinates cannot be used for placing popups within the application. Motif's internal code that places a popup uses `XtTranslateCoords()` instead of relying on the position resources.

11.1.8 Interacting With the Motif Window Manager

The application and *mwm* can communicate back and forth through properties stored on the server. The properties are associated with the top-level window of your application, so unlike selections, similar communications can be going on at the same time between different clients and the window manager without interference. The ICCCM, *Inter-Client Communication Conventions Manual*, defines a starting point for what information can be sent back and forth.‡ *mwm* also defines some other information it is willing to send and receive.

All Shell widgets handle the required communication with the window manager; this section concerns optional communication. Note that applications should not depend on this type of communication. An application may run under a different window manager that doesn't

---

†The *uwm* window manager doesn't decorate, but it is defunct as of R4 since it doesn't honor the current ICCCM.
‡The ICCCM is reprinted as an appendix of Volume Zero, *X Protocol Reference Manual*.

listen to this type of message. Furthermore, an application is not required to use this type of communication, because *mwm* runs fine without it. This type of communication is just icing on the cake. (If you want to know whether *mwm* is running anyway, use the `Xm-IsMotifWMRunning()` function.)

The next three sections describe the two major groups of protocols and a set of supplementary window manager hints. The first protocol group is defined by the ICCCM, and the second by Motif. You must include the header file *<X11/Protocols.h>* to use any of these features.

Before you can use these features, you must also prepare the required atoms. The type `Atom` is an ID for the string name for a property. All applications know the name of the property they will use for communication (such as WM_PROTOCOLS), but they don't know the ID for it since it changes each time the server is run. You can get the Atom for a property name by calling `XmInternAtom()`. This is called *interning* the atom. All the fully capitalized words used in this section are property names, and must be interned before use.

Both of the following sets of protocols work in the same way. You indicate interest in participating in one or more of them by calling `XmAddProtocols()`. Then you register a function, using `XmAddProtocolCallback()`, to be called when the window manager sends you a message on a particular protocol. Of course, it is possible to resign from any of the protocols whenever you want.

11.1.8.1 WM_PROTOCOLS

The WM_PROTOCOLS are messages sent to your application from the window manager that notify you of conditions requiring immediate action. There are currently three protocols defined in the ICCCM, but the list may expand.

WM_DELETE_WINDOW indicates that the user has just requested that one of your application's windows be destroyed. Your application should respond by destroying that window if possible without exiting. The idea behind this protocol is that some applications have multiple top-level windows, and if the window manager were simply to delete one without the application's cooperation, the application might not be able to recover. (You should participate in this protocol if you have multiple top-level windows.)

WM_SAVE_YOURSELF indicates that the user has just requested that your application be killed. You should save all data immediately in preparation. This should execute code equivalent to the code you have implemented for your application's quit feature, except that it does everything except exit. (You should participate in this protocol if you have data that could be lost by exiting abnormally.)

WM_TAKE_FOCUS indicates that your application has been given the keyboard focus. You would participate in this protocol if you wanted the keyboard focus to always start in one of your subwindows, instead of your main window.

11.1.8.2 _MOTIF_WM_MESSAGES

The user can configure *mwm*, using an *.mwmrc* file, to add one or more buttons to its system menu and then call your application when any of these buttons are pressed. (If you want this feature in your application, though, you'll have to provide the proper text to be added to the user's *.mwmrc*.)

You indicate interest in this protocol by calling `XmAddProtocols()` with the atom for _MOTIF_WM_MESSAGES. The leading underscore is intentional; it indicates a property not defined in the ICCCM. When the user presses one of the system menu buttons, your application receives notification in the form of an `ClientMessage` event. Motif will automatically dispatch this `ClientMessage` event to a function, if you have registered one using `XmAddProtocolCallback()`.

11.1.8.3 _MOTIF_WM_HINTS

The _MOTIF_WM_HINTS property is used in the opposite direction from the protocols described above. It is specified by the application and used by *mwm* if *mwm* is running. The property contains three hints about how the application would like to be treated: `decorations`, `functions`, and `input_mode`.

The value specified in the `decorations` field is combined (using AND) with the setting of the `XmNclientDecoration` shell resource. You can specify whether your application should have a border, resize button, title, window menu button, minimize button, or maximize button.

The `functions` field controls whether functions selected from *mwm* menus (that appear on the root window) should operate on your application. These operations consist of resizing, moving, minimizing, maximizing, and closing (exiting).

The `input_mode` field advises *mwm* to use various obscure focus management conventions when dealing with your application.

Note that *mwm* sets the _MOTIF_WM_INFO property on your application's main top-level shell. This property contains information about whether the *mwm* that is running has been customized (using *.mwmrc*) or if it is standard.

11.2 Selections: Widget-to-Widget Communication

Selections are a general mechanism for communicating information between two clients of the same server. The most familiar example of selections is selecting text from one *xterm* application and pasting it into another. This text can also be pasted into an *xmh* mail composition window, or into an *xedit* application.

In Xt applications, selection is normally implemented within widgets. For example, the Athena Text widget is used by *xmh* and *xedit*, and it is this widget that supports cutting and pasting of text in these applications. The application code of *xmh* and *xedit* does not play a part in the communication of selection data. The fact that selection is implemented in widgets also means that two widgets within the same application can communicate with each other through selections. For example, the Text widget is sometimes used to provide single-line input fields in an application. Since the Text widget supports selections, the user could select the text in one field and paste it into another field. This feature would be present without any code in the application. If the same widget class supports both copying and pasting, selections can be used to move data in a single widget. For example, selections allow you to copy text within an editor in *xterm* and paste the text in a new place (although some editors require keyboard commands to position the insertion point).

Motif provides a high-level interface to the selection mechanism that allows Motif applications or widgets to easily transfer data. See Section 11.3 for a description of this interface. The basic selection mechanism described in this section is valid for all widget sets, not just Motif.

The selection mechanism is not limited to text. It requires only that the sender and recipient have knowledge of the format of the data being transferred. Therefore, selections can be used to transfer graphics between widgets that can understand a common format for communicating graphics. Unfortunately, a standard format for graphics selections has not yet been agreed upon.

The selection mechanism uses properties for transferring data and uses the `Selection-Clear`, `SelectionNotify`, and `SelectionRequest` event types to synchronize the communication. Essentially, a property is common storage. Properties are stored in the server, and are named pieces of data associated with a window on that particular server, that any client of that server can read or write. Because the various clients may not be running on the same host, all communication between applications and between applications and the window manager must take place through the server using properties.†

The basic routines used to implement selections are part of Xlib. Xt provides an interface to the Xlib selection routines that makes selections easier to use in the context of widget code. Since there is a maximum size for the data stored in a single property, communication of large blocks of data using Xlib requires several partial transfers. Xt supplies routines that transparently perform the multiple partial transfers so that they appear to the application program like a single transfer, called an *atomic* transfer.

Xt also supplies a separate set of parallel routines that transfer a large selection one chunk at a time so that it appears as multiple small selections. This is called an *incremental* transfer. Incremental transfer can be preferable on systems with limited memory and more natural when the data is normally stored in small chunks.

The Toolkit selection routines also have built-in timeouts, so that one application won't wait forever for another to provide data.

---

†It is not practical to write your own networking routines in an application to communicate with other clients running on different hosts because your client may be communicating with the server using TCP/IP, and the other client may be using DECnet. Both may be the same X application that you wrote, but compiled with a version of Xlib that uses a different protocol layer underneath the X Protocol. When you communicate through the server using properties, the server takes care of the translation.

First we'll give you an overview of how an atomic selection transaction works, and then we'll discuss and demonstrate how to write the code to implement atomic selections in a widget. Following this is a discussion of how incremental selections work, and finally a discussion of the standard selection formats (known as target types).

If you are writing a custom widget that contains data that could be pasted into other instances of the widget or other widgets, you should read on to see how to implement selections. Otherwise, the rest of this chapter is probably only of academic interest to you.

11.2.1 How Atomic Selection Works

Selections communicate between an *owner* widget and a *requestor* widget.† The owner has the data and the requestor wants it. The owner is the widget in which the user has selected something, and the requestor is the widget in which the user has clicked to paste that something. Many widgets need to act as both owner and requester at different times. The code to handle each of the two roles is separate.

Here is a brief overview of the steps that take place during a single transfer of data from one widget to another. We'll assume we have two instances of the same widget class, which can operate either as the owner or the requestor. Initially, both widgets are in exactly the same state, neither having any text selected, and neither being the owner or requestor. We'll also assume that selections are implemented using actions tied to pointer buttons, as in existing widgets that use selections.

- The user selects an item in Widget *A*, and the widget highlights the item. An action, typically called in response to a `<Btn1Down>` translation, marks the start of a selection. A subsequent `<Btn1Motion>` event (that is, a motion event with button 1 held down) invokes another action to extend the highlighted selection.

- A `<Btn1Up>` event invokes a third action in Widget *A* that actually makes the selection. The action calls `XtOwnSelection()` to claim ownership of the PRIMARY selection for Widget *A*. This means that Widget *A* claims the sole right to use the `XA_PRIMARY` property for communication with other widgets, until some other widget claims ownership. (More about `XA_PRIMARY` below.) The call to `XtOwnSelection()` also registers three procedures, to be called by Xt in response to selection events. The *lose_ownership_proc* handles the case where Widget *A* loses the selection (because the user has made another selection elsewhere), the *convert_proc* converts the data in the selection to the target property type requested by Widget *B* (see below), and the optional *transfer_done_proc* prepares for the next selection request, if necessary (this function is often `NULL`).

---

†Note that since selections can be implemented in the application, as they are by non-Xt applications, the words "application" and "widget" are interchangeable in this section.

- The user pastes the item into Widget *B*, usually by clicking a pointer button. (By convention, a translation for `<Btn2Down>` invokes the action to do this.)

- The paste action in Widget *B* requests the value of the current selection by calling `XtGetSelectionValue()`; this specifies a *target* type, and a *requestor_callback* that will be invoked to actually paste the data when Widget *A* reports that the conversion has been successfully completed.

- The `XtGetSelectionValue()` call by Widget *B* also generates a `SelectionRequest` event. In response to this event, Xt invokes the *convert_proc* registered by the call to `XtOwnSelection()` in Widget *A*.

- The *convert_proc* in Widget *A* converts the selected item into the appropriate data type for the target property specified by *B*, if possible. The converted data is stored in the `XA_PRIMARY` property.

- Based on the return values from Widget *A*'s conversion procedure, Xt sends a `SelectionNotify` event to inform Widget *B* whether or not the data was successfully converted.

- The *requestor_callback* registered in Widget *B* reads the data from the property and displays it, or if Widget *A* reported that the conversion could not be made, Widget *B* beeps or otherwise indicates that the kind of data selected in Widget *A* cannot be pasted in Widget *B*, or that the kind of data requested by *B* cannot be supplied by *A*.

- Xt notifies Widget *A* that the selection has been transferred, so that the widget's *transfer_done_proc* can disown the selection if the selection is of a kind that can be transferred only once.

Figure 11-1 shows this procedure in graphic form.

The code to implement selections is divided logically into a number of functions within the widget. The next sections show the code necessary to implement both the owner and the requestor roles. The code for each role is separate and cannot share any widget variables with the other role because the transaction may be between two different widget instances.

As an example, we will add support for selections to the BitmapEdit widget described in Chapter 6, *Inside a Widget*, and Chapter 7, *Basic Widget Methods*. Little of the existing code in that widget needs to be changed. The examples show only the code added to implement selections, and describe where to add it.

We will start with the owner role, and then proceed to the requestor role, and then back to the owner role.

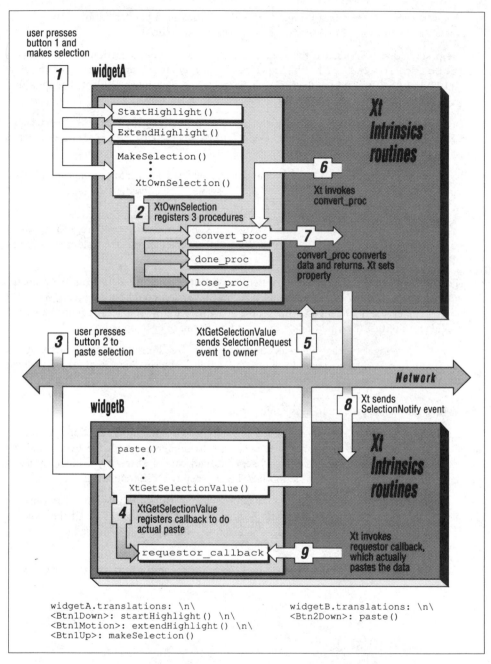

user presses
button 1 and
makes selection

1 **widgetA**

```
StartHighlight()
ExtendHighlight()
MakeSelection()
    ⋮
    XtOwnSelection()
```

**Xt
Intrinsics
routines**

6 Xt invokes
convert_proc

2 XtOwnSelection
registers 3 procedures

```
convert_proc
done_proc
lose_proc
```

7 convert_proc converts
data and returns. Xt sets
property

3 user presses
button 2 to
paste selection

XtGetSelectionValue
sends SelectionRequest
event to owner **5**

Network

widgetB

8 Xt sends
SelectionNotify event

```
paste()
    ⋮
    XtGetSelectionValue()
```

**Xt
Intrinsics
routines**

4 XtGetSelectionValue
registers callback to do
actual paste

```
requestor_callback
```
9

Xt invokes
requestor callback,
which actually
pastes the data

```
widgetA.translations: \n\
<Btn1Down>: startHighlight() \n\
<Btn1Motion>: extendHighlight() \n\
<Btn1Up>: makeSelection()
```

```
widgetB.translations: \n\
<Btn2Down>: paste()
```

Figure 11-1. The process of selection transfer

11.2.2 Highlighting the Selected Data (Owner)

The selection process begins when the user selects some text in Widget *A*. The widget code for the owner role must contain some code to identify the area or items selected and to highlight the text (or whatever) being selected. This user-interface portion of the owner role is carried out by actions added to the widget. Some event sequences that are not already in use must be mapped to these actions. In existing applications that support selections of text:

- A press of the first pointer button pins a starting point of the selection, dragging the first button extends and highlights the selection, and releasing the first button ends the selection. A subsequent press of the first button starts a new selection, unhighlighting the old one.

- A press of the second button pastes the selection.

- A button press or motion with the third button depressed repositions either end of the selected area.

It is a good idea to stick with existing conventions for the user interface of highlighting a selection, so that your application will operate in a familiar way. But since BitmapEdit already uses all three pointer buttons, unmodified, to set, unset, and toggle bitmap cells, we cannot use unmodified button presses to control selections. But we can (and will) use these same buttons modified by Shift.

A selection in BitmapEdit is any rectangular set of bitmap cells. Accordingly, BitmapEdit will use `Shift<Btn1Down>` to set the top-left corner of a selection rectangle, `Shift<Btn1Motion>` to follow dragging, and `Shift<Btn1Up>` to set the bottom right corner.† Each of these events will invoke a separate action routine, `StartHighlight`, `ExtendHighlight`, and `MakeSelection`, respectively. These translations are added to the widget's default translation table, and the actions are added to the actions table. Example 11-3 shows the action table, the translation table, and the three action routines.

Example 11-3. BitmapEdit: actions that highlight selection

```
static char defaultTranslations[ ] =
        "Shift<Btn1Down>:    StartHighlight()    \n\
        Shift<Btn1Motion>:   ExtendHighlight()   \n\
        Shift<Btn1Up>:       MakeSelection()     \n\
        Shift<Btn2Down>:     PasteSelection()    \n\
        ~Shift<Btn1Down>:    DoCell()            \n\
        ~Shift<Btn2Down>:    UndoCell()          \n\
        ~Shift<Btn3Down>:    ToggleCell()        \n\
        ~Shift<Btn1Motion>:  DoCell()            \n\
        ~Shift<Btn2Motion>:  UndoCell()          \n\
        ~Shift<Btn3Motion>:  ToggleCell()";

static XtActionsRec actions[ ] = {
    {"DoCell", DoCell},
    {"UndoCell", UndoCell},
    {"ToggleCell", ToggleCell},
```

---

†For simplicity, we won't copy the third button semantics used in text selections. This could easily be added.

Example 11-3. BitmapEdit: actions that highlight selection (continued)

```
    {"StartHighlight", StartHighlight},
    {"ExtendHighlight", ExtendHighlight},
    {"MakeSelection", MakeSelection},
    {"PasteSelection", PasteSelection},
};
    .
    .
    .
/*
 * User presses first button (by default), starting highlighting.
 */
static void
StartHighlight(w, event)
Widget w;
XButtonEvent *event;
{
    BitmapEditWidget cw = (BitmapEditWidget) w;
    cw->bitmapEdit.first_box = False;

    cw->bitmapEdit.select_start_x = (cw->bitmapEdit.cur_x + event->x)
            / cw->bitmapEdit.cell_size_in_pixels;
    cw->bitmapEdit.select_start_y = (cw->bitmapEdit.cur_y + event->y)
            / cw->bitmapEdit.cell_size_in_pixels;

    /* clear old selection */
    Redisplay(cw, NULL);
}

/*
 * MakeSelection is call when the first button is released (by
 * default).  This finishes the user's highlighting, and means
 * triggers ownership of the PRIMARY selection.
 */
static void
MakeSelection(w, event)
Widget w;
XButtonEvent *event;
{
    BitmapEditWidget cw = (BitmapEditWidget) w;
    int temp;

    cw->bitmapEdit.select_end_x = (cw->bitmapEdit.cur_x + event->x)
            / cw->bitmapEdit.cell_size_in_pixels;
    cw->bitmapEdit.select_end_y = (cw->bitmapEdit.cur_y + event->y)
            / cw->bitmapEdit.cell_size_in_pixels;

    if ((cw->bitmapEdit.select_end_x == cw->bitmapEdit.select_start_x)
            && (cw->bitmapEdit.select_end_y ==
            cw->bitmapEdit.select_start_y))  {
        Redisplay(cw, NULL);
        return; /* no selection */
    }

    /* swap start and end if end is greater than start */
    if (cw->bitmapEdit.select_end_x < cw->bitmapEdit.select_start_x) {
        temp = cw->bitmapEdit.select_end_x;
        cw->bitmapEdit.select_end_x = cw->bitmapEdit.select_start_x;
        cw->bitmapEdit.select_start_x = temp;
```

Example 11-3. BitmapEdit: actions that highlight selection (continued)

```
    }

    if (cw->bitmapEdit.select_end_y
            < cw->bitmapEdit.select_start_y) {
        temp = cw->bitmapEdit.select_end_y;
        cw->bitmapEdit.select_end_y =
                cw->bitmapEdit.select_start_y;
        cw->bitmapEdit.select_start_y = temp;
    }

    if (XtOwnSelection(cw, XA_PRIMARY, event->time, convert_proc,
            lose_ownership_proc, transfer_done_proc) ==
            False) {
        XtWarning("bitmapEdit: failed attempting to become
                selection owner; make a new selection.\n");
        /* Clear old selection, because lose_ownership_proc
         * isn't registered. */
        Redisplay(cw, NULL);
    }
}
/*
 * ExtendHighlight is called when the mouse is being dragged with
 * the first button down (by default).  During this time, the
 * bitmap cells that are selected (by crosses) are dynamically
 * changed as the mouse moves.
 */
static void
ExtendHighlight(w, event)
Widget w;
XMotionEvent *event;
{
    BitmapEditWidget cw = (BitmapEditWidget) w;
    static int last_drawn_x, last_drawn_y;
    int event_cell_x, event_cell_y;

    event_cell_x = cw->bitmapEdit.cur_x + (event->x /
            cw->bitmapEdit.cell_size_in_pixels);
    event_cell_y = cw->bitmapEdit.cur_y + (event->y /
            cw->bitmapEdit.cell_size_in_pixels);

    if ((event_cell_x == last_drawn_x) && (event_cell_y ==
            last_drawn_y))
        return;

    if (cw->bitmapEdit.first_box) {
        DrawBoxOfXs(cw, last_drawn_x, last_drawn_y, False);
        DrawBoxOfXs(cw, event_cell_x, event_cell_y, True);
    }
    else {
        DrawBoxOfXs(cw, event_cell_x, event_cell_y, True);
        cw->bitmapEdit.first_box = True;
    }

    last_drawn_x = event_cell_x;
    last_drawn_y = event_cell_y;
}
/*
```

Example 11-3. BitmapEdit: actions that highlight selection (continued)

```
 *   DrawBoxOfXs fills a rectangular set of bitmap cells with
 *   crosses, or erases them.
 */
static void
DrawBoxOfXs(w, x, y, draw)
Widget w;
Position x, y;
Bool draw;
{
    BitmapEditWidget cw = (BitmapEditWidget) w;
    Position start_pos_x, start_pos_y;
    Dimension width, height;
    GC gc;
    int i, j;

    start_pos_x = cw->bitmapEdit.cur_x +
            cw->bitmapEdit.select_start_x;
    start_pos_y = cw->bitmapEdit.cur_x +
            cw->bitmapEdit.select_start_y;

    /* swap start and end if end is greater than start */
    if (x < start_pos_x) {
        width = start_pos_x - x;
        start_pos_x = x;
    }
    else {
        width = x - start_pos_x;
    }

    if (y < start_pos_y) {
        height = start_pos_y - y;
        start_pos_y = y;
    }
    else {
        height = y - start_pos_y;
    }

    for (i=start_pos_x;i < start_pos_x + width;i++)
        for (j=start_pos_y;j < start_pos_y + height;j++)
            DrawX(cw, i, j, draw);
}
/*
 * DrawX draws an X in a bitmap cell, in white if a black cell, and
 * in black if a white cell.
 */
DrawX(cw, x, y, draw)
BitmapEditWidget cw;
Position x, y;
Bool draw;
{
    GC gc;
    if (cw->bitmapEdit.cell[x + y *
            cw->bitmapEdit.pixmap_width_in_cells] == DRAWN)
        if (draw)
            gc = cw->bitmapEdit.deep_undraw_gc;
        else
            gc = cw->bitmapEdit.deep_draw_gc;
```

Example 11-3. BitmapEdit: actions that highlight selection (continued)

```
    else
        if (draw)
            gc = cw->bitmapEdit.deep_draw_gc;
        else
            gc = cw->bitmapEdit.deep_undraw_gc;

    XDrawLine(XtDisplay(cw), XtWindow(cw), gc,
            x * cw->bitmapEdit.cell_size_in_pixels,
            y * cw->bitmapEdit.cell_size_in_pixels,
            (x + 1) * cw->bitmapEdit.cell_size_in_pixels,
            (y + 1) * cw->bitmapEdit.cell_size_in_pixels);

    XDrawLine(XtDisplay(cw), XtWindow(cw), gc,
            x * cw->bitmapEdit.cell_size_in_pixels,
            (y + 1) * cw->bitmapEdit.cell_size_in_pixels,
            (x + 1) * cw->bitmapEdit.cell_size_in_pixels,
            y * cw->bitmapEdit.cell_size_in_pixels);
}
```

The actions shown in Example 11-3 reference some new instance part fields we have added to *BitmapEditP.h* to store the state of the selection. Four of these variables are the x and y coordinates in cells of the top-left and bottom-right corners of the highlighted area: `select_start_x`, `select_start_y`, `select_end_x`, and **`select_end_y`**. These coordinates will be used throughout the owner code. (Because these fields are in units of bitmap cells, not pixels, their type is `int` rather than **`Position`**.)

The `StartHighlight` action is quite simple. It sets the upper-left corner instance part fields based on the button press position in the triggering event. It also clears the highlighting of the old selection, if one exists, and sets a flag to indicate that this is the beginning of a new selection. The `first_box` flag is added as an instance part field because it will be needed in the `ExtendHighlight` action.

`ExtendHighlight` is responsible for drawing Xs dynamically on the selected cells, much as the window manager draws the outline of a window while it is being moved. Xs are drawn on each cell in a rectangle of bitmap cells beginning from the cell selected in the `Start-Highlight` action and ending at the cell the pointer button was released in. `Extend-Highlight` is triggered by pointer motion events that occur while the first button is held down. It calculates which bitmap cell the pointer is in, and if the cell is not the same as the cell the pointer was in the last time `ExtendHighlight` was called, it erases the previous Xs and draws new ones. This is done using two different GCs—one for drawing in black and the other in white, so the color that contrasts with the current state of each cell can be used. The black GC is also used to copy the main pixmap to the screen, and the latter is just for doing the highlighting.

Code was added to the `initialize` method to create this latter GC. (See the example code distribution for this modified widget instance structure.)

The `MakeSelection` action is triggered when the button is released after dragging, indicating that the selection is complete. This action sets the `select_end_x` and `select_end_y` instance part variables to reflect the bottom-right corner of the selection, and then swaps the top-left and bottom-right coordinates if the end coordinate is to the left or above the start coordinate. If the start and end coordinates are the same, then the action returns, since no selection was made. If a selection was made, `MakeSelection` calls `Xt-OwnSelection()`.

11.2.3 Making the Selection with XtOwnSelection (Owner)

Once the area is highlighted, Widget *A* calls `XtOwnSelection()` to assert that it wants the right to set the value of a property that will be used to transfer information.

`XtOwnSelection()` is called with six arguments:

```
Boolean XtOwnSelection(widget, selection, time, convert_proc,
        lose_ownership_proc, transfer_done_proc)
    Widget widget;
    Atom selection;
    Time time;
    XtConvertSelectionProc convert_proc;
    XtLoseSelectionProc lose_ownership_proc;
    XtSelectionDoneProc transfer_done_proc;
```

The *selection* argument specifies an *Atom*—a number representing a property. Properties are arbitrarily named pieces of data stored on the server. To simplify communication with the server, a property is never referenced by name, but by a unique integer ID called an atom. Standard atoms are defined in *<Xatom.h>* using defined symbols beginning with `XA_`; nonstandard atoms can be obtained from the server by calling the Xlib function `Xt-InternAtom`.

Widgets that support one selection at a time pass the predefined `XA_PRIMARY` atom to `Xt-OwnSelection()`. The ICCCM also allows you to use the `XA_SECONDARY` and `XA_CLIPBOARD` atoms. `XA_SECONDARY` would be used by widgets implementing behavior involving more than one selection (for example, allowing the user to make two selections, and to exchange the data they contain). No current clients implement this behavior. The `XA_CLIPBOARD` atom should be used by a widget that allows the user to delete a selection. We'll talk more about the properties referenced by the `XA_SECONDARY` and `XA_CLIPBOARD` atoms in Section 11.3.

The purpose of the `XtOwnSelection()` call is to make sure that only one widget has the right to set the `XA_PRIMARY` selection property at a time, and to assert that this widget is prepared to honor requests for this data. Notice that when you select text with *xterm*, that text is highlighted only until you select a different area in a different window.

The next three arguments to `XtOwnSelection()` specify procedures that will carry out essential parts of the selection operation:

* The *convert_proc* is responsible for converting the selected data into the representation requested by the requestor in its call to `XtGetSelectionValue()`; this function is called by Xt when a `SelectionRequest` event arrives, as a result of the requestor calling `XtGetSelectionValue()`. The *convert_proc* is of type `Xt-ConvertSelectionProc`.

* The *lose_ownership_proc* clears the highlighted area when this widget has lost the selection (because some other widget has taken it); this routine is called by Xt when a

SelectionClear event arrives. The *lose_ownership_proc* is of type Xt-LoseSelectionProc.

- The *transfer_done_proc* is called by Xt when the requestor has successfully retrieved the converted value. If this selection is intended to be erased after being transferred once, this function should free any storage allocated in the transfer. If, instead, the owner remains ready for pasting the same selection into other widgets, this function pointer should be NULL. (For example, *xterm* does not clear its selection after pasting once.) The *transfer_done_proc* is of type XtSelectionDoneProc.

The XtOwnSelection() call also takes a *time* argument—this should be the time from the event that completed the highlighting, not the constant CurrentTime. If XtOwnSelection() returns False, it means that because of network conditions another client has called XtOwnSelection() with a more recent time argument.

XtOwnSelection() returns True or False to indicate whether Widget *A* has been granted ownership. If True, and if this widget was not already the owner, then the old owner (if any) will receive a SelectionClear event and will clear its highlighted area. The process may end here if the user never pastes the selected data anywhere. If the user selects a different piece of data, the selection owner will receive a SelectionClear itself before ever having converted the data for a requestor.

Otherwise the owner code waits to hear from the requestor that it is ready to paste the selection.

11.2.4 Requesting the Selection (Requestor)

When the user pastes the selection into Widget *B*, Widget *B* becomes the requestor and the second part of the process begins. First of all, Widget *B* needs a translation that maps a certain key or button event to an action that pastes data. This action calls XtGetSelectionValue().

XtGetSelectionValue() is called with six arguments:

```
void XtGetSelectionValue (widget, selection, target, callback,
    client_data, time)
Widget widget;
Atom selection;
Atom target;
XtSelectionCallbackProc callback;
XtPointer client_data;
Time time;
```

The *selection* argument is an atom specifying which property is being used to transfer the selection. This will typically be XA_PRIMARY, though in theory two widgets (or two instances of the same widget) could agree to transfer some particular data using other properties.

The *target* argument is another atom, this one specifying a target representation type in which the requestor wants the information. We'll talk more about the possible values for this atom in a moment.

The *callback* argument is a pointer to a callback procedure that actually pastes the data. Xt will call this procedure when the owner has converted the data. The `XtGet-SelectionValue()` call registers the callback with Xt, and sends a `Selection-Request` event to the owner.

When the selection owner has successfully converted the data, the owner sends back a `SelectionNotify` event to Xt. Xt then calls the requestor's callback procedure. The callback procedure must handle the pasting of the data into the widget's data structures, and it must handle the case where the data could not be converted into the requested representation. We'll discuss the responsibilities of this procedure in more detail once we've seen the owner's conversion procedure.

The *client_data* argument of `XGetSelectionValue()` is normally used to pass the event that triggered the pasting into the requestor callback. The callback will use the coordinates at which the event occurred as the location at which to paste the data.

As in the call to `XtOwnSelection()`, the *time* argument should be the time from the event that initiated the pasting, not the constant `CurrentTime`.

11.2.4.1 Possible Target Type Atoms

The *target* argument to `XtGetSelectionValue()` is an atom that the requestor uses to tell the owner what kind of information it is looking for from the selection.† This is not necessarily a conversion of the actual selection data. For example, it might be a timestamp on the data, or some characteristic of it, such as its size or font.

To take full advantage of the Xt selection mechanism, you need to understand what atoms can be used as selection targets. However, apart from some standard, predefined atoms, the atom for a property is not known by a client until it queries the server for the atom using an `XInternAtom()` call. This call specifies the string name of the property and returns the atom.

Some atoms needed by almost all applications are predefined in the header file *<X11/Xatom.h>*. These atoms are symbolic constants that can be used without an `XInternAtom()` call. The constants always start with the prefix `XA_`. See *<X11/Xatom.h>* for the complete list of predefined atoms.

Note that many of the predefined atoms have uses in X other than as target types, and not all are appropriate as selection targets. A few of those that might be useful as targets include:

```
XA_STRING
XA_INTEGER
XA_BITMAP
```

At present, the Athena widgets and the clients in the MIT core X distribution use only `XA_STRING` as a target. However, one can imagine uses for other targets as well. For example, `XA_FONT` might be used as a target to indicate that the requestor doesn't want the text of a selection, but wants only to know its font. `XA_TIMESTAMP` might be used to indicate that the requestor wants a timestamp for the data. Once the

---

†As described earlier, atoms (rather than strings) are always used in network transmissions to identify properties.

XtGetSelectionValue() request is made, a SelectionRequest event is generated, which Xt uses to invoke the owner widget's *convert_proc*. The *convert_proc* will need to branch according to the target type passed in by the requestor through Xt, and convert the data accordingly before transferring the selection to the requestor.

For selection of multiple data types to work correctly between any two arbitrarily chosen widgets, there must be conventions about which targets will be supported. As a step in the direction of interwidget selection compatibility, the ICCCM specifies a required target type of XA_TARGETS, to which the owner is supposed to respond by returning a list of the target types into which it is capable of converting data. We'll talk about how to work with this target in Section 11.2.9.

In a custom widget such as BitmapEdit, which has a custom data type not represented by a predefined atom, it is possible to obtain a custom atom using XInternAtom(), and use that as the target. Because the XInternAtom() call requires a round trip to the server, the best place to do this is in the widget's initialize method.† The returned atom can be stored in a field added to the widget's instance part. BitmapEdit's target type, "CELL_ARRAY," is unique to BitmapEdit. The atom is stored in an instance part field called target so that it is available in *convert_proc* and in the requestor role code. Example 11-4 shows the code added to the initialize method to get an atom for the string "CELL_ARRAY."

Example 11-4. BitmapEdit: getting the atom for a widget-specific target type

```
/* ARGSUSED */
static void
Initialize(request, new)
BitmapEditWidget request, new;
{
        .
        .
        .

    new->bitmapEdit.target_atom = XInternAtom(XtDisplay(new),
            "CELL_ARRAY," False);
```

The target type property name used by BitmapEdit is "CELL_ARRAY."

The third argument to XInternAtom() is a Boolean that indicates what to do if the atom doesn't already exist. If this argument is True, XInternAtom() will return None if no other client has already initialized this atom. This argument should always be False since your widget might be the first to try to make a selection using this target type atom. In a Motif application, one could use XmInternAtom() instead of XInternAtom().

---

†Since Xlib functions causing round-trip requests can impact performance, they should be called only once if possible, and where possible, during the set-up phase of the application as opposed to the event-loop phase. If XInternAtom() were called every time the user made a selection, it would slow the application. In addition, since atoms are server resources that are not freed until the server shuts down, it is important to use predefined atoms whenever possible.

Note that for repeated calls to `XInternAtom()` with the same string as an argument, even from different widgets, the returned atom will be the same. There will be only one atom created for any unique string interned on a given server. (Case is important: "Cell_Array" would return a different atom than "CELL_ARRAY".)

This `XInternAtom()` call occurs in every instance of the BitmapEdit widget, since all instances need to know the atom to participate in selections using that target type. Both the owner and requestor widgets, in separate applications, will get the same atom in return.

11.2.4.2 The Paste Action from BitmapEdit

To initiate the requestor role, you need to assign an event sequence to trigger the pasting, write an action that calls `XtGetSelectionValue()`, and write a callback function that inserts the returned data.

Traditionally, the action to paste data is triggered by a press of the second pointer button. BitmapEdit will use the shifted second button since it uses the unshifted button for other purposes. Example 11-5 shows the action mapped to `Shift<Btn2Down>`.

Example 11-5. BitmapEdit: action to paste a selection

```
static void
PasteSelection(w, event)
Widget w;
XButtonEvent *event;
{
    BitmapEditWidget cw = (BitmapEditWidget) w;
    XtGetSelectionValue(cw, XA_PRIMARY, cw->bitmapEdit.target_atom,
            requestor_callback, event,
            event->time);
}
```

This action can be dropped verbatim into your widget, replacing only the widget name and the name of the instance fields you are using to store the target atom.

11.2.5 Converting the Selection (Owner)

The real challenge in handling selections is writing the *convert_proc*, which converts data to the format specified by the requestor and prepares it for transfer.

As mentioned above, the widget's *convert_proc* is called by Xt when the requestor calls `XtGetSelectionValue()`. The procedure is passed the selection atom and the target atom, and is expected to return in its arguments the type, value, size, and format of the converted selection data.

To support the possibility of having to convert the data to any one of several targets, the code branches according to the value of the target passed in, and does its conversions accordingly. In the version of BitmapEdit's *convert_proc* shown here, only one target type is handled. Section 11.2.9 describes how to add more target types, including some that are required by the ICCCM such as TARGETS.

Once the conversion is made, the procedure sets the *value_return* argument passed in to a pointer to a block of memory, and *length_return* to the size of the block. This block of memory will be set into a property by Xt and passed to the requestor's callback in the same form—as a pointer to a block of memory and a length. This puts constraints on the formats that can be used for the data.

For text selections, the data is usually a simple character string. The *convert_proc* simply needs to set *value_return to a pointer to the string, and length_return to the length of the string. For BitmapEdit, however, the required data is a string (of bitmap cell states) *plus* width and height values. Since C provides easy ways to put numeric values into strings and to get them out again at the other end, we've chosen to handle this data by converting the numbers to characters and tacking them on to the beginning of the string.

If your selection is composed of a number of numeric values, you can create a structure containing the values and then pass a pointer to the structure. However, the structure cannot contain pointers, because the data pointed to by these pointers will not be set into the selection property. For example, BitmapEdit cannot pass a pointer to a structure containing a string pointer field and width and height fields because the block of memory pointed to by the string pointer will not be copied.

In this case, the *type_return* can simply be the target atom that was passed in, indicating that the data is of the requested type.

The *format_return* is the size in bits of each element in the array. Since we are passing a compound string, this value is 8. If we were passing a structure, *length_return* would be 1 and *format_return* would be 8 times the size of the structure in bytes.

Example 11-6 shows BitmapEdit's *convert_proc*.

Example 11-6. BitmapEdit: converting the selection value

```
static Boolean
convert_proc(w, selection, target, type_return, value_return,
        length_return, format_return)
Widget w;
Atom *selection;
Atom *target;
Atom *type_return;
XtPointer *value_return;
unsigned long *length_return;
int *format_return;
{
    BitmapEditWidget cw = (BitmapEditWidget) w;
    int x, y;
    int width, height;

    /* handle all required atoms, and the one that we use */
    /* Xt already handles MULTIPLE, no branch necessary */
    if (*target == XA_TARGETS(XtDisplay(cw))) {
        /* Required atom: see Example 10-10 */
            .
            .
            .
    }
    else if (*target == cw->bitmapEdit.target_atom) {
```

Example 11-6. BitmapEdit: converting the selection value (continued)

```
        char *data;

        width = cw->bitmapEdit.select_end_x -
                cw->bitmapEdit.select_start_x;
        height = cw->bitmapEdit.select_end_y -
                cw->bitmapEdit.select_start_y;

                /* 8 chars is enough for two 3-digit
                 * numbers and two delimiters */
        *length_return = ((width * height) + 8) * sizeof(char);

        data = XtMalloc(*length_return);

        sprintf(data, "%d@%d~", width, height);

        for (x = 0; x < width; x++) {
            for (y = 0; y < height; y++) {
                data[8 + x + (y * width)] = cw->bitmapEdit.cell[(x +
                        cw->bitmapEdit.select_start_x) +
                    ((y + cw->bitmapEdit.select_start_y) *
                    cw->bitmapEdit.pixmap_width_in_cells)];
            }
        }

        *value_return = data;

        *type_return = cw->bitmapEdit.target_atom;

        *format_return = 8;  /* number of bits in char */
        return(True);
    }
    else {
        /* code to handle standard selections: see Example 10-10 */
          .
          .
          .

    }
}
```

This code determines the width and height of the selected rectangle from the instance part
fields, and then allocates enough memory to fit a character array big enough to fit the width
and height values, delimiters, and a width by height character array. Then it copies the current contents of the selected area into the allocated character array. Finally, it sets
`*value_return` to point to the compound string, and sets `*length_return` to the
length of this string. `*format_return` is the size in bits of each element in the array,
which in this case is 8 bits.

11.2.6 Finally Pasting the Selection (Requestor)

When the owner's *convert_proc* returns, Xt sends a `SelectionNotify` event to the
requestor. The Xt code on the requestor side then invokes the callback routine the requestor
registered with the call to `XtGetSelectionValue()`.

The *requestor_callback* function is passed all the same arguments that the owner received in the *convert_proc*, plus the values that the owner returned through the argument of *convert_proc*. In the BitmapEdit widget, it sets instance part fields to paste the data.

Example 11-7 shows the requestor callback function from BitmapEdit.

Example 11-7. BitmapEdit: pasting selection in requestor_callback function

```
/* ARGSUSED */
static void
requestor_callback(w,client_data,selection,type,value,length,format)
Widget w;
XtPointer client_data;   /* cast to XButtonEvent below */
Atom *selection;
Atom *type;
XtPointer value;
unsigned long *length;
int *format;
{
    BitmapEditWidget cw = (BitmapEditWidget) w;
    if ((*value == NULL) && (*length == 0)) {
        XBell(XtDisplay(cw), 100);
        XtWarning("bitmapEdit: no selection or selection timed out:\
                try again\n");
    }
    else {
        XButtonEvent *event = (XButtonEvent *) client_data;
        int width, height;
        int x, y;
        int dst_offset_x, dst_offset_y;
        char *ptr;

        dst_offset_x = (cw->bitmapEdit.cur_x + event->x) /
                cw->bitmapEdit.cell_size_in_pixels;
        dst_offset_y = (cw->bitmapEdit.cur_y + event->y) /
                cw->bitmapEdit.cell_size_in_pixels;

        printf("dst offset is %d, %d\n", dst_offset_x, dst_offset_y);

        ptr = (char *) value;
        width = atoi(ptr);
        ptr = index(ptr, '@');
        ptr++;
        height = atoi(ptr);
        ptr = &value[8];

        for (x = 0; x < width; x++) {
            for (y = 0; y < height; y++) {
                /* range checking */
                if (((dst_offset_x + x) >
                        cw->bitmapEdit.pixmap_width_in_cells)
                        || ((dst_offset_x + x) < 0))
                    break;
                if (((dst_offset_y + y) >
                        cw->bitmapEdit.pixmap_height_in_cells)
                        || ((dst_offset_y + y) < 0))
                    break;
```

```
            cw->bitmapEdit.cell[ (dst_offset_x + x)
                + ((dst_offset_y + y) *
                cw->bitmapEdit.pixmap_width_in_cells) ]
                = ptr[ x + (y * width) ];
            if (cw->bitmapEdit.cell[ (dst_offset_x + x)
                + ((dst_offset_y + y) *
                cw->bitmapEdit.pixmap_width_in_cells) ]
                == DRAWN)
            DrawCell(cw, dst_offset_x + x,
                dst_offset_y + y,
                cw->bitmapEdit.draw_gc);
            else
            DrawCell(cw, dst_offset_x + x,
                dst_offset_y + y,
                cw->bitmapEdit.undraw_gc);
        }
    }
    /* Regardless of the presence of a
     * transfer_done_proc in the owner,
     * the requestor must free the data passed by
     * Xt after using it. */
    XtFree(value);
    Redisplay(cw, NULL);
    }
}
```

The *requestor_callback* first determines whether the conversion was a success by checking the value and data length. If it was not, it beeps and prints a message. This can happen if no selection has been made, or if there is some delay that causes the selection to have timed out before the owner could convert the data.

If the conversion was a success, the *requestor_callback* pastes the data. In Bitmap-Edit's case, the requestor must first convert the data into a more useful form. This means extracting the width and height values, and then setting the widget's cell array based on the data in the character array passed in. Note that the code should check to make sure that the data can be pasted in the desired position. BitmapEdit must make sure that no attempt is made to set a cell array member outside of the bitmap. The routine then updates the screen display of the widget.

The final responsibility of the *requestor_callback* is to free the memory passed in by Xt.

11.2.7 If the Selection is Lost (Owner)

If the owner loses the selection, either because the selection timed out or because the user made a different selection, the *lose_ownership_proc* that was registered with its call to **XtOwnSelection()** will be invoked. Typically, this function simply clears any high-lighting or other visual feedback about the selection, and resets to their initial state any internal variables used in handling selections.

Example 11-8 shows the *lose_ownership_proc* from the BitmapEdit widget.

Example 11-8. BitmapEdit: the lose_ownership_proc

```
/* ARGSUSED */
static void
lose_ownership_proc(w, selection)
Widget w;
Atom *selection;
{
    BitmapEditWidget cw = (BitmapEditWidget) w;

    /* clear old selection */
    cw->bitmapEdit.first_box = False;
    cw->bitmapEdit.select_start_x = 0;
    cw->bitmapEdit.select_start_y = 0;
    cw->bitmapEdit.select_end_x = 0;
    cw->bitmapEdit.select_end_y = 0;
    Redisplay(cw, NULL);
}
```

11.2.8 When the Selection Transfer is Complete (Owner)

The *transfer_done_proc*, registered in the call to XtOwnSelection(), is called when the transfer is complete. Its job is to do any processing necessary to get ready for the next selection request. In many cases no processing is necessary and this function can be NULL in the call to XtOwnSelection(). However, this function might clear variables or free memory. Some transfers are intended to be made only once to make sure that there is no duplication of information. In these cases, the *transfer_done_proc* would do a lot more, including erasing the visual selection, calling XtDisownSelection() (and perhaps even erasing the data that was selected).

11.2.9 ICCCM Compliance

For any two widgets to be able to transparently transfer different types of data, there must be agreement about the possible target types and their contents. The ICCCM suggests a list of possible target types, as shown in Table 11-2. If you can, use one of these target types since this will increase the chances that your widget will be able to communicate with widgets written by other people.

Table 11-2. Target Types Suggested in ICCCM

Atom	Type	Meaning
TARGETS	ATOM	List of valid target atoms
MULTIPLE	ATOM_PAIR	Look in the ConvertSelection property
TIMESTAMP	INTEGER	Timestamp used to acquire selection
STRING	STRING	ISO Latin 1 (+TAB+NEWLINE) text
TEXT	TEXT	Text in owner's encoding

Table 11-2. Target Types Suggested in ICCCM (continued)

Atom	Type	Meaning
LIST_LENGTH	INTEGER	Number of disjoint parts of selection
PIXMAP	DRAWABLE	Pixmap ID
DRAWABLE	DRAWABLE	Drawable ID
BITMAP	BITMAP	Bitmap ID
FOREGROUND	PIXEL	Pixel value
BACKGROUND	PIXEL	Pixel value
COLORMAP	COLORMAP	Colormap ID
ODIF	TEXT	ISO Office Document Interchange Format
OWNER_OS	TEXT	Operating system of owner
FILE_NAME	TEXT	Full path name of a file
HOST_NAME	TEXT	See WM_CLIENT_MACHINE
CHARACTER_POSITION	SPAN	Start and end of selection in bytes
LINE_NUMBER	SPAN	Start and end line numbers
COLUMN_NUMBER	SPAN	Start and end column numbers
LENGTH	INTEGER	Number of bytes in selection
USER	TEXT	Name of user running owner
PROCEDURE	TEXT	Name of selected procedure
MODULE	TEXT	Name of selected module
PROCESS	INTEGER, TEXT	Process ID of owner
TASK	INTEGER, TEXT	Task ID of owner
CLASS	TEXT	Class of owner—see WM_CLASS
NAME	TEXT	Name of owner—see WM_NAME
CLIENT_WINDOW	WINDOW	Top-level window of owner
DELETE	NULL	True if owner deleted selection
INSERT_SELECTION	NULL	Insert specified selection
INSERT_PROPERTY	NULL	Insert specified property

Because not every widget will support every possible target type, the ICCCM specifies a target type of **XA_TARGETS**, to which the owner is required to respond by returning a list of the target types into which it is capable of converting data.

Normally, a requestor would first call **XtGetSelectionValue()** for **XA_TARGETS**, and then in the callback determine which target it wants to request from the list, and then call **XtGetSelectionValue()** again for the desired target with a separate callback to process the actual data. This is really two separate selection transfers.

XA_TARGETS is not a predefined atom.† To use it, you must use the Xmu atom caching mechanism described in Section 11.2.9.1.

---

†The X Protocol defines all the predefined atoms. Therefore, even though XA_TARGETS would be convenient to have as a predefined atom, this can't be arranged with changing the protocol (albeit in a minor way). And the protocol is unlikely to be changed in even minor ways when there are workarounds, as in this case.

Fortunately, there is existing template code that you can copy to handle XA_TARGETS and some other standard target types that are required by the ICCCM.

This template code uses the Xmu routine XmuConvertStandardSelection. It also uses an Xmu atom-caching facility that eliminates the need for you to make XInternAtom() calls for each of the ICCCM standard target atoms.

11.2.9.1   Xmu Atom Caching

In a Motif application, you can use XmInternAtom() to cache atoms, so that when there are multiple instances of the same widget, only one query of the server will be done. However, Xmu provides an atom caching system that is somewhat more convenient for the atoms it supports.

Xmu's caching facility uses symbols similar to those defined in *<X11/Xatom.h>*, except that in this case they are macros that take an argument and call XmuInternAtom. For example, the macro for XA_TARGETS is defined as follows in *<X11/Xmu.h>*:

```
#define XA_TARGETS(d)          XmuInternAtom(d, _XA_TARGETS)
```

where d refers to a pointer to a Display structure. (This can be returned by the Xt-Display() macro.) The XmuInternAtom function first tries to get the atom for the string "XA_TARGETS" from Xmu's internal cache. If Xmu doesn't yet have a value for the atom, it calls XInternAtom() to make a server request. Because this facility makes only one query to the server, you can access the atoms in this way every time a selection is made without significant penalty. This allows you to place the XA_TARGETS() macro in your selection code instead of adding an instance part variable and setting it in the **initialize** method.

You might use this macro as follows in a *convert_proc* branch dedicated to handling the TARGETS target type:

```
if (*target == XA_TARGETS(XtDisplay(w))) { ...
```

The Xmu atom caching mechanism must be initialized before you can make calls of the form just shown. Example 11-9 shows the code that should be placed in the widget's **initialize** method to initialize this mechanism.

Example 11-9. BitmapEdit: initializing Xmu's atom caching mechanism in the initialize method

```
(void) XmuInternAtom( XtDisplay(new), XmuMakeAtom("NULL") );
```

11.2.9.2   Converting the Standard Selections

The Xmu routine XmuConvertStandardSelection can be used to respond to a TARGETS selection request, as well as to other standard targets defined by Xmu.

Example 11-10 shows the portion of the *convert_proc* for BitmapEdit that handles the standard targets.

This code is adapted from the standard client *xclipboard*, and can be copied almost directly into your widget.

Example 11-10. BitmapEdit: converting standard targets in the convert_proc

```
static Boolean
convert_proc(w, selection, target, type_return, value_return,
        length_return, format_return)
Widget w;
Atom *selection;
Atom *target;
Atom *type_return;
XtPointer *value_return;
unsigned long *length_return;
int *format_return;
{
    BitmapEditWidget cw = (BitmapEditWidget) w;
    int x, y;
    int width, height;
    XSelectionRequestEvent* req = XtGetSelectionRequest(w,
            *selection, (XtRequestId) NULL);

    /* handle all required atoms, and the one that we use */
    if (*target == XA_TARGETS(XtDisplay(cw))) {
        /* TARGETS handling copied from xclipboard.c */
        Atom* targetP;
        Atom* std_targets;
        unsigned long std_length;
        XmuConvertStandardSelection(cw, req->time, selection,
                target, type_return,
                (XtPointer*)&std_targets,
                &std_length, format_return);
        *value_return = XtMalloc(sizeof(Atom)*(std_length + 1));
        targetP = *(Atom**)value_return;
        *length_return = std_length + 1;
        *targetP++ = cw->bitmapEdit.target_atom;
        bcopy((char*)std_targets, (char*)targetP,
                sizeof(Atom)*std_length);
        XtFree((char*)std_targets);
        *type_return = XA_ATOM;
        *format_return = sizeof(Atom) * 8;
        return(True);
    }
    /* Xt already handles MULTIPLE, no branch necessary */
    else if (*target == cw->bitmapEdit.target_atom) {
        /* handle normal selection - code shown in Example 10-6 */
            .
            .
            .
    }
    else {
        if (XmuConvertStandardSelection(cw, CurrentTime, selection,
                target, type_return, value_return,
                length_return, format_return))
            return True;
```

Example 11-10. BitmapEdit: converting standard targets in the convert_proc (continued)

```
        else {
            XtWarning("bitmapEdit: requestor is requesting\
                        unsupported selection target type.\n");
            return(False);
        }
    }
}
```

Overall, this code handles the TARGETS atom in the first branch, the normal selection target in the second, and any remaining standard atoms and any unknown atoms as two cases in the third branch. For ICCCM-compliant code, you can copy this entire function into your widget and then write just the second branch. Note that branches that successfully provide the requested data return `True`, and branches that don't return `False`.†

In the first branch you will also need to change the reference to the instance part field that stores the target atom used for selections, `bitmapEdit.target_atom`. If your widget uses a predefined atom or one supported by the Xmu facility, you would reference that atom here instead of the instance part field. If you called `XInternAtom()` in `initialize` and stored the result in an instance part field, you specify that here.

Note that `XtGetSelectionRequest()` is used to get the time from the `Selection-Request` event that the owner received before Xt called the `convert_proc` function. `XtGetSelectionRequest()` was introduced in R4 for this specific reason; it needs to meet the current ICCCM and work around the fact that the `convert_proc` is defined without an event argument. (The `convert_proc` definition could not be changed because of the required backwards compatibility with R3.)

11.2.10 How Incremental Selection Works

An incremental selection is very similar to an atomic transfer, except that you use different set of routines and procedure types, and Xt calls the procedures you register multiple times instead of just once as in atomic transfers. Incremental transfers and atomic transfers are mutually exclusive—an owner can support both, but if the owner doesn't, a requestor cannot use the incremental routines to request a selection owned atomically, or vice versa.

As in an atomic transfer, the owner and the requestor in an incremental transfer only have to make one call each in order to initiate this multiple-section transfer. Here is the procedure:

• The owner calls `XtOwnSelectionIncremental()` in response to the user selecting something. `XtOwnSelectionIncremental()` returns `True` or `False` to

---

†The ICCCM also specifies that functions implementing selections must be able to respond to a MULTIPLE target value, which is used to handle selections too large to fit into a single property. However, the necessary handling is done by the Intrinsics. Your procedures do not need to worry about responding to the MULTIPLE target value; a selection request with this target type will be transparently transformed into a series of smaller transfers.

indicate whether ownership was granted. `XtOwnSelectionIncremental()` registers four callbacks:

```
XtConvertSelectionIncrProc convert_proc;
XtLoseSelectionIncrProc lose_selection_proc;
XtSelectionDoneIncrProc transfer_done_proc;
XtCancelConvertSelectionProc cancel_conversion_proc;
```

- The user pastes the selection in a widget, which causes that widget to request the selection with `XtGetSelectionValueIncremental()`. `XtGetSelectionValueIncremental()` registers one callback:

```
XtSelectionCallbackProc requestor_proc;
```

This callback receives the selection data. The *requestor_proc* is called once upon delivery of each segment of the selection value. It is called with type `XT_CONVERT_FAIL` when the transfer is aborted—the requestor has the option of keeping or disposing of the partial selection. `XtGetSelectionValuesIncremental()` is analogous except that it accepts multiple target/*client_data* pairs which must be received in the *requestor_proc*.

- The request for the selection causes Xt to call the *convert_proc*, which supplies the selection as described for atomic transfers, with the following exceptions. First, *convert_proc* is called repeatedly by Xt to get each segment. Therefore, it must keep track of what segments have been delivered. Second, when the last segment has been delivered, it should store a non-`NULL` value in *value* and zero in *length_return*. Third, the *convert_proc* must be ready to supply an additional requestor while it is still engaged in transferring segments to one requestor. The *convert_proc* is called with a *request_id* argument that identifies the request. You write the *convert_proc* to maintain a record of which segments have been delivered for each `request_id`. One easy way to do this is to use the Xlib context manager.

- When each segment is converted, Xt calls the *requestor_proc* (once for each segment), which extracts the data for the requestor and actually pastes it. This function may paste the data chunk-by-chunk or wait until the entire transfer is complete and then paste the entire selection.

- A zero-length segment terminates the transfer and results in Xt calling the *transfer_done_proc*.

This was the process of a successful transfer. All the remaining callback functions registered are for less common occurrences or unsuccessful transfers. The *cancel_callback* is called by Xt on timeout. This means that the transfer is considered complete even though it failed. In this process the owner frees memory allocated for the transfer.

Calls of the *lose_ownership_proc* do not indicate completion of in-progress transfers—these transfers should continue. It just means that the owner lost ownership of the selection, so that the owner should unhighlight what the user selected.

If *transfer_done_proc* is specified, the owner allocates and frees storage. If *transfer_done_proc* is NULL, *convert_proc* must allocate storage using Xt-Malloc(), XtCalloc() or XtRealloc(), but Xt will free that memory. The owner may use XtDisownSelection() to relinquish ownership. (This is the same routine used to relinquish ownership of an atomic selection.)

11.2.11 Miscellaneous Selection Routines

If the user deletes the information selected, the owner should call XtDisown-Selection(). XtSetSelectionTimeout() sets the time in which widgets must respond to one another. This is initially set by the XmNselectionTimeout resource, and defaults to 5 seconds. The selection timeout prevents hanging when the user pastes but the current owner is slow or hung. XtGetSelectionTimeout() reads the current selection timeout value. Widgets should not normally require these two calls, since the selection timeout should remain under the user's control.

If the requestor can request more than one target type, such as TARGETS and its normal selection target, it normally does so using separate actions. (Both actions can be invoked by the same triggering event, if desired.) Each action specifies a different target type and a different requestor callback. That way, each requestor callback handles only one type of target.

Beware: there is a danger in this approach. The selection owner might change between the repeated XtGetSelectionValue() calls. XtGetSelectionValues() (plural) can be used instead if the requestor would like to receive the data in more than one representation. The requestor's single callback function would then be called once for each representation. (The owner's *convert_proc* would also be called once per representation.)

11.3 Motif Cut and Paste Functions and the Clipboard

You've seen that Xt provides an underlying mechanism called *selections* that can transfer data from one widget instance to another, whether or not the instances are in the same application. The communication occurs through the server, using properties. Most widgets that display text already support selections.

You can also use selections in your application code to transfer data to other instances of your application or to or from any other widget or application that understands the format of the data. However, selections are quite cumbersome to implement.

Motif provides some easier-to-use functions that pass data to and from the clipboard. The *clipboard* is actually a property stored in the server, so that any client can read or write it. The clipboard can only hold one piece of data at a time.

Passing a large amount of data can take a few seconds. Therefore, the clipboard is set up so that the application does not actually pass data to the clipboard until the data has been requested by some other application or widget. Your application makes data available by registering a function that supplies the data, and Xt calls that function when the data is requested. Thus if there is any delay in sending the data, it occurs when the data is pasted, not when it is cut.

Motif provides about 15 functions that read and write this data. To copy data to the clipboard, you use the sequence of functions `XmClipboardStartCopy()`, `XmClipboardCopy()`, and `XmClipboardEndCopy()`. To retrieve data from the clipboard, you use `XmClipboardInquireLength()` and `XmClipboardRetrieve()`.

According to the ICCCM, if a widget or application allows the user to delete a selection, the selection owner code should place the deleted data on the CLIPBOARD selection. Since the CLIPBOARD selection is a list of selections, the most recent deletion should be pushed onto the stack of existing selections.

The standard X distribution includes a special client, *xclipboard*, that shows the current value of the CLIPBOARD property, and allows it to be manipulated. Except when a widget asserts ownership of the CLIPBOARD with `XtOwnSelection()` in order to place newly deleted data on it, the *xclipboard* client is the owner of this property. When it starts up, *xclipboard* asserts ownership of the CLIPBOARD selection. If it loses the selection (which will happen whenever a widget or client has newly deleted the contents of a selection), it obtains the contents of the selection from the new owner, then reasserts its own ownership of the selection.

Clients wishing to restore deleted data should request the contents of the CLIPBOARD, using the same techniques as we've shown for the PRIMARY selection. *xclipboard* will respond to these requests, returning the deleted data.

The use of *xclipboard* allows the value of a selection to survive the termination of the original selection owner.

12

Geometry Management

This chapter discusses how composite and constraint widgets manage the layout of widgets, and how to write your own simple composite and constraint widgets.

In This Chapter:

12
Geometry Management

Geometry managing widgets lay out your application's widgets on screen according to certain rules. You cannot hardcode the position of widgets in an application because X applications can be resized and they must reposition their widgets to take advantage of the available space. Because of the window manager, even the initial size of the application may not be the application's preferred size.

Chapter 3, *More Techniques for Using Widgets*, demonstrated how you can use existing composite widgets such as RowColumn and constraint widgets such as Form in the application. You can control widget layout rules with resources. However, you may find that no existing composite or constraint widget can be configured with resources to have the layout rules you need. In this case, you will need to write your own composite or constraint widget or modify an existing one. However, before embarking on writing one of these widgets, you should realize that composite and constraint widgets are complex. First investigate the alternatives! Perhaps you can find a composite or constraint widget from another widget set that has the layout characteristics you need. If you determine that you have no alternative but to write your own composite or constraint widget, you should keep it as simple as possible. It is much easier to write a special-purpose widget that handles a limited layout situation than it is to write a general-purpose composite or constraint widget like RowColumn or Form.

A *composite* widget is defined as any widget that is a subclass of the Xt-defined class Composite. A *constraint* widget is any widget that is a subclass of the Xt-defined class Constraint. Constraint is a subclass of Composite. As you may recall, a composite widget is the simplest kind of geometry-managing widget; it handles all its children equally, or handles each child in a fixed way. For example, the RowColumn widget handles all of its children equally. As an example of a special-purpose composite widget, Section 12.2 describes a composite widget called ScrollBox that manages two scrollbars and a main window. This widget requires that it have exactly three children added in a particular order.

A constraint widget has all the characteristics of composite widgets but maintains configurable data about each child so that it can cater to the needs of each child. By setting the constraint resources of a child of a constraint widget, you configure the constraint widget's layout policy for that child. Constraint widgets are inherently more powerful than composite widgets, but are also more complicated to write. A constraint widget requires all the code of a composite widget, plus code to handle the constraints of each child. Because of this complexity, you should hesitate even further before attempting to write a constraint widget. As an example of the code for a constraint widget, this section describes the Athena Form widget. (The Motif Form widget is too complex to be described here.)

Composite and constraint widgets can be used within widgets as well as within applications. For example, you may recall that the *xbitmap* application was implemented using the BitmapEdit widget that appeared inside a ScrolledWindow or MainWindow widget that in turn added scrollbars. We could rewrite the BitmapEdit widget to provide its own scrollbars, controllable through resources. Although this wouldn't be worth the effort, it could lead to better scrolling performance. This new widget, which might be called ScrolledBitmap, would be a composite widget and have three children: BitmapEdit and two ScrollBar widgets. This kind of *compound* widget is actually made up of several widgets, but to the application writer it should act like a single widget. The advantage of this rewrite would be that the application code would become simpler, and the bitmap editor with scrollbars could be easily used in other applications. The fourth major section of this chapter describes how to write a compound widget.

Chapter 13, *Menus, Gadgets, and Cascaded Popups*, describes how to write a widget capable of being the parent of gadgets, which are windowless widgets.

It is a good idea to define exactly what is meant by the *geometry* of a widget. The geometry of a widget is its position, its size, and its border width. These are the Core fields `x`, `y`, `width`, `height`, and `border_width`. Border width is included because window positions are measured from the origin of the parent (the top-left corner inside the border of the parent) to the top-left corner outside the border of the child. Therefore, changing the border width of a widget by 1 pixel moves the origin of that widget 1 pixel along both the x and y axes relative to its parent. This concept is shown in Figure 12-1.

Geometry management may also control the stacking order of a group of children (that is, which children appear to be on top). However, control of the stacking order requires more programmer effort than control of geometry, because it isn't completely built into Xt.

12.1 How Composite Management Works

Like simple widgets, the characteristics of composite widgets are defined by their methods. The key methods in a composite widget are the Core methods `resize` and `query_geometry` and the Composite methods `geometry_manager` and `change_managed`. We will discuss these methods first, and then move on to the other methods defined by Composite, `insert_child` and `delete_child`, which are infrequently used.

We'll begin with a summary of what these four most important methods do. In short, they handle interactions with the three generations of widgets involved in direct geometry interactions with a composite widget: the parent of the composite widget, the composite widget itself, and the children of the composite widget.

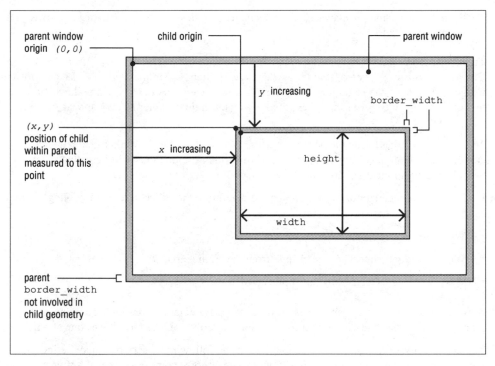

Figure 12-1. Role of border width in widget geometry

- The `resize` method moves and resizes the child widgets as necessary to fit within the composite widget's new size.

- The `query_geometry` method supplies a preferred geometry to a widget's parent when the parent calls `XtQueryGeometry()`. The parent makes this call in the process of determining a new layout for its children.

- The `geometry_manager` method handles resize requests from the child widgets. Usually, the only kind of child that will make a resize request to the parent is another composite or constraint widget. However, some simple widgets do request resizing. For example, when a Label widget's string is changed through resources, the Label widget increases its own size (this is allowed only in the `set_values` method). Xt then calls the parent's `geometry_manager` method, which must decide whether this new size is acceptable and then make any changes. When a child widget asks for more space and the composite widget doesn't have enough, the composite widget's `geometry_manager` may ask its own parent for more space by calling `XtMakeGeometryRequest()`.

- The `change_managed` method changes the layout of the children when a child is managed or unmanaged. A child is managed initially when `XtRealizeWidget()` is called (after children are created with `XtCreateManagedWidget()`) or when `Xt-ManageChild()` or `XtManageChildren()` is called to add an already-realized widget to a composite parent's managed set. (A widget can be unmanaged later to remove it from the screen without destroying it, and then managed again at any time.

Each time a child is managed or unmanaged, or destroyed, the `change_managed` method is called.)

The `resize` and `query_geometry` methods were already introduced in Chapter 7, *Basic Widget Methods*, as they are written in simple widgets. In composite widgets, they have the same job, but it is more complicated because they now have children to worry about. We will discuss these methods again in this chapter as they appear in composite widgets.

To write any of these four methods, you need to look at all the ways that geometry changes can occur, so that you know all the situations in which the methods will be called. Here are the four most important situations:

• During the negotiation that takes place to determine the initial size of each widget when an application starts up.

• When the user resizes the entire application.

• When a widget requests a size change from the application.

• When a widget is resized by the application.

As you can see, there are many cases. It helps to be systematic about understanding and programming for these cases. The next four sections describe each of these cases one at a time.

The complexity of the geometry negotiations in the following description may be intimidating. A truly general-purpose composite widget is a large, complex piece of software. You should leave this programming to the widget writers who write commercial widget sets, and concentrate on things that are more important in your application. The purpose of this description is to let you understand how complete composite widgets work, not to suggest that you should try to write one. However, it is possible to write small, special-purpose composite widgets that solve particular layout problems. Composite widgets are simpler when they are more authoritarian — when they don't do as much to try to satisfy the preferences of their children. Section 12.2 describes ScrollBox, a simple composite widget designed solely to manage a main widget and two scrollbars. Writing this kind of widget is manageable because the widget manages a fixed number of children and has simple layout rules.

12.1.1 Initial Geometry Negotiation

At least one geometry negotiation takes place in any application, even if the application is never resized. This geometry negotiation occurs when an application starts up.

Figure 12-2 shows the process of initial geometry negotiation in schematic form.

The call to `XtRealizeWidget()` initiates a two-step process. When `XtRealize-Widget()` is called on the top-level widget, most or all of the widgets have been created but windows have not been created for them. `XtRealizeWidget()` initiates a geometry negotiation that ripples through the widget hierarchy (as is described below). The widgets' `realize` methods (which create windows for the widgets) are not called until this process is complete.

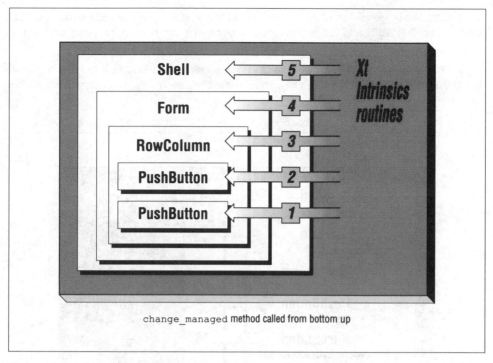

change_managed method called from bottom up

Figure 12-2. Initial geometry negotiation, assuming sufficient shell space

XtRealizeWidget() first calls the change_managed method of every composite widget in the application, beginning with the lowest widgets in the hierarchy (called a *post-order* traversal). Each change_managed method determines an initial size for each child and calls XtMoveWidget() and/or XtResizeWidget() for the child. All the change_managed methods are called until the one in the Shell widget. (Remember that the Shell widget is a composite widget that has only one child.) The child is also a composite widget (except in single-widget applications such as *xhello*). When the Shell widget is reached, the Shell widget size is set to the size of its child and the process stops unless the user has specified an initial geometry for the entire application through the resource database or command line.

A change_managed method can (but is not required to) determine each of its children's preferred geometry by calling XtQueryGeometry() for each child. This will result in the query_geometry method of each child being called. Instead of calling XtQuery-Geometry(), the change_managed method may use the child's Core width and height fields.

The change_managed method does not determine the composite widget's own size. That job is for the parent of the composite widget, which is another composite widget.

If the user-specified, top-level widget geometry is different from the geometry of the Shell widget's child after all the change_managed methods are called, then the Shell widget resizes its child to the user-specified size. This makes Xt call the resize method of the child composite, and this resize method reconsiders the layout of its children. This process proceeds down the chain of widgets to the bottom. At each stage the **resize** method can (but need not) call `XtQueryGeometry()` for each child to get each child's opinion of the intended geometry for that child.

Figure 12-3 shows the continued process of initial geometry negotiation if the user has specified the top-level geometry through resources rather than accepting the application's built-in defaults.

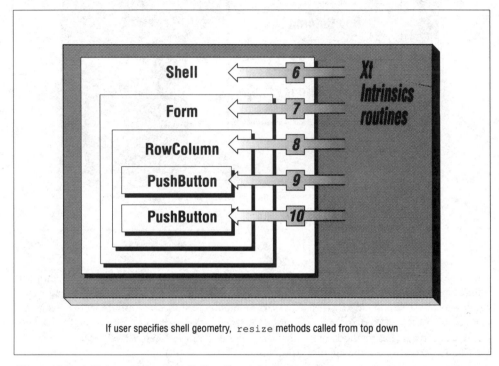

If user specifies shell geometry, `resize` methods called from top down

Figure 12-3. Initial geometry negotiation, if resizing is necessary

Note that this process and the methods involved are more complicated if the `change_managed` or `resize` methods call `XtQueryGeometry()`. `XtQueryGeometry()` calls a child widget's `query_geometry` method, as described in Section 12.2.5. When the `change_managed` or `resize` methods call `XtQueryGeometry()`, they need to propose a complete geometry for the child by setting fields in the arguments of the `XtQueryGeometry()` call, and then do different things depending upon which of the three different answers it receives from the child. The `XtGeometryAlmost` answer includes a suggested compromise. The `change_managed` or `resize` method will decide on a new size based on the compromise, and may or may not make another `Xt-QueryGeometry()` call to make this suggestion to the child. The code to perform all of this is extensive because the suggestions and answers are in the form of structures with several fields. Only the Frame, MainWindow, and ScrolledWindow classes in the Motif set call `XtQueryGeometry()`.

Notice that this process can result in the `resize, change_managed`, and possibly the `query_geometry` methods of every widget being called, but the `geometry_manager` method does not play a part.

Once this process is complete, `XtRealizeWidget()` calls the `realize` methods of all the widgets and actually creates windows for them. Up to this point, all the methods were simply changing the widget size and position parameters in Xt structures, not the sizes of actual windows. `XtRealizeWidget()` also maps all managed widgets.

12.1.2 User Resizes the Application

When `XtRealizeWidget()` returns, most applications call `XtAppMainLoop()`. Internally, this calls the Xlib call `XNextEvent()` which sends the batch of queued window creation and window map requests to the server.† Most window managers can intercept the mapping request for the top-level window and draw a rubber-band outline of the application on the screen, ready for the user to place or resize the application. With certain settings *mwm* can either place windows for you or allow you to place and size them. If the user simply places the application, no new geometry negotiation takes place. But if the user resizes the application, a new round of geometry negotiation takes place, identical to the process described above where the user specified a top-level widget geometry.

In other words, the process that occurs when the user resizes the application with the window manager is the same as when the user specifies top-level widget geometry with resources or the command line. This is also the same as when the user later resizes the existing application. This process was illustrated in Figure 12-2 and Figure 12-3.

This process uses all the methods except `geometry_manager`.

12.1.3 Widget Desires a Size Change

When an application sets a widget resource that affects what is displayed in the widget, it may be logical for the widget to ask its parent for a new size. This would occur in the `set_values` method of the widget. The widget sets its desired geometry into its Core geometry fields (`width, height, x, y,` and `border_width`). Xt finishes calling all the `set_values` methods (because they chain), and then calls `XtMakeGeometry-Request()` to ask the parent widget for a geometry change. Note that the `set_values` and `initialize` methods are the only place where widgets are allowed to set their own size directly. (In `set_values` they can do so only because of an `XtVaSetValues()` call to change a resource that affects geometry.)

Figure 12-4 shows what happens when a widget requests a size change.

---

†You can find out more about the network optimization done by Xlib in Volume One or Volume Zero.

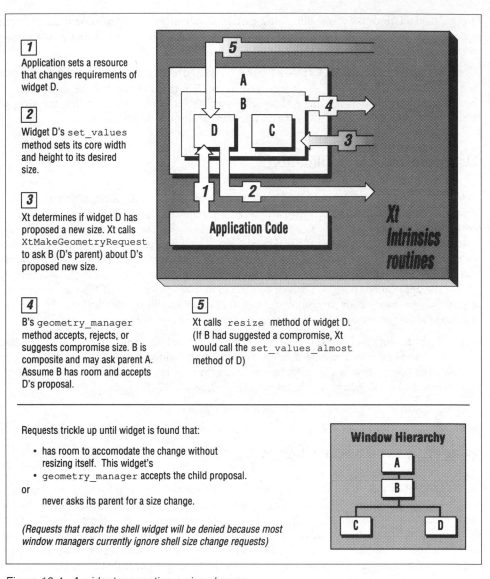

1

Application sets a resource that changes requirements of widget D.

2

Widget D's `set_values` method sets its core width and height to its desired size.

3

Xt determines if widget D has proposed a new size. Xt calls `XtMakeGeometryRequest` to ask B (D's parent) about D's proposed new size.

4

B's `geometry_manager` method accepts, rejects, or suggests compromise size. B is composite and may ask parent A. Assume B has room and accepts D's proposal.

5

Xt calls `resize` method of widget D. (If B had suggested a compromise, Xt would call the `set_values_almost` method of D)

Requests trickle up until widget is found that:

- has room to accomodate the change without resizing itself. This widget's
- `geometry_manager` accepts the child proposal.

or

never asks its parent for a size change.

(Requests that reach the shell widget will be denied because most window managers currently ignore shell size change requests)

Window Hierarchy

Figure 12-4. A widget requesting a size change

Of course, composite widgets often want a size change because their children have asked to be resized. The composite widget has no knowledge of what caused the child's size change. Therefore, composite widgets call **XtMakeGeometryRequest()** themselves to see if their parent will allow them to change size. Composite widgets should request such a change; otherwise their parent may have unused space or have other children that need more space. However, handling the variety of responses to the request is not trivial.

For both simple and composite widgets, Xt calls the `geometry_manager` method of the parent widget when `XtMakeGeometryRequest()` is called, and the method is responsible for deciding whether to except, reject, or compromise on the requested geometry. The `geometry_manager` method may have to ask its parent to decide whether it can accept its child's proposal. If so, it makes another `XtMakeGeometryRequest()` call. This can go on to arbitrary depth, and the final answer will trickle back down to the parent of the original requestor. The `XtMakeGeometryRequest()` call itself will change the child's geometry if the answer is yes. If the answer is no, the child gets this information and may try another geometry. If the answer is a compromise, then the child will get the compromise information returned in its call to `XtMakeGeometryRequest()` and make another request to be able to proceed. More on this interaction in Section 12.2.6.

This process uses only the `geometry_manager` methods of each widget. However, this method may call `XtQueryGeometry()` to determine the needs of each of its children before replying to the `XtMakeGeometryRequest()` request. When the process is finished, the `resize` method is called for any widgets that have been resized. However, the `change_managed` method is never involved.

12.1.4 Application Resizes a Widget

An application may change the size of a widget by setting the `XtNx`, `XtNy`, `XtNwidth`, `XtNheight`, or `XtNborderWidth` resources directly (as opposed to setting a resource which indirectly affects the size, as covered in the last section). If that widget has no children, the widget code does nothing, but Xt queries the parent with an `XtMakeGeometry-Request()`. The complete negotiation process as described for `XtRealizeWidget()` is repeated, except that the current top-level Shell size is used as a user-specified size (because ultimately it is).

Although the widget code did nothing, the `set_values` method sets the new values specified through resources into the Core fields. If the `XtMakeGeometryRequest()` request is denied by the parent, Xt sets these Core fields back to their original values. If the parent suggests a compromise, the `set_values_almost` method, which is described below, is called.

If the widget whose size is changed is a widget with children, the negotiation process is the same, except that when it is complete the children of the widget need to be laid out, and if the children have children they need to be laid out too, and so on.

12.2 Writing a Composite Widget

The process of writing a composite widget is the same as writing a simple widget. You copy the three files of some existing composite widget, perhaps Composite itself, make global name changes to make the files a skeleton for a distinct class, and then write new methods.

As mentioned earlier, writing a general-purpose composite widget is not a trivial task and should be done only when other options fail. Because composite widgets have no user interface, you may be able to find a composite widget with the proper characteristics from another widget set. There are several public domain widget sets to look in. Note, however, that commercial widget set vendors may design in a private protocol between their composite widgets and their children, which make the composite widgets unable to correctly manage widgets from other sets. And if you are writing a commercial product, you may have to pay a binary license fee to the commercial widget set vendor for each copy of your product. Especially for large software houses, it is a good idea to have at least one programmer adept at writing composite widgets and the `query_geometry` methods of simple widgets.

Small scale composite widgets that handle a small set of circumstances are not difficult to write, because you can make a number of simplifying assumptions. As an example, this section describes a very simple composite widget called ScrollBox, which is designed to manage a BitmapEdit widget (or any other main widget) and two ScrollBar widgets. It handles only these three widgets, and they must be added in a particular order. Because we know the geometry preferences of these three widgets (the bigger the better, but no size in particular), we can dispense with querying them about their preferred geometry. We also know that none of our children will request to be resized. Therefore, we do not need a `geometry_manager` method.

A ScrollBox widget is shown managing BitmapEdit and two scrollbars in Figure 12-5.†

The Athena Viewport widget does scrollbar management in a more general way than does ScrollBox. It is a subclass of Form that takes any main window as a child and creates scrollbars. It shows only a small portion of the main window and uses the scrollbars to determine which portion of the main window is shown. But Viewport doesn't work well with BitmapEdit because BitmapEdit has a built-in ability to display in a smaller window that conflicts with Viewport's efforts. Besides, Viewport is several times larger and more complicated than ScrollBox, because it includes the scrollbar callback functions and because it honors a child's geometry preferences. ScrollBox is a modest widget that manages the geometry of scrollbars, leaving their connection with the main window up to the application. This demonstrates the essential elements of a composite widget without too much complication.‡

The ScrollBox widget code, along with a version of *xbitmap* that uses it, is available in the example source in the *ch09* directory. It lays out its children by adjusting the width and height of the three children so that they fill the ScrollBox widget, while keeping the width of

---

†ScrollBox widens the borders of its children, for an unknown reason. It might as well be admitted that there is probably a bug in it somewhere!

‡It is worth noting that the Box widget fails miserably in managing scrollbars, while Form is adequate but has the annoying characteristic that it resizes the width of the scrollbars as well as their length, sometimes resulting in bloated or minuscule scrollbars.

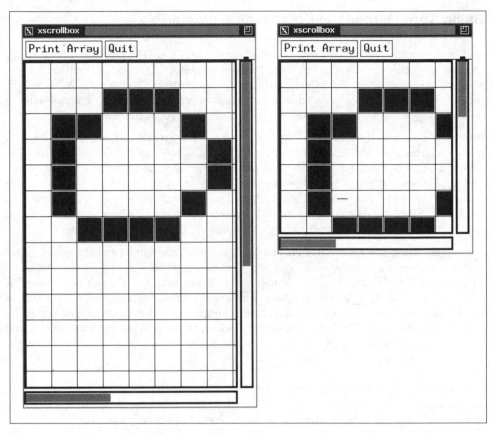

Figure 12-5. A ScrollBox widget at two different sizes

the Scrollbar widgets constant. The width of the Scrollbar widgets is set through their resources and is never modified by ScrollBox.

The first few sections below describe the methods that are used in ScrollBox and that are required in all composite widgets. First, we discuss the Core `initialize`, `realize`, `set_values`, `resize`, and `query_geometry` methods as they are used in composite widgets. Then, we discuss how the ScrollBox widget implements layout calculations in a common routine called by the `set_values`, `resize`, and `change_managed` values. This is followed by further discussion of the `change_managed` and `query_geometry` methods. Then, we go on to discuss the methods not used by ScrollBox, but that would be used in more complicated composite widgets, in particular `geometry_manager`. Finally, we briefly discuss the methods available in composite widgets but rarely needed: `set_values_almost`, `insert_child`, and `delete_child`.

12.2.1 Basic Core Methods in Composite Widgets

Both composite and constraint widgets are subclasses of Core. Therefore, they have all the Core methods described in Chapters 6 and 7. However, since composite and constraint widgets usually have no input and output semantics, the **expose** method is set to **NULL** and the widget has no default translation table or actions. As a result, all the event-oriented fields in the Core class structure become irrelevant to composite and constraint widgets.

But composite and constraint widgets do use the Core **initialize**, **realize**, and **set_values** methods. These methods have the same roles as for simple widgets. The **initialize** method initializes instance part variables and checks initial resource values. The **realize** method sets window attribute values and then creates a window for the widget. The **set_values** method updates any instance part fields that depend on resources. Since composite and constraint widgets don't need GCs, **initialize** and **set_values** don't contain code to create and change GCs as in simple widgets.

These three methods for ScrollBox are absolutely minimal, and call a common routine called **DoLayout** when any actual sizing or positioning of widgets is required. The **initialize** method simply sets the widget's default width and height, the **realize** method is inherited, and the **set_values** method changes the layout of children when either of ScrollBox's two resources is changed. These resources control the vertical and horizontal distance in pixels that will be left between the Scrollbar widgets and the main widget, and between each of these widgets and the borders of ScrollBox. Example 12-1 shows the **set_values** method of ScrollBox.

Example 12-1. ScrollBox: the set_values method

```
/* ARGSUSED */
static Boolean SetValues(current, request, new, args, num_args)
Widget current, request, new;
ArgList args;
Cardinal *num_args;
{
    ScrollBoxWidget sbwcurrent = (ScrollBoxWidget) current;
    ScrollBoxWidget sbwnew = (ScrollBoxWidget) new;

  /* need to relayout if h_space or v_space change */
    if ((sbwnew->scrollBox.h_space != sbwcurrent->scrollBox.h_space) ||
            (sbwnew->scrollBox.v_space !=
            sbwcurrent->scrollBox.v_space))
        DoLayout(sbwnew);

    return False;
}
```

Two more Core methods are used in composite widgets: **resize** and **query_geometry**. The **resize** method changes the layout of its children and is shown in Example 12-2.

Example 12-2. ScrollBox: the resize method

```
static void Resize(w)
Widget w;
{
    ScrollBoxWidget sbw = (ScrollBoxWidget) w;

    DoLayout(sbw);
}
```

The `query_geometry` method answers the parent's inquiry about a size change for this composite widget and is shown in Example 12-3.

Example 12-3. ScrollBox: the query_geometry method

```
/* ARGSUSED */
static XtGeometryResult QueryGeometry(w, request, reply_return)
Widget w;
XtWidgetGeometry *request, *reply_return;
{
    XtGeometryResult result;

    request->request_mode &= CWWidth | CWHeight;

    if (request->request_mode == 0)
    /* parent isn't going to change w or h, so nothing to
     * re-compute */
        return XtGeometryYes;

    /* if proposed size is large enough, accept it.  Otherwise,
     * suggest our arbitrary initial size. */

    if (request->request_mode & CWHeight) {
        if (request->height < INITIAL_HEIGHT) {
            result = XtGeometryAlmost;
            reply_return->height = INITIAL_HEIGHT;
            reply_return->request_mode |= CWHeight;
        }
        else
            result = XtGeometryYes;
    }

    if (request->request_mode & CWWidth) {
        if (request->width < INITIAL_WIDTH) {
            result = XtGeometryAlmost;
            reply_return->width = INITIAL_WIDTH;
            reply_return->request_mode |= CWWidth;
        }
        else
            result = XtGeometryYes;
    }

    return(result);
}
```

Although the `query_geometry` method has the same role in all widgets, composite and simple, a composite widget's size preference depends on its children. Normally this means the `query_geometry` method will query its children and try different layouts until it arrives at the geometry, or some approximation of it, suggested by its parent. This calculation is complicated because the widget may have any kind of child, and their responses to geometry suggestions are unpredictable. ScrollBox ignores this complexity because it knows exactly what kinds of children it will have and what their characteristics are. Therefore, its `query_geometry` method is basically the same as the `query_geometry` method of a simple widget.

To be more precise, what this `query_geometry` method does is accept any size suggested by the parent which is larger than the minimum useful size of the application. When the suggested size is too small, the `query_geometry` method uses the minimum useful size as a compromise. Note, however, that this is really hardcoding the characteristics of the child into our composite widget. It would be better to add resources to control the minimum useful size.

12.2.2 Laying Out Child Widgets

Composite widgets need to calculate a layout and manipulate their child widgets from `set_values`, from `resize`, and from `change_managed`. Therefore, in most composite widgets this common code is placed in a single routine called `DoLayout`. Example 12-4 shows the `DoLayout` routine from ScrollBox.

Example 12-4. ScrollBox: private routine to lay out child widgets

```
/* ARGSUSED */
static DoLayout(w)
Widget w;
{
    ScrollBoxWidget sbw = (ScrollBoxWidget) w;
    Widget main, vscroll, hscroll;
    Widget child;
    Dimension mw, mh; /* main window */
    Dimension vh;       /* vertical scrollbar length (height) */
    Dimension hw;       /* horizontal scrollbar length (width) */
    Position vx;
    Position hy;
    int i;

    if (sbw->composite.num_children != 3)
        XtAppError(XtWidgetToApplicationContext(sbw),
                "ScrollBox: must manage exactly three widgets.");

    for (i = 0; i < sbw->composite.num_children; i++) {
        child = sbw->composite.children[i];
        if (!XtIsManaged(child)) {
            XtAppError(XtWidgetToApplicationContext(sbw),
                "ScrollBox: all three widgets must be managed.");
        }
    }

    /* Child one is the main window, two is the vertical scrollbar,
     * and three is the horizontal scrollbar. */

    main = sbw->composite.children[0];
    vscroll = sbw->composite.children[1];
    hscroll = sbw->composite.children[2];

    /* Size all three widgets so that space is fully utilized. */
```

```
    mw = sbw->core.width - (2 * sbw->scrollBox.h_space) -
            vscroll->core.width - (2 * vscroll->core.border_width)
            - (2 * main->core.border_width);

    mh = sbw->core.height - (2 * sbw->scrollBox.v_space) -
            hscroll->core.height - (2 * hscroll->core.border_width)
            - (2 * main->core.border_width);

    vx = main->core.x + mw + sbw->scrollBox.h_space +
            main->core.border_width + vscroll->core.border_width;
    hy = main->core.y + mh + sbw->scrollBox.v_space +
            main->core.border_width + hscroll->core.border_width;

    vh = mh; /* scrollbars are always same length as main window */
    hw = mw;

    XtResizeWidget(main, mw, mh);

    XtResizeWidget(vscroll, vscroll->core.width, vh, 1);
    XtMoveWidget(vscroll, vx, vscroll->core.y);

    XtResizeWidget(hscroll, hw, hscroll->core.height, 1);
    XtMoveWidget(hscroll, hscroll->core.x, hy);
}
```

In general, DoLayout moves and resizes the child widgets according to its layout policy. This routine may query the children with XtQueryGeometry() before making decisions, but it is not required to. In this case, there is no need to because ScrollBox handles only two types of widgets with no size preferences.

DoLayout is passed only one argument, ScrollBox's own widget ID (a pointer to its widget instance structure). But the composite children field in ScrollBox's instance structure is an array of the IDs of all the children, and num_children is the number of children.†

When each child is added to a composite widget, its ID is added to the children field of the composite part of the instance structure, and the num_children field is incremented. Therefore, the code to lay out the children is usually a loop that treats each child one at a time. This often takes two passes, since the routine needs to know which children are managed before it can determine their final geometries. All children, even unmanaged ones, are listed in the children and num_children fields.

This particular DoLayout procedure makes sure that there are exactly three children and that they are all managed. Then, it calculates the positions and sizes for all the children so that they will fill all the available space in ScrollBox's own window. Finally, it calls Xt-ResizeWidget() and XtMoveWidget(), which check to see if there was any change before making Xlib calls to move and resize the windows.

---

†Incidentally, the children and num_children fields are resources. However, they are read-only from outside the widget code; the application should never set them with XtSetValues().

12.2.3 The change_managed Method

In every composite widget, the `change_managed` method is called once (and only once, even when there are multiple children) during the `XtRealizeWidget()` process to determine an application's initial layout. `change_managed` is also called when an application later unmanages a managed widget or manages an unmanaged widget (as long as the `Xt-NmappedWhenManaged` resource has its default value). Therefore, `change_managed` also calls `DoLayout`.

An application unmanages a widget to remove the widget from visibility without destroying it, and at the same time to tell the composite widget to change the layout of the remaining widgets to fill the gap. This is done by calling `XtUnmanageChild()` or `XtUnmanage-Children()`. The application can then make the composite widget redisplay the widget by calling `XtManageChild()` or `XtManageChildren()`. This response depends on the Core `XtNmappedWhenManaged` resource having its default value, `True`. When set to `False`, the management state has no effect on mapping, and the application must call `XtMapWidget()` and `XtUnmapWidget()` instead. Usually an application does this so that a widget will become invisible *without* triggering a re-layout to fill in the space it has vacated. Therefore, `change_managed` need not check the `XtNmapWhenManaged` resource of each child. Example 12-5 shows the `change_managed` method of ScrollBox.

Example 12-5. A basic change_managed method

```
static void ChangeManaged(w)
ScrollBoxWidget w;
{
    ScrollBoxWidget sbw = (ScrollBoxWidget) w;
    DoLayout(sbw);
}
```

12.2.4 The geometry_manager Method

The `geometry_manager` method responds to requests by the children to be resized. ScrollBox does not manage widgets that request to be resized, so theoretically it should not need a `geometry_manager`, but as of R4, Xt requires that all composite widgets have one. ScrollBox's geometry manager method is very simple, and is shown in Example 12-6.

Example 12-6. A simple geometry_manager method

```
static XtGeometryResult
GeometryManager(w, request, reply)
Widget w;
XtWidgetGeometry *request;
XtWidgetGeometry *reply;
{
    return XtGeometryYes;
}
```

Section 12.2.6 describes what would take place in a more complex `geometry_manager`, and Section 12.4.6 provides an example.

You have now seen all the code in ScrollBox! To summarize, a very basic composite widget such as ScrollBox has a standard `initialize` method, `resize` and `change_managed` methods that just call `DoLayout`, and a `set_values` method that calls `DoLayout` when any resource that affects layout is changed. The `DoLayout` routine actually lays out the children. The widget's `query_geometry` method is basically just like a simple widget's `query_geometry`. Now we'll move on to describe what may be added to this skeleton to make more fully-featured composite widgets.

12.2.5 XtQueryGeometry and the query_geometry Method

We have mentioned that `XtQueryGeometry()` calls a child's `query_geometry` method, but not the details of how this works. The `query_geometry` method for simple widgets is described in Chapter 7, *Basic Widget Methods*. The role of this method in composite widgets is the same, but the details of its job are different. You may recall that this method is passed pointers to two `XtWidgetGeometry` structures, one which specifies the parent's proposed geometry, and the other which is used by the child to return a compromise geometry. These two structures are allocated by the method that calls `XtQueryGeometry()` and passed as pointers to that call. The `XtGeometryResult enum` returned by the `query_geometry` method is passed right through as the returned value of `XtQueryGeometry()`.

Composite and constraint widgets play the role of both parent and child. When you write a composite widget, you may call `XtQueryGeometry()` in several places to get the child's response to your proposed size. You will also need to write a `query_geometry` method so that your composite can respond to its parent's `XtQueryGeometry()` request.

A `query_geometry` method in a composite widget should base its response on the size preferences of its children. It should calculate a new layout based on the proposed geometry passed in, and then query its children to get their opinions of their new geometry. If any of the children is a composite widget, they may query their children, and so on. Therefore, these requests tend to trickle down to the lowest widget in the hierarchy. ScrollBox took the biggest shortcuts in its `query_geometry` method. Not only didn't it query its children, but it hardcoded its response based on the characteristics of the kind of main window it expected. This would be the first place to begin improving ScrollBox.

Note, however, that a composite widget is allowed to be authoritarian and not ask its children whether they like the sizes they are about to be given. However, this kind of composite widget will not be suitable as a parent of a widget that really needs certain size preferences.

A parent must specify a complete proposed geometry when calling `XtQueryGeometry()`, not just the changes it intends to make.

12.2.6 XtMakeGeometryRequest and the geometry_manager Method

`XtMakeGeometryRequest()` calls are made for two reasons. First, when a composite widget honors its children's size preferences, it may find that its current size is inadequate to lay out its children. In this case, it should ask its parent to be resized by calling **XtMakeGeometryRequest()**. Second, Xt calls `XtMakeGeometryRequest()` for a widget when the application has changed a resource that affects geometry.

As mentioned above, `XtMakeGeometryRequest()` calls the parent's **geometry_ manager** method. The parent's `geometry_manager` has the job of deciding whether the size proposed by the child is acceptable. A subclass of Composite must either define a `geometry_manager` method, or set this field in the class structure to NULL, because there is no default method to inherit. The **XtInheritGeometryManager** symbol can be used only in subclasses of a class that defines a `geometry_manager` method. Any composite widget allowing its children to suggest resizing will require a `geometry_manager` method of its own.

The way the arguments and returned values are passed between **XtMakeGeometryRequest()** and the parent's `geometry_manager` method is almost exactly parallel to the way `XtQueryGeometry()` calls the child's `query_geometry` method. Both calls take pointers to two structures of the same types where one is used for a returned compromise. Both take no more arguments other than the widget ID. Both return an **enum** value of type `XtGeometryResult`. The returned value of the `geometry_manager` method is, generally speaking, passed through as the returned value of **XtMakeGeometryRequest()**. Review Section 7.6 so that these structures, their fields and values, and the returned values are fresh in your mind.

One difference between the way the `query_geometry` and `geometry_manager` methods are invoked is that the `geometry_manager` method can return a fourth **enum** value, XtGeometryDone (in addition to XtGeometryYes, XtGeometryNo, and XtGeometryAlmost). The return codes of the `geometry_manager` method are summarized in Table 12-1.

Table 12-1. Return Codes of geometry_manager Method

Code	Description
XtGeometryNo	Requested change is denied
XtGeometryAlmost	A compromise is suggested
XtGeometryYes	Requested change is accepted, let **XtMakeGeometryRequest()** make change
XtGeometryDone	Requested change is accepted, I have made change

XtGeometryDone means that `geometry_manager` approves of the change and has actually made the change. `XtMakeGeometryRequest()` never returns XtGeometryDone though; it returns XtGeometryYes when the `geometry_manager` returns XtGeometryYes or XtGeometryDone. When the `geometry_manager` returns XtGeometryYes, the `XtMakeGeometryRequest()` call itself makes the size change. All these shenanigans simply allow the parent to make the size change by calling its normal layout code or to let `XtMakeGeometryRequest()` do it, depending on which is most convenient.

The second difference is that `XtMakeGeometryRequest()` and the `geometry_manager` method interpret the `XtGeometryNo` returned value differently. For `XtMakeGeometryRequest()` and `geometry_manager`, it has its intuitive meaning that the requested change is denied. For `query_geometry` and `XtQuery-Geometry()`, the symbol should really be `XtGeometryNoChange`. Since this symbol doesn't exist, `XtGeometryNo` has to do double duty, meaning in this case that the proposed size and current size are the same.

The final difference is an additional mask for the `request_mode` field of the `Xt-WidgetGeometry` structure that contains the proposed change. In `XtMakeGeometry-Request()` requests, the mask `XtCWQueryOnly` can be ORed with the masks that identify which fields in the proposed geometry the child considers important. This indicates that the proposed change should not be made, but that the `geometry_manager` method should fill in the return structure with the changes it *would* have made. This flag is used whenever a widget is making an `XtMakeGeometryRequest()` from its `geometry_manager` method: these requests are intermediate (triggered by requests from children). The composite widget does not actually want to be resized until it has made a suggestion for its own size to its parent, received an answer from the parent, recalculated the layout of its children, and queried its children, if necessary, to see that the new size is adequate for everybody.

This also makes it obvious that the `geometry_manager` method you write for your composite widget must be prepared to handle the `XtCWQueryOnly` mask. It should calculate a layout but not actually move or resize any widgets.

ScrollBox does not need a `geometry_manager` method because it knows that its children will never make geometry requests. However, any composite widget that accepts all kinds of children requires a `geometry_manager` method. In Section 12.4.6 below, the `geometry_manager` method of the Form widget is shown and described.

Similar to `XtMakeGeometryRequest()`, but less general, is `XtMakeResize-Request()`. Instead of passing two structures, `XtMakeResizeRequest()` passes two width and height pairs. Otherwise, the results of this call are the same.

Shell widgets (which are a subclass of Composite) have an extension structure (see Section 14.13) that contains a `root_geometry_manager` field. This field is a pointer to a function which acts like the `geometry_manager` method that would exist in the composite parent of the Shell widget, if Shell had one. This method is needed because the only "parent" of Shell is the window manager. Since it is unlikely that you will need to write your own Shell widget, you are unlikely to have to write or even read a `root_geometry_manager` method.

12.2.7 The set_values_almost Method

As mentioned above, a child widget may request a geometry change for one of three reasons:

- The application just called `XtSetValues()` and set a geometry field. In this case, Xt makes the geometry request to the parent to allow the parent to overrule or modify the change.

- The application just called `XtSetValues()` and set a resource that affects geometry, like the string displayed in a Label widget. The `set_values` method of the child changes the geometry fields in the widget directly. Then Xt makes a geometry request to the parent, to allow the parent to overrule or modify the change.

- The child may decide it needs more or less room because of some kind of user input, or because its own children need more or less room. In this case, it calls `XtMake-GeometryRequest()` itself, and handles the various returned values itself. If the widget wants to use `set_values_almost` to make compromise suggestions (since it is designed for that purpose and may be there anyway), the widget will have to call the method itself.

In the first two cases, Xt calls `XtMakeGeometryRequest()`, while in the third case, the child must call the function itself. If the returned value is `XtGeometryYes`, the `Xt-MakeGeometryRequest()` call itself (or Xt) has resized the child.

When `XtMakeGeometryRequest()` is called by Xt, and its returned value is `Xt-GeometryAlmost` or `XtGeometryNo`, Xt calls the `set_values_almost` method of the widget whose geometry is changing. A return value of `XtGeometryNo` is like the parent saying: "I don't like the geometry you suggested, and I don't have any compromise to suggest." A return value of `XtGeometryAlmost` means "The geometry you suggested is not quite acceptable: would this compromise suit you?" The job of `set_values_almost` is to accept the compromise geometry proposed by the parent or to propose a different geometry to the parent. Once a new geometry is proposed by the `set_values_almost` method, Xt calls the parent's `geometry_manager` method again, and the cycle repeats until the `geometry_manager` returns `XtGeometryYes` or `XtGeometryDone`, or until the child gives up trying to change size. Figure 12-6 illustrates this process.

Most widgets inherit this method from the Core widget by specifying `XtInheritSet-ValuesAlmost` in the Core class part initialization. This inherited method always approves the suggestion made by the parent `geometry_manager` method. If your widget really depends on being certain sizes, however, you will need to write a `set_values_almost` method. You should never specify a NULL `set_values_almost` method because Xt will print a warning message when `set_values_almost` would have been called, and continue as if it had been called and had returned `XtGeometryYes`.

The `set_values_almost` method is passed pointers to two `XtWidgetGeometry` structures: `request` and `reply`. The `request` structure contains the child's original request and `reply` includes the `geometry_manager` method's compromise geometry if `geometry_manager` returned `XtGeometryAlmost`. To accept the compromise, the procedure must copy the contents of the reply geometry into the request geometry; to attempt an alternate geometry, the procedure may modify any part of the request argument; to termi-

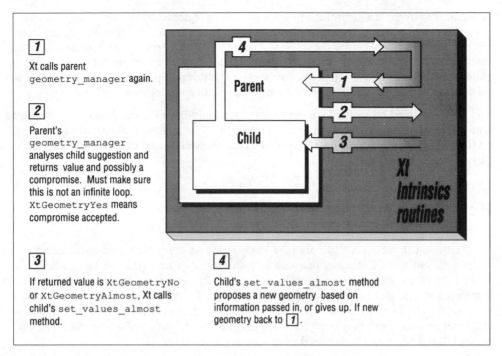

1

Xt calls parent
`geometry_manager` again.

2

Parent's
`geometry_manager`
analyses child suggestion and
returns value and possibly a
compromise. Must make sure
this is not an infinite loop.
`XtGeometryYes` means
compromise accepted.

3

If returned value is `XtGeometryNo`
or `XtGeometryAlmost`, Xt calls
child's `set_values_almost`
method.

4

Child's `set_values_almost` method
proposes a new geometry based on
information passed in, or gives up. If new
geometry back to **1**.

Figure 12-6. Geometry negotiation by the set_values_almost method

nate the geometry negotiation and retain the original geometry, the procedure must set
`request->request_mode` to zero.

If `geometry_manager` returned `XtGeometryNo`, it will not have generated a compromise. In this case, the `set_values_almost` method may suggest a new geometry, but it
is probably not worth it since the method has no information upon which to base its changes
to its previous suggestion. The `set_values_almost` method at this point should usually
just set `request->request_mode` to zero to terminate the geometry negotiation.

12.2.8 The insert_child and delete_child Methods

The Composite class has an instance part structure that contains an array of all the widget's
children (even those not currently managed), the current number of children, and the total
number of child slots available. The `insert_child` method inserts the ID of a child into
this array. It is called when the child is created by a call to `XtCreateWidget()` or `Xt-CreateManagedWidget()`. Most widgets inherit the `insert_child` method from
the Composite class by specifying the symbolic constant `XtInheritInsertChild` in
the class structure initialization. A class would replace the default `insert_child` method to control the position of each child added, or to limit the number or classes of widgets
that can be added.

A composite widget can control the position of each child added by calling a function whose pointer is stored in the instance part field `insert_position`. The function should return the number of widgets before the widget. The `XtNinsertPosition` resource sets this function pointer. The default `insert_position` function returns the current number of children. Of course, because this resource's value is a function pointer, it can be specified in the application only at run time, never through the resource files or command line.

The `delete_child` method removes the ID of a child from the child array and is called when the application calls `XtDestroyWidget()`. This method is almost always inherited from Composite by specifying the symbolic constant `XtInheritDeleteChild` in the class structure initialization.

12.3 How Constraint Management Works

The first thing to realize about constraint widgets is that everything said about composite widgets is still true. Because Constraint is a subclass of Composite, all the methods described above are still present and have the same tasks. However, constraint widgets also maintain a structure full of data attached to each child, set through resources. Every time it lays out the children, the constraint widget reads this data to determine how to handle that child. Of course, it still may query each children to get its opinion of a new size. The constraint information adds another level of complexity to the situation.

Like composite widgets, constraint widgets can be drastically simplified by reducing flexibility and features. The Athena Form widget, for example, never queries its children for their geometry input and never asks its parent for a size change. Furthermore, its constraints for each child are quite limited. This makes Form quite short and simple, but also means that it doesn't always do the right thing.

12.4 Writing a Constraint Widget

The following sections describe the portions of the Athena Form widget that relate to geometry management. We have chosen the Athena Form widget instead of the Motif Form widget because the Athena Form widget is less than one quarter the size and is much simpler to understand. The principles at work are similar, and an understanding of the Athena implementation should give you a good start towards understanding geometry management under Motif.

However, before we start, an introduction to the constraints of the Athena Form widget is in order. As you should remember, constraints appear to the user to be resources of the child widgets managed by the Form. Looking at these resources gives you a good idea of the kinds of things that can be done with Athena Form constraints.

• The resources `XtNhorizDistance` and `XtNfromHoriz` specify the widget position in terms of a specified number of pixels horizontally away from another widget in the form. As an example, `XtNhorizDistance` could equal 10 and `XtNfromHoriz` could be the widget ID of another widget in the Form. (When specified in a resource file,

XtNfromHoriz is set using the instance name of another widget in the form.) The new widget will always be placed 10 pixels to the right of the widget defined in **XtNfromHoriz**, regardless of the size of the Form. If **XtNfromHoriz** equals **NULL**, then **XtNhorizDistance** is measured from the left edge of the Form.

- Similarly, the resources **XtNvertDistance** and **XtNfromVert** specify the widget position in terms of a specified number of pixels vertically away from another widget in the Form. If **XtNfromVert** equals **NULL**, then **XtNvertDistance** is measured from the top of the Form.

  When set in the application, the values for **XtNfromHoriz** and **XtNFromVert** must be widget IDs. But in the resource database, widget names are used instead, since the actual widget ID changes each time the application is run. Athena uses an Xmu converter from widget name to widget ID, which is useful when setting constraints from resource files. However, Motif does not provide such a converter.

- The **XtNtop**, **XtNbottom**, **XtNleft**, and **XtNright** resources tell the Form where to position the child when the Form is resized. The values of these resources are specified by the **enum XtEdgeType**, which is defined in *<X11/Xaw/Form.h>*.

- The values **XtChainTop**, **XtChainBottom**, **XtChainLeft**, and **XtChainRight** specify that a constant distance is to be maintained from an edge of the child to, respectively, the top, bottom, left, and right edges of the Form.

- The value **XtRubber** specifies that a proportional distance from the edge of the child to the left or top edge of the Form is to be maintained when the Form is resized. The proportion is determined from the initial position of the child and the initial size of the Form. Form provides a **StringToEdgeType** conversion to allow the resize constraints to be easily specified in a resource file.

12.4.1 The Core Resource List

The Form widget has only one resource of its own, **XtNdefaultDistance**, as shown in Example 12-7. This resource is used only as the default for two of the Constraint resources, **XtNhorizDistance** and **XtNvertDistance**. **XtNdefaultDistance** is used to set the instance field **default_spacing**, which is used in only one place in the widget, in the Constraint **initialize** method described in Section 12.4.4.

Example 12-7. Form: the Core resource list

```
#define Offset(field) XtOffsetOf(FormRec, form.field)
static XtResource resources[ ] = {
    {
        XtNdefaultDistance,
        XtCThickness,
        XtRInt,
        sizeof(int),
        Offset(default_spacing),
```

Example 12-7. Form: the Core resource list (continued)

```
        XtRImmediate,
        (XtPointer)4
    }
};
#undef Offset
```

12.4.2 The Constraint Resource List

The Form widget has three groups of constraint resources. `XtNhorizDistance`, `XtNfromHoriz`, `XtNvertDistance`, and `XtNfromVert` together control the initial position of a child. `XtNtop`, `XtNleft`, `XtNbottom`, and `XtNright` govern repositioning of the child when Form is resized. The `XtNresizable` resource controls whether the `geometry_manager` of this widget will honor requests to change the geometry of this child. Note that `XtNresizable` does not control whether this constraint widget can resize a child—only whether or not it will do so because of a request from the child.†

For more details about how these constraint resources work, read about them on the reference page for the Form widget in Volume Five, *X Toolkit Intrinsics Reference Manual*.

Constraint resources are also called simply *constraints*, particularly because they are stored in a Core instance field called `constraints`. Example 12-8 shows Form's constraint resource list.

Example 12-8. Form: constraint resource list

```
static XtEdgeType defEdge = XtRubber;

#define Offset(field) XtOffsetOf(FormConstraintsRec, form.field)
static XtResource formConstraintResources[ ] = {
    {
    XtNhorizDistance,
    XtCThickness,
    XtRInt,
    sizeof(int),
    Offset(dx),
    XtRImmediate,
    (XtPointer)DEFAULTVALUE
    },
    {XtNfromHoriz, XtCWidget, XtRWidget, sizeof(Widget),
        Offset(horiz_base), XtRWidget, (XtPointer)NULL},
    {XtNvertDistance, XtCThickness, XtRInt, sizeof(int),
        Offset(dy), XtRImmediate, (XtPointer)DEFAULTVALUE},
    {XtNfromVert, XtCWidget, XtRWidget, sizeof(Widget),
        Offset(vert_base), XtRWidget, (XtPointer)NULL},

    {XtNtop, XtCEdge, XtREdgeType, sizeof(XtEdgeType),
        Offset(top), XtREdgeType, (XtPointer)&defEdge},
    {XtNbottom, XtCEdge, XtREdgeType, sizeof(XtEdgeType),
        Offset(bottom), XtREdgeType, (XtPointer)&defEdge},
```

---

†The fact that Form does not provide individual control over the resizability of each child is a major weakness.

Example 12-8. Form: constraint resource list (continued)

```
    {XtNleft, XtCEdge, XtREdgeType, sizeof(XtEdgeType),
        Offset(left), XtREdgeType, (XtPointer)&defEdge},
    {XtNright, XtCEdge, XtREdgeType, sizeof(XtEdgeType),
        Offset(right), XtREdgeType, (XtPointer)&defEdge},

    {XtNresizable, XtCBoolean, XtRBoolean, sizeof(Boolean),
        Offset(allow_resize), XtRImmediate, (XtPointer)False},
};
#undef Offset
```

The corresponding data structure that this resource list references, **FormConstraints**, is defined in the private include file for the widget. Its definition is shown in Example 12-9.

Example 12-9. Form: constraint data structure

```
typedef struct _FormConstraintsPart {
/*
 * Constraint Resources.
 */
    XtEdgeType   top, bottom,    /* where to drag edge on resize    */
                 left, right;
    int          dx;             /* desired horiz offset            */
    int          dy;             /* desired vertical offset         */
    Widget       horiz_base;     /* measure dx from here if non-null */
    Widget       vert_base;      /* measure dy from here if non-null */
    Boolean      allow_resize;   /* True if child may request resize */
/*
 * Private constraint variables.
 * These store the dimensions of the child prior to layout.
 */

    int          virtual_width, virtual_height;
/*
 * Size of this child as it would be if we did not impose the
 * constraint that its width and height must be greater than zero (0).
 */

    LayoutState layout_state;    /* temporary layout state */
} FormConstraintsPart;

typedef struct _FormConstraintsRec {
    FormConstraintsPart form;
} FormConstraintsRec, *FormConstraints;
```

The constraints part structure should be considered an instance part structure. This structure has public fields set through resources and private fields that hold state data, just like an instance part structure. Note also that the **FormConstraints** structure is built the same way as instance structures, by combining part structures for each class into a complete constraint structure. This allows subclasses of Form to create their own constraint part structure and add it after the Form constraint part.

When a widget is created as a child of a constraint widget, the constraint instance structure (**FormConstraintsRec**, in this case) is placed in the **constraints** field of the Core instance structure. Xt makes the constraint resources stored there settable, like resources defined by the child even though they are actually defined and used by the parent.

Note that the constraint resource list of a widget can be queried with `XtGet-ConstraintResourceList()`, although this is rarely needed in widget or application code.

12.4.3 Class Structure Initialization

The Form class is a subclass of Constraint. Therefore, its class structure contains class parts for Core, Composite, Constraint, and Form. Example 12-10 shows the class structure initialization of Form. Several methods referenced here have not been discussed so far in this book. They are the Core methods `class_initialize` and `class_part_init`, and the Constraint methods `initialize` and `set_values`. These and all the geometry management-related methods of Form are discussed in Section 12.4.6.

Example 12-10. Form: class structure initialization

```
FormClassRec formClassRec = {
  { /* Core class fields  */
    /* superclass          */    (WidgetClass) &constraintClassRec,
    /* class_name          */    "Form",
    /* widget_size         */    sizeof(FormRec),
    /* class_initialize    */    ClassInitialize,
    /* class_part_init     */    ClassPartInitialize,
    /* class_inited        */    False,
    /* initialize          */    Initialize,
    /* initialize_hook     */    NULL,
    /* realize             */    XtInheritRealize,
    /* actions             */    NULL,
    /* num_actions         */    0,
    /* resources           */    resources,
    /* num_resources       */    XtNumber(resources),
    /* xrm_class           */    NULLQUARK,
    /* compress_motion     */    True,
    /* compress_exposure   */    True,
    /* compress_enterleave */    True,
    /* visible_interest    */    False,
    /* destroy             */    NULL,
    /* resize              */    Resize,
    /* expose              */    XtInheritExpose,
    /* set_values          */    SetValues,
    /* set_values_hook     */    NULL,
    /* set_values_almost   */    XtInheritSetValuesAlmost,
    /* get_values_hook     */    NULL,
    /* accept_focus        */    NULL,
    /* version             */    XtVersion,
    /* callback_private    */    NULL,
    /* tm_table            */    NULL,
    /* query_geometry      */    PreferredGeometry,
    /* display_accelerator */    XtInheritDisplayAccelerator,
    /* extension           */    NULL
  },
  { /* Composite class fields */
    /* geometry_manager    */    GeometryManager,
    /* change_managed      */    ChangeManaged,
    /* insert_child        */    XtInheritInsertChild,
```

Example 12-10. Form: class structure initialization (continued)

```
    /* delete_child       */   XtInheritDeleteChild,
    /* extension          */   NULL
},
{ /* Constraint class fields */
    /* subresources       */   formConstraintResources,
    /* subresource_count  */   XtNumber(formConstraintResources),
    /* constraint_size    */   sizeof(FormConstraintsRec),
    /* initialize         */   ConstraintInitialize,
    /* destroy            */   NULL,
    /* set_values         */   ConstraintSetValues,
    /* extension          */   NULL
},
{ /* Form class fields */
    /* layout             */   Layout
}
};
WidgetClass formWidgetClass = (WidgetClass)&formClassRec;
```

Note that the Form class is the first widget we have shown that defines a class part field—a method of its own, called `layout`. Since this method is not known to Xt, Xt will never call it. The widget must invoke this method itself at the appropriate times (you will see this invocation in the methods below). This code is made into a method instead of just a private function only to make it possible for subclasses of this widget to inherit or replace the method. Having such a method requires that the widget have a `class_part_init` method to handle the inheritance if a subclass specifies the `layout` method with the symbolic constant `XtInheritLayout` (also defined in this class's private header file).

Section 12.2.1 described which Core and Composite methods are required for composite widgets, and how to initialize the other Core and Composite fields for a composite widget. The same is true for constraint widgets.

However, the Constraint part is probably new to you. The `ConstraintClassPart` structure contains seven fields. The first three fields are where the constraint resource list, the number of resources, and the size of the constraint instance structure are entered. This resource list and instance structure were described in the last section. These fields are analogous to the `resources`, `num_resources`, and `widget_size` fields in the Core class part.

The three next fields, `initialize`, `destroy`, and `set_values` are methods defined by the Constraint class. These methods have the same field names as methods of Core, but are fields of a different structure, and contain pointers to different functions that you may need to write. To differentiate Constraint methods from the Core methods, we will precede the names of Constraint fields with the word "Constraint" and the names of Core fields with the word "Core" throughout this chapter.

Two of the three Constraint methods will be described where they fit in below. We'll describe one of them, Constraint `destroy`, now, because it is not used in Form and is less likely to be needed in the constraint widgets you may write. The Constraint `destroy` method is called when a child is destroyed, just before the Core `destroy` method of the child. It is responsible for freeing any memory allocated by the constraint widget that was used to manage that child. However, like the Core `destroy` method, it does not need to free memory allocated by Xt, such as the constraint data structure for the child.

12.4.4 The Constraint initialize Method

The Constraint `initialize` method is called when a widget is created, soon after the Core `initialize` method. It has the same two responsibilities as the Core initialize method, and one additional responsibility. It must:

- Validate the ranges of resource settings, since they may be user-supplied.

- Compute the value of any private constraint instance part fields that depend on constraint resource values (public constraint instance part fields).

- Set child Core geometry fields to match the constraint resources. For example, if a constraint for the maximum height of a widget is set and the initial value set by the child is larger, the Constraint `initialize` method resets the height field in the Core instance structure.

However, like the Core `initialize` method, the Constraint `initialize` method is responsible only for constraint resources and for Core geometry resources. It need not handle any resources of superclasses (other than the Core geometry resources).

The Form widget performs only one of the tasks listed above, initializing constraint resources. In Form's case, the Constraint `initialize` method (shown in Example 12-11) simply sets the initial values of the **XtNvertDistance** and **XtNhorizDistance** constraint resources to the current value of the **XtNdefaultDistance** Form resource, unless the user has specified a value for either constraint resource. This is done only so that the application can set the Form resource once and have it apply to every child that does not override the value.

Form doesn't validate the values of any user-supplied resource values as it should. For example, the user may supply a negative value for the **XtNhorizDistance** or **XtNvert-Distance** resources. This would certainly make the layout look bad, but it could also cause the Form widget to go into an infinite loop on geometry negotiations. In general, all `initialize` methods in Core and Constraint should check for ranges of reasonable values of resources where this makes sense. Range checking eliminates a potential source of bugs. Range checking in **set_values** is also a good idea to give the programmer good warning messages).

Example 12-11. Form: the Constraint initialize method

```
#define DEFAULTVALUE -9999

/* ARGSUSED */
static void ConstraintInitialize(request, new)
    Widget request, new;
{
    FormConstraints form = (FormConstraints)new->core.constraints;
    FormWidget fw = (FormWidget)new->core.parent;

    form->form.virtual_width = (int) new->core.width;
    form->form.virtual_height = (int) new->core.height;


    if (form->form.dx == DEFAULTVALUE)
        form->form.dx = fw->form.default_spacing;
```

Example 12-11. Form: the Constraint initialize method (continued)

```
        if (form->form.dy == DEFAULTVALUE)
            form->form.dy = fw->form.default_spacing;
    }
```

Note that the Constraint instance part structure (**FormConstraints**) and the Form widget instance structure (**FormWidget**) are accessed by casting two different fields of the child's instance structure passed in.

The Constraint **initialize** method and the child's Core **initialize** are passed the same two copies of the child's instance structure: **request**, and **new**. The **request** widget is the widget as originally requested. The **new** widget starts with the values in the request, but it has already been updated by calling all superclass **initialize** methods.

12.4.5 The class_part_init Method

The **class_part_init** method should be present in a class that defines new methods in its class part structure. These new methods will never be called by Xt since Xt has no knowledge of when to call them. They can only be invoked directly from the widget code. The purpose of making them methods instead of just functions is to allow subclasses to inherit or replace the functions. The **class_part_init** method actually resolves this inheritance by setting each method field to the pointer provided by this class (the subclass is inheriting the method) or to the pointer provided by the subclass (the subclass is replacing the method). Example 12-12 shows a **class_part_init** method for a class that defines only one new method in its class part structure. This method is the Form widget's layout code.

Example 12-12. Form: the class_part_init method

```
static void ClassPartInitialize(class)
    WidgetClass class;
{
    register FormWidgetClass c = (FormWidgetClass) class;

    if (c->form_class.layout == XtInheritLayout)
        c->form_class.layout = Layout;
}
```

The **XtInheritLayout** symbol is defined in the private include file for any class that defines new class part methods (one for each new method). Its value is always **_XtInherit**.

Form itself sets the **layout** field to a pointer to its **Layout** function. When its **class_part_init** method is called when the first instance of Form is created, it does nothing because the **layout** field is not **XtInheritLayout**. When a subclass is defined that sets the **layout** field to a function, the same thing happens: Form's **class_part_init** method is called because it is chained downward (the **class_part_init** methods of all superclasses are called), and it still does nothing because the **layout** field is not **XtInheritLayout**. Thus, the subclass has replaced Form's method. But if the subclass sets the **layout** field to **XtInheritLayout**, Form's **class_part_init** method sets the field to its own **Layout** function. The subclass has inherited Form's method.

Usually, only the class that defines a particular new method resolves the inheritance by checking for the value of that field in its `class_part_init` method. There is no point in a subclass also checking for an `XtInherit` value, since the downward chaining means that the superclass will have already processed and replaced the `XtInherit` value before the subclass `class_part_init` method is called.

12.4.6 The geometry_manager Method

`geometry_manager` methods handle requests from the children to be resized. Therefore, they typically use the proposed geometry passed in from the child to calculate a new experimental layout, and actually move and resize the children if the new layout is acceptable. However, when the request is just a query, the method should be able to return the same values without actually moving or resizing anything.

The Form `geometry_manager` method is shown in Example 12-13. Note that Form uses the `allow_resize` field (the `XtNresizable` resource) to determine whether to even consider the resize request. Then, if the request specifies a width and height, Form will accept the change by returning `XtGeometryYes`. The `XtMakeGeometryRequest()` call that invoked the `geometry_manager` will actually make the geometry change before returning to the child's code. If the request specifies any other geometry change (border width, position, or stacking order), Form will deny the request. Finally, if the request was not a query, Form actually does the new layout. Note that Form never returns `XtGeometry-Done` since it never makes the geometry changes itself. Instead it returns `XtGeometry-Yes` when it agrees with the changes, and lets Xt make the changes.

Note that the `allowed` structure in this routine could be replaced by individual *width* and *height* variables. Also note that the `reply` structure is never filled; it is used only when the `geometry_manager` method wants to suggest a compromise.

Example 12-13. Form: the geometry_manager method

```
/* ARGSUSED */
static XtGeometryResult GeometryManager(w, request, reply)
    Widget w;
    XtWidgetGeometry *request;
    XtWidgetGeometry *reply;     /* RETURN */
{
    FormConstraints form = (FormConstraints)w->core.constraints;
    XtWidgetGeometry allowed;

    if ((request->request_mode & ~(XtCWQueryOnly |
            CWWidth | CWHeight)) ||
          !form->form.allow_resize)
        return XtGeometryNo;

    if (request->request_mode & CWWidth)
        allowed.width = request->width;
    else
        allowed.width = w->core.width;

    if (request->request_mode & CWHeight)
        allowed.height = request->height;
    else
```

Example 12-13. Form: the geometry_manager method (continued)

```
        allowed.height = w->core.height;

    if (allowed.width == w->core.width && allowed.height ==
            w->core.height)
        return XtGeometryNo;

    if (!(request->request_mode & XtCWQueryOnly)) {
        /* reset virtual width and height. */
        form->form.virtual_width = w->core.width = allowed.width;
        form->form.virtual_height = w->core.height = allowed.height;
        RefigureLocations( (FormWidget)w->core.parent );
    }
    return XtGeometryYes;
}
```

The `RefigureLocations` called from the `geometry_manager` method is a private
function analogous to the `DoLayout` routine used in ScrollBox, except that `Refigure-`
`Locations` calls Form's `layout` method that contains the actual layout code so that the
method can be inherited or replaced by subclasses. The `layout` method calculates a layout
and moves and resizes the children. `RefigureLocations` is also called from the
`change_managed` method, as described in Section 12.4.9. Example 12-14 shows the
`RefigureLocations` function and Form's `layout` method, which it calls. (The `if`
statement that branches depending on the value of the `no_refigure` field allows an application to turn relayout on and off, as described in Section 12.4.11.)

Example 12-14. Form: private functions: RefigureLocations and the layout method

```
static void RefigureLocations(w)
    FormWidget w;
{
    /* no_refigure supports the relayout recalculation
      delay described later in this chapter */
    if (w->form.no_refigure) {
        w->form.needs_relayout = True;
    }
    else {
        (*((FormWidgetClass)w->core.widget_class)->form_class.layout)
                ( w, w->core.width, w->core.height );
        w->form.needs_relayout = False;
    }
}

/* ARGSUSED */
static Boolean Layout(fw, width, height)
    FormWidget fw;
    Dimension width, height;
{
    int num_children = fw->composite.num_children;
    WidgetList children = fw->composite.children;
    Widget *childP;
    Position maxx, maxy;
    static void LayoutChild();
    Boolean ret_val;

    for (childP = children; childP - children < num_children;
            childP++) {
```

Geometry
Management

```
        FormConstraints form = (FormConstraints)
                (*childP)->core.constraints;
        form->form.layout_state = LayoutPending;
    }

    maxx = maxy = 1;
    /*
     * Layout children one at a time, and determine
     * necessary size for self
     */
    for (childP = children; childP - children
            < num_children; childP++) {
        /*
         * Layout child then find position of bottom right
         * outside corner of child
         */
        if (XtIsManaged(*childP)) {
            Position x, y;
            LayoutChild(*childP);
            x = (*childP)->core.x + (*childP)->core.width
                    + ((*childP)->core.border_width << 1);
            y = (*childP)->core.y + (*childP)->core.height
                    + ((*childP)->core.border_width << 1);
            if (maxx < x) maxx = x;
            if (maxy < y) maxy = y;
        }
    }

    fw->form.preferred_width = (maxx += fw->form.default_spacing);
    fw->form.preferred_height = (maxy += fw->form.default_spacing);

    /* Now ask parent to resize us.  If it says Almost, accept the
     * compromise.  If Almost and parent chose smaller size, or No
     * and we were smaller than necessary, children will be clipped,
     * not laid out again.
     */
    if (fw->form.resize_in_layout
            && (maxx != fw->core.width || maxy != fw->core.height)) {
        XtGeometryResult result;
        result = XtMakeResizeRequest( fw, (Dimension)maxx,
                (Dimension)maxy, (Dimension*)&maxx,
                (Dimension*)&maxy );
        if (result == XtGeometryAlmost)
            result = XtMakeResizeRequest( fw, (Dimension)maxx,
                    (Dimension)maxy, NULL, NULL );
        fw->form.old_width  = fw->core.width;
        fw->form.old_height = fw->core.height;
        ret_val = (result == XtGeometryYes);
    } else ret_val = False;

    return ret_val;
}
```

The `layout` method treats one child at a time, first initializing the `layout_state` private constraint instance field of each child to `LayoutPending`. The `LayoutChild` routine will start from this value. Next, it calls `LayoutChild` for each child, and at the same time keeps a running total of the sizes of the children so that when the loop is finished it knows how big to be to fit all the children. Finally, it requests of its parent that it be just big enough to fit its children. If the parent denies the request, the code makes no attempt to make another request. If the parent offers a compromise, it is accepted. The Form widget, in either case, may be too big or too small to fit its children. If it is too small, some of its children will be clipped.

The `LayoutChild` routine is shown in Example 12-15. What it does is simple, although it is a little hard to follow because it is called recursively. It moves the child according to the `XtNfromHoriz` and `XtNfromVert` constraint resources.† These resources specify that a child be placed to the right of or below another particular child.

Example 12-15. Form: the LayoutChild private function

```
static void LayoutChild(w)
    Widget w;
{
    FormConstraints form = (FormConstraints)w->core.constraints;
    Position x, y;
    Widget ref;

    switch (form->form.layout_state) {

        case LayoutPending:
                form->form.layout_state = LayoutInProgress;
                break;

        case LayoutDone:
                return;

        case LayoutInProgress:
                String subs[2];
                Cardinal num_subs = 2;
                subs[0] = w->core.name;
                subs[1] = w->core.parent->core.name;
                XtAppWarningMsg(XtWidgetToApplicationContext(w),
                        "constraintLoop","xawFormLayout",
                        "XawToolkitError", "constraint loop\
                        detected while laying out child\
                        '%s' in FormWidget '%s'",
                        subs, &num_subs);

                return;
    }

    x = form->form.dx;
    y = form->form.dy;

    if ((ref = form->form.horiz_base) != (Widget)NULL) {
        LayoutChild(ref);
        x += ref->core.x + ref->core.width +
                (ref->core.border_width
                << 1);
    }
    if ((ref = form->form.vert_base) != (Widget)NULL) {
        LayoutChild(ref);
```

---

†Form resizes children only when it is resized—never during normal layout.

Example 12-15. Form: the LayoutChild private function (continued)

```
        y += ref->core.y + ref->core.height +
              (ref->core.border_width
              << 1);
    }
    XtMoveWidget( w, x, y );
    form->form.layout_state = LayoutDone;
}
```

If neither `XtNfromHoriz` nor `XtNfromVert` are set for the child, it is simply placed the default distance from the top-left corner of the Form. When one child is set, the next child must be placed relative to that child. However, the other child may be later in the list and not properly positioned yet. Therefore, the code calls `LayoutChild` to lay out the child that this child is positioned relative to.

The `layout_state` field catches circular settings for the `XtNfromHoriz` and `XtNfromVert` resources. For example, if widget *A* is specified to the right of widget *B*, and widget *B* is specified to the right of widget *A*, there is no solution. `LayoutChild` would be caught in an infinite loop of calling itself. When first called from the `layout` method, the `layout_state` is `LayoutPending`. This is changed to `LayoutInProgress` in the `switch` statement. If the function is called again for the same child, this state will cause the warning message to be printed and the function to exit. The Form widget does not exit—it just gives up processing the invalid constraint resource setting and prints a warning message.

12.4.7 The resize Method

The `resize` method calculates a layout to fit in the new dimensions of Form and moves and resizes the children accordingly. Form's `resize` method is shown in Example 12-16. It consists of a loop that treats each managed child one at a time. The position and dimensions of each child are calculated with the help of the private function `TransformCoord` (also shown in Example 12-16) and the child is moved and resized. `TransformCoord` handles one parameter at a time, and uses a position, the size before resizing, the size after resizing, and the constraints settings to arrive at the appropriate value for the parameter. The old width and height of the Form widget are initialized in the Core `initialize` method and updated at the end of the `resize` method.

Example 12-16. Form: the resize method

```
static void Resize(w)
    Widget w;
{
    FormWidget fw = (FormWidget)w;
    WidgetList children = fw->composite.children;
    int num_children = fw->composite.num_children;
    Widget *childP;
    Position x, y;
    Dimension width, height;

    for (childP = children; childP - children < num_children;
            childP++) {
        FormConstraints form = (FormConstraints)
```

Example 12-16. Form: the resize method (continued)

```
                        (*childP)->core.constraints;
            if (!XtIsManaged(*childP)) continue;
            x = TransformCoord( (*childP)->core.x, fw->form.old_width,
                    fw->core.width, form->form.left );
            y = TransformCoord( (*childP)->core.y, fw->form.old_height,
                    fw->core.height, form->form.top );

            form->form.virtual_width =
                    TransformCoord((Position)((*childP)->core.x
                    + form->form.virtual_width
                    + 2 * (*childP)->core.border_width),
                    fw->form.old_width, fw->core.width,
                    form->form.right )
                    - (x + 2 * (*childP)->core.border_width);

            form->form.virtual_height =
                    TransformCoord((Position)((*childP)->core.y
                    + form->form.virtual_height
                    + 2 * (*childP)->core.border_width),
                    fw->form.old_height, fw->core.height,
                    form->form.bottom )
                    - ( y + 2 * (*childP)->core.border_width);

        width = (Dimension)
                    (form->form.virtual_width < 1) ? 1 :
                    form->form.virtual_width;
        height = (Dimension)
                    (form->form.virtual_height < 1) ? 1 :
                    form->form.virtual_height;

        XtConfigureWidget( *childP, x, y, (Dimension)width,
                    (Dimension)height, (*childP)->core.border_width);

    }
    fw->form.old_width = fw->core.width;
    fw->form.old_height = fw->core.height;
}

static Position TransformCoord(loc, old, new, type)
    register Position loc;
    Dimension old, new;
    XtEdgeType type;
{

    if (type == XtRubber) {
        if ( ((int) old) > 0)
            loc = (loc * new) / old;
    }
    else if (type == XtChainBottom || type == XtChainRight)
        loc += (Position)new - (Position)old;

    return (loc);
}
```

This **resize** method stores the new size of the children in the **virtual_width** and
virtual_height constraint part fields, and uses their previous values to arrive at the
new size. This is done because Form's **XtNtop**, **XtNbottom**, **XtNleft**, and **XtNright**
constraints specify the geometry of the child based on its previous geometry.

Notice that the `for` loop in this particular `resize` method loops through the children directly, using pointer arithmetic. This is equivalent to using a loop that increments an integer and then uses the integer to index the `children` array. For example, the first five lines of the loop could also be expressed as:

```
int i;

for (i = 0; i < num_children; i++) {
    FormConstraints form = (FormConstraints)
            (children[i])->core.constraints;
    if (!XtIsManaged(children[i])) continue;
    x = TransformCoord( (children[i])->core.x,
            fw->form.old_width, fw->core.width, form->form.left );
        .
        .
        .
}
```

12.4.8   The Core and Constraint set_values Methods

When the application calls `XtSetValues()` to set the resources of a child of a constraint widget, Xt calls the child's Core `set_values` method and then the parent's Constraint `set_values` method. Both methods are passed the same arguments. Constraint `set_values` validates the ranges of constraint resource settings and computes the value of any private constraint instance part fields that depend on constraint resource values. It should also set child Core geometry fields to match the changes in constraint resources. For example, if a constraint for the maximum height of a widget is changed to a value smaller than the widget's current height, then the Constraint `set_values` procedure should reset the height field in the widget.

Both Core and Constraint `set_values` must return **True** or **False** to indicate whether redisplay of the widget is necessary. For composite and constraint widgets, this value is usually meaningless because there is nothing to redisplay. But these might be useful if, for some reason, you write a composite widget that does have display semantics.

Form defines both the Core and Constraint `set_values` methods as empty functions that return **False**. An easier way to do this is to specify **NULL** for them in the class structure initialization.

12.4.9   The change_managed Method

The `change_managed` method is responsible for making the initial layout of an application and changing the layout when any child changes management state. Form's `change_managed` method (shown in Example 12-17) calls `RefigureLocations` to actually do a layout. (`RefigureLocations` is a private routine equivalent to **DoLayout** in ScrollBox, described in Section 12.4.6.) Form's `change_managed` method also stores the previous size of the children in the `virtual_width` and `virtual_height` constraint part fields for use in the `resize` method as described in Section 12.4.7.

Example 12-17. Form: the change_managed method

```
static void ChangeManaged(w)
    Widget w;
{
    FormWidget fw = (FormWidget)w;
    FormConstraints form;
    WidgetList children, childP;
    int num_children = fw->composite.num_children;
    Widget child;

    /*
     * Reset virtual width and height for all children.
     */

    for (children = childP = fw->composite.children;
            childP - children < num_children; childP++) {
        child = *childP;
        if (XtIsManaged(child)) {
            form = (FormConstraints)child->core.constraints;

            if ( child->core.width != 1)
                form->form.virtual_width = (int) child->core.width;
            if ( child->core.height != 1)
                form->form.virtual_height = (int) child->core.height;
        }
    }
    RefigureLocations( (FormWidget)w );
}
```

12.4.10 The query_geometry Method

Form's `query_geometry` method (shown in Example 12-18) is the minimal version, almost identical to the one described for simple widgets in Chapter 7, *Basic Widget Methods*. The `preferred_width` and `preferred_height` instance variables are set in the Form class `Layout` method to the size that just fits the current layout.

Example 12-18. Form: the query_geometry method

```
static XtGeometryResult PreferredGeometry( widget, request, reply  )
    Widget widget;
    XtWidgetGeometry *request, *reply;
{
    FormWidget w = (FormWidget)widget;

    reply->width = w->form.preferred_width;
    reply->height = w->form.preferred_height;
    reply->request_mode = CWWidth | CWHeight;
    if (  request->request_mode & (CWWidth | CWHeight) ==
            reply->request_mode & CWWidth | CWHeight
            && request->width == reply->width
            && request->height == reply->height)
        return XtGeometryYes;
    else if (reply->width == w->core.width && reply->height ==
            w->core.height)
        return XtGeometryNo;
```

Example 12-18. Form: the query_geometry method (continued)

```
    else
        return XtGeometryAlmost;
}
```

12.4.11 Delaying Geometry Recalculation

During an application's initial layout, the `change_managed` method of a composite widget is called only once even though many children may have been managed. However, after
that, `change_managed` is called once for every child that changes management state.
Many composite or constraint widgets, especially ones that have complicated layout code,
provide a public function (such as the one shown in Example 12-19) that the application can
call to turn off layout recalculation until a group of windows is managed or unmanaged, and
then call again to trigger recalculation once the whole group of children has been managed or
unmanaged.

To implement this delay, you need an instance variable to hold a Boolean value indicating
whether to delay or not (`no_refigure`, in this case). You set and unset this variable in
this public routine and you test it in `change_managed`.

Example 12-19. Form: the public function for delaying calls to change_managed

```
void XawFormDoLayout(w, doit)
Widget w;
Boolean doit;    /* False, don't recalculate; True, do */
{
    register FormWidget fw = (FormWidget)w;

    fw->form.no_refigure = !doit;

    if ( XtIsRealized(w) && fw->form.needs_relayout )
        RefigureLocations( fw );
}
```

12.5 Compound Widgets

A compound widget is a combination of widgets put together to make a higher-level, user-interface object. For example, a ScrolledWindow widget is itself a composite widget, but it
automatically creates its own ScrollBar children. Similarly, the code for MessageBox can
create its own Shell parent, and it creates PushButtonGadget children that read OK, Cancel,
and Help.

Compound widgets create their children in their `initialize` method, and set resources to
position them. Often they also provide resources of functions that make it easy for the application to configure some characteristics of their children. The application can manipulate the
children only through these resources, because it cannot access the widget IDs of the compound widget's subwidgets without breaking the rules of data hiding. Thus, compound widg-

ets are convenient for programming, but they make it more difficult to take advantage of all the configurable aspects of the subwidgets.

The main widget of the compound widget may be a subclass of Core, Composite, or Constraint. If it is a subclass of Core, the widget manages the positions and sizes of its children manually whenever it is resized. The success of this strategy is dependent on the children never trying to resize themselves and on the application never trying to resize the children directly.† The latter will not be a problem unless the application breaks the data-hiding rules by manipulating the child directly. The Text widget is an example of this kind of widget. It creates and manages its own scrollbar.

Compound widgets normally define only a few methods and inherit the rest. Compound widgets based on Core will move and resize their children manually in their `resize` method. If the widget is a subclass of Composite or Constraint, the normal geometry management facilities manage the position and size of the children. If it is a subclass of Constraint, the main widget sets the constraints of the children to control the geometry management process by providing a Constraint `initialize` method.

A compound widget always needs a `destroy` method that destroys the children it created. Compound widgets also need a `set_values` method to manage their resources.

12.6 Stacking Order

We promised earlier to say a bit more about how composite or constraint widgets can control the stacking order of their children. We noted that this must be done manually, because Xt doesn't provide much support for it. This is because most applications do not stack widgets—the whole concept of geometry management is based on each widget trying to lay out its children *without* stacking them. However, there are applications where it makes sense to stack widgets. For example, an application that provides note cards, where each card is a widget, would want to stack them showing only the corner of hidden cards.

There is no Core resource for stacking order, and therefore it can't be set with `XtSetValues()` unless you define the resources in your own widget class. Xt provides no call to restack windows; you must use the Xlib functions `XConfigureWindow()`, `XRestackWindows()`, `XRaiseWindow()`, or `XLowerWindow()`. When a widget suggests a stacking order for itself through its `query_geometry` method, Xt takes care of making the required Xlib call if the parent agrees with the change. However, stacking requests of unrealized widgets have no effect (so stacking order won't be set this way in the initial geometry negotiation). Therefore, the most robust method to handle stacking order is for your composite widget to make the appropriate Xlib calls directly to change the stacking order of its children. `XRestackWindows()` is probably the best call to use. Since restacking the windows doesn't change their requirements for screen space, it shouldn't affect either the parent or the children adversely. The appropriate place to call `XRestackWindows()`

---

†When a child of a simple widget calls `XtMakeGeometryRequest()` because it wants to change its size, `XtMakeGeometryRequest()` always makes the requested changes and returns `XtGeometryYes`. Therefore, a simple widget parent really has no control over its child if the child wants to resize itself. A simple widget cannot even tell that the child has resized itself.

depends on when you want to change the stacking order. (Note that the stacking change won't become visible until the next time Xt is waiting for an event.)

You can control the initial stacking order of a group of children by creating them in the desired order. The most recently created widget appears on the bottom. (This is the opposite of what you might expect if you know that newly created X windows appears on top of their siblings. The difference is due to the way a composite widget maintains its list of children.)

13

Menus, Gadgets, and
Cascaded Popups

This chapter begins by describing how to use Motif Popup and cascaded menus. Then it describes how menus actually work, and several ways to create menu widgets. One of these ways involves the use of windowless widgets, or gadgets. This chapter also describes how to use more advanced features of the Xt pop up mechanism, including modal cascades, to implement cascading pop up menus and dialog boxes.

In This Chapter:

13

Menus, Gadgets,
and Cascaded Popups

In Chapter 3, *More Techniques for Using Widgets*, we show a simple example that pops up a menu and a dialog box. We used Motif's widget creation functions to create these widgets and we let Motif handle their placement when they were popped up. We popped them up by creating a callback that called `XtManageChild()`. This chapter continues where Chapter 2 left off by describing how to create other types of menus, and how to create cascaded menus and dialog boxes with Motif.

Motif, however, is atypical since it hides the actual Xt mechanisms that support popup widgets. After describing how Motif handles popups, this chapter continues by exploring these underlying mechanisms. The examples in the second part of the chapter use the Athena widgets, since they expose Xt's underlying mechanisms effectively. Even though Motif hides these details, it is helpful to understand exactly what is happening underneath.

This chapter also discusses cascaded popups—popups that call other popups—and the event management necessary for them to shut out other input elsewhere in the application and system.

Finally, this chapter discusses windowless widgets called *gadgets*, which were originally designed to reduce X server memory consumption. Later improvements in the implementation of windows in the X server reduce the advantage of gadgets. Furthermore, gadgets greatly increase the network traffic caused by an application. Therefore, they should be avoided. However, Motif 1.1 and 1.2 still include gadgets for backwards compatibility, so for completeness they are covered here. Their most important use is to implement the panes in menu widgets. As an example of a widget that manages gadgets, we will show the R4 Athena SimpleMenu widget and its gadget children.

Also introduced in R4 is the *object*, which is another kind of windowless widget even simpler than a gadget. Objects are not usually used in menus, so we will reserve discussion of them until Chapter 14, *Miscellaneous Toolkit Programming Techniques*.

In this chapter, we use the term *menu* broadly to refer to any user-interface element that lists many options and allows the user to select one or more. A menu might consist of a list of commands, only one of which can be selected at a time, or a list of nonexclusive Boolean settings that can be turned on or off, or a list of exclusive choices (such as the colors or patterns for a paint palette). A menu that invokes commands will start in the same state each time, while the other two types may have different contents in any particular invocation, showing the settings invoked the previous time or all previous times, or a modified list of choices.

Menus are one of the most important user-interface elements in window-based applications. They offer the same feature as push buttons—a way for the user to invoke application functions or set parameters—but in a more organized and more easily accessible fashion when there are more than a few buttons.

Figure 13-1 compares a menu to a box full of buttons.

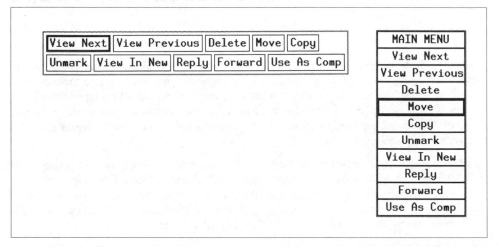

Figure 13-1. Athena Command widgets in an Athena Box widget, and the same commands as a SimpleMenu

The menu takes up less space because only its title is visible until it is called up.† As a result, you can have more menus than you could have permanent button boxes. Commands can be presented in smaller, more closely related groups. The user will spend less time searching for the desired command.

The commands in the menu are also easier to read because they are arranged one per row. The commands in the menu may even be easier to invoke because it is more natural to drag the mouse up and down than from side to side. And last but not least, menus avoid the worst problem with button boxes: when the application is resized, button boxes may place each command widget in a different position, making it more difficult for the user to find commands.‡

---

†Some menus don't even display a title—they simply pop up at the pointer position in response to a particular pointer button/keypress combination. This is the behavior of the menus provided by *xterm* and the system menu of *mwm*. However, this is not very desirable behavior from a user-interface point of view, since it gives the user no visual feedback that a menu is available or how to invoke it. The user needs the manual—something graphical user interfaces are designed to avoid.

‡ To be fair, there is something to be said for the fact that all the available commands are always visible in an application that uses button boxes. You can invoke a button in a box with just a button click, while in a menu it requires a press, a drag, and a release. When there are only a small number of commands, putting the command widgets in a box is probably better than using a menu.

Some of the applications in the core distribution from MIT use button boxes instead of menus because there was no menu widget in the Athena widget set until Release 4. And some of the applications that do use menus have implemented them directly with Xlib.

13.1 Menu Styles and Implementation

The conventions for the appearance and user interface of menus (look and feel) in widget sets probably varies more than any other aspect of the user interface.

There are several different styles of menus. As we've pointed out earlier, a button box is itself a style of menu. However, in this chapter we will be focusing on popup menus—menus that are not visible until the user presses a pointer button or a key-button combination.

There are several different styles of popup menu. Probably the most familiar is the pulldown menu popularized by the Apple Macintosh. A *pulldown menu* has a label permanently visible in the application, usually on a menu bar at the top. When the pointer is clicked on the label, and then dragged downwards, the menu is pulled down like a window shade, and remains displayed as long as the pointer button is depressed. The currently selected item (as indicated by the pointer position within the menu) is highlighted, and is executed when the pointer button is released.

The variation adopted by Motif and OPEN LOOK (possibly to avoid legal entanglements with Apple) is a menu in which the pointer need not be dragged down to display the menu. Instead, it appears below the menu title as soon as the button is depressed in the menu title. The distinction between pulldown and drop-down menus is a subtle one.

In some cases, selecting an item on the menu or moving off the right side of certain menu panes causes a second menu to appear next to the first (usually to the right). This is referred to as a *cascading menu*. (Another type of cascading popup is a dialog box that pops up another dialog box.)

Finally, there is the pure *spring-loaded popup menu* used by many of the standard X clients, which displays no menu label, and simply pops up at the pointer position, given the appropriate key or button press. For example, the menus in *xterm* pop up when you hold the Control key and press the first or second button while the pointer is anywhere in the *xterm* window. Motif calls this type of menu simply a *popup* menu (as opposed to pulldown or option menus). We will refer to these menus using the term spring-loaded since the term popup is too generic.

One can also imagine many other possible menu styles. For example, an effective user interface could be constructed using only horizontal menus, emulating the single-line menu popularized by Lotus for its character-based 1-2-3 spreadsheet. Any given button might either execute an action, or pop up a lower-level menu, which would overlay (and thus appear to replace) the first menu.

In this chapter, though, we will focus on the two styles of menu you are most likely to encounter in X applications: the pulldown menu and the pure spring-loaded popup menu.

In code, the difference between spring-loaded and pulldown menus is primarily the method by which the user invokes the menu and where the menu is placed; one menu widget class can usually work in either way. In Motif, both the pulldown and popup menu styles are actually RowColumn widgets inside Shell widgets, but they are popped up in slightly different ways.

All the differences described so far concern user-interface conventions. The Xt specification, however, classifies popups using a different criteria—while the menu is popped up, how is input dispatched to other parts of the application and to other applications? Also, is the menu subject to window management? The three styles are called modeless popups, modal popups, and spring-loaded popups.

Modeless popups are windows that, once popped up, are subject to window manager control, and for all intents and purposes act like regular applications in themselves. A help window that stayed up, and could be moved and resized like a regular window once popped up, is an example of this type of popup. It is referred to as "modeless" because it doesn't put the application into a special mode, in which only input to the popup is allowed.

A modal popup may or may not be visible to the window manager, but it always disables user-event processing by the application, except in the popup itself. A dialog box that requires the user to enter data or click on a button is an example of a modal popup. Input may still be possible to other applications.

As defined by Xt, a spring-loaded popup is invisible to the window manager and disables user input to all windows in all applications, except to the popup itself. The most important thing about spring-loaded popups is that they are invoked with a key or pointer button press, whereas another type of popup might be invoked as a routine part of application processing, or just because the pointer entered a particular window. Note that even though the term spring-loaded has been used in two different contexts above, both actually refer to the same kinds of widgets. The first use referred to a characteristic user-interface style, and the second to a characteristic absence of window management and disabling of input to other applications. Throughout this chapter, though, we use the term "spring-loaded popup" to refer to menus that pop up at the pointer position when a mouse button is pressed, such as that used by *xterm*, as opposed to popup or pulldown menus.

13.2 Using Motif Menus

Chapter 3, *More Techniques for Using Widgets*, showed how to create and use a Motif pull-down menu. This section demonstrates how to use a Motif popup menu, and then shows how to implement cascaded menus—menus that pop up other menus.

Volume Six, *Motif Programming Manual*, will describe more thoroughly how to use menus, such as how to add mnemonics and accelerators.

13.2.1 Popup Menus

Using a Motif popup menu is really not much different from using a Motif pulldown menu. The first difference, obviously, is that you use XmCreatePopupMenu() instead of Xm-CreatePulldownMenu(). The most significant difference, however, is that you are responsible for placing the popup. As you may recall, a pulldown menu is automatically positioned just below the button whose callback invoked the menu. A popup menu, on the other hand, is usually invoked by a button press in the custom window or main window of the application. The menu usually pops up at the pointer position.

A popup menu can be popped up in response to a button press in a particular widget only if the button press does not already have another meaning in that widget. For example, a Label widget can be used as the widget that will detect a button press and pop up a popup menu, because it doesn't otherwise use button presses for anything. Although a PushButton button widget could pop up a popup menu in its XmNactivateCallback, this would confuse the user because this callback is normally associated with executing a command.

Widgets that don't already use button presses usually don't have a callback triggered by them. Therefore, actions or event handlers are often used to place and to pop up menus. Example 13-1 shows the code to create, place, and pop up a popup menu using an event handler.

Example 13-1. Creating, placing, and popping up a popup menu

```
#include <Xm/Xm.h>

/*
 * Public include files for widgets used in this file.
 */
#include <Xm/RowColumn.h>
#include <Xm/PushB.h>
#include <Xm/Label.h>

/*
 * menu pane button callback function
 */
/*ARGSUSED*/
void PaneChosen(w, client_data, call_data)
Widget w;
XtPointer client_data;    /* cast to pane_number */
XtPointer call_data;
{
    int pane_number = (int) client_data;
    printf("Pane %d chosen.\n", pane_number);
}

static void
PostMenu (w, client_data, event)
Widget       w;
XtPointer    client_data;
XEvent       *event;
{
    Widget popup = (Widget) client_data;

    XmMenuPosition(popup, event);
    XtManageChild (popup);
```

Example 13-1. Creating, placing, and popping up a popup menu (continued)

```
}
main(argc, argv)
int argc;
char **argv;
{
    .
    .
    .
    Widget menu, label, menupane[10];
    .
    .
    .
    label = XtVaCreateManagedWidget(
        "label",                /* widget name */
        xmLabelWidgetClass,     /* widget class */
        box,                    /* parent widget */
        NULL                    /* terminate argument list */
        );

    menu = XmCreatePopupMenu(label, "menu", NULL, 0);

    XtAddEventHandler(label, ButtonPressMask, False, PostMenu, menu);

    for (i = 0; i < 10; i++) {
        sprintf(buf, "menupane%d", i);
            menupane[i] = XtVaCreateManagedWidget(buf, /* widget name */
                    xmPushButtonWidgetClass, menu, NULL);

        XtAddCallback(menupane[i], XmNactivateCallback,
                PaneChosen, i);
    }

    XtRealizeWidget(topLevel);

    XtAppMainLoop(app_context);
}
```

The standard way to place a popup menu is to call **XmMenuPosition()** just before calling **XtManageChild()** in the function that pops up the widget. This places the popup
with the center of its top edge at the pointer position, but forces the entire menu on the screen
(if part would otherwise extend off the screen).

Note that by default Motif will only pop up a popup menu in response to mouse button 3.
This can be changed by setting the **XmNmenuPost** resource of the popup menu.

13.2.2 Cascaded Menus

Cascaded menus in Motif are always pulldown menus, regardless of whether the parent menu
is popup or pulldown. The first step in implementing a submenu is to create it with **Xm-
CreatePulldownMenu()**. Next, you create a CascadeButtonWidget as a child of the
main menu, and set its **XmNsubMenuId** resource to the ID of the submenu. Then populate
the submenu with gadget entries and register their callback functions. Example 13-2 shows
the code needed to add a submenu to Example 13-1.

Example 13-2. Adding a cascading submenu

```
#include <Xm/CascadeB.h>

main(argc, argv)
int argc;
char **argv;
{
        .
        .
        .
    Widget menu, cascade, submenu, subentry[10];
        .
        .
        .
    /* create main menu */
        .
        .
        .
    submenu = XmCreatePulldownMenu(menu, "submenu", NULL, 0);

    cascade = XtVaCreateManagedWidget("cascade",
            xmCascadeButtonWidgetClass, menu,
            XmNsubMenuId, submenu,
            NULL);

    for (i = 0; i < 10; i++) {
        sprintf(buf, "subentry%d", i);
        subentry[i] = XtVaCreateManagedWidget(buf, /* widget name */
                xmPushButtonGadgetClass, submenu, NULL);
        XtAddCallback(subentry[i], XmNactivateCallback,
                PaneChosen, i);
    }
        .
        .
        .
}
```

Note that the submenu is created before the CascadeButtonWidget that will invoke the submenu. This makes it possible to set **XmNsubMenuId** while creating the CascadeButton-
Widget.

13.3 Basic Xt Popup Support

As mentioned above, Motif hides Xt's mechanisms that support popups. This section
exposes these mechanisms by describing how to create and use a menu using the Athena
widgets in two different menu styles: spring-loaded and pulldown. The purpose of this exercise is to expose some of the issues involved in event management of popups. Seeing how to
do the event management explicitly should help you to use popups more effectively.

The challenge of creating a popup with Box and Command buttons is to make it pop up and
down at the right times, and to control its event handling to fit the menu style. We will also
experiment with creating a cascaded menu, in which one menu pane in a main menu invokes
a submenu.

Finally, this section describes how to create a menu using the R4 Athena SimpleMenu widget
and its gadget children.

13.3.1 A Spring-loaded Menu: Pointer Grabbing

A spring-loaded menu should pop up when a button press occurs in a particular widget; usually the application's main window. The menu should stay visible as long as the user holds down that button, and disappear when the button is released. If the button is released in a menu pane, the function registered for that pane should be invoked. If the button is released outside the menu, no function should be invoked but the menu should still be popped down.

The only tricky part of implementing a spring-loaded menu is getting the menu to pop down when the button is released outside the menu. Since this occurs outside the menu and possibly outside the application, the X server will not send the button release event to the application unless a *grab* is in effect. Normally, user events are sent to the window that contains the pointer. But after an application makes a grab, the X server sends all events of particular types to the window that made the grab, even if the pointer is no longer in the window.

The X server defines several types of grab: keyboard grabs, pointer grabs, and server grabs. Keyboard and pointer grabs control only input from the indicated device, while server grabs make the server act on requests from one application exclusively. (Server grabs are mainly used by window managers.) Pointer grabs are used for controlling events in popups when a pointer button pops up the popup, and keyboard grabs are used when a key press pops up the popup. We will discuss pointer grabs since keyboard grabs are analogous (and keyboard-triggered popups are less common).

There are two types of pointer grabs: passive grabs and active grabs. An *active grab* is invoked directly with the Xt function `XtGrabPointer()`. This function tells the server that you want the grab to begin right away and to continue until specifically released with `XtUngrabPointer()`. Active grabs are not normally used for popups.†

A *passive grab* tells the server that you want a grab to begin when a certain key or button combination is pressed in a certain window (the combination that is to pop up the popup). The grab continues until the button in the combination is released. This is perfect for menus because we need the grab only until the button is released. (Also, as you'll see in the section on pulldown menus, you can register several passive grabs for the same key-button combination as long as each grab is initiated by a press in a different window. This technique lets you have as many pulldown menus as you want. Since spring-loaded popups are generally invoked by a press in the same window—the main window of the application—you will need to use a different key-button combination for each different menu.)

Passive grabs of a key or button and active grabs of the pointer or the keyboard we will call *global grabs*, since they affect not only this application but prevent distribution of the grabbed events to other applications running on the same server. This terminology is to distinguish the global grab from the effects of Xt's local *grab mode*, which simulates a global grab but requires no call to the server and affects only the distribution of events within the application. The Xt grab mode cannot commandeer events that occur outside the application

---

†One reason that `XtGrabPointer()` is rarely used for popups is that it requires that the window that will receive the grabbed events be visible. This is often not the case. In a menu, for example, the window that you want to grab the events may be hidden by the menu panes even when the menu is popped up. Another reason is that you need to call `XtUngrabPointer()` to release the grab when finished. Passive grabs match the task better.

like a global grab can. When an Xt grab is in effect, Xt redirects user events to the popups even if they occur somewhere else in the application. (Non-user events continue to be dispatched to widgets so that they can redraw themselves).

The Xt grab mode can be either exclusive or nonexclusive. Exclusive and nonexclusive Xt grabs differ only when a popup has popped up another popup—a so-called cascaded popup. An *exclusive* Xt grab redirects all user events that occur within the application to the latest popup in the cascade. A nonexclusive Xt grab redirects events to whichever popup the pointer is in, or the latest popup if the pointer is outside all the popups (but still in the application).

Here are examples of the two kinds of Xt grab modes. Consider an application that pops up a dialog box to get a filename from the user. The application wants to read the file. If the file can't be opened, the application pops up another dialog telling this to the user. This error popup takes no input, so input is still desired in the filename entry popup. This situation calls for a nonexclusive grab. By contrast, consider an application that uses the same filename entry popup to save a file. If the file exists, it would pop up a dialog that would ask whether the existing file should be overwritten. This popup must be answered before a new filename is chosen. This situation would call for an exclusive grab. In brief, an exclusive grab constrains input to the the latest widget in the cascade, while a nonexclusive grab allows input to any widget in the cascade. We'll talk more about the Xt grab mode in Section 13.3.3, when we talk about popup cascades.

Xt provides three ways of popping widgets up and down:

- There are three built-in callback functions: `XtCallbackNone()`, `XtCallback-Exclusive()`, and `XtCallbackNonexclusive()`. Each of these functions pops up a widget with a different type of Xt grab mode, as indicated by its name. `XtCallbackNone()` makes no grab at all. `XtCallbackExclusive()` makes an exclusive Xt grab, while `XtCallbackNonexclusive()` makes a nonexclusive grab.

  `XtCallbackPopdown()` is the corresponding built-in callback function to pop down a widget.

- There are two built-in actions, `XtMenuPopup()` and `XtMenuPopdown()`, that pop up or pop down a widget. You can use these actions in translation tables in the app-defaults file or application code. `XtMenuPopup()` always asserts an exclusive Xt grab and a passive global grab if the pointer or keyboard invoked it.

- There are three functions, `XtPopup()`, `XtPopupSpringLoaded()`, and `XtPopdown()`, that you can call directly in your application code to pop up or pop down a widget. `XtPopup()` has a *grab_kind* argument that lets you specify whether to assert an exclusive or nonexclusive grab mode, or no grab. `XtPopupSpringLoaded()` always asserts an exclusive Xt grab and makes an global pointer grab so that a button release outside a menu can be used to trigger the popping down of the menu.

Each of these ways is appropriate for different situations, and they are often used in combination. Each is described in the sections below.

Passive global grabs can be invoked directly using the Xt functions `XtGrabButton()` and `XtGrabKey()`. However, Xt takes care of making the appropriate passive global grab if you use `XtPopupSpringLoaded()` or the `XtMenuPopup()` action to pop up your shell widget. As we will see, the other ways to pop up a widget do not make any global grab, which makes them inappropriate for popping up main menus.† However, they are still useful for some types of dialog boxes and for cascading submenus, if the main menu has used `Xt-MenuPopup()` to assert an exclusive grab. We'll return to this subject in Section 13.3.3.

A popup menu globally grabs the pointer to force the user to make a menu choice before leaving the menu, or to pop down the menu if no choice is made. However, this global grab is necessary for another reason as well. The X server automatically grabs the pointer beginning at a button press and ending at the release of the same button. Since the initial button press pops up the menu, the next button release would also arrive at the same widget—the application main window or the menu title—even if the pointer were already in the menu. Furthermore, the application main window would get all `EnterNotify` and `Leave-Notify` events, so the Command widgets in the menu wouldn't get any of them. When the menu is popped up with `XtMenuPopup()` action, the passive global grab it makes cancels the automatic global grab. (Again, pointer grabs redirect only the events caused directly by the pointer; `ButtonPress`, `ButtonRelease`, `EnterNotify`, `LeaveNotify`, and `MotionNotify`. All other events (most notably `Expose` events) occur and are delivered normally.)

With that background, let's take a look at an application that provides a spring-loaded menu. The *xmenu1* application's permanent appearance is a variation of *xbox*; it displays a large Label widget that we are using to simulate an application's main window and a Command widget for quitting. Pressing any button in the Label widget calls up the menu, which operates as described at the beginning of this section. *xmenu1* is shown in Figure 13-2. As usual, we suggest you compile and run this example now.

The relevant code in *xmenu1* consists of an action routine to place the popup, code to add the action, a callback routine to handle when a menu item has been chosen, and code to create the Box populated with Command widgets that will act as the menu. Example 13-3 shows the complete code.

---

†With `XtPopupSpringLoaded()` you can write callback functions that are the equivalent of `XtCallback*`, except that they will pop up a menu with the necessary passive global grab. You can also write your own version of the `XtMenuPopup()` action if it doesn't do what you want. You will need `XtRegisterGrabAction()` to do this. This function tells Xt to automatically start a passive global grab whenever a certain action is invoked.

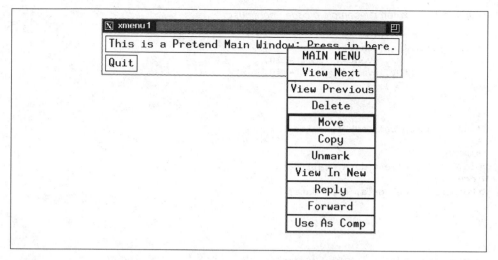

This is a Pretend Main Window: Press in here.

Quit

MAIN MENU
View Next
View Previous
Delete
Move
Copy
Unmark
View In New
Reply
Forward
Use As Comp

Figure 13-2. xmenu1: application with spring-loaded popup menu

Example 13-3. xmenu1: complete code

```
/*
 *  xmenu1.c - simple spring-loaded menu
 */

#include <stdio.h>

/*
 * Standard Toolkit include files:
 */
#include <X11/Intrinsic.h>
#include <X11/StringDefs.h>

#include <X11/Shell.h>

/*
 * Public include files for widgets used in this file.
 */
#include <X11/Xaw/Command.h>
#include <X11/Xaw/Box.h>
#include <X11/Xaw/Label.h>

/*
 * The popup shell ID is global because both dialog and pshell
 * are needed in the dialogDone callback, and both can't be
 * passed in without creating a structure.
 */
Widget pshell;

/*ARGSUSED*/
void PlaceMenu(w, event)
Widget w;
XButtonEvent *event;
{
    /* should make sure coordinates allow menu to fit on screen */

    /* move submenu shell to slightly left and above button
```

Example 13-3. xmenu1: complete code (continued)

```
        * press position */
    XtVaSetValues(pshell,
            XtNx, event->x_root - 10,
            XtNy, event->y_root - 10,
            NULL);
}
/*
 * quit button callback function
 */
/*ARGSUSED*/
void Quit(w, client_data, call_data)
Widget w;
XtPointer client_data, call_data;
{
    exit(0);
}

/*
 * menu pane button callback function
 */
/*ARGSUSED*/
void PaneChosen(w, client_data, call_data)
Widget w;
XtPointer client_data;    /* cast to pane_number */
XtPointer call_data;
{
    int pane_number = (int) client_data;
    printf("Pane %d chosen.\n", pane_number);
    XtPopdown(pshell);
}

main(argc, argv)
int argc;
char **argv;
{
    XtAppContext app_context;
    Widget topLevel, box, quit, label, menulabel, menubox,
            menupane[10];
    int i;
    String buf[50];

    static XtActionsRec trial_actions[] = {
        {"placeMenu", PlaceMenu},
    };

    XtSetLanguageProc(NULL, (XtLanguageProc)NULL, NULL);

    topLevel = XtVaAppInitialize(
        &app_context,         /* Application context */
        "XMenu1",             /* application class name */
        NULL, 0,              /* command line option list */
        &argc, argv,          /* command line args */
        NULL,                 /* for missing app-defaults file */
        NULL);                /* terminate varargs list */

    box = XtCreateManagedWidget(
        "box",                /* widget name */
        boxWidgetClass,       /* widget class */
```

Example 13-3. xmenu1: complete code (continued)

```
            topLevel,            /* parent widget */
            NULL,                /* argument list */
            0                    /* arglist size */
            );

    label = XtCreateManagedWidget(
            "label",             /* widget name */
            labelWidgetClass,    /* widget class */
            box,                 /* parent widget */
            NULL,                /* argument list */
            0                    /* arglist size */
            );

    quit = XtCreateManagedWidget(
            "quit",              /* widget name */
            commandWidgetClass,  /* widget class */
            box,                 /* parent widget */
            NULL,                /* argument list */
            0                    /* arglist size */
            );

    pshell = XtCreatePopupShell(
            "pshell",
            transientShellWidgetClass,
            topLevel,
            NULL,
            0
            );

    menubox = XtCreateManagedWidget(
            "menubox",           /* widget name */
            boxWidgetClass,      /* widget class */
            pshell,              /* parent widget */
            NULL,                /* argument list */
            0                    /* arglist size */
            );

    menulabel = XtCreateManagedWidget(
            "menulabel",         /* widget name */
            labelWidgetClass,    /* widget class */
            menubox,             /* parent widget */
            NULL,                /* argument list */
            0                    /* arglist size */
            );

    for (i = 0; i < 10; i++) {
        sprintf(buf, "menupane%d", i);
        menupane[i] = XtCreateManagedWidget(buf, /* widget name */
                commandWidgetClass, menubox, NULL, 0);

        XtAddCallback(menupane[i], XtNcallback, PaneChosen, i);
    }

    XtAppAddActions(app_context, trial_actions,
            XtNumber(trial_actions));
```

Gadgets and Popups

Example 13-3. xmenu1: complete code (continued)

```
    XtAddCallback(quit, XtNcallback, Quit, NULL);

    XtRealizeWidget(topLevel);

    XtAppMainLoop(app_context);
}
```

The **PlacePopup** action just places the popup slightly to the left and above the position where the pointer button that popped it up was clicked, using the coordinates reported in the button event. The offset of ten pixels from the pointer position simply helps to make sure that the pointer is inside the menu.† Remember that the window created by a popup shell widget is a child of the root window and therefore is placed relative to the root window. The **ButtonPress** event pointer coordinates relative to the root window are used.

The **PaneChosen** callback function is a stub function used in this example as the notify callback for all the menu panes. In this example, it simply prints the name of the chosen pane to *stdout* and then pops down the menu using **XtPopdown()**. In a real application, a different callback function would probably be registered for each pane.

Instead of calling **XtPopdown()** in each of these separate callback functions, you could write a single additional callback function that calls **XtPopdown()**, and then add it to the callback list for the Command widget that makes up each menu pane.

As usual, the popup is created by first creating a popup shell, then a Box widget as its child, and then a series of Label and Command widgets as children of Box. The popup shell and the box are invisible. As with all menus, what you actually see is the array of children.

Note that this program does not include any code that would pop up the menu. We've done that from the app-defaults file shown in Example 13-4. The translations we have defined for the Label widget invoke Xt's built-in **XtMenuPopup()** action.

Example 13-4. XMenu1: the app-defaults file

```
!
! Appearance Resources
!
*quit.label:     Quit
*label.label:    This is a Pretend Main Window; Press in here.
*menulabel.label:    MAIN MENU
!
! make all entries in menu same width
! (needs adjusting for longest entry)
!
*menulabel.width:    135
*menubox.Command.width:   135
!
! Pane Strings
!
```

---

†It is important to provide a consistent user interface, so you should use the same offset in all menus. Menus in commercial widget sets such as the OPEN LOOK widgets have carefully designed and documented policies about popup window placement. This allows the user's "pointer reflexes" to be trained, so that using menus becomes as automatic and easy as possible.

Example 13-4. XMenu1: the app-defaults file (continued)

```
*menupane0.label:    View Next
*menupane1.label:    View Previous
*menupane2.label:    Delete
*menupane3.label:    Move
*menupane4.label:    Copy
*menupane5.label:    Unmark
*menupane6.label:    View In New
*menupane7.label:    Reply
*menupane8.label:    Forward
*menupane9.label:    Use As Comp
!
! make Box leave no space around Command widgets in menu
!
*pshell.Box.hSpace: 0
*pshell.Box.vSpace: 0
!
! Functional Resources
!
*menubox.Command.translations:\
    <EnterWindow>:      highlight()                 \n\
    <LeaveWindow>:      reset()                     \n\
    <BtnUp>:        set() notify() unset()
*label.translations:\
    <BtnDown>: placeMenu() XtMenuPopup(pshell)
*pshell.translations:\
    <BtnUp>: XtMenuPopdown(pshell)
```

There are a number of settings designed to give the Box widget a characteristic menu appearance: all of the Command widgets are forced to have the same size (rather than the size of their label), and the Box widget is forced to leave no space between the command widgets.

However, it is the new translations that are the critical part of this app-defaults file. The Label widget must be given translations so that a button press will pop up the widget. The supplied translation maps a button press into a call to the application action **placeMenu** and then to Xt's predefined **XtMenuPopup()** action. The argument to **XtMenuPopup()** in the translation is the instance name of the popup shell. Xt converts this string name into the widget ID of the popup shell before it can pop up the widget.

We are replacing rather than overriding this widget's translations because it is a Label widget and has no default translations.

The menu panes are Command widgets, but we need to adjust their event response so that they will be triggered on a button release with no corresponding press (since the press that popped up the menu occurred in the application main window). We are replacing their translations to get rid of the translation for **ButtonPress** (which would still be present if we used the **#augment** directive, and we would have to create an action that did nothing in order to replace it with **#override**). The translation for **ButtonRelease** (abbreviated **BtnUp** in the translation table) calls all the actions that usually occur in Command widgets with both press and release.

Perhaps least obvious is the translation we have added to pop down the menu when the pointer button is released outside the menu. As mentioned earlier, Xt makes a passive global pointer grab on the popup shell (**pshell**) in the **XtMenuPopup()** action. When the pointer is inside the menu, the Command widgets intercept these grabbed events, because they are descendants of `pshell` and they have a translation for `ButtonRelease` events. This invokes the actions in the selected Command widget. But when the pointer is outside the menu, the grabbed events are sent directly to the widget that was specified in the grab call, namely `pshell`. Therefore, the translation to pop down the menu on button release must be added to `pshell`. (Again, this translation table is simply replaced because the popup shell normally has no translations.)

13.3.2 A Pulldown Menu

What are the desired characteristics of a pulldown menu? There is a Command widget or the like permanently visible in the application, with a label indicating some common characteristic of the items in the menu. When a button is pressed in this widget, the menu should pop up on or just below the button. Dragging the pointer down through the menu with the button still held should highlight the entry that is pointed to. Releasing the button in an entry should invoke or set that entry and pop down the menu. Moving out of the menu should not change this behavior, except that if the button is released anywhere outside of a menu pane, the menu should pop down without executing any entry.

If you compile and run *xmenu2* you can try out this style of menu. The appearance of this application is shown in Figure 13-3.

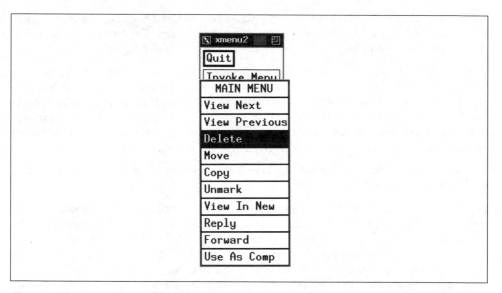

Figure 13-3. xmenu2: a pulldown menu

Invoking a menu as a pulldown is a simple enhancement of the spring-loaded invocation method just shown. We can do everything exactly the same as in the spring-loaded example, except that a pulldown menu should appear just below the `pressme` widget, not at the position of the pointer. Therefore, all we need to change is the placement code. However, since the coordinates in the event are not necessary for placing the popups, we can use a callback function instead of an action to place the popup. (In general, it is better to use an existing callback than to add an action to do the same thing.)

Popup shell widgets have **XtNpopupCallback** and **XtNpopdownCallback** callback resources; the functions on these callback lists are called whenever the popup is popped up or down using any of the Xt mechanisms.

In the last example we created an action called **PlaceMenu**, that moves the popup shell before it was actually popped up. We included it in a translation along with the standard action **XtMenuPopup( )**, which was actually used to pop up the widget. *xmenu2* also uses the standard action **XtMenuPopup( )** to pop up the widget, but it uses the **XtNpopup-Callback** resource to provide the code to place the widget. Using the callback saves having to reference the placement action in the translation table. This is preferable, since the placement code should almost always be hardcoded rather than user-configurable. Another advantage of the popup and popdown callbacks is that you may arrange for a popup to be popped up or down in more than one way, and it may be convenient to have certain code called automatically in all cases.

(You can also use the **XtNpopupCallback** resource to specify a callback function to create a popup widget the first time it is popped up, instead of at application startup. The one problem is that the functions on the callback list are invoked every time the widget is popped up. To make sure that your function callback creates the popup only once (the first time), the callback function should remove itself from the callback list by calling **XtRemove-Callback( )**.)

There is not enough difference between *xmenu1* and *xmenu2* to merit showing the complete code. All we have done is changed the **PlaceMenu** function from an action into a callback and changed its placement logic to place the popup relative to the invoking Command widget. We have then modified the app-defaults file accordingly. Example 13-5 shows the **PlaceMenu** routine (now a callback, not an action) and the code to register it as a callback.

Example 13-5. xmenu2: code to place pulldown menu

```
Widget pressme; /* button that invokes menu */
Widget pshell; /* menu shell */

/*ARGSUSED*/
void PlaceMenu(w, client_data, call_data)
Widget w;
XtPointer client_data;
XtPointer call_data;
{
    Position x, y;
    Dimension height;

    /*
     * translate coordinates in invoking Command widget
     * into coordinates from root window origin.
     */
    XtTranslateCoords(pressme,    /* Widget */
            (Position) 0,         /* x */
            (Position) 0,         /* y */
```

Example 13-5. xmenu2: code to place pulldown menu (continued)

```
            &x, &y);                /* coords on root window */

    /* get height of pressme so that menu is positioned below */
    XtVaGetValues(pressme,
            XtNheight, &height,
            NULL);

    /* move popup shell one pixel above and left of this position
     * (it's not visible yet) */
    XtVaSetValues(pshell,
            XtNx, x - 1,
            XtNy, y + height,
            NULL);
}

main(argc, argv)
int argc;
char **argv;
{
    .
    .
    .

    XtAddCallback(pshell, XtNpopupCallback, PlaceMenu, NULL);
    .
    .
    .

}
```

Xt calls the functions on the **XtNpopupCallback** list before it pops up the widget. This means that **PlaceMenu** is called before the **XtMenuPopup()** action, placing the widget before it is popped up.

Note that the **XtTranslateCoords()** routine determines the root window coordinates at the origin of the **pressme** widget. Because of the reparenting done by most window managers, this information cannot be obtained by using **XtGetValues()** to read the **XtNx** and **XtNy** resources.†

Example 13-6 shows the translation portion of the app-defaults file.

Example 13-6. XMenu2: translation portion of the app-defaults file

```
!
! Translation resources
!
*pressme.translations:\
   <EnterWindow>:      highlight()                \n\
   <LeaveWindow>:      reset()                    \n\
   <BtnDown>:          set() XtMenuPopup(pshell) reset()
!
*pshell.translations:\
```

---

†Incidentally, **XTranslateCoordinates()**, the Xlib equivalent of **XtTranslateCoords()**, gets the same information and a little more by querying the server. **XtTranslatCoords** does not have to make a server request because Xt stores this data locally. Each time a window in this application is moved, Xt receives this information as an event and updates its knowledge of the position of each window. This is an important optimization, because server queries are subject to network delays and tend to slow applications.

```
    <BtnUp>:                XtMenuPopdown(pshell)
!
*menubox.Command.translations:\
    <EnterWindow>:      set()                       \n\
    <LeaveWindow>:      unset()                     \n\
    <BtnUp>:            notify() unset()
```

These translations are different from those for *xmenu1* only in that **pressme** is a Command widget, which already has its own translation table, rather than a widget without existing translations such as Label (which we used as a fake main window). We have modified the translations of **pressme** to be suitable for this use. Note that the translation no longer calls **PlaceMenu** as an action because it is now a callback.

The translations for the menu pane Command widgets are also somewhat different from *xmenu1*, but only for cosmetic reasons. This iteration of the *xmenu* example uses the **set** and **unset** actions instead of **highlight** and **reset** or **unhighlight** to make the Command widgets highlight their entire box instead of just an area near the border. (Although this modification makes the menu look more like a typical menu, it also seems to make it slower.)

To create several menus you simply need to replicate the code shown here, changing the variable names for each menu. The passive global grabs invoked by Xt for each menu do not interfere with each other even if they specify the same key/button combination, because they specify different windows in which the key/button combination will begin the grab.

It is sometimes useful to be able to get a list of children in a menu, especially if you add and subtract menu entries. You can do this by querying the **XtNchildren** and **XtNnum-Children** resources of the parent. The value of **XtNchildren** is a list of the widget ID's of the children. This technique allows you to eliminate maintaining global variables for every pane of every menu.

13.3.3 Cascaded Menus

A cascaded menu is a menu in which one or more panes do not invoke functions but instead bring up additional menus.

The techniques used to bring up cascaded menus can also be used to have dialog boxes bring up other dialog boxes. However, cascaded menus are more challenging because they rely on the passive global pointer grab to receive the **ButtonRelease** event that occurs outside the menu and application.

You can implement a cascaded menu the same way for both spring-loaded and pulldown menus simply by adding to the code we've already written to implement a single menu. We'll show you *xmenu5*, the spring-loaded version, since it is slightly shorter. (*xmenu4* is the equivalent pulldown version.) Both are included in the example source code. In this example, only one menu pane will be used to invoke a submenu. However, this technique can be generalized to have additional panes bring up additional submenus.

Gadgets and Popups

First, let's describe exactly how we expect the cascaded menu to work. Figure 13-4 shows both menus popped up. (Compile the program and try it.)

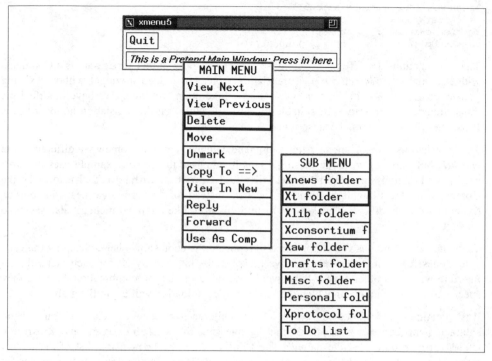

Figure 13-4. xmenu5: cascaded spring-loaded menus

The main menu works as described above. However, one of the panes—the one that brings up the submenu—has an arrow pointing to the right after its label. This pane does not highlight itself when the pointer moves inside (telling the user that this pane is different). Instead, when the user moves the pointer out through the right edge of the pane, the submenu pops up. The submenu operates just like the main menu. When the button is released inside either menu, the callback function associated with the chosen pane will be invoked. When the button is released outside of either menu, both menus pop down. If the pointer is moved back out of the submenu into the main menu, only the submenu pops down.

To create the submenu, we create a new popup shell, Box widget, and a set of Command widgets, and add callbacks for each function the submenu panes will invoke (in this example, one common callback). Then we write three actions: `PlaceMenu` (which you have already seen), `CheckRightAndPopupSubmenu` (which places and pops up the submenu if the pointer leaves the main menu pane through its right side), and `PopdownSubmenu` (which pops down the submenu if the pointer leaves the submenu). These actions are shown in Example 13-7.

```
/*ARGSUSED*/
void PlaceMenu(w, event, params, num_params)
Widget w;
XEvent *event;
String *params;
Cardinal *num_params;
{
    XButtonEvent *bevent = (XButtonEvent *) event;

    /* should make sure coordinates allow menu to fit on screen */

    /* move submenu shell to slightly left and above button
     * press position */
    XtVaSetValues(pshell,
            XtNx, bevent->x_root - 10,
            XtNy, bevent->y_root - 10,
            NULL);
}

/*ARGSUSED*/
void CheckRightAndPopupSubmenu(w, event, params, num_params)
Widget w;
XEvent *event;
String *params;
Cardinal *num_params;
{
    XLeaveWindowEvent *leave_event = (XLeaveWindowEvent *) event;
    Dimension height, width;

    XtVaGetValues(w,
        XtNheight, &height,
        XtNwidth, &width,
        NULL);

    if ((leave_event->x > width) && (leave_event->y > 0)
            && (leave_event->y < height)) {
        /* move submenu shell to start just right of pane,
         * using an arbitrary offset to place pointer in
         * first item. */
        XtVaSetValues(subshell,
                XtNx, leave_event->x_root,
                XtNy, leave_event->y_root - 12,
                NULL);
        XtPopup(subshell, XtGrabNonexclusive);
    }
}

/*ARGSUSED*/
void PopdownSubmenu(w, event, params, num_params)
Widget w;
XEvent *event;
String *params;
Cardinal *num_params;
{
    XtPopdown(subshell);
}
```

Gadgets and Popups

As usual, the app-defaults file specifies which events trigger these actions. We'll show this file in a moment, but for now you need to know just that `CheckRightAndPopup-Submenu` and `PopdownSubmenu` are triggered by `LeaveNotify` events. We want the submenu to pop up and down only when the pointer leaves through certain parts of certain sides of the widget—the entire right side of a pane for popping it up, and the part of the submenu touching the main menu on the left side for popping it down. These two actions are called in response to all `LeaveNotify` events, and they check if the pointer left through the correct parts before popping up and down the submenu.

As you may recall, we mentioned earlier that no matter what the arguments, `XtPopup()` and all other Xt facilities for grabbing, except `XtMenuPopup()` and `XtPopupSpring-Loaded()`, make no passive global grab, and therefore can't be used for spring-loaded or pulldown main menus. It turns out that for submenus the opposite is true—`XtPopup()` and `XtCallback*` work fine, but `XtMenuPopup()` is inappropriate because no new passive grab is needed. The original grab directs events normally to all widgets in the application, including the submenu, and directs all events that occur outside the application to `pshell`.

The `CheckRightAndPopupSubmenu` action calls `XtPopup()` with a grab mode of `XtGrabNonexclusive`. This grab mode controls Xt's event dispatching within the application—it has nothing to do with the passive global grab that Xt makes from the `Xt-MenuPopup()` action. `XtGrabNonexclusive` means that widgets in the cascade but outside of the submenu will continue to get events normally. The grab mode specified in the call to `XtPopup()`, or specified by the standard popup callback function selected (`Xt-CallbackExclusive()` or `XtCallbackNonexclusive()`) merely control the event dispatching within the application.

As an exercise, you may want to modify the example so that `CheckRightAndPopup-Submenu` calls `XtPopup()` with a grab mode of `XtGrabExclusive`, and see how the menus work as a result. The `XtGrabExclusive` mode means that only the most recent popup popped up will get events, while `XtGrabNonexclusive` means that all popups in a popped-up cascade will get events. In this case, when the submenu is popped up, it alone will get pointer events if you use grab mode `XtGrabExclusive`, while both it and the main menu will get pointer events if you use grab mode `XtGrabNonexclusive`. Because of the logic that pops down the submenu when the pointer leaves it through the portion adjoining the main menu, you can see this difference only if you move out through another part of the submenu and then around into the main menu again. (In the example code distribution, *xmenu5.c* uses `XtGrabNonexclusive` and *xmenu4.c* uses `XtGrab-Exclusive`, so that you can compare the results of these two flags.)

The user-interface conventions for a particular widget set usually specify which kinds of pop-ups should have exclusive grabs and which nonexclusive. Note that the effect of these two grab modes is the same unless there is more than one popup widget in a cascade visible.

`CheckRightAndPopupSubmenu` places the submenu itself (instead of using a separate action) because the menu should be placed only when it is first popped up. If the placement code were a separate action, it would be called every time a `LeaveWindow` event arrived, even if not through the correct border of the widget. (Remember that this code is in an action rather than a callback because it uses the contents of the event.)

The translation portion of the app-defaults file for *xmenu5* is shown in Example 13-8.

Example 13-8. XMenu5: translation portion of app-defaults file

```
!
! Appearance resources
!
*menupane5.label:  Copy To ==>
    .
    .   (other appearance resources not shown)
    .
!
! Translation resources
!
!  popping down both menus
*pshell.translations:\
    <BtnUp>: XtMenuPopdown(subshell) XtMenuPopdown(pshell)
!
!  popping up main menu
*label.translations:\
    <BtnDown>: placeMenu() XtMenuPopup(pshell)
!
!  popping down submenu
*menubox.menupane5.translations:\
    <LeaveWindow>:      checkRightAndPopupSubmenu()
!
! Main Menu translations
*menubox.Command.translations:\
    <EnterWindow>:      highlight()             \n\
    <LeaveWindow>:      reset()                 \n\
    <BtnUp>:            set() notify() unset()
!
! Sub Menu translations
*subbox.translations:\
    <LeaveWindow>:      popdownSubmenu(subbox)
*subbox.Command.translations:\
    <EnterWindow>:      highlight()             \n\
    <LeaveWindow>:      reset()                 \n\
    <BtnUp>:            set() notify() unset()
```

The first three translation tables handle popping up the main menu and making the menu Command widgets work as expected. We've seen these in previous examples.

The translation table for `pshell` pops down one or both menus; no error or warning is caused if only the main menu is up. This translation table works because the button release is sent to `pshell` if it occurs outside a menu regardless of whether just the main menu or both menus are up.

In this case, menu pane 5 is the pane that will pop up the submenu. The label for this pane is shown at the top of Example 13-8. The translation for this pane replaces all the normal translations for highlighting and notifying with a single translation for `LeaveWindow` events. These events in this widget trigger the `CheckRightAndPopupSubmenu` action which has already been described.

The translations for the **subbox** widget invoke **PopdownSubmenu** action to check whether the pointer left the submenu. In this case, the submenu is popped down, but the original popup remains visible.

The pane that will pop up the submenu and its event handling characteristics is controlled from the app-defaults file. Therefore, it may seem like you can change which menu pane invokes the submenu simply by changing the app-defaults file. This is true here, because the menu actions are nonfunctional and simply call a common callback. But it would not be possible if each pane invoked its own callback. To give the user the freedom to rearrange the menu, you would have to use actions instead of callbacks.

Note that you can define accelerators for any of the menus shown up to this point simply by placing settings for the **XtNaccelerators** resource in the app-defaults file. You would set this resource for every Command widget in the menus. This provides keyboard shortcuts for popping up the menu and choosing a pane. However, remember to make sure that each key combination is unique.

For completeness, here are some rules that apply when multiple cascaded popups are invoked with specified grab modes.

- When a grab is removed, all grabs added after that one are also removed.

- When a shell is popped up with **XtGrabExclusive** or **XtGrabNonexclusive** a grab is added to the list.

- When a shell is popped down, its grab is removed from the list - hence removing all the later shell grabs.

- When the later shells are popped down, they are no longer on the grab list but the grab is attempted to be removed.

13.3.4 Using the R4 SimpleMenu Widget

Once you have R4, you can use a real menu widget: the R4 SimpleMenu widget. The internals of this widget and its children, which are gadgets, are described later. This section describes a simple application that uses the SimpleMenu widget.

R4 supplies three types of panes to be used with the SimpleMenu widget: SmeBSB (an entry composed of a bitmap, a string, and another bitmap), SmeLine (a horizontal line between entries), and Sme (a blank entry). The SimpleMenu widget is itself a subclass of the popup shell widget, and therefore no separate popup shell needs to be created.

R4 also provides a MenuButton widget, which is a subclass of Command with built-in placement and popup code. Using a MenuButton to invoke a menu makes it even simpler to implement a pulldown menu, since the popup and placement code can be eliminated from the application.

The *xmenu7* application shown in Example 13-9 creates a SimpleMenu widget with panes of all three types. The menu is invoked in pulldown style using the R4 MenuButton widget.†

---

†This example was written by Chris Peterson of MIT Project Athena and modified only slightly by the authors.

As an additional enhancement, the menu marks or unmarks each item when it is selected in addition to calling a callback function. This iteration marks entries with the X logo, which is available as a standard bitmap in */usr/include/X11/bitmaps* (on UNIX systems).

Figure 13-5 shows the appearance of the program.

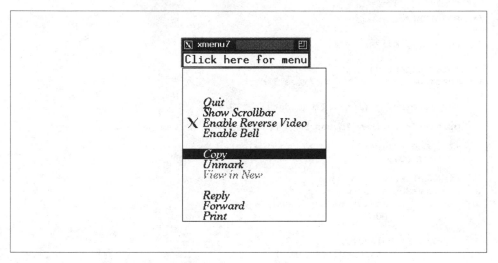

Figure 13-5. xmenu7: a menu using the Athena SimpleMenu widget

Example 13-9. xmenu7: using the SimpleMenu widget and its children

```
/* xmenu7.c */

#include <stdio.h>

#include <X11/Intrinsic.h>
#include <X11/StringDefs.h>
#include <X11/bitmaps/xlogo16>

#include <X11/Xaw/MenuButton.h>
#include <X11/Xaw/SimpleMenu.h>
#include <X11/Xaw/SmeBSB.h>
#include <X11/Xaw/SmeLine.h>

#define NUM_MENU_ITEMS 12
static String menu_entry_names[ ] = {
    "quit",
    "item1",
    "item2",
    "item3",
    "line",
    "item5",
    "item6",
    "item7",
    "blank",
    "menu1",
```

```
    "menu2",
    "menu3",
};

static Boolean status[NUM_MENU_ITEMS];
static Pixmap mark;

/* ARGSUSED */
static void
MenuSelect(w, client_data, garbage)
Widget w;
XtPointer client_data;
XtPointer garbage;           /* call_data */
{
    int pane_num = (int) client_data;

    printf("Menu item %s has been selected.\n", XtName(w));

    if (pane_num == 0)       /* quit selected. */
        exit(0);

    if (status[pane_num])
        XtVaSetValues(w,
                XtNleftBitmap, None,
                NULL);
    else
        XtVaSetValues(w,
                XtNleftBitmap, mark,
                NULL);

    status[pane_num] = !status[pane_num];
}

void
main(argc, argv)
char **argv;
int argc;
{
    XtAppContext app_context;
    Widget topLevel, menu, button, entry;
    int i;
    Arg arglist[1];

      XtSetLanguageProc(NULL, (XtLanguageProc)NULL, NULL);

    topLevel = XtVaAppInitialize(
        &app_context,          /* Application context */
        "XMenu7",              /* Application class */
        NULL, 0,               /* command line option list */
        &argc, argv,           /* command line args */
        NULL,                  /* for missing app-defaults file */
        NULL);                 /* terminate varargs list */

    button = XtCreateManagedWidget("menuButton",
            menuButtonWidgetClass, topLevel,
            arglist, (Cardinal) 0);

    menu = XtCreatePopupShell("menu", simpleMenuWidgetClass,
            button, NULL, 0);

    for (i = 0; i < NUM_MENU_ITEMS; i++) {
```

```
        String item = menu_entry_names[i];

        if (i == 4)   /* use a line pane */
            entry = XtCreateManagedWidget(item,
                    smeLineObjectClass, menu,
                    NULL, 0);
        else if (i == 8) /* blank entry */
            entry = XtCreateManagedWidget(item, smeObjectClass, menu,
                    NULL, 0);
        else {
            entry = XtCreateManagedWidget(item, smeBSBObjectClass,
                    menu, NULL, 0);

            XtAddCallback(entry, XtNcallback, MenuSelect,
                    (XtPointer) i);
        }
    }

    mark = XCreateBitmapFromData(XtDisplay(topLevel),
            RootWindowOfScreen(XtScreen(topLevel)),
            xlogo16_bits, xlogo16_width, xlogo16_height);

    XtRealizeWidget(topLevel);
    XtAppMainLoop(app_context);
}
```

You will notice that each pane has an **XtNleftBitmap** resource, which is alternately set to the X logo or to nothing each time that item is selected.

The app-defaults file for *xmenu7* is shown in Example 13-10.

Example 13-10. XMenu7: app-defaults file

```
!
! For Color workstations only.
!
*SimpleMenu*foreground:          SteelBlue
*SimpleMenu*menuLabel.foreground:    Gold
*SimpleMenu*line.foreground:     Grey

*MenuButton.label:          Click here for menu

*SimpleMenu*menuLabel.vertSpace:     100
*SimpleMenu*menuLabel.leftMargin:    70
*SimpleMenu.label: Main Menu
*SimpleMenu*item1*label: Show Scrollbar
*SimpleMenu*item2*label: Enable Reverse Video
*SimpleMenu*item3*label: Enable Bell
*SimpleMenu*item4*label: Disable Auto-Repeat
*SimpleMenu*item5*label: Copy
*SimpleMenu*item6*label: Unmark
*SimpleMenu*item7*label: View in New
*SimpleMenu*menu1*label: Reply
*SimpleMenu*menu2*label: Forward
*SimpleMenu*menu3*label: Print
*SimpleMenu*quit*label:          Quit
*SimpleMenu*RowHeight:           16
*SimpleMenu*item7*sensitive:     off
```

Gadgets and Popups

Example 13-10. XMenu7: app-defaults file (continued)

```
*SimpleMenu*HorizontalMargins:    30
! Just for fun:
*font: *times*medium*18*iso8859-1
!*item7*font: *helv*medium*24*iso8859-1
!*item8*font: *helv*bold*24*iso8859-1

*quit*accelerators:\
    <Key>q: notify()
*item1*accelerators:\
    <Key>1: notify()
*item2*accelerators:\
    <Key>2: notify()
*item3*accelerators:\
    <Key>3: notify()
*item5*accelerators:\
    <Key>5: notify()
*item6*accelerators:\
    <Key>6: notify()
*item7*accelerators:\
    <Key>7: notify()
*menu1*accelerators:\
    <Key>m: notify()
```

This file simply sets various cosmetic features of the menu. (See Appendix C, *Naming Conventions*, for information on font-naming conventions.) Naturally, you could easily set the strings for each menu entry in this file. Note that there are no translation tables in this file because MenuButton and SimpleMenu are doing exactly what they were designed to do.

Accelerators can be defined for menus with gadget children, but not in the usual sense. They cannot be defined to invoke the actions of the gadget children, but they can invoke global application actions, which for menus is usually good enough. For example, in the R4 *xmh*, one item on one of the menus incorporates new mail. From the widget, the **notify** action of the menu pane gadget calls the **DoIncorporateNewMail** callback function. The **XtNaccelerators** resource for the SimpleMenu widget itself (not the gadgets) maps a Meta-I key event into a call to the **XmhIncorporateNewMail** global action. **XmhIncorporateNewMail** then calls **DoIncorporateNewMail**. This use of accelerators depends on having both a callback and an action form of each function.

13.3.5 Delayed Popup Creation

As we've seen, a popup may consist of a single widget, or it may be a shell widget which contains a composite widget which contains a number of children. In the latter case, creating all those widgets (or gadgets) takes time. It may be beneficial to create those widgets using idle time in the application instead of delaying startup. In either case, it may make sense to create the popup only when it is needed, to minimize wasted resources.

If your goal is to speed startup, and you want all menus created even if some are never used, you can register a work procedure to create each popup, as described in Section 8.5. As you may recall, a work procedure uses idle time in the application to call a function, which must return swiftly. If you use this technique, you add one work procedure for each popup you need to create, and you need to add code to make sure that the popup has been created before the user is allowed to use it.

If your goal is to create only the required popups, you can create the popup in a callback function or action routine that you have registered to place or pop up the popup. In this case, you would have a static variable in the callback or action to make sure that the popup widgets are only created the first time the popup is popped up. You need to have created the popup shell before this can work.

There is also another way to create only the required popups. Shell widgets have an `Xt-NcreatePopupChildProc` resource which you can set to a function that creates the Shell's children. See `XtCreatePopupChildProc(2)` in Volume Five, *X Toolkit Intrinsics Reference Manual*, for the calling sequence of this function type. The Xt specification does not say whether an `XtCreatePopupChildProc` is called just once when the shell is first popped up or every time it is popped up. But the MIT implementation of Xt calls it every time the shell is popped up, so you will again need a static variable to make sure the children are only created once.

13.4 About Dialog Boxes

Although we have been talking so far exclusively about menus, much that has been said is also true of dialog boxes. Both menus and dialog boxes that get user input usually need to get that input before other application functions can be invoked. Of course, one way to disable all other application functions is to make all other widgets insensitive with `XtSet-Sensitive()` (passing it `False`). Setting the sensitivity of one common ancestor does this efficiently, but even this is too slow because all the widgets redraw themselves dimmed or grayed. It is much faster to use a global grab. Unlike menus, which require the global grab in order to get button release events outside the application so they can pop down properly, dialog boxes do not, strictly speaking, need a grab. But they sometimes make the grab anyway to disable other application functions.

Dialog boxes can also invoke other dialog boxes. For example, a dialog box that gets input might check the validity of the input before popping down the dialog, and if incorrect, pop up a message telling the user the problem with the input. Cascaded dialog boxes are implemented the same way as cascaded menus. Note that, as a general rule, sub-dialog boxes are popped up with grab mode `XtGrabExclusive`, which means that the user must satisfy the most deeply nested dialog first. However, it is often desirable to leave a Help dialog on the screen until after the dialog it provides help for has been removed.

Some popups do not need to disable other application functions. For example, imagine a dialog box that informed the user of some fact without requiring confirmation. This kind of popup would be popped up with grab mode `XtGrabNone`, allowing the user to continue with other application functions.

We pointed out earlier that the built-in callback functions for popping up a widget are not useful for menus because they make no passive global pointer grab. However, they come in handy for dialog boxes. The functions `XtCallbackNone()`, `XtCallback-`

Gadgets and Popups

Exclusive(), and XtCallbackNonexclusive() can be used to pop up dialog boxes, as long as the position of the dialog box need not depend on information in an event.

We haven't shown how to use Xt's standard callback for popping down a widget: Xt-CallbackPopdown(). Instead of calling XtPopdown() in the callback functions for each menu entry, we can add XtCallbackPopdown() to the callback list after the existing callback function. XtCallbackPopdown() requires an XtPopdownId structure to be passed as the *client_data* argument. This structure must contain the popup shell and the widget that invoked the popup (the MenuButton or Command widget).

All three of the standard popup callbacks set the invoking widget to insensitive mode before popping up the widget. XtCallbackPopdown() resets the invoking widget to sensitive mode. Therefore, if you use XtCallbackNone(), XtCallbackNonexclusive(), or XtCallbackExclusive() without also using XtCallbackPopdown(), remember to set the widget to sensitive mode yourself. This feature is useless but also harmless when the popup is spring-loaded, because the invoking widget is often the main application window and that widget rarely responds to sensitivity.

In certain rare cases, you may want to use XtAddGrab() and XtRemoveGrab() directly to append a widget to or remove a widget from the current popup cascade. These functions are called internally by the Xt facilities that pop widgets up and down, and should not be necessary on their own. Note that these functions never make a request to the server to start or release a passive global pointer grab—they affect only Xt's internal event dispatching. (However, the functions XtGrabKey(), XtGrabKeyboard(), XtGrab-Button(), and XtGrabPointer() do initiate global grabs. These functions are described in Chapter 14, *Miscellaneous Toolkit Programming Techniques*.)

13.5 Gadgets

When an application includes many different menus with many fields each, the server memory consumption of having separate widgets for every menu pane was once thought to be a problem. So the window-less widget, called a *gadget*, was invented. A gadget depends on special behavior of its parent to get events and operate much like a widget. (Gadgets also consume slightly less client-side memory.)

Now that the server implementation has been improved, the memory consumption of a window is much less significant now. In fact, the use of Motif Button gadgets in particular greatly increases network traffic during the crucial user-interaction phase of the application. This is because the Motif Button gadget parent requires MotionNotify events to track whether the pointer has entered or left a gadget (since gadgets have no window to cause EnterNotify events). These MotionNotify events allow the gadget to highlight its border when the pointer enters, just like a regular widget. A gadget is fully configurable using the resource database just like a widget, and can have its own callback list.

This network traffic problem is much more serious than the memory problem gadgets were originally thought to improve. Therefore, gadgets should be avoided in uses where they cause this problem.

Gadgets also have other limitations. Gadgets have to draw on their parent's window, and they share this space with the parent and with all other gadget children. The gadgets and the parent must agree to draw in certain areas only. For this reason, gadgets must be used with a special composite widget parent that is prepared to manage them properly.

The Athena SimpleMenu widget is such a parent. It is a composite widget designed to manage gadget children. The gadgets it is designed to manage are Sme, SmeBSB, and SmeLine (where Sme stands for Simple Menu Entry). These provide a blank entry (and generic menu entry superclass), an entry which can contain a bitmap, a string, and another bitmap (thus BSB), and an entry that draws a horizontal line. We will use and describe this widget and these gadgets both to show how menu widgets are built and to demonstrate how the parent and the gadgets work together.

Gadgets do not handle events automatically as widgets do, and because they have no windows, the server does not handle overlapping between them. This places certain demands on the parent. All the gadgets that are children of a particular parent share that parent's window. The parent is responsible for coordinating the gadget children, telling them about events by calling their functions. Therefore, the composite widget that manages a group of gadgets must be specially designed for that purpose, not a general-purpose composite or constraint widget such as Box or Form. It is possible for a composite widget to manage both gadget and widget children, but its code has to be more involved to do this.

Like normal widgets, gadgets provide their own code to redraw themselves in their expose method. However, since gadgets do not receive events, they depend on the parent to directly call their expose method. The parent keeps track of the geometry of each child, and when the parent's expose method is called, this method calculates whether the area exposed overlaps any of the gadget children. If the area exposed does overlap a gadget, the parent's expose method calls that gadget's expose method, which redraws the area.

A gadget's actions also have to work differently from widget actions because of the fact that gadgets don't get events. A gadget defines its actions as methods—as fields in its class part structure—instead of in an action list and translation table. It initializes these fields directly to pointers to functions during class initialization. The parent widget has corresponding actions that are defined and operate like normal actions, except that they determine which gadget the event that invoked the action occurred in and call the gadget method corresponding to that action. In other words, the parent has actions that operate the gadget children.

One weakness of a menu composed of gadget panes is that gadgets cannot have an accelerator table. Therefore, accelerators cannot be used to provide a keyboard equivalent that would invoke each menu pane.

The parent of gadgets has to position the gadget children so that they do not overlap, or take care of the consequences if they do overlap. Since the gadgets draw on the parent's window, if they did overlap they would draw over each other's graphics, with unpredictable results. The parent would have to calculate the area of overlap between two gadgets, and clear this area before letting one of the gadgets draw itself. (A gadget could clear its own area before drawing, but this would be unnecessary in many cases, and would cause flashing.)

Gadgets are subclasses of RectObj, one of the invisible superclasses of Core that we have so far ignored because for widgets it is safe to assume that Core is the top of the widget class hierarchy.† The actual class hierarchy leading up to Core is shown in Figure 13-6.

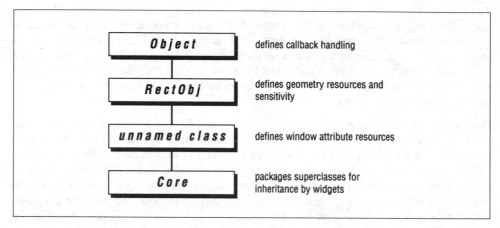

Figure 13-6. Class hierarchy derivation of Core

The "unnamed class" actually has a name (WindowObj) but this class is intentionally undocumented in the Xt specification so that its characteristics can be changed in later releases without compatibility problems. You should never create subclasses directly from the unnamed class.

The superclasses of Core are not real classes in the sense that they do not play by all the rules we have described in Chapter 6, *Inside a Widget*. For one thing, each shares what we call the Core class structure instead of adding its own part structure. Applications are never intended to create instances of these superclasses—they are really just part of the implementation of Xt. Instead of developing all the characteristics of widgets in one large base class Core, it made more sense to implement Xt in object-oriented fashion by dividing the implementation into separate pseudo-classes. It is important to know what each early class defines simply so that you know what characteristics are available in gadgets and which are available only in widgets. Each class defines the following features:

- Object defines only the `XtNdestroyCallback` resource and the underlying support for callbacks in general.

- RectObj defines the geometry resources (`XtNx`, `XtNy`, `XtNwidth`, `XtNheight`, and `XtNborder_width`) and the resources that control sensitivity: `XtNancestor-Sensitive` and `XtNsensitive`. RectObj itself doesn't use the sensitivity resources. They are provided at this level in the hierarchy so that sensitivity can be set for gadgets. Gadgets draw themselves according to these resources (gray if insensitive),

---

†Only the header files for RectObj are public, so that you can write and compile gadgets.

and check these resources in their action routines (stored in their class part methods), invoking their callback function only if sensitive.

- The unnamed class (WindowObj) adds many window-oriented resources: ones that control window attributes such as the background pixmap, permanent window features such as the window depth, and event resources such as translations and accelerators. It also includes the `XtNmappedWhenManaged` resource. This class is known as the unnamed class because it never appears in widget, gadget, or application code. Widgets are subclassed from Core, while gadgets are subclassed from RectObj. The exact features of unnamed class are subject to change and should not be relied upon.

The Core class structure actually is inherited all the way from RectObj. Therefore, the class structure in gadgets is the Core class structure you are already familiar with. All the event-related fields in the Core class part structure of gadgets are unused. The only exception is the `expose` method, which is present, but draws on the parent's window and is not called in the usual way by Xt because the gadget receives no events. The remaining non-event-related fields have the same purpose as for widgets, including all the remaining methods.

Without further ado, let's take a look at a gadget, and then at a gadget parent.

13.5.1 Inside a Gadget

Many portions of a gadget's code are exactly the same as those of a widget, as described in Chapter 6, *Inside a Widget*. This section summarizes the parts that are identical so that you know that nothing is left out, and describes the differences in detail.

The code for gadgets and widgets includes the same three implementation files with the same naming conventions. As in Chapter 6, we'll take the three implementation files one at a time, beginning with the private header file, then the code file, and then the public header file.

As in widget code, many of the conventions described here are automatically taken care of for you when you are writing a new gadget if you copy all three files of an existing gadget and then globally change the gadget class name.

The Athena menu pane gadgets are implemented in two class levels:

- Sme (Simple Menu Entry) defines the callback for an entry, the actions to highlight, unhighlight, and notify, and the code that allows subclasses to inherit or replace these actions (because they are defined as methods). The actual functions for highlight and unhighlight are empty, while the notify action calls the callback. The `expose` method of this gadget is also empty. This gadget can be used by itself to create a blank entry.

- SmeBSB and SmeLine are each subclasses of Sme. SmeLine replaces only the `expose` method of its superclass. SmeBSB replaces both the `expose` method and the highlight and unhighlight actions of the superclass. (Sme can be subclassed to create new types of menu entries.)

The following sections describe both Sme and SmeBSB.

13.5.2 Private Header File

The private header file for a gadget is identical in format to the private header file for a widget. It defines a class part structure for this class of gadget and then a complete class structure including the class parts of superclasses and this class. The only difference is that a gadget inherits its features from Object and RectObj, whereas a widget inherits from Core. Example 13-11 shows the complete class structure of the R4 Athena Sme gadget.

Example 13-11. Sme gadget: class part and complete class structure declaration

```
typedef struct _SmeClassPart {
    void (*highlight)();
    void (*unhighlight)();
    void (*notify)();
    XtPointer extension;
} SmeClassPart;

/* Full class record declaration */
typedef struct _SmeClassRec {
    RectObjClassPart    rect_class;
    SmeClassPart  sme_class;
} SmeClassRec;

#define XtInheritHighlight     ((_XawEntryVoidFunc) _XtInherit)
#define XtInheritUnhighlight XtInheritHighlight
#define XtInheritNotify        XtInheritHighlight
```

Notice that the complete class structure declaration does not include the class part for the Object class, even though it is a superclass. This is because all the superclasses of Core share the same class part structure.

The class part structure for Sme defines three methods—these are essentially the gadget's actions, but they will be invoked by the gadget parent's actions, not directly by Xt. The **extension** field allows fields to be added to this structure in a future version while retaining binary compatibility. In a future version this field could be changed to point to an extension structure.†

Any class that defines methods must provide code to allow them to be inherited or replaced by subclasses. The Sme class therefore must define the **XtInherit** constants that allow the methods to be inherited. The .c code file provides the **class_part_init** method that allows them to be replaced. (See Section 12.4.5.)

In the private header file for SmeBSB, the class part structure would contain only the extension field, because SmeBSB will be using the highlight, unhighlight, and notify fields defined by Sme. However, the .c file will initialize these fields to point to its own functions.

---

†Note that the **extension** field is defined as type **XtPointer**. In R4, all occurrences of **caddr_t** have been replaced with **XtPointer**. On most systems, **XtPointer** will be defined to be **caddr_t**. But for some architectures, **caddr_t** is too small to hold a pointer to a function. On such systems, **XtPointer** will be defined to be larger. The **caddr_t** type will continue to work on most systems, but you are advised to use **XtPointer** instead for maximum portability.

The instance part structure and complete instance structure of Sme are shown in Example 13-12.

Example 13-12. Sme gadget: instance part and complete instance structure declaration

```
typedef struct {
    /* resources */
    XtCallbackList callbacks;    /* The callback list */
} SmePart;

typedef struct _SmeRec {
    ObjectPart     object;
    RectObjPart    rectangle;
    SmePart   sme;
} SmeRec;
```

The `SmePart` adds a `callbacks` resource. The complete `SmeRec` includes the prior elements in the widget hierarchy: `ObjectPart` and `RectObjPart`. Note that unlike the class structure, the Object class does appear in the complete instance structure, because the superclasses of Core do not share instance structures.

The instance part structure for SmeBSB includes the usual fields to maintain the graphics state of the entry, including the label, colors, font, GCs, and positioning information. The complete instance structure for SmeBSB is the same as the one for Sme but with the Sme-BSBPart structure added at the end.

13.5.3 The Gadget Source File

The source file for a gadget is identical in form to a widget source file. The only differences are that the superclass of a gadget in the class structure initialization is `rectObjClass-Rec`, and the complete instance structure type is called `SmeObject` for a gadget where it would have been `SmeWidget` if the entry was a true widget. Therefore, `SmeObject` is the type into which you cast the pointer to the instance structure before accessing the structure's fields in all the widget methods.

In addition, several of the Core class structure fields that might be used in a widget are never used in gadgets. The following is the complete list of fields that are always initialized to a certain value in a gadget:

- `realize` set to NULL
- `actions` set to NULL
- `num_actions` set to 0 (zero)
- `compress_motion` set to False
- `compress_exposure` set to False
- `compress_enterleave` set to False
- `visible_interest` set to False

- `resize` set to `NULL`

- `display_accelerators` set to `NULL`

Setting these fields otherwise (of the right type) probably won't cause the gadget to crash, but won't accomplish anything useful either.

Gadgets, like widgets, should always define the `query_geometry` method, and either define `set_values_almost` or initialize it to `XtInheritSetValuesAlmost`. The remainder of the fields and methods have the same purpose and are used in the same way as for widgets.

There are, however, slight differences in the code for certain gadget methods. The `expose` method checks not only its own sensitivity but also its parent's sensitivity before deciding whether to draw the entry in normal colors or grayed. When creating GCs using `XCreate-GC()` or creating any other server resources from the `initialize` method using an Xlib call, you must remember to use the parent's window, since the gadget has no window. (`Xt-Window()` is not smart enough to give you the parent's window ID in the case of gadgets.) Also, the parent's resource values, such as `background_pixel`, may be used to provide data in common among all instances of a subclass like SmeBSB.

13.5.4 The Public Header File

The only difference in the public header file between widgets and gadgets is that what would have been `Widget` for a widget is `Object` for a gadget. As mentioned previously, if you are writing a gadget you should start by copying the files for an existing gadget and then globally change names. Then you will start with the proper conventions already in place.

13.5.5 The Gadget Parent

A gadget parent is a composite widget designed to manage gadget children. Gadget parents perform all the geometry management tasks that all composite widgets perform, which are described in Chapter 12, *Geometry Management*. Gadgets also follow all the rules of normal widget children. However, gadget parents also have the added responsibility of managing the overlap of gadgets or making sure they don't overlap, and of handling events for the gadgets and calling gadget code. This section describes the gadget-managing role of the gadget parent.

The Athena SimpleMenu widget is designed to manage the gadget children already described, Sme, SmeLine, and SmeBSB (and any other subclass of Sme that is written later). It forms a vertical menu with horizontal panes. It is quite a large widget because it contains all the geometry management code in addition to code for managing events for the gadgets. We'll concentrate just on the code that manages events for the gadgets, since the geometry management code is described in Chapter 12, *Geometry Management*.

Let's begin with the `expose` method. SimpleMenu's `expose` method does no drawing of its own. It simply calls the `expose` methods of the gadget children. However, it compares the region passed into its **expose** method to determine which gadgets need redrawing. Example 13-13 shows SimpleMenu's **expose** method.

Example 13-13. SimpleMenu: expose method calling gadget children's expose methods

```
#define ForAllChildren(smw, childP) \
    for ( (childP) = (SmeObject *) (smw)->composite.children ; \
        (childP) < (SmeObject *) ( (smw)->composite.children + \
        (smw)->composite.num_children );   (childP)++ )

/* ARGSUSED */
static void
Redisplay(w, event, region)
Widget w;
XEvent * event;
Region region;
{
    SimpleMenuWidget smw = (SimpleMenuWidget) w;
    SmeObject * entry;
    SmeObjectClass class;

    if (region == NULL)
        XClearWindow(XtDisplay(w), XtWindow(w));

    /*
     * Check and Paint each of the entries - including the label.
     */

    ForAllChildren(smw, entry) {
        if (!XtIsManaged ( (Widget) *entry))
            continue;

        if (region != NULL)
            switch(XRectInRegion(region, (int) (*entry)->rectangle.x,
                    (int) (*entry)->rectangle.y,
                    (unsigned int) (*entry)->rectangle.width,
                    (unsigned int) (*entry)->rectangle.height)) {
                case RectangleIn:
                case RectanglePart:
                    break;
                default:
                    continue;
            }
        class = (SmeObjectClass) (*entry)->object.widget_class;

        if (class->rect_class.expose != NULL)
            (class->rect_class.expose)((Widget) *entry, NULL, NULL);
    }
}
```

Note that this **expose** method is also called from elsewhere in the widget code (specifically, from the **resize** and **geometry_manager** methods) to redraw the gadgets. In these cases, the region passed in is set to NULL, and the method clears its window and redraws all the gadgets.

Also note how this **expose** method invokes the **expose** methods of its children. All **expose** methods (and in fact all methods) are stored in the class structure, not the instance structure. Composite widgets keep only a list of the instance structures of their children. However, one field in each instance structure points to the class structure for that child. This

Gadgets and Popups

is the `widget_class` field of the Object instance part.† In this example, the *entry* counter variable is a pointer to the gadget ID (opaque pointer to the instance structure) of one of the children. Another variable, *class*, declared as a pointer to the `SmeObjectClass` class structure (the expected class of the children), is set to the `widget_class` field in the instance structure of one of the children. Then the `expose` field of this class structure is checked to see if it is `NULL`, and if not it is invoked.

Note that the class of the children is hardcoded in this method. This widget can manage only Sme widgets and its subclasses.

The `resize` method of SimpleMenu must resize the children when it is resized itself. (Actually, this is unlikely, since the SimpleMenu widget itself is a subclass of Shell and is therefore not managed by any parent.) This method is invoked only when the user resizes the menu using the window manager. Since this widget has the authority to determine the geometry of its children, it can simply resize them. This particular resize method (shown in Example 13-14) simply sets their width to be the same as its own.

Example 13-14. SimpleMenu: resize method

```
static void
Resize(w)
Widget w;
{
    SimpleMenuWidget smw = (SimpleMenuWidget) w;
    SmeObject * entry;

    if ( !XtIsRealized(w) ) return;

    ForAllChildren(smw, entry)  /* reset width of all entries. */
        if (XtIsManaged( (Widget) *entry))
            (*entry)->rectangle.width = smw->core.width;

    Redisplay(w, (XEvent *) NULL, (Region) NULL);
}
```

Notice that this `resize` method invokes the `expose` method (`Redisplay`) because the gadgets don't have `resize` methods, and will not redraw themselves in response to their size change.‡

Now let's look at SimpleMenu's actions. Their only purpose is to call the gadgets' actions when the appropriate events arrive. These actions are added in the usual way: they are declared at the top of the .c file, then registered with an action list that is entered into the class structure initialization, and then defined. One of the three actions is shown in Example 13-15.

---

†The Core instance part structure (not complete) is the concatenation of the instance parts of the three superclasses Object, RectObj, and the unnamed class. Therefore, it also includes a `widget_class` field. Since composite widgets do not normally need to invoke the methods of their children, you shouldn't need to access this field.

‡The gadget children could have `resize` methods, and this resize method could call the children's `resize` methods. The gadget's `resize` methods would simply call their `expose` method. However, this does exactly the same thing as the code shown while being more complicated.

Example 13-15. SimpleMenu: the Notify action routine

```
/* ARGSUSED */
static void
Notify(w, event, params, num_params)
Widget w;
XEvent * event;
String * params;
Cardinal * num_params;
{
    SimpleMenuWidget smw = (SimpleMenuWidget) w;
    SmeObject entry = smw->simple_menu.entry_set;
    SmeObjectClass class;

    if ( (entry == NULL) || !XtIsSensitive((Widget) entry) )
        return;

    class = (SmeObjectClass) entry->object.widget_class;
    (class->sme_class.notify)( (Widget) entry );
}
```

This action determines whether the chosen entry is sensitive and, if so, calls the **notify** method of that gadget. As described above in the section on the gadget children, gadgets define their actions as methods so that they can conveniently be called by their parent. Since these methods are stored in the class structure not the instance structure, this is done using the technique described above for the **expose** method.

Although not critical to its handling of gadgets, SimpleMenu does one more interesting thing. It registers the **PositionMenuAction** action in the global application action list (as opposed to the internal widget action list) so that the application or app-defaults file can refer to this action in translation tables without needing to register the action. This action can be triggered by any type of event in the widget and positions the menu according to data in the event type. (SimpleMenu has a resource that controls whether this placement process makes sure that the menu is not off the screen.)

A widget can add an action to the global action list by calling **XtAddAction()** just like an application would, but from its **class_initialize** method.

Any composite widget that is capable of managing gadgets must declare a Composite extension structure in the *.c* file and set the **accepts_objects** field of that structure to **True**. It must then set the pointer to the extension structure into the Composite class part structure in the **class_part_initialize** method. Extension structures were introduced in Chapter 6, *Inside a Widget*, and are discussed further in Chapter 14, *Miscellaneous Toolkit Programming Techniques*. Example 13-16 shows this code from *SimpleMenu.c*.

Example 13-16. SimpleMenu.c: Setting accepts_objects in the Composite extension structure

```
CompositeClassExtensionRec extension_rec = {
    /* next_extension */   NULL,
    /* record_type */      NULLQUARK,
    /* version */          XtCompositeExtensionVersion,
    /* record_size */      sizeof(CompositeClassExtensionRec),
    /* accepts_objects */  True,
};

static void
ClassPartInitialize(wc)
```

Example 13-16. SimpleMenu.c: Setting accepts_objects in the Composite extension structure (continued)

```
WidgetClass wc;
{
    SimpleMenuWidgetClass smwc = (SimpleMenuWidgetClass) wc;
/*
 * Make sure that our subclass gets the extension rec too.
 */

    extension_rec.next_extension = smwc->composite_class.extension;
    smwc->composite_class.extension = (XtPointer) &extension_rec;
}
```

This code, with names changed, will appear in all gadget parents.

14

Miscellaneous Toolkit
Programming Techniques

This chapter describes various Xt functions that have not been treated else-where in the book.

In This Chapter:

☞

Miscellaneous

14

Miscellaneous Toolkit Programming Techniques

This chapter discusses various Xt facilities that didn't fit neatly into any other chapter. Many of them are functions provided mostly because Xt uses them internally, and they are unlikely to be useful in application or widget code. Some of them are quite important for accomplishing certain tasks. You should scan the contents of this chapter to familiarize yourself with these facilities so that you will be aware of them.

The topics covered are errors and warning messages, objects, a description of all of Xt's macros and functions for getting information, the Core `accept_focus` method, how to interpret key events, Xt's facilities for memory management, making global grabs, file finding and internationalization, multiple application contexts, multiple top-level shells, and connecting to multiple servers.

14.1 Errors and Warnings

There are several broad categories of errors that may occur in Xt applications. One is the X server error, which is a form of event that tells the client that some parameter in an earlier request was illegal, or that no more server memory is available. A second is the connection failure error generated by Xlib when the connection with the server fails (usually due to a system crash or network interruption). Xlib provides the `XSetErrorHandler()` and `XSetIOErrorHandler()` functions to allow the application to provide a routine to handle these two types of errors. Xt provides no interface to these routines—Toolkit applications must use the Xlib routines to customize these error handlers (Xlib uses default error handlers when the application does not use these routines to specify them). For a description of these error handlers and the routines for changing them, see Volume One, *Xlib Programming Manual*.

A third category is made up of error and warning messages that Xt reports when function parameters are specified improperly, when a translation is incorrectly specified, and for many other reasons. For a complete listing of all errors and warnings that can be generated by Xt, see Volume Five, *X Toolkit Intrinsics Reference Manual*, Appendix D, *Standard Errors and Warnings*. Xt provides separate parallel routines for errors and for warnings. The difference between Xt errors and Xt warnings is that errors are fatal and the application exits after print-

Miscellaneous

ing the error, while warnings are nonfatal and the application continues. The main purpose of these facilities is to generate consistent messages.

Two levels of interface are provided:

- A high-level interface that takes an error name and class and looks the error up in an error resource database. The high-level fatal error handler is invoked by a call to **XtApp-ErrorMsg( )**; the high-level nonfatal error handler is invoked by a call to **XtApp-WarningMsg( )**. The high-level functions construct a string and pass it to the lower-level interface.

- A low-level interface that takes a simple string, which is printed out as the error message. The low-level fatal error handler is invoked by a call to **XtAppError( )**; the low-level nonfatal error handler is invoked by a call to **XtAppWarning( )**.

These error-reporting interfaces are used internally by Xt, but widget or application code can also use them. For example, when a resource is given an illegal value in a resource file, the widget or application can report the error or warning to the user (which depends on whether the widget or application can continue after the error—most widgets issue only warnings and then fall back on their default value).

The low-level handlers are much easier to use, but they do not support internationalization (alternate languages) at all since the messages are hardcoded in the application. The high-level handlers can potentially support internationalization, but not as elegantly as the normal resource database since Xt searches for the error database file in a fixed location, not using the language string. If you want your application or widget to run in more than one language, you should use the high-level handlers, but only one database for one language can be installed on a system at a time. This is likely to be improved in later releases of Xt.

To use the low-level handlers, you specify the string message as the sole argument to **Xt-AppError( )** or **XtAppWarning( )**.

Contrary to what you might expect, the high-level handlers **XtAppErrorMsg( )** and **Xt-AppWarningMsg( )** are actually harder to use than the low-level handlers. You must pass six arguments to the calls that generate the errors or warnings, and then to take advantage of their benefits you must set up an error resource database. The first three arguments are the name, type, and class of the error. The use of these three arguments is not yet standardized since they are not widely used. However, in Xt itself, the name identifies the error message, and the type identifies the task that was in progress when the error occurred (or the section of code). The class, within Xt, is always **XtToolkitError**. The three remaining arguments of **XtAppErrorMsg( )** and **XtAppWarningMsg( )** are a default message, a parameter list, and the number of parameters. The default message will be printed only if no matching message is found in the database. Because Xt does not define or install any error database, it uses these default messages only, and ignores the name, type, and class information. (Xt uses the high-level handlers so that an error resource file can be installed to print all the errors in a foreign language.) The parameter list is used together with the message in the database. The message may be in standard *printf* format, and the parameters are used to fill in any variable fields.

Example 14-1 shows one of the rare cases where `XtAppErrorMsg()` is invoked in the Athena widgets.

Example 14-1. How to invoke XtAppErrorMsg (from AsciiSrc.c)

```
if (src->ascii_src.string == NULL)
    XtAppErrorMsg(XtWidgetToApplicationContext(src),
            "NoFile", "asciiSourceCreate", "XawError",
            "Creating a read only disk widget and no file \
            specified.", NULL, 0);
```

The error resource database is stored in a file, */usr/lib/X11/XtErrorDB*, under most UNIX-based operating systems. The MIT distribution does not include an *XtErrorDB* database, but you can define one. Since this database is made up of one file, you must append the resource settings you need to this file rather than replacing it. The resource name searched for in the database is the concatenation of the *name* and *type* arguments specified in the calls to `Xt-AppErrorMsg()` or `XtAppWarningMsg()`.

You can redefine the routine that prints the message in order to change the fixed part of the message or to add features like logging of errors and warnings. Use `XtAppSetError-MsgHandler()` and `XtAppSetWarningMsgHandler()` (if you are using the high-level handlers) or `XtAppSetErrorHandler()` and `XtAppSetWarning-Handler()` (if you are using the low-level handlers). See the reference pages for `Xt-ErrorMsgHandler`(2) and `XtErrorHandler`(2) in Volume Five, *X Toolkit Intrinsics Reference Manual*, for a description of how to define a new error or warning handler. The default error and warning messages printed are:

```
X Toolkit Error:   message.        (for errors)
X Toolkit Warning: message.        (for warnings)
```

Remember that Xt itself uses these messages (not just your widget code), so that they must remain appropriate when called from anywhere in the Xt, widget, or application code. If you want the message to identify the name of the widget set or widget, you must include this information in the part of the message filled in from the string you pass or from the resource database.

Table 14-1 summarizes Xt's calls for issuing errors and warnings and for modifying the messages issued.

Table 14-1. Xt Error and Warning Message Utilities

Message	Low Level	High Level
Issue Error	XtAppError	XtAppErrorMsg
Issue Warning	XtAppWarning	XtAppWarningMsg
Set Error Handler	XtAppSetErrorHandler	XtAppSetErrorMsgHandler
Set Warning Handler	XtAppSetWarningHandler	XtAppSetWarningMsgHandler

Note, however, that for the high-level routines that use the error and warning resource database, there is only one database common to all application contexts, at least in the sample implementation of Xt provided by MIT in R4 and R5.

When writing a high-level error or warning handler you will need to call **XtGetError-Database()** to get a pointer to the error resource database and **XtGetError-DatabaseText()** to get the message for a particular set of arguments passed to **XtApp-ErrorMsg()** or **XtAppWarningMsg()**. For details on how to use these functions, see the reference pages in Volume Five, *X Toolkit Intrinsics Reference Manual*.

XtDisplayStringConversionWarning() is a convenience routine to be used in resource type converters that convert from **XmRString** to any representation type. It calls **XtAppWarningMsg()** with the appropriate arguments to issue a suitable warning. Note however, that the class used is **XtToolkitError**. It may be better to use a class that describes the widget or widget set that defines the converter.

14.2 Objects

Most of this book describes how to use widgets, which are subclasses of the Core widget class. Chapter 13, *Menus, Gadgets, and Cascaded Popups*, also discusses using gadgets, which are subclasses of the RectObj widget class. As described there, gadgets are windowless widgets that are especially useful for menu panes, because they cut back on the overhead that would be required to implement the same thing using a widget for each pane.

The third and final Xt class you can subclass is the Object widget class. Objects are windowless widgets like gadgets, but they lack geometry resources, sensitivity resources, and the **expose** method. They provide support for resources and callbacks, and that is all.

The primary use of objects is to create replaceable subparts of a widget. For example, the R4 Athena Text widget uses objects to implement its source and sink, which control the storage and the display of the data respectively. By replacing the source and sink, you could develop a multi-color or multi-font editor without having to rewrite the central widget which implements all the editing commands.

An object has the following methods: **class_initialize**, **class_part _initialize**, **set_values**, and **get_values_hook**. All these methods have the same purposes as in widgets.

While a gadget uses part of its parent's window, an object shares its parent's entire window, and is not managed at all by its parent since it has no geometry. The parent of an object is normally a widget that is a subclass of Core but not Composite or Constraint (unlike gadget parents).

But like gadgets, objects depend on cooperation by their parent, and require a specially designed parent. The object parent's methods make calls to functions defined by the object child instead of doing the work themselves. The object child's functions can be either semipublic functions or they can be class methods defined by the object. The latter is done so that subclasses of the object can replace the functions.

As an example, let's look at how the Athena Text widget handles drawing. The drawing is done by the TextSink object, and its subclass AsciiSink. Although an object has no **expose** method, it provides an equivalent function that draws on the parent. This function is either a semi-public function (public to its parent but not to the application writer), or it is a class method. The Text widget uses both techniques. TextSink provides a semi-public function `XawTextSinkDisplayText()`, which is called by Text whenever drawing is needed.

`XawTextSinkDisplayText()` calls one of TextSink's class methods called Display-Text. DisplayText is a class method so that subclasses of TextSink can replace it or inherit it. AsciiSink does replace this method with code that draws the text in a single constant-width font, in the foreground and background colors. So in order to write a Text widget that draws in more than two colors, you would just have to write an object that is a new subclass of Text-Sink.

When Text calls `XawTextSinkDisplayText()`, this function calls one of TextSink's class methods called DisplayText. DisplayText is a class method so that subclasses of Text-Sink can replace it or inherit it. AsciiSink does replace this method with code that draws the text in a single constant-width font, in the foreground and background colors. So in order to write a Text widget that draws in more than two colors, you would just have to write an object that is a new subclass of TextSink.

An object may assume that it should draw on its parent, but this is not necessarily the case, since an object could have an object as its parent. An object also has no idea of its own size, since it has no geometry data in its instance structure, and therefore doesn't by itself know what size window it is drawing into. To solve both these problems, `XawTextSink-DisplayText()` passes the parent's widget ID and the parent's size into the objects drawing code.

14.3 Macros For Getting Information

Xt provides several macros and functions for getting information about widgets. Some of these, such as `XtIsRealized()` and `XtIsManaged()`, you have seen before in the context of widget methods.

Some of these are macros and some are functions, and some are macros when used in widget code and functions when used in application code. This does not affect how they can be used, so we won't bother to specify which can be both functions and macros. We will use the term "macro" for all of these informational routines. In Volume Five, *X Toolkit Intrinsics Reference Manual*, they are listed alphabetically, together with all of the Intrinsics functions.

Xt provides two basic macros for determining the class of a widget: `XtIsComposite()` and `XtIsSubclass()`. These are primarily used internally by Xt to implement geometry management, but you may find a use for them. For example, you might write a composite widget that uses `XtIsComposite()` to treat composite children differently than simple children, or uses `XtIsSubclass()` to treat constraint children or one of your own classes uniquely. There are lots of convenience functions for `XtIsSubclass()` that determine if a widget is a subclass of a particular class. These are `XtIsObject()`, `XtIsRect-Obj()`, `XtIsWidget()`, `XtIsComposite()`, `XtIsConstraint()`, `Xt-`

IsShell(), XtIsOverrideShell(), XtIsWMShell(), XtIsVendor-
Shell(), XtIsTransientShell(), XtIsTopLevelShell(), and Xt-
IsApplicationShell().

You have already seen **XtIsManaged()** used in composite widgets. See Chapter 12, *Geometry Management*.

You have also already seen **XtIsRealized()** used in various methods to make sure a widget has a window before operations are attempted on the window. For example, the **expose** method calls **XtIsRealized()** before drawing into the window.

XtIsSensitive() checks the value of the **XmNsensitive** resource for a widget and its ancestors. If any of them is **False**, it returns **False**. Remember that sensitivity controls whether a widget responds to user events.

XtHasCallbacks() lets you tell whether a widget class has a callback of a certain resource name, and whether any callback functions have actually been added to it. It returns the **enum** value **XtCallbackNoList** if there is no callback list, **XtCallbackHasNone** if there is a callback list with no functions on it, and **XtCallbackHasSome** if there is a callback list containing functions pointers.

XtNameToWidget() searches a hierarchy for the widget ID of the specified widget instance name. Its primary use from the application is to get the IDs of the child widgets of a compound widget such as Dialog, so that their resources can be set directly. This is a violation of the rules of data hiding, however, and is not recommended. In widget code, **XtNameToWidget()** is used to provide a layer of abstraction so that widgets can be identified using string names. For example, it is used by the converter defined by Form that allows widget names to be specified in resource files. The opposite function, which returns a widget instance name given the widget ID, is **XtName()** (which perhaps should have been called "XtWidgetToName").

XtWindowToWidget() gives you the **Widget** which corresponds to the specified X window ID. This is used mainly by Xt, but you may find a use for it.

XtDisplayOfObject(), **XtScreenOfObject()**, and **XtWindowOfObject()** search the parental hierarchy of an object to discover the closest windowed ancestor and then return a pointer to a **Display** structure, a pointer to a **Screen** structure, or a **Window** ID. These macros are useful for making Xlib calls from within code that implements a subclass of Object.

XtGetApplicationNameAndClass() returns the name and class strings of an application. The name is usually **argv[0]** stripped of any directories, while the class is the string passed as the second argument of **XtAppInitialize()**. These are the name and class used by Xt to look up resources for the application and its widgets. You are not likely to need this function.

14.4 The accept_focus Method and the Keyboard Focus

The keyboard focus is the window to which the server sends keyboard events. The window manager controls which top-level window gets the keyboard focus (using either a click-to-type or pointer-following model). Once an application's top-level window gets the focus, it can set the focus to one of its children; that's the way Motif's keyboard traversal code works. As described in Chapter 5, *More About Motif*, within a Motif application, you can have either a click-to-type or pointer-following model, although keyboard operation is only possible if the click-to-type model is used.

The Core class part structure includes a field for the **accept_focus** method. Theoretically, this method lets a widget set the keyboard focus to one of its children when it gets the keyboard focus. A typical example is an application that wants to set the keyboard focus to the text entry child of a dialog box whenever the dialog box is given the keyboard focus by the window manager. This would be done so that the user can type with the pointer anywhere in the dialog widget instead of just with the pointer in the text entry widget.

To implement this example, the text entry child would need an **accept_focus** method that would set the keyboard focus to itself using the Xlib call **XSetInputFocus()**. The dialog box would need an **accept_focus** method that called **XtCallAccept-Focus()** on the text entry widget child. The application can call **XtCallAccept-Focus()** on the dialog widget in response to **FocusIn** events to start this process, and set the focus back to **PointerRoot** on **FocusOut** events. For details on these events, see Volume Two, *Xlib Reference Manual*. This procedure for giving the child of a dialog the keyboard focus is necessary because the application can't find out the name of the child that should have the focus without breaking widget encapsulation rules.

In reality, none of the Motif widgets (and none of the Athena widgets, for that matter) use the **accept_focus** method. The keyboard traversal code is implemented separately.

An **accept_focus** method should return a Boolean value to report whether it succeeded in setting the keyboard focus, and **XtCallAcceptFocus()** returns this same value.

The **XtSetKeyboardFocus()** function redirects keyboard events that occur within an application to any widget within that application. This is different from **XSetInput-Focus()** in that no request to the server is made, and the redirection of keyboard events is handled entirely by Xt's event dispatching mechanism. However, **XtSetKeyboard-Focus()** should not be used in Motif applications, since it interferes with the keyboard traversal code.

Miscellaneous

14.5 Keyboard Interpretation

Keyboard handling in X is designed so that you can write a program that will operate on systems with widely different physical keyboards. To accomplish this, there are several layers of mappings:

- The first mapping is between physical keys and keycodes (a number for each key), and varies between servers. A **KeyPress** event includes only the keycode and information about what other keys and buttons were being held at the time of the keypress. Programs that interpret keycodes directly will operate on only one type of system.

- The next mapping is between keycodes and keysyms, which are symbolic constants beginning with **XK_** that represent the meaning of a key press. This mapping takes into account whether Shift or other modifier keys were being held during the press. Xlib provides the routine **XLookupString()** that converts the keycode in a key event to the appropriate keysym. Internationalized programs use the **XmbLookupString** or **XwcLookupString** versions which can figure out the keysym resulting from key sequences entered into an input method. Portable programs use keysyms to interpret key events. The keycode to keysym mapping is server-wide. It can be changed, but this is normally done only to accomplish radical changes in the placement of keys such as changing a QWERTY style keyboard to DVORAK.

- The final mapping is between keysyms and strings. For printing characters, **XLookupString()** also returns a string representation of the interpretation of the key pressed. For example, if the key marked *A* was pressed with no other keys held down, the string returned would be *a*. A text entry widget, for example, would append this string to the string being displayed, but modify the string in other ways to handle keysyms that do not have a string representation such as **XK_Backspace**. The values of keysyms are arranged logically so that all printing characters have a particular range.

Motif adds virtual key bindings to this model, as described in Section 5.9.

When you write an action that accepts key events, you will usually need to interpret the meaning of the key pressed. Xt provides its own interface to **XLookupString()**: **XtTranslateKeycode()**. You pass several fields of the key event to **XtTranslateKeycode()**, and it returns the keysym. However, **XtTranslateKeycode()** does not return the string interpretation of the key event that would be returned by **XLookupString()**. If you need that string, you will have to call **XLookupString()**.

Xt provides **XtTranslateKeycode()** because Xt also provides routines for changing the way the translation returned by **XtTranslateKeycode()** is done. **XtSetKeyTranslator()** allows you to specify your own procedure to convert from the key event information to a keysym. The default key event translation procedure is **XtTranslateKey()**, and so you can restore the default translator if necessary, and so that you can call it from your own translator to get default translations (you need to add only the code that makes the translations not done by the default translator). See **XtKeyProc** in Volume Five, *X Toolkit Intrinsics Reference Manual*, for details on providing a key event translation procedure.

Among these routines for modifying the interpretation of key events is a facility for changing the handling of capitalization. For example, most keyboards have the question mark (*?*) symbol over the slash (/) symbol on one key. The standard case converter converts a press of this key with the Shift key held down to the `XK_question` keysym. In rare cases a keyboard may have a different symbol over / and put *?* somewhere else. Also, some keyboards have two or more symbols on a single key, some of which are not represented at all by standard keysyms. The case converter handles these situations. The case converter is usually called from the key translator described above. To call the case converter, use `XtConvert-Case()`, and to change the case converter, call `XtRegisterCaseConverter()`. See *XtCaseProc* in Volume Five, *X Toolkit Intrinsics Reference Manual*, for details on writing a case converter procedure.

Note that the translation manager uses these same key translation and case converter routines to interpret translation tables. Therefore, make sure that you add features only to them, keeping existing features.

Xt also provides two routines that may help in interpreting key events: `XtGetKeysym-Table()` and `XtKeysymToKeycodeList()`. The former returns the entire mapping of keycodes to keysyms for the server, while the latter tells you what keycodes are listed for the specified keysym. Neither function is necessary for routine keyboard handling.

From within an action routine, you can call `XtGetActionKeysym()` to get the keysym that resulted in the action being called. This can be very useful, since the event passed to the action contains only the keycode of the key that was pressed. However, there is another way to achieve a similar result. You can use string parameters of actions to pass in the keysym that you specified in the translation table. For example, if you provide the translation `:<Key>q : Quit(q)`, the Quit action will be passed the string "q" in its *params* argument. However, `XtGetActionKeysym()` is very useful if you translate a wide range of key events to one action, and then want to distinguish between them in the action.

14.6 Memory Allocation

Xt provides routines for performing routine memory allocation and deallocation. The routines `XtMalloc()`, `XtCalloc()`, `XtRealloc()`, and `XtFree()` are equivalents of the standard C routines `malloc`, `calloc`, `realloc`, and `free` but they add error checking and reporting. The allocation routines make sure the allocation succeeded, and if it did not, they print a (fatal) error message. `XtFree()` makes sure the passed pointer is not `NULL` before calling `free`.

`XtNew()` is a macro which allocates storage for one instance of the passed type and returns a pointer. For example, `XtNew(XtCallbackList)` allocates storage for one callback list structure. `XtNewString()` is a macro that allocates storage for a string, copies the string into the new storage, and returns the pointer. For example, a string can be copied into new storage using the following:

```
static String buf[ ] = "How do you do?";
String p;

p = XtNewString(buf);
```

After this sequence, p points to a separate string that contains "How do you do?" Then **buf** can be changed without affecting p.

14.7 Action Hooks and Calling Actions Directly

Xt allows you to register any number of functions to be called whenever any action in an application context is invoked. This is done with `XtAppAddActionHook()`. Note that there is just one "action hook" in the application context, so that all the action hook functions registered for that application context are called whenever *any* of the actions in that application context are invoked. The registration does not specify any particular action or any particular widget.

The main reason for registering an action hook is to record all the actions that were invoked in an application, so that they can be played back later using `XtCallActionProc()`. An action hook function is called with all the same arguments that are passed to an action, plus the string name of the action. The action hook function would store this information as a unit each time it was called. When it comes time to play back the recorded actions, it would pass all the information in each unit to `XtCallActionProc()`.

An action hook can be removed with `XtRemoveActionHook()`.

14.8 Xt Grabbing Functions

Grabs are used mostly for popup menus and dialog boxes. As described in Chapter 13, *Menus, Gadgets, and Cascaded Popups*, Xt has its own *grab mode* that controls the distribution of events within one application, which can be used to restrict events to one popup in a cascade or allow events to go to any popup in a cascade. As also described there, popup menus in particular need a passive global grab of the pointer in order to detect button releases that occur completely outside the application so that menus can be popped down properly. A passive global grab actually instructs the server to redirect events to a certain window. All the grabbing needs of popups are satisfied by the built-in action `XtMenu-Popup()`, or by the function `XtPopupSpringLoaded()`, which can be used in a callback function. If necessary, you can write your own version of `XtMenuPopup()` and register it with `XtRegisterGrabAction()` so that the appropriate passive global grab is in effect.

The above facilities should be quite sufficient for your needs in the area of popups. However, it is possible that you may need an global grab for some other purpose. Perhaps you need all keyboard events in one window for a short time and don't want to change existing translations or accelerators for keyboard events in other widgets. This is only one plausible scenario.

The Xlib functions for grabbing are `XGrabKey()`, `XGrabButton()`, `XGrab-Keyboard()`, and `XGrabPointer()`. Each of these functions has an analogue for ungrabbing. But Xt provides its own version of all eight of these functions. You should use the Xt versions because they are integrated into Xt and take care of things like making sure the widget that is to get the grab has been realized. In other words, if you do need the server to redirect events for you using a grab, use the following functions: `XtGrabKey()`, `Xt-GrabButton()`, `XtGrabKeyboard()`, `XtUngrabKeyboard()`, and `XtUngrab-Pointer()`. For more on global grabs, see Chapter 8 in Volume One, *Xlib Programming Manual*.

14.9 File Finding and Internationalization

Xt's facilities for allowing an application to run in different languages are mostly built into the resource database mechanism. Where Xt searches for resource files depends on a language string, which can be set within resources at run time or with an environment variable to affect one user's environment. This is described in Chapter 10, *Resource Management and Type Conversion*. In R5 and later, Xt also uses the value of the `XtNcustomization` resource to set the path it uses when looking for application defaults and other files. `Xt-Ncustomization` is normally used to supply separate sets of resources for color and monochrome screens.

The functions that Xt uses to implement its search for resource files are also available to you for searching for application files. This allows you to provide separate data files for each language for a help system, for example. The primary function you would use to do this is `Xt-ResolvePathname()`, since it searches directories in a standard order based on X/Open Portability Guide conventions.

If you want to find a file but are not interested in internationalization, you can use `XtFind-File()`. This function can simplify code that reads files, since it helps handle differences in file systems.

14.10 Application Contexts

The introduction to application contexts in Section 3.9 described their use in 99 percent of applications. As you may recall, their purpose is chiefly to attain portability to certain systems that do not provide a separate address space for each process.

Xt provides parallel versions of many routines—one set that uses the default application context, and one set that has an explicit application context argument. The routines that use the default application context are remnants of an earlier release when application contexts did not work properly. To achieve the desired portability, you must now use the versions with the explicit argument. We have done this throughout this book. In Volume Five, *X Toolkit Intrinsics Reference Manual*, the reference pages for all the functions that use the default application context note the fact that they should no longer be used.

Table 14-2 shows the complete list of routines that have two versions.

Table 14-2. Xt Routines That Use Default and Explicit Application Contexts

Default	Explicit
(registering functions)	
XtAddActions()	XtAppAddActions()
XtAddConverter()	XtAppAddConverter()
XtAddInput()	XtAppAddInput()
XtTimeOut()	XtAppTimeOut()
XtWorkProc()	XtAppWorkProc()
(creating shells)	
XtCreateApplicationShell()	XtAppCreateShell()
(event dispatching)	
XtMainLoop()	XtAppMainLoop()
XtNextEvent()	XtAppNextEvent()
XtPeekEvent()	XtAppPeekEvent()
XtPending()	XtAppPending()
XtProcessEvent()	XtAppProcessEvent()
(error and warning messages)	
XtError()	XtAppError()
XtErrorMsg()	XtAppErrorMsg()
XtGetErrorDatabase()	XtAppGetErrorDatabase()
XtGetErrorDatabaseText()	XtAppGetErrorDatabaseText()
XtSetErrorHandler()	XtAppSetErrorHandler()
XtSetErrorMsgHandler()	XtAppSetErrorMsgHandler()
XtSetWarningHandler()	XtAppSetWarningHandler()
XtSetWarningMsgHandler()	XtAppSetWarningMsgHandler()
XtWarning()	XtAppWarning()
XtWarningMsg()	XtAppWarningMsg()
(selection timeouts)	
XtGetSelectionTimeout()	XtAppGetSelectionTimeout()
XtSetSelectionTimeout()	XtAppSetSelectionTimeout()
(action hooks)	
(no equiv)	XtAppAddActionHook()
(toolkit initialization)	
(no equiv)	XtAppInitialize()
(resources)	
(no equiv)	XtAppSetFallbackResources()
XtSetTypeConverter()	XtAppSetTypeConverter()
(no equiv)	XtAppReleaseCacheRefs()

Note that **XtCreateApplicationShell()** and **XtAppCreateShell()** have names that don't follow the example set by all the rest.

14.10.1 Multiple Application Contexts

The use of more than one application context in a single program presents possibilities that you might wish to explore. Having more than one application context in the same program allows you to have one program that when run looks like two or more independent programs. This approach saves disk space and memory on systems that don't provide shared libraries, since the grouped programs can share a single copy of the libraries.†

Having two application contexts makes each sub-application more separate than if they were just under different top-level Shell widgets. Each widget class has an action list, and each application context has a separate context-wide action list. When the translation manager looks for an action, it looks in the widget class action list first, and then the application context action list. Therefore, each sub-application could add an action to its application context without conflict with another sub-application adding a different action of the same name.

On parallel processing machines, each separate application context could run in parallel. However, it is difficult to write portable code to take advantage of this, since each architecture has different conventions for indicating parallelisms in C code.

14.10.2 Rewriting XtAppMainLoop for Multiple Application Contexts

To use multiple application contexts, you need to write your own equivalent of `XtApp-MainLoop()` to dispatch events to your multiple application contexts. This is necessary because `XtAppMainLoop()` dispatches events only from one application context, and it never returns so you can't call it again for the other.

The available tools are `XtAppNextEvent()`, `XtAppPeekEvent()`, `XtApp-Pending()`, `XtAppProcessEvent()`, and the Xlib functions `XFlush()` and `XSync()`. Rewriting `XtAppMainLoop()` for two or more application contexts is tricky, because you don't want to let the dispatching of any one application context get behind. It is not as simple as dispatching events from each application context alternately, since the events might not occur alternately. It is easy to get stuck waiting for events in one application context while events queue up at the other. There is little experience in how this should be done properly, and no examples in the distribution from MIT. However, hypothetically, the following describes how it could work.

To do this properly, you have to understand how Xlib's network optimization works. Xlib buffers up many types of requests and sends (flushes) them to the server as a group.‡ A flush is most commonly caused by a routine such as `XtAppNextEvent()` that waits for an event if none are available. It is because `XtAppNextEvent()` waits forever for an event

---

†In SunView, many of the basic applications were grouped in a single binary probably for this reason. The Xlib and Xt libraries are quite large. For example, on a Sony NWS-841 workstation, the executable image of a "hello, world" application written with Xt and the Athena widget set uses 450K of disk space. One of the most complicated existing X applications, *xterm*, uses 600K of disk space on this system. Therefore, the various libraries account for about three-quarters of the disk space used, even for a fairly large program.

‡For a detailed discussion of Xlib's network optimization and its effects, see the introduction to Volume Zero, *X Protocol Reference Manual*.

that the routine could get locked waiting for events in one application context while the user types frantically in the other.

The answer is to use `XtAppPending()` to determine whether an event is available on a particular application context, and then call `XtAppProcessEvent()` if there is an event to process. Then continue to do the same on each other application context. However, this alone is not enough. Neither `XtAppPending()` nor `XtAppProcessEvent()` called in this manner cause Xlib's buffer of requests to be sent to the server. Therefore, periodic calls to `XSync()` or `XFlush()` are necessary to flush the output buffer. The difficult part is to call these enough to flush the buffer when necessary, but not so much as to eliminate the advantages of the buffering. There is no ideal solution to this problem.

On multi-tasking systems it is perhaps possible to `fork` so that each application context runs in a separate process.

14.10.3 Functions Used with Multiple Application Contexts

`XtWidgetToApplicationContext()` and `XtDisplayToApplication-Context()` could be useful if you use more than one application context in an application. `XtWidgetToApplicationContext()` is also useful in widget code, to call error-issuing routines that require an application context argument, such as `XtAppWarning()` and `XtAppWarningMsg()`.

14.11 Multiple Top-level Shells

A single application can have more than one top-level window. In other words, you are not restricted to containing your application's entire user interface in a single rectangle. If you have one section of the application that is most appropriate as a long, thin vertical window that looks like a long, permanent menu, and another section that is a long, horizontal bar such as a ruler, each of these could be a separate top-level window. That way, not only is less screen space wasted than if these two windows were placed within a single rectangle, but the user can move the two windows around separately using the window manager. The user can also iconify them separately when not needed.

To create additional top-level application shell widgets, you call `XtAppCreateShell()` or `XtVaAppCreateShell()`. (`XtCreateApplicationShell()` is now superceded.) The class specified in the call should be `topLevelShellWidgetClass`.

As you may know, a single server may have several screens attached. At present, all shells created will appear on the default screen. There is no way for the application to specify that a shell be created on a particular screen, but then again, doing this is usually unwise anyway because not many users actually have more than one screen. The user can specify which screen is considered the default screen using the –*display* command-line option.

14.12 Connecting to Multiple Servers

One of the great features of the server-client model is that a single program can connect to several servers to display on the screens of several users. For example, this would allow you to create an X-based version of the UNIX utility *wall* in which one user can make a message appear on all user's screens throughout a network. You could also create a conferencing program in which each user has a window on their screen in which they can type and view typing by others in real time, and their typing will appear on all the other user's screens.

The Xt application opens a connection with a server using `XtOpenDisplay()` (this routine requires an explicit application context argument). Once you have opened the connection, you will want to create a shell widget on the server's default screen using `XtCreateApplicationShell()` or `XtAppCreateShell()`. Then, you create widgets for each server simply by using the appropriate Shell widget as parent. Thereafter, `XtAppMainLoop()` dispatches events from all the connections to the appropriate widget.

14.13 Class Extension Structures

X Consortium standards, once adopted, can only be changed in ways that are binary and source compatible with the original standard specification. Xt became an X consortium standard in Release 3. Therefore, Release 4 and later releases are required to be source and binary compatible with Release 3. *Source compatibility* means that properly coded applications and widgets written to the R3 specification should compile and work under R4 and later releases. Source compatibility is maintained by keeping all programming interfaces intact while adding features with new interfaces. *Binary compatibility* means that widgets written and compiled with R3 must be able to be linked with R4 or R5 Xt and Xlib libraries and still run. Source compatibility is necessary but not sufficient for binary compatibility. The major addition requirement of binary compatibility is that fields added to structures must be added to the end of the structure.

In Chapter 6, *Inside a Widget*, you saw how a class structure for a widget class is built by nesting the class part structures of all its superclasses into one big structure, the class record. The X consortium could not simply add fields to the class part structures of the basic Xt classes without breaking binary compatibility with existing subclasses because the class parts of basic Xt classes appear in the middle of the class record of subclasses. Therefore, they used extension structures to add these fields.

Class extension structures allowed the X consortium to add to the class structures of basic Xt classes. The last field of each basic Xt class is called **extension**. This field can be set to a pointer to the class's extension structure, which contains its added fields. New features that required additional class structure fields were added to the Composite and Constraint classes in R4. Therefore, these two classes now have extension structures.

Some classes, such as Core, do not have an extension structure because no additional class fields have yet been necessary. They still have the **extension** field, but it is not used.

A class extension structure is defined in the private header file of a widget class. The extension structure for Composite is called `CompositeClassExtensionRec` as shown in Example 14-2.

Example 14-2. Common fields in a class extension record

```
typedef struct {
    XtPointer next_extension;/* 1st 4 mandated for all ext rec */
    XrmQuark record_type;     /* NULLQUARK; on CompositeClassPart */
    long version;             /* must be XtCompositeExtensionVersion */
    Cardinal record_size;     /* sizeof(CompositeClassExtensionRec) */
    Boolean accepts_objects;
} CompositeClassExtensionRec, *CompositeClassExtension;
```

All extension structures start with the same four fields. The only field in this structure actually used by Composite is `accepts_objects`, the use of which is described in Section 12.4.5. The `accepts_objects` field is only used by Composite widgets that have the code necessary to accept gadget children. When a widget class needs an extension feature, the widget class initializes the extension structure in its *.c* file, and then in the `class_initialize` method sets the `extension` field to point to the extension structure.

When a widget class does not need an extension feature—for example, a Composite widget that does not accept gadget children—the widget class does not provide code in the `class_initialize` method to set the `extension` field.

The *.c* file of all widget classes should initially set all `extension` fields to `NULL`. The difference between classes that use extension features and those that don't is only the presence or absence of code in `class_initialize` to set the `extension` fields.

The four required fields in an extension structure are:

`next_extension` Specifies the next record in the list, or `NULL`.

`record_type`   Specifies the particular structure declaration to which each extension
                  record instance conforms.

`version`   Specifies a symbolic constant supplied by the definer of the structure.

`record_size`   Specifies the total number of bytes allocated for the extension record.

When you initialize an extension structure of a given class in the *.c* file, you always set these four fields to the same values. Example 14-3 shows how to initialize the Composite extension structure. The first two fields are usually `NULL` and `NULLQUARK`. The reference page for each class that has an extension structure will document how to initialize the third and fourth fields.

```
    CompositeClassExtensionRec extension_rec = {
        /* next_extension */  NULL,
        /* record_type */     NULLQUARK,
        /* version */         XtCompositeExtensionVersion,
        /* record_size */     sizeof(CompositeClassExtensionRec),
        /* accepts_objects */ True,  /* only new field */
    };
```

The `next_extension` field implies correctly that you can nest extension structures. Perhaps a later release of Xt will require the addition of more Composite class fields. These could be added to the end of the existing extension structure, or a new extension structure could be defined and a pointer to it placed in `next_extension`. This allows additions to be made to a class structure without breaking binary compatibility.

You may be wondering whether you should use extension structures when extending your own widgets. Probably not. Because you are likely to release your set of widgets as a package, you have no need for binary compatibility with previous releases (of your own). Binary compatibility would only be an advantage if you wanted to replace a few widgets from a former release and save users who may have subclassed the widgets you have replaced from recompiling their widgets. For the trouble involved, the benefit is very small.

14.14 Using Editres in Xt Programming†

editres is a tool for viewing the structure of X Toolkit applications, finding and setting resources, and dynamically see the results of such settings. *editres* can help programmers create an app-default file and fallback resources and test custom Xt widgets. This section describes how to add support to Motif applications, and how to use *editres* as an aid in debugging widgets and applications.

14.14.1 A Tour of editres

The *editres* application is part of the core distribution in Release 5. This section is a brief tour of the *editres* resource editor. It will illustrate how to use *editres* to customize an X Toolkit application. When the user starts *editres* it looks like Figure 14-1.

---

†This section was written by Chris Peterson, and originally appeared in *The X Resource*, Issue 0.

Miscellaneous

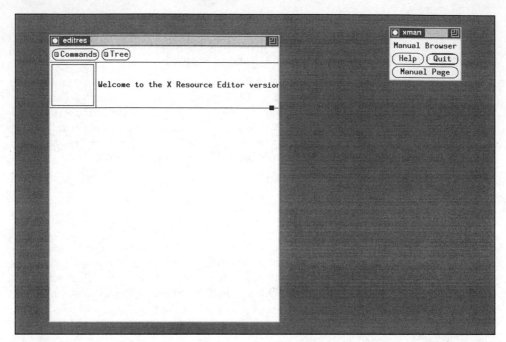

Figure 14-1. editres immediately after startup

The *editres* application contains four areas; The Menu Bar, the Panner, the Message Area, and the Tree Display (which is initially empty). You begin by choosing Get Widget Tree from the Command menu and, following the instructions in the Message Area, select an X Toolkit application by clicking a pointer button. Figure 14-2 shows the result of selecting the *xman* application. (Note that the application must have support for *editres*. All applications written using the Athena widget set have that support built in as of R5. Applications written using Motif need to have support added, as shown later.)

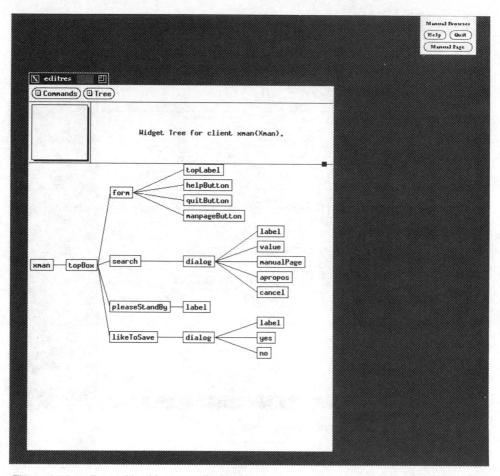

Figure 14-2. editres with widget tree displayed

The Tree Display now contains the widget hierarchy of *xman*, displayed graphically. You can now see the name of each widget in the application, and the parent-child relationship of each of these widgets. By using the Tree menu or a keyboard accelerator the user can also see the Class names, Widget ID's, or Window ID's. Figure 14-3 shows the same *xman* application, but with the Window ID's displayed instead of the widget names.

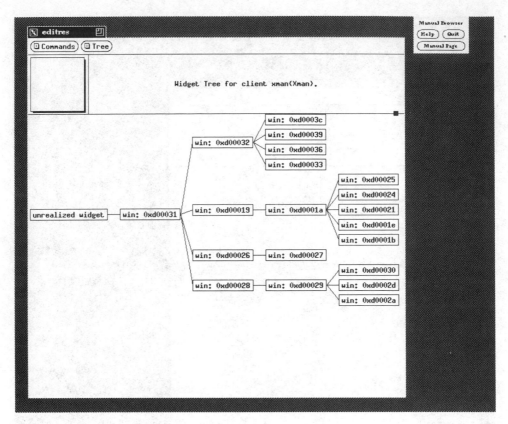

Figure 14-3. editres display window IDs of widget tree

By selecting "Select Widget in Client" from the Tree menu you can click a pointer button anywhere in the application, and *editres* will highlight the corresponding widget in the Tree Display. Figure 14-4 shows the result of clicking in the topLabel widget of the *xman* application. Editres can also do the inverse of this; selecting the "Flash Active Widgets" command from the Tree menu will show you (by flashing widgets in the application) which widgets are currently selected in the Tree Display.

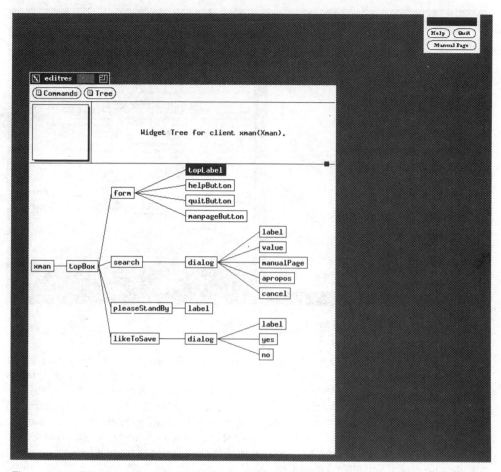

Figure 14-4. Flashing widget in application by selecting it in editres

With these two commands you can easily determine the correspondence between the application itself and the Tree Display representation of it. Because a resource specification is simply a description of the widget's locations in the Tree Display and can be constructed by concatenating the names of the widget and it ancestors, *editres* can easily construct valid resource specifications that apply to the widgets selected. For example, the fully specified resource name of the topLevel widget is xman.topBox.form.topLabel.

Once you find the widget you want to modify you can select the Show Resource Box command to bring up a dialog box that will allow you to set the resource of that widget. A Resource Box is shown in Figure 14-5, as it would look after changing the topLabel widget's resource to "Testing, Testing."

Miscellaneous

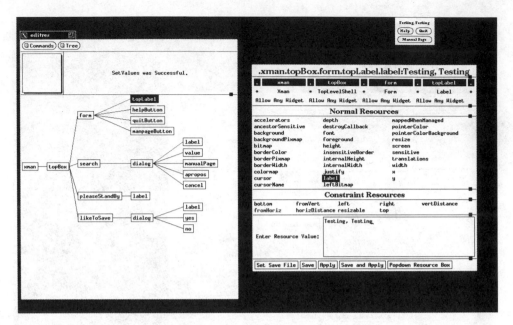

Figure 14-5. Resource box for the selected Label widget

At the top of the Resource Box is the resource line currently being edited. This is the actual string that will be inserted into the resource file if you decide to save a change. Below this is an area that allows you to modify the widgets to be affected by this change. This area allows you to substitute class names for instance names, and asterisks for periods in the left hand side of the resource specification. These changes will loosen the binding of the resource specification allowing this one resource line to apply to more and more widgets (see Figure 14-6). Note that no matter how the bindings are modified (by changing periods to asterisks) the original widget will always match the specification.

When taken to the extreme, the resource specification can apply to every widget in the application. As you change the bindings of the resource specification, the Tree Display is updated to highlight all the widgets that will be affected by the resource line displayed. When this is combined with the Show Highlighted Widgets command, which flashes the widgets in the application that correspond to those highlighted in the Tree Display, you can quickly determine which widgets will match a given resource specification.

The next area contains a complete list of normal and constraint resources that are available for the originally selected widget. This area is used to select the name of the resource that the user wishes to modify. Foreground, for example, will set the foreground color. Below this area is simply a text field to allow the user to enter the string that will represent the resource value. The resource value that is entered here should be exactly what would be entered into a resource file, thus all new lines should be escaped by a backslash (\) and backslash-n (\n) should be used to add a new line to the resource value.

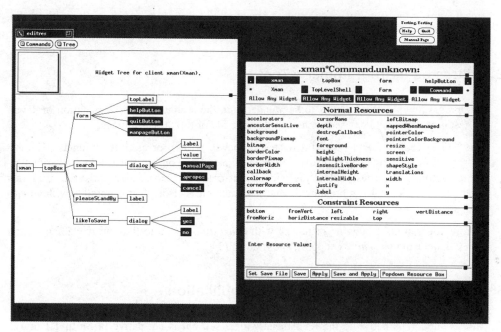

Figure 14-6. Generalizing the widgets affected by the resource specification

Since *editres* specifies all resources as strings, it can only set those resources that can be set from resource files. Motif 1.1 and 1.2 do not provide support for certain resources to be set in resource files. One example is the **XmNleftWidget** resource of the Form widget.)

The commands at the bottom of the Resource Box allows the user to select the file the resources will be written into, write the resources to the file, apply the resource immediately to the application, or just popdown the resource box.

Note that applying the resource to the application will not always have the same effect as restarting the application with the resource added to the user's customization file. This is a design constraint of the X Toolkit. Some resources are designed to be read once at startup, and trying to coerce them into a dynamic resource editor is problematic. The basic problem is that the *editres* support in the application uses **XtSetValues()** to change the resource of the selected widgets. An **XtSetValues()** call after startup will override any *hard-coded* application defaults (but not application defaults specified in files or as fallback resources), whereas the same resource specification in a resource file will not. Therefore, the results of applying a resource setting using *editres* are only a guide.

Those are the basic features of *editres*. You can see there is much work to be done, but the basic task of finding and setting resource values is much simpler with this tool. This brief tour should give you an idea of the capabilities of the resource editor, and hopefully stir your

Miscellaneous

imagination a bit. I will next describe the method *editres* uses to communicate with the applications.

14.14.2 editres as a Programmer's Tool

The programmer can use editres to help understand the structure of the application or develop resource settings to be used as the app-defaults file or fallback resources.

The *editres* tool can also be useful for testing newly written or modified widgets. The test program can be written generically and then *editres* lets you see the results of various resource settings. The tests allow the widget's `geometry_manager` and `set_values` methods to be debugged more quickly and with much less effort than is possible without *editres*.

Before you can do debugging or testing with *editres*, you need to find out if the application you will be using has *editres* support, and if not, add it.

14.14.3 Adding editres Support to an Xt Application

editres support is native to the R5 Athena widget set, but is not native in Motif 1.1 or 1.2. When the support is not available, only a few lines of code need to be added to an Xt application to link in the *editres* communication routines. Also note that if you use custom widgets with a widget set that supports *editres*, the custom widgets are automatically included and no code needs to be added. If you know the widget set you use already supports *editres*, you can skip to the next section.

First check that *editres* is not supported by the widget set you are using, by invoking the "Get Widget Tree" command from the *editres* command menu, and then clicking on your application. If editres is not supported, the command will fail resulting in no tree display and the message "It appears that this client does not understand the Editres Protocol." This message will be displayed only after the *editres* command has timed out, a process that may take up to sixty seconds.

The R5 Xmu library provides an event handler that can send and receive the *editres* protocol. To add *editres* support to an Xt based application, you need only to register this event handler on at least one shell widget in the application. But to allow the user to select any window in the application and activate *editres*, you must add it to every shell widget in the application. Here is the code needed to add the event handler to one shell widget:

Example 14-3. Adding editres support in an application
```
#include <X11/Xmu/Editres.h>

XtAddEventHandler(shell, (EventMask) 0, True, _XEditResCheckMessages, NULL);
```

This code can be added anywhere after the shell widget has been created. The X11R5 Xmu library must be linked into the application to provide the routines that actually decode the protocol and process the *editres* events. Because Xmu depends upon Xt and X11, the order of linking is important. The link command for the application should be:

```
% cc <objects> —lwidget set library –lXmu –lXt –lX11 –lXext
```

Once the application has been recompiled and relinked *editres* support should be available. If the **_XEditResCheckMessages()** handler was added to only one shell in the application, be sure to select that shell or one of its normal (non-popup) children when *editres* prompts you to "Click the mouse pointer on any Xaw client."

14.14.4 Using editres to Understand the Structure of an Application

Picking up maintenance of an X application that was written by someone else can be an exercise in patience. Because of the event driven nature of X applications there is no single flow of control. In order to find out what is happening it is often necessary to locate the place where a widget on the screen is created in the code and then use this information to find its widget ID and display the data contained in that widget. *editres* can make this task much simpler.

To find the place where a widget is created, use the "Select widget in client" command, and click the pointer on the widget of interest within the target application. This will highlight that widget in editres's tree display. The tree display will show the name of the widget, which makes finding where it was created easier, usually a simple matter of using *grep*(1). You can also view the widget's class name, widget ID and window ID by selecting various commands from the Tree menu, or using the keyboard accelerators described below.

Table 14-3. editres accelerators

Accelerator	Description
N	Show widget name
C	Show widget class
I	Show widget ID (in hex)
W	Show widget's window

If the pointer is over a widget when the accelerator is used then only that one widget is affected. If the pointer is over the tree background then all widgets in the application are affected.

When viewing the widget windows, the programmer is also informed if the widget is unrealized or if the widget in question is a non-windowed object, such as an Object or a Motif Gadget. This information is often useful when attempting to decipher an X protocol error, since it contains the XID of the offending widget. The class names can be useful to help understand the behavior, and geometry constraints of the current application's window layout. Widget ID's are mainly useful when used in concert with a symbolic debugger such as *dbx* or CodeCenter (formerly Saber-C), since the values in the widget structure can be viewed in the debugger by de-referencing this widget pointer.

Miscellaneous

To provide a permanent hard copy of the widget hierarchy of an application, either for future reference, or for inclusion in the application's documentation, *editres* provides a command called "Dump Widget Tree to a File." The output is dumped in an outline format and includes both the name and class of each widget currently in the application. Note that this command will only show those widgets that had been created the last time a "Get Widget Tree", or "Refresh Current Widget Tree" command was executed.

In addition to allowing the programmer to understand the structure of an application, *editres* can be used to add entries to an application defaults resource file. To use *editres* as an aid simply use the "Set Save File" button at the bottom of the Resource Box, and then use the "Save and Apply" button to add entries to the application defaults file. *editres* immediately applies the resource change to the application.

14.14.5 Using editres to Test or Debug a Widget

The programmer can also use *editres* to test some of the dynamic characteristics of a widget. Since a widget's most common interface to the outside world is through the setting of resources, the "Apply" action in *editres*'s resource box window provides a very convenient mechanism for testing and debugging widget resources. This mechanism can be used to test the widget's set_values and Constraint set_values procedures, as well as the widget's geometry_manager.

editres gets its list of resources for a widget by sending a message to the application. The *editres* support code in the application that receives the message then calls the Xt functions `XtGetResourceList()` and `XtGetConstraintResourceList()` to get the list of resources supported. Xt does not provide functions for getting the list of resources for application resources, objects that are not Xt children or Xt popup children, and subresources, so they are not visible to *editres*. This limitation appears in most Text widgets, because they use either objects or subparts that have subresources, and *editres* cannot find these resources.

Editres passes only string values across to the application to set resources. Therefore, the *editres* support code in the application uses a StringTo<*something*> converter to actually set the widget resource. If no such converter is available, *editres* will not be able to set the resource. Since these converters are required to allow the resource to be set in the app-defaults file or user resource file, your widget should have them anyway, so you should not need to add any special code to your widget in order to debug it using *editres*.

14.14.5.1 Testing a Widget's set_values Procedures

To test a widget's `set_values` procedure you must first pop up the resource box associated with that widget. The resource box is popped up by selecting the widget in question and selecting the "Show Resource Box" command. This will pop up a window that shows all the resources available to this widget. Selecting a resource, entering a value, and hitting the Apply button at the bottom of the Resource Box window allows the programmer to test each resource of this widget to verify that it is responding to them correctly.

Note that each widget must register a type converter from String to each new type of resource it created, since *editres* sends all values as strings. Writing and registering these converters is a good idea in any case, since it allows each widget resource to be specified in the app-defaults file or another resource file as well as through the `set_values` mechanism.

It is important to note that changes to a resource defined by the superclass may often require support from the subclass. If your new widget, which is a subclass of an existing widget, has added some additional functionality to a resource that is not new to this widget, but was defined by its superclass, you must test this resources as well (e.g., a Label widget will need to test the sensitivity resource, since it added support for stippling the text when it becomes insensitive). Programmers should be sure to modify the value of each resource, not just those new resources added to this widget,

To test the Constraint `set_values` procedure of a widget the Resource Box of a child of this widget must be popped up. This Resource Box window will list the constraint resources separately from the normal resources. These resources can be tested with the apply button in the same fashion as normal resources.

14.14.5.2 Testing a Widget's geometry_manager

Although it is not obvious at first, *editres* can be used to test a widget's geometry manager. Since the size and location of every widget are stored in resources they can be modified on-the-fly with *editres*.

First identify the widget whose geometry manager is to be tested. I will call this widget the "parent." To test its geometry manager we must make a request to change the geometry of one of its children. Therefore, use *editres* to select one of the children of the "parent" widget and pop up its Resource Box. This will allow the child's size and location to be changed by modifying the x, y, width and height resources. Changing these attributes will in turn call upon the geometry manager of the parent widget, allowing the programmer to see if the proper behavior is occurring. By placing several different kinds of children in the parent and seeing how changes to the geometry of each child affects the others, extensive testing can be performed in a short period of time.

Since two resources cannot be modified in a single *editres* command there is no direct way to make a simultaneous width and height change to a widget. But if a Xaw Label or XmLabel widget is used as a child then a change to the font will often cause a change to both the width and height of the widget. The effects of such a change can then be tested in the parent's geometry manager.

Editres may be expanded to include additional features.

14.15 Internationalization in the X Toolkit

In X11R5, Xt was modified to better support internationalization. An internationalized application reads the user's language (called a locale) from the environment or a resource file and operates in that language without changes to its binary. X internationalization is based on the ANSI-C internationalization model. The concepts and implementation of X internationalization are described in the Third Edition of Volume One, *Xlib Programming Manual*. Xt support of internationalization is trivial in most applications: the only code needed is a call to `XtSetLanguageProc()` just before the call to `XtAppInitialize()`. However, if your program directly manipulates text from widgets, or you need to write widgets that accept text input or draws text, you'll need to understand Xlib's internationalization features.

14.15.1 String Encoding and Locale Dependencies in Xt

The X Toolkit specification has not been so thoroughly revised as the Xlib spec to make explicit the expected encodings of all strings. Generally, it will be true that Xt variables or arguments of type `String` should be in the encoding of the locale, but caution is necessary: the widget name passed to `XtCreateWidget()` is of type `String`, for example, but since it may be used in resource specifications it should be in the Host Portable Character Encoding if the application is to operate in more than a single locale. Neither is the specification explicit about such things as the encoding of translation tables or the localized behavior of resource converters like `XtCvtStringToBoolean`. None of these are critical problems; the Xt programmer who wishes to write internationalized applications should be aware, however, that there are internationalization issues in Xt that remain to be worked out.

14.15.2 Establishing Locale in an Xt Application

Resource specifications in X11R5 are parsed in the current locale, which means that an application should have established its locale before reading its app-defaults file and creating its resource database. However, it should be possible to specify the locale for an application using a resource, which means that the resources should be read before the locale is set. The Intrinsics as of X11R5 resolves this catch-22 by parsing resources in two steps: first it scans the command line and per-display resource string for the setting of the locale, then, once the locale is set, it fully parses all the resource specifications.

The locale and resource initialization sequence is as follows:

1. The application starts up in the default locale. The programmer does not call `setlocale`, but registers a *language procedure* by calling `XtSetLanguageProc()`. This language procedure will later be called to set the locale.

2. The application then typically calls `XtInitialize()` or `XtAppInitialize()` or `XtOpenDisplay()`. These initialization routines call `XtDisplayInitialize()` which scans (but doesn't actually parse—this scan is done in a way that is independent of the initial locale of the process) the command line and the `RESOURCE_MANAGER` property on the root window of the default screen for the value of the

xnlLanguage resource. (The class of this resource is **XnlLanguage**, and it can be set from the command line using the –xnlLanguage option. The "nl" stands for "native language.") The *language string* obtained from this resource (or the empty string if the resource doesn't exist) is passed to the language procedure registered with **XtSet-LanguageProc()**. If no language procedure was registered, **XtDisplay-Initialize()** continues exactly as it did in X11R4.

3. The language procedure uses the passed string to set the locale. Note that the language procedure can pass the empty string directly to **setlocale** which will take it as a signal to set the locale based on the value of the appropriate operating system environment variable. The language procedure should also call **XSupportsLocale()** to verify that the locale is supported and **XSetLocaleModifiers()** to set any locale modifiers. Finally, the language procedure must return the name of the locale it set (which is the return value of **setlocale**).

4. Now **XtDisplayInitialize()** saves the return value of the language procedure for use by **XtResolvePathname()** as a pathname substitution when searching for the appropriate application defaults file for the locale.

Note that **XtDisplayInitialize()** could make the call to **setlocale** itself, but that this was deemed inappropriate by the designers. If no language procedure is registered, **XtDisplayInitialize()** behaves as it did in X11R4, and the locale is never set. For most applications the default language procedure will be sufficient: it calls **setlocale**, **XSupportsLocale()**, and **XSetLocaleModifiers()** and it returns the name of the locale it set. Note that the default procedure is not actually registered by default; you must explicitly register it or you will get X11R4 behavior. To register it, call **XtSet-LanguageProc()** with a procedure argument of **NULL**. Example 14-4 shows how to initialize Xt using the default language procedure to correctly set the locale.

Example 14-4. Establishing the locale in an Xt application

```
main(argc, argv)
int argc;
char **argv;
{
    Widget toplevel;

    /* register the default language proc */
    /* no app-context, no function, no tag */
    XtSetLanguageProc(NULL, (XtLanguageProc)NULL, NULL);

    /* this function invokes XtDisplayInitialize which
     * will call the language procedure. */
    toplevel = XtAppInitialize(...);
        .
        .
        .
```

14.15.3 XFontSet Resources

The **XFontSet** abstraction defined by X11R5 Xlib for internationalized text output will be an important resource for any internationalized widget that draws text. The purpose of the **XFontSet** is as follows. An application needs more than one X font in order to operate in a language like Japanese. In Japanese, any useful text-based application needs a Kanji font (final symbols), a Katakana font (phonetic font used in typing), and an English font (for specialized terms) at the same time. So these are grouped together and called one **XFontSet**.

The X11R5 Xt Intrinsics give **XFontSet** almost the same support they give the **XFontStruct**. They define:

- **XtNfontSet**, a name for an **XFontSet** resource.

- **XtCFontSet**, a class for an **XFontSet** resource.

- **XtRFontSet**, the representation type for an **XFontSet** resource.

- A pre-registered String-to-XFontSet converter.

- **XtDefaultFontSet**, a string constant guaranteed to work with the pre-registered String-to-XFontSet converter.

When the constant **XtDefaultFontSet** is passed to the pre-registered String-to-XFont-Set converter, it queries the resource database for the value of a resource with name **xtDefaultFontSet** and class **XtDefaultFontSet**. If this resource exists and has a valid value, the **XFontSet** is created using the resource value as the base font name list. If the resource doesn't exist or no font set can be created from it, the converter falls back onto an implementation-defined default font set list.

Unfortunately there is no standard command-line option analogous to **-font** defined by the Xt Intrinsics which will set this **xtDefaultFontSet** resource. Applications can provide this command-line option themselves, or a user can specify a font set with the **-xrm** option:

```
imail -xrm "*xtDefaultFontSet: -*-*-*-R-*-*-*-140-100-100-*-*-*-*"
```

14.15.4 Other Xt Changes for Internationalization

The three other changes to Xt for internationalization are as follows:

- To allow the localization of error messages, the high-level Xt error and warning handling routines are no longer required to use the single file */usr/lib/X11/XtErrorDB* (on POSIX systems) as the error message database. Unfortunately, the app-context based design of the error and warning handlers means that these handers are not passed a handle to the Display that the error occurred on. This implies that they cannot use **XtResolvePathname()** (which requires the display to look up the language string to use in path substitutions) to find an appropriate error database for the locale. For this reason X11R5 does not specify a standard error database search path, but simply states that the source of the error and warning message text is implementation-dependent. What this means to the programmer of internationalized applications is that you cannot portably rely on the default high-level Xt warning and error handlers to find the localized text of your error messages. You should register an error handler of your own or display your error messages through some entirely different mechanism.

- X11R4 specified that the language string obtained from the **xnlLanguage** resource should be in the form:

  language[*_territory*][*.codeset*]

  This was deemed an unnecessary restriction, and for X11R5 the specification has been changed to state that the language string (obtained from the **xnlLanguage** resource or returned by the new language procedure) has a "language part," a "territory part," and a "codeset part," but that the format of the string is implementation-dependent.

- The internationalization of X text input with input methods (see Xlib) requires that an input method have a way to intercept X events before they are processed by the application. An input method does this by registering an event filter, and all applications that perform internationalized text input are required to call the function **XFilterEvent()** each time they receive an event. To support internationalized input, **XtDispatchEvent()** has been modified to make this required call to **XFilterEvent()**. Furthermore, if an event arrives that triggers a grab registered by **XtGrabButton()** or **XtGrabKey()**, and that event is filtered by **XFilterEvent()**, then **XtDispatchEvent()** breaks the grab by calling **XtUngrabPointer()** or **XtUngrabKeyboard()** with the timestamp of the event. This is done because when an input method filters an event, the application should behave as if that event never arrived.

14.15.5 Internationalization in Motif 1.2

Since Motif 1.2 is built upon the R5 version of the Xt Intrinsics, it has the same internationalization features. In addition, however, Motif widgets that handle text have been reimplemented to support wide character and multi-byte strings.

14.15.6 Text Output

The Motif 1.2 **XmFontList** can contain **XFontSet**s as well as **XFontStruct**s. The 1.2 **XmString** drawing functions use the new X11R5 internationalized Xlib text drawing functions when they encounter an **XFontSet** in an **XmFontList**. In this way, text display in all Motif widgets except Text and TextField has been internationalized. Note that **XmString**s can only be created from multi-byte strings; there is no wide-character **XmString** creation function.

The **XmString** and **XmFontList** API have changed; see below.

14.15.7 Text Input

The Text and TextField widgets have been extensively re-written in Motif 1.2 to support internationalized text input and output based on the X11R5 mechanisms. Fortunately, the complexity of Xlib internationalization is almost entirely hidden by these widgets.

The text widgets have a new resource `XmNvalueWcs` which expects a wide-character string value, and also support a number of new callbacks which return text in wide-character form. The existing resources and callbacks remain to support multi-byte strings. Programmers may use whichever style is more convenient for their application.

Much of the interaction with the X Input Method is handled by the Motif VendorShell widget. It supports two new resources, `XmNinputMethod` and `XmNpreeditType`, which specify locale modifiers with which to select the input method and the preedit interaction style desired. When input method preedit or status information must be displayed in "off-the-spot" style at the bottom of the application window, the VendorShell widget provides and manages this space.

14.15.8 Compound Text Conversion

Compound Text is the X Consortium standard for inter-client communication of internationalized text. When performing cut-and-paste or drag-and-drop in an internationalized application, it may be necessary to convert between `XmStrings` and Compound Text. Motif 1.2 provides 2 new functions to do this: `XmCvtXmStringToCT()` and `XmCvtCTToXmString()`.

14.15.9 _XmGetLocalized()

Motif 1.2 contains a new function, `_XmGetLocalized()` intended for use by widget writers to obtain localized equivalents for common strings such as "Ok", "Cancel", and "Help".

14.15.10 Summary

Motif 1.2 makes internationalization nearly transparent. To write an internationalized application with Motif, do the following:

- Place all strings and pixmaps in resource or UIL files.

- Specify a generic font set in your `XmFontList`s.

- Do not use multiple charset tags in your `XmString`s.

- Call `XtSetLanguageProc(NULL, NULL, NULL);` to establish locale, before calling `XtAppInitialize()`.

- Don't expect internationalization to work or to work well on existing generic US platforms. Operating system support for locales and internationalization is also required.

A

Athena, OPEN LOOK, and Motif

This appendix gives an overview of the widgets available in the Sun's OPEN LOOK widget set (also known as OLIT, the OPEN LOOK Intrinsics Toolkit) and the OSF/Motif widget set. It gives a sense of the look and feel of applications developed with each set, and provides the inheritance hierarchy and overview of the available widgets.

In This Appendix:

A
Athena, OPEN LOOK, and Motif

This section provides an overview and comparison of the widgets in MIT's Athena widget set, Sun's OPEN LOOK widget set (also known as OLIT), and the Open Software Foundation's Motif.†

As we've already discussed, the Athena widgets were developed to test and demonstrate the Xt Intrinsics. They are used as the basis for some of the standard MIT clients and many public domain applications, but are not expected to be used for most commercial applications because Xaw is not a complete environment.

A number of vendors have developed proprietary widget sets. For example, Sony Microsystems offers S-windows, a widget set for its News workstations. However, given that one of the purposes of widgets is to provide a common look and feel for X applications, it is natural there should be a shakeout as vendors align themselves with one or two major contenders.

As it has turned out, the two major contenders for a graphical user-interface standard, OPEN LOOK and Motif, are put forth by the two major contenders for an underlying UNIX operating system standard, AT&T and the Open Software Foundation.

It is theoretically possible to write an application that will run under either of these widget sets, using one set of source code interspersed with `#ifdef` symbols for conditional compilation. This becomes difficult when you use any of the Xt-level features Motif alone provides, however.

OPEN LOOK is somewhat unusual in that it started out not as a set of widgets, but as a user-interface specification. The specification, originally developed by Sun Microsystems with AT&T backing, was widely circulated for comment before any implementations were begun. The objective was to develop a graphical user-interface standard for UNIX workstations—one that would be implementation-independent, and, it was hoped, implemented separately by many different vendors.

At present, the two major implementations of OPEN LOOK are Sun's XView toolkit (which is not based on Xt, but instead provides an application-programmer's interface similar to Sun's proprietary SunView windowing system), and AT&T's OPEN LOOK Xt-based widget set. XView is on the R4 distribution from MIT. Both of these toolkits will be available to all AT&T UNIX System V Release 4 licensees. In our discussions, we are referring specifically

---

†OPEN LOOK is a registered trademark of AT&T and Motif is a registered trademark of Open Software Foundation, Inc.

to AT&T's OPEN LOOK toolkit, which does not necessarily include every OPEN LOOK feature. Nor should its implementation be considered the only way to provide features called for by OPEN LOOK.

The Open Software Foundation's Motif toolkit is based on a combination of widget sets originally developed by two OSF sponsors, Digital and Hewlett Packard. The look and feel of the widget set was proposed by HP/Microsoft. It is designed to emulate the look and feel of the IBM/Microsoft Presentation Manager standard widely expected to be adopted in the microcomputer world. Motif 1.1 is fully compatible with the MIT Release 4 Intrinsics. Motif 1.2 is fully compatible with the MIT Release 5 Intrinsics. Motif 1.2, released in May 1992, is described here.

Table A-1 compares the widgets available in Athena, AT&T OPEN LOOK set, and Motif.

Table A-1. Comparison of Athena, OPEN LOOK, and Motif Widgets

Simple widgets (mostly controls):

Athena	OPEN LOOK	Motif	Description
Command	OblongButton	PushButton	Invokes a command
—	—	DrawnButton	Invokes a command
Toggle	RectButton	ToggleButton	Chooses a setting
—	CheckBox*	CheckBox, RadioBox	Alternate way of choosing a setting
MenuButton	ButtonStack	CascadeButton	Invokes a menu, displays label
—	AbbrevStack	OptionMenu	Invokes a menu, displays default
—	—	ArrowButton	Reverses direction of movement
—	ScrollingList*	List	Displays a list of selectable strings
Scrollbar	Scrollbar	ScrollBar	Scrolls through an associated window
—	Slider	Scale*	Sets (or displays) an analog value
Grip	—	—	Resize point for panes in VPaned
Label	StaticText	Label	Displays a fixed string
Text	Text	Text	Displays editable text
—	TextField	TextField	Displays a single line of editable text
—	—	Separator	Displays a line or other separator

*CheckBox, ScrollingList, and Scale are technically composite widgets.

Table A-1. Comparison of Athena, OPEN LOOK, and Motif Widget (continued)

Popups (subclasses of shell):

Athena	OPEN LOOK	Motif	Description
SimpleMenu	Menu	MenuShell	Parents a popup menu
—	Notice	DialogShell	Displays a dialog requiring input
—	PopupWindow	MessageBox	Displays a more complex dialog
—	Help	MessageBox	Displays a help window

Composite and Constraint Widgets:

Athena	OPEN LOOK	Motif	Description
—	BulletinBoard	BulletinBoard	Free-form placement area
—	—	DrawingArea	Free-form drawing area
Box	—	—	Displays children in order added
—	ControlArea	RowColumn	Arranges children in rows or columns
Form	Form	Form	Manages children relative to each other
—	Exclusives	RadioBox	Makes RectButton children exclusive
—	Nonexclusives	CheckBox	Makes RectButton children nonexclusive
—	FooterPanel	—	Provides a consistently-sized message area
—	—	Frame	Gives consistent border to enclosed widgets
—	ScrollingList*	SelectionBox	Provides a selectable list of strings, plus a text area for entering a new value
—	—	Command	Provides a selectable list of commands
—	—	FileSelectionBox	Provides a selectable list of filenames
—	Caption	—	Displays a label and one child widget
Viewport	ScrollingWindow	ScrolledWindow	Displays a scrollable child window
—	—	MainWindow	ScrolledWindow with special appearance
VPaned	—	PanedWindow	Displays panes resizable in one direction

*Checkbox, ScrollingList, and Scale are technically composite widgets.

Comparable widgets share a line in the table. Widgets for which no equivalent occurs in a given set are indicated by a hyphen in the appropriate column. Note that comparisons are approximate only, since widgets have complex behavior that may distinguish them significantly from another widget with an ostensibly similar purpose.

The following sections provide an overview of the widgets available in the OPEN LOOK and Motif widget sets. Throughout, we contrast them with the Athena widgets, which have been used as examples in this book, to give you an idea of the additional features provided by the commercial widget sets.

Keep in mind that the look and feel of an application is controlled by the window manager as well as by the widget set. Both AT&T and OSF supply window managers to complement their widgets.

Note that both widget sets make additions to the basic X Toolkit API. In the AT&T OPEN LOOK widget set, these API additions are rather minor. There is one essential function, `Ol-Initialize`, which sets initial values needed by other routines and by certain widgets. `OlInitialize` creates a base window, which from the programmer's point of view is identical to the Intrinsics-supplied TopLevelShell widget class, but which automatically handles certain features of the OPEN LOOK interface. There are also several convenience functions, mostly having to do with conversions between pixel sizes and various standard units. More importantly, there is a facility for registering help screens for each element in an application.

In addition, Motif makes heavy use of convenience functions. Rather than using `Xt-CreateManagedWidget()` to create each widget, there is a separate creation routine for each widget. In some cases, a convenience routine creates more than one widget. Rather than using separate calls to `XtCreatePopupShell()` and `XtCreateManaged-Widget()` to create a popup shell and the dialog box it displays, you might call a function such as `XmCreateMessageDialog()` to create both widgets at once. Some convenience routines create special configurations of a single, complex widget (e.g., a composite widget with specific children.)

In Motif, all resources are referred to by names beginning with **XmN** or **XmC** rather than the familiar **XtN** and **XtC**.

Motif also uses the `call_data` argument of callback functions extensively. Almost every widget has a structure defined as *widgetclass*`CallbackStruct` (e.g., **XmToggle-ButtonCallbackStruct**). This struct contains different fields for each widget, but each contains a field called **reason**. The **reason** field defines which callback has been called. So using this feature allows you to have a single piece of code to handle all callbacks for a widget.

Both Motif and OPEN LOOK offer clear advantages over Xaw. Unfortunately, however, the choice of which one to use may depend on company marketing goals and politics rather than on clear technical merit. We encourage independent developers to try both and to base your opinions on the ease of programming and the preferences of your users, rather than on marketing hype by one side or the other. Both Motif and OPEN LOOK come with their own window manager and have defined their own protocols for communication between their Shell widgets and their window manager. By setting resources of Shell widgets you can control some aspects of how these window managers will handle your application.

A.1 The AT&T OPEN LOOK Widgets

Figure A-1 shows the overall look and feel of an OPEN LOOK application.

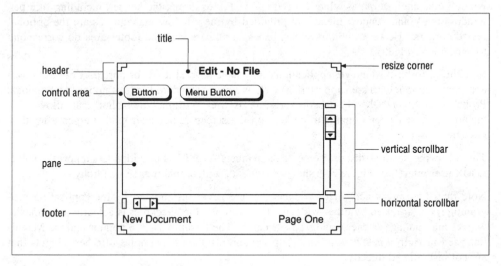

Figure A-1. An OPEN LOOK application

The base window of an application always has these elements:

- A title bar, or header, with a title supplied by the application centered in the bar. The title might be the application name, or the name of a file being edited. If the application doesn't provide a title, the title bar displays the string "Untitled."

- A "window mark" on the left side of the title bar. If the user clicks on this mark with the first (leftmost) pointer button, the window closes.

- A window menu that comes up automatically when you click on the title bar with the third (rightmost) pointer button.

- One or more panes for input and display of application data.

- One or more control areas, containing buttons that invoke application actions or menus containing additional actions. Control areas can be horizontal, vertical, or both.

Optional elements include resize corners (which allow the user to resize the application by dragging them with the first pointer button), horizontal and/or vertical scrollbars, and a footer area for displaying messages.

Some of these elements do not correspond to widgets, but are produced by the OPEN LOOK window manager, *olwm*, as window decoration. For example, the header, including title bar, window mark and window menu, are provided by the window manager, as are the optional resize corners. However, control areas, panes, scrollbars, and the footer area do correspond to particular widgets.

In addition to base windows, applications may have several kinds of popup. Both pulldown and pure popup menus are supported, as well as several standard kinds of notices and dialogs. Probably OPEN LOOK's best-known feature is the "pushpin" metaphor that allows frequently-accessed popup menus to be kept on the screen rather than hidden again after they have been used.

The following sections discuss some of the widgets AT&T has provided to support the OPEN LOOK user interface. Figure A-2 shows the overall widget inheritance hierarchy.

Note that there are a number of widgets that are never instantiated by the application programmer, but are used by other widgets. For example, the checkbox is actually a composite widget that manages a check widget as its child! The Pushpin used in popups and the Magnifier used in Help windows (and the Help window itself) are examples of other widgets that are not instantiated directly.

A.1.1 Application Controls

Most applications will have at least one control area, with pointer-selectable buttons that invoke commands or menus, or choose settings.

One of the areas where OPEN LOOK clearly stands out over the Athena widgets is in the rich set of controls it provides. Athena has one kind of Command widget; OPEN LOOK has six.

A.1.1.1 Command Buttons

The Athena Command widget implements one of the most basic user-interface idioms—a button that invokes an action when you click on it with the pointer. The Athena widgets include a subclass of Command, the MenuButton widget, which includes code for placing a popup menu.

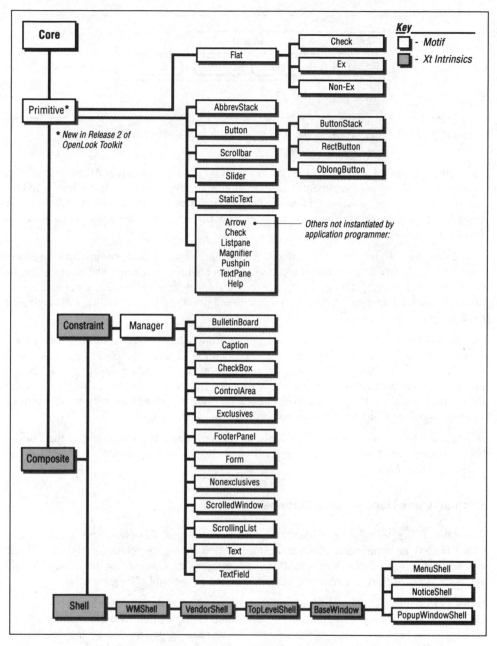

Figure A-2. Class inheritance hierarchy of the AT&T OPEN LOOK widgets

The OPEN LOOK widget set implements similar functions using the OblongButton and ButtonStack widgets. Figure A-3 shows a Control Area containing OblongButton and ButtonStack widgets.

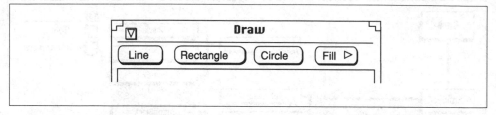

Figure A-3. An OPEN LOOK ControlArea with OblongButton and ButtonStack widgets

The OblongButton widget provides many niceties lacking from the Athena Command widget. One of the most important is that OblongButton has a resource that allows one button among several to be designated as the default, in which case the button is bordered by a double line, to give the user immediate visual feedback about which button to choose when several are available.

The OblongButton also has the notion of a "busy" state in which it cannot perform the action because it is already doing it. (This is different from a widget that is insensitive (meaning its function is unavailable), though in practice the effect is quite similar.) The label and border of an insensitive button are dimmed; the background of a busy button is filled with a stippled pattern.

The ButtonStack widget is similar to the OblongButton but invokes a menu rather than a single command. Clicking on it with one mouse button (usually Button 3) pops up a menu (which may in turn include other ButtonStack widgets, for cascading popups.) Clicking on the ButtonStack with another mouse button (usually Button 1) activates the default item for the menu. Visually, a ButtonStack is differentiated from an OblongButton by the presence of an arrowhead that points in the direction that the menu will pop up.†

In addition, there is an AbbrevStack widget, which performs similar functions as the Button-Stack widget, but shows up only as a small unlabelled box with the default choice for the menu displayed beside it.

A.1.1.2 Exclusive and Nonexclusive Settings

The Athena Toggle widget provides the concept of a button that establishes a setting (for example, sets an application resource) instead of performing an action. It highlights itself when selected, but remains highlighted until selected again. However, in the Athena Widget set, there is no visual distinction between a Command widget and a Toggle widget.

OPEN LOOK provides such a distinction. In contrast to OblongButton, which always indicates that an action will be performed, a RectButton indicates that an option setting will be chosen. This setting may be exclusive or nonexclusive, as determined by the RectButton widget itself, depending on whether the widget is managed by an Exclusives, or Nonexclusives composite widget. The RectButton widget class will not work correctly unless

---

†In an earlier implementation of the toolkit, a ButtonStack widget had a double border on its bottom half, giving it the appearance of a stack of regular buttons. Hence its name, which is now merely historical.

X Toolkit Intrinsics Programming Manual, Motif Edition

managed by one of these two composite widgets. The Exclusives and Nonexclusives widgets are themselves usually children of a Menu or ControlArea widget.

In an Exclusives widget, RectButton widgets are laid out side by side in one or more columns. One or none of the RectButton widgets is chosen as the default, which is indicated by a double border. Once a RectButton is selected, it is shown with a dark border. The Exclusives widget makes sure that no more than one RectButton is selected at a time.

In a Nonexclusives widget, RectButtons are displayed with separation between each button. As when used in an Exclusives widget, a dark border indicates that the option has been chosen. However, more than one button may be chosen at a time.

Figure A-4 shows examples of exclusive and nonexclusive settings on menus. Note that, like the OblongButton, a RectButton may display a pixmap instead of a label. This makes the RectButton useful for a palette in a paint program.

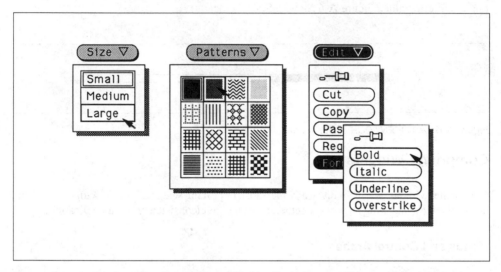

Figure A-4. OPEN LOOK RectButtons controlled by Exclusives and Nonexclusives widgets

The CheckBox widget provides an alternate way to display nonexclusive settings to the user. It displays a small box next to the label and displays a checkmark in the box when the option is selected. Checkboxes appear in ControlAreas rather than on menus. Figure A-5 shows examples of CheckBox widgets.

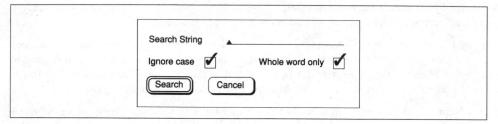

Figure A-5. An OPEN LOOK CheckBox widget

A.1.1.3 Analog Controls

In addition to the various kinds of buttons outlined above, OPEN LOOK provides an analog control called a Slider. A Slider widget is used analogously to a Scrollbar but is used for setting a numeric value. Figure A-6 shows a Slider widget.

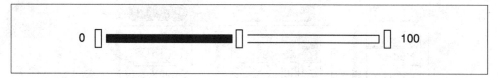

Figure A-6. An OPEN LOOK Slider widget

A.1.2 Composite Widgets

Composite widgets are in many ways the most important widgets in any widget set. They define the way that widgets work together, and they give consistency to an application.

A.1.2.1 Menus and Control Areas

As we've already discussed, command buttons of any kind are usually displayed as part of a menu or control area.

Menus can either pop up below a ButtonStack or an AbbrevStack, or if the button is itself displayed on a menu, to the right, in a menu cascade. Figure A-4 showed examples of menus.

The Menu widget is a popup widget created with `XtCreatePopupShell()`. It has a single child, which is a ControlArea widget.

The ControlArea widget places its children in rows or columns. Resources allow the application to specify a fixed width and/or height, or a fixed number of rows or columns. Control-Area widgets are usually used as the parent of OblongButton, ButtonStack, Exclusives, or Nonexclusives widgets (which in turn manage RectButton widgets, as described in the next section).

A.1.2.2 General Purpose Composite Widgets

We've already discussed the Composite widgets relating to control areas and menus. However, there are several general-purpose composite widgets in the OPEN LOOK set as well.

The BulletinBoard widget provides a free-form area for placing subwindows. Widgets can be placed on a BulletinBoard at arbitrary x and y coordinates; if no coordinates are specified, they appear in the upper left corner. The BulletinBoard provides no management of its children, and is often used to establish the base frame for an application, since it allows the application programmer to place the major components of the application, rather than having to go by some Composite widget's arbitrary placement decisions.

A BulletinBoard is often used as the main window of an application.

The Form widget is a constraint widget similar to the Athena Form widget. It allows the placement of widgets to be specified relative to each other, and with rules governing their separation or relative position.

The Caption widget is like an Athena Label widget turned inside out. Like the Label widget, it prints a string. However, while the label widget's string is printed inside a visible widget border, a Caption string appears outside a bordered area. Caption is a composite widget class, and its label typically refers to a child widget of any size, which the Caption widget manages. The label can be aligned on either the right, left, top or bottom of the child widget.

The FooterPanel widget provides a consistent method for placing a footer along the bottom of another window. The footer panel takes two children. The top child is typically the main composite widget of the application; the bottom widget may contain a control or message area. The basic feature of the FooterPanel widget is that when the widget is resized, it applies all the change in the vertical direction to the top child, maintaining the bottom child at a constant height.

A.1.2.3 Scrollbars and Scrollable Windows

OPEN LOOK scrollbars use the visual metaphor of an elevator on a cable, but functionally they are similar to the Athena Scrollbar widget. The drag area (the thumb in an Athena Scrollbar widget) doesn't change size; instead, as shown in Figure A-7, there is a separate area that indicates the proportion of the data that is currently being displayed.

Scrollbars may be oriented either horizontally or vertically.

Scrollbars are used as a component of a ScrolledWindow widget, which, like the Athena Viewport widget, provides a scrollable view of a data area in a child widget. The child widget is typically larger than the view area, but only the area in the parent's view area can be seen at any one time. Figure A-1 showed a ScrolledWindow widget as the main application pane. The ScrollingList widget displays a scrollable list of editable text fields, and provides facilities for choosing and displaying one of the fields as "currently selected." Items can be selected from the list, changed, copied, and so on. This widget is useful for providing an interface to select a file for reading or writing.

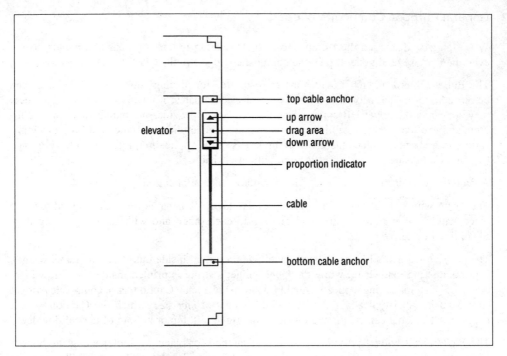

Figure A-7. An OPEN LOOK Scrollbar

Figure A-8 shows a ScrollingList widget.

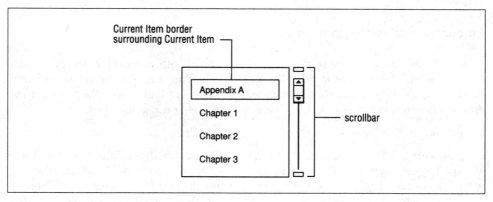

Figure A-8. An OPEN LOOK ScrollingList widget

A.1.3 Popups

In addition to Menu widgets, the OPEN LOOK widget set contains three other special types of popup widgets: Notices, PopupWindows, and Help windows. A Notice is used to request confirmation or other information from the user. The widget contains a text area, where the message to the user is displayed, and a control area containing one or more buttons, one of which must be the default button.

Figure A-9 shows an OPEN LOOK Notice widget.

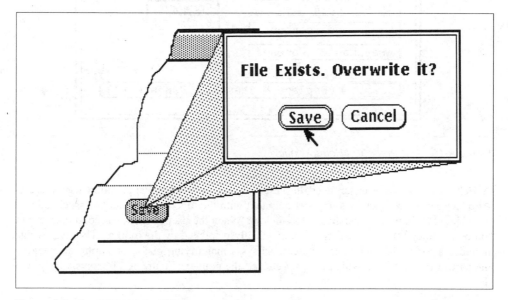

Figure A-9. An OPEN LOOK Notice

A Notice grabs the pointer. The only input allowed is to the Notice. Once the user has clicked a button, the Notice disappears.

The second special popup type is a PopupWindow, which can be used for more complex popups. Unlike a Notice, which is a subclass of OverrideShell, a PopupWindowShell is a subclass of WMShell, and so is decorated by the window manager. It has all the visual attributes of a top-level window, including resize corners, etc. In addition, it displays a pushpin in the upper left corner. If the user clicks on the pushpin with the pointer, the menu doesn't go away when its action has been performed, but stays on the screen. This allows the user to keep menus (and other frequently-referenced popups, such as help screens) "pinned" on the display, where they can be moved like regular windows. (Menus can also display a pushpin; its presence or absence is controlled by a widget resource.)

A PopupWindow typically contains an upper control area that may include menus, and a lower control area that may be used for buttons invoking widget actions. Resources allow for automatic creation of several buttons, including a "reset to factory" button, a "set defaults" button, and several other ways of setting standard properties for an application.

Figure A-10 shows a PopupWindow.

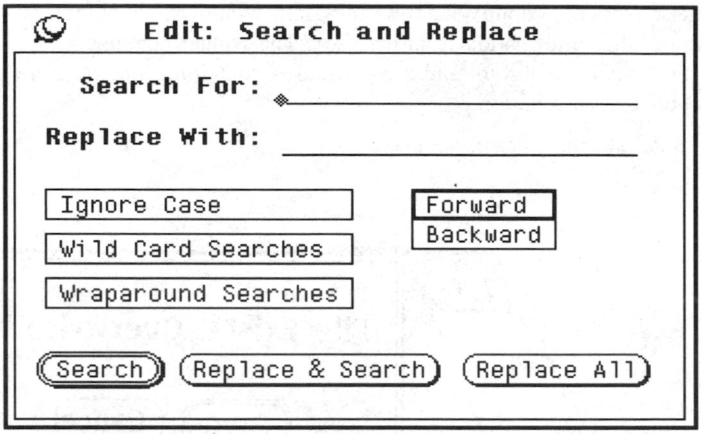

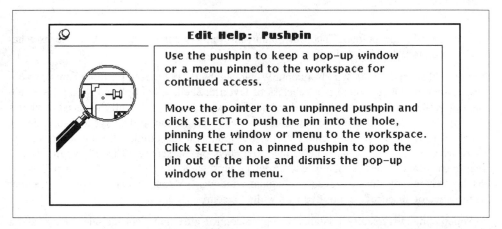

Figure A-10. An OPEN LOOK PopupWindow

A Help window is not instantiated in the usual way. Instead, an application uses the `Ol-RegisterHelp` function to register help text with the toolkit. Text can be associated with a widget class, a widget instance, or a window. When the user clicks the second pointer button on an object, the Help widget is automatically displayed by the toolkit. The Help widget includes a Magnifier subwidget, which displays a magnifying glass containing an image of the part of the screen on which the user clicked the pointer. Figure A-11 shows a Help window.

Figure A-11. An OPEN LOOK Help window

A.1.4 Text Widgets

OPEN LOOK offers three separate text widgets. The StaticText widget is similar to the Athena Label widget in that it displays a fixed text string. However, it can handle longer strings by using wordwrapping to break the string onto multiple lines.

The OPEN LOOK Text widget is very similar to the Athena Text widget. It provides a general-purpose editable text widget, with editing commands customizable via a translation table.

One of the annoying weaknesses of the Athena Text widget is that it is difficult and inefficient to use as a single-line editable field. (A program can add translations for the Return key to limit the text to a single line.) OPEN LOOK addresses this need with the TextField widget, useful for developing form-driven applications. TextField widgets were shown in Figure A-11.

The TextField widget provides simple editing commands, and scrolling if the string is too long to be displayed. When the keyboard focus leaves the widget, or when the Tab or Return key is pressed, it passes the data in the field to the application for validation.

A.1.5 Drawing Areas

Like the Athena widget set, the AT&T OPEN LOOK widgets provide no widget explicitly labeled as a drawing area. As described in this book, one is expected either to create a custom widget for an application's main window, or to use a very basic widget class, and add actions for drawing.

The AT&T OPEN LOOK widget set does include a Stub widget class (which is not documented in the manual, but is included in the source), which is useful for providing a window for drawing.

A.2 The OSF/Motif Widgets

Figure A-12 shows the general look of a Motif application, the Motif Reference Editor, *mre*. *mre*, developed by Mitch Trachtenberg, was OSF demo software in Motif 1.1, but is no longer provided in the Motif distribution.

As with the AT&T OPEN LOOK widget set, some of the features of a main application window are actually decoration provided by the window manager, *mwm*. As shown in Figure A-11, these include the title bar, which displays:

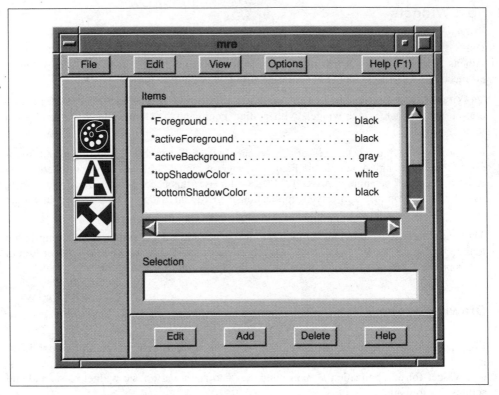

Figure A-12. Look of a Motif application

- The title provided by the application.

- A Menu button, which drops down a menu containing basic window manipulation commands.

- A "Minimize" button, which iconifies the application.

- A "Maximize" button, which causes the application window to fill the entire screen.

You will also recognize Motif's version of many of the common controls discussed in the section on the AT&T OPEN LOOK widget set.

Figure A-13 shows the inheritance hierarchy of the Motif widgets. The Intrinsics-supplied widget classes are shaded grey.

The Primitive and Manager widgets are not generally instantiated and exist only to provide resources and other features inherited by other widgets.

In addition, Motif supports a Gadget class, which, as described in Chapter 13, *Menus, Gadgets, and Cascaded Popups*, is subclassed from RectObj rather than Core. Gadget equivalents exist for the Label widget, some classes of Button widgets, and the Separator widget. Gadgets are not shown in Figure A-13.

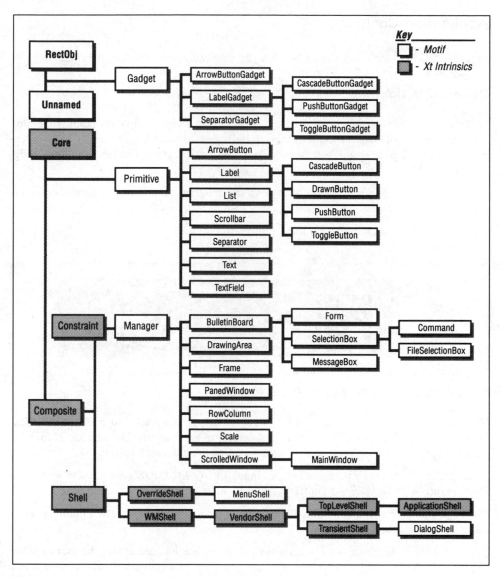

Figure A-13. Class inheritance hierarchy of the Motif widget set

A.2.1 Application Controls

Like OPEN LOOK, Motif has a much richer set of application controls than Athena.

A.2.1.1 Command Buttons

Motif's PushButton is equivalent to Athena's Command widget and OPEN LOOK's Oblong-Button. It has a 3-D appearance and seems to be depressed when clicked on. It invokes separate callbacks for button up, button down, and button click, much like the equivalent widgets in other sets.

The DrawnButton works similarly, but allows the programmer to provide a pixmap for the appearance of the button.

Figure A-14 shows a DrawnButton and a PushButton.

Figure A-14. Motif DrawnButton and PushButton widgets

The CascadeButton is similar in effect to OPEN LOOK's ButtonStack—it can have a particular appearance that indicates that a menu is invoked, rather than a single callback. Typically, this is simply an arrow pointing in the direction where the menu will appear.

A ToggleButton is used for option setting, much like OPEN LOOK's RectButton or Check-Box. Figure A-16 shows a box containing a set of ToggleButtons.

The Separator widget can be used to draw a line or other separator between a group of widgets in a menu or other box. It is typically used in menus.

The List widget displays a list of strings set by the application and allows the user to select one or more of the strings. The selected data is passed to a callback function. (We'll talk more about this widget in the section on scrolling.)

A.2.1.2 Analog Controls

Motif's Scale widget is similar to OPEN LOOK's Slider but is more powerful since it can be used to display as well as to control analog values.

A.2.2 Composite Widgets

As with OPEN LOOK, we've divided the discussion of Composite widgets into three areas: Menus and Control Areas, General-Purpose Composite Widgets, and Scrollable Windows. These distinctions are somewhat arbitrary and with menus the sections overlap with the one on popups, which appears later.

A.2.2.1 Menus and Control Areas

Motif provides a special Shell widget class called MenuShell for managing popup menus. However, most actual menu displays are managed by the RowColumn composite widget, which, like OPEN LOOK's ControlArea, displays buttons in rows or columns.

Through resources, the RowColumn widget can be configured to create such specialized, predefined elements as a MenuBar (which can only accept CascadeButton widgets as children), several different styles of pulldown or popup menu panes, and several preconfigured control areas, such as a "Radio Box" containing multiple exclusive ToggleButton gadgets.

Here you can begin to see the wide divergence in programming style made possible by the Xt Intrinsics. It is possible to create a hierarchy of relatively simple widgets to perform separate parts of a task, or a single, very complex widget which is highly configurable. In one of its incarnations, the RowColumn widget is equivalent to an OPEN LOOK ControlArea plus an Exclusives widget; in another, a ControlArea plus a Nonexclusives.

In general, Motif widgets are more complex and have many more resources than widgets provided in other widget sets. To simplify their use, though, Motif provides numerous convenience functions. For example, `XmCreateRadioBox()` will create a RowColumn widget with one specialized set of resources, while `XmCreateMenuBar()` will create one that is entirely different in appearance and function.

Figure A-15 shows a RowColumn widget configured as a MenuBar and Figure A-16 shows one configured as a RadioBox (each with appropriate children).

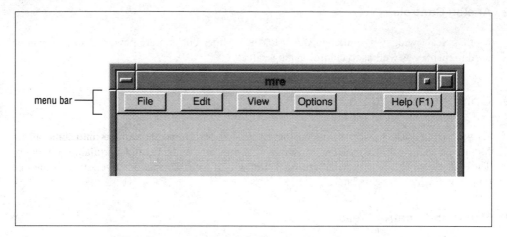

Figure A-15. A Motif RowColumn widget configured as a MenuBar

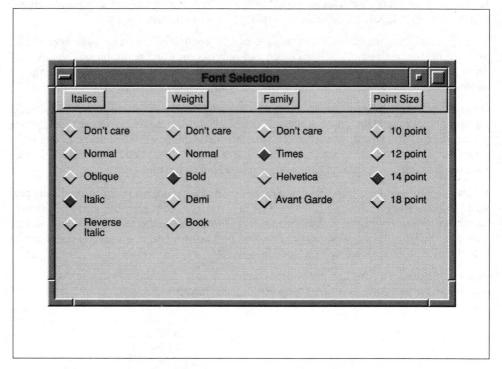

Figure A-16. A Motif RowColumn widget configured with four RadioBoxes

Figure A-17 shows a RowColumn widget implementing a pulldown menu.

Items on Motif menus can be selected by dragging the pointer down the menu and releasing it when the chosen item is highlighted. Alternately, the pointer can simply be clicked on the menu title to drop down the menu. Clicking on an item in the menu selects it; clicking any-where other than in the menu pops the menu down without executing any item.

Note also that as a general feature, Motif menus support accelerators. That is, there are key-board equivalents for every menu item. These keyboard accelerators are listed after the menu label, as shown above. In addition, typing the underlined letter in any menu item label when the pointer is in the menu will select that menu item. These underlined letters are called "mnemonics."

The items on a menubar or menu pane simply appear as labels but when selected take on the 3-D appearance of a PushButton.

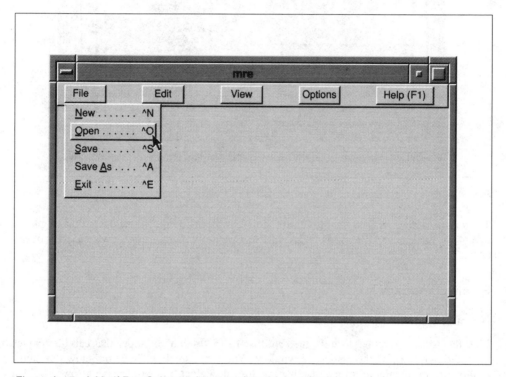

Figure A-17. A Motif RowColumn widget configured as a drop-down window

A.2.2.2 General Purpose Composite Widgets

The BulletinBoard widget provides simple composite management, allowing widgets to be placed arbitrarily anywhere within its confines. The only constraint is that they are not allowed to overlap.

The Form widget is a subclass of BulletinBoard that, like the widgets of the same name in other sets, allows children to be laid out relative to each other or to one or another of the sides of the Form. The children will thus always maintain their proper relative position when the application is resized.

Figure A-18 shows a fully configured Form.

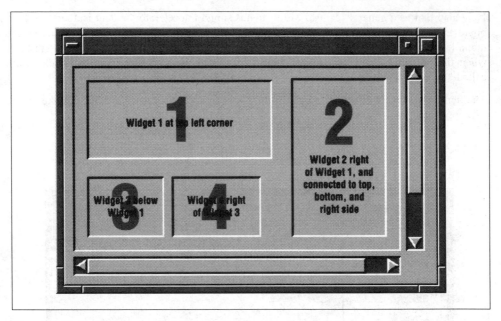

Figure A-18. A Motif Form widget and children

The Frame widget is used simply to provide a consistent border for widgets that might not otherwise have one. One use is to give a RowColumn widget a border with a 3-D appearance.

A.2.2.3 Scrollable Windows

A Motif ScrollBar is illustrated in Figure A-19.

Like the Athena Scrollbar widget, the scrollbar has a "thumb" or slider that can be dragged up and down to scroll the associated window. You can also click above or below the thumb to move it a screenful at a time. Unlike the Athena widget, it also displays arrows at either end that can be used to scroll line by line. The associated window scrolls in the indicated direction as long as the pointer button is held down in one of the arrows.

There are several different types of scrolling windows. The ScrolledWindow widget, like Athena's Viewport, provides a general mechanism for attaching scrollbars to some other window.

The MainWindow widget is a subclass of ScrolledWindow with a special appearance reserved for application main windows. Figure A-14 showed a MainWindow widget.

Using the `XmCreateScrolledList()` function, a List widget can be created as a child of a ScrolledWindow, giving the effect of a simple scrolled list. In addition, there are several

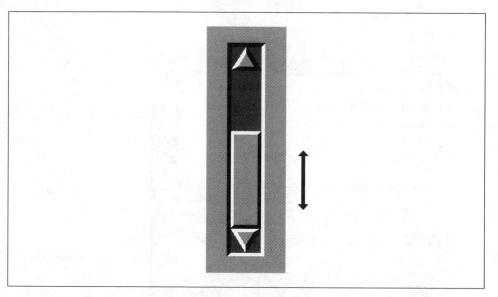

Figure A-19. A Motif ScrollBar

flavors of more complex scrolling lists. These include the SelectionBox widget, and its two subclasses, Command and FileSelectionBox.

A general-purpose SelectionBox is akin to a ScrolledWindow/List combination, but adds a Text widget for entering additional data not on the list. The SelectionBox also adds at least three buttons labeled by default *OK*, *Cancel*, and *Help*.

Figure A-20 shows a SelectionBox.

A FileSelectionBox is a SelectionBox specially designed to present a list of filenames for selections. A Command widget is a special kind of SelectionBox whose list consists of the history of commands entered in the Text widget. Each time a new command is entered, it is added to the history list.

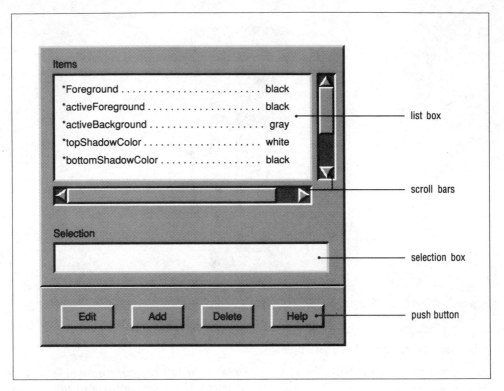

Figure A-20. A Motif SelectionBox

A.2.3 Popups

Motif defines two classes of Shell widgets: DialogShell, which is used for parenting Dialog boxes, and MenuShell, which is used for menus. These classes are rarely instantiated directly, but are instead created by convenience functions that also create their composite children.

For example, functions exist to create a DialogShell with a variety of pre-configured MessageBox widgets as the visible child.

As we've already discussed, a specially configured RowColumn widget is used to create a menu pane as the visible child of a MenuShell widget.

A.2.4 Text Widgets

Like Athena and the AT&T OPEN LOOK widgets, Motif provides a Text widget that supports a complete editing command set. Like Athena, and unlike AT&T's OPEN LOOK widget set, both single- and multiline editing is supported by a single widget. But arranging for single-line editing is easier with Motif than with Athena.

A.2.5 Drawing Areas

As you may recall, to do drawing in the Athena widgets we either created a custom widget or instantiated a Core widget in order to obtain a window for drawing. The Motif DrawingArea widget class answers this need in Motif. It provides a window for drawing and provides very simple, bulletin-board like composite management of children.

Though the name of this widget class sounds promising, you should be aware that Motif really provides no more sophisticated drawing capabilities than Athena or the AT&T OPEN LOOK widget set. In each case, once you have selected the widget to draw on, you simply draw in its window using Xlib calls.

B

Specifying Fonts and Colors

This appendix describes the possible values for color, font, and geometry specifications. It also describes the font service and scalable font capabilities added in Release 5.

In This Appendix:

Specifying Fonts and Colors

This appendix describes the possible values for color, font, and geometry specifications. For fonts, it first describes basic font naming, and then the font service and scalable font capabilities added in Release 5.

B.1 Color Specification

Many clients have resources and command-line options that allow you to specify the color of the window background, foreground (the color that text or graphic elements will be drawn in), or window border. For example, the following resources might be set for a Label widget:

```
*background:    orange    set the background color to orange
*foreground:    black     set the foreground color to black
*borderColor:   black     This must be Halloween!
```

The corresponding command-line options have the form:

–bg `color`   sets the background color

–fg `color`   sets the foreground color

–bd `color`   sets the border color

Some clients allow additional options to specify color for other elements, such as the cursor, highlighting, and so on.

By default, the background is usually white and the foreground black, even on color workstations. You can specify a new color using either the names in the X Window System's color name database or hexadecimal values.

B.1.1 Color Names

The *rgb.txt* file, usually located in */usr/lib/X11* on UNIX systems, is supplied with X and consists of predefined colors assigned to specific (but not necessarily intuitive) names.†

---

† A corresponding compiled file called *rgb.pag* contains the definitions used by the server; the *rgb.txt* file is the human-readable equivalent.

The following are some of the default color names that come with the X Window System. (See Appendix A, *System Management*, in Volume Three, *X Window System User's Guide, Motif Edition*, for information on customizing color name definitions.) This file is not part of the X standard, so vendors are free to modify it. However, most will just add to it, or redefine the values associated with each color name for better effects on their display hardware.

aquamarine	mediumaquamarine	black	blue
cadetblue	cornflowerblue	darkslateblue	lightblue
lightsteelblue	mediumblue	mediumslateblue	midnightblue
navyblue	navy	skyblue	slateblue
steelblue	coral	cyan	firebrick
gold	goldenrod	mediumgoldenrod	green
darkgreen	darkolivegreen	forestgreen	limegreen
mediumforestgreen	mediumseagreen	mediumspringgreen	palegreen
seagreen	springgreen	yellowgreen	darkslategray
darkslategray	dimgray	dimgray	lightgray
lightgray	khaki	magenta	maroon
orange	orchid	darkorchid	mediumorchid
pink	plum	red	indianred
mediumvioletred	orangered	violetred	salmon
sienna	tan	thistle	turquoise
darkturquoise	mediumturquoise	violet	blueviolet
wheat	white	yellow	greenyellow

A number zero through three can be appended to each of these names in order to get various intensities of each color. In addition, a complete range of grays are provided by using the name *gray* or *gray* followed by a number from zero through 100.

For example, the command line:

```
% xterm -bg lightblue -fg darkslategray -bd plum &
```

creates an *xterm* window with a background of light blue, foreground of dark slate gray, and border of plum. Note that the RGB values in the color database provided by MIT are correct for only one type of display; you may find that the color you get is not exactly what you expect given the name. To combat this, vendors may have corrected the RGB values to give colors closer to what the name implies. Or they may provide a device-independent color database. See Volume One, *Xlib Programming Manual* or *The X Color Management System* for more on device-independent color specification.

At the command line, a color name should be typed as a single word (for example, **darkslategray**). However, you can type the words comprising a color name separately if you enclose them in quotes, as in the following command line:

```
% xterm -bg "light blue" -fg "dark slate gray" -bd plum &
```

B.1.2 Hexadecimal Color Specification

You can also specify colors more exactly using a hexadecimal color string. You probably won't use this method unless you require a color not available by using a color name. This method is not recommended in R5 and later: use the device-independent style specification instead. Moreover, you shouldn't use this method unless necessary because it tends to discourage the sharing of colors between applications. In order to understand how this works, you may need a little background on how color is implemented on most workstations.

B.1.2.1 The RGB Color Model

Most color displays on the market today are based on the RGB color model. Each pixel on the screen is actually made up of three phosphors: one red, one green, and one blue. Each of these three phosphors is excited by a separate electron beam. When all three phosphors are fully illuminated, the pixel appears white to the human eye. When all three are dark, the pixel appears black. When the illumination of each primary color varies, the three phosphors generate a subtractive color. For example, equal portions of red and green, with no admixture of blue, makes yellow.

As you might guess, the intensity of each primary color is controlled by a three-part digital value—and it is the exact makeup of this value that the hexadecimal specification allows you to set.

Depending on the underlying hardware, different servers may use a larger or smaller number of bits (from 4 to 16 bits) to describe the intensity of each primary. To insulate you from this variation, clients are designed to take color values containing anywhere from 4 to 16 bits (1 to 4 hex digits), and the server then scales them to the hardware. As a result, you can specify hexadecimal values in any one of the following formats:

```
#RGB
#RRGGBB
#RRRGGGBBB
#RRRRGGGGBBBB
```

where R, G, and B represent single hexadecimal digits and determine the intensity of the red, green, and blue primaries that make up each color.

When fewer than four digits are used, they represent the most significant bits of the value. For example, #3a6 is the same as #3000a0006000.

What this means concretely is perhaps best illustrated by looking at the values that correspond to some colors in the color name database. We'll use 8-bit values (two hexadecimal digits for each primary) because that is the way they are defined in the *rgb.txt* file:

```
#000000       black
#FCFCFC       white
#FF0000       red
#00FF00       green
#0000FF       blue
#FFFF00       yellow
#00FFFF       cyan
#FF00FF       magenta
#5F9F9F       cadet blue
#42426F       cornflower blue
#BFD8D8       light blue
#8F8FBC       light steel blue
#3232CC       medium blue
#23238E       navy blue
#3299CC       sky blue
```

```
#007FFF        slate blue
#236B8E        steel blue
```

As you can see from the colors given above, pure red, green, and blue result from the corresponding bits being turned full on. All primaries off yields black, while all nearly full on gives white. Yellow, cyan, and magenta can be created by pairing two of the other primaries at full intensity. The various shades of blue shown above are created by varying the intensity of each primary—sometimes in unexpected ways.

The bottom line here is that if you don't intimately know the physics of color, the best you can do is to look up existing colors from the color name database and experiment with them by varying one or more of the primaries till you find a color you like. Unless you need precise colors, you are probably better off using color names.

If you do specify a color using a hexadecimal value, try to use the same value for several applications so that they will share a color cell.

In R5, the recommended way to specify specific RGB values is:

RGB:*<red>*/*<green>*/*<blue>*

Where *red*, *green*, and *blue* are each between 1 and 4 hexadecimal digits. Different primaries may be specified with different numbers of digits. If fewer than 4 digits are specified, they do not simply represent the most significant bits of the value; instead they represent a fraction of the maximum value. So the single digit 0xA does not mean 0xA000, but 10/15ths of 0xFFFF, or 0xAAAA.

This form is now understood by all the Xlib functions that accept color strings.

B.1.2.2   How Many Colors are Available?

The number of distinct colors available on the screen at any one time depends on the amount of memory available for color specification.

A color display uses multiple bits per pixel (also referred to as multiple planes or the *depth* of the display) to select colors. Programs that draw in color use the value of these bits as a pointer to a lookup table called a *colormap,* in which each entry (or *colorcell*) contains the RGB values for a particular color.† As shown in Figure B-1, any given pixel value is used as an index into this table—for example, a pixel value of 16 will select the sixteenth colorcell.

This implementation explains several issues that you might encounter in working with color displays.

First, the range of colors possible on the display is a function of the number of bits available in the colormap for RGB specification. If 8 bits are available for each primary, then the range of possible colors is 256^3 (somewhere over 16 million colors). This means that you can create incredibly precise differences between colors.

---

†There is a type of high-performance display in which pixel values are used directly to control the illumination of the red, green, and blue phosphors, but far more commonly, the bits per pixel are used indirectly, with the actual color values specified independently, as described here.

However, the number of different colors that can be displayed on the screen at any one time is a function of the number of planes. A four-plane system can index 2^4 colorcells (16 distinct colors); an eight-plane system can index 2^8 colorcells (256 distinct colors); and a 24-plane system can index 2^{24} colorcells (over 16 million distinct colors).

If you are using a four-plane workstation, the fact that you can precisely define hundreds of different shades of blue is far less significant than the fact that you can't use them all at the same time. There isn't space for all of them to be stored in the colormap at one time.

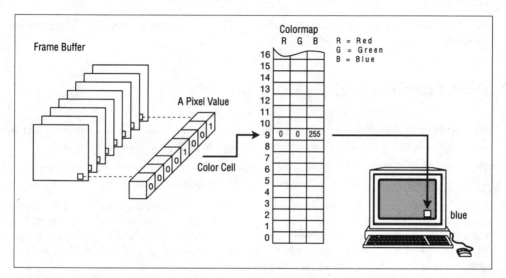

Figure B-1. Multiple planes used to index a colormap

This limitation is made more significant by the fact that X is a multiclient environment. When X starts up, usually no colors are loaded into the colormap. As clients are invoked, certain of these cells are allocated. But when all of the free colorcells are used up, it is no longer possible to request new colors. When this happens, you will usually be given the closest possible color from those that have already been allocated. However, you may instead be given an error message and told that there are no free colorcells.

In order to minimize the chance of running out of colorcells, many programs use "shared" colorcells. Shared colorcells can be used by any number of applications, but they can't be changed by any of them. They can be deallocated only by each application that uses them, and when all applications have deallocated the cell, it is available for setting again. Shared cells are most often used for background, border, and cursor colors.

Alternately, some clients have to be able to change the color of graphics they have already drawn. This requires another kind of cell, called private, which can't be shared. A typical use of a private cell would be for the palette of a color mixing application. Such a program might have three bars of each primary color, and a box which shows the mixed color. The primary bars would use shared cells, while the mixed color box would use a private cell.

In summary, some programs define colorcells to be read-only and shareable, while others define colorcells to be read/write and private.

To top it off, there are even clients that may create a whole private colormap of their own, which will be swapped in by the window manager. Because of the way color is implemented, if this happens, all other applications will be displayed in unexpected colors.

In order to minimize such conflicts, you should request precise colors only when necessary. By preference, use color names or hexadecimal specifications that you specified for other applications.

For more information on color, see Chapter 7, *Color*, in Volume One, *Xlib Programming Manual*.

B.2 Font Specification

Most widgets that display text allow you to specify the font to be used in displaying text in the widget, via either the `XtNfont` resource, or the *–fn* and *–font* command-line options.

The X Window System supports many different display fonts, with different sizes and type styles. (These are *screen* fonts and are not to be confused with *printer* fonts.)

Adobe Systems, Inc., Digital Equipment Corporation, and others have contributed five families of screen fonts (Courier, Helvetica, New Century Schoolbook, Symbol and Times) in a variety of sizes, styles, and weights for 75 dots per inch monitors. Bitstream, Inc. contributed its Charter font family in the same sizes, styles, and weights for both 75 and 100 dots per inch monitors, plus outline versions of the same fonts.

By default, standard fonts are stored in three directories:

Directory	Contents
/usr/lib/X11/fonts/misc	Six fixed-width fonts (also available in Release 2), the cursor font.
/usr/lib/X11/fonts/75dpi	Fixed- and variable-width fonts, 75 dots per inch.
/usr/lib/X11/fonts/100dpi	Fixed- and variable-width fonts, 100 dots per inch.

These three directories (in this order) comprise X's default font path. The font path can be changed with the *fp* option to the *xset* client, as described in Volume Three, *X Window System User's Guide, Motif Edition*. (The font path, together with a great deal of other information about the server defaults, can be listed with *xset query*.) The font path may include font servers, which supply fonts over the network. All fonts in the font path can be listed with *xlsfonts* and *fslsfonts*, and the characters in a font can be displayed on the screen with *xfd*.

The names of each font file in the font directories has a filename extension of *.snf*, which stands for *server natural format*. Fonts are distributed in *binary distribution format* (*bdf*) in Release 4, and need to be compiled for a given server. Fonts are distributed in portable compiled format (*pcf*) in Release 5, and do not need compiling.

B.2.1 Font Naming Conventions

If you do a listing of any of the current font directories, you'll notice that the filenames have *.snf* or *.pdf* extensions. However, font names are not determined by the names of the files in which they are stored.

Now, a font's name is determined by the contents of the font property named FONT† rather than the name of the file in which the font is stored.

If you run *xlsfonts*, you'll get an intimidating list of names similar to the one shown in Figure B-2. names are defined by the X Logical Font Description convention, also known as XLFD. The complete XLFD is reprinted in Volume Zero, *X Protocol Reference Manual*. Upon closer examination and XLFD name contains a great deal of useful information:

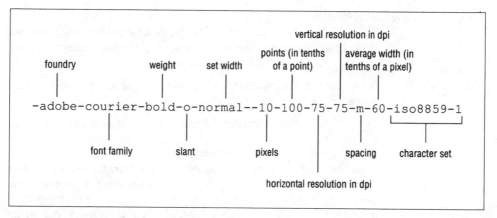

Figure B-2. A font name

This rather verbose line is actually the name of the font stored in the file *courBO10* (in the *75dpi* directory). This font name specifies the foundry (Adobe), the font family (Courier), weight (bold), slant (Oblique), set width (normal), size of the font in pixels (10), size of the font in tenths of a point (100—measured in tenths of a point, thus equals 10 points), horizontal resolution (75dpi), vertical resolution (75dpi), spacing (m, for monospace), average width in tenths of a pixel (60—measured in tenths of a pixel, thus equals 6 pixels) and character set (iso8859-1).

The meaning of many of these statistics is obvious. Some of the less obvious information is explained below.

---

†A property is a piece of information associated with a window or a font. See Volume One, *Xlib Programming Manual*, for more information about properties.

Foundry	The type foundry (in this case, Adobe) that digitized and supplied the font.
Set width	A value describing a font's proportionate width, according to the foundry. Typical set widths include: normal, condensed, narrow, double width. All of the newer fonts have the set width *normal*.
Pixels and points	Type is normally measured in points, a printer's unit equal to 1/72 of an inch. The size of a font in pixels depends on the resolution of the display font in pixels. For example, if the display font has 100 dots per inch (dpi) resolution, a 12 point font will have a pixel size of 17, while with 75 dpi resolution, a 12 point font will have a pixel size of 12.
Spacing	Either m (monospace, i.e., fixed-width) or p (proportional, i.e., variable-width).

Horizontal and vertical resolution
> The resolution in dots per inch that a font is designed for. Horizontal and vertical figures are required because a screen may have different capacities for horizontal and vertical resolution.

Average width	Mean width of all characters in the font, measured in tenths of a pixel, in this case 6 pixels.
Character set	ISO, the International Standards Organization, has defined character set standards for various languages. The iso8859-1 in Figure B-2 represents the ISO Latin 1 character set, which is used by all of the fonts in the *75dpi* and *100dpi* directories. The ISO Latin 1 character set is a superset of the standard ASCII character set, which includes various special characters used in European languages other than English. See Appendix H of Volume Two, *Xlib Reference Manual*, for a complete listing of the characters in the ISO Latin 1 character set.

This font-naming convention is intended to allow for the unique naming of fonts of any style, resolution and size. It is powerful, but unwieldy.

To create a label widget that displays text in the font stored in the file *courBO10*, you could use the resource setting:

```
*label:  -adobe-courier-bold-o-normal--10-100-75-75-m-60-iso8859-1
```

Developers can specify default fonts using a complete font name. However, requiring users to type a font name of this length is neither desirable nor practical. The X Window System developers have provided two alternatives: wildcarding and aliasing.

B.2.2 Font Name Wildcarding

Any unnecessary part of a font name can be "wildcarded" by specifying a question mark (*?*) for any single character and an asterisk (*) for any group of characters.

For example, using a wildcarded font name, the resource specification above could be written:

```
*label:  *courier-bold-o-*-100*
```

(Note that when using wildcards with the *–fn* command line option, you must take care to quote the font names, since the UNIX shell has special meanings for the wildcard characters * and ?. This can be done by enclosing the entire font name in quotes, or by escaping each wildcard character by typing a backslash before it.)

If more than one font in a given directory matches a wildcarded font name, the server chooses the font to use. If fonts from *more than one directory* match the wildcarded name, the server will always choose a font from the directory that is earlier in the font path. Thus, if a wildcarded font name matches a font from both the *75dpi* and *100dpi* directories, and the *75dpi* directory comes first in the font path, the server chooses the font from that directory.

In creating a wildcarded font name, you need to decide which parts of the standard font name must be explicit and which parts can be replaced with wildcards. As the previous example illustrates, you can use a single wildcard character for multiple parts of the font name. For instance, the final asterisk in the example stands for the sequence:

```
-75-75-m-60-iso8859-1
```

in the explicit font name. The idea is to specify enough parts of the font name explicitly so that the server gives you the font you have in mind.

It's helpful to familiarize yourself with the available font families, weights, slants, and point sizes. The following list gives these statistics for the fonts in the directories *75dpi* and *100dpi* in the standard X distribution from MIT.† (The fonts in the *misc* directory are holdovers from Release 2 and have short, manageable names that should not require wildcarding.)

Font families	Charter, Courier, Helvetica, New Century Schoolbook, Symbol, Times
Weights	Medium, bold
Slants	Roman (r), an upright design
	Italic (i), an italic design slanted clockwise from vertical
	Oblique (o), an obliqued upright design, slanted clockwise from vertical
Point sizes	8, 10, 12, 14, 18, 24

If you're unfamiliar with the general appearance of a particular font family, try displaying one of the fonts with *xfd*, as described in Volume Three, *X Window System User's Guide, Motif Edition*.

As a general rule, we suggest you type the following parts of a font name explicitly:

• Font family

• Weight

---

†For fonts other than those shipped by MIT, other families, weights, slants, point sizes, etc., may apply.

- Slant

- Point size

Note that it's better to match the point size field, which is measured in tenths of a point (the 100 in the previous example, equal to 10 points), than the pixel field (the 10). This allows your wildcarded font name to work properly with monitors of different resolutions. For example, say you use the following name to specify a 24 point (size), medium (weight), Italic (slant) Charter (family) font:

```
*charter-medium-i-*-240-*
```

This will match either of the following two font names (the first for 75 dpi monitors and the second for 100 dpi monitors):

```
-bitstream-charter-medium-i-normal--25-240-75-75-p-136-iso8859-1
-bitstream-charter-medium-i-normal--33-240-100-100-p-136-iso8859-1
```

depending on which directory comes first in your font path. Specifying font size explicitly in pixels (25 for the first or 33 for the second) rather than in points would limit you to matching only one of these fonts.

Given the complexity of font names and the rules of precedence used by the server, you should use wildcards carefully.

B.2.3 Font Name Aliasing

Another way to abbreviate font names is by aliasing—that is, by associating them with alternative names. You can create a file (or files) called *fonts.alias*, in any directory in the font search path, to set aliases for the fonts in that directory. The X server uses both *fonts.dir* files (see Section B.2.5) and *fonts.alias* files to locate fonts in the font path.

Be aware that when you create or edit a *fonts.alias* file, the server does not *automatically* recognize the aliases in question. You must make the server aware of newly created or edited alias files by resetting the font path with *xset*.

The *fonts.alias* file has a two-column format similar to the *fonts.dir* file (described in a moment): the first column contains aliases, the second contains the actual font names. If you want to specify an alias that contains spaces, enclose the alias in double quotes. If you want to include double quotes or other special characters as part of an alias, precede each special symbol with a backslash.

When you use an alias to specify a font in a command line, the server searches for the font associated with that alias in every directory in the font path. Therefore, a *fonts.alias* file in one directory can set aliases for fonts in other directories as well. You might choose to create a single alias file in one directory of the font path to set aliases for the most commonly used fonts in all the directories. Example B-1 shows a sample *fonts.alias* file.

Example B-1. Sample fonts.alias file

```
xterm12    -adobe-courier-medium-r-normal--12-120-75-75-m-70-iso8859-1
xterm14    -adobe-courier-medium-r-normal--14-140-75-75-m-90-iso8859-1
xterm18    -adobe-courier-medium-r-normal--18-180-75-75-m-110-iso8859-1
```

As the names of the aliases suggest, this sample file contains aliases for three fonts (of different point sizes) that are easily readable in *xterm* windows.

You can also use wildcards within the font names in the right hand column of an alias file. For instance, the alias file above might also be written:

```
xterm12    *courier-medium-r-*-120*
xterm14    *courier-medium-r-*-140*
xterm18    *courier-medium-r-*-180*
```

Once the server is made aware of aliases, you can specify an alias in resource specifications or on the command line:

```
xterm.font: xterm12
```

or:

```
% xterm -fn xterm12
```

If you are accustomed to the Release 2 font naming convention (each font name being equivalent to the name of the file in which it is stored, without the *.snf* extension), there is a way to emulate this convention using alias files. In each directory in the font path, create a *fonts.alias* file containing only the following line:

```
FILE_NAMES_ALIASES
```

Each filename (without the *.snf* extension) will then serve as an alias for the font the file contains. Note that an alias file containing this line applies only to the directory in which it is found. To make every font name equivalent to the name of the file in which it is stored, you need to create a *fonts.alias* file such as this in every font directory.

If you've specified FILE_NAMES_ALIASES in an alias file, you can choose the fonts in that directory by means of their filenames, as we did in the resource example at the end of Chapter 2, *Introduction to the X Toolkit and Motif.*

B.2.4 Making the Server Aware of Aliases

After you create (or update) an alias file, the server does not automatically recognize the aliases in question. You must make the server aware of newly created or edited alias files by "rehashing" the font path with *xset*. Enter:

```
% xset fp rehash
```

on the command line. The *xset* option *fp* (font path) with the **rehash** argument causes the server to reread the *fonts.dir* and *fonts.alias* files in the current font path. You need to do this every time you edit an alias file. (You also need to use *xset* if you add or remove fonts. See Volume Three, *X Window System User's Guide, Motif Edition*, for details.)

B.2.5 The fonts.dir Files

In addition to font files, each font directory contains a file called *fonts.dir*. The *fonts.dir* files serve, in effect, as databases for the X server. When the X server searches the directories in the default font path, it uses the *fonts.dir* files to locate the font(s) it needs.

Each *fonts.dir* file contains a list of all the font files in the directory with their associated font names, in two-column form. (The first column lists the font file and the second column lists the actual font name associated with the file.) The first line in *fonts.dir* lists the number of entries in the file (i.e., the number of fonts in the directory).

Example B-2 shows the *fonts.dir* file from the directory */usr/lib/X11/fonts/100dpi*. As the first line indicates, the directory contains 24 fonts.

Example B-2. a portion of the fonts.dir file in /usr/lib/X11/fonts/100dpi

```
24
charBI08.snf  -bitstream-charter-bold-i-normal--11-80-100-100-p-68-iso8859-1
charBI10.snf  -bitstream-charter-bold-i-normal--14-100-100-100-p-86-iso8859-1
charBI12.snf  -bitstream-charter-bold-i-normal--17-120-100-100-p-105-iso8859-1
charBI14.snf  -bitstream-charter-bold-i-normal--19-140-100-100-p-117-iso8859-1
charR08.snf   -bitstream-charter-medium-r-normal--11-80-100-100-p-61-iso8859-1
charR10.snf   -bitstream-charter-medium-r-normal--14-100-100-100-p-78-iso8859-1
charR12.snf   -bitstream-charter-medium-r-normal--17-120-100-100-p-95-iso8859-1
charR14.snf   -bitstream-charter-medium-r-normal--19-140-100-100-p-106-iso8859-1
charR18.snf   -bitstream-charter-medium-r-normal--25-180-100-100-p-139-iso8859-1
charR24.snf   -bitstream-charter-medium-r-normal--33-240-100-100-p-183-iso8859-1
```

The *fonts.dir* files are created by the *mkfontdir* client when X is installed. *mkfontdir* reads the font files in directories in the font path, extracts the font names, and creates a *fonts.dir* file in each directory. If *fonts.dir* files are present on your system, you probably won't have to deal with them, or with *mkfontdir*, at all. If the files are not present, or if you have to load new fonts or remove existing ones, you will have to create files with *mkfontdir*. Refer to Volume Three, *X Window System User's Guide, Motif Edition*, for details.

B.3 Font Service

If you have worked with X at a site with workstations from several vendors, you may have encountered frustrating problems with the use of fonts. If fonts have different names on one host than they do on another, an application that performs normally on one display will abort with a "Can't load font" error on another. Or you may have had to maintain separate defaults files for use on different displays.

Ideally, the site administrator could simply place fonts in a directory of a networked file system that is accessible to all hosts at the site. Unfortunately, no binary format for font data has been standardized, and the X servers supplied by different vendors expect data in mutually incompatible formats. If a vendor wishes to support several font formats, the server must include code to parse each one.

R5 provides an elegant solution to these problems in the form of a networked font service. Under this new model, an X server can obtain font data in a simple bitmap format from a *font server* process running somewhere on the network. The font server does the work of parsing font files for any supported format and exports font data in a bitmap format standardized by the X Font Service Protocol (reprinted in Volume Zero, *X Protocol Reference Manual* as of late 1992). X servers that take advantage of font service no longer need to do the work of parsing fonts themselves. In the near future, however, it is likely that workstation-based X servers and X terminals will continue to support file-based fonts along with their support for font servers.

The Font Service Protocol was designed by Jim Fulton of Network Computing Devices. The font server in the MIT distribution was implemented primarily by Dave Lemke, also of NCD. In addition, Apple Computer has donated a font server (which runs only on the Apple Macintosh computer) to export the Apple bitmap fonts, and, if available, the Apple TrueType fonts as well.

Typically, a font server will run on one host per site and will export all the fonts available at the site, but there are a variety of other ways that font service can be configured. A large site may choose to have multiple font servers to prevent overloading of a single server or to protect against service outages caused by network trouble or server crashes. A font server could export fonts parsed from a variety of formats, or a separate server could be used for each format. A vendor of fonts with a custom format might provide a special font server to export those fonts, and might use the special server to implement licensing policies—restricting the maximum number of simultaneous users of a font, for example. Finally, note that in the terminology of X font service, the X server is a *font client*, and that it is perfectly legal to have other font clients such as printer drivers. Figure B-3 shows a font server providing service to a workstation, an X terminal, and a printer driver.

R5 font service and scalable font support consists of the following components:

- The X Font Service Protocol, a standardized, extensible protocol for communication between a font server and font clients, such as an X display server. This protocol also standardizes the format used for the communication of font data between font server and font client.

- Additions to the X server to allow it to participate in the font service protocol.

- A convention for the naming and inclusion of font servers in the X server font path.

- A bitmap and outline font-scaling algorithm in the X server.

- A set of scalable outline fonts (in Charter and Courier typefaces) from Bitstream, Inc.

- A font server capable of scaling and exporting the new outline fonts as well as the standard X bitmap fonts.

- A font server that runs on an Apple Macintosh computer to export the Apple bitmap fonts and, if available, scaled Apple TrueType fonts to any X servers on the network.

- A respecification of the X server's handling of `XListFonts()`, `XLoadFont()`, and `XLoadQueryFont()` to allow pattern matching for scalable fonts. These functions are used by Xt.

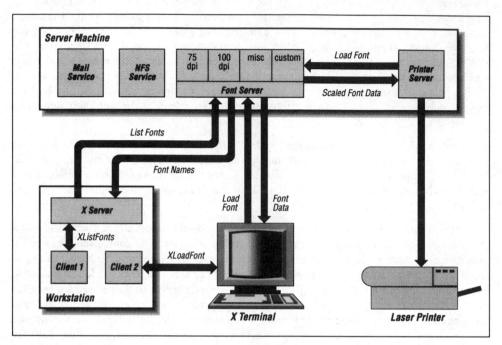

Figure B-3. A typical font server configuration

- An addition to the *X Logical Font Description Conventions* (XLFD) to handle pattern matching for scalable fonts.

There are no new or changed Xlib or Xt functions for the support of font service or scalable fonts. There are new conventions for naming and listing scalable fonts, however, and applications that want to make explicit use of scalable fonts will have to follow these conventions. Note that R5 defines a new abstraction, the **XFontSet**, which is used in internationalized applications, but that this has nothing whatsoever to do with font service.

B.4 Scalable Fonts

Another new feature in R5 is font scaling. In previous releases, each font was available only in a limited number of standard point sizes and resolutions. In the MIT distribution of R5, both the X server and the font server implement a simple bitmap font-scaling algorithm that allows fonts to be obtained at any desired point size and resolution. Bitmap fonts are easily scalable, but the resulting scaled font is generally jagged and difficult to read. Fortunately, R5 also provides a set of outline fonts. Outline fonts scale nicely, but the scaling process requires significant computation, so an X server might freeze for several seconds while scaling a large Asian font. This is one of the problems that font servers are intended to address. The fonts and the scaling code were donated by Bitstream, Inc.

Until Release 5, X relied exclusively on non-scalable bitmap fonts. If there was no installed font in the point size and resolution you wanted, then you were out of luck—it is obviously not feasible to provide every font in every point size and for every possible resolution. Bitmap fonts do not scale well, because their pixel-by-pixel specification can only be made smaller by omitting pixels or made larger by making pixels bigger, resulting in a jagged, low-resolution font. The fonts shipped by MIT for Release 5 include several "outline fonts" which describe characters by their component curves rather than by individual pixels. This description allows for successful scaling to any desired point size and resolution. The font server shipped by MIT in Release 5 has the capability to read and scale these outline fonts, and therefore the number of fonts available to the user is greatly increased. (Note, however, that a good bitmap font that is "hand-tuned" to a particular point size and screen resolution will generally be better looking than an outline font scaled to that size and resolution. Font design is an art, and the human touch is still important.)

The following two sections apply equally to all scalable and scaled fonts, whether outline or bitmap, from the X server or the font server.

B.4.1 Finding Scalable Fonts

Supporting scalable fonts raises some important questions about the behavior of the Xlib function `XListFonts()`. First, since there are (theoretically) an infinite number of point sizes and resolutions that a font could be scaled to, it is no longer possible to list all available fonts in *all* available sizes. So some special syntax is needed to indicate that a font is scalable and is available in any desired size, even if that size is not listed. But backwards compatibility is also an issue—the new point sizes provided by scalable fonts should not be hidden from existing pre-R5 applications.

These seemingly contradictory goals are resolved by changing the semantics of the call to `XListFonts()` and by extending the *X Logical Font Description Conventions* slightly.†
In R5, scalable fonts are returned by `XListFonts()` with the string "0" in the PIXEL_SIZE, POINT_SIZE, and AVERAGE_WIDTH fields (the seventh, eighth, and twelfth fields of the 14-field XLFD font name). Non-scalable fonts will never have these three fields zero, and therefore these fields are sufficient to distinguish scalable from non-scalable fonts. Most font servers will list a few specific *derived instances* of each scalable font at standard sizes and resolutions for the benefit of older X applications that expect to find font names in this form.

The X server and font server are only required to match scalable fonts when the font name pattern they are passed is a *well-formed* one. A well-formed font name is one that contains all 14 hyphens specified in the XLFD convention. Wildcards are permitted for any field, but may not replace multiple fields—all fields must be present in the name. For example,

```
*-helvetica-bold-o-*-*-*-120-*
```

---

†The XLFD Conventions are printed as Appendix M of *X Protocol Reference Manual*, Volume Zero of the O'Reilly & Associates series of X books.

is not a well-formed name, but

```
-*-helvetica-bold-o-*-*-*-120-75-75-*-*-iso8859-1
```

is well-formed. Shortcut names specified as in the first example have come into common use, but with the increasing variety of display resolutions and fonts with non-standard charsets, it is good practice to specify these extra fields, even if you are not interested in using scaled fonts. If `XListFonts()` is passed a pattern that is not well-formed, it may not include scalable fonts in the search at all.

To list scalable fonts, call `XListFonts()` with a well-formed pattern with "0" or "*" in its PIXEL_SIZE, POINT_SIZE, and AVERAGE_WIDTH fields. Example B-3 shows some queries that will return scalable fonts. You can quickly try them out by replacing the call to `XList-Fonts()` with the client `xlsfonts`.

Example B-3. Listing scalable fonts

```
/* List all Latin-1 fonts.  Returned names of scalable fonts will have
 * "0" for pixel size, point size, and average width
 */
fonts = XListFonts(dpy, "-*-*-*-*-*-*-*-*-*-*-*-*-iso8859-1", 1000, &count);

/* List all scalable courier fonts.  Non-scalable fonts will
 * not be listed.
 */
list = XListFonts(dpy,"-*-courier-*-*-*-*-0-0-*-*-*-0-*-*", 200, &count);
```

B.4.2 Finding Derived Instances of Scalable Fonts

A scalable font name with a point size (and pixel size and average width) of zero is not very useful by itself. If you call `XLoadFont()` on this font name without a size (or specify such a font name for a font resource), you will get some implementation-defined default size. Instead of listing scalable Helvetica fonts, for example, you will more often want to list all Helvetica fonts at some particular point size. The list you get may contain non-scaled bitmap fonts as well as derived instances of scalable fonts. In order to include derived instances of scalable fonts in a search, it is necessary to specify some of the size fields explicitly. There are five *scalable fields* in an XLFD font name: PIXEL_SIZE, POINT_SIZE, RESOLUTION_X, RESOLUTION_Y, and AVERAGE_WIDTH (fields 7, 8, 9, 10, and 12.) In order for `XList-Fonts()` to list a particular scaled size of a scalable font, enough of these scalable fields must be specified so that the font name pattern matches exactly one derived instance of the font. If too few of the scalable fields are specified, there will be no unique match, and if too many are specified, there may not be any possible scaling that meets all of those specified criteria.

When searching for fonts at a particular size, you will typically wildcard the pixel size and average width by setting those fields to "*" and explicitly specify the point size you want along with the x- and y-resolutions of your screen. (You can calculate screen resolutions with macros like `DisplayWidth` and `DisplayWidthMM`, as shown in a later example.) These three fields specify all that is needed to correctly scale the font. You need not (and should not) specify the pixel size, because the point size and y-resolution of the screen determine the desired pixel size. You need not specify the average width because the point size and x-resolution of the screen, together with the height to width ratio implicit to the font, determine the desired width. It is also possible to name a single derived instance of a scalable font by specifying a pixel size plus x- and y-resolutions. There are also other combinations of fields that will work, but none are particularly useful in practice. Example B-4 shows font name patterns that will match derived instances of scalable fonts.

Example B-4. Finding derived instances of scalable fonts

```
/* Load a 12-point bold helvetica font defined at a 100x100 dpi
 * resolution.  The actual font loaded might be a derived instance of a
 * scalable font, or it might be a bitmap font--there is no way to
 * distinguish them.
 */
font = XLoadFont(dpy, "-*-helvetica-bold-r-*-*-*-120-100-100-*-*-iso8859-1");

/* Load a 20 pixel high helvetica font defined at 100x100 dpi */
font2 = XLoadFont(dpy, "-*-helvetica-medium-r-*-*-20-*-100-100-*-*-iso8859-1");

/* List all 13-point Latin-1 helvetica fonts defined at a 106x97 dpi
 * resolution.  This pattern will match derived instances of scalable
 * fonts, and will probably only match derived instances of scalable
 * fonts, because there are not likely to be bitmap fonts defined at this
 * particular size and resolution.
 */
list = XListFonts(dpy,"-*-helvetica-*-*-*-*-*-130-106-97-*-*-iso8859-1",
          50, &count);
```

There are a number of reasons that a font name pattern could fail to match derived instances of scalable fonts. It is difficult to devise an algorithm that will correctly match scalable fonts against any font name pattern. For this reason, the X server or font server is not required to include scalable fonts in its search if the pattern it is given is not well-formed. A well-formed pattern must contain 14 hyphens. Note in particular that the first character in a well-formed name must be a hyphen.

An underspecified font name will not match any derived instances of scalable fonts. This is because your font name could match any number of derived instances, and it is not possible to list them all. When only the point size and pixel size are specified, for example, they are enough together to determine the desired y-resolution for the font, but any x-resolution (and therefore any average width) is still possible. To uniquely match a derived instance, you'd have to specify the x-resolution of your screen or a desired average width for the font. The MIT implementation, however, makes reasonable guesses for unspecified resolution values, so underspecified font names do not occur. If only point size is specified, then default resolutions (75 or 100 dpi) are used. If both point and pixel size are specified as above, then the y-resolution they specify is used for both x- and y-resolution fields.

Similarly, an overspecified font name, one with point size, pixel size, and x- and y-resolutions, for example, may not match any derived instances of scalable fonts: if the specified y-resolution is different from the y-resolution implicitly defined by the combination of point size and pixel size, then there is no way that the font can be scaled to satisfy your request. Example B-5 shows font name patterns that will fail to match any derived instances of scalable fonts.

```
/* List 15-point bold oblique helvetica fonts.  Derived instances of
 * scalable fonts will probably not be included in the list because the
 * pattern does not have all 14 fields.
 */
helvbold15 = XListFonts(dpy,"*-helvetica-bold-o-*-*-*-150-*", 50, &count);

/* List all 17-point, 17-pixel bold oblique helvetica fonts defined at
 * 100dpi x- and y-resolutions.  This pattern will not match any derived
 * instances of scalable fonts (nor any font) because a 17 point font
 * at 100dpi is not 17 pixels high.
 */
helvbold17 = XListFonts(dpy,"-*-helvetica-bold-o-*-*-17-170-100-100-*-*-
                             iso8859-1",50, &count);
```

B.4.3 Using Scalable Fonts

Many applications use only a small number of fonts, that are opened at startup and never changed. These applications may leave the choice of fonts to the user. If the user overrides the default with a font that doesn't exist, the application may simply print an error message and exit. Applications such as this need no modification to work with scalable fonts. Users who want to take advantage of scalable fonts, must provide a well-formed and correctly specified font name. Other applications, such as word processors or presentation graphics packages, may allow the user to select fonts from a menu or list at runtime. This kind of application will have to be modified to recognize and make use of scalable fonts. Example B-6 and Example B-7 demonstrate one approach.

Example B-6 shows a procedure that determines whether or not a given font name represents a scalable font. This procedure is intended to be called once for each font returned by XListFonts().

Example B-6. Determining if a font is scalable

```
/*
 * This routine returns True if the passed name is a well-formed
 * XLFD style font name with a pixel size, point size, and average
 * width (fields 7,8, and 12) of "0".
 */
Bool IsScalableFont(name)
char *name;
{
    int i, field;

    if ((name == NULL) || (name[0] != '-')) return False;

    for(i = field = 0; name[i] != '\0'; i++) {
        if (name[i] == '-') {
            field++;
            if ((field == 7) || (field == 8) || (field == 12))
                if ((name[i+1] != '0') || (name[i+2] != '-'))
                    return False;
        }
    }
```

```
    if (field != 14) return False;
    else return True;
}
```

Example B-7 shows a procedure that takes a scalable font name and a desired point size and loads the derived instance of that font at the requested size and at the precise resolution of the screen. It is intended to be called with a scalable font name as returned by **XList-Fonts()**.

Example B-7. Loading a derived instance of a scalable font

```
/*
 * This routine is passed a scalable font name and a point size.  It returns
 * an XFontStruct for the given font scaled to the specified size and the
 * exact resolution of the screen.  The font name is assumed to be a
 * well-formed XLFD name, and to have pixel size, point size, and average
 * width fields of "0" and arbitrary x-resolution and y-resolution fields.
 * Size is specified in tenths of points.  Returns NULL if the name is
 * malformed or no such font exists.
 */
XFontStruct *LoadQueryScalableFont(dpy, screen, name, size)
Display *dpy;
int screen;
char *name;
int size;
{
    int i,j, field;
    char newname[500];     /* big enough for a long font name */
    int res_x, res_y;      /* resolution values for this screen */

    /* catch obvious errors */
    if ((name == NULL) || (name[0] != '-')) return NULL;

    /* calculate our screen resolution in dots per inch. 25.4mm = 1 inch */
    res_x = DisplayWidth(dpy, screen)/(DisplayWidthMM(dpy, screen)/25.4);
    res_y = DisplayHeight(dpy, screen)/(DisplayHeightMM(dpy, screen)/25.4);

    /* copy the font name, changing the scalable fields as we do so */
    for(i = j = field = 0; name[i] != '\0' && field <= 14; i++) {
        newname[j++] = name[i];
        if (name[i] == '-') {
            field++;
            switch(field) {
            case 7:  /* pixel size */
            case 12: /* average width */
                /* change from "-0-" to "-*-" */
                newname[j] = '*';
                j++;
                if (name[i+1] != '\0') i++;
                break;
            case 8:  /* point size */
                /* change from "-0-" to "-<size>-" */
                sprintf(&newname[j], "%d", size);
                while (newname[j] != '\0') j++;
                if (name[i+1] != '\0') i++;
                break;
```

```
          case 9:  /* x-resolution */
          case 10: /* y-resolution */
              /* change from an unspecified resolution to res_x or res_y */
              sprintf(&newname[j], "%d", (field == 9) ? res_x : res_y);
              while(newname[j] != '\0') j++;
              while((name[i+1] != '-') && (name[i+1] != '\0')) i++;
              break;
          }
      }
  }
  newname[j] = '\0';

  /* if there aren't 14 hyphens, it isn't a well formed name */
  if (field != 14) return NULL;

  return XLoadQueryFont(dpy, newname);
}
```

B.5 Window Geometry

All clients that display in a window take a geometry option that specifies the size and location of the client window.† The syntax of the geometry option is:

    -geometry geometry

The –geometry option can be (and often is) abbreviated to –g, unless there is a conflicting option that begins with g.

The corresponding resource is XtNGeometry, which can be set in a resource file as follows:

    *mywidget.geometry: geometry_string

The argument to the geometry option (geometry), referred to as a "standard geometry string," has the form:

    widthxheight±xoff±yoff

The variables width and height, are values in pixels for many clients. However, application developers are encouraged to use units that are meaningful to the application. For example, xterm uses columns and rows of text as width and height values in the xterm window. xoff (x offset), and yoff (y offset) are always in pixels.

You can specify any or all elements of the geometry string. Incomplete geometry specifications are compared to the resource manager defaults and missing elements are supplied by the values specified there. If no default is specified there, and uwm is running, the window manager will require you to place the window interactively.

---

†The Release 2 syntax:

    =geometry

is no longer supported.

The values for the *x* and *y* offsets have the following effects:

Table B-1. Geometry Specification: x and y Offsets

Offset Variables	Description
+*xoff*	A positive *x* offset specifies the distance that the left edge of the window is offset from the left side of the display.
+*yoff*	A positive *y* offset specifies the distance that the top edge of the window is offset from the top of the display.
−*xoff*	A negative *x* offset specifies the distance that the right edge of the window is offset from the right side of the display.
−*yoff*	A negative *y* offset specifies the distance that the bottom edge of the window is offset from the bottom of the display.

For example, the command line:

```
% xclock —geometry 125x125—10+10 &
```

places a clock 125×125 pixels in the upper-right corner of the display, 10 pixels from both the top and the right edge of the screen.

For *xterm*, the size of the window is measured in characters and lines. (80 characters wide by 24 lines long is the default terminal size.) If you wanted to use the vt100 window in 132-column mode, with 40 lines displayed at a time, you could use the following geometry options:

```
% xterm —geometry 132x40—10+350 &
```

This will place an *xterm* window 132 characters wide by 40 lines long in the lower-right corner, 10 pixels from the right edge of the screen and 350 pixels from the top of the screen.

Some clients may allow you to specify geometry strings for the size and position of the icon or an alternate window, usually through resources (in an *.Xdefaults* or other resource file). See the appropriate client reference pages in Part Three of Volume Three, *X Window System User's Guide, Motif Edition*, for a complete list of available resources.

You should be aware that, as with all user preferences, you may not always get exactly what you ask for. Clients are designed to work with a window manager, which may have its own rules for window or icon size and placement. However, priority is always given to specific user requests, so you won't often be surprised.

C

Naming Conventions

This appendix describes a suggested set of conventions for naming widgets, and elements within widget code.

C
Naming Conventions

This appendix proposes a set of conventions for naming certain elements of widget code.† If the naming conventions used in all widget sets are consistent, there will be several benefits:

- It will be much easier for programmers to move from toolkit to toolkit without needing to constantly refer to manuals to figure out how to properly name various items.

- It will be easier to mix widgets from different widgets sets in one application.

- It will make it possible for automatic code generators to work with lots of widgets without making special modifications for any toolkit.

These conventions are common between the OPEN LOOK and Motif widget sets with a few minor differences. However, the Athena widget set currently does not follow the conventions described.

It is important to note that these suggestions are in no way blessed (or damned) by the X Consortium—they are simply a guideline that we suggest you follow in the interests of promoting the benefits listed above. We will use Motif as an example.

A toolkit uses a special prefix with all its widgets. In the case of Motif, this prefix is *m*. Using that prefix and a hypothetical Label widget as an example, the conventions are as follows:

Toolkit library name	*libXm.a*
Widget class name	`XmLabel`
Include directives	`<Xm/Label.h>`
`class_name` field in the core structure	`Label`
Enumerated resource values	`XmCAPITALIZED_WORDS`
Public function names	`XmLabelFunctionName()`

---

†This appendix is based on a *comp.windows.x* network news posting by Gene Dykes of Cornell University.

Truncated include file names	Strip the lowercase letters a word at a time until the basename is nine characters or fewer (but strip as few letters as possible from the initial word). Thus:

`<Xm/VeryLongWidgetName.h>`

becomes:

`<Xm/VeryLWN.h>`

but:

`<Xm/Verylongwidgetname.h>`

becomes:

`<Xm/Verylongw.h>`

(Note difference in **VeryLong** (two words) and **Very-long** (one word).)

Macro names for preprocessor in include files	`#ifndef XM_LABEL_H`

This is to prevent header files from being included more than once.

If a widget has a corresponding gadget, then **Gadget** is appended to the widget name, so **XmLabelGadget** is the gadget class name.

Widget class pointer	`xmLabelWidgetClass`
Gadget class pointer	`xmLabelGadgetClass`
Create function for widgets or gadgets	`Widget XmCreateLabel (parent, name,` `    arglist, argcount)`

This is a shortcut to using **XtCreateWidget()**. However, in the case of top-level widgets (menus, dialogs, MainWindow), it also creates the shell widget and creates the requested widget within it.

The special Create functions can also be used as convenience routines for specialized widget instances. For example, **XmCreateWorkingDialog()** and **Xm-CreateWarningDialog()** actually create a MessageBox whose **XmDialogType** resources are respectively **XmDIALOG_WARNING** and **Xm-DIALOG_WORKING**.

OPEN LOOK uses conventions similar to Motif, but leaves the prefixes off the widget class name. We recommend that you supply a prefix for any widgets you write, especially if there is any chance that some other widget set may use the same class name. In other words, if we wrote a new Label widget, we might call it OraLabel, not just Label, so that we could still use the Athena Label widget in the same application.

D

Release Notes

This appendix summarizes the changes between Release 4 and Release 5 of the X Toolkit, and between Motif 1.1 and 1.2.

In This Appendix:

D
Release Notes

This appendix summarizes the changes to the Xt Intrinsics between Release 4 and Release 5, and provides a table listing the obsolete Motif 1.1 functions and their 1.2 counterparts.

D.1 R4 to R5

`XtSetLanguageProc()` is a new function designed to set the function that sets the locale for internationalization. Most applications should call it just before `XtApp-Initialize()`, using three `NULL` arguments. This instructs Xt to use the default locale-setting function.

The X11R5 Xt Intrinsics make use of permanently-allocated strings for quarks, and the Translation Manager was reimplemented to save memory and speed execution for the most common uses.

There is a new client, *editres*, which allows a user or programmer to interactively edit the widget resources of any running application that participates in the Editres protocol. See Chapter 14.

The functions `XtAppInitialize()`, `XtVaAppInitialize()`, `XtOpen-Display()`, `XtDisplayInitialize()`, and `XtInitialize()` all require a pointer to a number of command line arguments (i.e., `&argc`). In X11R4 these functions expected this argument to be of type `Cardinal *` which, to guarantee portability, required an annoying typecast: `(Cardinal *)&argc`. In X11R5, these functions were changed to expect an argument of type `int *`. This does not affect the binary compatibility of clients, but programs which perform the explicit cast to `Cardinal *` will need to be changed to avoid compilation warnings with the X11R5 Xt header files. The `Cardinal *` type continues to be used in a number of places, including the `XtAppErrorMsg()` and `Xt-AppWarningMsg()` functions, type converter functions, and the `initialize` and `set_values` widget methods.

Prior to X11R5, the Xt string constants (the `XtN`, `XtC`, and `XtR` names) were macros for constant strings. With many compilers, each occurrence of a constant string is compiled into the object file, even when there are multiple instances of the same string. In the X11R5 MIT implementation of Xt, these macros have been changed to pointers into a single large array of characters (with embedded null characters dividing the array into individual strings). Under this new scheme, all of the Xt strings are embedded in every application once, but none more than once. For many applications this will result in an overall memory savings.

Prior to X11R5, the MIT implementation of *<X11/Intrinsic.h>* included the file *<X11/Xos.h>*. This inclusion was a violation of the specification, and the file is no longer included. *<X11/Xos.h>* defines System V and BSD-style string indexing functions (**index** and **strchr**), includes the appropriate time-handling header file, and hides other, more obscure, operating system dependencies. The most likely problem to result from this change in *<X11/Intrinsic.h>* is that programs that unknowingly relied on macro definitions of **index** or **strchr** from *<X11/Xos.h>* will now fail to compile. These programs may be compiled with the **-DXT_BC** flag which will restore the pre-X11R5 behavior. Substantial effort has been put into the MIT X11R5 implementation to make it comply with ANSI-C and POSIX standards. New standard header files have been defined that make it easier to write portable X applications. They are *<X11/Xfuncs.h>*, *<X11/Xfuncproto.h>*, and *<X11/Xosdefs.h>*. See the Third Edition of Volume One, *Xlib Programming Manual* for more information on these files.

D.2 Motif 1.1 to 1.2

The following tables are only partial lists of changes from Motif 1.1 to 1.2. For more information, see the Second Edition of Volume Six, *Motif Programming Manual*, due to be published in late 1992. Table D-1 lists the functions that are obsolete as of Motif 1.2, and their replacements.

Table D-1. Motif 1.1 Obsolete Functions and Replacements

Obsolete Function	New Function
MrmOpenHierarchy()	MrmOpenHierarchyPerDisplay()
XmAddTabGroup()	set XmNnavigationType to XmEXCLUSIVE_TAB_GROUP
XmCvtStringToUnitType()	converter uses RepType facility
XmFontListAdd()	XmFontListAppendEntry()
XmFontListCreate()	XmFontListAppendEntry()
XmFontListGetNextFont()	XmFontListNextEntry()
XmGetMenuCursor()	get XmScreen resource XmNmenuCursor
XmRemoveTabGroup()	set XmNnavigationType to XmNONE
XmSetFontUnit()	set XmScreen resources XmNhorizontalFontUnit and XmNverticalFontUnit
XmSetFontUnits()	set XmScreen resources XmNhorizontalFontUnit and XmNverticalFontUnit
XmSetMenuCursor()	set XmScreen resource XmNmenuCursor
XmStringCreateSimple()	XmStringCreateLocalized()
XmTrackingLocate()	XmTrackingEvent()

The following are resources that were used in Motif 1.1 but should not be used in Motif 1.2:

Table D-2. Obsolete Motif 1.1 Resources

Widget	Resource
`VendorShell`	`defaultFontList, buttonFontList, labelFontList, textFontList`
`MenuShell`	`defaultFontList, buttonFontList, labelFontList`
`RowColumn`	`whichButton, menuPost`

The following are enumerated values that were used in Motif 1.1 and their replacements to be used in Motif 1.2:

Table D-3. Obsolete Enumerated Values

Obsolete Value	New Value
`XmSTRING_COMPONENT_CHARSET`	`XmSTRING_COMPONENT_FONTLIST_ELEMENT_TAG`
`XmSTRING_DEFAULT_CHARSET`	`XmFONTLIST_DEFAULT_TAG`

D.2.1 Widget Changes

XmText. Besides internationalization, there are a number of other changes to the XmText widget. In 1.2 the text widget has changed significantly enough that any subclasses may need to be re-written.

* `XmTextDisableRedisplay()` and `XmTextEnableRedisplay()` are public; use them when making batched updates.

* `XmTextFindString()` searches for a string within the text widget.

* `XmTextGetSubstring()` get just a portion of the text value. This can save memory for large text widgets because the entire value does not need to be duplicated.

* There is now an overstrike mode, and an action procedure `toggle-overstrike()` to toggle between insert and overstrike modes.

* The annoying caret-cursor ("destination cursor") has been dropped.

* There is a new internal data structure, which makes scrolling of long files much faster.

XmTextField. The 1.2 XmTextField widget has a substring function, `XmTextFieldGet-Substring()`, and no longer has a destination cursor.

XmList. The XmList widget now has items that are selectable with drag-and-drop. There are a number of new convenience routines for adding, removing, and replacing items, as well as setting and querying the position of the keyboard traversal cursor, etc.

XmMessageBox and XmSelectionBox. The XmMessageBox and XmSelectionBox widgets now allow the programmer to add a menubar and additional button children. There is a new convenience dialog creation routine, `XmCreateTemplateDialog()` which creates an XmMessageBox containing only a separator gadget. The XmSelectionBox widget now uses an XmTextField widget rather than an XmText widget.

XmScrollBar. There is now an action procedure that cancels a drag in progress.

XmScrolledWindow. There is a new callback list invoked when the user attempts to traverse to a widget that is not currently visible. There is a new function, `XmScrollVisible()` which will adjust the XmScrolledWindow to make one of its widget children visible.

XmFrame. The XmFrame widget now supports an additional child (usually a label) to serve as the "title" for the frame.

XmRowColumn. The XmRowColumn widget supports a new resource `XmNvertical-Alignment` which controls the vertical alignment of its children.

VendorShell. The Motif VendorShell widget now has resources to control input methods and provides geometry management for input method preedit and status areas, when needed. It also supports a new resource `XmNaudibleWarning` which controls whether a beep should accompany warning messages. Text widgets determine the default value of their `Xm-NverifyBell` resource from this VendorShell resource.

D.2.2 New Display and Screen Objects

Motif 1.2 now automatically creates an XmDisplay object to hold display-specific data and XmScreen object to hold screen-specific data. These objects may be obtained for a specific display or screen with the functions `XmGetXmDisplay()` and `XmGetXmScreen()`. The XmScreen object has resources such as `XmNlightThreshold` and `XmNdark-Threshold` which control the automatic selection of colors, and resources such as `Xm-NdefaultSourceCursorIcon` which control default drag-and-drop visuals.

D.2.3 Default Colors

The XmScreen object now has resources that allow fine control over the procedures that automatically generate shadow colors and a contrasting foreground color based on the background color. A new function `XmChangeColor()` changes all the colors for a specified widget. There is a new interface to the pixmap cache: `XmGetPixmapByDepth()` which allows pixmaps to be obtained for Visuals of other than the default depth.

D.2.4 Insensitive Visuals

The XmList, XmText, XmTextField, XmScrollBar, and XmArrowButton widgets now provide visual feedback when they have been made insensitive.

D.2.5 Baseline Alignment

Two new functions `XmWidgetGetBaselines()` and `XmWidgetGetDisplayRect()` allow precise alignment of text within widgets of different classes or with different margins.

D.2.6 Geometry Management

Geometry management code has been overhauled in Motif 1.2. This should result in more uniform interactions between primitive and manager widgets.

D.2.7 Traversal

Motif 1.2 provides better support for programmers who need to explicitly manage traversal. There are five new public functions: `XmGetFocusWidget()`, `XmGetTabGroup()`, `XmIsTraversable()`, `XmIsVisible()`, and `XmGetVisibility()`.

In addition, the XmManager widget has a new resource, `XmNinitialFocus` which specifies which child will be the first to receive keyboard focus. This is independent of the XmBulletinBoard resource `XmNdefaultButton`.

`XmTrackingLocate()` has been improved to handle keyboard events as well as mouse button events.

D.2.8 Representation Type Convenience Functions

Motif 1.2 supports `XmRepTypeRegister()` and a series of other `XmRepType*()` functions that allow the simple registration of resource converters for enumerated types. With these functions it is no longer necessary to write a resource converter procedure for every enumerated type.

D.2.9 caddr_t Changed to XtPointer

All references to the type `caddr_t` have been changed to `XtPointer` because `caddr_t` is not part of the ANSI-C standard.

D.2.10 Mwm

In Motif 1.2, mwm supports the non-rectangular window SHAPE extension, supports opaque moves of windows, has the concept of window "families" with their own internal stacking order, and allows the user to specify the location of the feedback window. There are a number of other minor changes.

D.2.11 UIL and Mrm

In Motif 1.2, the UIL compiler has been internationalized. Invoking it with the "–s" option will cause it to call `setlocale()` and run in the current locale. There are new primitives that allow the creation of wide character strings and font sets from UIL. The Mrm library contains a new function `MrmOpenHierarchyPerDisplay()` which supports different UID file search paths for each display.

E

The xbitmap Application

This appendix shows the complete code for the BitmapEdit widget and a relatively complex version of xbitmap, *which is described in Chapter 4,* An Example Application.

In This Appendix:

The xbitmap Application

This appendix shows the complete code for the BitmapEdit widget (without selections), and for an advanced version of the *xbitmap* application (*xbitmap5* in the example distribution) which is similar to *xbitmap3* described in Chapter 4 except that it both reads and writes X11 bitmap files (*xbitmap3* was capable of writing them only).

All source code from this book is available free from numerous sources, as described in the Preface.

E.1 The BitmapEdit Widget

Example E-1. BitmapEdit: complete widget code

```
/*
 * BitmapEdit.c - bitmap editor widget.
 */

#include <Xm/XmP.h>
#include <X11/StringDefs.h>

#include <stdio.h>

#include "BitmapEdiP.h"

#define INTERNAL_WIDTH     2
#define INTERNAL_HEIGHT 4

#define DEFAULT_PIXMAP_WIDTH    32  /* in cells */
#define DEFAULT_PIXMAP_HEIGHT   32  /* in cells */

#define DEFAULT_CELL_SIZE   30  /* in pixels */

/* values for instance variable is_drawn */
#define DRAWN 1
#define UNDRAWN 0

/* modes for drawing */
#define DRAW 1
#define UNDRAW 0

#define MAXLINES 1000    /* max of horiz or vertical cells */
#define SCROLLBARWIDTH 15

#define DEFAULTWIDTH 300  /* widget size when show_all is False */
```

```
#define offset(field) XtOffsetOf(BitmapEditRec, field)

static XtResource resources[ ] = {
/* not needed in Motif - already defined by Primitive.
*    {
*    XtNforeground,
*    XtCForeground,
*    XtRPixel,
*    sizeof(Pixel),
*    offset(bitmapEdit.foreground),
*    XtRString,
*    XtDefaultForeground
*      },
*/
      {
    XtNtoggleCallback,
    XtCToggleCallback,
    XtRCallback,
    sizeof(XtPointer),
    offset(bitmapEdit.callback),
    XtRCallback,
    NULL
      },
      {
    XtNcellSizeInPixels,
    XtCCellSizeInPixels,
    XtRInt, sizeof(int),
    offset(bitmapEdit.cell_size_in_pixels),
    XtRImmediate,
    (XtPointer)DEFAULT_CELL_SIZE
      },
      {
    XtNpixmapWidthInCells,
    XtCPixmapWidthInCells,
    XtRDimension,
    sizeof(Dimension),
    offset(bitmapEdit.pixmap_width_in_cells),
    XtRImmediate,
    (XtPointer)DEFAULT_PIXMAP_WIDTH
      },
      {
    XtNpixmapHeightInCells,
    XtCPixmapHeightInCells,
    XtRDimension,
    sizeof(Dimension),
    offset(bitmapEdit.pixmap_height_in_cells),
    XtRImmediate,
    (XtPointer)DEFAULT_PIXMAP_HEIGHT
      },
      {
    XtNcurX,
    XtCCurX,
    XtRInt,
    sizeof(int),
    offset(bitmapEdit.cur_x),
    XtRImmediate,
```

```
    (XtPointer) 0
     },
     {
    XtNcurY,
    XtCCurY,
    XtRInt,
    sizeof(int),
    offset(bitmapEdit.cur_y),
    XtRString,
    (XtPointer) NULL
     },
     {
    XtNcellArray,
    XtCCellArray,
    XtRString,
    sizeof(String),
    offset(bitmapEdit.cell),
    XtRImmediate,
    (XtPointer) 0
     },
     {
    XtNshowEntireBitmap,
    XtCShowEntireBitmap,
    XtRBoolean,
    sizeof(Boolean),
    offset(bitmapEdit.show_all),
    XtRImmediate,
    (XtPointer) True
     },
};

/* Declaration of methods */

static void Initialize();
static void Redisplay();
static void Destroy();
static void Resize();
static Boolean SetValues();
static XtGeometryResult QueryGeometry();

/* these Core methods not needed by BitmapEdit:
 *
 * static void ClassInitialize();
 * static void Realize();
 */

/* the following are private functions unique to BitmapEdit */
static void DrawPixmaps(), DoCell(), ChangeCellSize();

/* the following are actions of BitmapEdit */
static void DrawCell(), UndrawCell(), ToggleCell();

/* The following are public functions of BitmapEdit, declared extern
 * in the public include file: */
char *BitmapEditGetArray();

static char defaultTranslations[ ] =
    "<Btn1Down>:    DrawCell()              \n\
    <Btn2Down>:    UndrawCell()            \n\
```

```
    <Btn3Down>:     ToggleCell()            \n\
    <Btn1Motion>:   DrawCell()              \n\
    <Btn2Motion>:   UndrawCell()            \n\
    <Btn3Motion>:   ToggleCell()";

static XtActionsRec actions[ ] = {
        {"DrawCell", DrawCell},
        {"UndrawCell", UndrawCell},
        {"ToggleCell", ToggleCell},
};

/* definition in BitmapEdit.h */
static BitmapEditPointInfo info;

BitmapEditClassRec bitmapEditClassRec = {
    {
    /* core_class fields */
    /* superclass          */ (WidgetClass) &xmPrimitiveClassRec,
    /* class_name          */ "BitmapEdit",
    /* widget_size         */ sizeof(BitmapEditRec),
    /* class_initialize    */ NULL,
    /* class_part_initialize */ NULL,
    /* class_inited        */ False,
    /* initialize          */ Initialize,
    /* initialize_hook     */ NULL,
    /* realize             */ XtInheritRealize,
    /* actions             */ actions,
    /* num_actions         */ XtNumber(actions),
    /* resources           */ resources,
    /* num_resources       */ XtNumber(resources),
    /* xrm_class           */ NULLQUARK,
    /* compress_motion     */ True,
    /* compress_exposure   */ XtExposeCompressMultiple,
    /* compress_enterleave */ True,
    /* visible_interest    */ False,
    /* destroy             */ Destroy,
    /* resize              */ Resize,
    /* expose              */ Redisplay,
    /* set_values          */ SetValues,
    /* set_values_hook     */ NULL,
    /* set_values_almost   */ XtInheritSetValuesAlmost,
    /* get_values_hook     */ NULL,
    /* accept_focus        */ NULL,
    /* version             */ XtVersion,
    /* callback_private    */ NULL,
    /* tm_table            */ defaultTranslations,
    /* query_geometry      */ QueryGeometry,
    /* display_accelerator */ XtInheritDisplayAccelerator,
    /* extension           */ NULL
    },
    { /* Primitive class fields */
    /* border_highlight    */      _XtInherit,
    /* border_unhighlight  */      _XtInherit,
    /* translations        */      XtInheritTranslations,
    /* arm_and_activate    */      NULL,
    /* syn resources       */      NULL,
    /* num_syn_resources   */      0,
```

```
    /* extension          */      NULL,
    },
    {
    /* extension          */      0,
    },
};

WidgetClass bitmapEditWidgetClass = (WidgetClass) & bitmapEditClassRec;

static void
GetDrawGC(w)
Widget w;
{
    BitmapEditWidget cw = (BitmapEditWidget) w;
    XGCValues values;
    XtGCMask mask = GCForeground | GCBackground | GCDashOffset |
            GCDashList | GCLineStyle;

    /*
     * Setting foreground and background to 1 and 0 looks like a
     * kludge but isn't.  This GC is used for drawing
     * into a pixmap of depth one.  Real colors are applied with a
     * separate GC when the pixmap is copied into the window.
     */
    values.foreground = 1;
    values.background = 0;
    values.dashes = 1;
    values.dash_offset = 0;
    values.line_style = LineOnOffDash;

    cw->bitmapEdit.draw_gc = XCreateGC(XtDisplay(cw),
            cw->bitmapEdit.big_picture, mask, &values);
}

static void
GetUndrawGC(w)
Widget w;
{
    BitmapEditWidget cw = (BitmapEditWidget) w;
    XGCValues values;
    XtGCMask mask = GCForeground | GCBackground;

    /* this looks like a kludge but isn't.  This GC is used for drawing
     * into a pixmap of depth one.  Real colors are applied as the
     * pixmap is copied into the window.
     */
    values.foreground = 0;
    values.background = 1;

    cw->bitmapEdit.undraw_gc = XCreateGC(XtDisplay(cw),
            cw->bitmapEdit.big_picture, mask, &values);
}

static void
GetCopyGC(w)
Widget w;
{
    BitmapEditWidget cw = (BitmapEditWidget) w;
    XGCValues values;
```

```
    XtGCMask mask = GCForeground | GCBackground;

    values.foreground = cw->primitive.foreground;
    values.background = cw->core.background_pixel;

    cw->bitmapEdit.copy_gc = XtGetGC(cw, mask, &values);
}

/* ARGSUSED */
static void
Initialize(treq, tnew, args, num_args)
Widget treq, tnew;
ArgList args;
Cardinal *num_args;
{
    BitmapEditWidget new = (BitmapEditWidget) tnew;
    new->bitmapEdit.cur_x = 0;
    new->bitmapEdit.cur_y = 0;

    /*
     * Check instance values set by resources that may be invalid.
     */

    if ((new->bitmapEdit.pixmap_width_in_cells < 1) ||
            (new->bitmapEdit.pixmap_height_in_cells < 1)) {
        XtWarning("BitmapEdit: pixmapWidth and/or pixmapHeight is too\
                small (using 10 x 10).");
        new->bitmapEdit.pixmap_width_in_cells = 10;
        new->bitmapEdit.pixmap_height_in_cells = 10;
    }

    if (new->bitmapEdit.cell_size_in_pixels < 5) {
        XtWarning("BitmapEdit: cellSize is too small (using 5).");
        new->bitmapEdit.cell_size_in_pixels = 5;
    }

    if ((new->bitmapEdit.cur_x < 0) || (new->bitmapEdit.cur_y < 0)) {
        XtWarning("BitmapEdit: cur_x and cur_y must be non-negative\
                (using 0, 0).");
        new->bitmapEdit.cur_x = 0;
        new->bitmapEdit.cur_y = 0;
    }

    if (new->bitmapEdit.cell == NULL)
        new->bitmapEdit.cell = XtCalloc(
                new->bitmapEdit.pixmap_width_in_cells *
                new->bitmapEdit.pixmap_height_in_cells, sizeof(char));
    else
        new->bitmapEdit.user_allocated = True;/* user supplied cell array */

    new->bitmapEdit.pixmap_width_in_pixels =
            new->bitmapEdit.pixmap_width_in_cells *
            new->bitmapEdit.cell_size_in_pixels;

    new->bitmapEdit.pixmap_height_in_pixels =
            new->bitmapEdit.pixmap_height_in_cells *
            new->bitmapEdit.cell_size_in_pixels;

    /*
     * Motif Primitive sets width and height to provide enough room for
     * the highlight and shadow around a widget.  BitmapEdit
```

```
         * doesn't use these features.  A widget that did use these
         * features would *add* its desired dimensions to those set
         * by Primitive.  To use this widget with another widget set, remove
         * the following two lines.
         */
        new->core.width = 0;
        new->core.height = 0;

        if (new->core.width == 0) {
            if (new->bitmapEdit.show_all == False)
                new->core.width = (new->bitmapEdit.pixmap_width_in_pixels
                        > DEFAULTWIDTH) ? DEFAULTWIDTH :
                        (new->bitmapEdit.pixmap_width_in_pixels);
            else
                new->core.width = new->bitmapEdit.pixmap_width_in_pixels;
        }

        if (new->core.height == 0) {
            if (new->bitmapEdit.show_all == False)
                new->core.height =
                        (new->bitmapEdit.pixmap_height_in_pixels >
                        DEFAULTWIDTH) ? DEFAULTWIDTH :
                        (new->bitmapEdit.pixmap_height_in_pixels);
            else
                new->core.height = new->bitmapEdit.pixmap_height_in_pixels;
        }

        /* tell Primitive not to allow tabbing to this widget */
        XtVaSetValues(new,
                XmNtraversalOn, False,
                NULL);

        CreateBigPixmap(new);

        GetDrawGC(new);
        GetUndrawGC(new);
        GetCopyGC(new);

        DrawIntoBigPixmap(new);
}

/* ARGSUSED */
static void
Redisplay(w, event)
Widget w;
XExposeEvent *event;
{
    BitmapEditWidget cw = (BitmapEditWidget) w;
    register int x, y;
    unsigned int width, height;
    if (!XtIsRealized(cw))
        return;

    if (event) {  /* called from btn-event or expose */
        x = event->x;
        y = event->y;
        width = event->width;
        height =  event->height;
    }
```

xbitmap Application

```
    else {          /* called because complete redraw */
        x = 0;
        y = 0;
        width = cw->bitmapEdit.pixmap_width_in_pixels;
        height = cw->bitmapEdit.pixmap_height_in_pixels;
    }

    if (DefaultDepthOfScreen(XtScreen(cw)) == 1)
        XCopyArea(XtDisplay(cw), cw->bitmapEdit.big_picture,
                XtWindow(cw), cw->bitmapEdit.copy_gc, x +
                cw->bitmapEdit.cur_x, y + cw->bitmapEdit.cur_y,
                width, height, x, y);
    else
        XCopyPlane(XtDisplay(cw), cw->bitmapEdit.big_picture,
                XtWindow(cw), cw->bitmapEdit.copy_gc, x +
                cw->bitmapEdit.cur_x, y + cw->bitmapEdit.cur_y,
                width, height, x, y, 1);

}

/* ARGSUSED */
static Boolean
SetValues(current, request, new, args, num_args)
Widget current, request, new;
ArgList args;
Cardinal *num_args;
{
    BitmapEditWidget curcw = (BitmapEditWidget) current;
    BitmapEditWidget newcw = (BitmapEditWidget) new;
    Boolean do_redisplay = False;

    if (curcw->primitive.foreground != newcw->primitive.foreground) {
        XtReleaseGC(curcw, curcw->bitmapEdit.copy_gc);
        GetCopyGC(newcw);
        do_redisplay = True;
    }

    if ((curcw->bitmapEdit.cur_x != newcw->bitmapEdit.cur_x) ||
            (curcw->bitmapEdit.cur_y != newcw->bitmapEdit.cur_y))
        do_redisplay = True;

    if (curcw->bitmapEdit.cell_size_in_pixels !=
            newcw->bitmapEdit.cell_size_in_pixels) {
        ChangeCellSize(curcw, newcw->bitmapEdit.cell_size_in_pixels);
        do_redisplay = True;
    }

    if (curcw->bitmapEdit.pixmap_width_in_cells !=
            newcw->bitmapEdit.pixmap_width_in_cells) {
        newcw->bitmapEdit.pixmap_width_in_cells =
                curcw->bitmapEdit.pixmap_width_in_cells;
        XtWarning("BitmapEdit: pixmap_width_in_cells cannot be set\
                by XtSetValues.\n");
    }

    if (curcw->bitmapEdit.pixmap_height_in_cells !=
            newcw->bitmapEdit.pixmap_height_in_cells) {
        newcw->bitmapEdit.pixmap_height_in_cells =
                curcw->bitmapEdit.pixmap_height_in_cells;
        XtWarning("BitmapEdit: pixmap_height_in_cells cannot be set\
```

```
                  by XtSetValues.\n");
    }

    return do_redisplay;
}

static void
Destroy(w)
Widget w;
{
    BitmapEditWidget cw = (BitmapEditWidget) w;
    if (cw->bitmapEdit.big_picture)
        XFreePixmap(XtDisplay(cw), cw->bitmapEdit.big_picture);

    if (cw->bitmapEdit.draw_gc)
        XFreeGC(XtDisplay(cw), cw->bitmapEdit.draw_gc);

    if (cw->bitmapEdit.undraw_gc)
        XFreeGC(XtDisplay(cw), cw->bitmapEdit.undraw_gc);

    if (cw->bitmapEdit.copy_gc)
        XFreeGC(XtDisplay(cw), cw->bitmapEdit.copy_gc);

    /* Free memory allocated with Calloc.  This was done
     * only if application didn't supply cell array.
     */
    if (!cw->bitmapEdit.user_allocated)
        XtFree(cw->bitmapEdit.cell);
}

static void
DrawCell(w, event)
Widget w;
XEvent *event;
{
    BitmapEditWidget cw = (BitmapEditWidget) w;
    DrawPixmaps(cw->bitmapEdit.draw_gc, DRAW, cw, event);
}

static void
UndrawCell(w, event)
Widget w;
XEvent *event;
{
    BitmapEditWidget cw = (BitmapEditWidget) w;
    DrawPixmaps(cw->bitmapEdit.undraw_gc, UNDRAW, cw, event);
}

static void
ToggleCell(w, event)
Widget w;
XEvent *event;
{
    BitmapEditWidget cw = (BitmapEditWidget) w;
    static int oldx = -1, oldy = -1;
    GC gc;
    int mode;
    int newx, newy;

    /* This is strictly correct, but doesn't
```

```
       * seem to be necessary */
      if (event->type == ButtonPress) {
          newx = (cw->bitmapEdit.cur_x + ((XButtonEvent *)event)->x) /
          cw->bitmapEdit.cell_size_in_pixels;
          newy = (cw->bitmapEdit.cur_y + ((XButtonEvent *)event)->y) /
          cw->bitmapEdit.cell_size_in_pixels;
      }
      else {
          newx = (cw->bitmapEdit.cur_x + ((XMotionEvent *)event)->x) /
          cw->bitmapEdit.cell_size_in_pixels;
          newy = (cw->bitmapEdit.cur_y + ((XMotionEvent *)event)->y) /
          cw->bitmapEdit.cell_size_in_pixels;
      }

      if ((mode = cw->bitmapEdit.cell[newx + newy *
              cw->bitmapEdit.pixmap_width_in_cells ]) == DRAWN) {
          gc = cw->bitmapEdit.undraw_gc;
          mode = UNDRAW;
      }
      else {
          gc = cw->bitmapEdit.draw_gc;
          mode = DRAW;
      }
      if (oldx != newx || oldy != newy) {
          oldx = newx;
          oldy = newy;
          DrawPixmaps(gc, mode, cw, event);
      }
  }
}

static void
DrawPixmaps(gc, mode, w, event)
GC gc;
int mode;
Widget w;
XButtonEvent *event;
{
    BitmapEditWidget cw = (BitmapEditWidget) w;
    int newx = (cw->bitmapEdit.cur_x + event->x) /
            cw->bitmapEdit.cell_size_in_pixels;
    int newy = (cw->bitmapEdit.cur_y + event->y) /
            cw->bitmapEdit.cell_size_in_pixels;
    XExposeEvent fake_event;

    /* if already done, return */
    if (cw->bitmapEdit.cell[newx + newy *
            cw->bitmapEdit.pixmap_width_in_cells ] == mode)
        return;

    /* otherwise, draw or undraw */
    XFillRectangle(XtDisplay(cw), cw->bitmapEdit.big_picture, gc,
            cw->bitmapEdit.cell_size_in_pixels*newx + 2,
            cw->bitmapEdit.cell_size_in_pixels*newy + 2,
            (unsigned int)cw->bitmapEdit.cell_size_in_pixels - 3,
            (unsigned int)cw->bitmapEdit.cell_size_in_pixels - 3);

    cw->bitmapEdit.cell[newx + newy *
```

```
                    cw->bitmapEdit.pixmap_width_in_cells ] = mode;
        info.mode = mode;
        info.newx = newx;
        info.newy = newy;

        fake_event.x = cw->bitmapEdit.cell_size_in_pixels * newx -
                cw->bitmapEdit.cur_x;
        fake_event.y = cw->bitmapEdit.cell_size_in_pixels * newy -
                cw->bitmapEdit.cur_y;
        fake_event.width = cw->bitmapEdit.cell_size_in_pixels;
        fake_event.height = cw->bitmapEdit.cell_size_in_pixels;

        Redisplay(cw, &fake_event);
        XtCallCallbacks(cw, XtNtoggleCallback, &info);
}

CreateBigPixmap(w)
Widget w;
{
        BitmapEditWidget cw = (BitmapEditWidget) w;
        /* always a 1 bit deep pixmap, regardless of screen depth */
        cw->bitmapEdit.big_picture = XCreatePixmap(XtDisplay(cw),
                RootWindow(XtDisplay(cw), DefaultScreen(XtDisplay(cw))),
                cw->bitmapEdit.pixmap_width_in_pixels + 2,
                cw->bitmapEdit.pixmap_height_in_pixels + 2, 1);
}

DrawIntoBigPixmap(w)
Widget w;
{
        BitmapEditWidget cw = (BitmapEditWidget) w;
        int n_horiz_segments, n_vert_segments;
        XSegment segment[MAXLINES];
        register int x, y;

        XFillRectangle(XtDisplay(cw), cw->bitmapEdit.big_picture,
                cw->bitmapEdit.undraw_gc, 0, 0,
                cw->bitmapEdit.pixmap_width_in_pixels
                + 2, cw->bitmapEdit.pixmap_height_in_pixels + 2);

        n_horiz_segments = cw->bitmapEdit.pixmap_height_in_cells + 1;
        n_vert_segments = cw->bitmapEdit.pixmap_width_in_cells + 1;

        for (x = 0; x < n_horiz_segments; x++) {
            segment[x].x1 = 0;
            segment[x].x2 = (short) cw->bitmapEdit.pixmap_width_in_pixels;
            segment[x].y1 = (short) cw->bitmapEdit.cell_size_in_pixels * x;
            segment[x].y2 = (short) cw->bitmapEdit.cell_size_in_pixels * x;
        }
        XDrawSegments(XtDisplay(cw), cw->bitmapEdit.big_picture,
                cw->bitmapEdit.draw_gc, segment, n_horiz_segments);

        for (y = 0; y < n_vert_segments; y++) {
            segment[y].x1 = (short) y * cw->bitmapEdit.cell_size_in_pixels;
            segment[y].x2 = (short) y * cw->bitmapEdit.cell_size_in_pixels;
            segment[y].y1 = 0;
            segment[y].y2 = (short) cw->bitmapEdit.pixmap_height_in_pixels;
        }
```

xbitmap Application

```
        XDrawSegments(XtDisplay(cw), cw->bitmapEdit.big_picture,
                cw->bitmapEdit.draw_gc, segment, n_vert_segments);

    /* draw current cell array into pixmap */
    for (x = 0; x < cw->bitmapEdit.pixmap_width_in_cells; x++) {
        for (y = 0; y < cw->bitmapEdit.pixmap_height_in_cells; y++) {
            if (cw->bitmapEdit.cell[x + (y *
                    cw->bitmapEdit.pixmap_width_in_cells)] == DRAWN)
                DoCell(cw, x, y, cw->bitmapEdit.draw_gc);
            else
                DoCell(cw, x, y, cw->bitmapEdit.undraw_gc);
        }
    }
}

/* A Public function, not static */
char *
BitmapEditGetArray(w, width_in_cells, height_in_cells)
Widget w;
int *width_in_cells, *height_in_cells;
{
    BitmapEditWidget cw = (BitmapEditWidget) w;

    *width_in_cells = cw->bitmapEdit.pixmap_width_in_cells;
    *height_in_cells = cw->bitmapEdit.pixmap_height_in_cells;
    return (cw->bitmapEdit.cell);
}

/* ARGSUSED */
static void
Resize(w)
Widget w;
{
    BitmapEditWidget cw = (BitmapEditWidget) w;
    /* resize does nothing unless new size is bigger than entire pixmap */
    if ((cw->core.width > cw->bitmapEdit.pixmap_width_in_pixels) &&
            (cw->core.height > cw->bitmapEdit.pixmap_height_in_pixels)) {
        /*
         * Calculate the maximum cell size that will allow the
         * entire bitmap to be displayed.
         */
        Dimension w_temp_cell_size_in_pixels, h_temp_cell_size_in_pixels;
        Dimension new_cell_size_in_pixels;

        w_temp_cell_size_in_pixels =
                cw->core.width / cw->bitmapEdit.pixmap_width_in_cells;
        h_temp_cell_size_in_pixels =
                cw->core.height / cw->bitmapEdit.pixmap_height_in_cells;

        if (w_temp_cell_size_in_pixels < h_temp_cell_size_in_pixels)
            new_cell_size_in_pixels = w_temp_cell_size_in_pixels;
        else
            new_cell_size_in_pixels = h_temp_cell_size_in_pixels;

        /* if size change mandates a new pixmap, make one */
        if (new_cell_size_in_pixels != cw->bitmapEdit.cell_size_in_pixels)
            ChangeCellSize(cw, new_cell_size_in_pixels);
    }
}
```

```
static void
ChangeCellSize(w, new_cell_size)
Widget w;
int new_cell_size;
{
    BitmapEditWidget cw = (BitmapEditWidget) w;
    int x, y;

    cw->bitmapEdit.cell_size_in_pixels = new_cell_size;

    /* recalculate variables based on cell size */
    cw->bitmapEdit.pixmap_width_in_pixels =
            cw->bitmapEdit.pixmap_width_in_cells *
            cw->bitmapEdit.cell_size_in_pixels;

    cw->bitmapEdit.pixmap_height_in_pixels =
            cw->bitmapEdit.pixmap_height_in_cells *
            cw->bitmapEdit.cell_size_in_pixels;

    /* destroy old and create new pixmap of correct size */
    XFreePixmap(XtDisplay(cw), cw->bitmapEdit.big_picture);
    CreateBigPixmap(cw);

    /* draw lines into new pixmap */
    DrawIntoBigPixmap(cw);

    /* draw current cell array into pixmap */
    for (x = 0; x < cw->bitmapEdit.pixmap_width_in_cells; x++) {
        for (y = 0; y < cw->bitmapEdit.pixmap_height_in_cells; y++) {
            if (cw->bitmapEdit.cell[x + (y *
                    ppcw->bitmapEdit.pixmap_width_in_cells)] == DRAWN)
                DoCell(cw, x, y, cw->bitmapEdit.draw_gc);
            else
                DoCell(cw, x, y, cw->bitmapEdit.undraw_gc);
        }
    }
}

static void
DoCell(w, x, y, gc)
Widget w;
int x, y;
GC gc;
{
    BitmapEditWidget cw = (BitmapEditWidget) w;
        /* otherwise, draw or undraw */
    XFillRectangle(XtDisplay(cw), cw->bitmapEdit.big_picture, gc,
            cw->bitmapEdit.cell_size_in_pixels * x + 2,
            cw->bitmapEdit.cell_size_in_pixels * y + 2,
            (unsigned int)cw->bitmapEdit.cell_size_in_pixels - 3,
            (unsigned int)cw->bitmapEdit.cell_size_in_pixels - 3);

}

static XtGeometryResult QueryGeometry(w, proposed, answer)
Widget w;
XtWidgetGeometry *proposed, *answer;
{
    BitmapEditWidget cw = (BitmapEditWidget) w;
```

```
        /* set fields we care about */
        answer->request_mode = CWWidth | CWHeight;

        /* initial width and height */
        if (cw->bitmapEdit.show_all == True)
            answer->width = cw->bitmapEdit.pixmap_width_in_pixels;
        else
            answer->width = (cw->bitmapEdit.pixmap_width_in_pixels >
                    DEFAULTWIDTH) ? DEFAULTWIDTH :
                    cw->bitmapEdit.pixmap_width_in_pixels;

        if (cw->bitmapEdit.show_all == True)
            answer->height = cw->bitmapEdit.pixmap_height_in_pixels;
        else
            answer->height = (cw->bitmapEdit.pixmap_height_in_pixels >
                    DEFAULTWIDTH) ? DEFAULTWIDTH :
                    cw->bitmapEdit.pixmap_height_in_pixels;

        if (   ((proposed->request_mode & (CWWidth | CWHeight))
                == (CWWidth | CWHeight)) &&
                proposed->width == answer->width &&
                proposed->height == answer->height)
            return XtGeometryYes;
        else if (answer->width == cw->core.width &&
                answer->height == cw->core.height)
            return XtGeometryNo;
        else
            return XtGeometryAlmost;
}
```

E.2 The BitmapEdiP.h Private Header File

Example E-2. BitmapEdiP.h: complete private header file

```
/*
 * BitmapEditP.h - Private definitions for BitmapEdit widget
 */

#ifndef _ORABitmapEditP_h
#define _ORABitmapEditP_h

/*
 * Include private header file of superclass.
 */
#include <Xm/PrimitiveP.h>

/*
 * Include public header file for this widget.
 */
```

```
#include "BitmapEdit.h"

/* New fields for the BitmapEdit widget class record */

typedef struct {
    int make_compiler_happy;      /* keep compiler happy */
} BitmapEditClassPart;

/* Full class record declaration */
typedef struct _BitmapEditClassRec {
    CoreClassPart       core_class;
    XmPrimitiveClassPart    primitive_class;
    BitmapEditClassPart     bitmapEdit_class;
} BitmapEditClassRec;

extern BitmapEditClassRec bitmapEditClassRec;

/* New fields for the BitmapEdit widget record */
typedef struct {
    /* resources */
    Pixel    foreground;
    XtCallbackList callback;/* application installed callback function(s) */
    Dimension     pixmap_width_in_cells;
    Dimension     pixmap_height_in_cells;
    int cell_size_in_pixels;
    int cur_x, cur_y;       /* position of visible corner in big pixmap */
    char *cell;             /* array for keeping track of array of bits */
    Boolean show_all;       /* whether bitmap should display entire bitmap */

    /* private state */
    Dimension     pixmap_width_in_pixels;
    Dimension     pixmap_height_in_pixels;
    Pixmap big_picture;
    GC       draw_gc;       /* one plane, for drawing into pixmap */
    GC       undraw_gc;     /* one plane, for drawing into pixmap */
    GC       copy_gc; /* defaultdepthofscreen, for copy'g pixmap into window */
    Boolean user_allocated; /* whether user allocated cell array */
} BitmapEditPart;

/*
 * Full instance record declaration
 */
typedef struct _BitmapEditRec {
    CorePart            core;
    XmPrimitivePart     primitive;
    BitmapEditPart      bitmapEdit;
} BitmapEditRec;

#endif /* _ORABitmapEditP_h */
```

E.3 The BitmapEdit.h Public Header File

Example E-3. BitmapEdit.h: complete public header file

```
#ifndef _ORABitmapEdit_h
#define _ORABitmapEdit_h

/* BitmapEdit Widget public include file */

/*
 * The public header file for the immediate superclass normally
 * must be included.  However, not in this case because the public
 * header file for Primitive is in Xm.h, which is already included
 * in all Motif applications.
 */

/* #include <Xm/Superclass.h>  */

/*
 * This public structure is used as call_data to the callback.
 * It passes the x, y position of the cell toggled (in units of
 * cells, not pixels) and a mode flag that indicates whether the
 * cell was turned on (1) or off (0).
 */
typedef struct {
    int mode;
    int newx;
    int newy;
} BitmapEditPointInfo;

#define XtNtoggleCallback "toggleCallback"
#define XtNcellSizeInPixels "cellSizeInPixels"
#define XtNpixmapWidthInCells "pixmapWidthInCells"
#define XtNpixmapHeightInCells "pixmapHeightInCells"
#define XtNcurX "curX"
#define XtNcurY "curY"
#define XtNcellArray "cellArray"
#define XtNshowEntireBitmap "showEntireBitmap"

#define XtCToggleCallback "ToggleCallback"
#define XtCCellSizeInPixels "CellSizeInPixels"
#define XtCPixmapWidthInCells "PixmapWidthInCells"
#define XtCPixmapHeightInCells "PixmapHeightInCells"
#define XtCCurX "CurX"
#define XtCCurY "CurY"
#define XtCCellArray "CellArray"
#define XtCShowEntireBitmap "ShowEntireBitmap"

extern char *BitmapEditGetArray(); /* w */
    /* Widget w; */

/* Class record constants */
extern WidgetClass bitmapEditWidgetClass;

typedef struct _BitmapEditClassRec *BitmapEditWidgetClass;
typedef struct _BitmapEditRec      *BitmapEditWidget;

#endif /* _ORABitmapEdit_h */
/* DON'T ADD STUFF AFTER THIS #endif */
```

E.4 xbitmap5

Example E-4. xbitmap5: complete application code

```
/*
 * Copyright 1989 O'Reilly and Associates, Inc.
 * See ../Copyright for complete rights and liability information.
 */

/*
 *  xbitmap5.c - bitmap in main window with small pixmaps
 */

/*
 *  So that we can use fprintf:
 */
#include <stdio.h>

/*
 * Standard Toolkit include files:
 */
#include <X11/Intrinsic.h>
#include <Xm/Xm.h>

/*
 * Public include files for widgets used in this file.
 */
#include <Xm/PanedW.h>     /* paned window */
#include <Xm/PushB.h>      /* push button */
#include <Xm/MessageB.h>   /* message box */
#include <Xm/CascadeB.h>   /* cascade button */
#include <Xm/RowColumn.h>  /* row column (for menus) */
#include <Xm/DrawingA.h>   /* drawing area */
#include <Xm/Form.h>       /* pixmap box */
#include <Xm/Frame.h>      /* frame */
#include <Xm/ScrolledW.h>  /* scrolled window */

#include "BitmapEdit.h"

#define DRAWN 1
#define UNDRAWN 0

struct {
    GC draw_gc, undraw_gc, invert_gc;
    Pixmap normal_bitmap, reverse_bitmap;
    Widget showNormalBitmap, showReverseBitmap;
    String filename;     /* filename to read and write */
    Dimension pixmap_width_in_cells, pixmap_height_in_cells;
} bitmap_stuff;

static Boolean file_contained_good_data = False;

static void CellToggled(), SetUpThings();

/*ARGSUSED*/
static void
RedrawSmallPicture(w, client_data, call_data)
Widget w;
XtPointer client_data;
XtPointer call_data;
{
```

```
    Pixmap pixmap;

    if (w == bitmap_stuff.showNormalBitmap)
        pixmap = bitmap_stuff.normal_bitmap;
    else
        pixmap = bitmap_stuff.reverse_bitmap;

    if (DefaultDepthOfScreen(XtScreen(w)) == 1)
        XCopyArea(XtDisplay(w), pixmap, XtWindow(w),
                DefaultGCOfScreen(XtScreen(w)), 0, 0,
                bitmap_stuff.pixmap_width_in_cells,
            bitmap_stuff.pixmap_height_in_cells,
                0, 0);
    else
        XCopyPlane(XtDisplay(w), pixmap, XtWindow(w),
                DefaultGCOfScreen(XtScreen(w)), 0, 0,
                bitmap_stuff.pixmap_width_in_cells,
            bitmap_stuff.pixmap_height_in_cells,
                0, 0, 1);
}
/*
 * The printout routine writes the data into a standard X11 bitmap file.
 */
/* ARGSUSED */
static void
PrintOut(widget, client_data, call_data)
Widget widget;
XtPointer client_data;   /* unused */
XtPointer call_data;     /* unused */
{
    XWriteBitmapFile(XtDisplay(widget), bitmap_stuff.filename,
            bitmap_stuff.normal_bitmap,
            bitmap_stuff.pixmap_width_in_cells,
            bitmap_stuff.pixmap_height_in_cells, 0, 0);
}

String
FillCell(w)
Widget w;
{
    String cell;
    int x, y;
    XImage *image;

    cell = XtCalloc(bitmap_stuff.pixmap_width_in_cells
            * bitmap_stuff.pixmap_height_in_cells, sizeof(char));

    /* Convert pixmap into image, so that we can
     * read individual pixels */
    image = XGetImage(XtDisplay(w), bitmap_stuff.normal_bitmap, 0, 0,
                bitmap_stuff.pixmap_width_in_cells,
                bitmap_stuff.pixmap_height_in_cells,
                AllPlanes, XYPixmap);

    for (x = 0; x < bitmap_stuff.pixmap_width_in_cells; x++) {
        for (y = 0; y < bitmap_stuff.pixmap_height_in_cells; y++) {
            cell[x + (y * bitmap_stuff.pixmap_width_in_cells)] =
                        XGetPixel(image, x, y);
```

```
        }
    }
    return(cell);
}

/*
 * callback to pop up help dialog widget
 */
/*ARGSUSED*/
void ShowHelp(w, client_data, call_data)
Widget w;
XtPointer client_data;
XtPointer call_data;
{
    Widget dialog = (Widget) client_data;
    XtManageChild(dialog);
}

/*
 * quit button callback function
 */
/*ARGSUSED*/
void Quit(w, client_data, call_data)
Widget w;
XtPointer client_data, call_data;
{
    exit(0);
}

main(argc, argv)
int argc;
char **argv;
{
    XtAppContext app_context;
    Widget topLevel, mainWindow, menuBar;
    Widget fileButton, fileMenu, quit, helpButton, helpMenu,
                 help, helpBox;
    Widget temp;
    Widget bigBitmap, output, smallPixmapBox;
    Widget scrolledWin, frame1, frame2;
    Arg args[5];
    int i;
    unsigned int width, height;
    int junk;
    String cell;

    /* never call a Widget variable "exit"! */
    extern exit();

    static XrmOptionDescRec table[] = {
        {"-pw",            "*pixmapWidthInCells",    XrmoptionSepArg, NULL},
        {"-pixmapwidth",   "*pixmapWidthInCells",    XrmoptionSepArg, NULL},
        {"-ph",            "*pixmapHeightInCells",   XrmoptionSepArg, NULL},
        {"-pixmapheight",  "*pixmapHeightInCells",   XrmoptionSepArg, NULL},
        {"-cellsize",      "*cellSizeInPixels",      XrmoptionSepArg, NULL},

    };

    XtSetLanguageProc(NULL, (XtLanguageProc)NULL, NULL);
```

xbitmap Application

```
    topLevel = XtVaAppInitialize(
            &app_context,               /* Application context */
            "XBitmap5",                 /* Application class */
            table, XtNumber(table),     /* command line option list */
            &argc, argv,                /* command line args */
            NULL,                       /* for missing app-defaults file */
            NULL);                      /* terminate varargs list */

    if (argv[1] != NULL)
        bitmap_stuff.filename = argv[1];
    else {
        fprintf(stderr, "xbitmap: must specify filename on command line\n");
        exit(1);
    }

    /* create main window */
    mainWindow = XtVaCreateManagedWidget(
            "mainWindow",                   /* widget name */
            xmPanedWindowWidgetClass,       /* widget class */
            topLevel,                       /* parent widget */
            NULL);                          /* terminate varargs list */

    /* create menu bar along top inside of main window */
    menuBar = XmCreateMenuBar(
            mainWindow, /* parent widget */
            "menuBar",  /* widget name */
            NULL,       /* no arguments needed */
            0);         /* no arguments needed */
    XtManageChild(menuBar);

    scrolledWin = XtVaCreateManagedWidget("scrolledWin",
            xmScrolledWindowWidgetClass, mainWindow,
            NULL);

    switch (XReadBitmapFile(XtDisplay(topLevel),
            RootWindowOfScreen(XtScreen(topLevel)), bitmap_stuff.filename,
            &width, &height, &bitmap_stuff.normal_bitmap, &junk, &junk)) {
    case BitmapSuccess:
        file_contained_good_data = True;
        if ((bitmap_stuff.pixmap_width_in_cells != width) ||
                    (bitmap_stuff.pixmap_height_in_cells != height)) {
            i = 0;
            XtSetArg(args[i], XtNpixmapWidthInCells, width);    i++;
            XtSetArg(args[i], XtNpixmapHeightInCells, height);   i++;
            bitmap_stuff.pixmap_width_in_cells = width;
            bitmap_stuff.pixmap_height_in_cells = height;
            cell = FillCell(topLevel);
            XtSetArg(args[i], XtNcellArray, cell);   i++;
        }
        break;
    case BitmapOpenFailed:
        fprintf(stderr,
          "xbitmap: could not open bitmap file, using fresh bitmap.\n");
        i = 0;
        file_contained_good_data = False;
        break;
    case BitmapFileInvalid:
```

```
        fprintf(stderr, "xbitmap: bitmap file invalid.\n");
        exit(1);
    case BitmapNoMemory:
        fprintf(stderr,
          "xbitmap: insufficient server memory to create bitmap.\n");
        exit(1);
    default:
        fprintf(stderr, "xbitmap: programming error.\n");
        exit(1);
    }

    bigBitmap = XtCreateManagedWidget("bigBitmap",
            bitmapEditWidgetClass, scrolledWin, args, i);

    XtAddCallback(bigBitmap, XtNtoggleCallback, CellToggled, NULL);

    if (!file_contained_good_data) {
        XtVaGetValues(bigBitmap,
            XtNpixmapWidthInCells, &bitmap_stuff.pixmap_width_in_cells,
            XtNpixmapHeightInCells, &bitmap_stuff.pixmap_height_in_cells,
            NULL);
    }

    /*
     *  CREATE FILE MENU AND CHILDREN
     */
    /* create button that will pop up the menu */
    fileButton = XtVaCreateManagedWidget(
            "fileButton",              /* widget name */
            xmCascadeButtonWidgetClass, /* widget class */
            menuBar,                    /* parent widget */
            NULL);                      /* terminate varargs list */

    /* create menu (really a Shell widget and RowColumn widget combo) */
    fileMenu = XmCreatePulldownMenu(
            menuBar,   /* parent widget */
            "fileMenu", /* widget name */
            NULL,      /* no argument list needed */
            0);        /* no argument list needed */

    /*
     *  CREATE BUTTON TO OUTPUT BITMAP
     */
    /* create button that will pop up the menu */
    output = XtVaCreateManagedWidget(
            "output",                 /* widget name */
            xmPushButtonWidgetClass,   /* widget class */
            fileMenu,                  /* parent widget */
            NULL);                     /* terminate varargs list */

    XtAddCallback(output, XmNactivateCallback, PrintOut, 0);

    /* create the quit button up in the menu */
    quit = XtVaCreateManagedWidget(
            "quit",                   /* widget name */
            xmPushButtonWidgetClass,   /* widget class */
            fileMenu,                  /* parent widget */
            NULL);                     /* terminate varargs list */

    /*
```

xbitmap Application

```
     * Specify which menu fileButton will pop up.
     */
    XtVaSetValues(fileButton,
            XmNsubMenuId, fileMenu,
            NULL);

    /* arrange for quit button to call function that exits. */
    XtAddCallback(quit, XmNactivateCallback, Quit, 0);

    /*
     *   CREATE HELP BUTTON AND BOX
     */
    /* create button that will bring up help menu */
    helpButton = XtVaCreateManagedWidget( "helpButton",
        xmCascadeButtonWidgetClass, menuBar, NULL);

    /* tell menuBar which is the help button (will be specially positioned) */
    XtVaSetValues(menuBar,
            XmNmenuHelpWidget, helpButton,
            NULL);

    /* create menu (really a Shell widget and RowColumn widget combo) */
    helpMenu = XmCreatePulldownMenu( menuBar,
            "helpMenu", NULL, 0);

    /* create the help button up in the menu */
    help = XtVaCreateManagedWidget( "help",
            xmPushButtonWidgetClass, helpMenu, NULL);

    /*
     * Specify which menu helpButton will pop up.
     */
    XtVaSetValues(helpButton,
            XmNsubMenuId, helpMenu,
            NULL);

    /* create popup that will contain help */
    helpBox = XmCreateMessageDialog(
            help,        /* parent widget */
            "helpBox",   /* widget name   */
            NULL,        /* no arguments needed */
            0);          /* no arguments needed */

    temp = XmMessageBoxGetChild (helpBox, XmDIALOG_CANCEL_BUTTON);
    XtUnmanageChild (temp);
    temp = XmMessageBoxGetChild (helpBox, XmDIALOG_HELP_BUTTON);
    XtUnmanageChild (temp);

    /* arrange for getHelp button to pop up helpBox */
    XtAddCallback(help, XmNactivateCallback, ShowHelp, helpBox);

    smallPixmapBox = XtVaCreateManagedWidget("smallPixmapBox",
            xmFormWidgetClass, mainWindow,
            NULL);

    frame1 = XtVaCreateManagedWidget("frameNormal",
            xmFrameWidgetClass, smallPixmapBox,
            XmNleftAttachment, XmATTACH_FORM,
            NULL);

    SetUpThings(topLevel);
```

```
    bitmap_stuff.showNormalBitmap = XtVaCreateManagedWidget("showNormalBitmap",
            xmDrawingAreaWidgetClass, frame1,
            XmNwidth, bitmap_stuff.pixmap_width_in_cells,
            XmNheight, bitmap_stuff.pixmap_height_in_cells,
            NULL);

    frame2 = XtVaCreateManagedWidget("frameReverse",
            xmFrameWidgetClass, smallPixmapBox,
            XmNleftAttachment, XmATTACH_WIDGET,
            XmNleftWidget, frame1,
            NULL);

    bitmap_stuff.showReverseBitmap = XtVaCreateManagedWidget("showReverseBitmap",
            xmDrawingAreaWidgetClass, frame2,
            XmNwidth, bitmap_stuff.pixmap_width_in_cells,
            XmNheight, bitmap_stuff.pixmap_height_in_cells,
            NULL);

    XtAddCallback(bitmap_stuff.showNormalBitmap, XmNexposeCallback,
            RedrawSmallPicture, NULL);

    XtAddCallback(bitmap_stuff.showReverseBitmap, XmNexposeCallback,
            RedrawSmallPicture, NULL);

    XtRealizeWidget(topLevel);

    XtAppMainLoop(app_context);
}

static void
SetUpThings(w)
Widget w;
{
    XGCValues values;

    if (!file_contained_good_data) {
      bitmap_stuff.normal_bitmap = XCreatePixmap(XtDisplay(w),
            RootWindowOfScreen(XtScreen(w)),
            bitmap_stuff.pixmap_width_in_cells,
            bitmap_stuff.pixmap_height_in_cells, 1);
    }

    values.foreground = 1;
    values.background = 0;
    /* note that normal_bitmap is used as the drawable because it
     * is one bit deep.  The root window may not be one bit deep */
    bitmap_stuff.draw_gc = XCreateGC(XtDisplay(w),
            bitmap_stuff.normal_bitmap,
            GCForeground | GCBackground, &values);

    values.foreground = 0;
    values.background = 1;
    bitmap_stuff.undraw_gc = XCreateGC(XtDisplay(w),
            bitmap_stuff.normal_bitmap,
            GCForeground | GCBackground, &values);

    bitmap_stuff.reverse_bitmap = XCreatePixmap(XtDisplay(w),
            RootWindowOfScreen(XtScreen(w)),
            bitmap_stuff.pixmap_width_in_cells,
            bitmap_stuff.pixmap_height_in_cells, 1);
```

xbitmap Application

```
        if (file_contained_good_data) {
            XImage *image;
            int x, y;

            image = XGetImage (XtDisplay(w), bitmap_stuff.normal_bitmap, 0, 0,
                bitmap_stuff.pixmap_width_in_cells,
                bitmap_stuff.pixmap_height_in_cells,
                AllPlanes, XYPixmap);

            for (x = 0; x < bitmap_stuff.pixmap_width_in_cells; x++) {
                for (y = 0; y < bitmap_stuff.pixmap_height_in_cells; y++) {
                    XDrawPoint(XtDisplay(w), bitmap_stuff.reverse_bitmap,
                            ((XGetPixel(image, x, y) == DRAWN) ?
                            bitmap_stuff.undraw_gc :
                            bitmap_stuff.draw_gc), x, y);
                }
            }
        }
        else {
        /* pixmaps must be cleared - may contain garbage */
          XFillRectangle(XtDisplay(w),
                bitmap_stuff.reverse_bitmap, bitmap_stuff.draw_gc,
                0, 0, bitmap_stuff.pixmap_width_in_cells + 1,
                bitmap_stuff.pixmap_height_in_cells + 1);
          XFillRectangle(XtDisplay(w),
                bitmap_stuff.normal_bitmap, bitmap_stuff.undraw_gc,
                0, 0, bitmap_stuff.pixmap_width_in_cells + 1,
                bitmap_stuff.pixmap_height_in_cells + 1);
        }
}

/* ARGSUSED */
static void
CellToggled(w, client_data, call_data)
Widget w;
XtPointer client_data;   /* unused */
XtPointer call_data;     /* will be cast to cur_info */
{
    /* cast pointer to needed type: */
    BitmapEditPointInfo *cur_info = (BitmapEditPointInfo *) call_data;
    /*
     * Note, BitmapEditPointInfo is defined in BitmapEdit.h
     */

    XDrawPoint(XtDisplay(w), bitmap_stuff.normal_bitmap,
            ((cur_info->mode == DRAWN) ? bitmap_stuff.draw_gc :
            bitmap_stuff.undraw_gc), cur_info->newx, cur_info->newy);
    XDrawPoint(XtDisplay(w), bitmap_stuff.reverse_bitmap,
            ((cur_info->mode == DRAWN) ? bitmap_stuff.undraw_gc :
            bitmap_stuff.draw_gc), cur_info->newx, cur_info->newy);

    RedrawSmallPicture(bitmap_stuff.showNormalBitmap,
            cur_info->newx, cur_info->newy);
    RedrawSmallPicture(bitmap_stuff.showReverseBitmap,
            cur_info->newx, cur_info->newy);
}
```

F

Sources of Additional Information

This appendix describes where you can get more information about Xlib and about X in general, including other books on the subject and the various ways to get the source code for X.

In This Appendix:

Sources of Additional Information

This appendix lists a few of the official and unofficial sources for information about the X
Window System and associated software.

Note that some of this detailed information may become dated rather quickly. The best
source of current information is the *comp.windows.x* network news group, described later in
this appendix.

F.1 Getting the X Software

At this writing, the current public release level is Release 5. This book documents Release 4
and Release 5. Many people will continue to use R4 for a while, since there is a considerable
lag time between the date that MIT distributes a new release and the date by which vendors
integrate that release into their own products and issue updates. All changes to Xlib in R5
are backwards compatible, although there are many new interfaces that provide additional
capabilities.

You can get the X software directly from MIT on three 9-track 1600-BPI magtapes written in
UNIX *tar* format or on one 9-track 6250-BPI magtape, along with printed copies of MIT's
manuals, by sending a check in U.S. currency for U.S. $400 to:

> MIT Software Distribution Center
> Technology Licensing Office
> MIT E32-300
> 77 Massachusetts Avenue
> Cambridge, MA 02139

Their telephone number is (617) 253-6966, and the "X Ordering Hotline" is (617) 258-8330.
If you want the tapes and manuals shipped overseas, the price is $500. The manual set alone
is $125, including U.S. shipping, or $175, including overseas shipping.

Other distribution media or formats are not available from the MIT Software Distribution
Center but are from other independent vendors such as ICS, mentioned later. The Release
tape comes with source code for sample servers for Apollo, DEC, HP, IBM, Sony, Sun, and
several other workstations, source code for clients written by MIT, sources for the toolkits
Xt, XView, Interviews, and Andrew, contributed software written outside MIT, and sources
and Postscript files for all MIT's documentation. Note that the servers supplied are sample

servers only; commercial vendors typically release optimized (faster) servers for the same machines.

Sites that have access to the Internet can retrieve the distribution from the following machines using anonymous *ftp*. Here are the current sites:

Location	Hostname	Address	Directory
Western USA	*gatekeeper.dec.com*	16.1.0.2	*pub/X11/R5*
Eastern USA	*ftp.uu.net*	192.48.96.9	*X/R5*
		137.39.1.9	*X/R5*
Northeastern USA	*export.lcs.mit.edu*	18.24.0.12	*pub/R5*
	crl.dec.com	192.58.206.2	*pub/X11/R5*
Central USA	*mordred.cs.purdue.edu*	128.10.2.2	*pub/X11/R5*
	giza.cis.ohio-state.edu	128.146.8.52	*pub/X.V11R5*
Southern USA	*wuarchive.wustl.edu*	129.252.135.4	*packages/X11R5*
UK (Janet)	*src.doc.ic.ac.uk*	146.169.2.1	*X*
Australia	*munnari.oz.au*	128.250.1.21	*X.V11/R5*
		192.43.207.1	*X.V11/R5*

DO NOT do anonymous *ftp* during normal business hours, and please use the machine nearest you.

The distribution is also available by UUCP from UUNET for sites without Internet access. The files are split up to be small enough for UUCP distribution.

F.1.1 Bug Fixes

Critical bug fixes as well as a limited number of important new features are available from the archive server *xstuff@expo.lcs.mit.edu*. Electronic mail sent to this address is forwarded to a program which responds with the requested information. The rest of this section and the two sections that follow it explain how to use *xstuff*.

The *xstuff* server is a mail-response program. This means that you mail it a request and it mails back the response.

The *xstuff* server is a very dumb program. It does not have much error checking. If you do not send it commands that it understands, it will just answer "I don't understand you."

The *xstuff* server reads your entire message before it does anything, so you can have several different commands in a single message. It treats the "Subject:" header line just like any other line of the message. You can use any combination of upper and lowercase letters in the commands.

The archives are organized into a series of directories and subdirectories. Each directory has an index, and each subdirectory has an index. The top-level index gives you an overview of what is in the subdirectories, and the index for each subdirectory tells you what it contains.

If you are bored with reading documentation and just want to try something, then send the server a message containing the line:

```
send index fixes
```

When you get the index back, it will contain the numbers of all of the fixes and batches of fixes in the archive. Then you can send the server another message asking it to send you the fixes that you want:

```
send fixes 1 5 9 11-20
```

If you are using a mailer that understands "@" notation, send to *xstuff@expo.lcs.mit.edu*. If your mailer deals in "!" notation, try sending to *{someplace}!eddie!expo.lcs.mit.edu!xstuff*. For other mailers, you're on your own.

The server has four commands. Each command must be the first word on a line.

help   The command *help* or *send help* causes the server to send you the help file. No other commands are honored in a message that asks for help (the server figures that you had better read the help message before you do anything else).

index   If your message contains a line whose first word is *index*, then the server will send you the top-level index of the contents of the archive. If there are other words on that line that match the names of subdirectories, then the indexes for those sub-directories are sent instead of the top-level index. For example, you can say:

```
index
```

or:

```
index fixes
```

You can then send back another message to the *xstuff* server, using a *send* command (see below) to ask it to send you the files whose names you learned from that list.

index fixes and *send index fixes* mean the same thing: you can use *send* instead of *index* for getting an index.

If your message has an *index* or a *send index* command, then all other *send* commands will be ignored. This means that you cannot get an index and data in the same request. This is so that index requests can be given high priority.

send   If your message contains a line whose first word is *send*, then the *xstuff* server will send you the item(s) named on the rest of the line. To name an item, you give its directory and its name. For example:

```
send fixes 1-10
```

Once you have named a category, you can put as many names as you like on the rest of the line. They will all be taken from that category. For example:

```
send fixes 1-10 11-20 21-30
```

Each *send* command can reference only one directory. If you would like to get one fix and one of something else, you must use two *send* commands.

You may put as many *send* commands as you like into one message to the server, but the more you ask for, the longer it will take to receive. See Section F.1.1.2 for an explanation. Actually, it is not strictly true that you can put as many *send* commands as you want into one message. If the server must use UUCP mail to send your files, then it cannot send more than 100K bytes in one message. If you ask for more than it can send, then it will send as much as it can and ignore the rest.

path   The *path* command exists to help in case you do not get responses from the server when you mail to it.

Sometimes the server is unable to return mail over the incoming path. There are dozens of reasons why this might happen, and if you are a true wizard, you already know what those reasons are. If you are an apprentice wizard, you might not know all the reasons, but you might know a way to circumvent them.

If you put in a *path* command, then everything that the server mails to you will be mailed to that address rather than to the return address on your mail. The server host *expo.lcs.mit.edu* does not have a direct UUCP connection to anywhere; you must go through *mit-eddie* (the UUCP name of *eddie.mit.edu*) or somewhere else.

F.1.1.1 Notes

The *xstuff* server acknowledges every request by return mail. If you do not get a message back in a day or two, you should assume that something is going wrong and perhaps try a *path* command.

The *xstuff* server does not respond to requests from users named *root*, *system*, *daemon*, or *mailer*. This is to prevent mail loops. If your name is "Bruce Root" or "Jane Daemon" and you can document this, we will happily rewrite the server to remove this restriction. Yes, we know about Norman Mailer and Waverley Root. Norman doesn't use netmail and Waverley is dead.

F.1.1.2 Fairness

The *xstuff* server contains many safeguards to ensure that it is not monopolized by people asking for large amounts of data. The mailer is set up so that it will send no more than a fixed amount of data each day. If the work queue contains more requests than the day's quota, then the unsent files will not be processed until the next day. Whenever the mailer is run to send its day's quota, it sends the shortest requests out first.

If you have a request waiting in the work queue and you send in another request, the new request is added to the old one (thereby increasing its size) rather than being filed anew. This prevents you from being able to send in a large number of small requests as a way of beating the system.

The reason for all of these quotas and limitations is that the delivery resources are finite, and there are many people who would like to make use of the archive.

F.2 Netnews

The Usenet network newsgroup and mailing lists are probably the most valuable source of information abouta X. The current list of public mailing lists that discuss X is as follows:

News Group	Description
motif@lobo.gsfc.nasa.gov	People interested in the OSF's Motif X toolkit. This mailing list is also gatewayed to the Usenet newsgroup *comp.windows.x.motif*. If you receive that newsgroup, you don't need to get this mailing list.
x11-3D@x.org	People interested in X and 3-D graphics.
x-ada@x.org	X and ada.
ximage@x.org	People interested in image processing and X.
xpert@x.org	General discussion of X. This mailing list is also gatewayed to the Usenet newsgroup *comp.windows.x*. If you receive that newsgroup, you don't need to get this mailing list.
openlook@unify.com	Discussion of the OPEN LOOK graphical user interface and its various implementations. This mailing list is also gatewayed to the Usenet newsgroup *comp.windows.openlook*. If you receive that newsgroup, you don't need to get this mailing list.
xvideo@x.org	Discussion of video extensions for X.

First ask your site administrator whether you can get these news groups locally. Requests to have the Motif mailing list mailed directly to you should be sent to *motif-request@lobo.gsfc.nasa.gov*. Requests to have the OPEN LOOK mailing list mailed directly to you should be sent to *openlook-request@unify.com*. Requests for all the other lists should be sent to *mailing-list-name-request@x.org*, or *uunet!x.org!mailing-list-name-request* (for example, to join the ximage mailing list, send mail to *ximage-request@x.org*).

The newsgroup *comp.window.x* (which is the same as *xpert*), is where users and developers around the world ask and answer questions.

F.3 Training, Consulting, and Support

Numerous independent vendors provide courses on X programming. Several sources that we are aware of include:

- *Integrated Computer Solutions*, 201 Broadway, Cambridge, MA 02139; (617) 621-0060. Courses on Xlib, Motif, strategic overviews of X. Also provides consulting services and manages an X user's group.

- *Hands-On Learning*, 27 Cambridge Street, Burlington, MA 01803; (617) 272-0088. Courses on Xlib and Xt.

- X tutorials are now a regular feature of UNIX conventions, such as the UNIX EXPO, Usenix, Uniforum, Xhibition, and the annual X conference at MIT. Also contact hardware vendors for information on courses they offer.

- Dyksen Associates offers training in X including courses on Xlib, the Intrinsics, the Motif toolkit, and the OPEN LOOK toolkit. Contact them at (317) 497-7613.

- Gary O'Neal, GHG Corporation, 1300 Hercules, Suite 111, Houston, TX 77058, (713)-488-8806.

Training companies wishing to be listed here should send us information on the courses they offer.

There are currently no telephone support lines at the X Consortium, because X was developed by a university, not a system manufacturer or software house. Some vendors such as OSF offer support for a fee.

F.4 The X Consortium

The X Consortium can be reached at:

X Consortium
One Memorial Drive
PO Box 546
Cambridge, MA 02142-0004

The Consortium's telephone number is (617) 374-1000.
The fax number is (617) 374-1025.

Its current members are shown below.

Table F-1. Consortium Members

Apple Computer, Inc.	Eastman Kodak Company
AT&T UNIX System Laboratories	Kubota Pacific
BULL	Matsushita Electric Industrial CO., LTD.
Control Data Corporation	Mitsubishi
Convex Computer Corporation	Motorola, Inc.
Cray Research, Inc.	NCR Corporation
Data General	NEC Corporation
Digital Equipment Corporation	Network Computing Devices, Inc.
Du Pont Imaging Systems	Nippon Telegraph and Telephone Corporation
Fujitsu America, Inc.	Oki Electric Industry Co., Ltd.
Hewlett-Packard Company	Olivetti Systems & Networks
Hitachi	OMRON Corp.
Hughes Aircraft Co.	Prime Computer Inc.
IBM Corporation	The Santa Cruz Operation, Inc.
Intergraph Corporation	Sequent Computer Systems Inc.

Table F-1. Consortium Members (continued)

Siemens Nixdorf Informationssysteme AG
Silicon Graphics Computer Systems
Sony Corporation
Sun Microsystems, Inc.
Tandberg Data A/S

Tektronix, Inc.
Texas Instruments, Inc.
Unisys Corp.
Xerox Corporation

Table F-2. Consortium Affiliates

Adobe Systems
AGE Logic, Inc.
Aptronix, Inc.
ASTEC, Inc.
Athenix Corp.
Bitstream, Inc.
CETIA
Chromatics
Codonics, Inc.
Industrial Technology Research
  Institute (China)
Data Connection Ltd.
Evans & Sutherland
Frame Technology Corp.
GIPSI S.A. (France)
GfxBase
HaL Computer Systems, Inc.
Institute for Information
  Industry (Taiwan)
Integrated Computer Solutions, Inc.
Interactive Systems Corp.
Ithaca Software
IXI Limited
Japan Computer Corporation
Jupiter Systems
KAIST (Korea Advanced Institute
  of Science and Technology)
Labtam Australia
Liant Software Corp.
Locus Computing Corporation

Megatek Corp.
Metro Link, Inc.
Metheus Corp.
MIPS Computer Systems
Mitre Corp.
Objectivity, Inc.
Open Software Foundation
O'Reilly & Associates, Inc.
PCS Computer Systeme GmbH (Germany)

Peritek Corp.
PsiTech, Inc.
Quarterdeck Office Systems
Ramtek Corp.
Samsung Software America
ShoGraphics, Inc.
Snitily Graphics Consulting Services

Solbourne Computer Inc.
SOUM Corporation (Japan)
SPARC International
SpectraGraphics Corp.
Stanford University
Strategic Research Institute Inc. (Japan)
Sumitomo Electric Workstation Corp.

Tatung Science and Technology
Tyan Computer
Unipalm XTech
University of Lowell

VisionWare Ltd.   Visual Technology, Inc.
Visix Software, Inc.   Widget, Inc. (Japan)
Visual Information Technologies, Inc.   X/Open Company Ltd.

Most of these companies have or are preparing products based on X.

F.5 Finding Out for Yourself

X is unusual in that the source code is freely copyable by anyone as long as the copyright
notices are observed. It should be possible for most X programmers to get a copy of the X
source code from the sources listed above. Once you understand how the code is organized,
you can look up certain details about how X works as long as you have a good knowledge of
C and a little persistence. In "Star Wars," the saying was "Use the Force, Luke." In X, it is
"Use the Source, Luke."

Xlib and the server are two distinct chunks of code. Each contains code for sending and
receiving information to and from the other over the network using protocol requests, replies,
events, and errors. The source tree as supplied on the X distribution tape places the Xlib
source in the directory *mit/lib/X*, where *mit* is the top of the entire source tree. Their server
source is placed in *mit/server*.

The procedure for finding out something about an Xlib routine is normally to search for the
routine in the Xlib code and then figure out what it does. Sometimes the answer can be found
there. Many of the routines, however, simply place their arguments in a protocol request and
send it to the server. Then you will have to look in the server code for the answer. To find
the correct place in the server code, you will need the symbol for the protocol request, which
is the first argument in the GetReq call.

The server code is more involved than Xlib. The device-dependent portions are in
mit/server/ddx; the device-independent portions are in *mitserver/dix*. The device-independent code should be your first stop, because here protocol requests from Xlib arrive and are
dispatched to the appropriate code. Search for the protocol request symbol you found in
Xlib. It will appear in several source files. Start with the occurrence in *dispatch.c*, and try to
figure out what the code does. This will require following leads to other routines.

If you do not find a routine in *mit/server/dix*, then it must be in the device-dependent code.
mit/server/ddx has one directory in it for each brand of hardware to which a sample server
has been ported. It also contains the directories */cfb*, */mfb*, */mi*, and */snf*, which contain routines used in writing the sample server device-dependent code. Note that servers may
include code ostensibly for other machines. For example, the Sun sample server appears to
use code in several of the directories for other servers such as *dec* and *hp*.

Xlib and the X protocol are both defined by specification documents, not by any particular
implementation. Never depend on the implementation details of the Xlib or server code. If
you do, your code may not run on a machine that has optimized X software. This manual
documents only those features of Xlib and X in general that are governed by X Consortium
standard specifications. If you follow the guidance you find in this volume and the details in
Volume Two, *Xlib Reference Manual*, you will be in good shape.

Glossary

X uses many common terms in unique ways. A good example is "children." While most, if not all, of these terms are defined where they are first used in this manual, you will undoubtedly find it easier to refresh your memory by looking for them here.

Glossary

This glossary is an expanded version of the glossary from Volume One, *Xlib Programming Manual* (which in turn is based on the glossary in the *Xlib–C Language X Interface*, by Jim Gettys, Ron Newman, and Bob Scheifler). As such, it contains definitions of many Xlib terms not actually used in this book, but which you might come across in other reading, or in comments in code. In some cases, these Xlib terms may be used in the definitions of the Xt terms given in this glossary. Any term used in a definition, for which another entry exists in the glossary, is generally shown in italics.

accelerator

> An *accelerator* is a *translation* that maps events in one widget to actions in another. The name is based on the most frequent use for this feature, namely to provide keyboard shortcuts to invoke application or widget functions that would otherwise have only a pointer-driven interface.

accept_focus method

> The *accept_focus method* of a child is invoked when a parent offers the *keyboard focus* to a child by calling `XtCallAcceptFocus()`. This method is part of the Core widget class.

access control list

> X maintains lists of hosts that are allowed access to each server controlling a display. By default, only the local host may use the display, plus any hosts specified in the *access control list* for that display. This access control list can be changed by clients on the local host. Some server implementations may implement other authorization mechanisms in addition to or instead of this one. The list can currently be found in */etc/X#.hosts* where # is the number of the display, usually 0 (zero). The access control list is also known as the host access list.

action

> An *action* is a function bound by a *translation*, to be invoked in response to a user event.

actions table

> An *actions table* is an array of function pointers and corresponding strings by which *actions* can be referenced in a *translation table*. The use of actions requires a widget to define both an actions table and a translation table.

active grab

> A grab is *active* when the pointer or keyboard is actually owned by a single grabbing client. See also *grab*.

ancestor

        If window *W* is an *inferior* of window *A*, then *A* is an *ancestor* of *W*. The *parent* window, the parent's parent window, and so on are all ancestors of the given window. The *root window* is the ancestor of all windows on a given screen.

application context

        An *application context* specifies a connection to a server. When an application program has connections to multiple servers, the application context coordinates events and their dispatching, so all connections get processed.

argument list

        An *argument list* is used in a call to create a widget in order to "hardcode" the value of widget resources, and also in calls to `XtSetValues()` or `XtGet-Values()`. It consists of an array of `Arg` structures, each consisting of a resource name and the value to which it should be set.

Athena widget

        MIT distributes a set of widgets developed by MIT's Project Athena in the *Athena Widget* library, Xaw. The include files for Athena widgets usually reside in */usr/include/X11/Xaw*.

atom   An *atom* is a unique numeric ID corresponding to a string name. Atoms are used to identify properties, types, and selections in order to avoid the overhead of passing arbitrary-length strings over the network. See also *property*.

background

        Windows may have a *background*, consisting of either a solid color or a tile pattern. If a window has a background, it will be repainted automatically by the server whenever there is an `Expose` event on the window. If a window does not have a background, it will be transparent. By default, a window has a background. See also *foreground*.

backing store

        When a server maintains the contents of a window, the off-screen saved pixels are known as a *backing store.* This feature is not available on all servers. Even when available, the server will not maintain a backing store, unless told to do so with a window attribute. Use the `DoesBackingStores` Xlib macro to determine if this feature is supported.

bit gravity

        When a window is resized, the contents of the window are not necessarily discarded. It is possible to request the server (though no guarantees are made) to relocate the previous contents to some region of the resized window. This attraction of window contents for some location of a window is known as *bit gravity.* For example, an application that draws a graph might request that the contents be moved into the lower-left corner, so that the origin of the graph will still appear in the lower-left corner. See also *window gravity*.

bit plane

On a color or gray scale display, each pixel has more than one bit defined. Data in display memory can be thought of either as pixels (multiple bits per pixel) or as bit planes (one bit plane for each usable bit in the pixel). The *bit plane* is an array of bits the size of the screen.

bitmap   A *bitmap* is a pixmap with a depth of one bit. There is no bitmap type in X11. Instead, use a pixmap of depth 1. See also *pixmap*.

border   A window can have a border that is zero or more pixels wide. If a window has a border, the border can have a solid color or a tile pattern, and it will be repainted automatically by the server whenever its color or pattern is changed or an `Expose` event occurs on the window.

button grabbing

A pointer grab that becomes active only when a specified set of keys and/or buttons are held down in a particular window is referred to as a *button grab*.

byte order

The order in which bytes of data are stored in memory is hardware-dependent. For pixmaps and bitmaps, *byte order* is defined by the server, and clients with different native byte ordering must swap bytes as necessary. For all other parts of the protocol, the byte order is defined by the client, and the server swaps bytes as necessary.

callback   A *callback* is an application function registered with a widget by the application using either of the calls `XtAddCallback()` or `XtAddCallbacks()` or through an argument list. A widget declares one or more *callback lists* as resources; applications add functions to these lists in order to link widgets to applications code.

change_managed method

When a parent should change its managed widgets, the *change_managed method* is invoked, at which time a parent reorganizes its children. The `change_managed` method is part of the Composite widget class.

child, children

1) A widget created by `XtCreateWidget()` is a *child* of the widget specified as its *parent*. The parent controls the layout of its children.

2) The *children* of a window are its first-level subwindows. All of these windows were created with the same window as parent. A client creates its top-level window as a child of the root window.

Glossary

class   1) (X Toolkit) A widget's *class* determines what methods will be called for it and what instance variables it has. For widget users, a widget's class is declared in the *.h* file for the widget.

2) (Xlib) There are two uses of the term *class* in X: window class and visual class. The window class specifies whether a window is `InputOnly` or `Input-Output`. The visual class specifies the color model that is used by a window. See the classes `DirectColor`, `GrayScale`, `PseudoColor`, `StaticColor`, `StaticGray`, and `TrueColor`. Both window class and visual class are set permanently when a window is created.

class_initialize method

This method—part of the Core widget—is invoked when a widget class is initialized. That is, it is called when the first instance of a particular class is created.

client   An application program connects to the window system server by an interprocess communication (IPC) path, such as a TCP connection or a shared memory buffer. This program is referred to as a *client* of the window system server. More precisely, the client is the IPC path itself; a program with multiple paths open to one or more servers is viewed by the protocol as multiple clients. X Resources are available only as long as the connection remains intact, not as long as a program remains running. Normally the connection and the program terminate concurrently, but the client's resources may live on if `XChangeCloseDownMode( )` has been called.

clipping region

In many graphics routines, a bitmap or list of rectangles can be specified to restrict output to a particular region of the window. The image defined by the bitmap or rectangles is called a *clipping region*, or clip mask. Output to child windows is automatically clipped to the borders of the parent unless `subwindow_mode` of the GC is `IncludeInferiors`. Therefore the borders of the parent can be thought of as a clipping region.

colorcell   An entry in a colormap is known as a *colorcell*. An entry contains three values specifying red, green, and blue intensities. These values are always 16-bit unsigned numbers, with zero being minimum intensity. The values are truncated or scaled by the server to match the display hardware. See also *colormap*.

colormap

A *colormap* consists of a set of colorcells. A pixel value indexes into the colormap to produce intensities of Red, Green, and Blue to be displayed. Depending on hardware limitations, one or more colormaps may be installed at one time, such that windows associated with those maps display with true colors. Regardless of the number of installable colormaps, any number of virtual colormaps can be created. When needed, a virtual colormap can be installed and the existing installed colormap might have to be uninstalled. The colormap on most systems is a limited resource that should be conserved by allocating read-only colorcells whenever possible, and by selecting RGB values from the predefined color database. Read-only cells may be shared between clients. See also *colorcell*, *DirectColor*, *GrayScale*, *PseudoColor*, *StaticColor*, *StaticGray*, and *TrueColor*.

Composite widget

A *Composite widget* is designed to manage the geometry of children; that is, a Composite widget instance can be passed in the parent argument to `XtCreate-Widget()`.

connection

The communication path between the server and the client is known as a *connection*. A client usually (but not necessarily) has only one connection to the server over which requests and events are sent.

Constraint widget

The *Constraint widget* is a subclass of Composite. A Constraint widget has more information about each child than a Composite widget.

constraints

A Constraint widget provides a list of resources, or *constraints*, for its children. The constraints give the Constraint widget information about how each child should be laid out.

containment

A window *contains* the pointer if the window is viewable and if the hotspot of the cursor is within a visible region of the window or a visible region of one of its inferiors. The border of the window is included as part of the window for containment. The pointer is in a window if the window contains the pointer but no inferior contains the pointer.

coordinate system

The *coordinate system* has x horizontal and y vertical, with the origin (0, 0) at the upper-left. Coordinates are discrete, and in terms of pixels. Each window and pixmap has its own coordinate system. For a window, the origin is inside the border, if there is one. The position of a child window is measured from the origin of the parent to the outside corner of the child (not the child's origin).

Core widget

The *Core widget* is the basic class in the Toolkit. All widgets that can be displayed are subclasses of Core.

cursor
A *cursor* is the visible shape of the pointer on a screen. It consists of a hotspot, a shape bitmap, a mask bitmap, and a pair of pixel values. The cursor defined for a window controls the visible appearance of the pointer when the pointer is in that window.

delete_child method
The *delete_child method* is invoked on a parent after its child is deleted. This method is part of the Composite widget and is usually inherited.

depth
The *depth* of a window or pixmap is the number of bits per pixel.

dereference
To access the contents of a pointer, you must *dereference* it.

descendants
See *inferiors*.

destroy method
The *destroy method* is invoked when a widget has been destroyed. This method is part of the Core widget and is used to deallocate memory and GCs.

device
Keyboards, mice, tablets, track-balls, button boxes, etc. are all collectively known as input *devices*.

DirectColor
DirectColor is a visual class in which a pixel value is decomposed into three separate subfields for colormap indexing. One subfield indexes an array to produce red intensity values; the second subfield indexes a second array to produce blue intensity values; and the third subfield indexes a third array to produce green intensity values. The RGB (red, green, and blue) values in the colormap entry can be changed dynamically. This visual class is normally found on high-performance color workstations.

display
A *display* is a set of one or more *screens* that are driven by a single X server. The Xlib `Display` structure contains all information about the particular display and its screens as well as the state that Xlib needs to communicate with the display over a particular connection. In Xlib, a pointer to a `Display` Structure is returned by `XOpenDisplay()`. In most Xt applications, the `Display` is part of the *application context*, and need not be referenced directly. If necessary, a display can be opened directly with a call to `XtOpenDisplay()`, and a pointer to the currently open display can be returned by the `XtDisplay()` macro.

drawable
Both windows and pixmaps may be used as destinations in graphics operations. These are collectively known as *drawables*.

encapsulation
Encapsulation is a key concept in object-oriented programming. Objects are defined in such a way that their internals are hidden from the programs that use them; the only way to access an object should be through its published interfaces.

event   An X *event* is a data structure sent by the server that describes something that just happened that may be of interest to the application. There are two major categories of events: user input and window system side effects. For example, the user pressing a keyboard key or clicking a mouse button generates an event; a window being moved on the screen also generates events—possibly in other applications as well if the movement changes the visible portions of their windows. It is the server's job to distribute events to the various windows on the screen.

event compression

Event compression is an Xt feature that allows some events to be ignored or repackaged before they are given to a widget. This happens on the client side, rather than in the server.

event handler

An *event handler* is a function that is called by Xt when a particular event is received. Event handlers have the same purpose as translations and actions—to call a function in response to an event—but event handlers have lower overhead and are not user-configurable.

event mask

Events are requested relative to a window or widget. The set of event types a client requests relative to a window is described using an *event mask*, a bitwise OR of defined symbols specifying which events are desired.

The `event_mask` is a window attribute, which can be set in Xlib with `XSelectInput()`, and is also specified in calls that grab the pointer or keyboard. The `do_not_propagate_mask` attribute is also an event mask, and it specifies which events should not be propagated to ancestor windows. In Xt, you never need to set a window's `event_mask` or `do_not_propogate_mask` directly. The translation manager automatically selects the required events.

event propagation

Device-related events *propagate* from the source window to ancestor windows until a window that has selected that type of event is reached, or until the event is discarded explicitly in a `do_not_propagate_mask` attribute.

event source

The smallest window containing the pointer is the *source* of a device-related event.

expose method

When `Expose` events are received, the Intrinsics invoke the *expose method*. A widget should perform its redisplay activities in this method. The `expose` method is part of the Core widget class.

exposure

Window *exposure* occurs when a window is first mapped, or when another window that obscures it is unmapped, resized, or moved. Servers do not guarantee to preserve the contents of windows when windows are obscured or reconfigured. `Expose` events are sent to clients to inform them when contents of regions of windows have been lost and need to be regenerated.

extension

Named *extensions* to the core protocol can be defined to extend the system. Extension to output requests, resources, and event types are all possible, and expected. Extensions can perform at the same level as the core Xlib.

font A *font* is an array of characters or other bitmap shapes such as cursors. The protocol does no translation or interpretation of character sets. The client simply indicates values used to index the font array. A font contains additional metric information to determine intercharacter and interline spacing.

foreground

The pixel value that will actually be used for drawing pictures or text is referred to as the *foreground*. The foreground is specified as a member of a graphics context. See also *background*.

frozen events

Clients can *freeze* event processing while they change the screen, by grabbing the keyboard or pointer with a certain mode. These events are queued in the server (not in Xlib) until an **XAllowEvents()** call with a counteracting mode is given.

GC The term *GC* is used as a shorthand for graphics context. See *graphics context*.

geometry management

A Composite parent controls its children through *geometry management*, thereby manipulating the size and placement of widgets within a window on the display.

get_values_hook method

The *get_values_hook method* is invoked by the Intrinsics when someone calls **Xt-GetValues()**. This method is part of the Core widget class. Its role is to get the resource values of a subpart using **XtGetSubvalues()**.

glyph A *glyph* is an image, usually of a character in a font, but also possibly of a cursor shape or some other shape.

grab Keyboard keys, the keyboard, pointer buttons, the pointer, and the server can be *grabbed* for exclusive use by a client, usually for a short time period. In general, these facilities help implement various styles of user interface. Popup widgets generally make a *passive grab*. Server grabs are generally used only by window managers.

graphics context

Various information for interpreting graphics primitives is stored in a *graphics context* (GC), such as foreground pixel, background pixel, line width, clipping region, etc. Everything drawn to a window or pixmap is modified by the GC used in the drawing request.

graphics primitive

A *graphics primitive* is an Xlib call that sends a protocol request to the server, instructing the server to draw a particular shape at a particular position. The graphics context specified with the primitive specifies how the server interprets the primitive.

gravity See *bit gravity* and *window gravity*.

GrayScale

> *GrayScale* is a visual class in which the red, green, and blue values in any given colormap entry are equal, thus producing shades of gray. The gray values can be changed dynamically. `GrayScale` can be viewed as a degenerate case of `PseudoColor.`

hint Certain properties, such as the preferred size of a window, are referred to as *hints*, since the window manager makes no guarantee that it will honor them.

host access list

> See *access control list*.

hotspot A cursor has an associated *hotspot* that defines the point in the cursor which corresponds to the coordinates reported for the pointer.

identifier

> Each server resource has an *identifier* or *ID*, a unique value that clients use to name the resource. Any client can use a resource if it knows the resource ID.

inferiors

> The *inferiors* of a window are all of the subwindows nested below it: the children, the children's children, etc. The term *descendants* is a synonym.

inheritance (single vs. multiple)

> *Inheritance* is the ability to obtain methods from a *superclass*. Multiple inheritance, which is not supported by Xt, would allow a class to obtain methods from multiple unrelated superclasses.

initialize method

> The *initialize method* is invoked when a widget is created. It initializes instance variables and checks resource values. This method is part of the Core widget class.

initialize_hook method

> The *initialize_hook method* is called just after the initialize method, and is responsible for initializing subpart instance variables and checking subpart resource values. This method is part of the Core widget class.

input focus

> See *keyboard focus*.

InputOnly window

> A window that cannot be used for graphics requests is called an *InputOnly* window. `InputOnly` windows are invisible and can be used to control such things as cursors, input event distribution, and grabbing. `InputOnly` windows cannot have `InputOutput` windows as inferiors.

InputOutput window

> The normal kind of window that is used for both input and output is called an *InputOutput* window. It usually has a background. `InputOutput` windows can have both `InputOutput` and `InputOnly` windows as inferiors.

input manager

Control over keyboard input may be provided by an *input manager* client. This job is more often done by the window manager.

insert child method

A widget's *insert child method* is invoked when someone specifies it as a parent in an `XtCreateWidget()` call. This method is part of the Composite widget class. This method is usually inherited.

instance An *instance* is a particular widget that has a class. An instance ID is returned by `XtCreateWidget()`.

instantiate

When you *instantiate* a class, you create an instance of it.

Intrinsics

The X Toolkit defines functions and datatypes called *Intrinsics*.

key grabbing

A keyboard grab that occurs only when a certain key or key combination is pressed is called a *key grab*. This is analogous to button grabbing. Both are forms of passive grabs.

keyboard focus

The *keyboard focus* is the window that receives main keyboard input. By default the focus is the root window, which has the effect of sending input to the window that is being pointed to by the mouse. It is possible to attach the keyboard input to a specific window with `XSetInputFocus()`. Events are then sent to the window independent of the pointer position.

keyboard grabbing

All keyboard input is sent to a specific window (or client, depending on `owner_events`) when the *keyboard* is *grab*bed. This is analogous to mouse grabbing. This is very much like a temporary keyboard focus window.

keycode A *keycode* is a code in the range 8-255 inclusive that represents a physical or logical key on the keyboard. The mapping between keys and keycodes cannot be changed, and varies between servers. A list of keysyms is associated with each keycode. Programs should use keysyms instead of keycodes to interpret key events.

keysym A *keysym* is a `#define`'d symbol which is a portable representation of the symbol on the cap of a key. Each key may have several keysyms, corresponding to the key when various modifier keys are pressed. You should interpret key events according to the keysym returned by `XLookupString()` or `XLookup-Keysym()`, since this translates server-dependent keycodes into portable keysyms.

listener A *listener* style window manager sets the keyboard focus to a particular window when that window is clicked on with a pointer button. This is the window manager style used with the Apple Macintosh. This style is also referred to as click-to-type.

locale   The international environment of a computer program defining the "localized" behavior of that program at run-time. This information can be established from one or more sets of localization data. ANSI C defines locale-specific processing by C system library calls. See ANSI C and the X/Open Portability Guide specifications for more details. In this specification, on implementations that conform to the ANSI C library, the "current locale" is the current setting of the LC_CTYPE `set-locale` category. Associated with each locale is a text encoding. When text is processed in the context of a locale, the text must be in the encoding of the locale. See the glossary in Volume One, *Xlib Programming Manual*, for related terms.

loose binding

A *loose binding* refers to the use of an asterisk (*) wildcard in a *resource specification* to indicate that the specification applies to zero or more hierarchy levels of widget instances or classes.

mapping

A window is said to be *mapped* if an `XMapWindow()` or `XMapRaised()` call has been performed on it. Unmapped windows are never viewable. Mapping makes a window eligible for display. The window will actually be displayed if the following conditions are also met:

1) All its ancestors are mapped.

2) It is not obscured by siblings.

3) The window manager has processed the request, if for a top-level window.

message   In object-oriented programming, a *message* is used to invoke an object's methods. In Xt, you can think of the Intrinsics functions used to create, destroy, and set resource values as sending messages to widget classes.

method   A *method* is a function internal to widget class that the Intrinsics invoke under specified conditions. Methods are provided as pointers to functions in widget class records.

modal popup

A *modal popup* is a popup widget that grabs the pointer when a mouse button is pressed in a particular window.

modeless popup

A *modeless popup* is a popup widget that doesn't grab the pointer on a mouse button.

modifier keys

Shift, Control, Meta, Super, Hyper, Alt, Compose, Apple, Caps Lock, Shift Lock, and similar keys are called *modifier keys*.

monochrome

A *monochrome* screen has only two colors: black and white. Monochrome is a special case of the `StaticGray` visual class, in which there are only two colormap entries.

non-maskable event

A *non-maskable event* is an event that is not selected by the application or widget via an event mask, but is instead sent automatically by the X server. The non-maskable events are `MappingNotify`, `ClientMessage`, `Selection-Clear`, `SelectionNotify`, and `SelectionRequest`.

object   In object-oriented programming, an *object* is a self-contained program unit containing both data and procedures.

object-oriented programming

Object-oriented programming is a way of defining classes and creating instances so that objects respond to messages with methods. One of its major benefits is the encapsulation of code.

obscure   Window *A obscures* window *B* if *A* is higher in the global stacking order, and the rectangle defined by the outside edges of *A* intersects the rectangle defined by the outside edges of *B*. See *occlude*.

occlude   Window *A occludes* window *B* if both are mapped, if *A* is higher in the global stacking order, and if the rectangle defined by the outside edges of *A* intersects the rectangle defined by the outside edges of *B*. The (fine) distinction between the terms *obscures* and *occludes* is that for *obscures*, the windows have to be mapped, while for *occludes* they don't. Also note that window borders are included in the calculation. Note that `InputOnly` windows never obscure other windows but can occlude other windows.

padding   Some bytes are inserted in the data stream to maintain alignment of the protocol requests on natural boundaries. This *padding* increases ease of portability to some machine architectures.

parent   A *parent* is a Composite widget instance specified as the parent argument in `Xt-CreateWidget()`. Parents control a child's layout.

parent window

Each new window is created with reference to another previously-created window. The new window is referred to as the *child*, and the reference window as the *parent*. If *C* is a child of *P*, then *P* is the parent of *C*. Only the portion of the child that overlaps the parent is viewable.

passive grab

A *passive grab* is a grab that will become active only when a specific key or button is actually pressed in a particular window.

pixel value

A *pixel value* is an N-bit value, where *N* is the number of bit planes used in a particular window or pixmap. For a window, a pixel value indexes a colormap to derive an actual color to be displayed. For a pixmap, a pixel value will be interpreted as a color in the same way when it has been copied into a window.

pixmap   A *pixmap* is a three-dimensional array of bits. A pixmap is normally thought of as a two-dimensional array of pixels, where each pixel can be a value from 0 to $(2^N - 1)$, where N is the depth (z-axis) of the pixmap. A pixmap can also be thought of as a stack of N bitmaps. A pixmap may have only one plane. Such a pixmap is often referred to as a bitmap, even though there is no bitmap type in X11. See also *bitmap*.

plane   When a pixmap or window is thought of as a stack of bitmaps, each bitmap is called a *plane*.

plane mask
Graphics operations can be restricted to affect only a subset of bit planes in a drawable. A *plane mask* is a bit mask describing which planes are to be modified.

pointer   The *pointer* is the pointing device currently attached to the cursor, and tracked on the screens. This may be a mouse, tablet, track-ball, or joystick.

pointer grabbing
A client can actively *grab* control of the pointer, causing button and motion events to be sent to that client rather than to the client the pointer indicates.

pointing device
A *pointing device* is typically a mouse or tablet, or some other device with effective two-dimensional motion, that usually has buttons. There is only one visible cursor defined by the core protocol, and it tracks whatever pointing device is currently attached as the pointer.

popup   A *popup* is a widget outside the normal parental hierarchy of geometry management. It is a child window of the root window that is popped up temporarily to give the user a piece of information, or to get some information from the user.

post-order traversal
When a tree structure is subject to *post-order traversal*, its root is visited last; for example, a function might process the left descendant, the right descendant, and then the root.

pre-order traversal
When a tree structure is subject to *pre-order traversal*, its root is visited first; for example, a function might process the root, and then the left and right descendant.

private header file
A *private header file* contains the internal class definitions of a widget. For example, the Label widget's internal class definitions are contained in the private header file *LabelP.h*. This file is included only in the widget *.c* file of this class and any subclasses, never in the application.

property

Windows may have associated *properties*, each consisting of a name, a type, a data format, and some data. The protocol places no interpretation on properties; they are intended as a general-purpose data storage and intercommunication mechanism for clients. There is, however, a list of predefined properties and property types so that clients might share information such as resize hints, program names, and icon formats with a window manager via properties. In order to avoid passing arbitrary-length property-name strings, each property name is associated with a corresponding integer value known as an atom. See also *atom*.

PseudoColor

PseudoColor is a visual class in which a pixel value indexes the colormap entry to produce independent red, green, and blue values. That is, the colormap is viewed as an array of triples (*RGB values*). The RGB values can be changed dynamically.

public header file

A *public header file* contains the declarations (e.g., class widget pointer) necessary to use a widget. For example, `labelWidgetClass` declarations are contained in the public header file *label.h*. This header file is included in the widget *.c* file and in the application source file.

quark   A *quark* is an integer ID that identifies a string. In the context of Xt, this string is usually a name, class, or type string for the resource manager. Like atoms and resource IDs, quarks eliminate the need to pass strings of arbitrary length over the network. The quark type is `XrmQuark`, and the types `XrmName`, `XrmClass`, and `XrmRepresentation` are also defined to be `XrmQuark`.

query geometry method

Parents call `XtQueryGeometry()` to invoke the child's *query geometry method* to find out a child's preferred geometry. This method is part of the Core widget class.

raise   Changing the stacking order of a window so as to occlude all sibling windows is to *raise* that window.

real estate

The window management style characterized by the input being sent to whichever window the pointer is in is called *real-estate-driven*. This is the most common style of input management used in X.

realize method

The *realize method* creates a window on the display and is part of the Core widget class.

rectangle

A *rectangle* specified by [x,y,w,h] has an (infinitely thin) outline path with corners at [x,y], [x+w,y], [x+w,y+h], and [x,y+h]. When a rectangle is filled, the lower-right edges are not drawn. For example, if w=h=0, nothing would be drawn when drawing the rectangle, but a single pixel when filling it. For w=h=1, a single pixel would be drawn when drawing the rectangle, four pixels when filling it.

redirect Window managers (or other clients) may wish to enforce window layout policy in various ways. When a client attempts to change the size or position of a window, or to map one, the operation may be *redirected* to the window manager, rather than actually being performed. Then the window manager (or other client that redirected the input) is expected to decide whether to allow, modify, or deny the requested operation before making the call itself. See also *window manager*.

reparenting

The window manager often *reparents* the top-level windows of each application in order to add a title bar and perhaps resize boxes. In other words, a window with a title bar is inserted between the root window and each top-level window. See also *save-set*.

reply Information requested from the server by a client is sent back to the client in a *reply*. Both events and replies are multiplexed on the same connection with the requests. Requests that require replies are known as round-trip requests, and, if possible, should be avoided since they introduce network delays. Most requests do not generate replies. Some requests generate multiple replies. Xt caches frequently-used data on the client side of the connection in order to minimize the need for round-trip requests. See Volume Zero, *X Protocol Reference Manual*, for a detailed discussion of the X Protocol.

representation type

A symbolic constant beginning with *XtR*, which is defined in *<X11/StringDefs.h>* or an application or widget header file, and which is used to define the data type of a resource. Xt automatically converts between resource settings, which are strings, and various representation types.

request A command to the server is called a *request*. It is a single block of data sent over the connection to the server. See Volume Zero, *X Protocol Reference Manual*, for a detailed discussion of the X Protocol.

resize method

The *resize method* of a widget is called when the widget's parent has changed its size. This method is part of the Core widget class. In composite widgets, this method calculates a new layout for the children. In simple widgets, this method recalculates instance variables so that the **expose** method can redraw the widget properly.

Glossary

resource

1) A widget or application variable whose value can be set by the user or application programmer via the *Resource Manager*.

2) In the X Protocol and server documentation, windows, pixmaps, cursors, fonts, graphics contexts, and colormaps are known as *resources*. They all have unique identifiers (IDs) associated with them for naming purposes.

resource database

The *resource database* is the collection of possible places where resource specifications can be made. The most important of these are the *app-defaults file*, where the programmer specifies resource defaults, the **RESOURCE_MANAGER** server *property*, which the user can set with *xrdb*, and the *.Xdefaults* file in the user's home directory, where he or she specifies local resource preferences.

Resource Manager

The *Resource Manager* is a part of Xlib that merges a database consisting of several ASCII files, a server property, and values hardcoded by the application, and determines a unique value for each resource of each widget. It resolves conflicts between multiple settings for the same resource according to its internal precedence rules, and provides the widget or application with the resulting value.

resource setting

A *resource setting* is the actual value of a resource variable.

resource specification

A *resource specification* describes a "pathname" to a widget resource, using widget class and/or instance names, resource class or instance names, and optional wildcards. For example, the resource specification:

```
xbox.box.quit.label: Quit
```

specifies that the label resource of the quit widget, which is contained in the box widget in the *xbox* application, should be set to "Quit." The specification:

```
*Command.background: blue
```

which uses wildcards and widget classes, specifies that the background (color) resource of all Command widgets in any application should be set to "blue." It is up to the Resource Manager to resolve differences between resource specifications, which may have varying levels of specificity in the various locations that make up the resource database.

RGB values

See *colorcell*.

root

The *root* of a window, pixmap, or graphics context (GC) is the same as the root window of whatever drawable was specified in the call to create the window, pixmap, or GC. These resources can be used only on the screen indicated by this window. See *root window*.

root window

Each screen has a *root window* covering it. It cannot be reconfigured or unmapped, but otherwise acts as a full-fledged window. A root window has no parent.

round-trip request

A request to the server that generates a reply is known as a *round-trip request*. See *reply*.

save-set

The *save-set* of a client is a list of other clients' windows which, if they are inferiors of one of the client's windows at connection close, should not be destroyed, and which should be reparented and remapped if the client is unmapped. Save-sets are typically used by window managers to avoid lost windows if the manager should terminate abnormally. See *reparenting* for more background information.

scan line

A *scan line* is a list of pixel or bit values viewed as a horizontal row (all values having the same y coordinate) of an image, with the values ordered by increasing x coordinate values.

scan line order

An image represented in *scan line order* contains scan lines ordered by increasing y coordinate values.

screen

A *screen* may not have physically independent monitors. For instance, it is possible to treat a color monitor as if it were two screens, one color and the other black and white or to have two separate color and monochrome screens controlled by one server. There is only a single keyboard and pointer shared among the screens. A `Screen` structure contains the information about each screen and the list is a member of the `Display` structure.

scrollbar

A *scrollbar* is an area on a window that allows a user to view different portions of a window's information by scrolling, or moving.

selection

Selections are a means of communication between clients using properties and events. From the user's perspective, a selection is an item of data which can be highlighted in one instance of an application and pasted into another instance of the same or a different application. The client that highlights the data is the owner, and the client into which the data is pasted is the requestor. Properties are used to store the selection data and the type of the data, while events are used to synchronize the transaction and to allow the requestor to indicate the type it prefers for the data and to allow the owner to convert the data to the indicated type if possible.

server

The *server* provides the basic windowing mechanism. It handles IPC connections from clients, demultiplexes graphics requests onto the screens, and multiplexes input back to the appropriate clients. It controls a single keyboard and pointer and one or more screens that make up a single display.

server grabbing

> The *server* can be *grabbed* by a single client for exclusive use. This prevents processing of any requests from other client connections until the grab is complete. This is typically a transient state for such tasks as rubber-banding, or to execute requests indivisibly.

set_values method

> The Intrinsics invoke a widget's *set_values method* when one of the widget's resource values is changed. This method should return **TRUE** or **FALSE** to indicate whether the widget's **expose** method should be invoked.

set_values_almost method

> The *set_values_almost method* is invoked when a parent rejects a widget's geometry request, but the parent sends back a compromise. This method is part of the Core widget class.

set_values_hook method

> A widget can provide a *set_values_hook method* to allow the application to set resources of subparts.

sibling   Children of the same parent window are known as *sibling* windows.

spring-loaded popup

> When a button press triggers a popup, the popup is called a *spring-loaded popup*.

stacking order

> Sibling windows may stack on top of each other, obscuring lower windows. This is similar to papers on a desk. The relationship between sibling windows is known as the *stacking order*. The first window in the stacking order is the window on top.

StaticColor

> The *StaticColor* visual class represents a multiplane color screen with a predefined and read-only hardware colormap. It can be viewed as a degenerate case of **PseudoColor**. See *PseudoColor*.

StaticGray

> The *StaticGray* visual class represents a multiplane monochrome screen with a predefined and read-only hardware colormap. It can be viewed as a degenerate case of **GrayScale**, in which the gray values are predefined and read-only. Typically, the values are linearly increasing ramps. See *GrayScale*.

stipple   A *stipple* is a single plane pixmap that is used to tile a region. Bits set to 1 in the stipple are drawn with a foreground pixel value; bits set to 0, with a background pixel value. The stipple and both pixel values are members of the GC.

status   Many Xlib functions return a *status* of **TRUE** or **FALSE**. If the function does not succeed, its return arguments are not disturbed.

subclass

A widget *subclass* has its own features plus many of the features of its superclasses. For example, since Composite is a subclass of Core, Composite has all the fields in Core plus its own unique fields. A subclass can inherit or replace most superclass features.

superclass

One widget is a *superclass* of a second widget when the second widget includes the first, or the Core widget is a *superclass* of the Composite widget because the Composite widget's definition depends on, or includes, the Core widget.

tight binding

A *tight binding* refers to the use of a dot (.) in a *resource specification* to indicate that the widget class or instance on the right side of the dot is a child of the widget whose class or instance name is on the left side of it.

tile

A pixmap can be replicated in two dimensions to *tile* a region. The pixmap itself is also known as a *tile*.

time

A *time* value in X is expressed in milliseconds, typically since the last server reset. Time values wrap around (after about 49.7 days). One time value, represented by the constant `CurrentTime`, is used by clients to represent the current server time.

top-level window

A child of the root window is referred to as a *top-level window*.

translation

A *translation* maps an event or event sequence into an action name. Once a translation is installed in a widget, the named action function will be invoked when the specified event sequence occurs in the widget. Translations are specified as ASCII strings.

translation table

A *translation table* lists one or more translations.

TrueColor

The *TrueColor* visual class represents a high-performance multiplane display with predefined and read-only RGB values in its hardware colormap. It can be viewed as a degenerate case of `DirectColor`, in which the subfields in the pixel value directly encode the corresponding RGB values. Typically, the values are linearly increasing ramps. See *DirectColor*.

type property

A *type property* is used to identify the interpretation of property data. Types are completely uninterpreted by the server; they are solely for the benefit of clients.

viewable

A window is *viewable* if it and all of its ancestors are mapped. This does not imply that any portion of the window is actually visible, since it may be obscured by other windows.

visible A region of a window is *visible* if someone looking at the screen can actually see it; that is, the window is viewable and the region is not obscured by any other window.

visual The specifications for color handling for a window, including visual class, depth, RGB/pixel, etc., are collectively referred to as a *visual*, and are stored in a structure of type `Visual`.

visual class

Visual class refers to `DirectColor`, `GrayScale`, `PseudoColor`, `StaticColor`, `StaticGray`, or `TrueColor`. It is a definition of the colormap type but not its depth.

widget The basic object in a toolkit, a *widget* includes both code and data, and can therefore serve as an input or output object.

window gravity

When windows are resized, subwindows may be repositioned automatically by the server, relative to an edge, corner, or center of the window. This attraction of a subwindow to some part of its parent is known as *window gravity*. Window gravity is a window attribute. See also *bit gravity*.

window manager

The user manipulates windows on the screen using a *window manager* client. The window manager has authority over the arrangement of windows on the screen, and the user interface for selecting which window receives input. See also *redirect*.

XYPixmap

The data for an image is said to be in *XYPixmap* format if it is organized as a set of bitmaps representing individual bit planes. This applies only to the server's internal data format for images. It does not affect normal programming with pixmaps.

ZPixmap

The data for an image is said to be in *ZPixmap* format if it is organized as a set of pixel values in scan line order. This applies only to the server's internal data format for images. It does not affect normal programming with pixmaps.

zoomed window

Some applications have not only a normal size for their top-level window and an icon, but also a *zoomed window* size. This could be used in a painting program (similar to the MacPaint fat bits). The zoomed window size preferences can be specified in the window manager hints.

Master Index

The master index provides a thorough, combined index to Volume Four
(Motif Edition) and Volume Five, making it easy to look up all appropriate references to a topic in either volume. You will find main entries in boldface
type. Page numbers are marked with a volume number to indicate which
book the pages refer to. Page numbers preceded by a "IV" refer to Volume
Four, X Toolkit Intrinsics Programming Manual, Motif Edition. Those that are
preceded by a "V" refer to Volume Five, X Toolkit Intrinsics Reference Manual.

Master Index

Master Index

Athena widgets, (see also Box widget (cont'd)
    Sme object; SmeBSB object;
    SmeLine object; StripChart
    widget; Template widget; Text
    widget; Toggle widget;
    Viewport widget.)"
atoms
    about, IV:364, 604
    for protocols
        _MOTIF_WM_MESSAGES,
        IV:354
        WM_DELETE_WINDOW,
        IV:353
        WM_PROTOCOLS, IV:353
        WM_SAVE_YOURSELF,
        IV:353
        WM_TAKE_FOCUS, IV:353
        _MOTIF_WM_HINTS, IV:354
        _MOTIF_WM_INFO, IV:354
    obtaining
        example, IV:367
    predefined, IV:366
    standard, IV:375
augmenting translations
    IV:136-137
AVERAGE_WIDTH
    IV:546

B

background
    about, IV:604
    option (–background, –bg),
        IV:97-98
    pixmap, IV:52
    processing, IV:290
    resources, IV:52
    window attribute, IV:207
background processing
    XtAppAddWorkProc, V:80
backing_store
    about, IV:604
    window attribute, IV:207, 327
binding
    tight vs. loose, IV:303
bit
    bit gravity window attribute,
        IV:207, 604
    bit plane, IV:604

bitmap
    about, IV:351, 605
    files, IV:114
    fonts, IV:545
    font-scaling algorithm, IV:543
BitmapEdit widget
    IV:66, 113-148, 114, 230, 392,
        567
    BitmapEditClassRec,
        IV:188-189, 288
    BitmapEditRec example,
        IV:190
    class hierarchy of, IV:187
    instance part and record, IV:189
bitwise OR
    combining mask symbols, V:65
Boolean values
    IV:322
border
    about, IV:605
    border option (–border, –bd),
        IV:98
    bordercolor option (–border-
        color), IV:98
    borderwidth option (–bor-
        derwidth, –bw), IV:98
    pixmap, IV:52
    resources, IV:52
    width, IV:384
    window attribute, IV:207
border crossing events
    V:822-827
bounding box
    IV:224
Box widget
    IV:262
    geometry management,
        V:621-623
    resources, V:621-623
BulletinBoard widget
    IV:158, 513
button
    mapping, V:845
ButtonPress event
    IV:251, 434
    V:807-809
ButtonRelease event
    IV:251, 434
    V:807-809
buttons
    IV:508
    grabbing, IV:605
    (see also command buttons.)

byte order
 IV:605
%C
 IV:320

C

caching
 old size, IV:232
 resource, IV:329-330
 standard atoms, IV:375
 Xmu
  initializing, IV:375
 XtCacheAll constant, V:794
 XtCacheByDisplay constant,
  V:794
 XtCacheNone constant, V:794
 XtCacheRefCount constant,
  V:794
callbacks
 V:421-423, 476
 about, IV:27, 31, 41-42, 41, 605
  V:794
 adding, IV:43-44
  more than one, IV:90
  to callback list, V:52-54
  to callback resource,
  V:50-51
 arguments to, IV:44, 88
 as resources, IV:41
 callback list, IV:89
  deleting method, V:322-323
  determining status, V:234
  executive methods, V:126
  popping down widget,
  V:133-134
  popping up widget,
  V:130-132
  XtCallbackExclusive, V:130
  XtCallbackNone, V:131
  XtCallbackNonexclusive,
  V:132
  XtCallbackPopdown,
  V:133-134
  XtCallCallbacks, V:126
  XtHasCallbacks, V:234
  XtRemoveCallback, V:322
  XtRemoveCallbacks, V:323
 contrasted with actions, IV:133
 format, IV:44
 naming conventions, IV:45
 passing data, IV:86-88

 procedure, V:421-423
 reasons, IV:28
 structure, IV:88
 XtAddCallback, V:50-51
 (see also XtCallbackProc
  XtTimerCallbackProc.)
callbacks order of
 IV:89
Caption widget
 IV:513
Cardinal *
 IV:559
cascading popups
 about, IV:425, 427, 443-448
 example, IV:444-445
case converter
 IV:255
 XtRegisterCaseConverter,
  V:316
chained methods
 (see inheritance)
change_managed method
 IV:384-386, 398-399
  V:548
 in constraint widgets,
  IV:418-419
CheckBox widget
 IV:155
CirculateNotify event
 V:810
CirculateRequest event
 V:811
class
 about, IV:20, 605
 class_initialize method, IV:204,
  328, 408, 463, 482
  V:550-551
 class_part_initialize method,
  IV:205, 408, 411, 463
  V:552
 extension structure, IV:481
 hierarchy, IV:187
  Athena widgets, IV:204
  gadgets, IV:456-458
  (see also widget classes.)
 name
  defined in Core class part,
  IV:201
  matching widgets, IV:64
 part, IV:188
  combining into class record,
  IV:188
 record, IV:187

converters (cont'd)
  string to orientation, IV:328
  string to Position, IV:323
  string to short, IV:323
  string to translation table,
    IV:323
  widget name to widget ID,
    IV:328
  XColor to Pixel, IV:324
  (see also XtAppAddConverter
    XtSetTypeConverter.)
converters; old-style
  registering, V:74-76
coordinate system
  IV:5, 607
Core
  V:503
  Core widget, V:696
Core class fields
  accept_focus, V:508
  actions, V:507
  callback_private, V:509
  class_inited, V:506
  class_initialize, V:506
  class_name, V:506
  class_part_initialize, V:506
  compress_enterleave, V:507
  compress_exposure, V:507
  compress_motion, V:507
  destroy, V:508
  display_accelerator, V:509
  expose, V:508
  extension, V:509
  get_values_hook, V:508
  initialize, V:507
  initialize_hook, V:507
  num_actions, V:507
  num_resources, V:507
  query_geometry, V:509
  realize, V:507
  resize, V:508
  resources, V:507
  set_values, V:508
  set_values_almost, V:508
  set_values_hook, V:508
  superclass, V:506
  tm_table, V:509
  version, V:509
  visible_interest, V:508
  widget_size, V:506
  xrm_class, V:507

Core widget
  IV:17, 121, 187, 201, 247
    V:551
  about, IV:17, 23, 51, 607
  class part
    initializing, IV:199-202,
    199-200
  class structure
    in gadgets, IV:457
  CoreClassPart structure, IV:189
  CorePart structure, IV:189
  drawing into from application,
    IV:122
  fields, IV:201
    compress_enterleave,
    IV:201, 293
    compress_exposure, IV:201,
    225, 293
    compress_motion, IV:201,
    293
    display_accelerator, IV:201
    extension, IV:202
    superclass, IV:201
    tm_table, IV:201
    version, IV:202
    visible_interest, IV:202, 288
    widget_size, IV:201
    xrm_class, IV:201
    (see also methods, set_val-
    ues_hook.)
  hidden superclasses, IV:206
  instance record
    height field, IV:387
    width field, IV:387
  resources, IV:51
  superclasses, IV:456
  (see also methods.)
counter incrementing
  inside XtSetArg, IV:50
CreateNotify event
  V:819-820
Ctrl key
  IV:252
  (see also modifiers.)
cursor
  about, IV:208, 322, 607
  hotspot, IV:611
  window attribute, IV:208
customization
  IV:477

customization resource
  IV:306
customizations
  resources, IV:320
  specifying multiple, IV:320
cut and paste
  (see selections)

D

data
  data transfer completion
    method, V:472
  data types, V:787
  database, V:158
    obtaining for display, V:158
  (see also XtDatabase.)
database
  of screen, V:340
debugging
  IV:58
DECnet
  IV:355
decoration
  IV:33, 352
default
  multiple click timing, IV:257
  size, IV:233
delete_child method
  IV:384
    V:554
depth
  IV:52, 222, 607
derived instances
  IV:546
  of scalable fonts, IV:545-546
descendants
  IV:607
destroy method
  IV:206, 217, 236
    V:556
  about, IV:236
  Constraint, IV:409
  example from BitmapEdit,
    IV:236
DestroyNotify event
  V:821
destructors
  IV:330

details in translations
  (see translations)
device
  IV:608
dialog boxes
  IV:453
  cascading, IV:453
  creating, IV:80
  grabs in, IV:453
  without grabs, IV:453
Dialog widget
  IV:421
    V:628-630
  adding children, V:630
  resources, V:628-629
Dialog widgets
  different kinds of, IV:158-159
DirectColor
  IV:608
directories
  font, IV:536
display
  V:171
  about, IV:6, 608
  adding
    XtOpenDisplay, V:288-290
  closing, V:140
  connecting to multiple displays,
    IV:481
  depth, IV:534
  display lists, V:562
  display_accelerator method,
    IV:268
    V:560
  initializing, V:171-175
  lists, IV:224
  option (–display), IV:98
  pointer
    returning for widget, V:170
  XtCloseDisplay, V:140
  (see also XtDisplayInitialize.)
DISPLAY environment variable
  IV:52
distributed processing
  IV:7
DoesBackingStore Xlib macro
  IV:207
DoesSaveUnders Xlib macro
  IV:208
double clicks
  IV:256-257

events, KeyPress (cont'd)
    V:840-842
    KeyRelease, IV:248, 251
        V:840-842
    LeaveNotify, IV:250-251, 293,
        434
        V:822-827
    list of types and structure
        names, IV:280-281
    MapNotify, V:843-844
    MappingNotify, V:845-846
    MapRequest, V:847
    mocking up from action, IV:224
    MotionNotify, IV:251, 257,
        273, 293, 434
        V:848-850
    NoExpose, IV:247
        V:836-837
    nonmaskable, IV:245, 264,
        275-277, 613
        example of handlers, IV:245,
        264, 275
    processing one event
        XtProcessEvent, V:306
    propagation, IV:263
    PropertyNotify, V:851-852
    ReparentNotify, V:853
    ResizeRequest, V:854
    returning next event, V:101,
        283
    selecting, IV:263
    SelectionClear, IV:355, 365
        V:855
    SelectionNotify, IV:355, 366,
        370
        V:856-857
    SelectionRequest, IV:355, 357,
        366
        V:858
    structures, V:806
    translation table abbreviations,
        IV:246-247
    UnmapNotify, V:843-844
    using inside actions or event
        handlers, IV:278-279
    VisibilityNotify, IV:202, 247
        V:859-860
    XEvent
        example, IV:279
        union, V:805
    XtAppNextEvent, V:101
    XtAppPending, V:103, 301
    (see also expose.)

expo.lcs.mit.edu
    IV:36
expose
    Expose events, IV:25, 217, 226,
        434
        V:59
    exposure, IV:11
        compression, IV:225, 293
        XtAddExposureToRegion,
        V:59
        (see also events, Expose.)
    method, IV:203, 217, 224-226,
        224, 277
        V:561-566
        example from BitmapEdit,
        IV:224
        in gadgets, IV:455, 460-461
Expose event
    V:828-829
extensions
    about, IV:12, 609
    structures, IV:463, 481

F

fallback resources
    IV:312
fatal error
    (see error)
file, .Xdefaults, IV:305
    .Xdefaults-hostname, IV:305
    XtErrorDB, IV:496
File menu
    creating, IV:76-77
    example, IV:79
files
    character limit in filenames,
        IV:186
    file events
        (see XtInputCallbackProc)
    file input, IV:282-284
        registering file, V:77-78
        source masks, IV:282
        XtAppAddInput, V:77-78
    including in resource files,
        IV:308
    paths to resource, IV:307
    resource, IV:477
    searching for, V:182

Master Index

grabs
    about, IV:432, 603, 610
        V:797
    active vs. passive, IV:432
    adding or removing explicitly,
        IV:454
    exclusive vs. nonexclusive,
        IV:433, 446
    global, IV:432
    grab modes, IV:446
    in dialog boxes, IV:453
    keyboard, IV:432
    passive, IV:432, 614
    pointer, IV:432
    reasons for in menus, IV:434
    XtAddGrab, V:60-62
    XtRemoveGrab, V:326
graphics contexts
    V:68, 160, 199, 319
    about, IV:124, 190, 208, 610
    caching, IV:218, 222
    changing, IV:222, 229
    creating, IV:218, 221-223
    deallocating, V:319
    destroying, V:160
    exclusive or logical function,
        IV:363
    freeing, IV:229, 236
        V:160
    hardcoding values in, IV:223
    obtaining, V:68-70, 199-200
    read-only, IV:222
    reasons for, IV:124
    setting with resources, IV:223
    sharable, V:199-200
    sharable and modifiable,
        V:68-70
    (see also XtAllocateGC
        XtDestroyGC; XtGetGC;
        XtReleaseGC.)
graphics primitive
    IV:610
GraphicsExpose event
    IV:277
        V:59, 836-837
gravity
    IV:610
GravityNotify event
    V:806, 838
GrayScale
    IV:610

Grip widget
    resources, V:635-636

H

hand-tuned fonts
    IV:545
hardcoding
    resources, IV:40, 103, 105-106
    translations, IV:136
header files
    IV:31, 48, 53, 186, 283, 456,
        556
    not included twice, IV:189
    private, IV:615
    public, IV:616
height
    IV:387
    checking in initialize method,
        IV:219
help
    Help button
        creating, IV:77-84
    Help dialogue box
        creating, IV:77-84
    help text, IV:84
hexadecimal color specification
    IV:532
hints
    about, IV:342-354, 610
    icon position, IV:346
    position, IV:56
    size, IV:346
    size increment, IV:346
hooks
    IV:476
host access list
    IV:610
Hyper key
    IV:252
    (see also modifiers.)

I

ICCCM
    IV:12, 341, 364, 367, 373-377
icon
    creating pixmap, IV:351
    iconic option, (–iconic), IV:98
    popups, IV:345
    setting

icon, setting (cont'd)
    name, IV:350
      pixmap, IV:341, 351
    size and position, IV:551
    starting application as, IV:345
identifier
    IV:611
ifndef statement
    IV:189
image caching
    IV:168-169
Imakefile
    writing, IV:321
implementation file
    (see widget)
include files
    IV:31, 48, 53, 186, 189
    in widget implementation,
      IV:192
#include files
    IV:308
incremental selections
    IV:377
inferiors
    IV:611
inheritance
    about, IV:21, 45, 54, 199-209,
      611
    adding features to superclass,
      IV:209
    among Motif Widgets, IV:21
    among Motif widgets, IV:503
    among OPEN LOOK widgets,
      IV:503, 509
    in widget class and instance
      record, IV:187-188
    of chained methods, IV:203
    of conflicting methods, IV:209
    of Core resources, IV:51, 53
    of self-contained methods,
      IV:203
    of superclass method, IV:206
    resources, IV:193, 195-196
    styles, IV:202-204
    using XtInherit constants,
      IV:203
    widget not using resource
      value, IV:56
initial size
    IV:387

initialization
    XtToolkitInitialize, V:368
initialization procedure
    registering, V:739
initialize method
    IV:217, 219-223, 367, 394
      V:579-582
    about, IV:219
    Constraint, IV:410
    creating GCs in, IV:221
    example from BitmapEdit,
      IV:221
initialize_hook method
    IV:337
initializer functions
    calling, V:740
input
    focus, IV:611
    from file, IV:282-284
    from pipe, IV:284-285
    input events method, V:446-447
    InputOnly window, IV:611
    InputOutput window, IV:204,
      611
    manager, IV:611
    queue
      determining events, V:103,
      301
        examining head, V:102, 300
        XtAppNextEvent, V:101
        XtAppPeekEvent, V:102
        XtAppPending, V:103, 301
        XtPeekEvent, V:300
    source masks, IV:282
input methods
    and text internationalization,
      IV:497
InputOutput window
    V:828
insert_child method
    IV:384
      V:586
insert_position
    V:461
instance
    about, IV:20, 611
    record, IV:187
      adding variables to, IV:190
      allocating storage, IV:191
      BitmapEdit widget,
       IV:189-190
      contents, IV:187
    structures, IV:187-213, 219

Master Index

methods, resize (cont'd)
   in constraint widget,
      IV:416-417
      in gadget parent, IV:462
   resources and set_values,
      IV:227-230
   root_geometry_manager, V:601
   set_values, IV:205, 217-218,
      227-230, 389, 391, 394, 418
      V:603-608
      about, IV:620
   set_values_almost, IV:205, 391,
      402-403
      V:612-614
      about, IV:620
      in gadgets, IV:460
   set_values_hook, IV:205,
      337-338
      V:615
      about, IV:620
   vs. actions, IV:30
minimal useful size
   IV:396
mkfontdir
   IV:542
mnemonics
   IV:267
Mod keys
   IV:252
   (see also modifiers.)
modal cascade
   IV:428
modal popups
   IV:428
modifiers, !, IV:255
   adding, IV:253
   and event sequences, IV:258
   case-specifics, IV:255
   colon, IV:255-256
   displaying list, IV:253
   for button events, IV:258
   keys, IV:251-256, 613
      V:870-877
   matching exactly, IV:255
   negating, IV:254
   None, IV:255
mono vs. color
   IV:477
monochrome
   IV:613

Motif
   application's look and feel,
      IV:517
   popup widgets, IV:526
Motif converters
   IV:324
Motif Style Guide
   IV:81
Motif widgets
   IV:38, 66-67, 69, 517-527
   about, IV:19
   command, IV:520
   DrawingArea, IV:527
   inheritance among, IV:21
   Text, IV:527
   (see also Form widget
      Label widget; PanedWindow
      widget; PushButton widget;
      RowColumn widget;
      Scrollbar widget.)
_MOTIF_WM_HINTS
   IV:354
_MOTIF_WM_INFO
   IV:354
_MOTIF_WM_MESSAGES
   IV:354
motion compression
   IV:293
MotionNotify event
   IV:251, 273, 293, 434
      V:848-850
multi-click time
   setting, V:202
multiple
   click timing, IV:257
   toplevel shells, IV:480
mwm
   interclient communication,
      IV:353
   keyboard focus in, IV:348
   .mwmrc file, IV:341, 354
   use of input hint, IV:347

                    N

name option (−name)
   IV:98
naming conventions
   for widgets, IV:555

native language option
IV:494
netnews
IV:597
networked font service
(see font service)
newlines
in translations, IV:244
NoExpose event
V:836-837
nonfatal error
IV:247
V:118
registering method, V:117
(see also error handling
errors.)
nonmaskable events
(see events)
notify method
IV:463
notify modes
(see translations)

O

Object
V:511
objects
about, IV:29, 614
Object class, IV:456
ObjectClass, V:511
ObjectClassRec, V:511
object-oriented programming,
IV:xxvi, 29-30, 277, 614
ObjectPart, V:512
ObjectRec, V:512
obscure
IV:614
occlude
IV:614
OOP
(see objects, object-oriented
programming)
OPEN LOOK
application's look and feel,
IV:507
popup widgets, IV:515
OPEN LOOK widgets
IV:507-517
command, IV:508-510
text, IV:517

optimization
IV:139, 232, 479
options
abbreviating, IV:97
argument styles, IV:100
−background, IV:97-98, 531
−border, IV:98, 531
−bordercolor, IV:98
−borderwidth, IV:98
command line, IV:96
styles, IV:100
custom, IV:305
defining your own, IV:98
−display, IV:98
−font, IV:98
−foreground, IV:98, 531
−geometry, IV:346, 550-551
handling errors in, IV:102
−iconic, IV:98, 345
options table example, IV:100
overriding standard, IV:102
−rv/+rv, IV:98
−selectionTimeout, IV:98
standard, IV:97
−synchronous, IV:98
−title, IV:98
−xrm, IV:97, 305
OR operator
V:65
order of
callbacks, IV:89
outline fonts
IV:543, **545**
OverrideShell
V:515
OverrideShell widget
IV:77, 345
overriding
redirect, IV:345
window attribute, IV:208
standard options, IV:102
translations, IV:136-137
overspecified font names
IV:547

P

padding
IV:614

Paned widget
V:650-656
about, IV:68
change height settings, V:655
child resources, V:652
disabling auto-reconfiguring,
V:655
disabling resources, V:650-652
enabling auto-reconfiguring,
V:655
enabling/disabling pane resizing, V:654
getting height settings, V:655
PanedWidgetClass, V:650-656
PanedWindow widget
IV:67, 158
Panner widget
V:657
parent
about, IV:614
window, IV:614
parsing
command-line arguments,
IV:98-102
translations, IV:137
part (vs. record)
IV:188
passive grab
IV:432
path resources
IV:306
paths
to resource files, IV:307
pipe input
IV:284-285
pixel values
about, IV:126, 614
PIXEL_SIZE
IV:546
pixmap
about, IV:53, 224, 614
built-in, IV:169
freeing, IV:236
XYPixmap format, IV:622
ZPixmap format, IV:622
plane
IV:615
(see also bit plane.)
plane mask
IV:615

pointer
IV:432
about, IV:3, 615
dereferencing, IV:607
device, IV:615
events (see events or translations)
grabbing, IV:615
(see also grabs.)
POINT_SIZE
IV:546
popup menus
example, IV:434, 438
popup widgets
IV:505
Motif, IV:526
OPEN LOOK, IV:515
popups
V:151
about, IV:17, 77, 615
cascading, IV:425
creating, IV:77, 80
V:151-152
before popping up, IV:84
in work procedure, IV:291;
V:488
example, IV:83
from callback function, IV:84
linking group, IV:345
mapping, V:303-304
menus, IV:425
menus, spring-loaded using
Box widget, IV:434, 438-439
modal, IV:428
about, IV:613
modeless, IV:428
about, IV:613
OverrideShell, IV:345
sensitivity, IV:454
spring-loaded, IV:428, 620
unmapping, V:302
when application is iconified,
IV:345
(see also XtCreatePopupShell.)
portability
IV:106, 282, 458, 474, 477-478
Porthole widget
V:663
position
about, IV:56, 323
hints, IV:346

position (cont'd)
    relative to root window, IV:352
    setting with resources, IV:55
PRIMARY selection
    IV:356
Primitive widget
    IV:23, 121
    PrimitiveClassPart, IV:189
    PrimitivePart, IV:189
printer fonts
    (see fonts)
private header file
    BitmapEdiP.h, IV:187-191
private instance variables
    IV:190
process input
    XtAppMainLoop, V:99
program structure
    IV:31
properties
    about, IV:355, 615
    and atoms, IV:364
property
    RESOURCE_MANAGER,
        IV:305-306
    SCREEN_RESOURCES, IV:305
PropertyNotify event
    V:851-852
protocol, _MOTIF_WM_MES-
        SAGES atom, IV:354
    network, IV:6
    WM_DELETE_WINDOW atom,
        IV:353
    WM_PROTOCOLS atom, IV:353
    WM_SAVE_YOURSELF atom,
        IV:353
    WM_TAKE_FOCUS atom,
        IV:353
Protocols.h header file
    IV:353
PseudoColor
    IV:616
public
    functions, IV:115, 118, 209
    header file, IV:31, 460
        BitmapEdit.h, IV:186,
        209-211
    instance variables (see
        resources)
    routines, IV:420

pulldown menu
    IV:427, 440
    creating, IV:78
    example, IV:442
    vs. spring-loaded, IV:428
push buttons
    IV:15
PushButton widget
    IV:15, 23, 42-44, 64, 66, 134
PushButtonGadget
    IV:64
    example using, IV:118

                Q

quarks
    IV:335, 616
query_geometry method
    IV:206, 233-235, 460
        V:589
    about, IV:233
    example from BitmapEdit,
        IV:235
    gadgets, IV:419-420, 460
querying
    scalable fonts, IV:549

                R

R5
    new features
        font service, IV:543
RadioBox widget
    IV:155
raise
    IV:616
raw event handlers
    IV:278
        V:64-65
    (see also events.)
realization
    IV:35, 225, 229
realize method
    IV:203, 206, 208, 347, 394
        V:594-597
reason
    in callbacks, IV:28
rectangle
    IV:616

resources (cont'd)

XmNaccelerators (Core), IV:52

XmNallowShellResize (Shell), IV:344

XmNancestorSensitive (Core), IV:52

XmNargc (Shell), IV:344-345

XmNargv (Shell), IV:344-345

XmNbackground (Core), IV:52

XmNbackgroundPixmap (Core), IV:52

XmNbaseHeight (Shell), IV:344, 346

XmNbaseWidth (Shell), IV:344, 346

XmNborderColor (Core), IV:52

XmNborderPixmap (Core), IV:52

XmNborderWidth (Core), IV:52

XmNclientDecoration (Shell), IV:354

XmNcolormap (Core), IV:52

XmNdepth (Core), IV:52

XmNdestroyCallback (Core), IV:42, 52

XmNgeometry (Shell), IV:344-346

XmNheight (Core), IV:52

XmNheightInc (Shell), IV:344, 346

XmNiconic (Shell), IV:344-345

XmNiconMask (Shell), IV:344

XmNiconName (Shell), IV:344, 350

XmNiconPixmap (Shell), IV:344, 351

XmNiconWindow (Shell), IV:344

XmNiconX (Shell), IV:344, 346

XmNiconY (Shell), IV:344, 346

XmNinitialState (Shell), IV:344

XmNinput (Shell), IV:347-349

XmNmappedWhenManaged (Core), IV:52

XmNmaxAspectX (Shell), IV:344, 346

XmNmaxAspectY (Shell), IV:344, 346

XmNmaxHeight (Shell), IV:344, 346

XmNmaxWidth (Shell), IV:344, 346

XmNminAspectX (Shell), IV:344, 346

XmNminAspectY (Shell), IV:344, 346

XmNminHeight (Shell), IV:344, 346

XmNminWidth (Shell), IV:344, 346

XmNoverrideRedirect (Shell), IV:344-345

XmNsaveUnder (Shell), IV:344

XmNscreen (Core), IV:52

XmNsensitive (Core), IV:52

XmNtitle (Shell), IV:344, 350

XmNtransient (Shell), IV:344-345

XmNtranslations (Core), IV:52, 133, 137

XmNwaitForWm (Shell), IV:344-345

XmNwidth (Core), IV:52

XmNwidthInc (Shell), IV:344, 346

XmNwindowGroup (Shell), IV:344-345

XmNwmTimeout (Shell), IV:344-345

XmNx (Core), IV:52

XmNy (Core), IV:52

xnlLanguage, IV:309

XtGetResourceList, V:203

XtNdefaultDistance (Form), IV:405

XtNhorizDistance (Constraint), IV:405

XtNinsertPosition (Composite), IV:404

XtNmappedWhenManaged (Core), IV:398

XtNpopdownCallback (Shell), IV:441

XtNpopupCallback (Shell), IV:441-442

XtNvertDistance (Constraint), IV:405

reverse option (–rv/+rv) IV:98

Master Index

underspecified font names
IV:547
units of measurement
setting, IV:170
unmanaging widget
IV:398
UnmapNotify event
V:843-844
upward chaining
IV:203
Usenet network news
see netnews, IV:597
user interface language
(see UIL)
uunet
IV:36
uwm
IV:426

V

varargs interfaces
advantages and disadvantages,
IV:108
VendorShell
V:533
VendorShell widget
IV:348
Viewport widget
IV:392
V:733-735
destroying, V:735
removing child, V:735
resources, V:733-735
ViewportWidgetClass,
V:733-735
virtual colormaps
IV:208, 349
virtual crossing
V:824
visibility interest
IV:202, 288-289
VisibilityNotify event
V:859-860
visual class
IV:622

W

Warning
Cannot convert . . . , IV:71
warning handler
V:119, 404
calling high-level, V:119-120,
404
(see also XtAppWarningMsg
XtWarningMsg.)
warnings
IV:467
listing, V:861
(see also error handling.)
WCL toolkit aid
IV:181
well-formed font names
IV:545
widget
V:628, 631, 635, 638, 641, 646,
677, 693, 704, 724
creating
custom widget, V:696-703,
697
displaying non-editable string,
V:638-640
displaying real-time graphic
chart, V:693-695
dragging
attachment point,
V:635-637
management
row-column geometry,
V:641-645
resizing
reasons for, IV:402
scrolling viewing area in
another widget, V:670-676
source file, V:700
text-editing widget, V:704-723
Window widget, V:698
(see also Dialog widget
Form widget; Grip widget;
Label widget; List widget;
MenuButton widget; Simple
widget; StripChart widget;
Text widget; Toggle widget.)
widget class
Core, V:503
Object, V:511
RectObj, V:517
Shell, V:522
TransientShell, V:530

widget class (cont'd)
  VendorShell, V:533
  WMShell, V:536
widget nodes
  initializing arrays of, V:762
  looking up by name, V:764
widgets
  IV:61
  about, IV:9, 15, 19, 622
  accept_focus method, V:123
  actions example, IV:237, 239
  adding to parent list, IV:16
    V:270-272
  as data types, IV:35
  callback list
    (see callbacks)
  child widget
    creating/managing, IV:61,
    385; V:150
    layout of, IV:396-397
  class
    determining subclass (XtIs-
    Subclass), V:255
    obtaining (XtClass), V:139
    verifying (XtCheckSub-
    class), V:138
    XtIsComposite, V:246
    XtIsConstraint, V:247
    XtIsShell, V:254
    XtIsSubclass, V:255
  converting (R4 to R5), IV:559
  converting strings to, V:756
  creating, IV:31, 90
    V:82, 149-150, 153-155, 153
    additional top-level, V:149
    independent widget trees,
    V:82-83
    Motif vs. Xt, IV:74
    window, V:156-157
    (see also XtAppCreateShell;
    XtCreateApplicationShell;
    XtCreateMgdWidget;
    XtCreateWidget.)
  declaring class record pointer,
    IV:206
  default size, IV:233
  defining conventions, IV:186,
    303
    summary, IV:212
  destroying, IV:28, 236
    V:161-162

  determining number of
    resources inherited, V:759
  display pointer, V:170
  Exclusives and Nonexclusives,
    IV:511
  framework of code, IV:185-213
  geometry (see geometry man-
    agement)
  hierarchy, IV:84
    creating, IV:63
  implementation file
    actions table, IV:196-198
    declaration of methods,
    IV:198-199
    resources, IV:193, 195-196
    translation table, IV:196-198
  implementation files, IV:186,
    191-209
  include files, IV:186
  inheritance among (Motif),
    IV:21
  installing accelerators (see
    accelerators)
  instance structure, IV:219
  internals, IV:185-213
  macros for, IV:471
  management, IV:61, 233-235
    V:248, 270-271
    child, IV:219-223
    XtIsManaged, V:248
    (see also XtManageChild;
    XtManageChildren.)
  mapping, IV:53
    changing map_when_man-
    aged field, V:351
    to display, V:273
    windows, IV:35
    XtSetMappedWhen-
    Managed, V:351
  merging translations, V:121
  modal widget
    XtAddGrab, V:60-62
    XtRemoveGrab, V:326
  moving (XtMoveWidget),
    V:277
  moving/resizing, IV:52
    V:141
    XtConfigureWidget, V:141
  name defined, IV:201
  naming conventions, IV:555

Master Index

Master Index

Master Index

Master Index

Master Index

Master Index

About the Authors

Adrian Nye is a senior technical writer at O'Reilly & Associates. In addition to the X Window System programming manuals, he has written user's manuals for data acquisition products, and customized UNIX documentation for Sun Microsystems and Prime. Adrian has also worked as a programmer writing educational software in C, and as a mechanical engineer designing offshore oilspill cleanup equipment. He has long-term interests in using his technical writing skills to promote recycling and other environmentally sound technologies. He graduated from the Massachusetts Institute of Technology in 1984 with a B.S. in Mechanical Engineering.

Tim O'Reilly is founder and president of O'Reilly & Associates, publisher of the X Window System series and the popular Nutshell Handbooks on UNIX. Tim has had a hand in writing or editing many of the books published by O'Reilly & Associates.

Tim's long-term vision for the company is to create a vehicle where creative people can support themselves by exploring interesting ideas. Technical book publishing is just the first step. Tim graduated cum laude from Harvard in 1975 with a B.A. in Classics.

More Titles from O'Reilly

X Window System Programming

Volume 0: X Protocol Reference Manual

VOLUME 0

Edited by Adrian Nye
4th Edition January 1995
458 pages, ISBN 1-56592-083-X

This manual describes the X Network Protocol, which underlies all software for Version 11 of the X Window System. It not only provides a practical demonstration of what is involved in a client session, but also an extensive set of reference pages for each protocol request and event. Reference pages, alphabetized for easy access, include encoding of requests and replies.

The fourth edition of *X Protocol Reference Manual* includes protocol clarifications of X11 Release 6 and can be used with any release of X. Note: This edition does not contain the Inter-Client Communication Conventions Manual (ICCCM) or the X Logical Font Description Convention (XLFD). This material will be included in an upcoming O'Reilly book.

Volume 1: Xlib Programming Manual

VOLUME 1

By Adrian Nye
3rd Edition July 1992
824 pages, ISBN 1-56592-002-3

Covering X11 Release 5, the *Xlib Programming Manual* is a complete guide to programming the X library (Xlib), the lowest level of programming interface to X. It includes introductions to internationalization, device-independent color, font service, and scalable fonts.

Includes chapters on:

- X Window System concepts
- A simple client application
- Window attributes
- The graphics context
- Graphics in practice
- Color
- Events
- Interclient communication
- Internationalization
- The Resource Manager
- A complete client application
- Window management
- Other programming techniques

This manual is a companion to Volume 2, *Xlib Reference Manual*.

Volume 2: Xlib Reference Manual

VOLUME 2

By Adrian Nye
3rd Edition June 1992
1138 pages, ISBN 1-56592-006-6

Volume 2, *Xlib Reference Manual*, is a complete programmer's reference for Xlib. Covers X11 Release 4 and Release 5.

Contents Include:

- Reference pages for Xlib functions
- Reference pages for event types
- Permuted index to Xlib functions
- Description of macros and reference pages for their function versions
- Listing of the server-side color database
- Alphabetical index and description of structures
- Alphabetical index and description of defined symbols
- KeySyms and their meaning
- Illustration of the standard cursor font
- Function group index to the right routine for a particular task
- Reference pages for Xlib-related Xmu functions (miscellaneous utilities)
- Four single-page reference aids for the GC and window attributes
- Index

New features in the third edition include:

- Over 100 new man pages covering Xcms, internationalization, and the function versions of macros.
- Updating to the R5 spec.
- New "Returns" sections on all the functions which return values, making this information easier to find.

Volume 5: X Toolkit Intrinsics Reference Manual

VOLUME 5

Edited by David Flanagan
3rd Edition April 1992
916 pages, ISBN 1-56592-007-4

The X Toolkit Intrinsics Reference Manual is a complete programmer's reference for the X Toolkit. This volume is based on Xt documentation from the X Consortium and has been reorganized and expanded for X11 Release 5. It provides reference pages for each of the Xt functions, as well as the widget classes defined by Xt and the Athena widgets, and many useful appendices.

This manual is a companion to Volume 4M, X Toolkit Intrinsics Programming Manual.

O'REILLY®

TO ORDER: **800-998-9938** • *order@oreilly.com* • *http://www.oreilly.com/*
OUR PRODUCTS ARE AVAILABLE AT A BOOKSTORE OR SOFTWARE STORE NEAR YOU.
FOR INFORMATION: **800-998-9938** • **707-829-0515** • *info@oreilly.com*

X Window System Programming

Volume 6A: Motif Programming Manual

By Dan Heller, Paula Ferguson & David Brennan
2nd Edition February 1994
1016 pages, ISBN 1-56592-016-3

The Motif Programming Manual is a source for complete, accurate, and insightful guidance on Motif application programming. There is no other book that covers the ground as thoroughly or as well as this one.

The Motif Programming Manual describes how to write applications using the Motif toolkit from the Open Software Foundation (OSF). The book goes into detail on every Motif widget class, with useful examples that will help programmers to develop their own code. Anyone doing Motif programming who doesn't want to have to figure it out alone needs this book.

In addition to information on Motif, the book is full of tips about programming in general and about user interface design. It includes a tutorial on UIL; coverage of drag-and-drop, tear-off menus, and internationalization as implemented in the Motif widgets such as Text and TextField; plus the entire book has been checked for accuracy with Motif 1.2 (while remaining usable with Motif 1.1). Complements Volume 6B, Motif Reference Manual.

Volume 6B: Motif Reference Manual

By Paula Ferguson & David Brennan
1st Edition June 1993
920 pages, ISBN 1-56592-038-4

The *Motif Reference Manual* is a complete programmer's reference for the Motif toolkit from the Open Software Foundation (OSF). Motif has become the standard user interface for X Window System applications, and the Motif toolkit makes it easy for programmers to build applications that conform with the Motif "look and feel."

This book provides reference pages for the Motif functions and macros, the Motif and Xt widget classes, the Mrm functions, the Motif clients, and the UIL file format, data types, and functions. The reference material has been expanded from the appendices of the first edition of Volume 6 and covers Motif 1.2. This book is designed to be used with Volume 6A, *Motif Programming Manual*, which describes how to build applications using the Motif toolkit and provides a complete tutorial with programming examples.

Java

Java Network Programming

By Elliotte Rusty Harold
1st Edition February 1997
442 pages, ISBN 1-56592-227-1

The network is the soul of Java. Most of what is new and exciting about Java centers around the potential for new kinds of dynamic, networked applications. *Java Network Programming* teaches you to work with Sockets, write network clients and servers, and gives you an advanced look at the new areas like multicasting, using the server API, and RMI. Covers Java 1.1.

Java in a Nutshell, Second Edition

By David Flanagan
2nd Edition May 1997
628 pages, ISBN 1-56592-262-X

This second edition of the bestselling Java book describes all the classes in the Java 1.1 API, with the exception of the still-evolving Enterprise APIs. And it still has all the great features that have made this the Java book most often recommended on the Internet: practical real-world examples and compact reference information. It's the only quick reference you'll need.

Java Distributed Computing

By Jim Farley
1st Edition January 1998
384 pages, ISBN 1-56592-206-9

Java Distributed Computing offers a general introduction to distributed computing, meaning programs that run on two or more systems. It focuses primarily on how to structure and write distributed applications and, therefore, discusses issues like designing protocols, security, working with databases, and dealing with low bandwidth situations.

Java

Java in a Nutshell, DELUXE EDITION

By David Flanagan, et al.
1st Edition June 1997
628 pages, includes CD-ROM & book
ISBN 1-56592-304-9

Java in a Nutshell, Deluxe Edition, brings together on CD-ROM five volumes for Java developers and programmers, linking related info across books. *Exploring Java, 2nd Edition*, covers Java basics. *Java Language Reference, 2nd Edition, Java Fundamental Classes Reference*, and *Java AWT Reference* provide a definitive set of documentation on the Java language and the Java 1.1 core API. *Java in a Nutshell, 2nd Edition*, our bestselling quick reference, is included both on the CD-ROM and in a companion desktop edition. This deluxe library is an indispensable resource for anyone doing serious programming with Java 1.1.

Java Cryptography

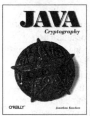

By Jonathan B. Knudsen
1st Edition May 1998
362 pages, ISBN 1-56592-402-9

Java Cryptography teaches you how to write secure programs using Java's cryptographic tools. It includes thorough discussions of the java.security package and the Java Cryptography Extensions (JCE), showing you how to use security providers and even implement your own provider. It discusses authentication, key management, public and private key encryption, and includes a secure talk application that encrypts all data sent over the network. If you work with sensitive data, you'll find this book indispensable.

Java Security

By Scott Oaks
1st Edition May 1998
474 pages, ISBN 1-56592-403-7

This essential Java 1.2 book covers Java's security mechanisms and teaches you how to work with them. It discusses class loaders, security managers, access lists, digital signatures, and authentication and shows how to use these to create and enforce your own security policy.

Java Virtual Machine

By Jon Meyer & Troy Downing
1st Edition March 1997
452 pages, includes diskette
ISBN 1-56592-194-1

This book is a comprehensive programming guide for the Java Virtual Machine (JVM). It gives readers a strong overview and reference of the JVM so that they may create their own implementations of the JVM or write their own compilers that create Java object code. A Java assembler is provided with the book, so the examples can all be compiled and executed.

Java Threads

By Scott Oaks and Henry Wong
1st Edition January 1997
268 pages, ISBN 1-56592-216-6

With this book, you'll learn how to take full advantage of Java's thread facilities: where to use threads to increase efficiency, how to use them effectively, and how to avoid common mistakes like deadlock and race conditions. Covers Java 1.1.

Java

Java Examples in a Nutshell

By David Flanagan
1st Edition September 1997
414 pages, ISBN 1-56592-371-5

From the author of *Java in a Nutshell*, this companion book is chock full of practical real-world programming examples to help novice Java programmers and experts alike explore what's possible with Java 1.1. If you learn best by example, this is the book for you.

Java Language Reference, Second Edition

By Mark Grand
2nd Edition July 1997
492 pages, ISBN 1-56592-326-X

This book helps you understand the subtle nuances of Java—from the definition of data types to the syntax of expressions and control structures—so you can ensure your programs run exactly as expected. The second edition covers the new language features that have been added in Java 1.1, such as inner classes, class literals, and instance initializers.

Java Servlet Programming

By Jason Hunter with William Crawford
1st Edition November 1998
528 pages, ISBN 1-56592-391-X

Java servlets offer a fast, powerful, portable replacement for CGI scripts. *Java Servlet Programming* covers everything you need to know to write effective servlets. Topics include: serving dynamic Web content, maintaining state information, session tracking, database connectivity using JDBC, and applet-servlet communication.

Java Fundamental Classes Reference

By Mark Grand & Jonathan Knudsen
1st Edition May 1997
1114 pages, ISBN 1-56592-241-7

The *Java Fundamental Classes Reference* provides complete reference documentation on the core Java 1.1 classes that comprise the *java.lang, java.io, java.net, java.util, java.text, java.math, java.lang.reflect,* and *java.util.zip* packages. Part of O'Reilly's Java documentation series, this edition describes Version 1.1 of the Java Development Kit. It includes easy-to-use reference material and provides lots of sample code to help you learn by example.

Java Swing

By Robert Eckstein, Marc Loy & Dave Wood
1st Edition September 1998
1252 pages, ISBN 1-56592-455-X

The Swing classes eliminate Java's biggest weakness: its relatively primitive user interface toolkit. Java Swing helps you to take full advantage of the Swing classes, providing detailed descriptions of every class and interface in the key Swing packages. It shows you how to use all of the new components, allowing you to build state-of-the-art user interfaces and giving you the context you need to understand what you're doing. It's more than documentation; Java Swing helps you develop code quickly and effectively.

How to stay in touch with O'Reilly

1. Visit Our Award-Winning Web Site

http://www.oreilly.com/

★ "Top 100 Sites on the Web" —*PC Magazine*
★ "Top 5% Web sites" —*Point Communications*
★ "3-Star site" —*The McKinley Group*

Our web site contains a library of comprehensive product information (including book excerpts and tables of contents), downloadable software, background articles, interviews with technology leaders, links to relevant sites, book cover art, and more. File us in your Bookmarks or Hotlist!

2. Join Our Email Mailing Lists

New Product Releases

To receive automatic email with brief descriptions of all new O'Reilly products as they are released, send email to:
listproc@online.oreilly.com
Put the following information in the first line of your message (*not* in the Subject field):
subscribe oreilly-news

O'Reilly Events

If you'd also like us to send information about trade show events, special promotions, and other O'Reilly events, send email to:
listproc@online.oreilly.com
Put the following information in the first line of your message (*not* in the Subject field):
subscribe oreilly-events

3. Get Examples from Our Books via FTP

There are two ways to access an archive of example files from our books:

Regular FTP

- ftp to:
  ftp.oreilly.com
  (login: anonymous
  password: your email address)
- Point your web browser to:
  ftp://ftp.oreilly.com/

FTPMAIL

- Send an email message to:
  ftpmail@online.oreilly.com
  (Write "help" in the message body)

4. Contact Us via Email

order@oreilly.com
To place a book or software order online. Good for North American and international customers.

subscriptions@oreilly.com
To place an order for any of our newsletters or periodicals.

books@oreilly.com
General questions about any of our books.

software@oreilly.com
For general questions and product information about our software. Check out O'Reilly Software Online at **http://software.oreilly.com/** for software and technical support information. Registered O'Reilly software users send your questions to: **website-support@oreilly.com**

cs@oreilly.com
For answers to problems regarding your order or our products.

booktech@oreilly.com
For book content technical questions or corrections.

proposals@oreilly.com
To submit new book or software proposals to our editors and product managers.

international@oreilly.com
For information about our international distributors or translation queries. For a list of our distributors outside of North America check out:
http://www.oreilly.com/www/order/country.html

O'Reilly & Associates, Inc.
101 Morris Street, Sebastopol, CA 95472 USA
TEL   707-829-0515 or 800-998-9938
       (6am to 5pm PST)
FAX   707-829-0104

O'REILLY®

TO ORDER: **800-998-9938** • **order@oreilly.com** • **http://www.oreilly.com/**
OUR PRODUCTS ARE AVAILABLE AT A BOOKSTORE OR SOFTWARE STORE NEAR YOU.
FOR INFORMATION: **800-998-9938** • **707-829-0515** • **info@oreilly.com**

International Distributors

UK, EUROPE, MIDDLE EAST AND AFRICA (EXCEPT FRANCE, GERMANY, AUSTRIA, SWITZERLAND, LUXEMBOURG, LIECHTENSTEIN, AND EASTERN EUROPE)

INQUIRIES
O'Reilly UK Limited
4 Castle Street
Farnham
Surrey, GU9 7HS
United Kingdom
Telephone: 44-1252-711776
Fax: 44-1252-734211
Email: josette@oreilly.com

ORDERS
Wiley Distribution Services Ltd.
1 Oldlands Way
Bognor Regis
West Sussex PO22 9SA
United Kingdom
Telephone: 44-1243-779777
Fax: 44-1243-820250
Email: cs-books@wiley.co.uk

FRANCE

ORDERS
GEODIF
61, Bd Saint-Germain
75240 Paris Cedex 05, France
Tel: 33-1-44-41-46-16 (French books)
Tel: 33-1-44-41-11-87 (English books)
Fax: 33-1-44-41-11-44
Email: distribution@eyrolles.com

INQUIRIES
Éditions O'Reilly
18 rue Séguier
75006 Paris, France
Tel: 33-1-40-51-52-30
Fax: 33-1-40-51-52-31
Email: france@editions-oreilly.fr

GERMANY, SWITZERLAND, AUSTRIA, EASTERN EUROPE, LUXEMBOURG, AND LIECHTENSTEIN

INQUIRIES & ORDERS
O'Reilly Verlag
Balthasarstr. 81
D-50670 Köln
Germany
Telephone: 49-221-973160-91
Fax: 49-221-973160-8
Email: anfragen@oreilly.de (inquiries)
Email: order@oreilly.de (orders)

CANADA (FRENCH LANGUAGE BOOKS)

Les Éditions Flammarion ltée
375, Avenue Laurier Ouest
Montréal (Québec) H2V 2K3
Tel: 00-1-514-277-8807
Fax: 00-1-514-278-2085
Email: info@flammarion.qc.ca

HONG KONG

City Discount Subscription Service, Ltd.
Unit D, 3rd Floor, Yan's Tower
27 Wong Chuk Hang Road
Aberdeen, Hong Kong
Tel: 852-2580-3539
Fax: 852-2580-6463
Email: citydis@ppn.com.hk

KOREA

Hanbit Media, Inc.
Sonyoung Bldg. 202
Yeksam-dong 736-36
Kangnam-ku
Seoul, Korea
Tel: 822-554-9610
Fax: 822-556-0363
Email: hant93@chollian.dacom.co.kr

PHILIPPINES

Mutual Books, Inc.
429-D Shaw Boulevard
Mandaluyong City, Metro
Manila, Philippines
Tel: 632-725-7538
Fax: 632-721-3056
Email: mbikikog@mnl.sequel.net

TAIWAN

O'Reilly Taiwan
No. 3, Lane 131
Hang-Chow South Road
Section 1, Taipei, Taiwan
Tel: 886-2-23968990
Fax: 886-2-23968916
Email: benh@oreilly.com

CHINA

O'Reilly Beijing
Room 2410
160, FuXingMenNeiDaJie
XiCheng District
Beijing, China PR 100031
Tel: 86-10-86631006
Fax: 86-10-86631007
Email: frederic@oreilly.com

INDIA

Computer Bookshop (India) Pvt. Ltd.
190 Dr. D.N. Road, Fort
Bombay 400 001 India
Tel: 91-22-207-0989
Fax: 91-22-262-3551
Email: cbsbom@giasbm01.vsnl.net.in

JAPAN

O'Reilly Japan, Inc.
Kiyoshige Building 2F
12-Bancho, Sanei-cho
Shinjuku-ku
Tokyo 160-0008 Japan
Tel: 81-3-3356-5227
Fax: 81-3-3356-5261
Email: japan@oreilly.com

ALL OTHER ASIAN COUNTRIES

O'Reilly & Associates, Inc.
101 Morris Street
Sebastopol, CA 95472 USA
Tel: 707-829-0515
Fax: 707-829-0104
Email: order@oreilly.com

AUSTRALIA

WoodsLane Pty., Ltd.
7/5 Vuko Place
Warriewood NSW 2102
Australia
Tel: 61-2-9970-5111
Fax: 61-2-9970-5002
Email: info@woodslane.com.au

NEW ZEALAND

Woodslane New Zealand, Ltd.
21 Cooks Street (P.O. Box 575)
Waganui, New Zealand
Tel: 64-6-347-6543
Fax: 64-6-345-4840
Email: info@woodslane.com.au

LATIN AMERICA

McGraw-Hill Interamericana
Editores, S.A. de C.V.
Cedro No. 512
Col. Atlampa
06450, Mexico, D.F.
Tel: 52-5-547-6777
Fax: 52-5-547-3336
Email: mcgraw-hill@infosel.net.mx

O'REILLY®